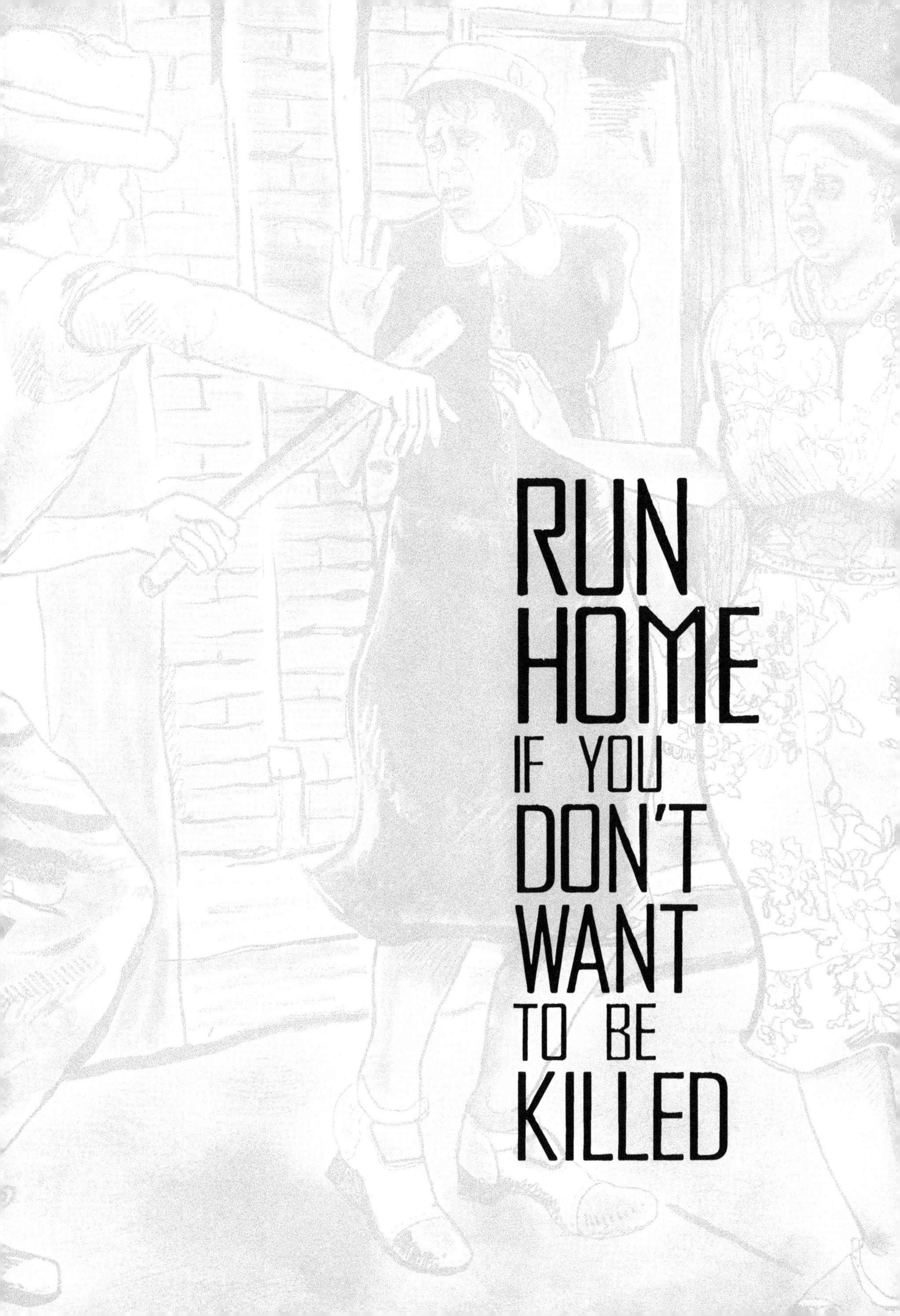

RUN HOME IF YOU DON'T WANT TO BE KILLED

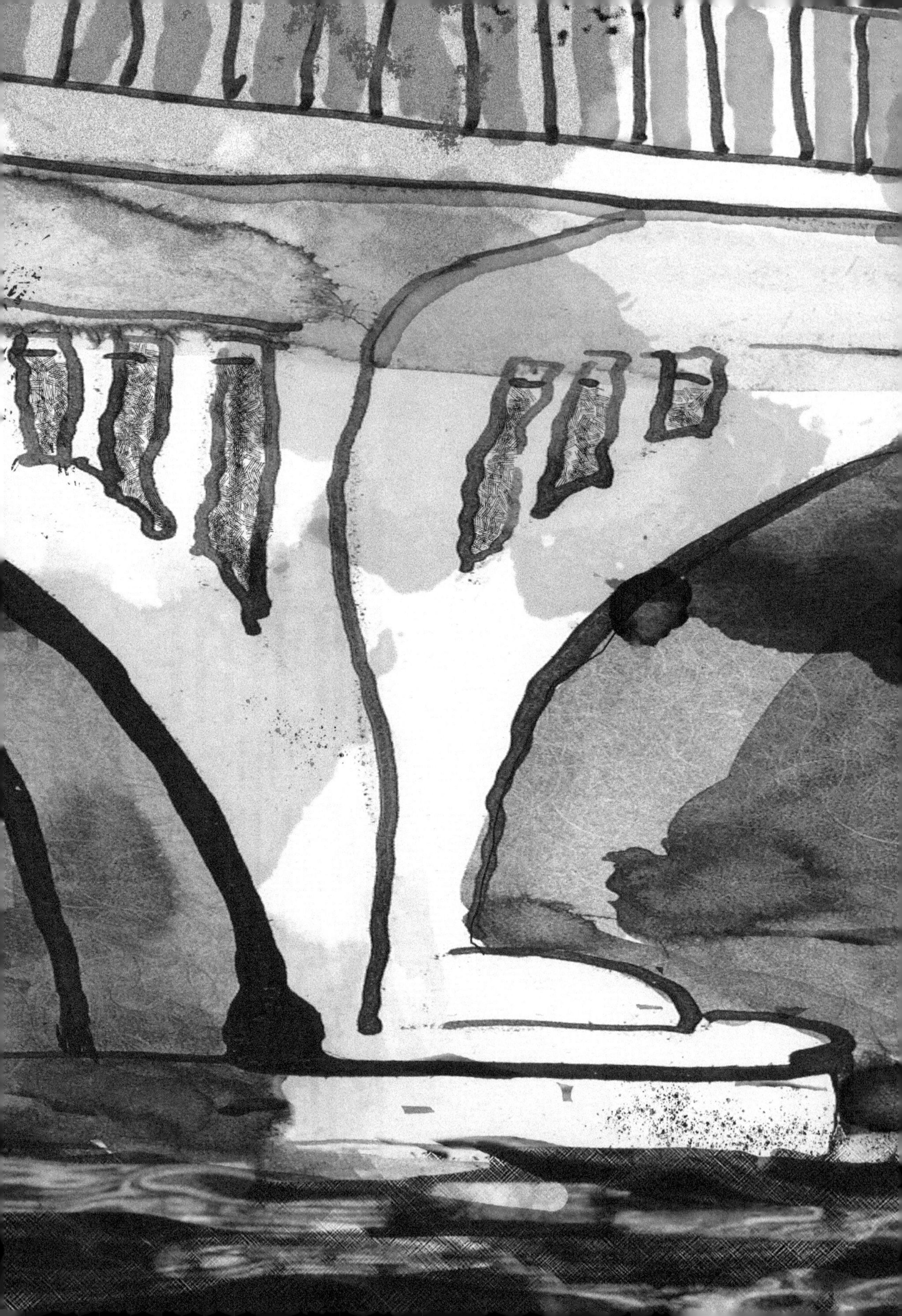

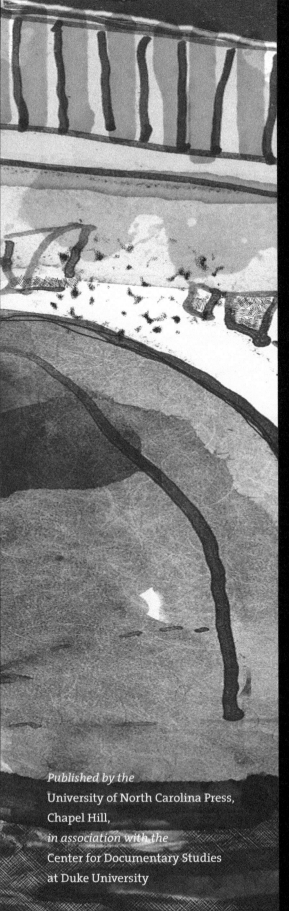

RUN HOME IF YOU DON'T WANT TO BE KILLED

The Detroit Uprising of 1943

Written and Illustrated by

RACHEL MARIE-CRANE WILLIAMS

Published by the
University of North Carolina Press,
Chapel Hill,
in association with the
Center for Documentary Studies
at Duke University

Designed by Rachel Marie-Crane Williams. Set in The Serif by Rebecca Evans and Kim Bryant. Manufactured in the United States of America. The University of North Carolina Press has been a member of the Green Press Initiative since 2003.

LIBRARY OF CONGRESS CATALOGING-IN-PUBLICATION DATA
Names: Williams, Rachel Marie-Crane, 1972– author, artist. | Duke University. Center for Documentary Studies, publisher.
Title: Run home if you don't want to be killed: the Detroit uprising of 1943 / written and illustrated by Rachel Marie-Crane Williams.
Other titles: Documentary arts and culture.
Description: Chapel Hill: University of North Carolina Press; [Durham, NC]: in association with the Center for Documentary Studies at Duke University, 2021. | Series: Documentary arts and culture | Include bibliographical references and index.
Identifiers: LCCN 2020037026 | ISBN 9781469663265 (cloth) | ISBN 9781469663272 (paperback) | ISBN 9781469663289 (ebook)
Subjects: LCSH: Detroit Race Riot, Detroit, Mich., 1943—Comic books, strips, etc. | Detroit Race Riot, Detroit, Mich., 1943—Personal narratives. | African Americans—Michigan—Detroit—Social conditions—20th century—Comic books, strips, etc. | Racism—Michigan—Detroit—Comic books, strips, etc. | Detroit (Mich.)—Race relations—Comic books, strips, etc. | LCGFT: Nonfiction comics. | Historical comics.
Classification: LCC F574.D49 N4878 2021 | DDC 305.8009774/340904—dc23
LC record available at https://lccn.loc.gov/2020037026

Documentary Arts and Culture

EDITED BY ALEXA DILWORTH, WESLEY HOGAN, AND TOM RANKIN OF THE CENTER FOR DOCUMENTARY STUDIES AT DUKE UNIVERSITY

In a time when the tools of the documentary arts have become widely accessible, this series of books, published in association with the Center for Documentary Studies at Duke University, explores and develops the practice of documentary expression. Drawing on the perspectives of artists and writers, this series offers new and important ways to think about learning and doing documentary work while also examining the traditions and practice of documentary art through time.

Center for Documentary Studies at Duke University
https://documentarystudies.duke.edu

Rachel Williams's *Run Home If You Don't Want to Be Killed* immerses us in the Detroit uprising of 1943, using hand-drawn images based on a decade-plus of research to connect us with testimony and witness from sources on hard-to-reach library shelves or squirreled away in digital archives. Books in the Documentary Arts and Culture series feature artists working across mediums to demonstrate the power of the long view; they have addressed aesthetic, cultural, political, and philosophical issues to provide a more substantial critical literature for documentary studies. As the series' inaugural book of graphic non-fiction, *Run Home* invites readers to reconsider how images and words together work to expand our view of an appalling shared history. Williams shows us people in various parts of their day-to-day: on the streets, in their bedrooms, at their kitchen tables, at work, in the civic square. The Detroit uprising "was a large event composed of smaller individual decisions," Williams notes, "many of which caused harm, some of which showed deep compassion and bravery." At its core, this work is by a white artist who hopes to unveil white supremacy more fully, who knows that we must "know and remember the truth of events in order to understand our present reality." A profound way of rendering this reality is through invention, the documentary imagi-nation visualized to its fullest. Art has many purposes; one, she says, "is to act as a mirror." Another is to envision the possibility of a more just future. We bring this book forward in the spirit of both.

—ALEXA DILWORTH, WESLEY HOGAN, and TOM RANKIN
    Editors, Documentary Arts and Culture series

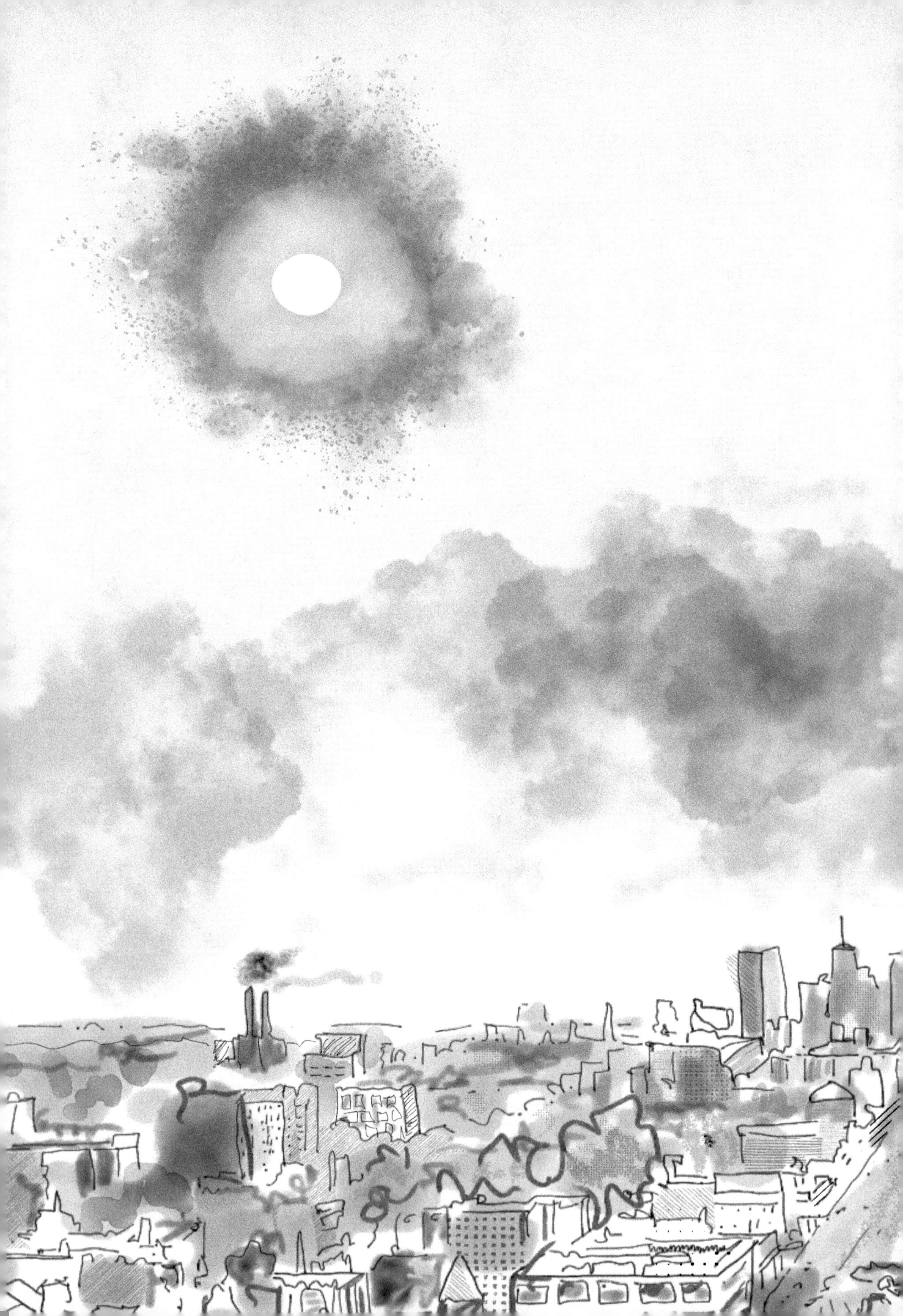

DEDICATED WITH LOVE

to the city of Detroit, historians, librarians, archivists, comic geeks, my friends, and my family, especially Rylie, Jack, and Don. Thank you for putting up with hours of drawing, frozen pizza, the Photoshop and InDesign rabbit holes, research trips, piles of papers and books, and twelve years of work. Your love and support made it possible.

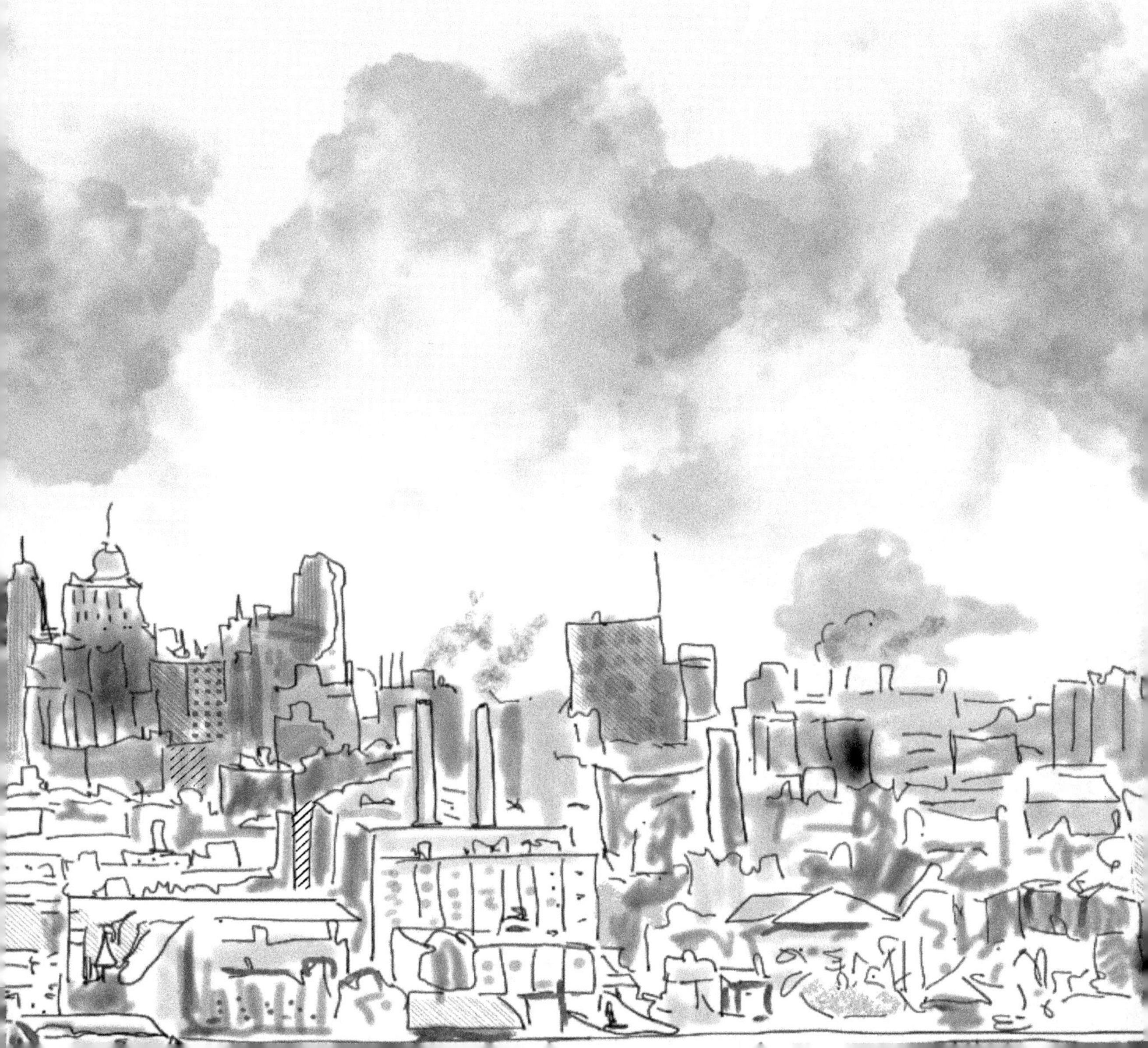

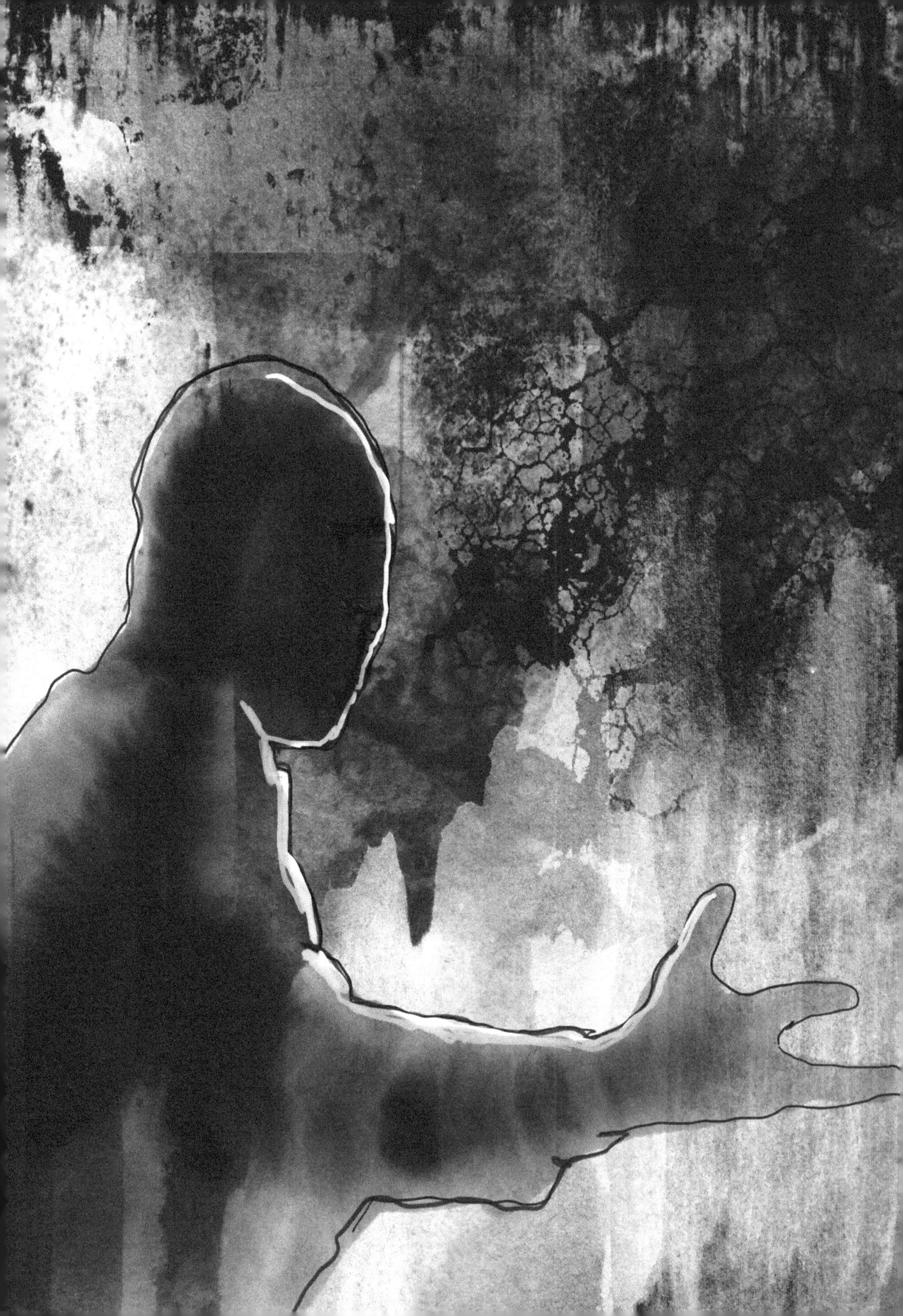

And I must say tonight that a riot is the language of the unheard. And what is it America has failed to hear? It has failed to hear ... that large segments of white society are more concerned about tranquility and the status quo than about justice and humanity.

— MARTIN LUTHER KING JR.
  March 14, 1968

CONTENTS

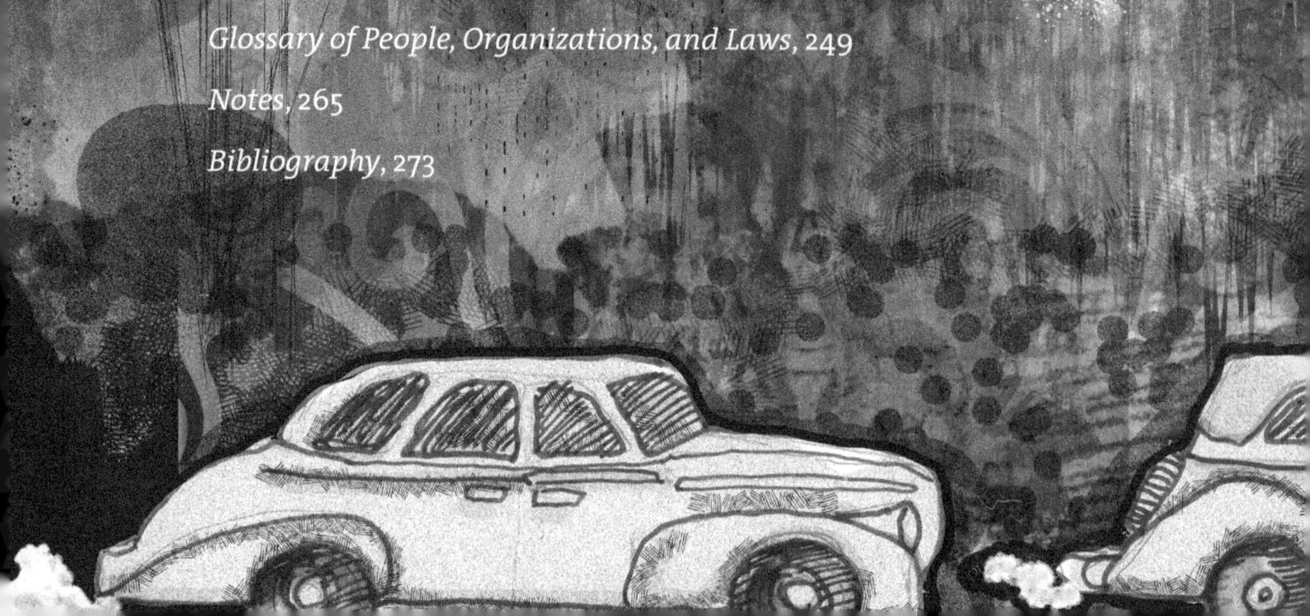

A NOTE ON LANGUAGE

This book is about violence, rebellion, and racism. It is based on primary historical documents and secondary sources and includes quotes from these sources, and this means that you are going to encounter the word "Negro." You will also encounter offensive racial slurs such as "ofay," "nigger," and "cracker."

I am a white woman who grew up in the South. From a very early age I understood that polite, decent, well-mannered people never *ever* used these words. Despite my discomfort, as an author, I made the decision to quote historical figures as accurately as possible and share images of historical documents that include offensive language. In the history of the United States there has always been intense state-sponsored oppression, racism, and support for the ongoing violence of white supremacy; people have openly called each other terrible names. We can't pretend that these words are not an important part of our history because they hurt our hearts or jar our senses when we read them. In 1963, twenty years after the rebellion in Detroit, James Baldwin wrote in *The Fire Next Time*, "An invented past can never be used; it cracks and crumbles under the pressures of life like clay in a season of drought." I could not invent a past in which people didn't use these words when there was clear evidence, in black and white, that they did.

Many of these words are painful. They were painful to read and painful to illustrate. The N-word was especially difficult. It is a word I wish were not part of our cultural lexicon. On July 9, 2007, the NAACP opened their annual convention in Detroit by holding a mock funeral for the N-word. While this gesture was reassuring for many liberals and activists interested in practicing respectability politics, it also resulted in criticism. People wanted the NAACP to acknowledge that there were more important things to do than choreograph a symbolic spectacle. In a critical response to this gesture, the African American writer David H. Bradley penned a eulogy for the word:

> Take Nigger out of American history; all that's left is indentured servitude. Change "Nigger Hollow" to "Freedom Road" and the Underground Railroad might as well be Amtrak. Take Nigger out of American literature; *Huckleberry Finn* is "What I Did on My Summer Vacation" and *Native Son* is a bad crime novel: Bigger not only does not rhyme, he does not get born. Take Nigger out of music; you've got no rags, no blues, no spirituals, probably no From the New World symphony and definitely no American String Quartet. Take Nigger out of social policy; all that's left is progressive jazz.

If that word didn't appear in these pages, the depth of the racial hate that sparked the rebellion in Detroit in 1943 would be shrouded and obscured. We should not sanitize history lest we forget how people's responses to hatred have shaped our current society, expanded civil rights, made art more powerful, and made life more tolerable. My decision to include racial slurs in quotes is not about who can say what; I get no secret pleasure from using or drawing or writing these words. It's about openly showing what has been already said and what using these words led to.

In 2013 Ta-Nehisi Coates wrote in an opinion column in the *New York Times*, "'Nigger' is the border, the signpost that reminds us that the old crimes don't disappear. It tells white people that, for all their guns and all their gold, there will always be places they can never go."

As a white woman I know that there is a bright line held taut by that word and all that it represents.

"Negro" is another word that you will encounter in this book. As a college professor I have seen students grow angry when reading texts with this word. I chose to use this word in order to accurately represent language of the 1930s and 1940s. The term "Negro" became popular in the 1920s after W. E. B Du Bois and Booker T. Washington began to advocate for it to replace the word "colored." In 1928, a high school student named Roland Barton wrote a letter to *The Crisis*, the NAACP's official magazine, lamenting that it used the word "Negro" instead of "American." In his response, Du Bois said:

> Do not at the outset of your career make the all too common error of mistaking names for things. Names are only conventional signs for identifying things. Things are the reality that counts. If a thing is despised, either because of ignorance or because it is despicable, you will not alter matters by changing its name. If men despise Negroes, they will not despise them less if Negroes are called "colored" or "Afro-Americans." . . .
>
> A Negro by any other name would be just as black and just as white; just as ashamed of himself and just as shamed by others, as today. It is not the name—it's the Thing that counts.

I'm white, and in creating this book, I worried about the use of labels such as "Negro," "Black," "white," and "African American." I fretted. But in 1943, "Negro" was the word that was commonly used. It appears in documents from the United Auto Workers and the NAACP, in newspapers, and in speeches by both Black and white leaders. My friends who are historians warned me against changing quotes and putting words in real people's mouths. For them, such a change would be unholy—if there is ugliness, they argued, we must show it. The word "Negro" did not begin to fall out of vogue until October 1966, when activist Stokely Carmichael coined the term "Black Power" in a speech at the University of California, Berkeley:

> Now we are now engaged in a psychological struggle in this country, and that is whether or not black people will have the right to use the words they want to use without white people giving their sanction to it. And that we maintain, whether they like it or not, we gonna use the word "Black Power" and let them address themselves to that; but that we are not goin' to wait for white people to sanction Black Power. We are tired of waiting; every time black people move in this country, they're forced to defend their position before they move. It's time that the people who are supposed to be defending their position do that. That's white people. They ought to start defending themselves as to why they have oppressed and exploited us.

It is important to acknowledge that white people have always used derogatory words for people who are not white. For example, the word "Jap," which also appears in this book, is a term that was cemented in U.S. culture as a racial slur during World War II. Some white people use these terms openly; others do it only in the company of other people who (they assume) are white. Using racial slurs is a way for white people to assert some false sense of divine dominion, which has been used as a tool of mental distancing and oppression since whites encountered Indigenous people on the shores of what later became the United States. Using these words makes it easier for oppressors, colonizers, and racists to see others as less than human, to enslave, kill, maim, lynch, deport, incarcerate, and oppress people with more melanin. When people read these slurs, they may feel enraged or uncomfortable. They may want to distance themselves from the words or from people who use such words. In truth, we can't deny these facts by swapping words around for comfort. We have to bear witness to our past and present by not turning away. We have to examine our discomfort in order to confront evil and ignorance.

I write this only to warn and remind you, if you didn't know already through experience, circumstance, and generational trauma, that history can be ugly and violent and discomforting. We must know and remember the truth of events in order to understand our present reality. We have to confront over and over the cyclical violence, myths, misdeeds, and murders that take place in our communities until they stop. Take your time reading this. Reflect. Discuss what you are feeling if it helps. Art has many purposes. One is to act as a mirror. In this capacity, it is meant to provoke and to make people see things they might not have recognized or known about themselves or their culture. I hope this book brings a lot of feelings to the surface. I hope you want to share the book and your feelings with others.

—RACHEL MARIE-CRANE WILLIAMS

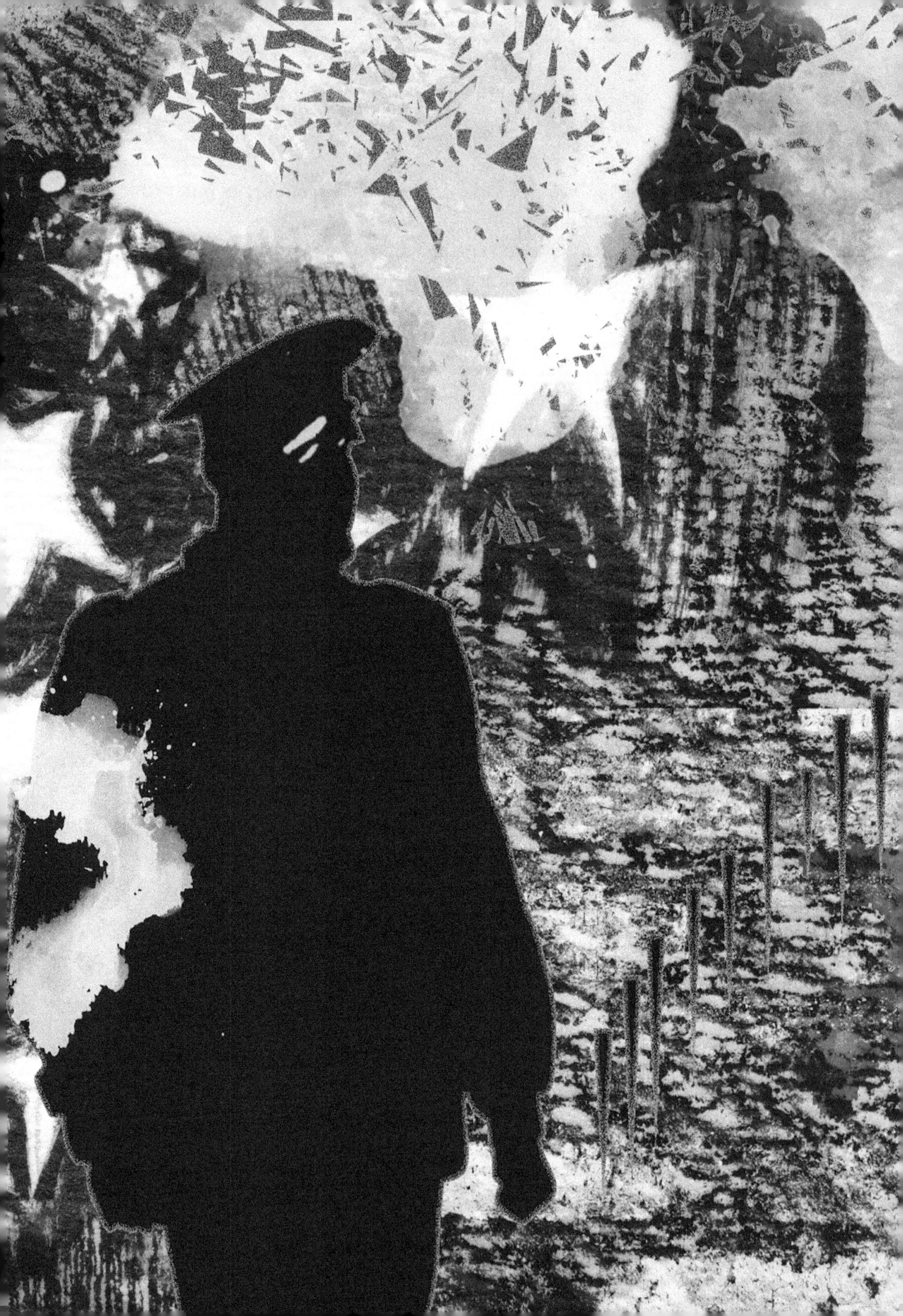

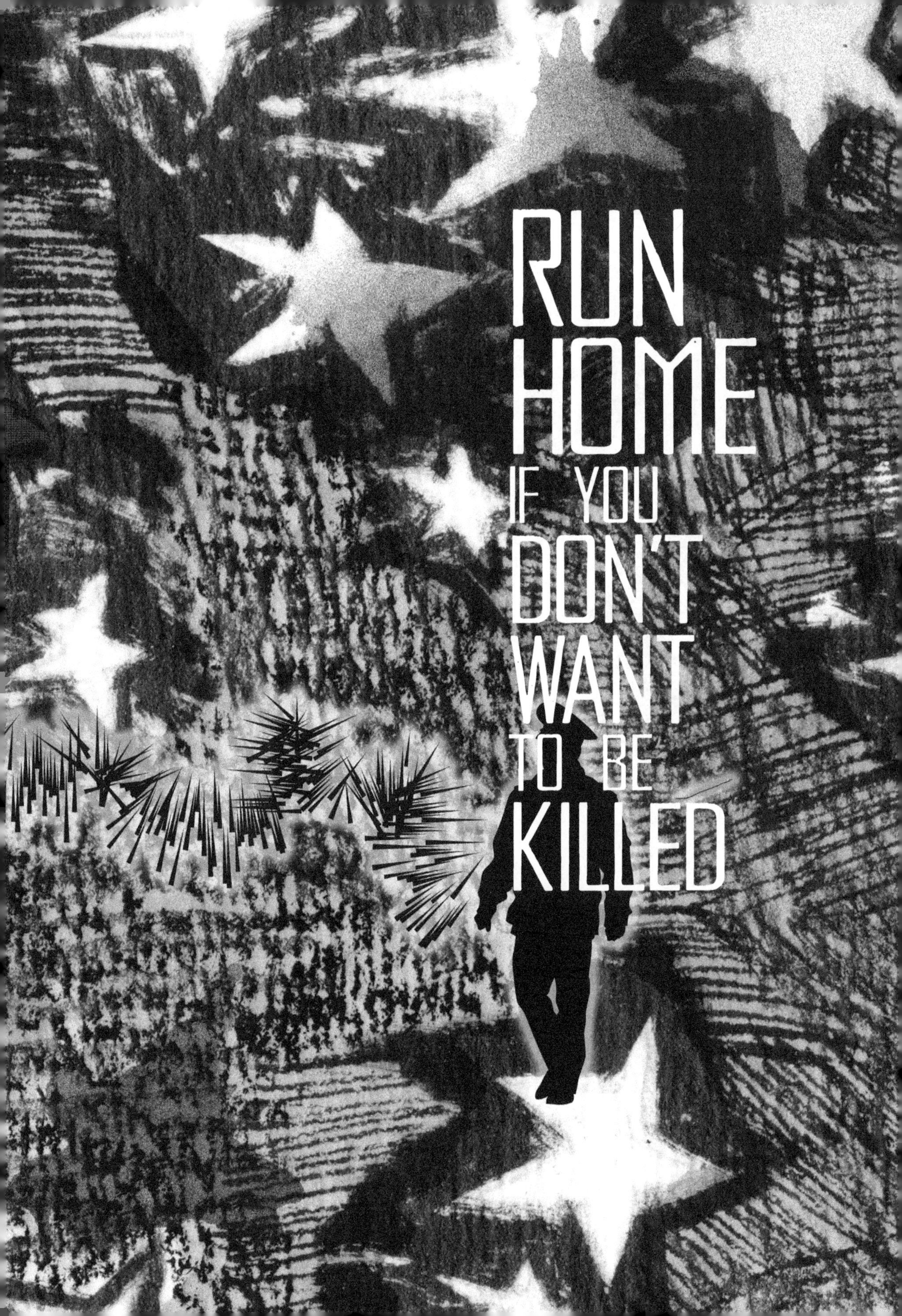
RUN
HOME
IF YOU
DON'T
WANT
TO BE
KILLED

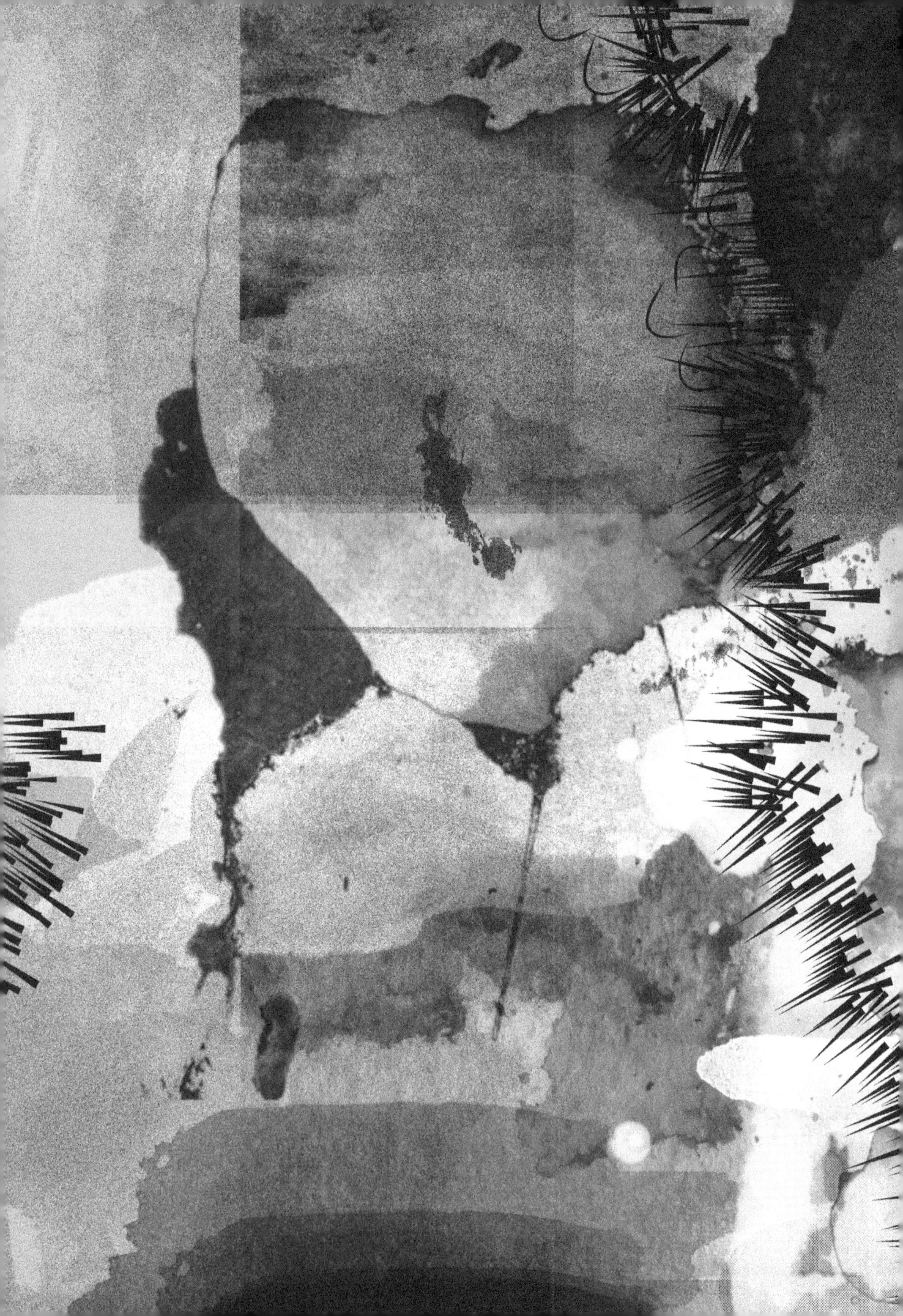

PROLOGUE

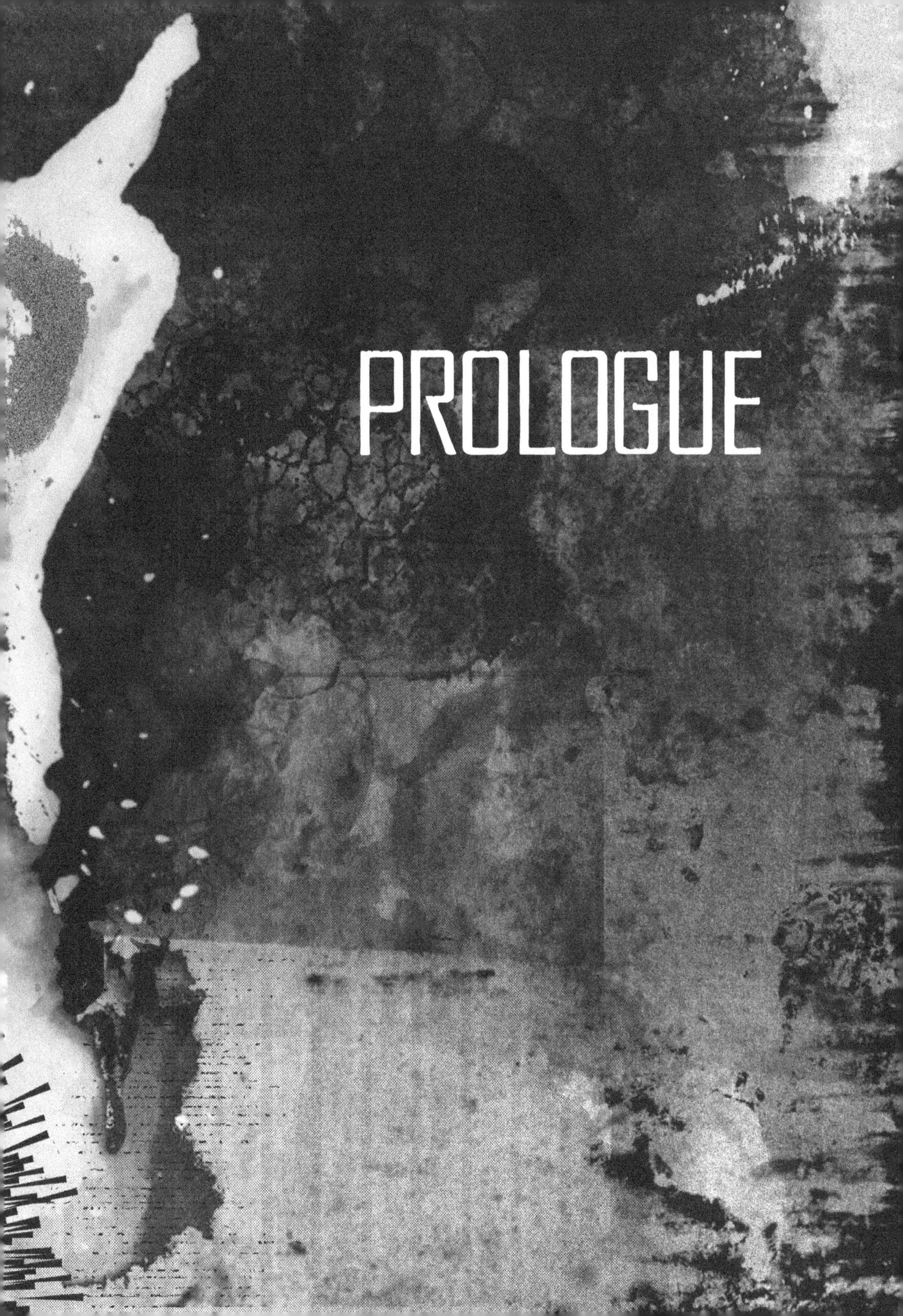

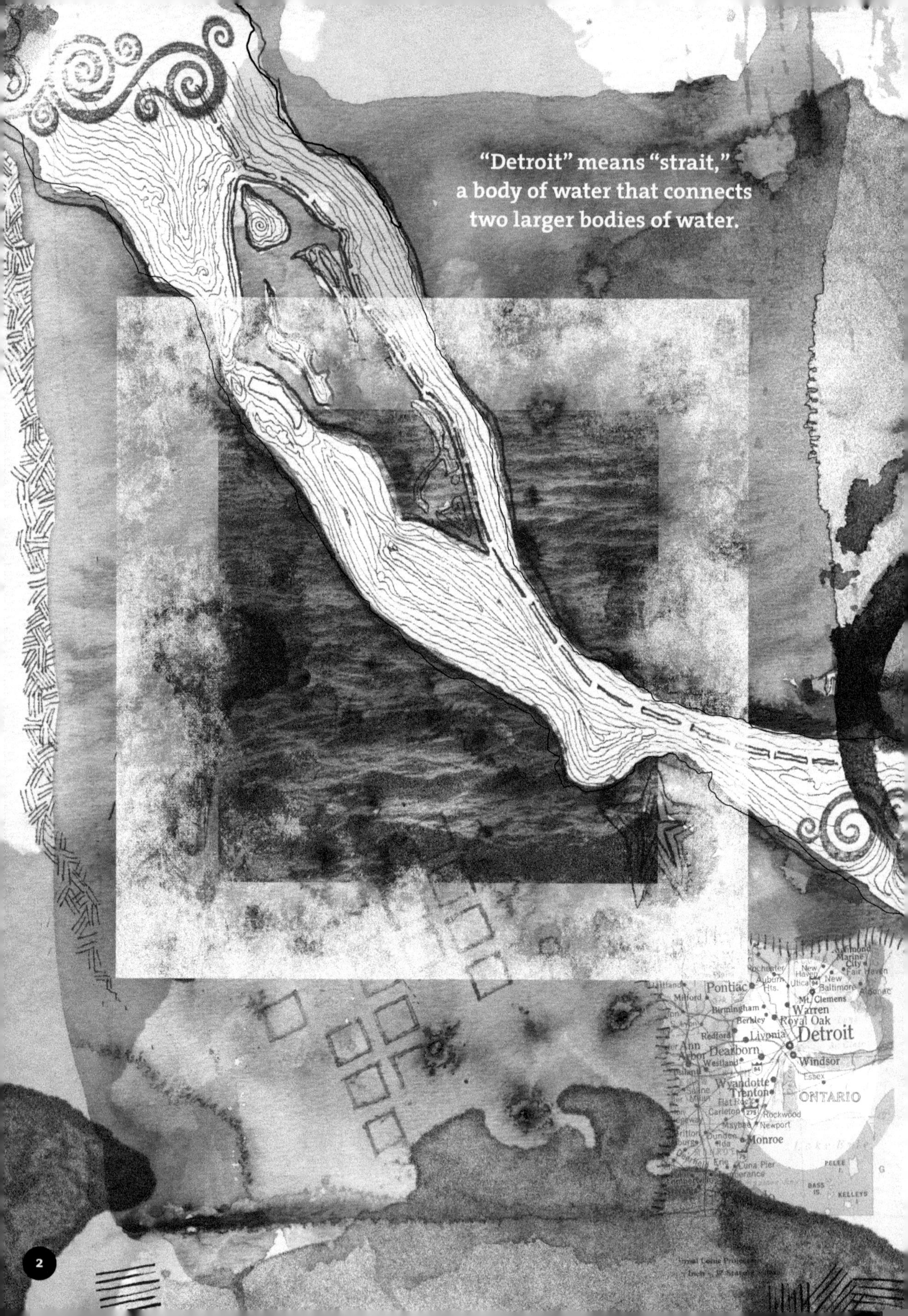
"Detroit" means "strait,"
a body of water that connects
two larger bodies of water.
Pontiac
Detroit
Windsor
Dearborn
Livonia
Royal Oak
Warren
Mt. Clemens
Birmingham
Redford
Westland
Wyandotte
Trenton
Monroe
ONTARIO

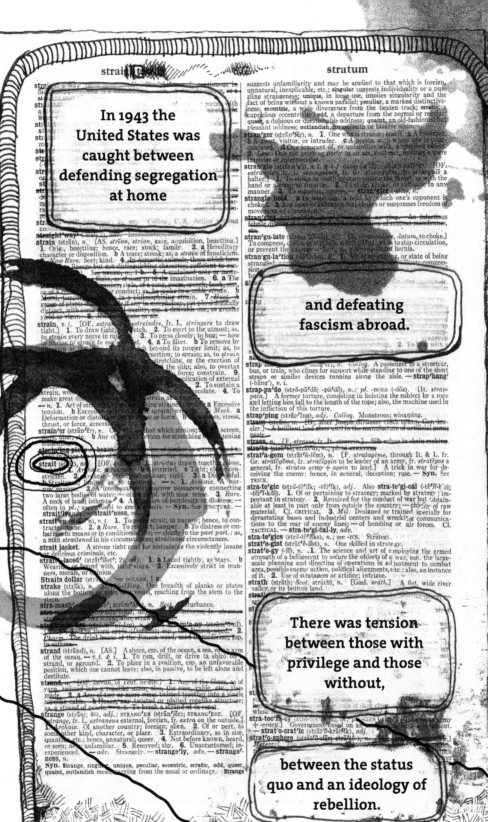

In 1943 the United States was caught between defending segregation at home

and defeating fascism abroad.

There was tension between those with privilege and those without,

between the status quo and an ideology of rebellion.

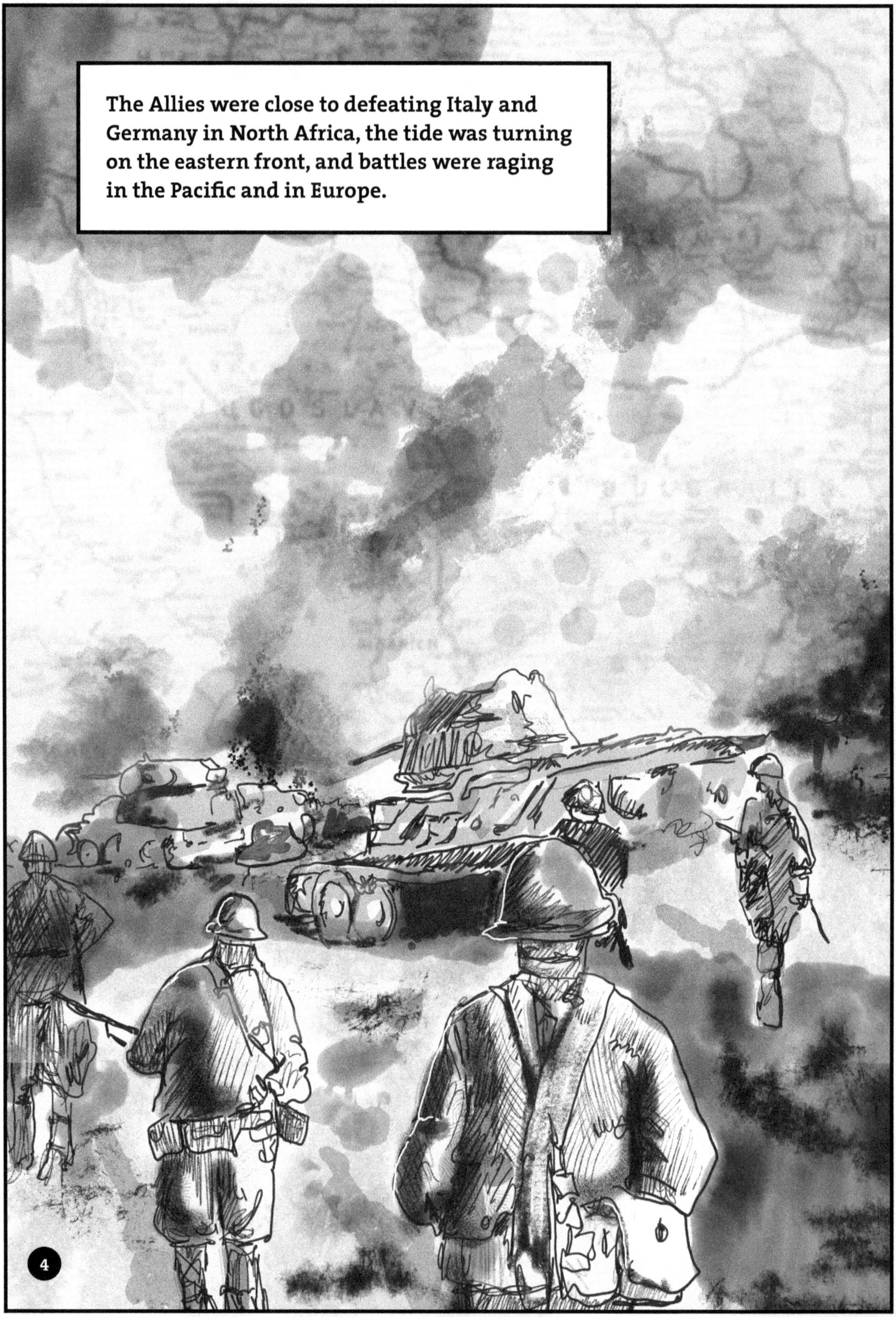
The Allies were close to defeating Italy and Germany in North Africa, the tide was turning on the eastern front, and battles were raging in the Pacific and in Europe.

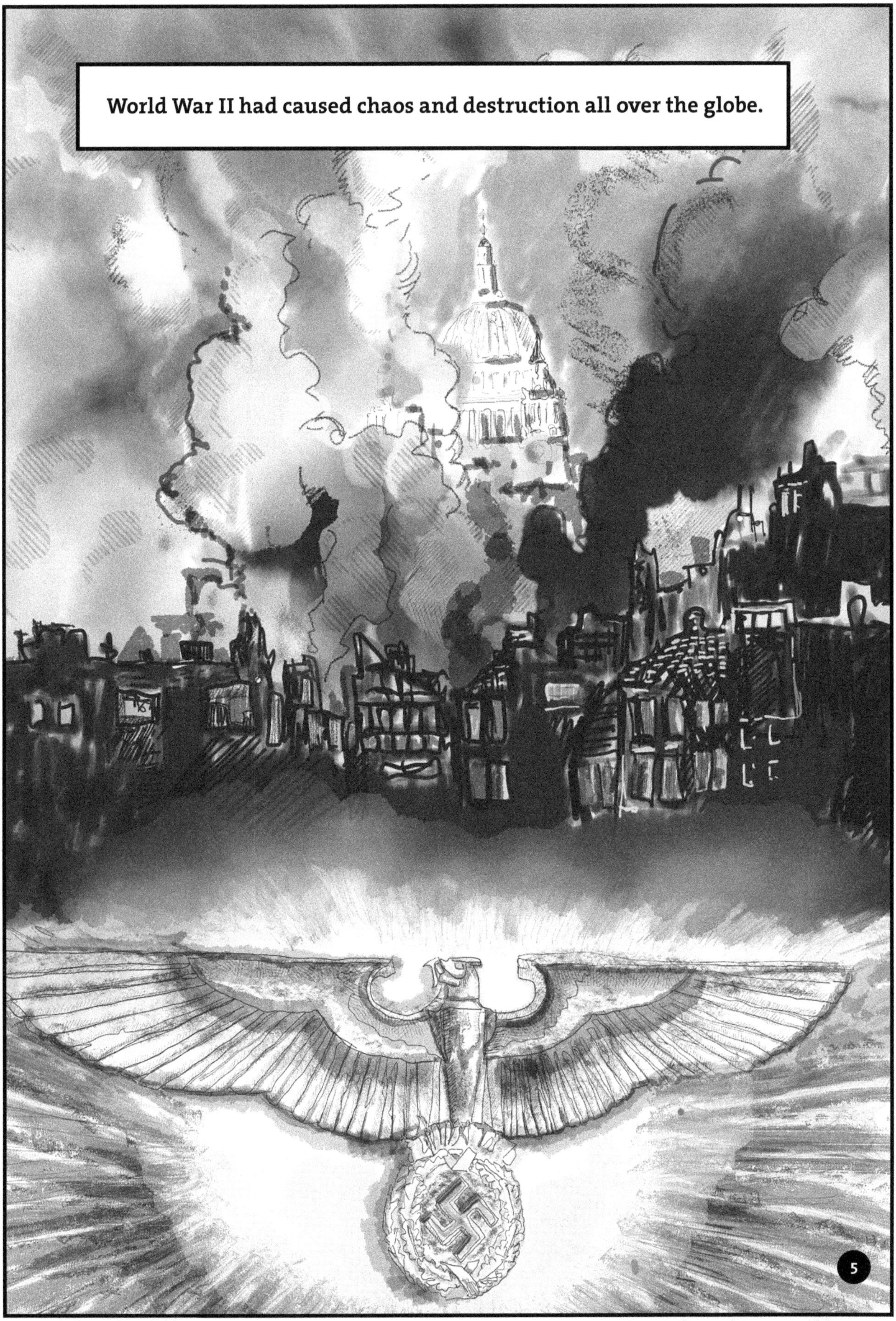
World War II had caused chaos and destruction all over the globe.

"V" for Victory
Victory over aggression, slavery, and tyranny
—JAMES THOMPSON, letter to the editor, *Pittsburgh Courier*, January 31, 1942

E PLURIBUS UNUM

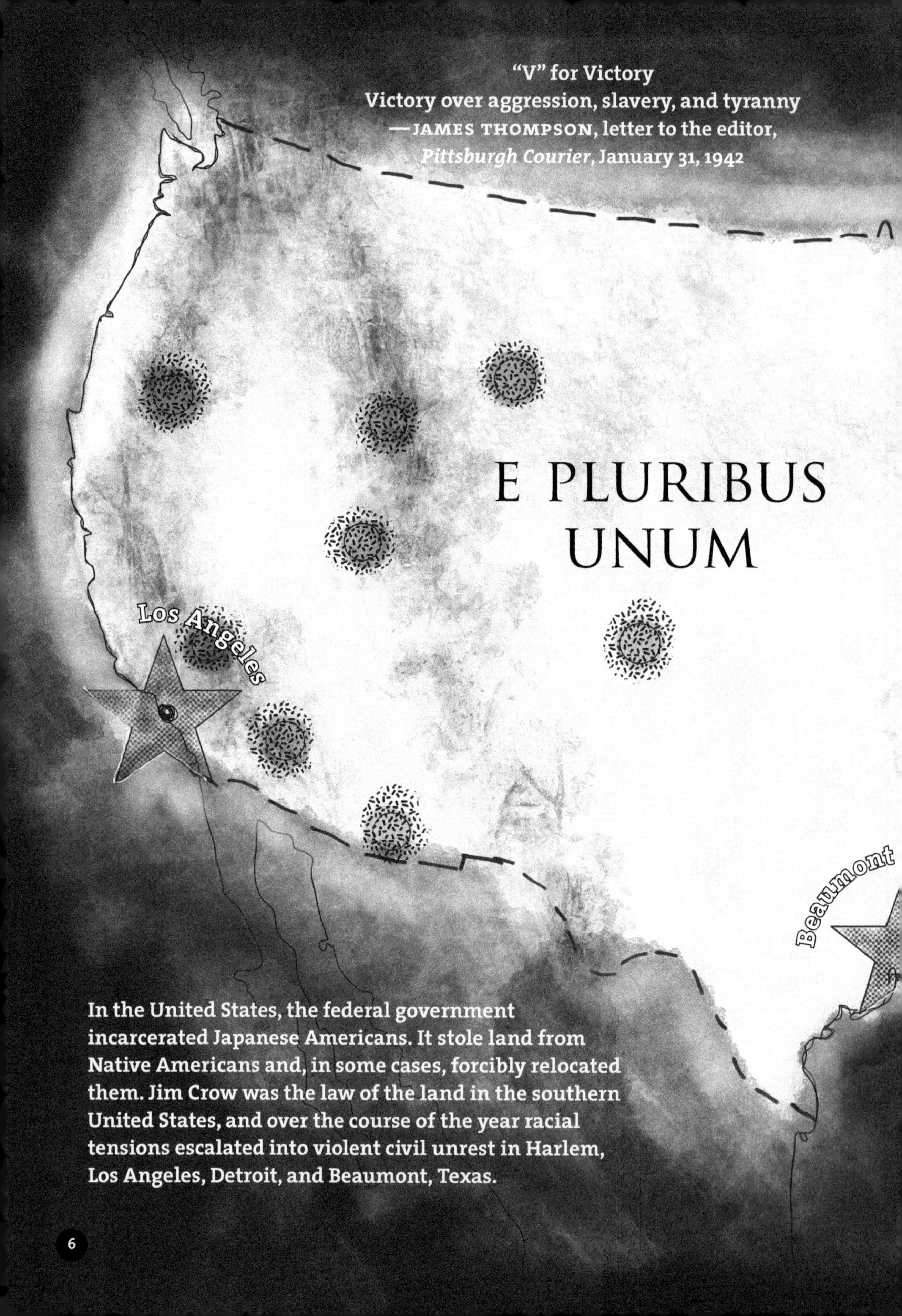
Los Angeles
Beaumont

In the United States, the federal government incarcerated Japanese Americans. It stole land from Native Americans and, in some cases, forcibly relocated them. Jim Crow was the law of the land in the southern United States, and over the course of the year racial tensions escalated into violent civil unrest in Harlem, Los Angeles, Detroit, and Beaumont, Texas.

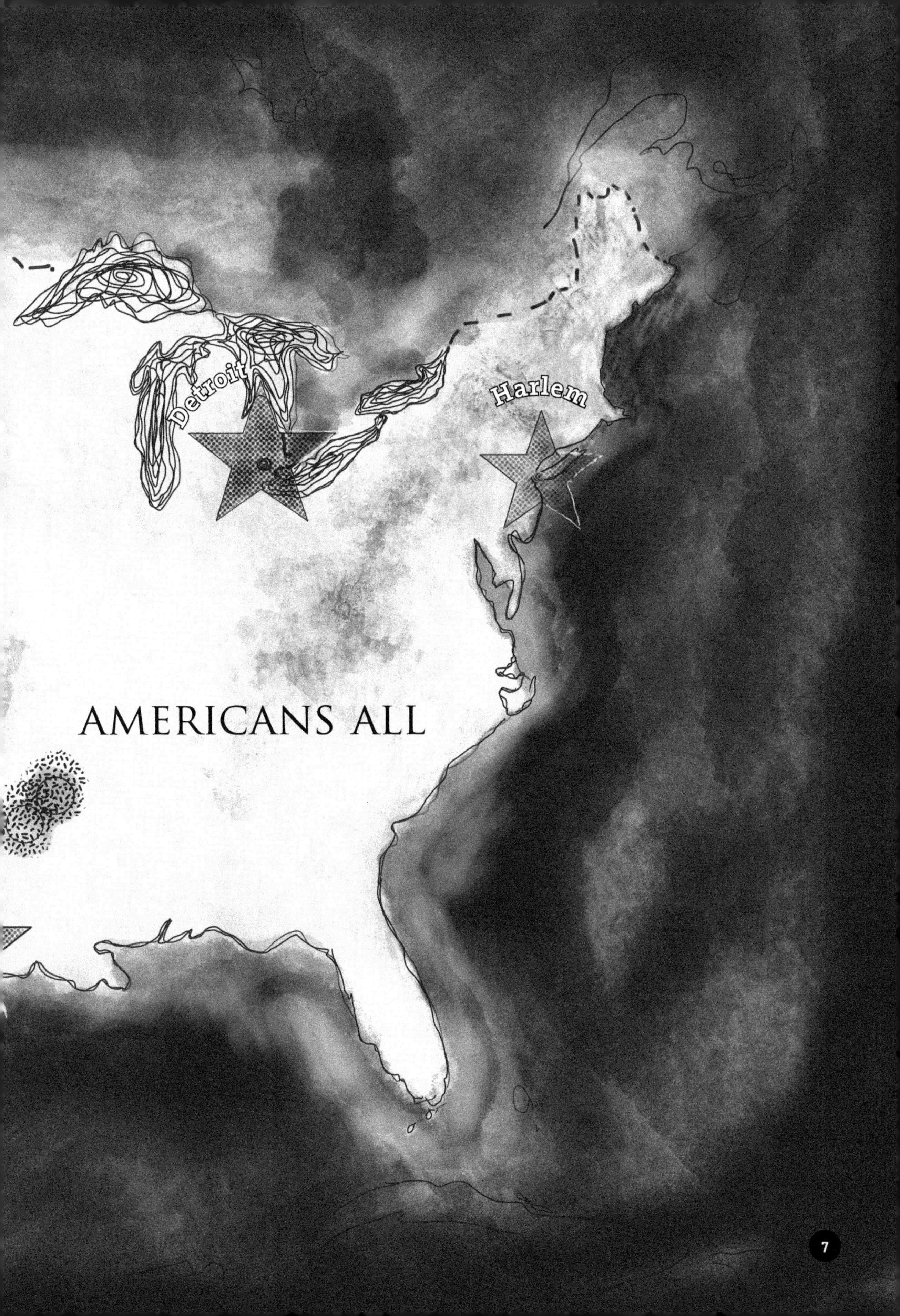
Detroit
Harlem

AMERICANS ALL

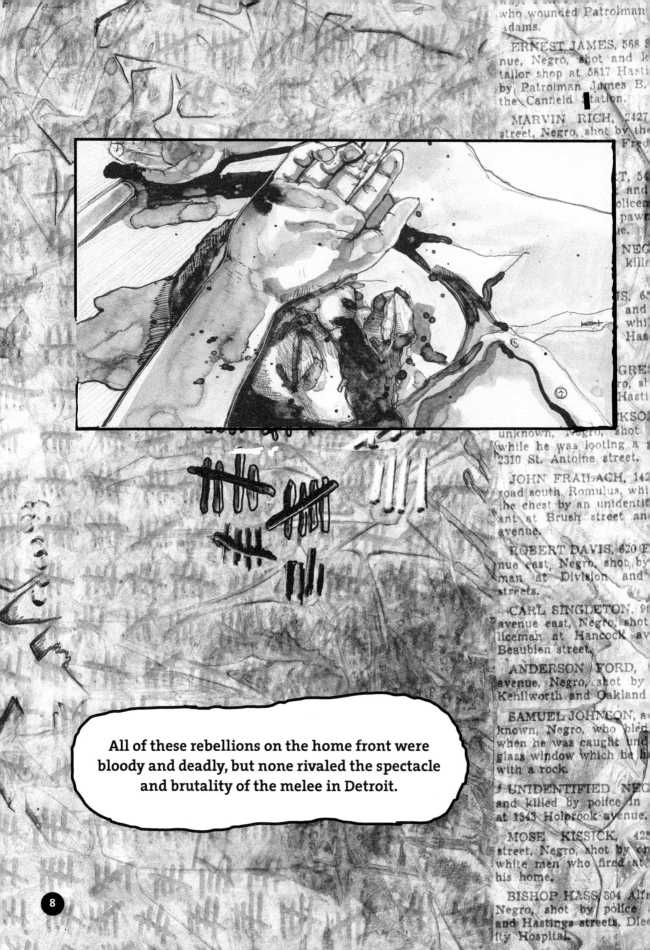

All of these rebellions on the home front were bloody and deadly, but none rivaled the spectacle and brutality of the melee in Detroit.

1
No Forgotten Men, No Forgotten Races

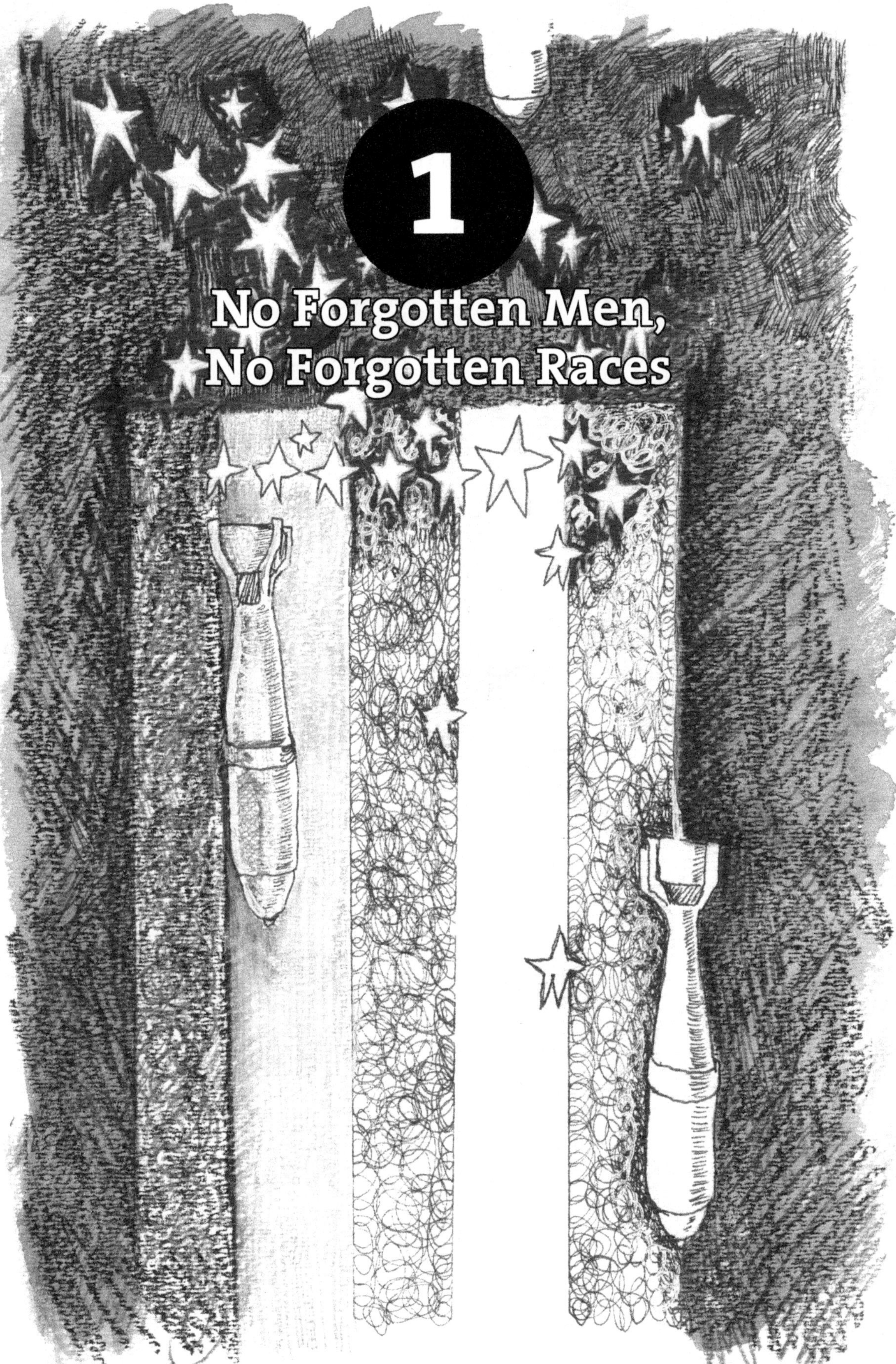

In the fall of 1940, A. Philip Randolph, from the Brotherhood of Sleeping Car Porters; Walter White, from the NAACP; and T. Arnold Hill, from the National Urban League, met with President Roosevelt, Secretary of the Navy Frank Knox, and Under Secretary of War Robert Patterson to discuss integrating the defense industries and the military.

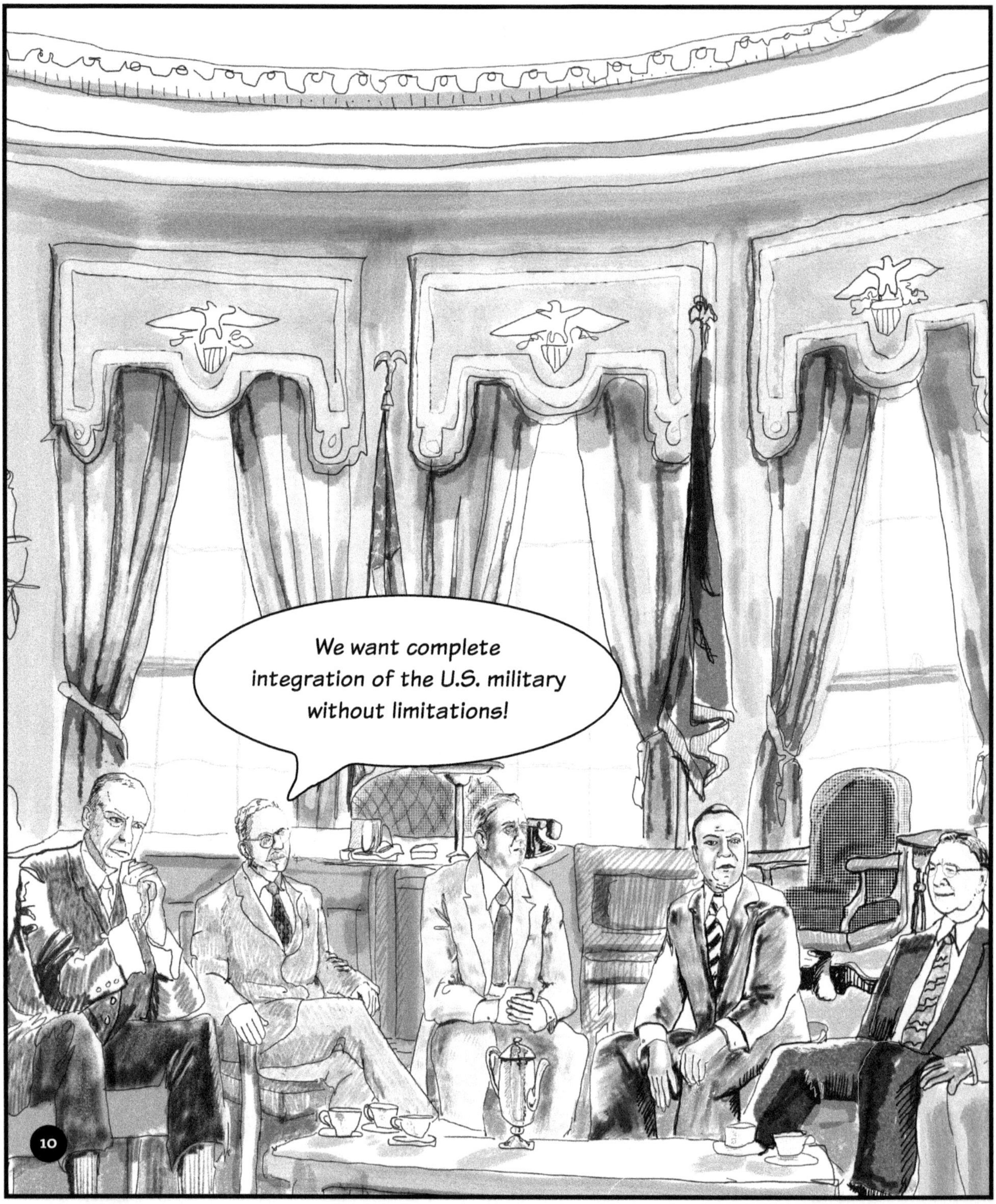
We want complete integration of the U.S. military without limitations!

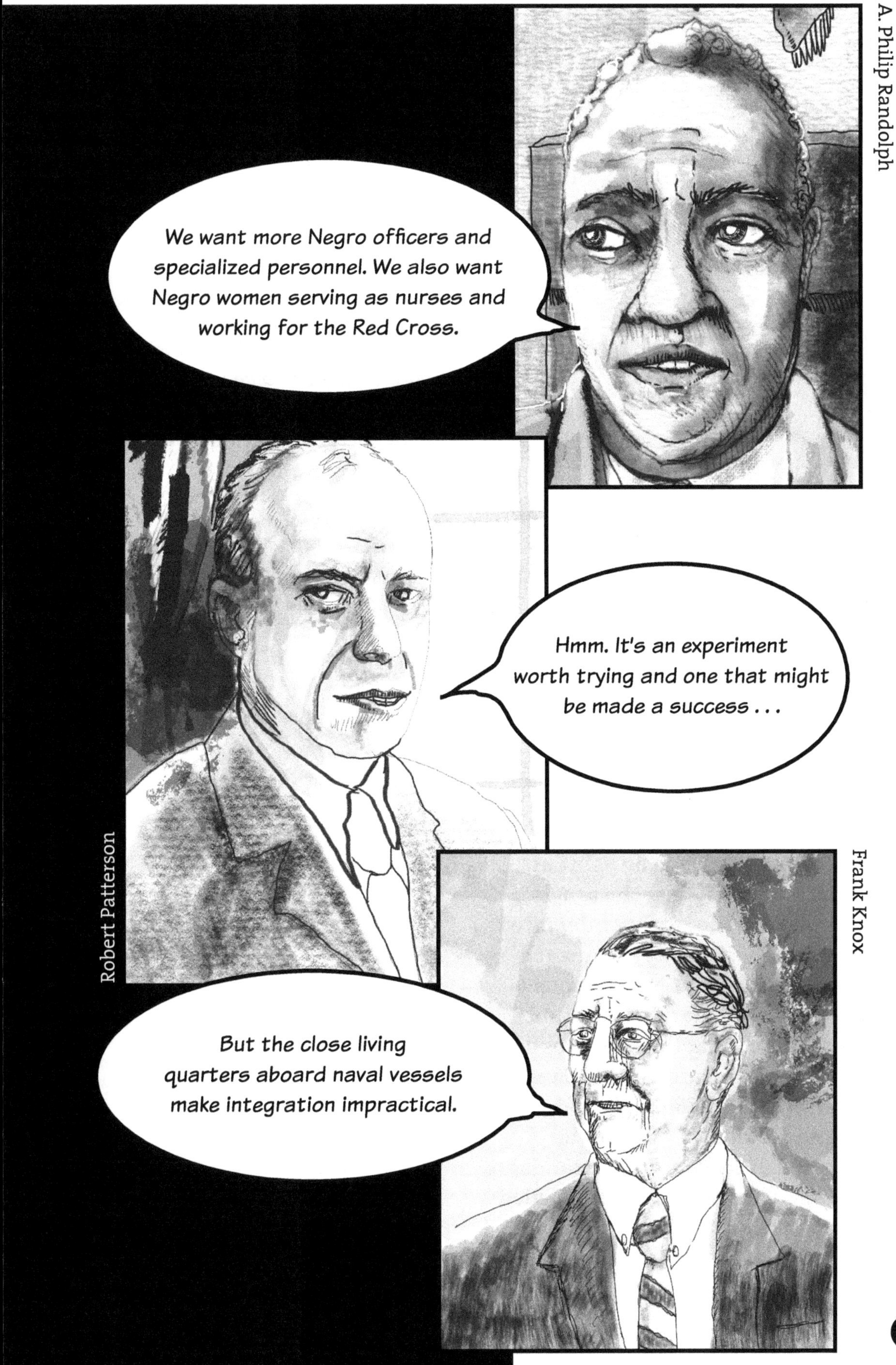
A. Philip Randolph
We want more Negro officers and specialized personnel. We also want Negro women serving as nurses and working for the Red Cross.
Robert Patterson
Hmm. It's an experiment worth trying and one that might be made a success . . .
Frank Knox
But the close living quarters aboard naval vessels make integration impractical.

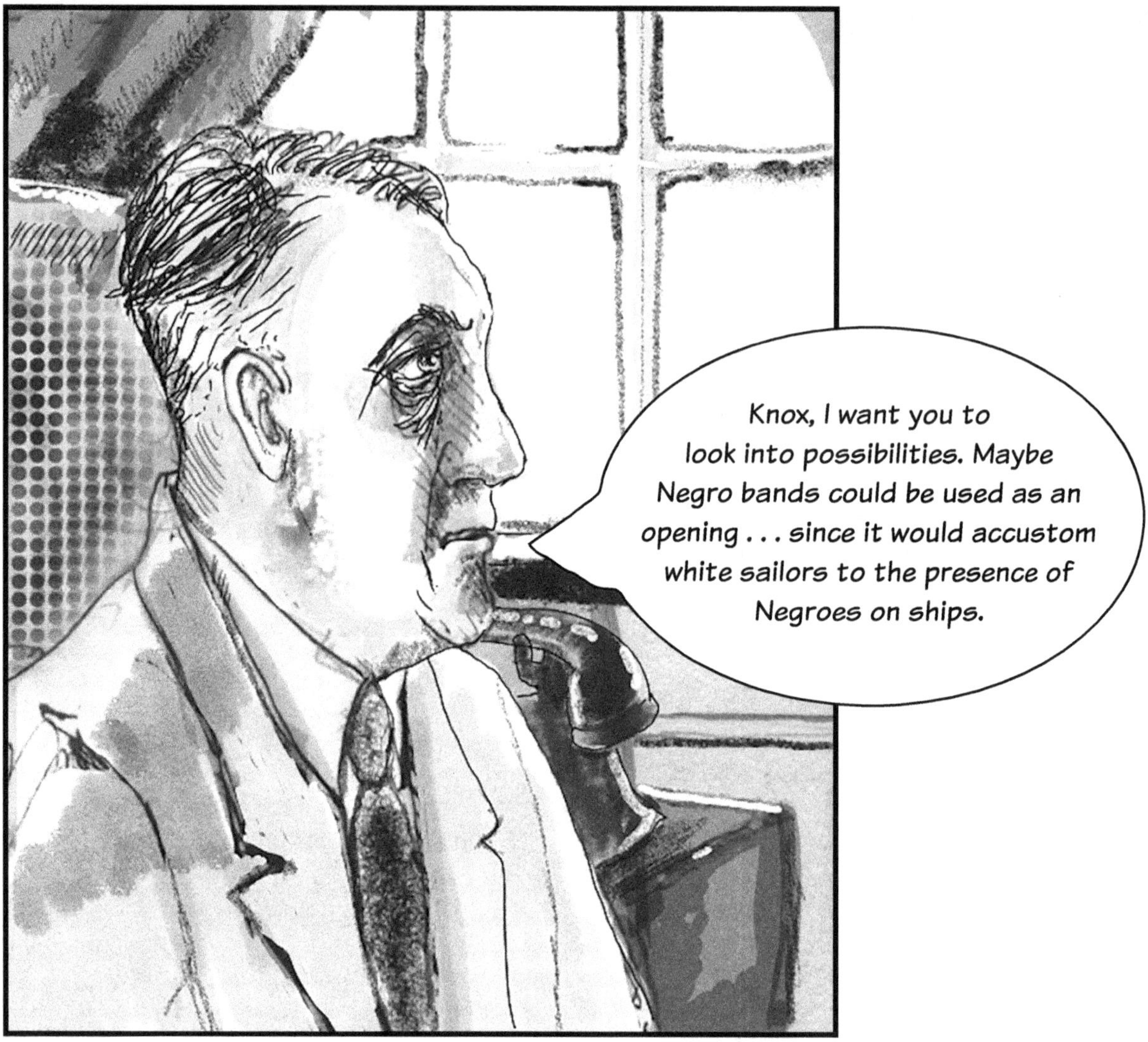
Knox, I want you to look into possibilities. Maybe Negro bands could be used as an opening . . . since it would accustom white sailors to the presence of Negroes on ships.

The meeting proved to be pointless, and the outcome—that the armed forces wouldn't be further integrated in any meaningful way—damaged the relationship that had tenuously existed between Black leaders and the White House. What followed was a White House misinformation campaign claiming that Randolph, Arnold, and White had endorsed the plan for segregated units. This understandably angered Black leaders and compelled them to take a different approach to integration of the armed forces.

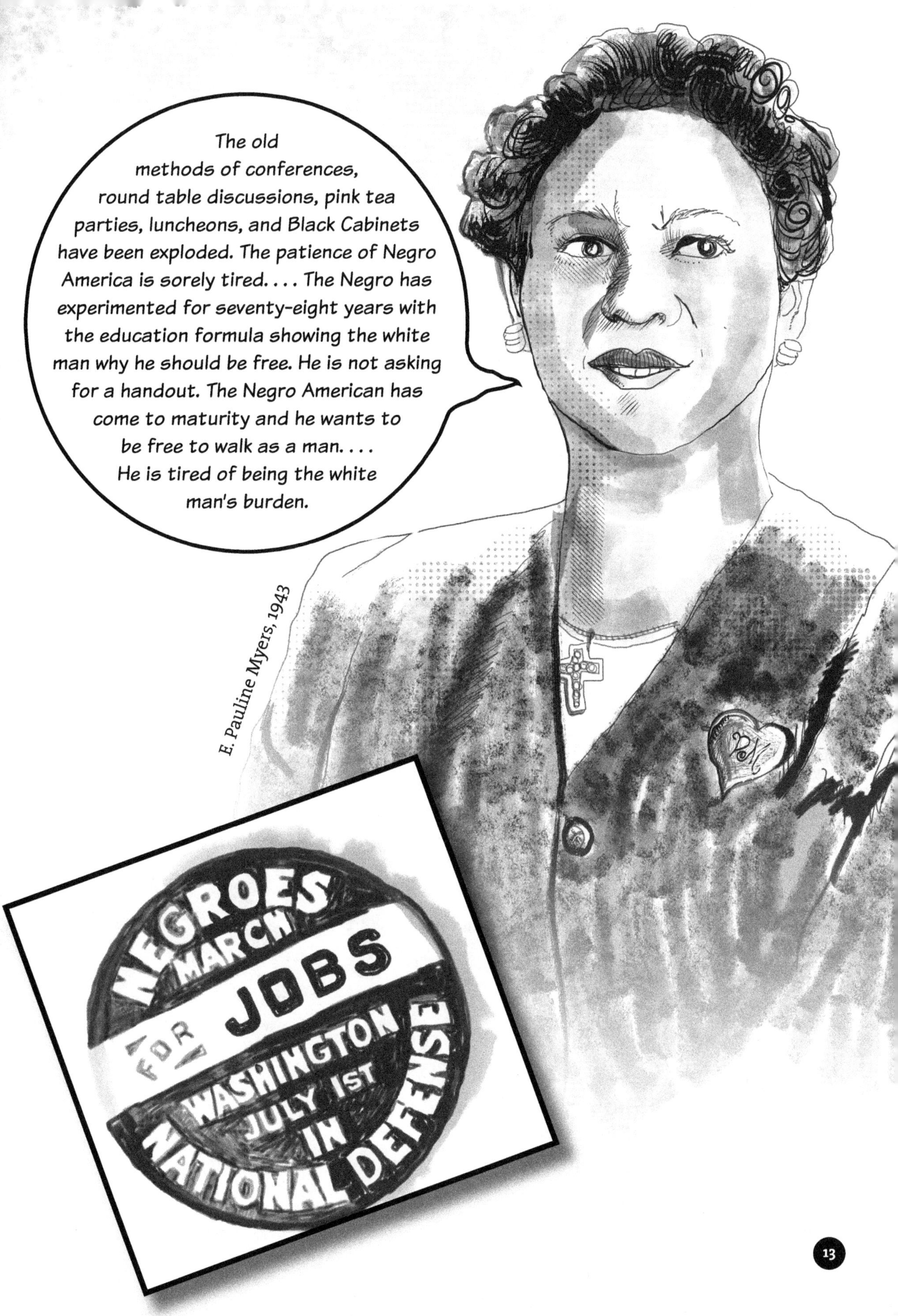

The old methods of conferences, round table discussions, pink tea parties, luncheons, and Black Cabinets have been exploded. The patience of Negro America is sorely tired. . . . The Negro has experimented for seventy-eight years with the education formula showing the white man why he should be free. He is not asking for a handout. The Negro American has come to maturity and he wants to be free to walk as a man. . . . He is tired of being the white man's burden.
NEGROES
MARCH
FOR
JOBS
WASHINGTON
JULY 1ST
IN
NATIONAL DEFENSE

E. Pauline Myers, 1943

2

The
FOUR FREEDOMS
Executive Order 8802

On January 6, 1941, Franklin Delano Roosevelt delivered the State of the Union address to members of the Seventy-Seventh Congress. He identified four freedoms that everyone should have: freedom of speech, freedom of worship, freedom from want, and freedom from fear. He also said, "Just as our national policy in internal affairs has been based upon a decent respect for the rights and dignity of all our fellow men within our gates, so our national policy in foreign affairs has been based on a decent respect for the rights and dignity of all nations, large and small. And the justice of morality must and will win in the end."

Despite these words, within the gates of the nation, turmoil and unrest brewed from the East Coast to the West Coast. Racial tension within the nation grew as people migrated to escape poverty, seek better housing, and create opportunities that would lead to brighter futures for their families.

Discrimination was rampant. In cities everywhere it was evident that within the United States there was a racial caste system that suppressed opportunity for Black and brown people.

A Democratic congressman from Illinois, Arthur W. Mitchell, listened to the president's speech. He was the only African American serving in the House of Representatives at the time. There had not been a Black senator since 1881.

The voices of people of color had been stifled and ignored. Roosevelt's speech expressed a series of ideals that the United States was not putting into practice. This was especially true for freedom from want and freedom from fear.

"In the future days, which we seek to make secure, we look forward to a world founded upon four essential human freedoms."

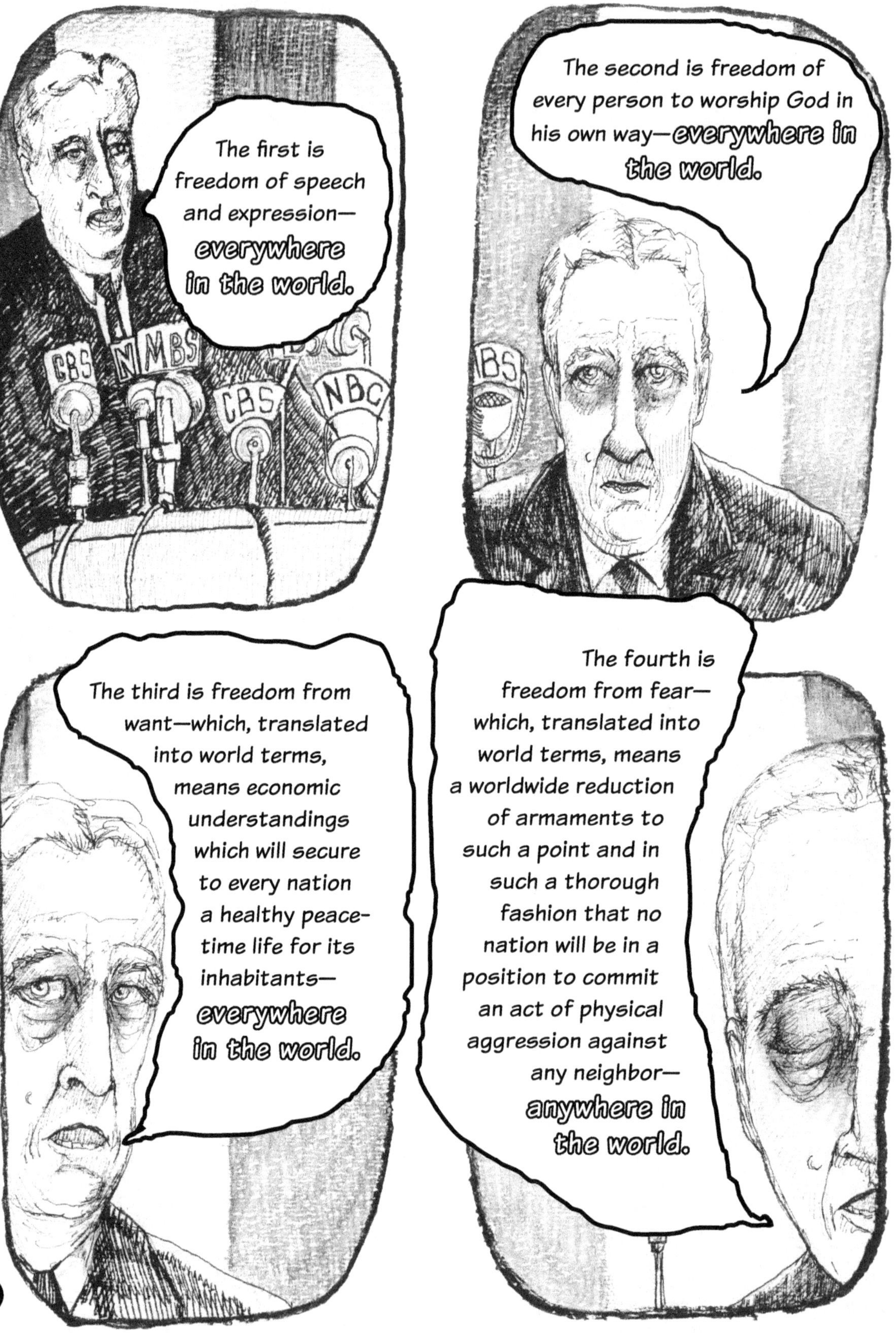
The first is freedom of speech and expression—everywhere in the world.
The second is freedom of every person to worship God in his own way—everywhere in the world.
The third is freedom from want—which, translated into world terms, means economic understandings which will secure to every nation a healthy peace-time life for its inhabitants—everywhere in the world.
The fourth is freedom from fear—which, translated into world terms, means a worldwide reduction of armaments to such a point and in such a thorough fashion that no nation will be in a position to commit an act of physical aggression against any neighbor—anywhere in the world.

January 6, 1941

While FDR spoke of the Four Freedoms, Black Americans still were not free from fear or want. The prosperous economy had not made the lives of many African Americans better. They were unable to gain employment in the defense industries, couldn't live where they wanted, and weren't treated fairly by the law or the military. After the 1940 meeting, a number of Black leaders—including A. Philip Randolph, Walter White, Ella Baker, T. Arnold Hill, E. Pauline Myers, and Layle Lane—called for action.

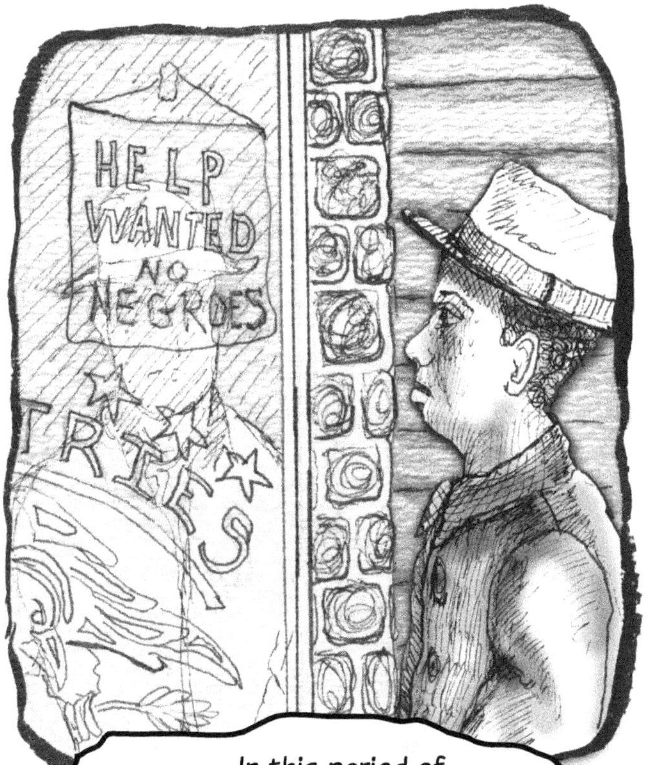
HELP WANTED NO NEGROES

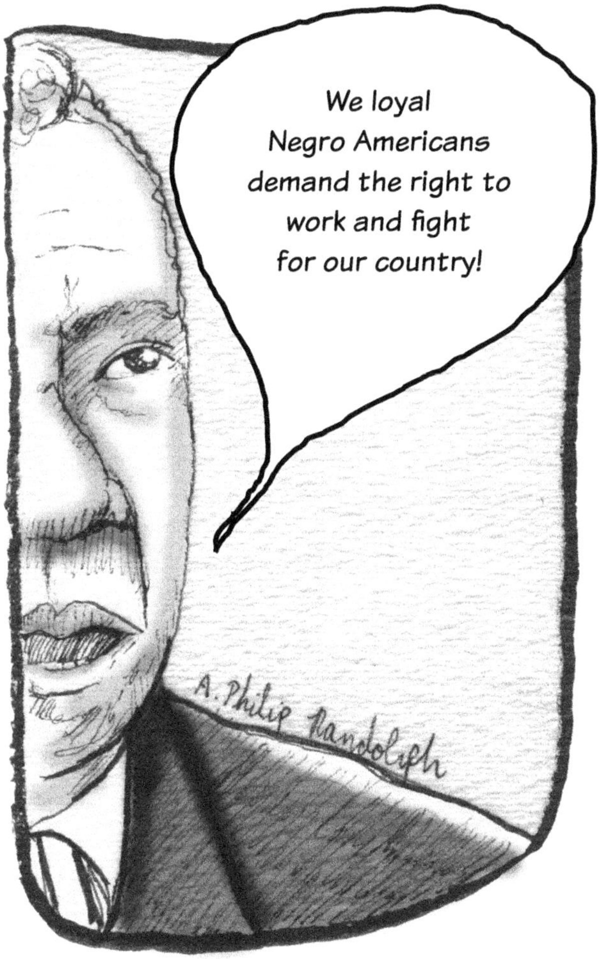
We loyal Negro Americans demand the right to work and fight for our country!
A. Philip Randolph

January 15, 1941

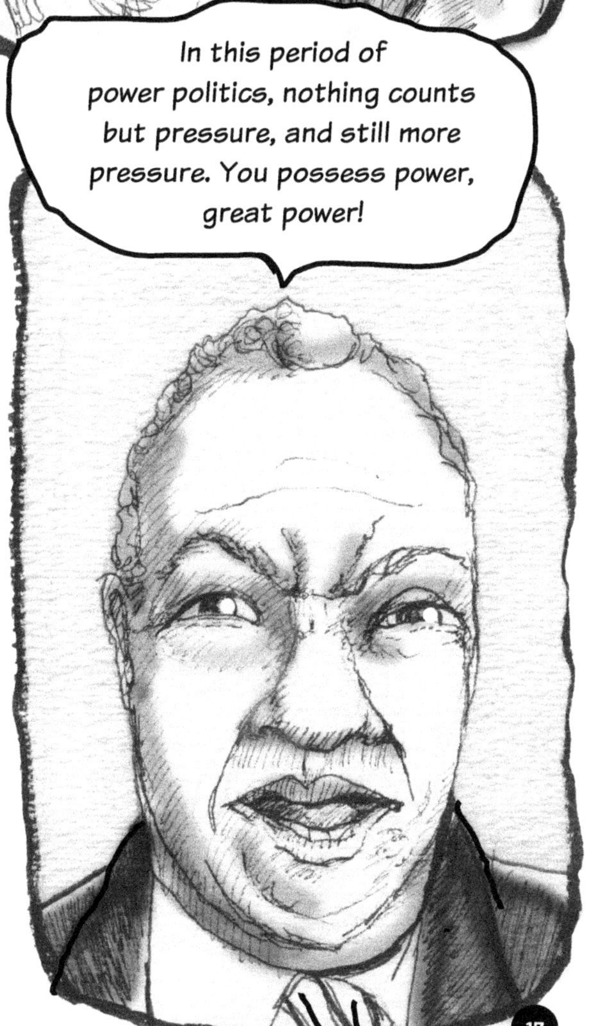
In this period of power politics, nothing counts but pressure, and still more pressure. You possess power, great power!

January 25, 1941

Black Americans were tired of hearing rhetoric from people in positions of power that did not reflect their lived experience and the segregation and discrimination they faced on a daily basis. At the 1941 NAACP annual convention there was a call for complete integration and an end to segregation.

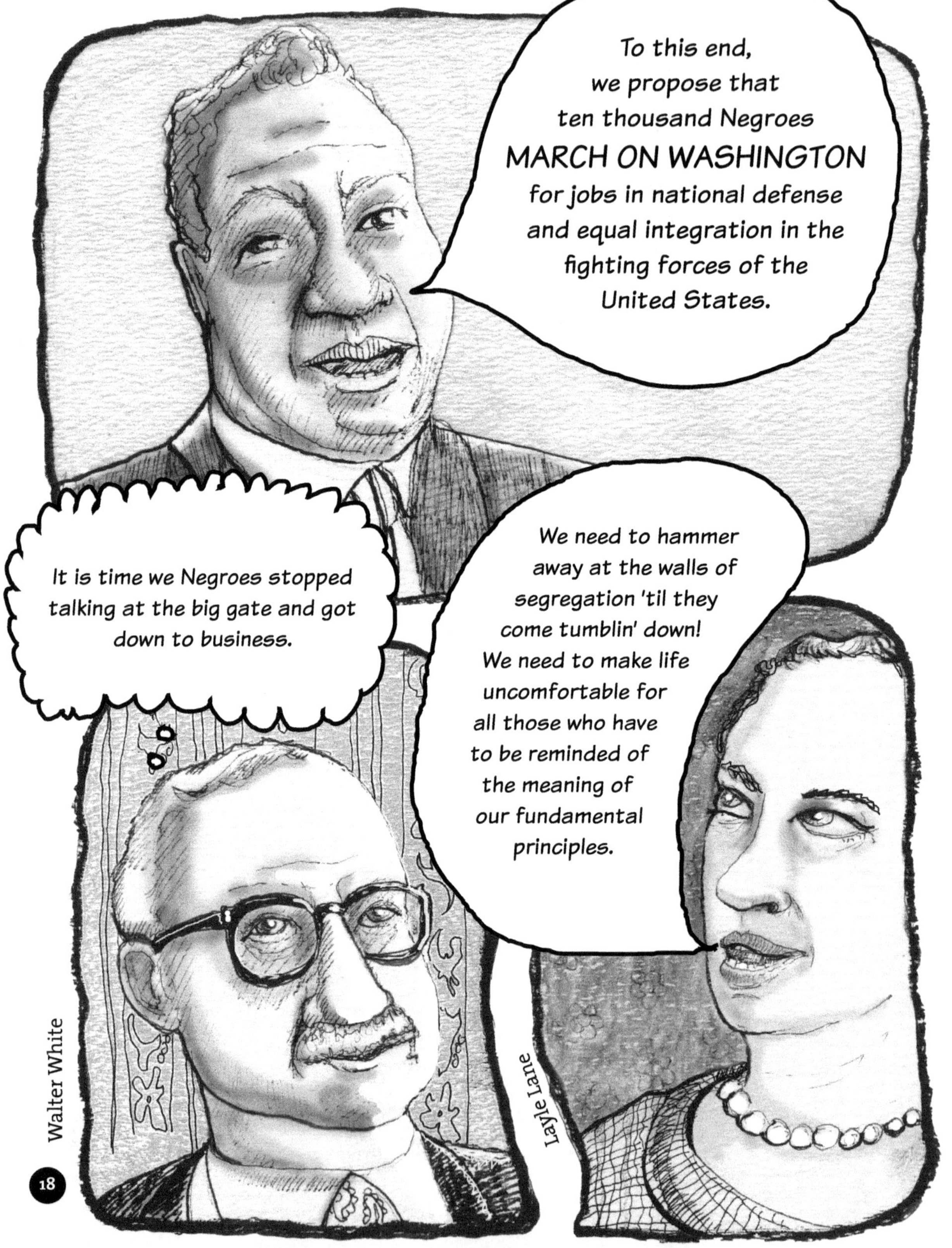
To this end, we propose that ten thousand Negroes MARCH ON WASHINGTON for jobs in national defense and equal integration in the fighting forces of the United States.
It is time we Negroes stopped talking at the big gate and got down to business.
We need to hammer away at the walls of segregation 'til they come tumblin' down! We need to make life uncomfortable for all those who have to be reminded of the meaning of our fundamental principles.
Walter White
Layle Lane

Many white people felt these tactics were unpatriotic.

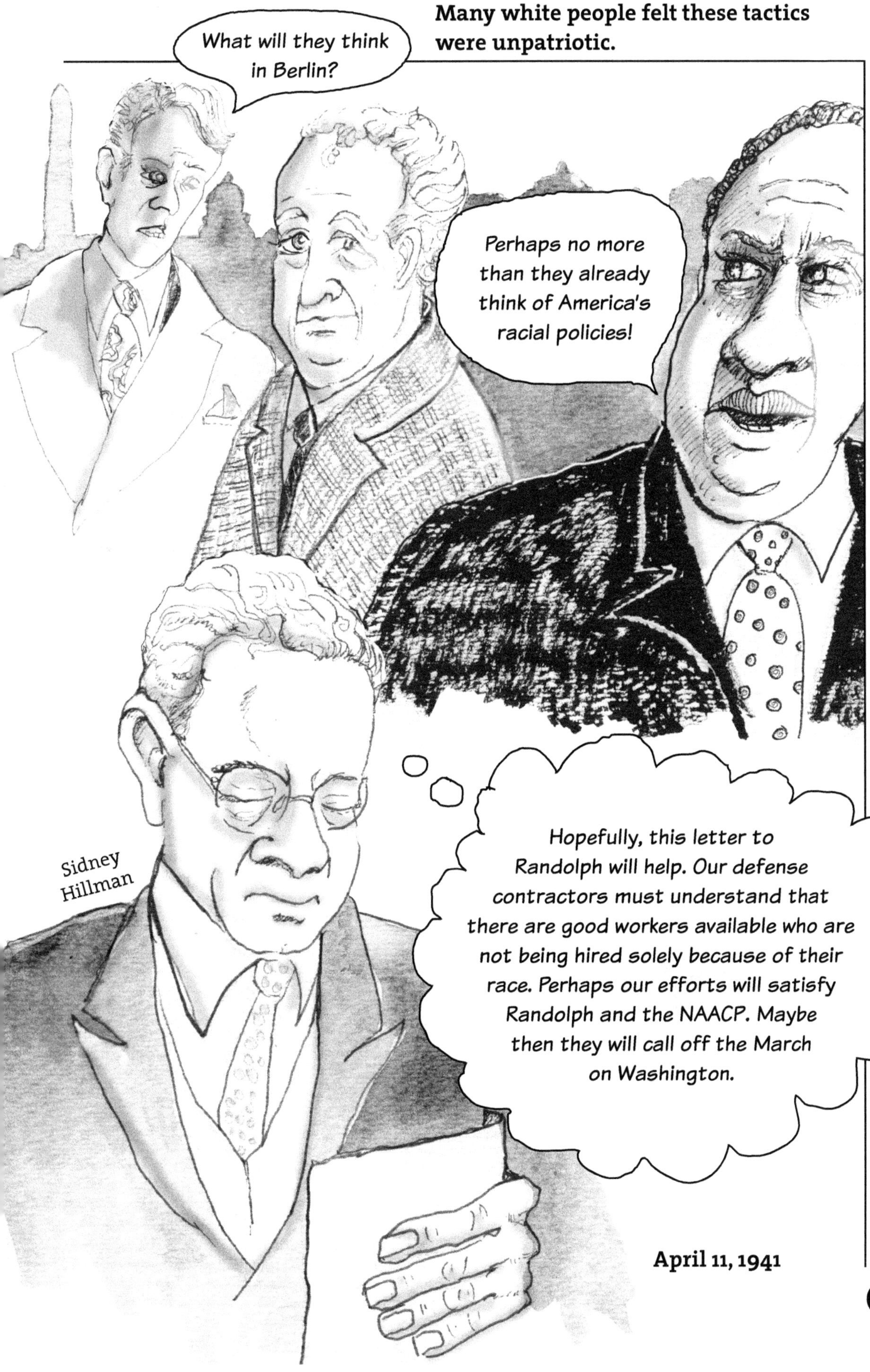
What will they think in Berlin?
Perhaps no more than they already think of America's racial policies!
Sidney Hillman
Hopefully, this letter to Randolph will help. Our defense contractors must understand that there are good workers available who are not being hired solely because of their race. Perhaps our efforts will satisfy Randolph and the NAACP. Maybe then they will call off the March on Washington.
April 11, 1941

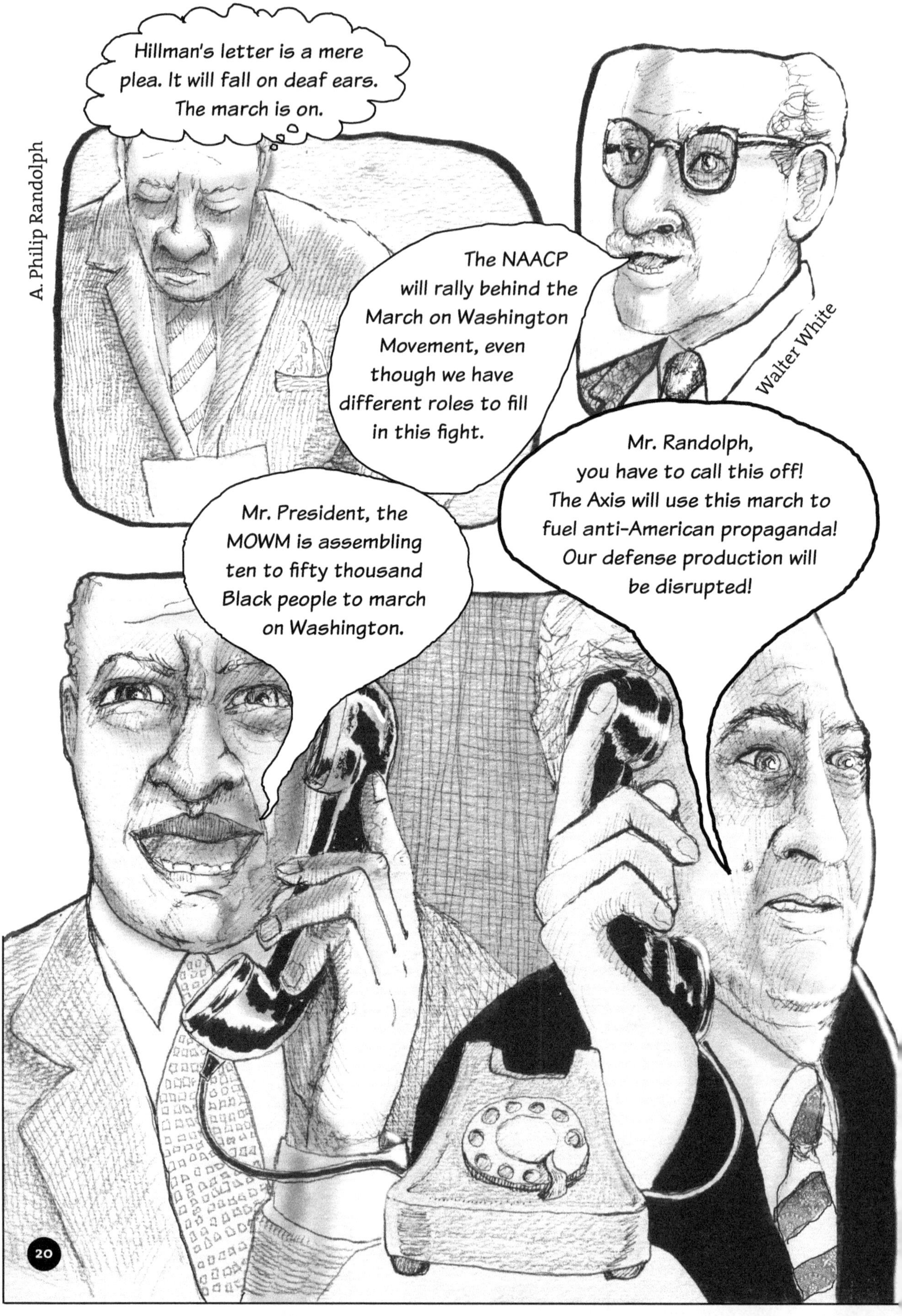
Hillman's letter is a mere plea. It will fall on deaf ears. The march is on.
A. Philip Randolph
The NAACP will rally behind the March on Washington Movement, even though we have different roles to fill in this fight.
Walter White
Mr. President, the MOWM is assembling ten to fifty thousand Black people to march on Washington.
Mr. Randolph, you have to call this off! The Axis will use this march to fuel anti-American propaganda! Our defense production will be disrupted!

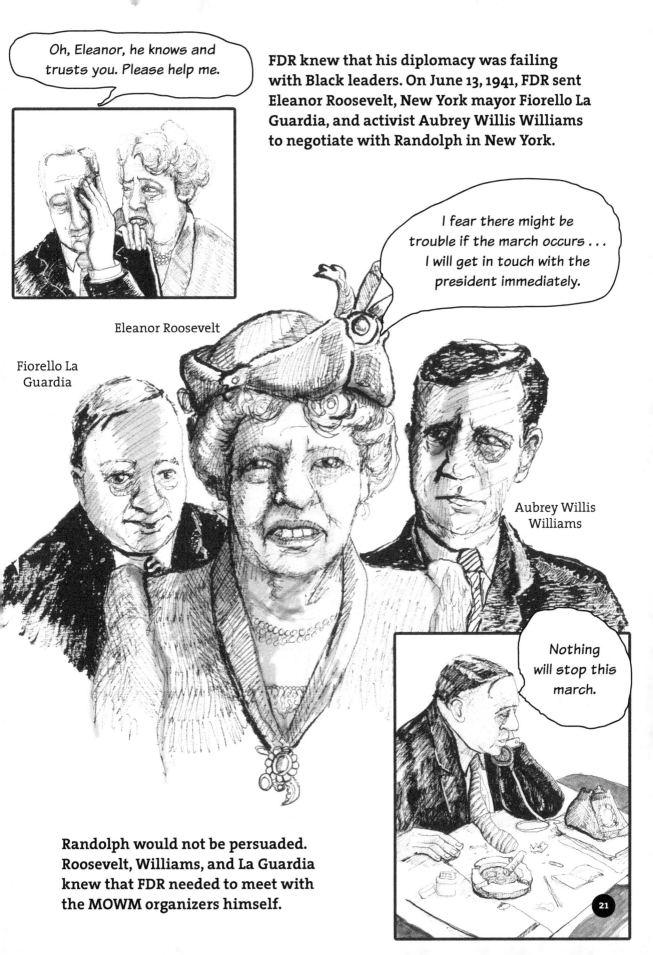

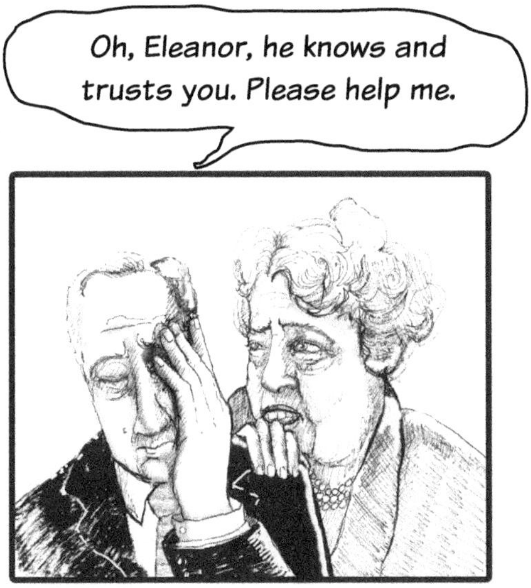
Oh, Eleanor, he knows and trusts you. Please help me.

FDR knew that his diplomacy was failing with Black leaders. On June 13, 1941, FDR sent Eleanor Roosevelt, New York mayor Fiorello La Guardia, and activist Aubrey Willis Williams to negotiate with Randolph in New York.

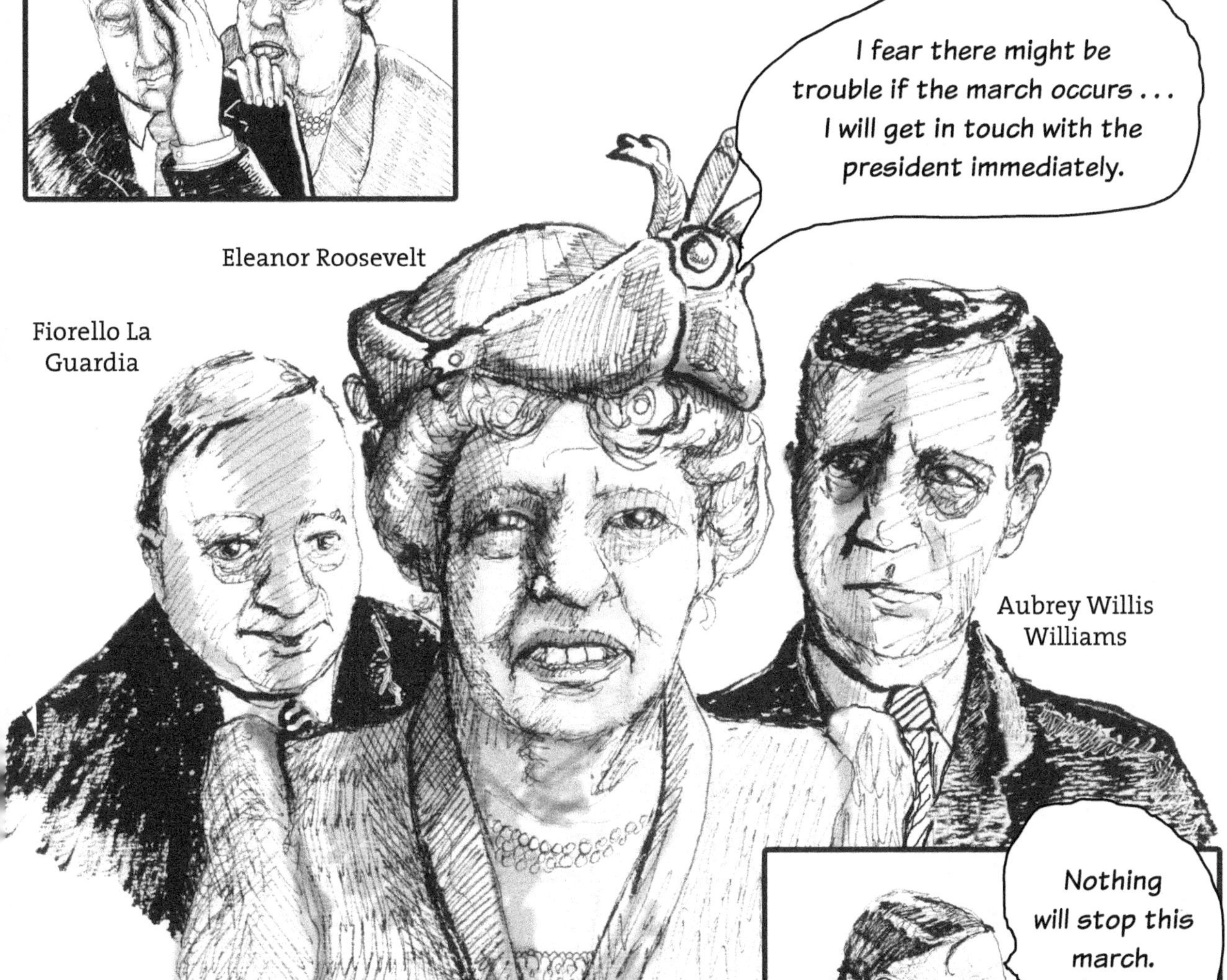
I fear there might be trouble if the march occurs . . . I will get in touch with the president immediately.
Eleanor Roosevelt
Fiorello La Guardia
Aubrey Willis Williams

Randolph would not be persuaded. Roosevelt, Williams, and La Guardia knew that FDR needed to meet with the MOWM organizers himself.

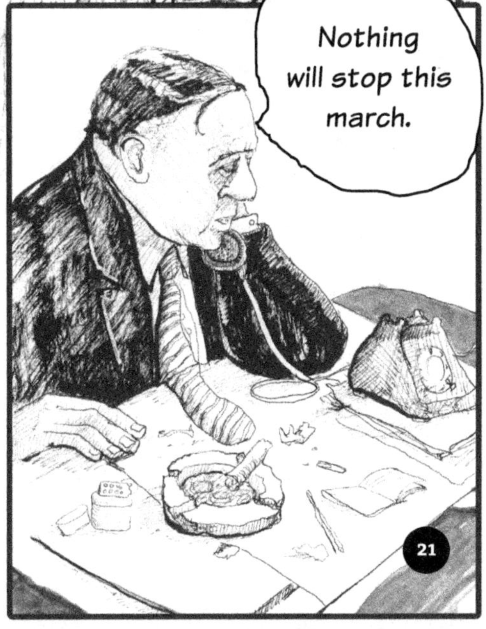
Nothing will stop this march.

On June 18, 1941, a group of leaders including A. Philip Randolph, Walter White, Franklin D. Roosevelt, and Fiorello La Guardia met at the White House.

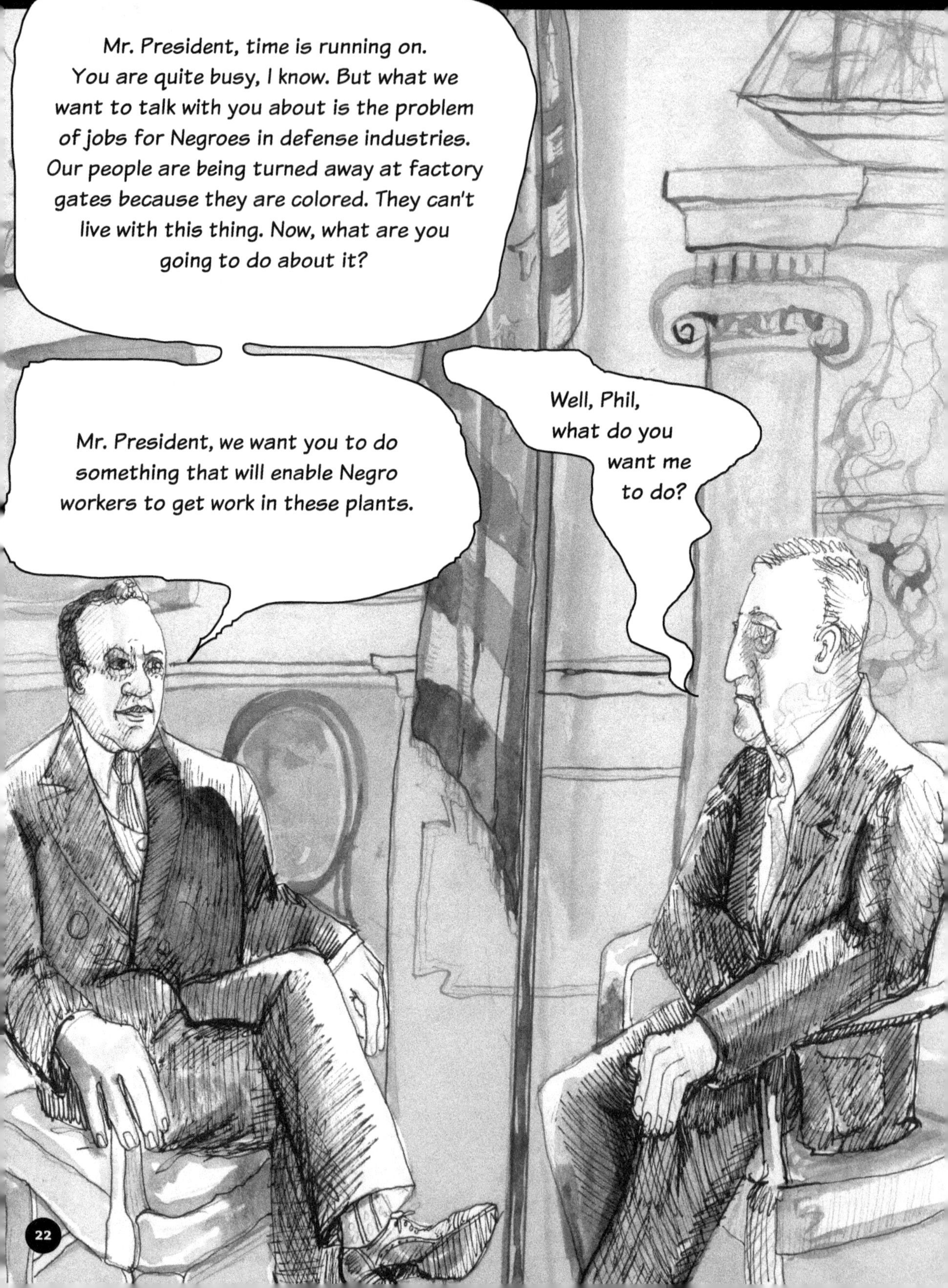
Mr. President, time is running on. You are quite busy, I know. But what we want to talk with you about is the problem of jobs for Negroes in defense industries. Our people are being turned away at factory gates because they are colored. They can't live with this thing. Now, what are you going to do about it?
Mr. President, we want you to do something that will enable Negro workers to get work in these plants.
Well, Phil, what do you want me to do?

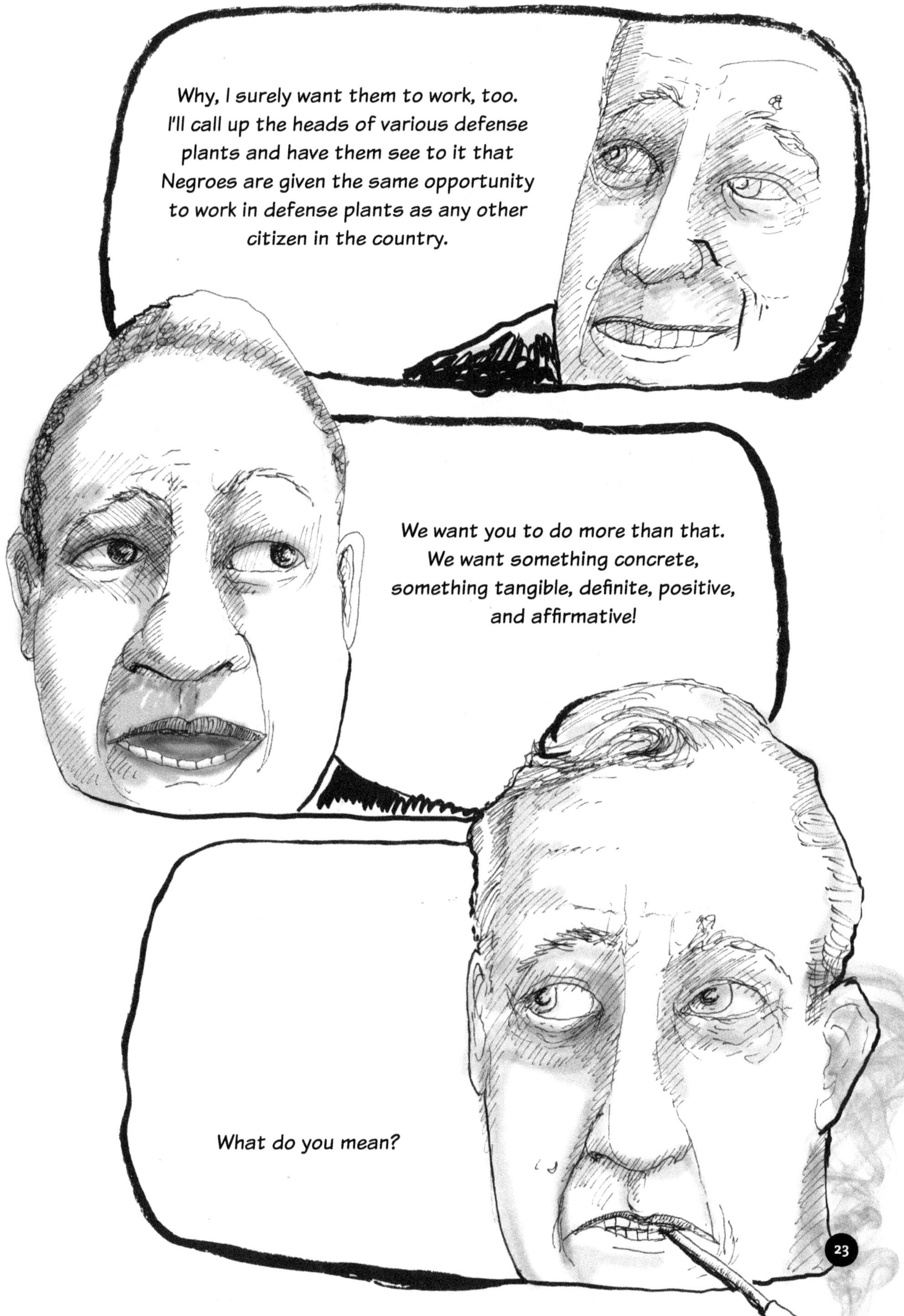
Why, I surely want them to work, too. I'll call up the heads of various defense plants and have them see to it that Negroes are given the same opportunity to work in defense plants as any other citizen in the country.
We want you to do more than that. We want something concrete, something tangible, definite, positive, and affirmative!
What do you mean?

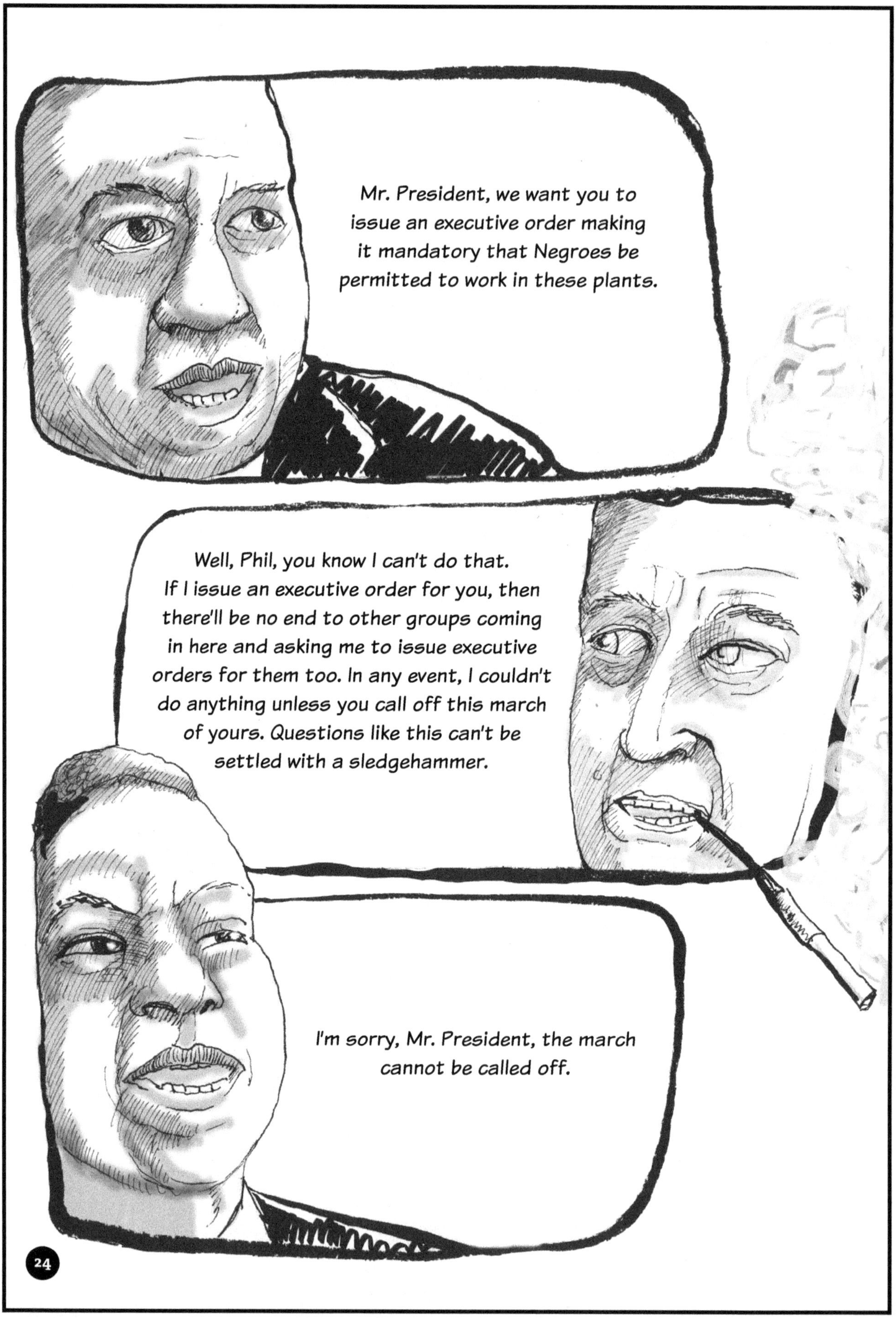
Mr. President, we want you to issue an executive order making it mandatory that Negroes be permitted to work in these plants.
Well, Phil, you know I can't do that. If I issue an executive order for you, then there'll be no end to other groups coming in here and asking me to issue executive orders for them too. In any event, I couldn't do anything unless you call off this march of yours. Questions like this can't be settled with a sledgehammer.
I'm sorry, Mr. President, the march cannot be called off.

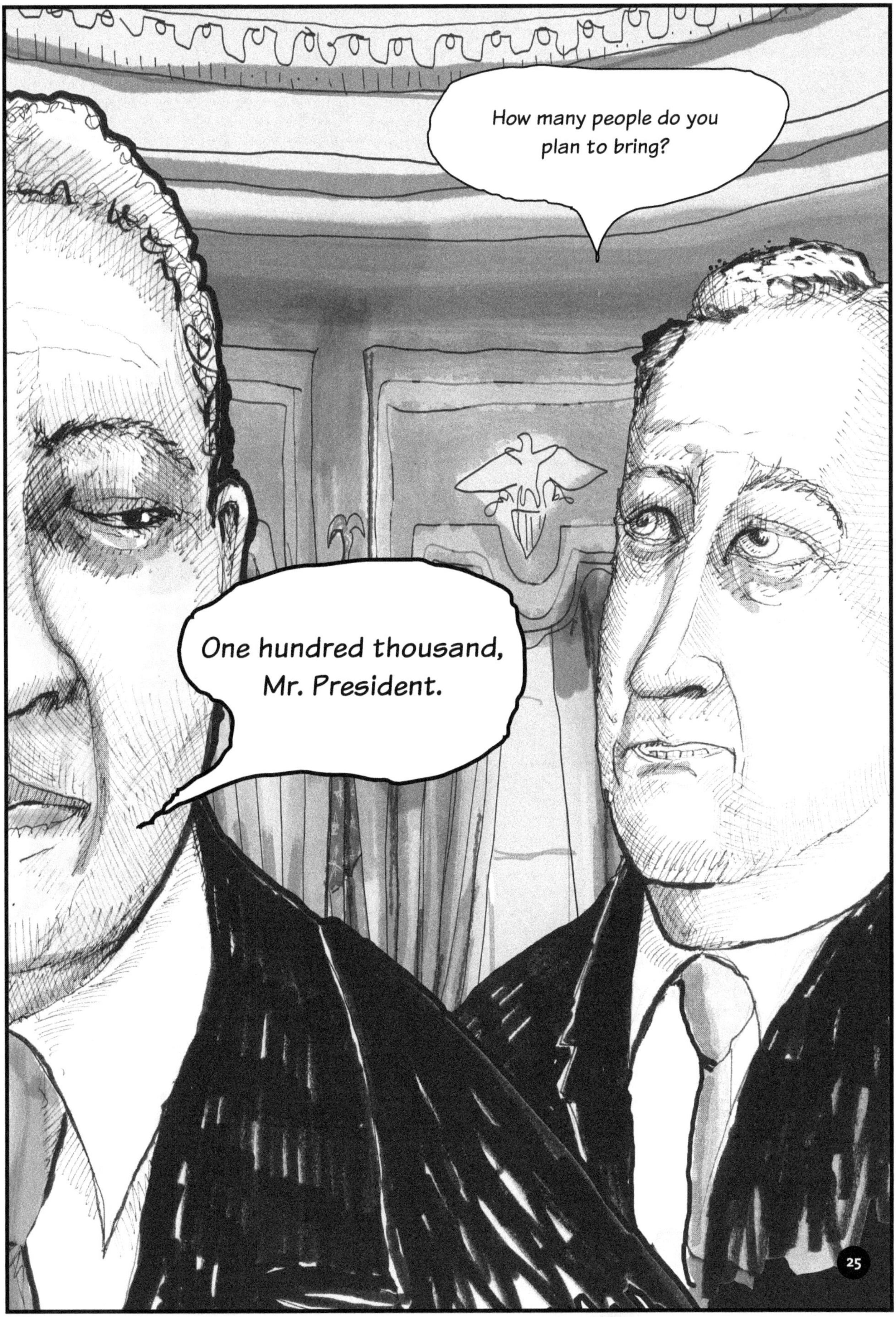
How many people do you plan to bring?
One hundred thousand, Mr. President.

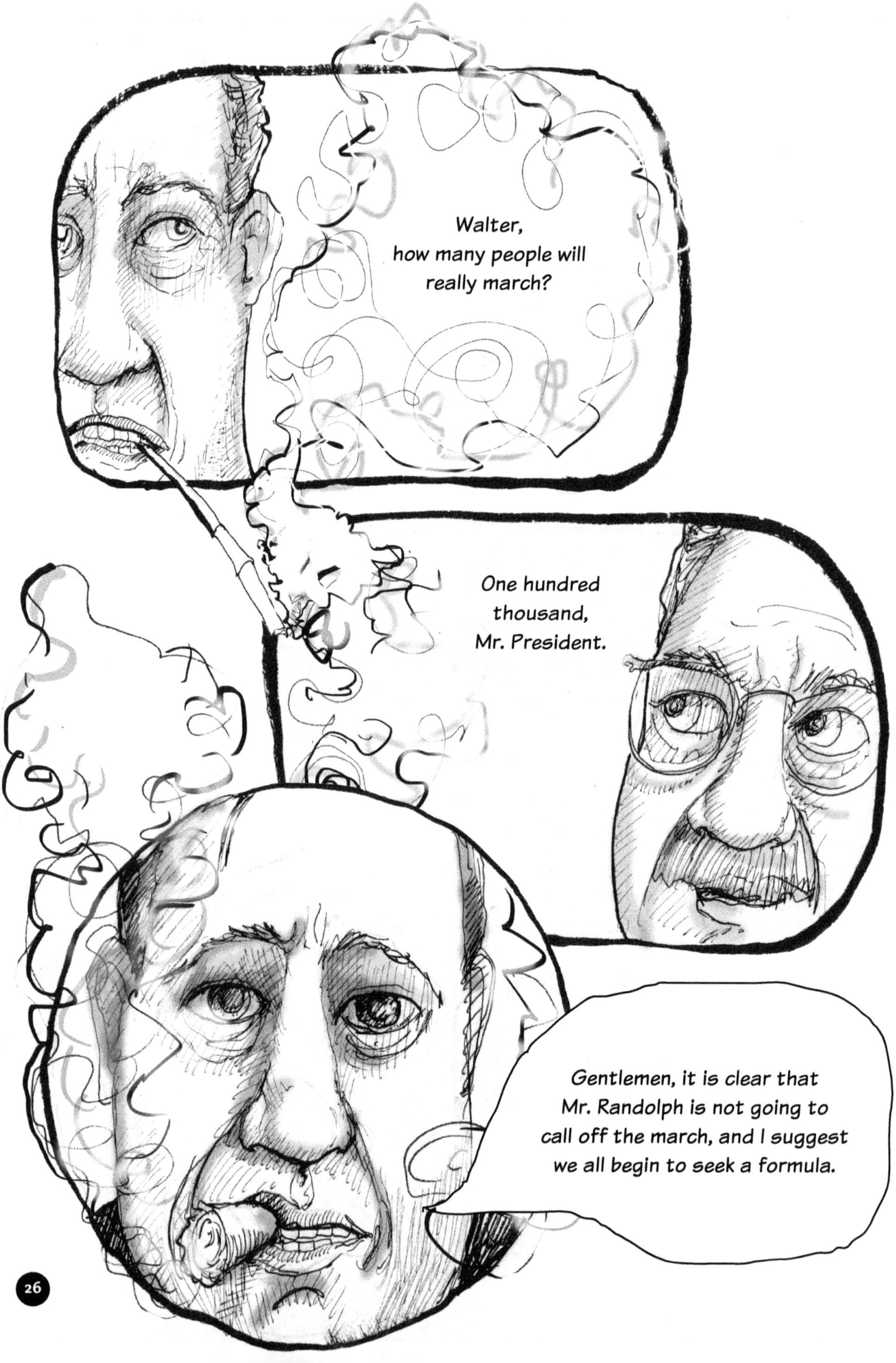
Walter, how many people will really march?
One hundred thousand, Mr. President.
Gentlemen, it is clear that Mr. Randolph is not going to call off the march, and I suggest we all begin to seek a formula.

On June 25, 1941, President Franklin D. Roosevelt signed Executive Order 8802, which prohibited racial and ethnic discrimination in the defense industries. Desegregation of the armed forces would not happen until 1948.

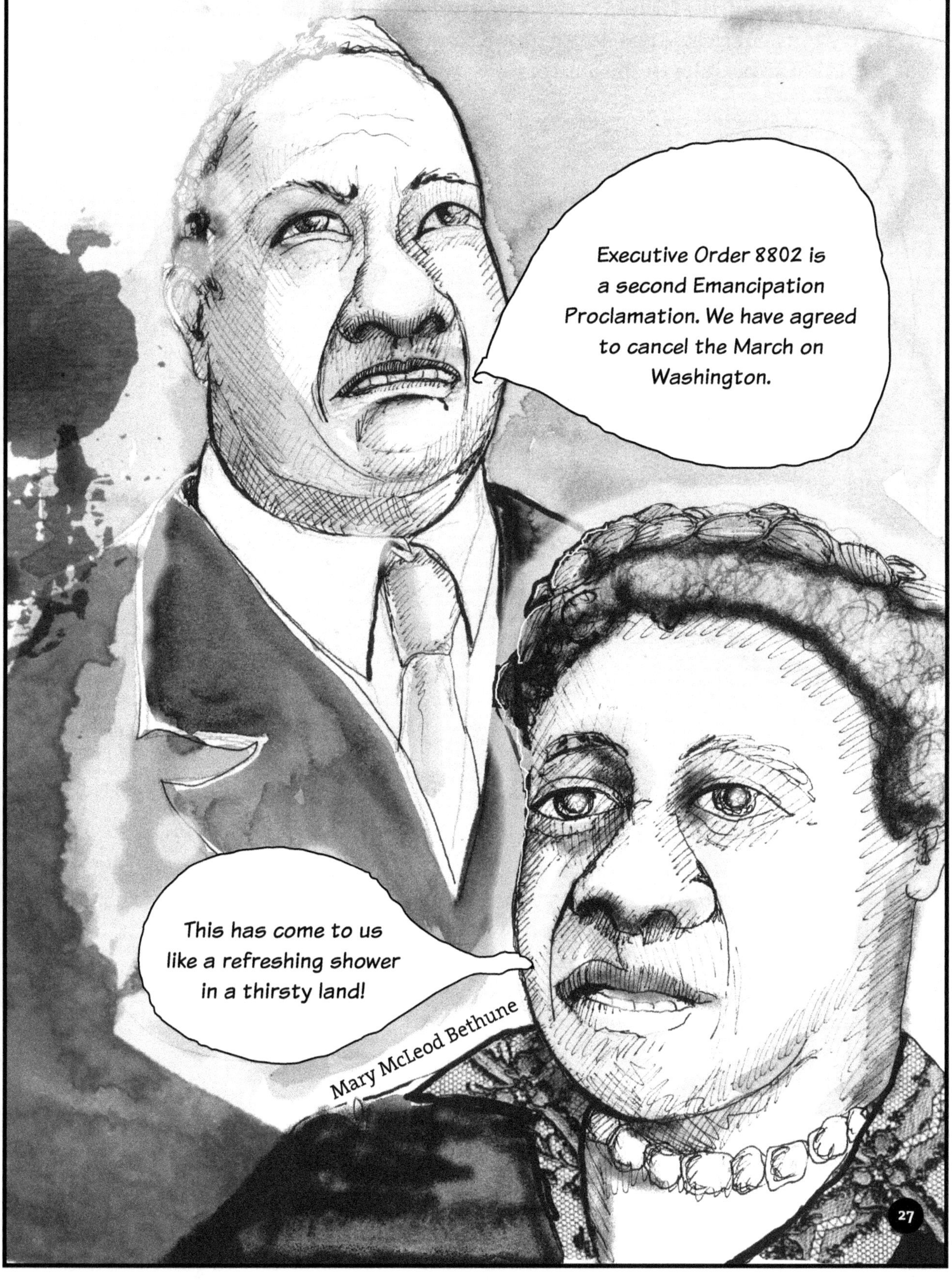

Executive Order 8802 is a second Emancipation Proclamation. We have agreed to cancel the March on Washington.
This has come to us like a refreshing shower in a thirsty land!
Mary McLeod Bethune

Despite the success of the MOWM organizers, Executive Order 8802 did not change the way that patriotic Black Americans were allowed to serve their country. While Black men were putting their lives on the line for democracy at home and abroad, the United States government still treated them like second-class citizens. Black soldiers wrote home from boot camp about racism and segregation, especially in the South.

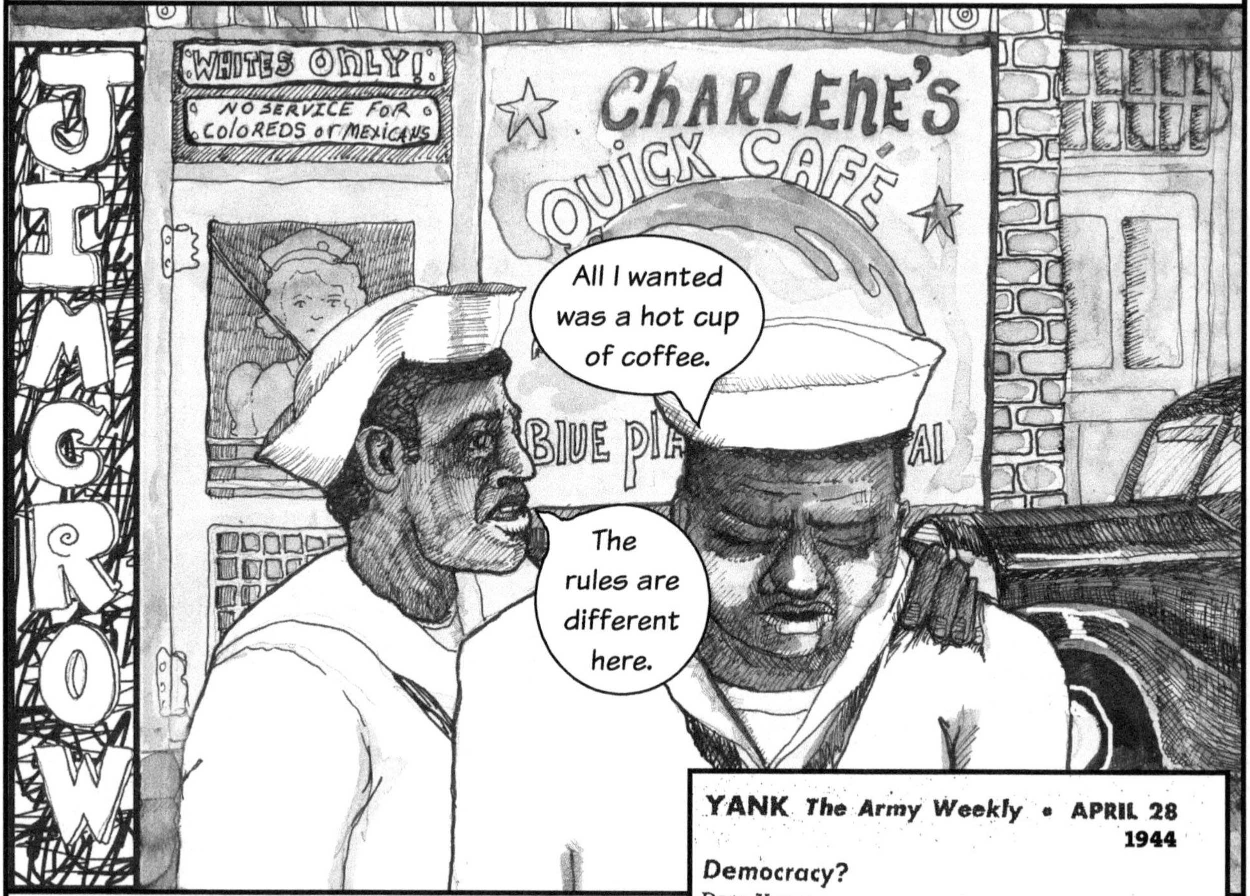
JIM CROW
WHITES ONLY!
NO SERVICE FOR COLOREDS or MEXICANS
CHARLENE'S
QUICK CAFÉ
All I wanted was a hot cup of coffee.
The rules are different here.

African Americans could join one of four units in the army, and some were accepted into the navy to perform menial jobs in segregated units; they were not allowed to join the marines until 1942. The daily experiences of African Americans continued to be demarcated by the color line, even as American soldiers fought against the Nazis, a regime rooted in racist ideology.

YANK *The Army Weekly* • **APRIL 28 1944**

Democracy?

Dear YANK:

Here is a question that each Negro soldier is asking. What is the Negro soldier fighting for? On whose team are we playing? Myself and eight other soldiers were on our way from Camp Claiborne, La., to the hospital here at Fort Huachuca. We had to lay over until the next day for our train. On the next day we could not purchase a cup of coffee at any of the lunchrooms around there. As you know, Old Man Jim Crow rules. The only place where we could be served was at the lunchroom at the railroad station but, of course, we had to go into the kitchen. But that's not all; 11:30 A.M. about two dozen German prisoners of war, with two American guards, came to the station. They entered the lunchroom, sat at the tables, had their meals served, talked, smoked, in fact had quite a swell time. I stood on the outside looking on, and I could not help but ask myself these questions: Are these men sworn enemies of this country? Are they not taught to hate and destroy . . . all democratic governments? Are we not American soldiers, sworn to fight for and die if need be for this our country? Then why are they treated better than we are? Why are we pushed around like cattle? If we are fighting for the same thing, if we are to die for our country, then why does the Government allow such things to go on? Some of the boys are saying that you will not print this letter. I'm saying that you will. . . .

Fort Huachuca, Ariz. —Cpl. RUPERT TRIMMINGHAM

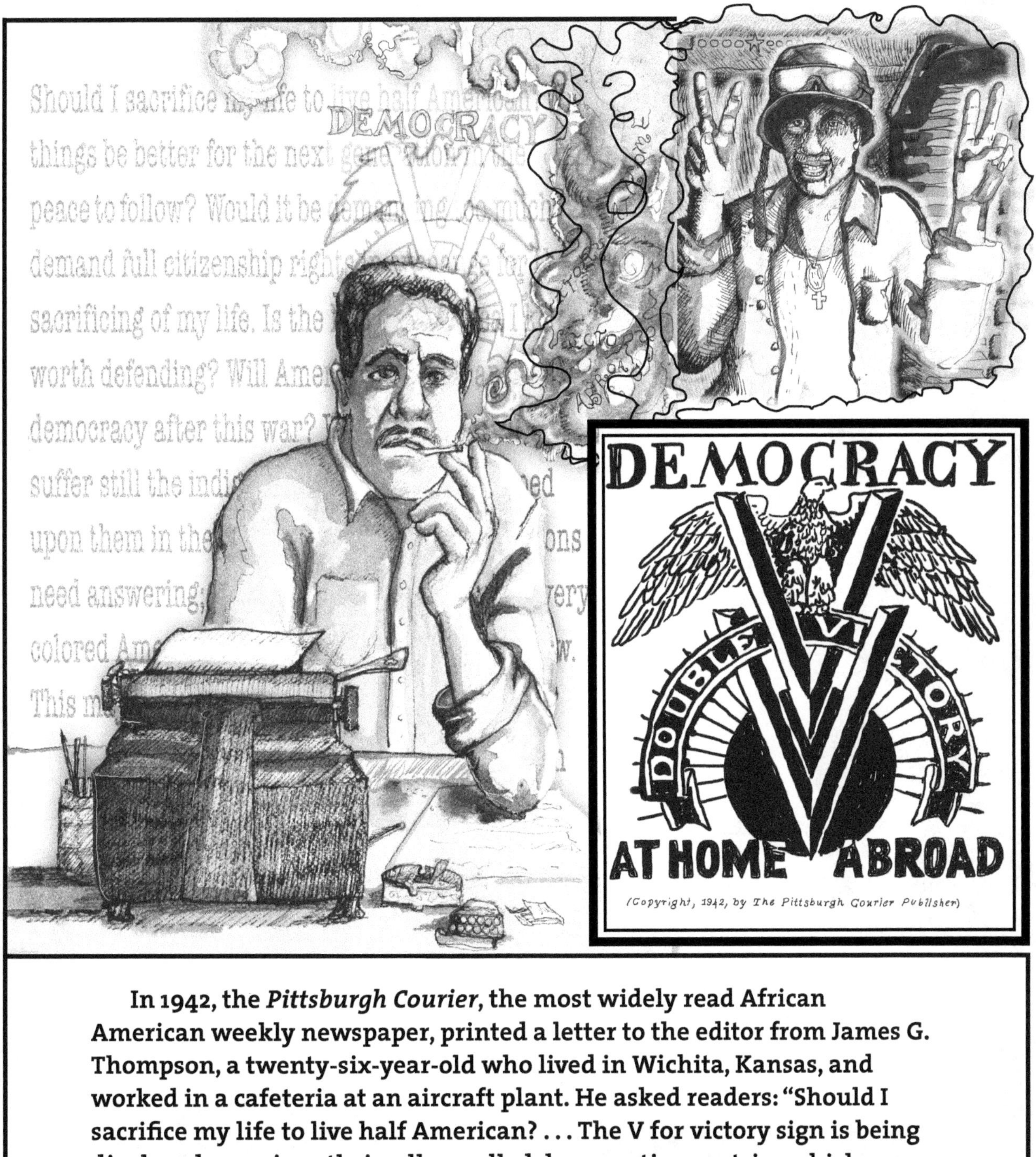
DEMOCRACY
DOUBLE VICTORY
AT HOME ABROAD
(Copyright, 1942, by The Pittsburgh Courier Publisher)

In 1942, the *Pittsburgh Courier*, the most widely read African American weekly newspaper, printed a letter to the editor from James G. Thompson, a twenty-six-year-old who lived in Wichita, Kansas, and worked in a cafeteria at an aircraft plant. He asked readers: "Should I sacrifice my life to live half American? . . . The V for victory sign is being displayed prominently in all so-called democratic countries which are fighting for victory over aggression, slavery and tyranny. . . . Let we colored Americans adopt the double VV for a double victory. The first V for victory over our enemies from without, the second V for victory over our enemies from within. For surely those who perpetrate these ugly prejudices here are seeking to destroy our democratic form of government just as surely as the Axis forces."

This was how the famous "Double V for Victory at Home and Abroad" campaign was born. Wilbert L. Holloway, a staff artist at the *Pittsburgh Courier*, designed the logo.

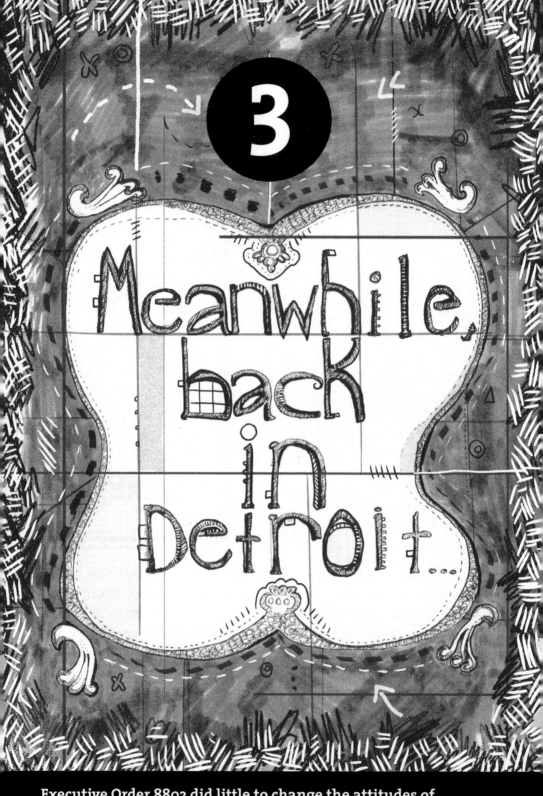

3

Meanwhile, back in Detroit...

Executive Order 8802 did little to change the attitudes of working-class whites, employers in the defense industry, landlords, and municipal governments.

Northern cities like Detroit experienced a rapid influx of workers from the South. Their arrival stoked racial tensions as competition increased for precious resources like housing, jobs, transportation, and recreational spaces.

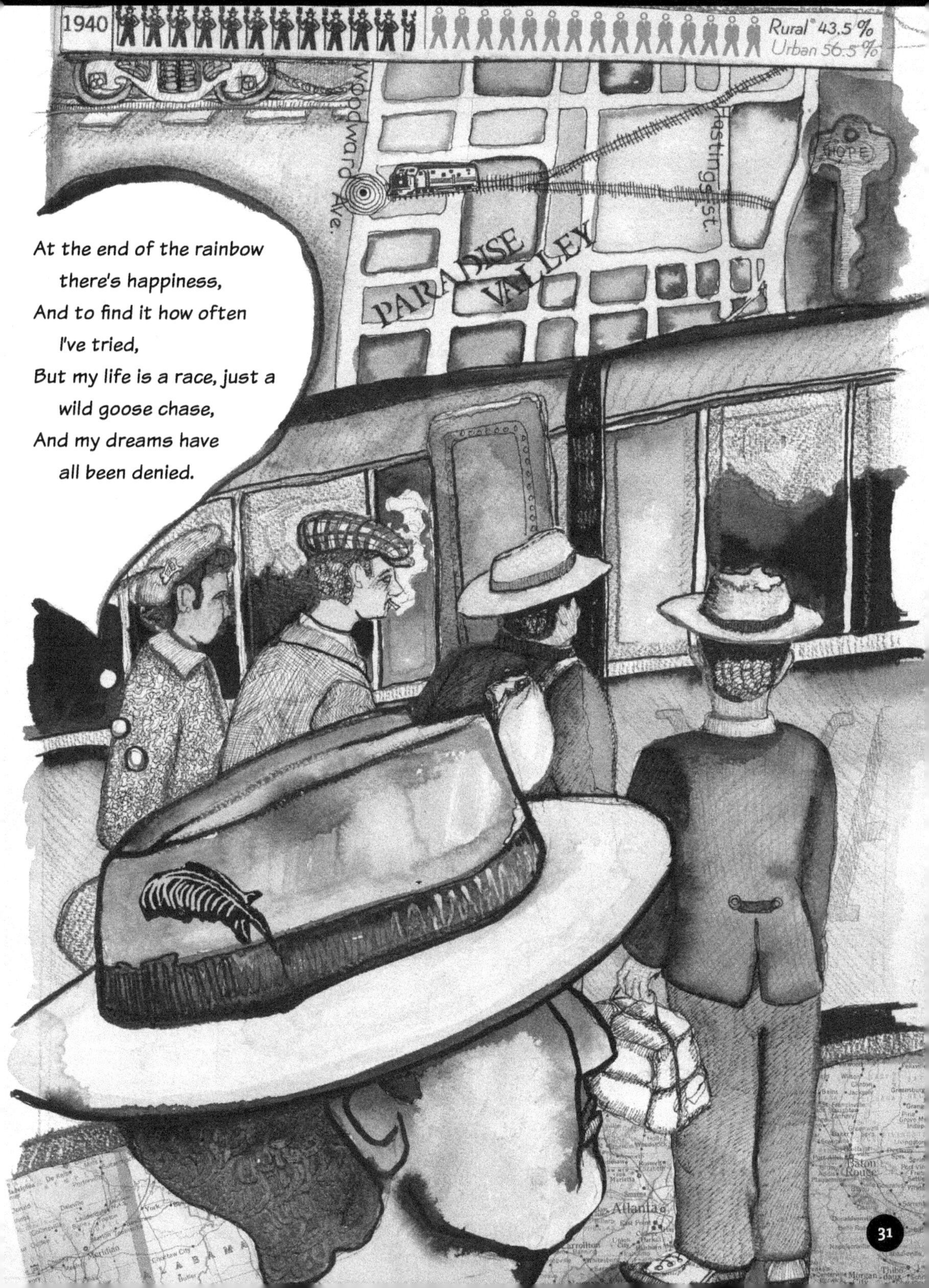

1940
Rural 43.5 %
Urban 56.5 %
Woodward Ave.
Hastings st.
PARADISE VALLEY
HOPE
At the end of the rainbow there's happiness,
And to find it how often I've tried,
But my life is a race, just a wild goose chase,
And my dreams have all been denied.
Atlanta
Baton Rouge

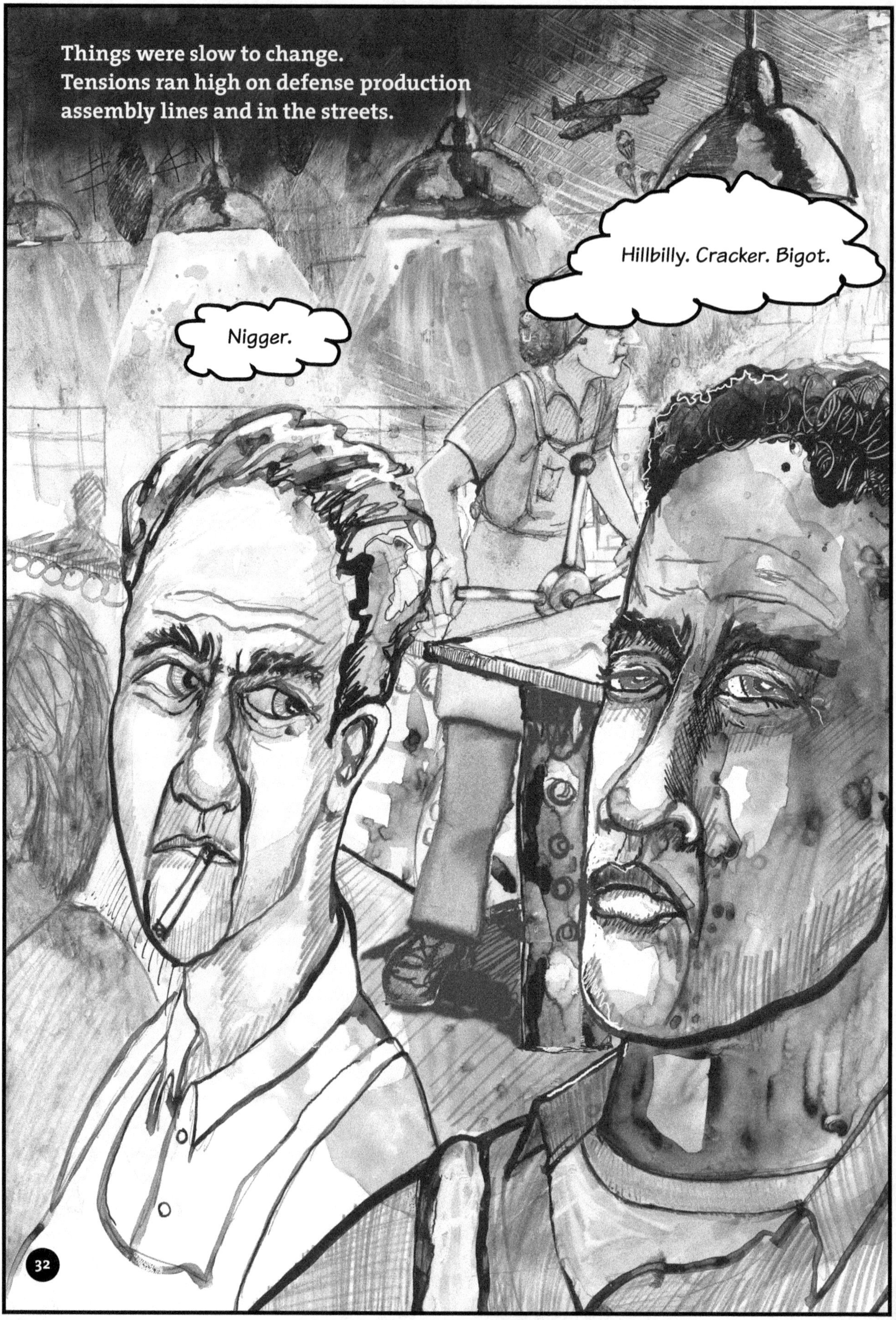
Things were slow to change.
Tensions ran high on defense production assembly lines and in the streets.
Nigger.
Hillbilly. Cracker. Bigot.

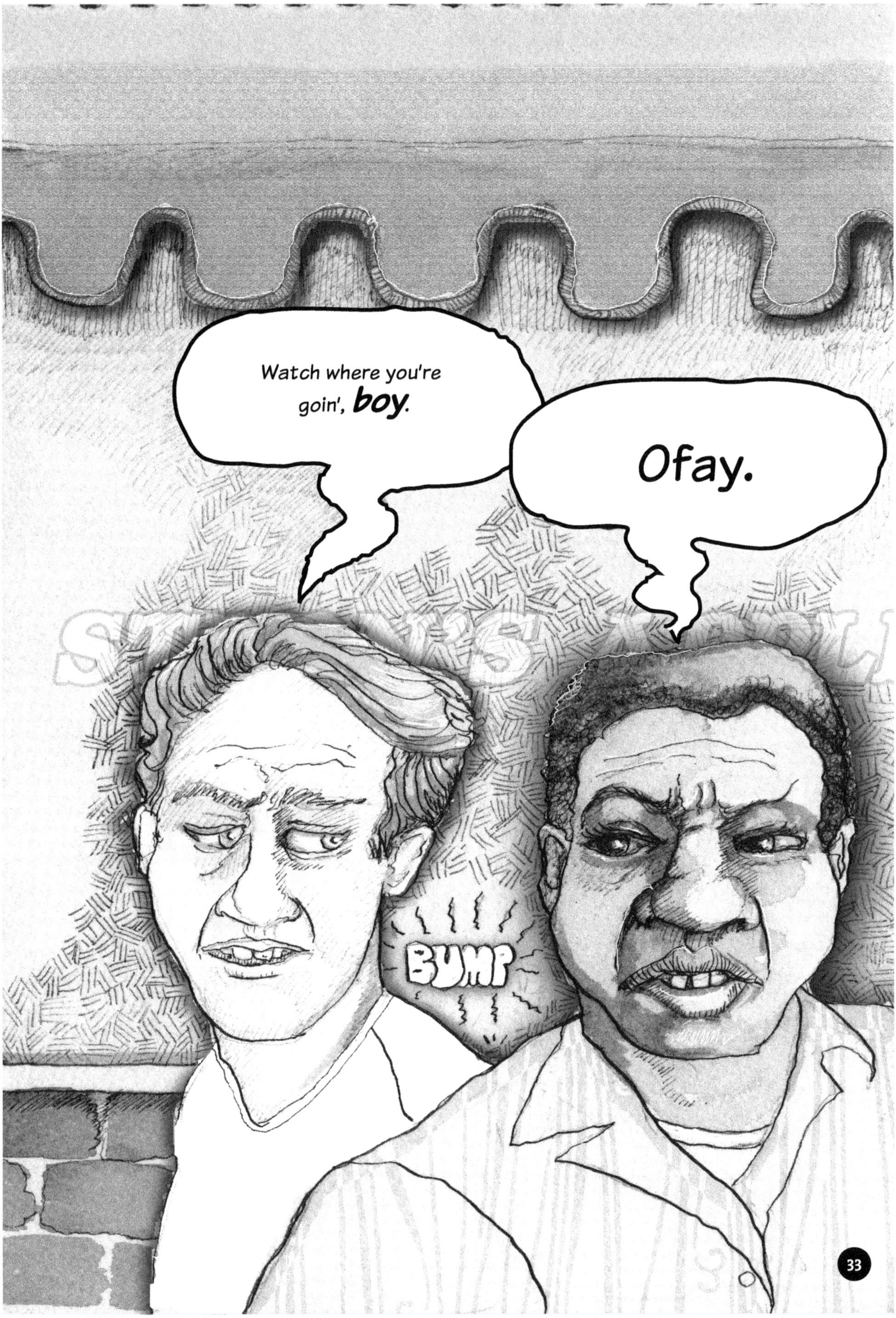
Watch where you're goin', **boy**.
Ofay.
BUMP

In 1942, in a kitchen somewhere in Detroit's Black Bottom neighborhood, two friends drink coffee.

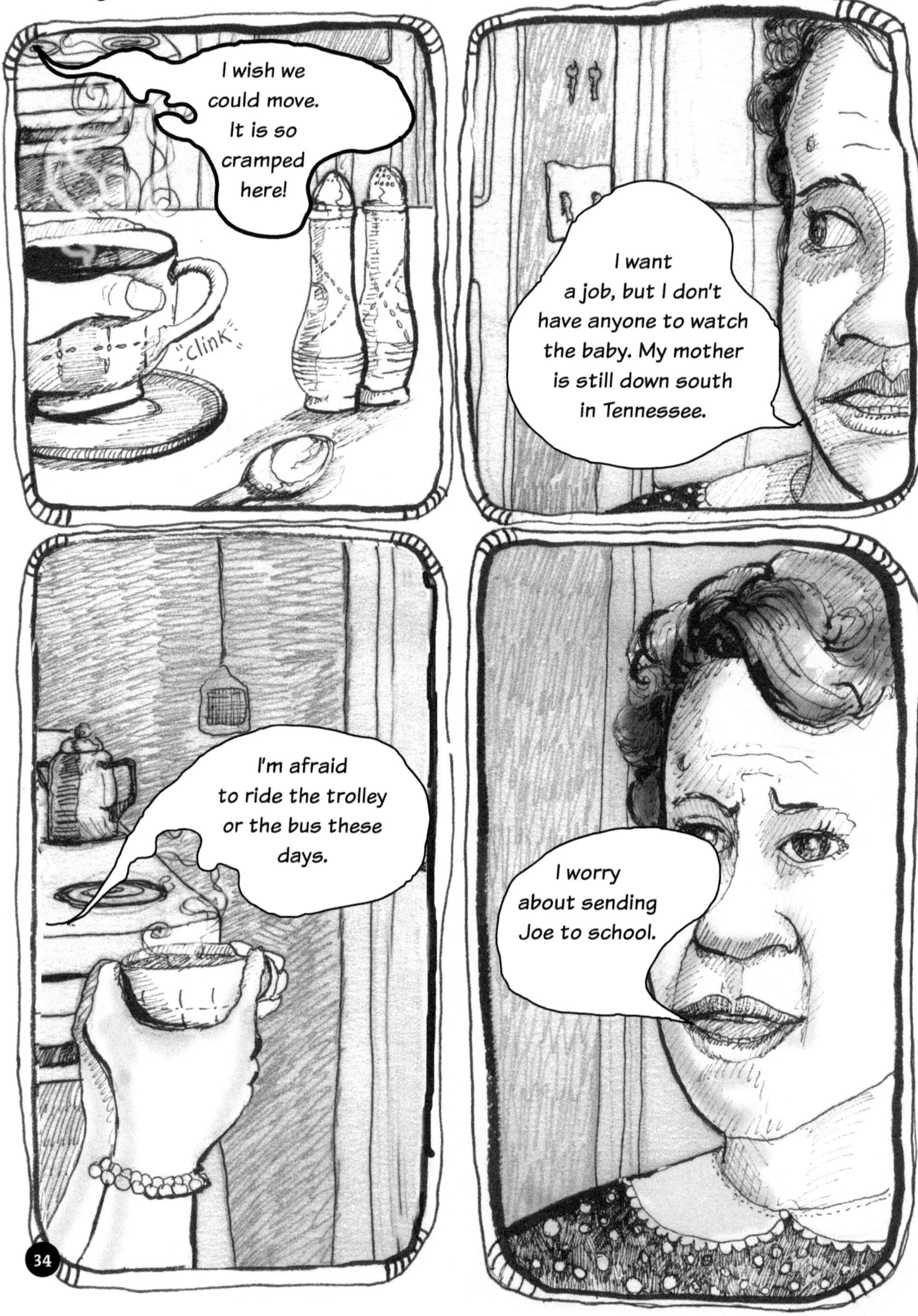
I wish we could move. It is so cramped here!
"clink"
I want a job, but I don't have anyone to watch the baby. My mother is still down south in Tennessee.
I'm afraid to ride the trolley or the bus these days.
I worry about sending Joe to school.

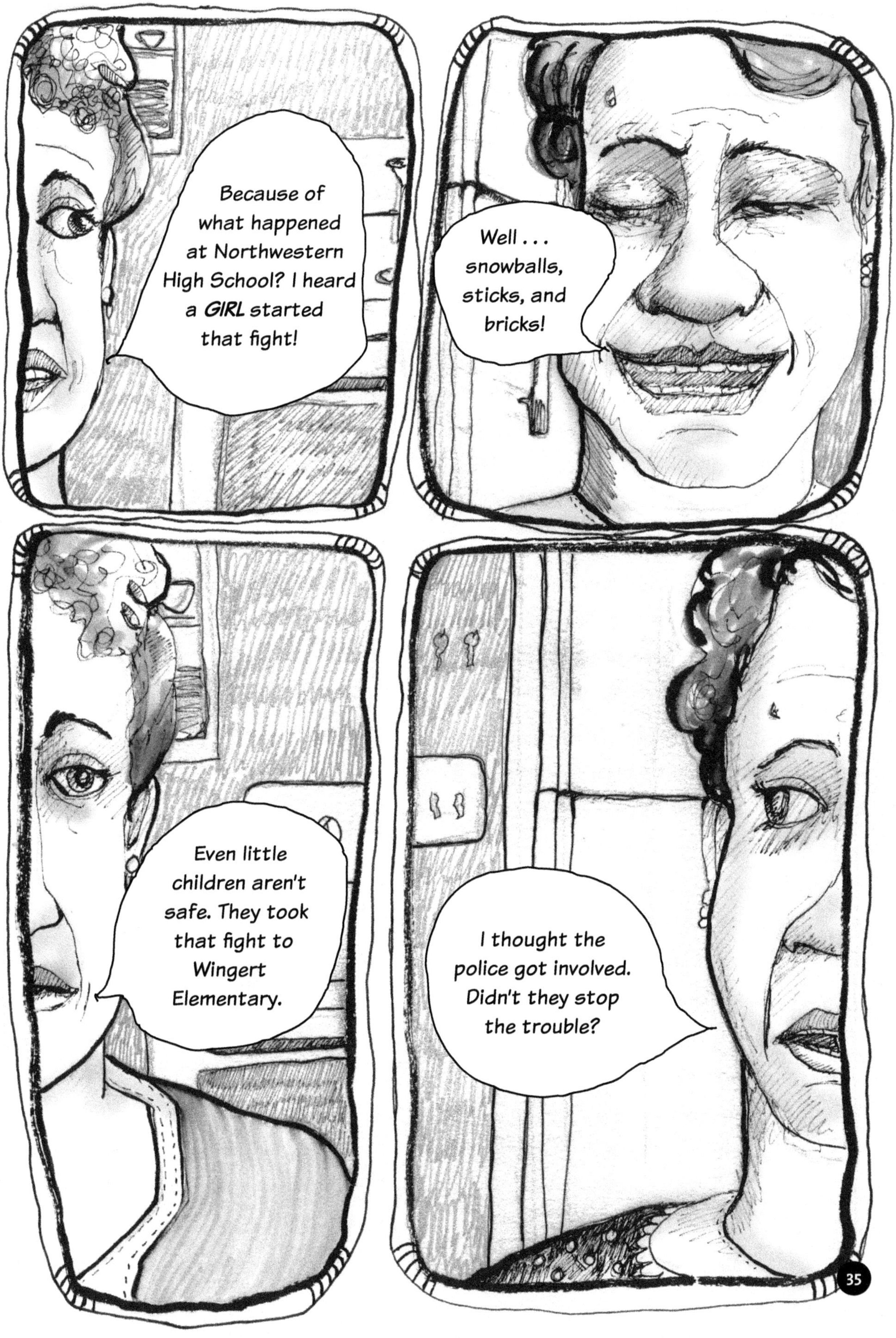
Because of what happened at Northwestern High School? I heard a *GIRL* started that fight!
Well . . . snowballs, sticks, and bricks!
Even little children aren't safe. They took that fight to Wingert Elementary.
I thought the police got involved. Didn't they stop the trouble?

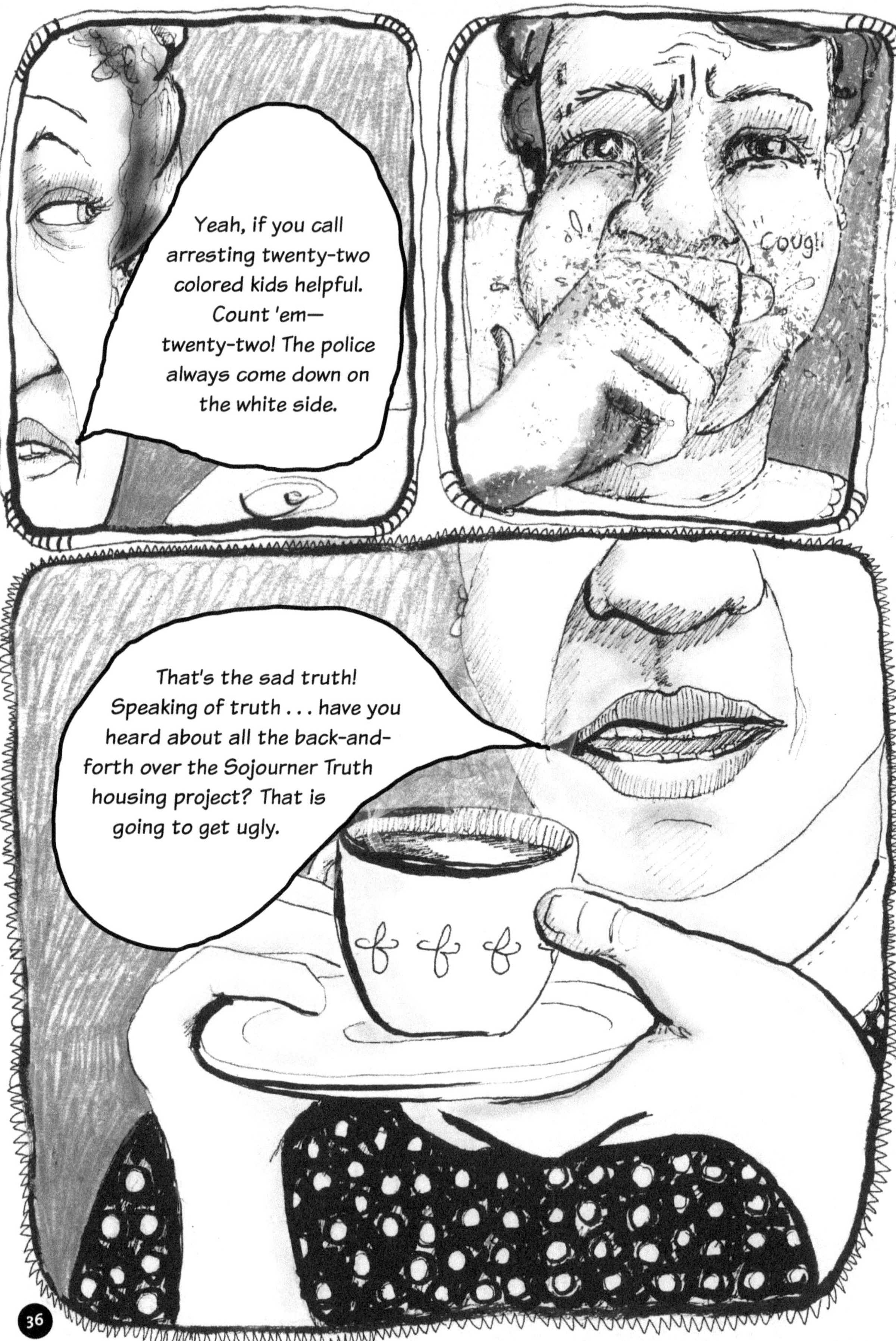
Yeah, if you call arresting twenty-two colored kids helpful. Count 'em— twenty-two! The police always come down on the white side.
COUGH
That's the sad truth! Speaking of truth . . . have you heard about all the back-and-forth over the Sojourner Truth housing project? That is going to get ugly.

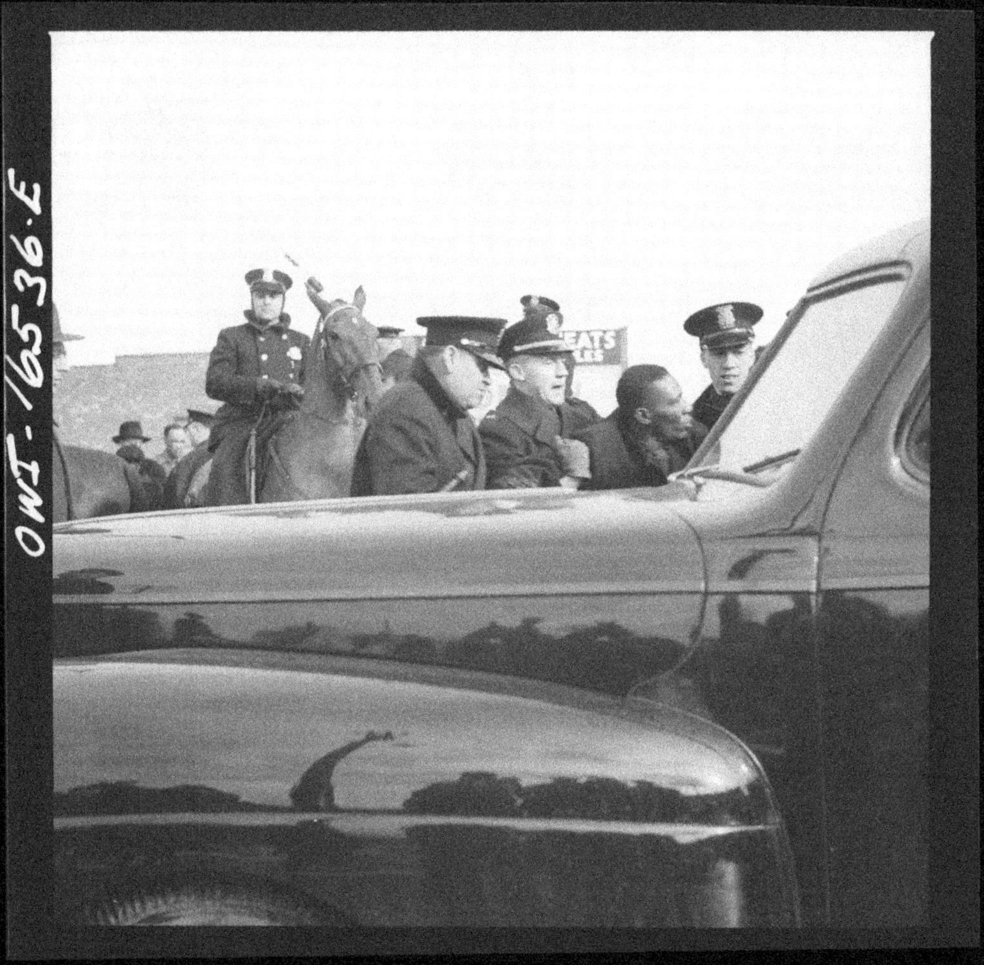
OWI-16536-E

Detroit police arresting an African American man at the site of the Sojourner Truth housing project in February 1942, when white protesters prevented Black families from moving into their newly built homes.

Photograph by Arthur Siegel, February 1942, Library of Congress, Prints and Photographs Division, LC-USW3- 016536-E [P&P] LOT 661.

In 1941 and 1942 violence escalated between Black and white people over housing. There was a tremendous housing shortage in Detroit. The influx of newcomers overwhelmed the housing market. Both Black and white families suffered in poor living conditions, but the African American population expanded at a higher rate and had fewer housing options. Black families were limited to the neighborhoods of Paradise Valley, Black Bottom, Eight Mile Wyoming, and parts of the West Side. Rent was exorbitant and living conditions were crowded and substandard.

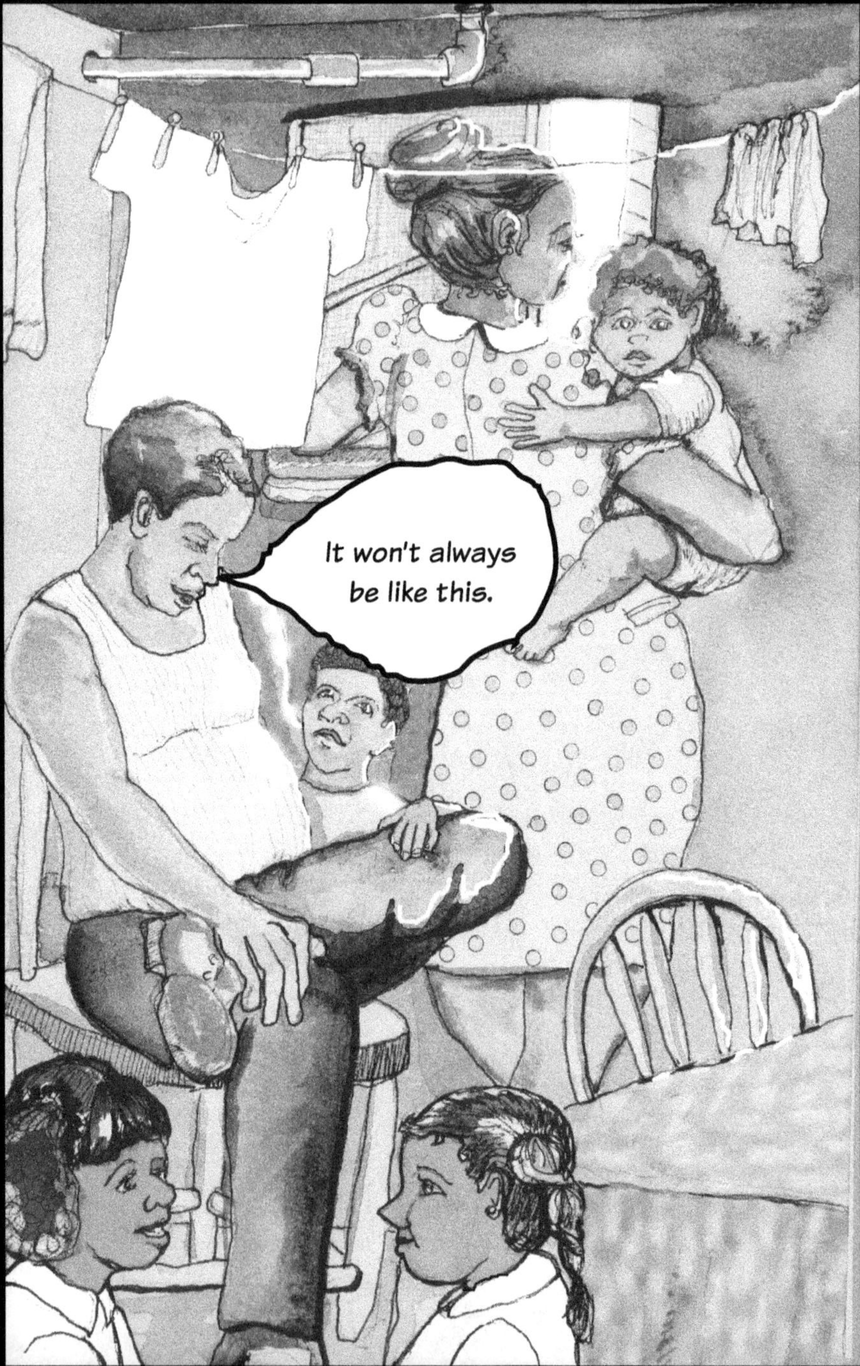
It won't always be like this.

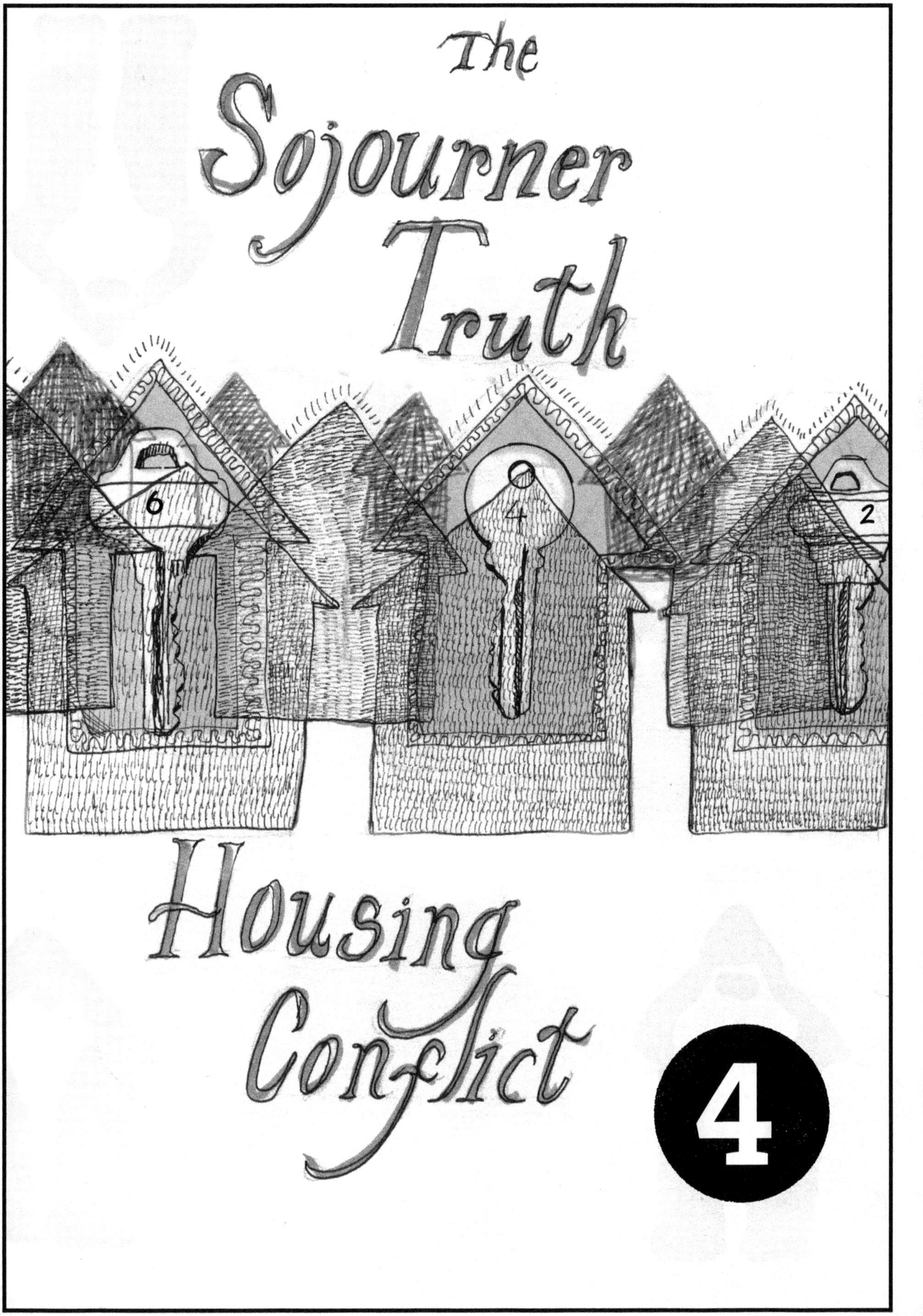
The Sojourner Truth
Housing Conflict
4

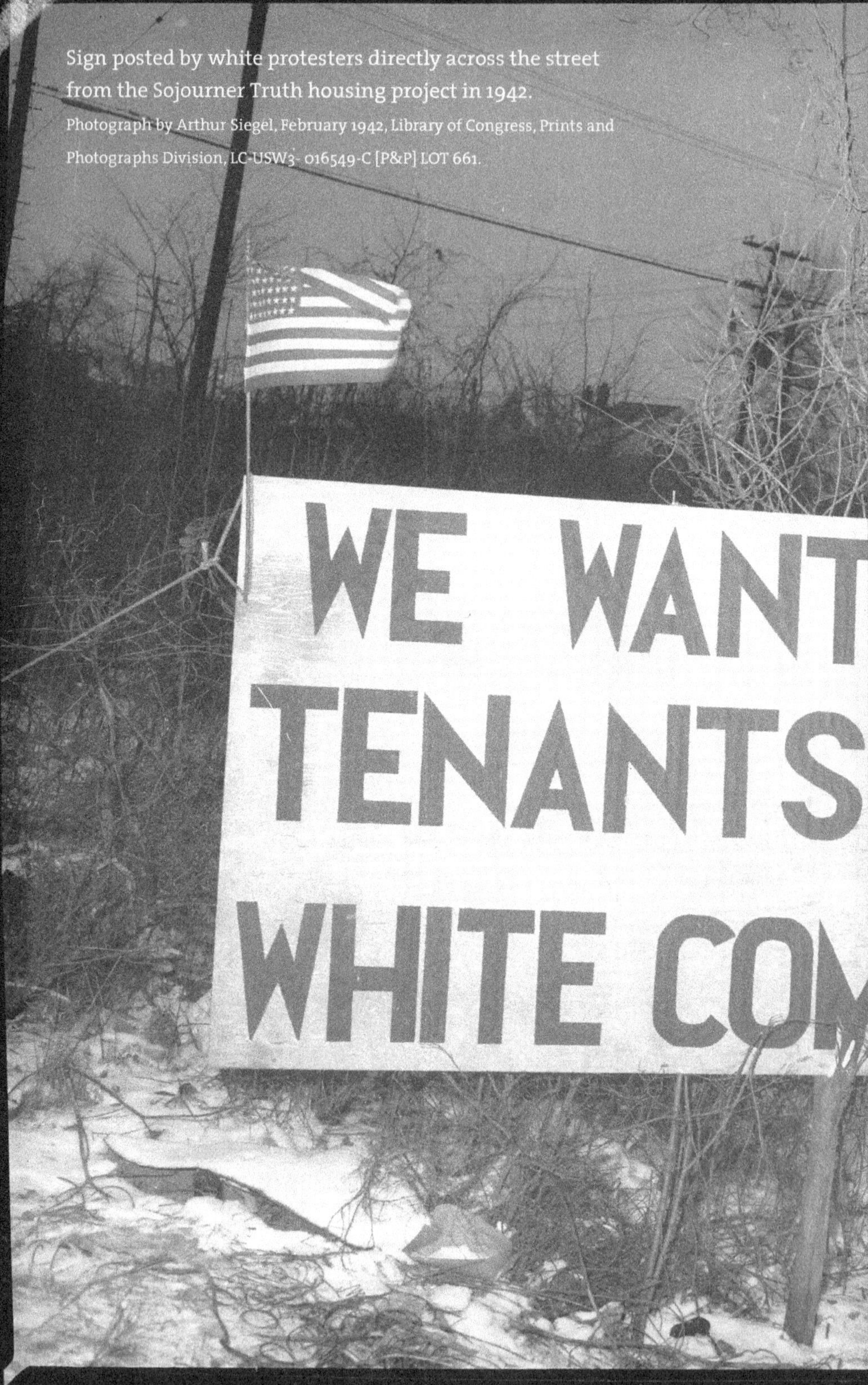
WE WANT
TENANTS
WHITE CO

Sign posted by white protesters directly across the street from the Sojourner Truth housing project in 1942.

Photograph by Arthur Siegel, February 1942, Library of Congress, Prints and Photographs Division, LC-USW3- 016549-C [P&P] LOT 661.

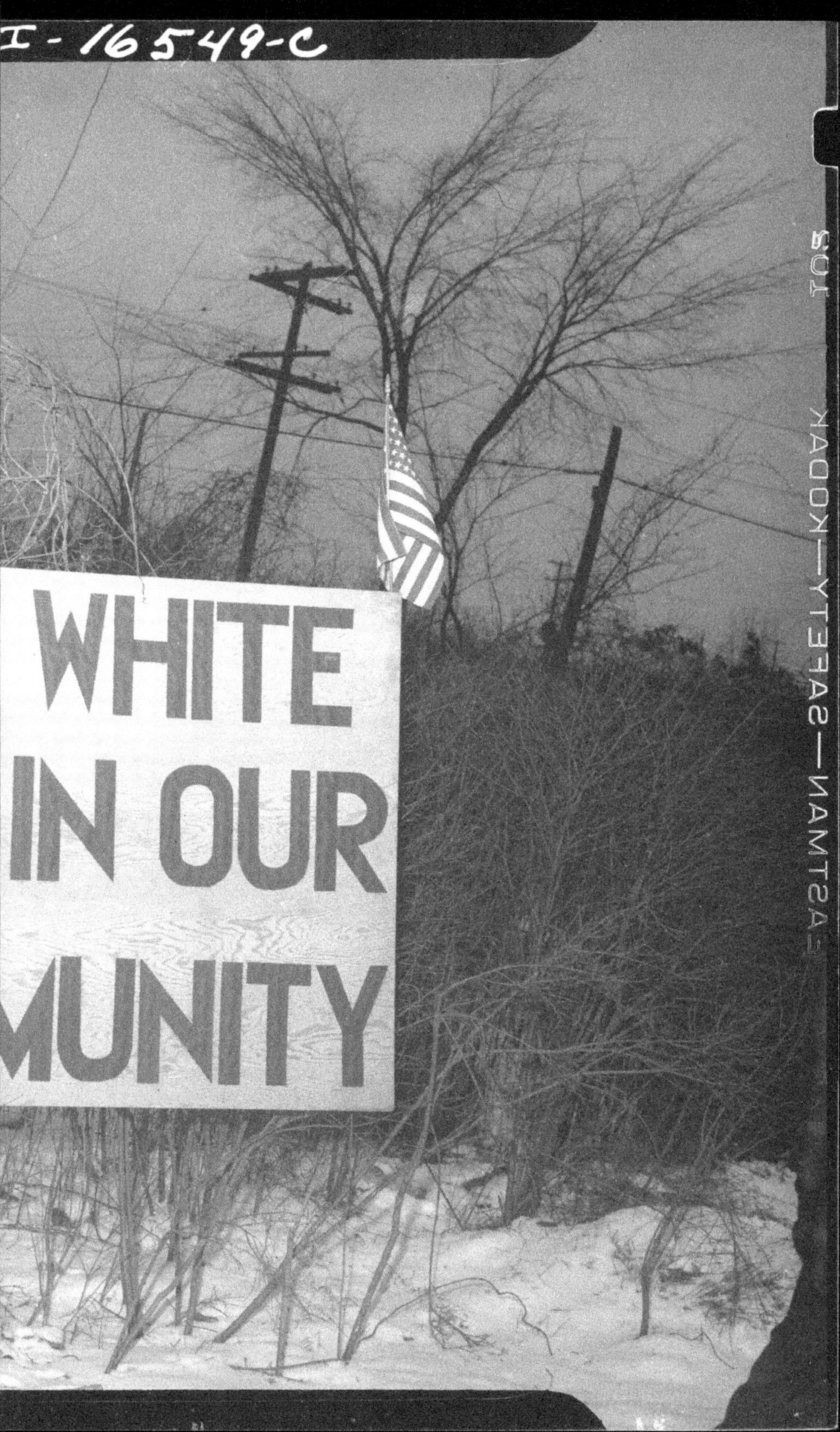
I-16549-C
WHITE
IN OUR
MUNITY

Defense Housing Coordinator Charles F. Palmer had a mandate to create wartime housing.

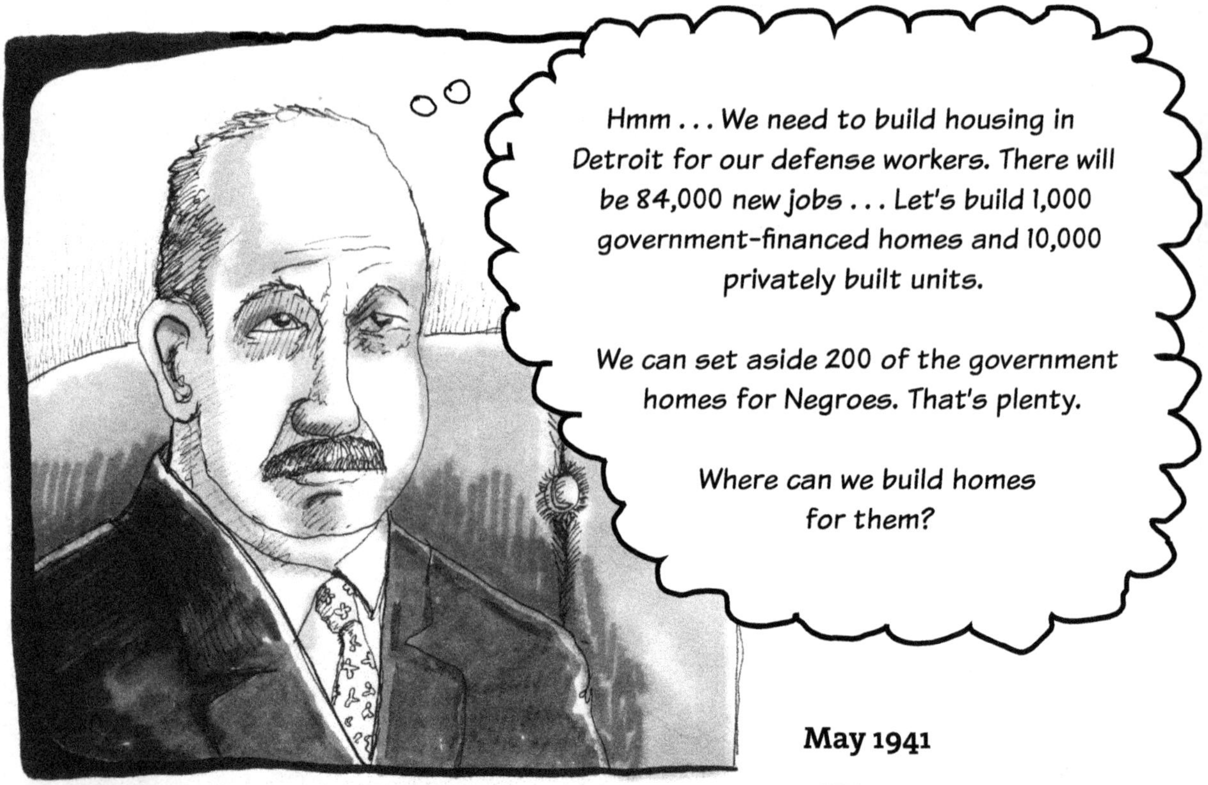
Hmm . . . We need to build housing in Detroit for our defense workers. There will be 84,000 new jobs . . . Let's build 1,000 government-financed homes and 10,000 privately built units.
We can set aside 200 of the government homes for Negroes. That's plenty.
Where can we build homes for them?

May 1941

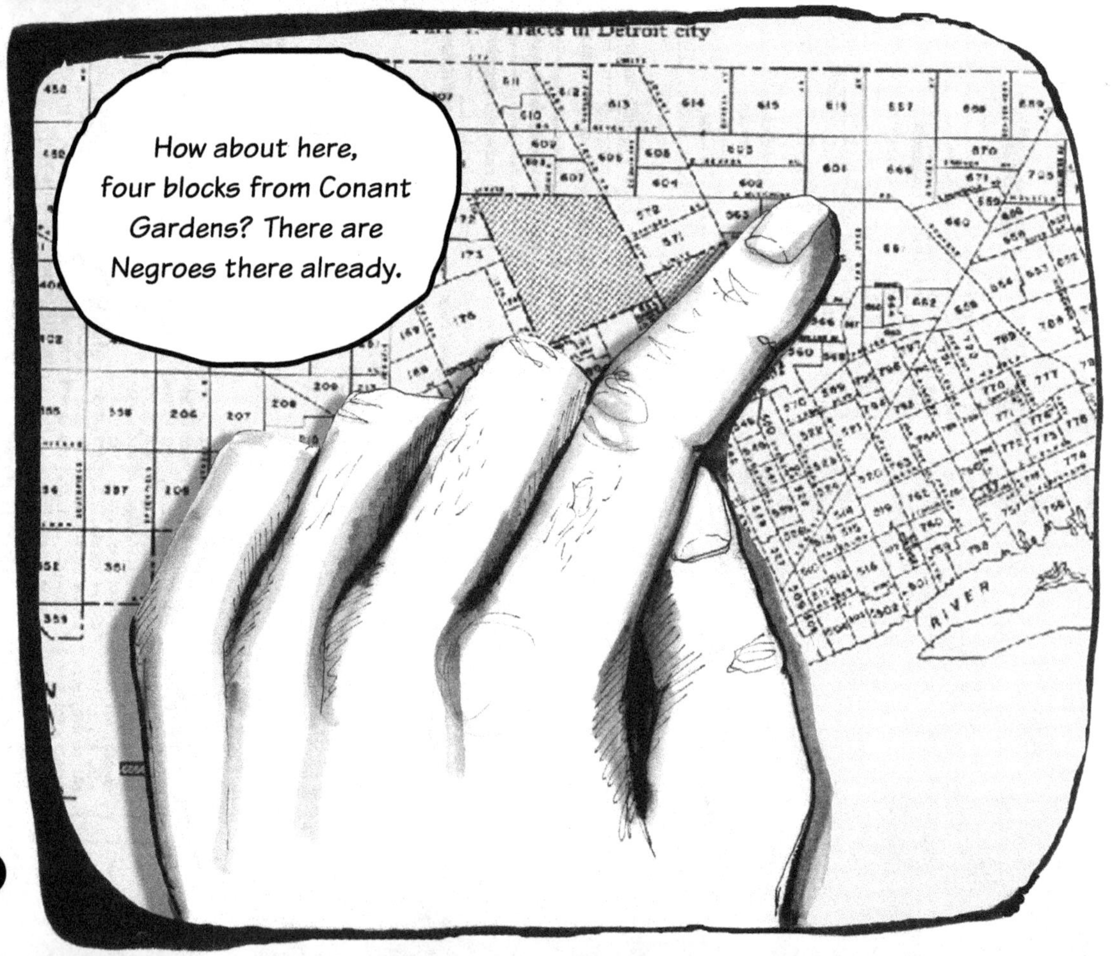
Tracts in Detroit city
How about here, four blocks from Conant Gardens? There are Negroes there already.
RIVER

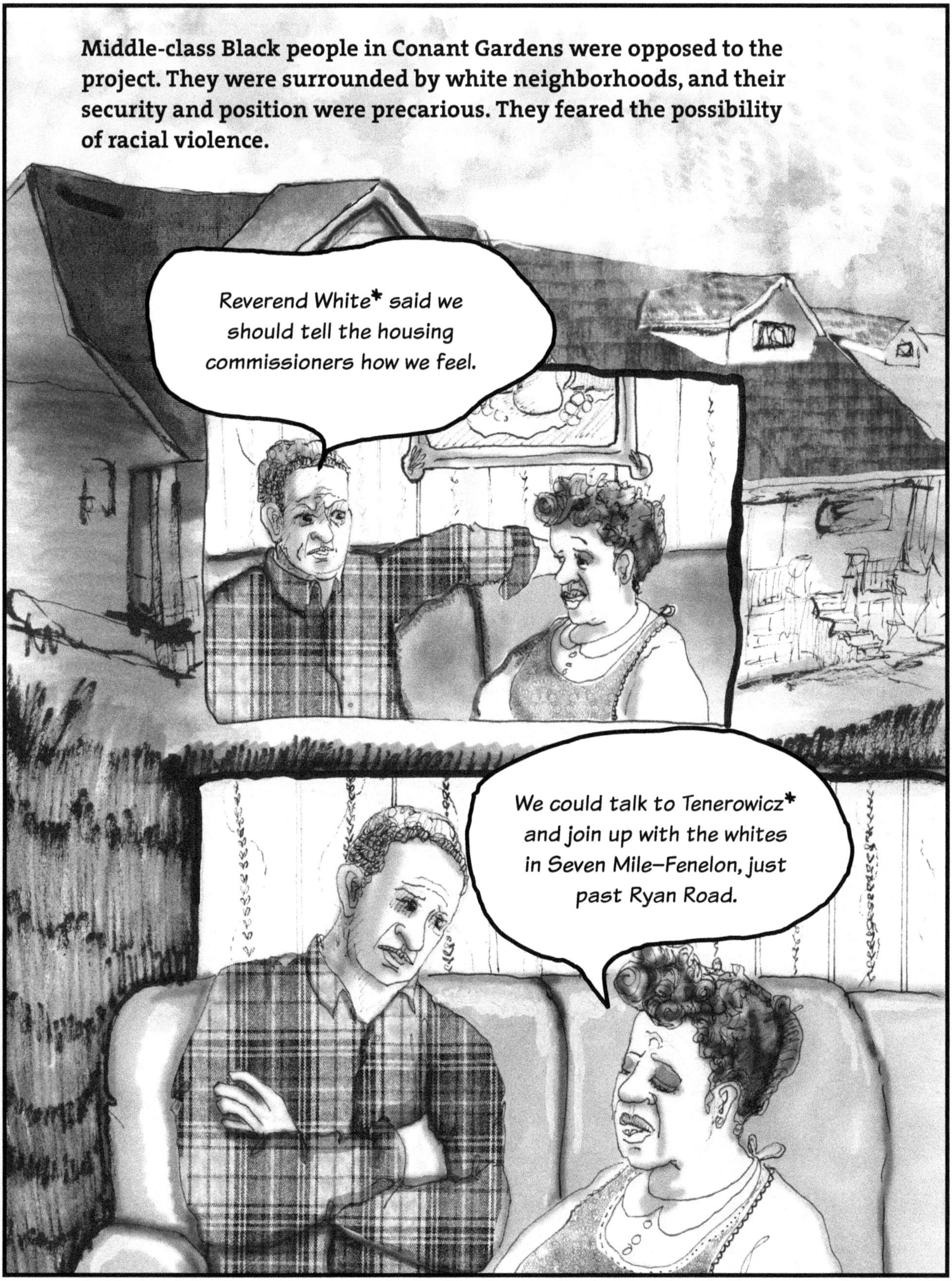
Middle-class Black people in Conant Gardens were opposed to the project. They were surrounded by white neighborhoods, and their security and position were precarious. They feared the possibility of racial violence.
Reverend White* said we should tell the housing commissioners how we feel.
We could talk to Tenerowicz* and join up with the whites in Seven Mile–Fenelon, just past Ryan Road.

*Reverend Horace White was the Black leader of the Plymouth United Church of Christ. Rudolph Tenerowicz was a local politician who supported making the Sojourner Truth Homes for white families only.

White homeowners in the Seven Mile–Fenelon area were outraged.

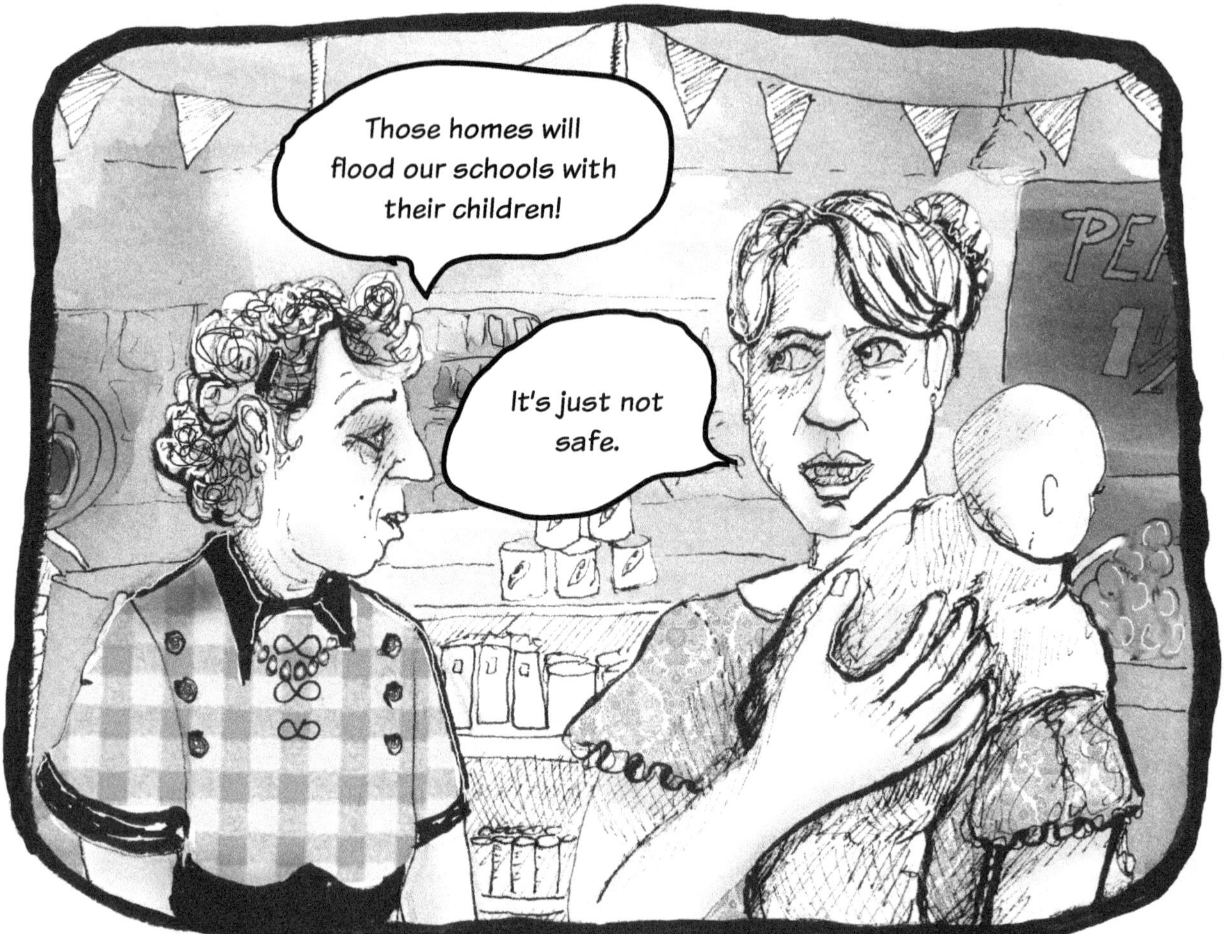
Those homes will flood our schools with their children!
It's just not safe.

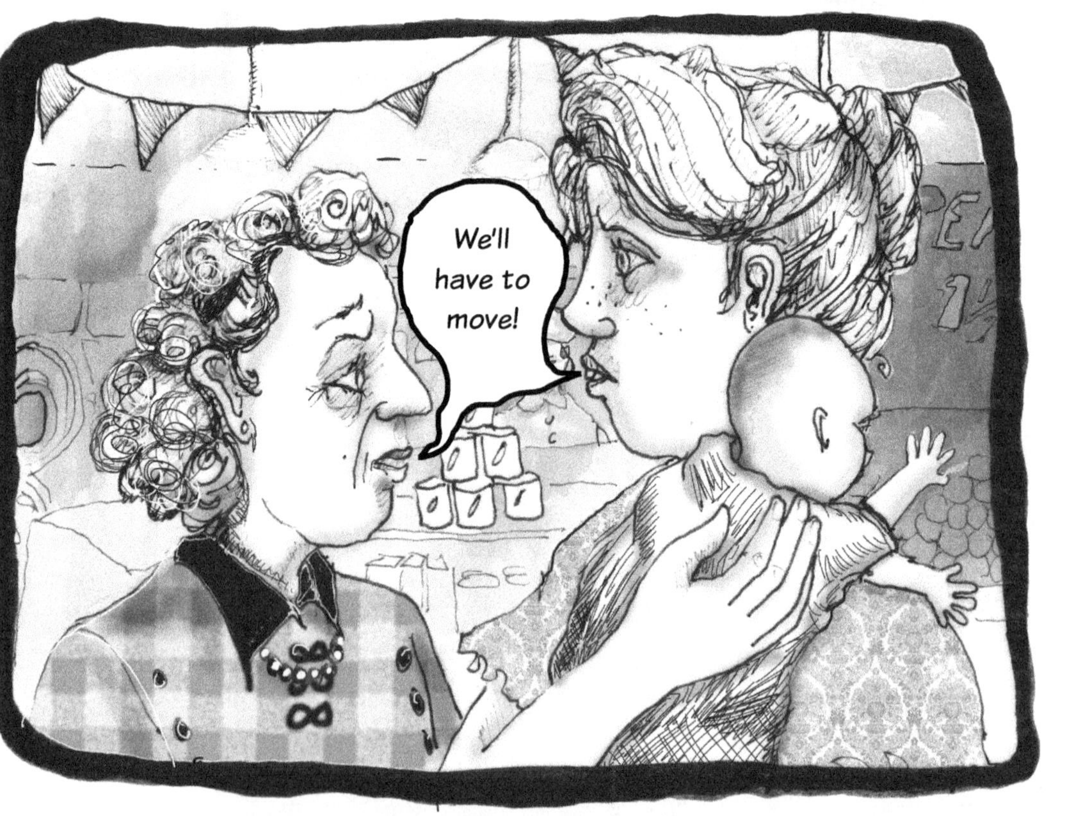
We'll have to move!

Black and white religious leaders like the Reverend Horace White, the Reverend Charles A. Hill, and the Reverend Constantine Dzink were deeply involved in discussions within their local communities and with federal and city authorities. Most whites were deeply opposed to the housing project, while the Black churches of Detroit rallied around the issue of expanded housing opportunities. They were joined by progressive white religious leaders in their struggle for equality.

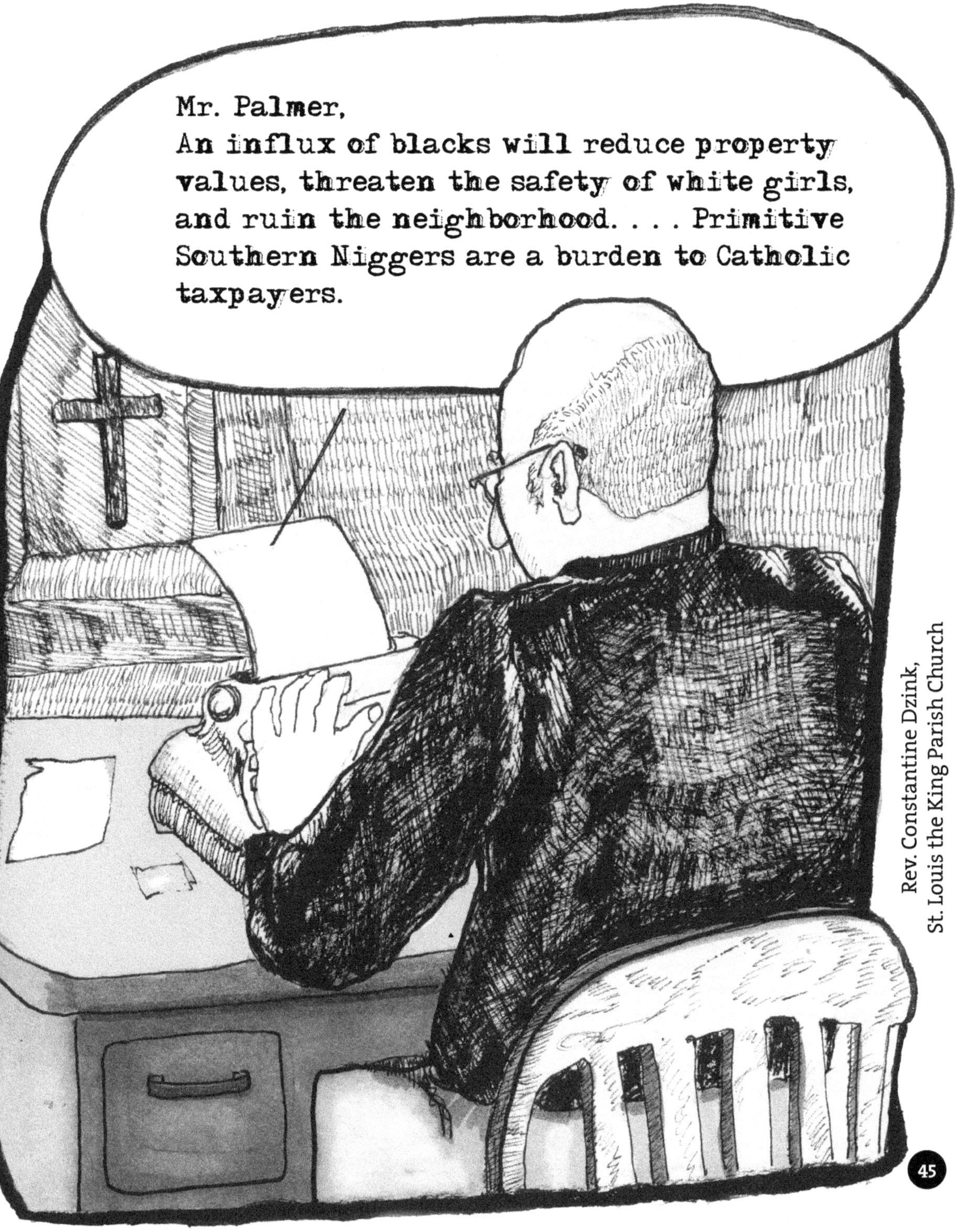
Mr. Palmer,
An influx of blacks will reduce property values, threaten the safety of white girls, and ruin the neighborhood. . . . Primitive Southern Niggers are a burden to Catholic taxpayers.
Rev. Constantine Dzink, St. Louis the King Parish Church

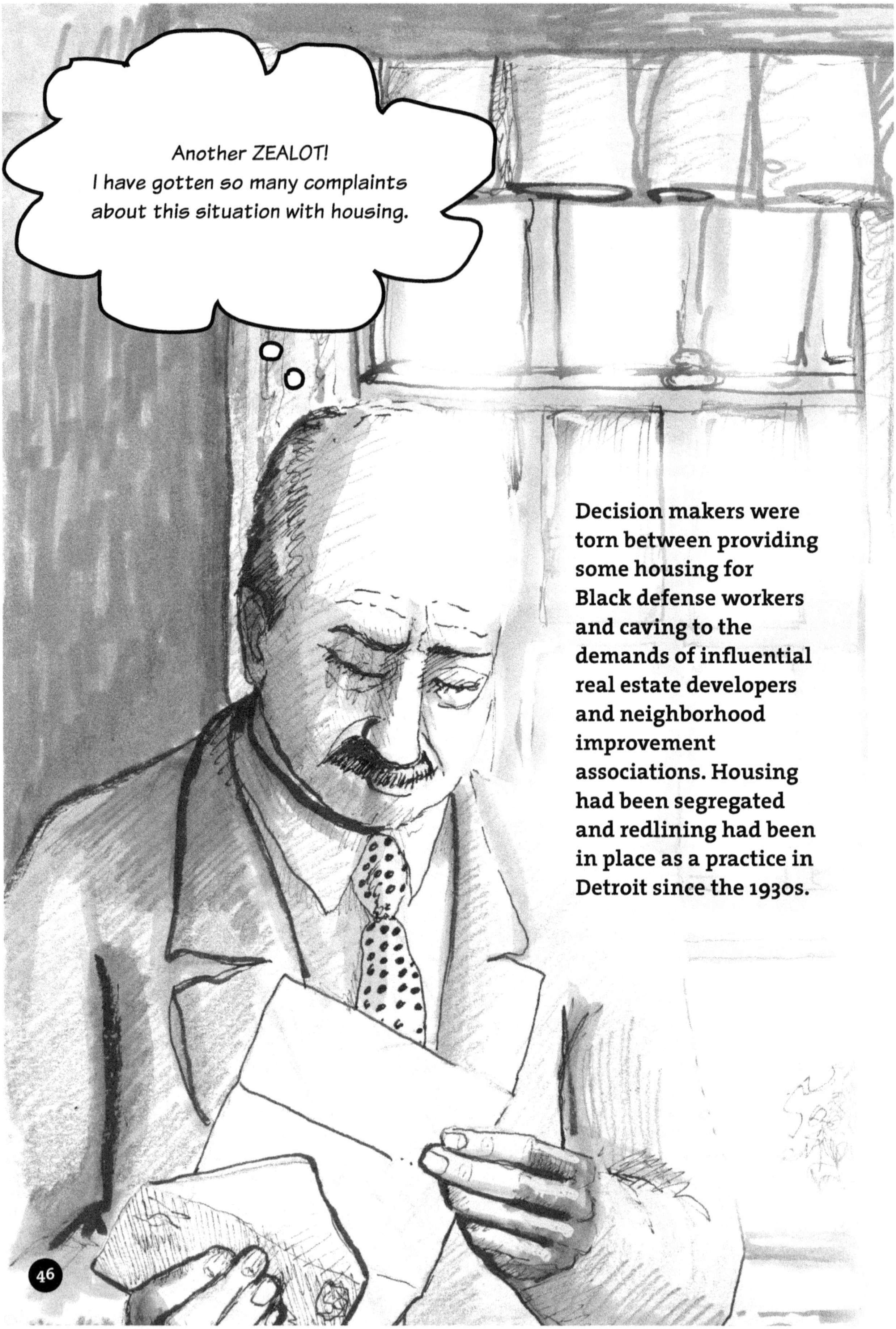
Another ZEALOT!
I have gotten so many complaints about this situation with housing.
Decision makers were torn between providing some housing for Black defense workers and caving to the demands of influential real estate developers and neighborhood improvement associations. Housing had been segregated and redlining had been in place as a practice in Detroit since the 1930s.

In September 1941, the situation looked promising for Black families.

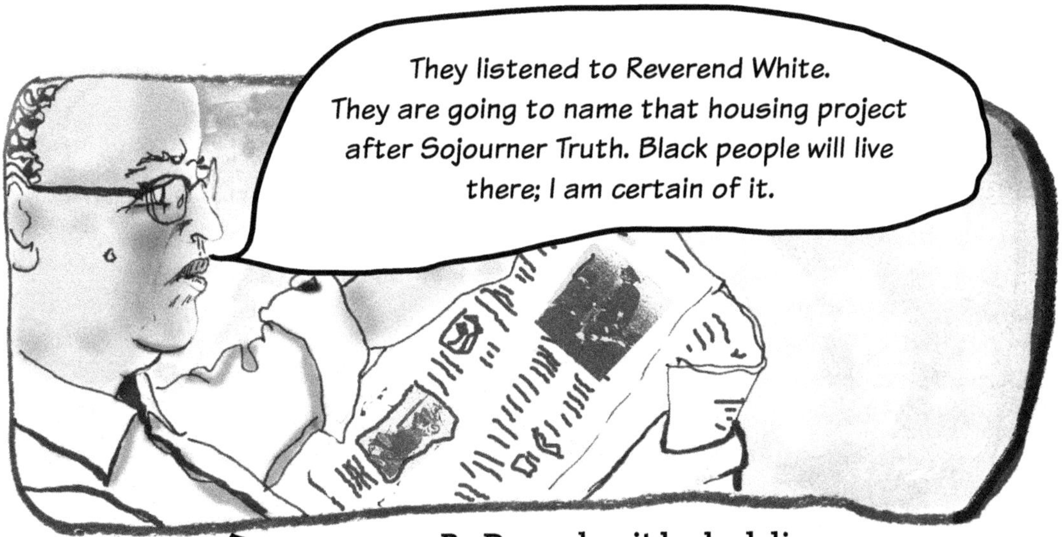
They listened to Reverend White. They are going to name that housing project after Sojourner Truth. Black people will live there; I am certain of it.

By December it looked dire.

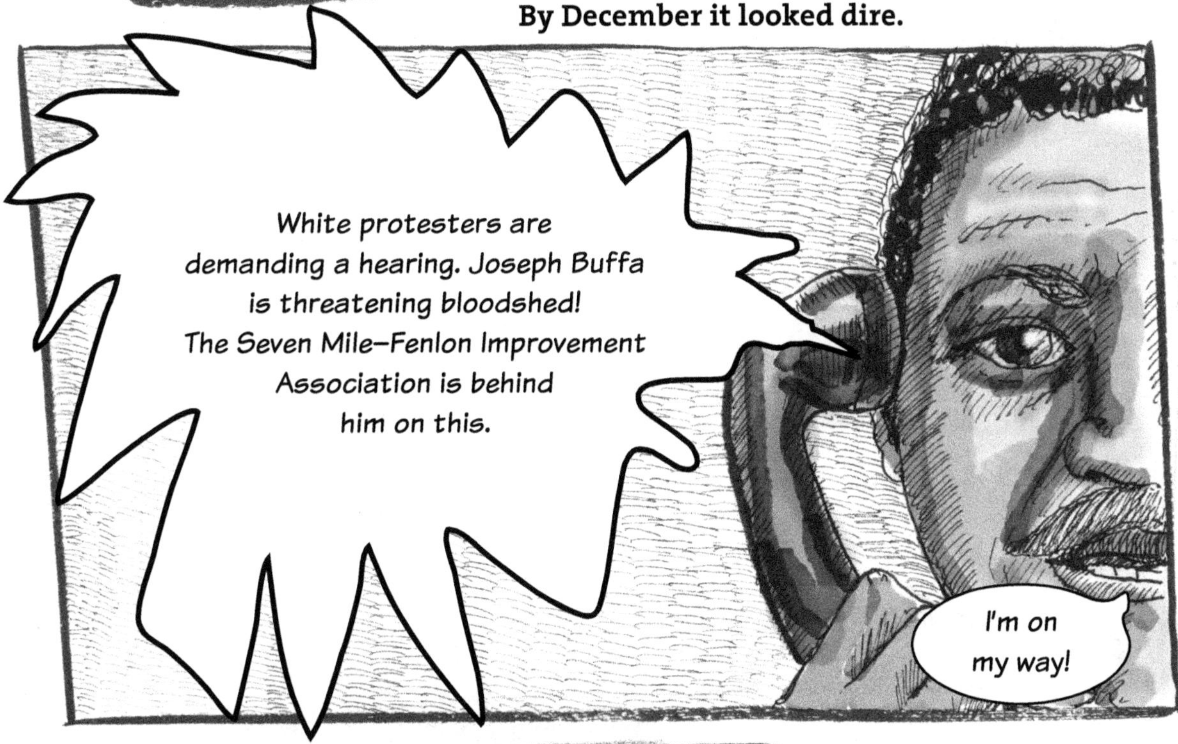
White protesters are demanding a hearing. Joseph Buffa is threatening bloodshed! The Seven Mile–Fenlon Improvement Association is behind him on this.
I'm on my way!

Dr. James J. McClendon

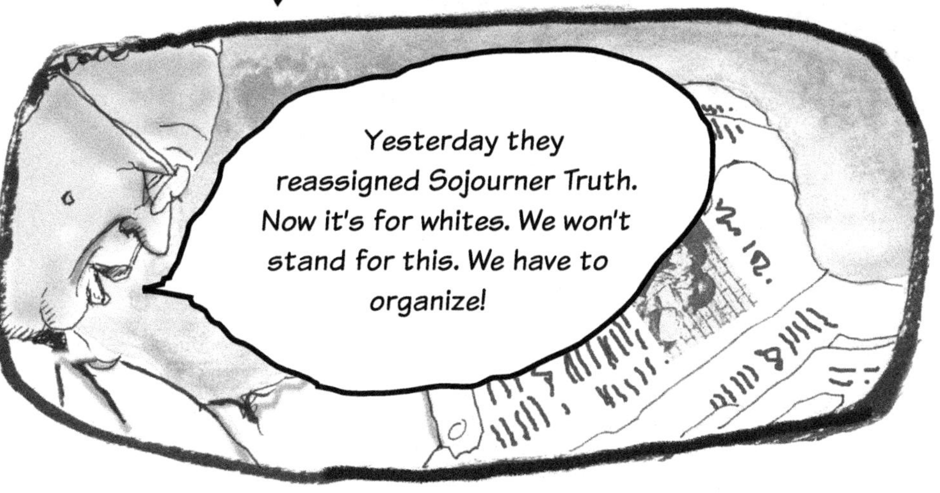
Yesterday they reassigned Sojourner Truth. Now it's for whites. We won't stand for this. We have to organize!

By January 1942, the tide had turned.

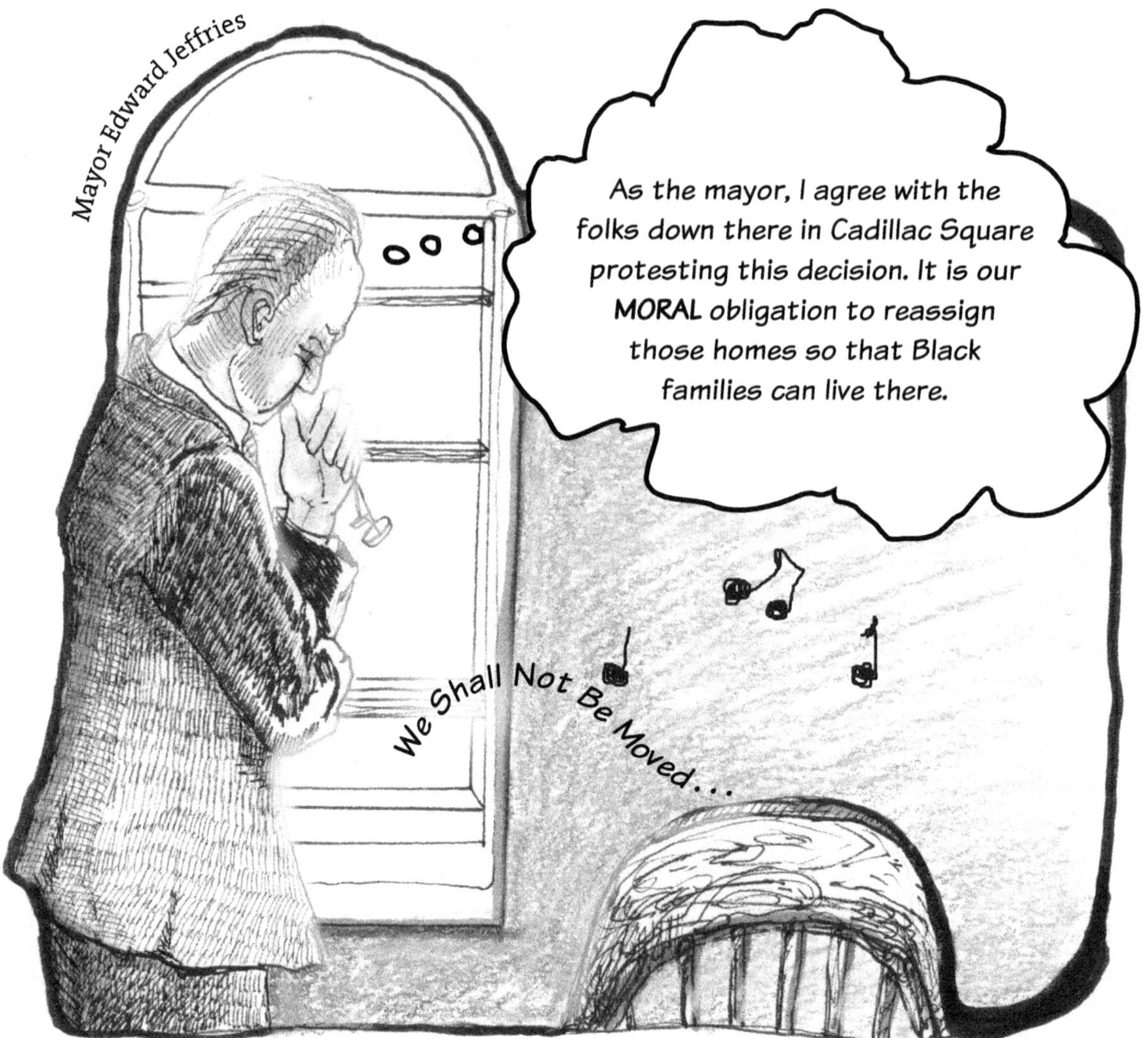
Mayor Edward Jeffries
As the mayor, I agree with the folks down there in Cadillac Square protesting this decision. It is our MORAL obligation to reassign those homes so that Black families can live there.
We Shall Not Be Moved . . .

January 28, 1942

February 2, 1942

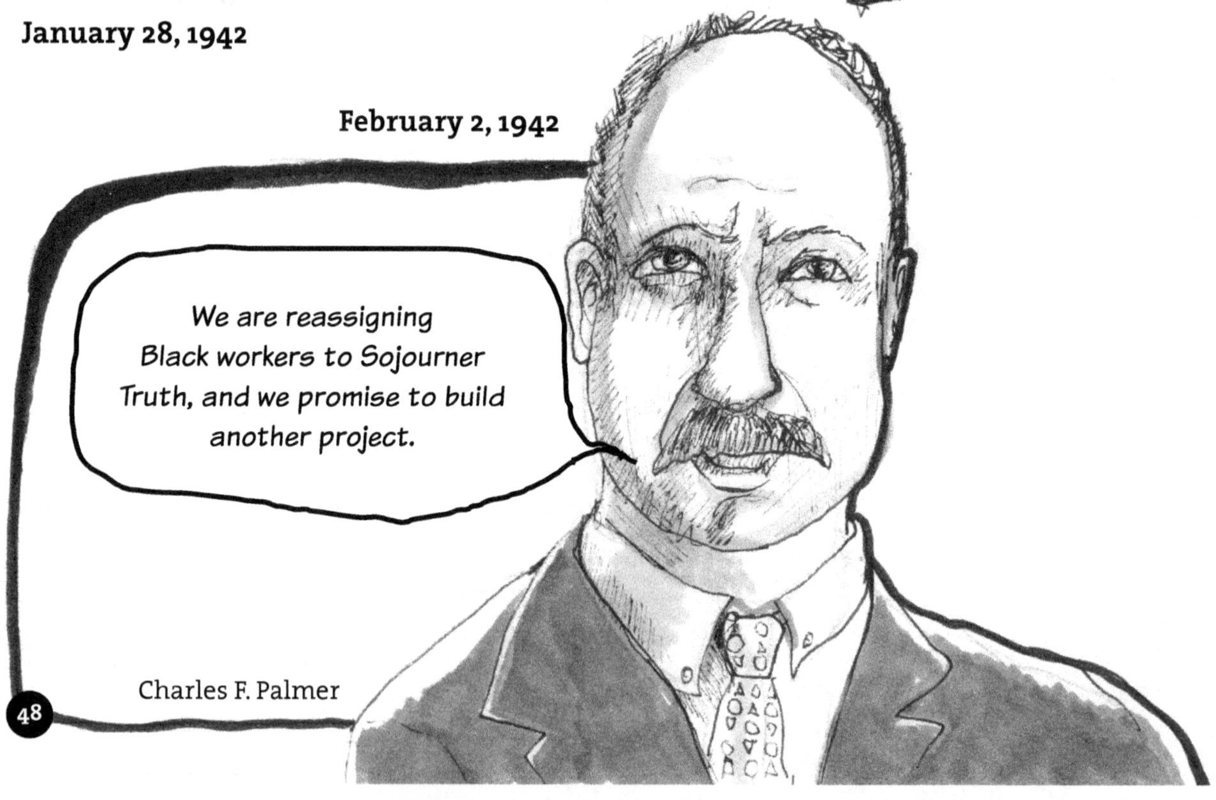
We are reassigning Black workers to Sojourner Truth, and we promise to build another project.
Charles F. Palmer

Fearful white residents in the area were furious with the decision to allow Black workers to occupy the new houses. They decided to protest. Men, women, and children picketed the project.

February 16, 1942

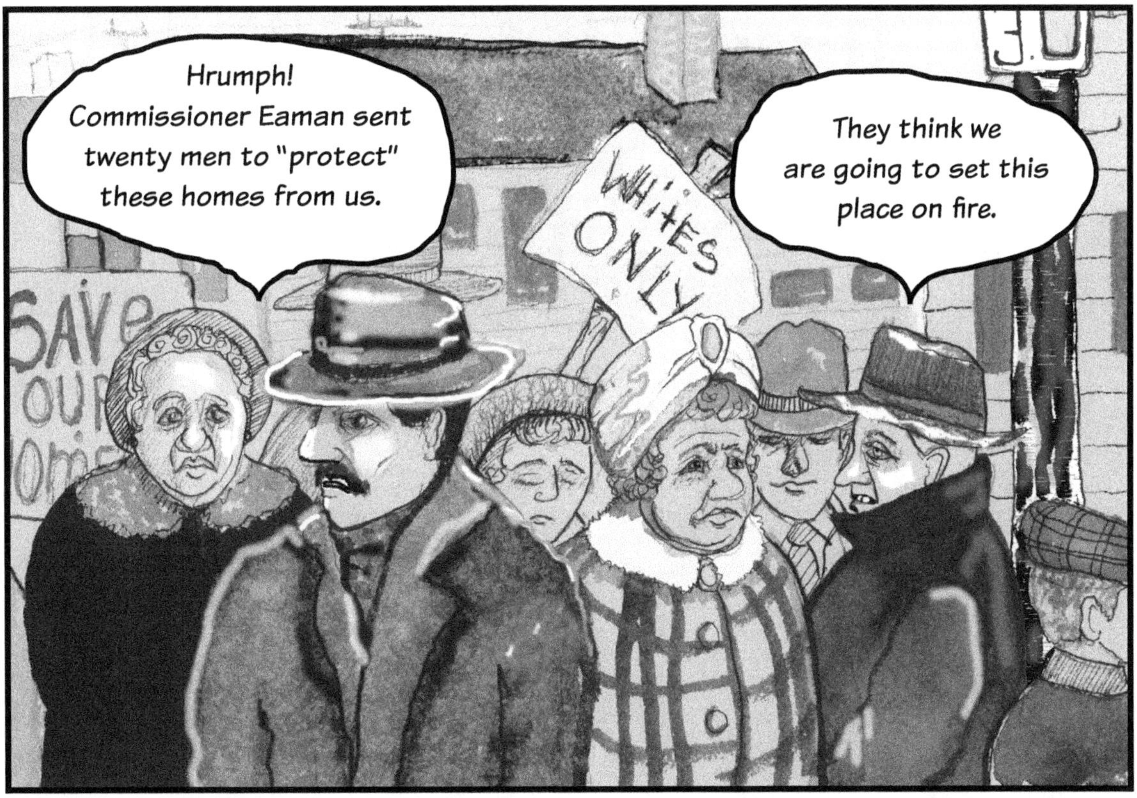

Hrumph! Commissioner Eaman sent twenty men to "protect" these homes from us.
They think we are going to set this place on fire.
WHITES ONLY
SAVE OUR

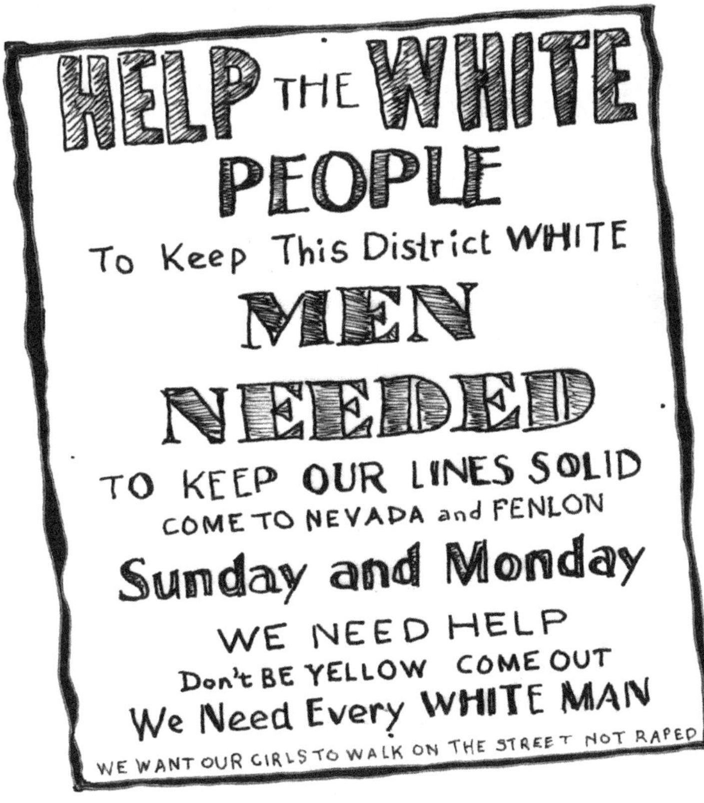

HELP THE WHITE PEOPLE
To Keep This District WHITE
MEN NEEDED
TO KEEP OUR LINES SOLID
COME TO NEVADA and FENLON
Sunday and Monday
WE NEED HELP
Don't BE YELLOW COME OUT
We Need Every WHITE MAN
WE WANT OUR GIRLS TO WALK ON THE STREET NOT RAPED

Peaceful protests and flyers were not the only tactics white people used. On February 27, 1942, at 11:00 p.m., a burning cross was sighted blazing close to the new homes, an unmistakable harbinger of violence.

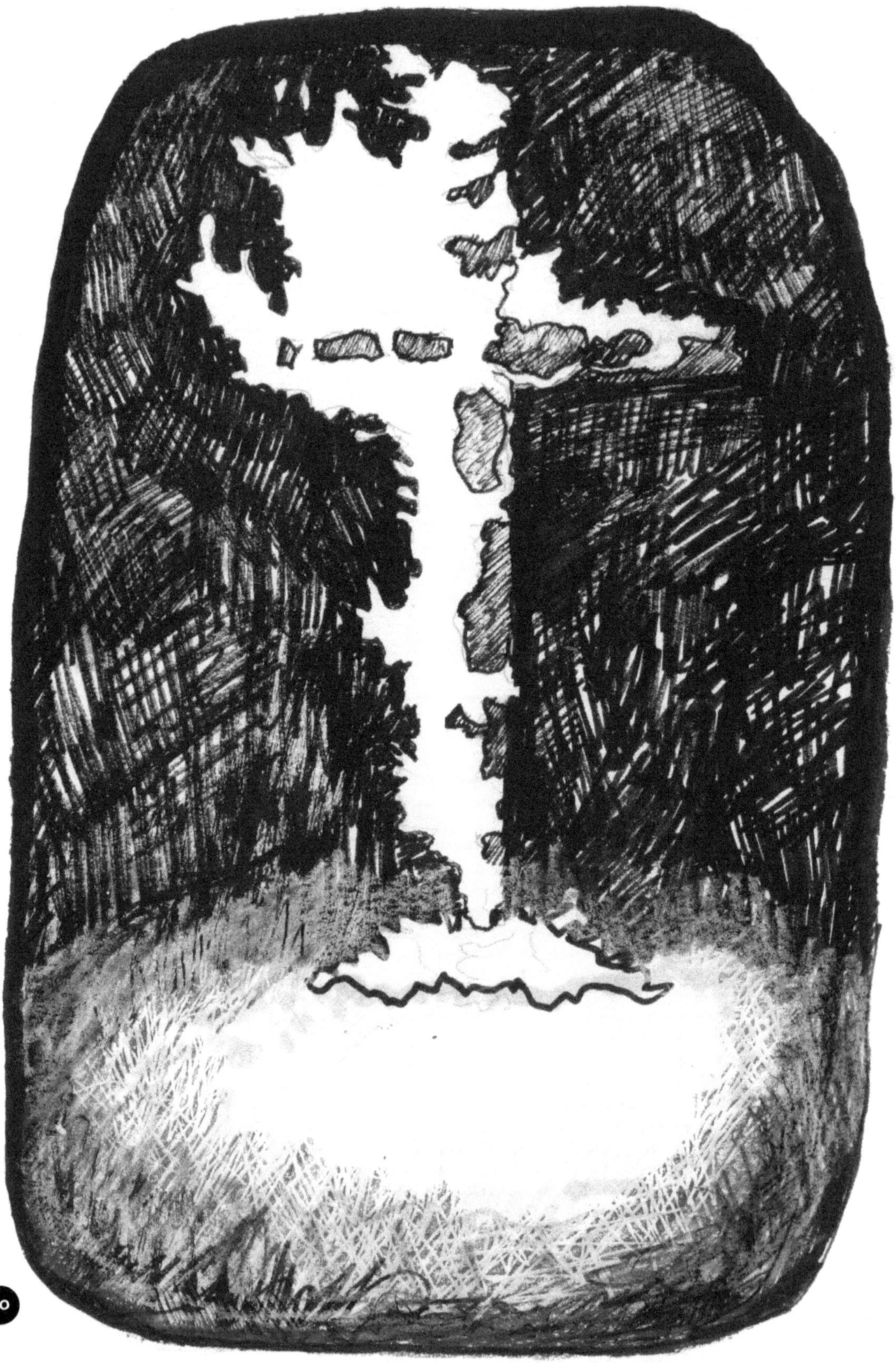

On February 28, 1942, the first day Black families could move into their homes, at approximately 6:00 a.m., a large crowd of white picketers, mostly women and boys, stood directly in front of the new homes.

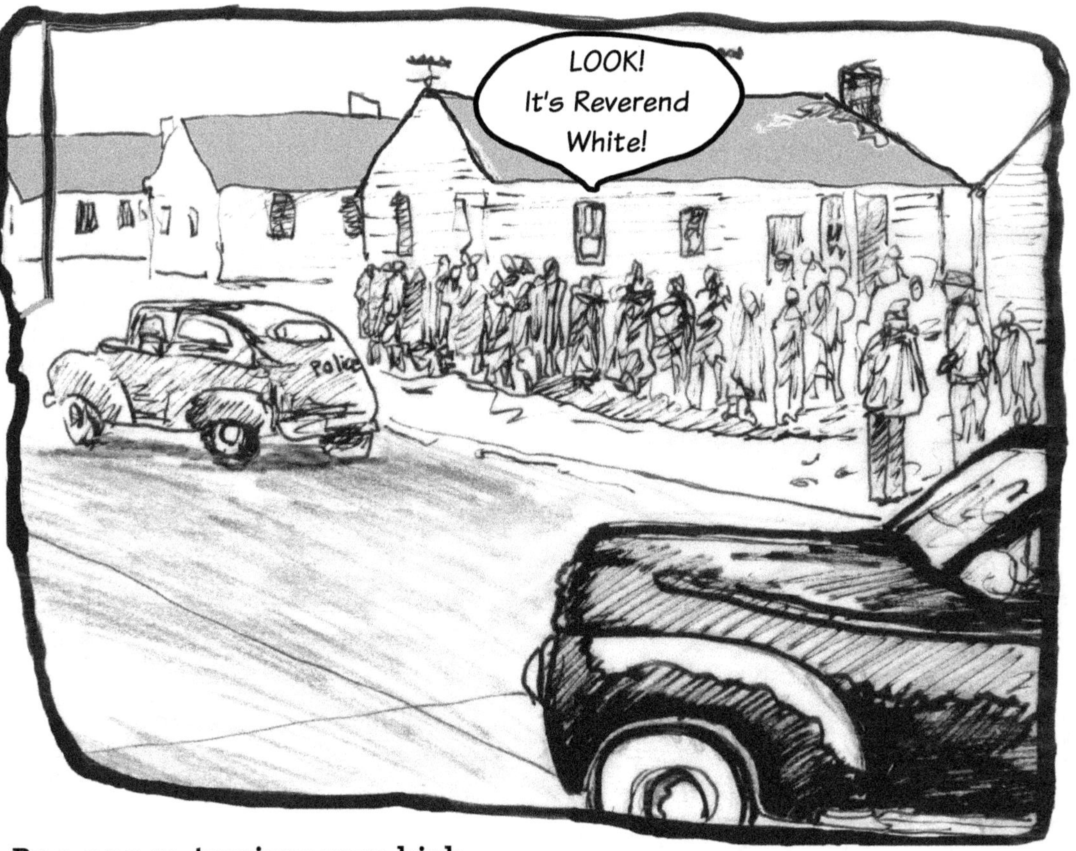

LOOK! It's Reverend White!
Police

By 9:00 a.m. tensions were high.

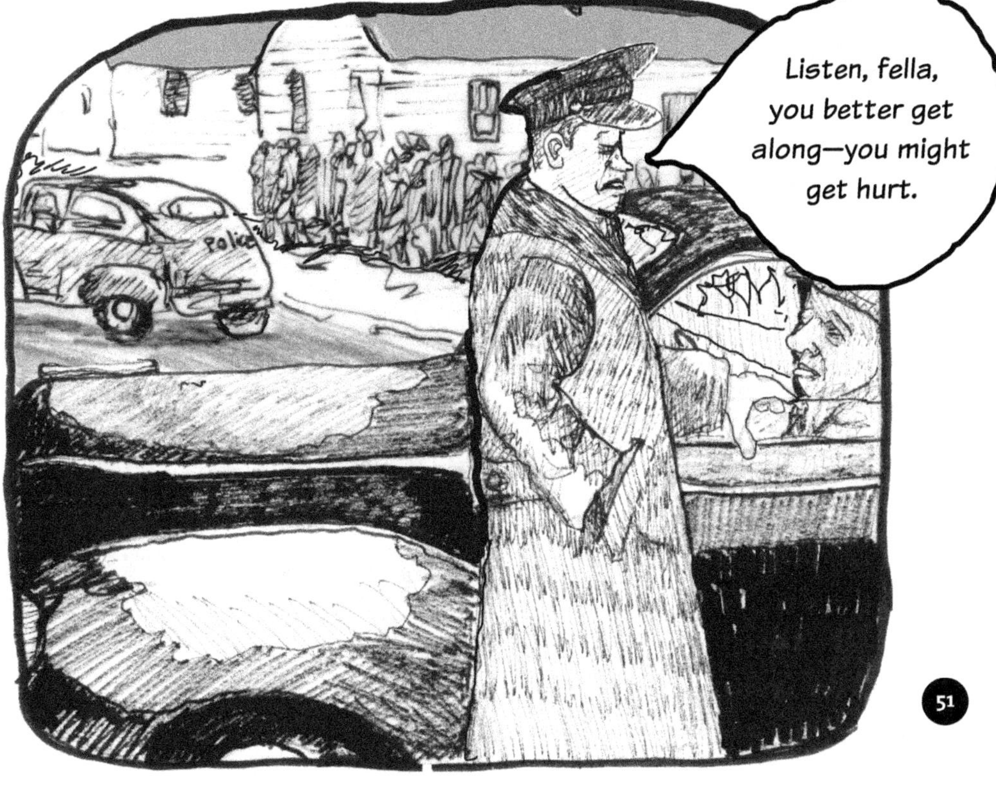

Police
Listen, fella, you better get along—you might get hurt.

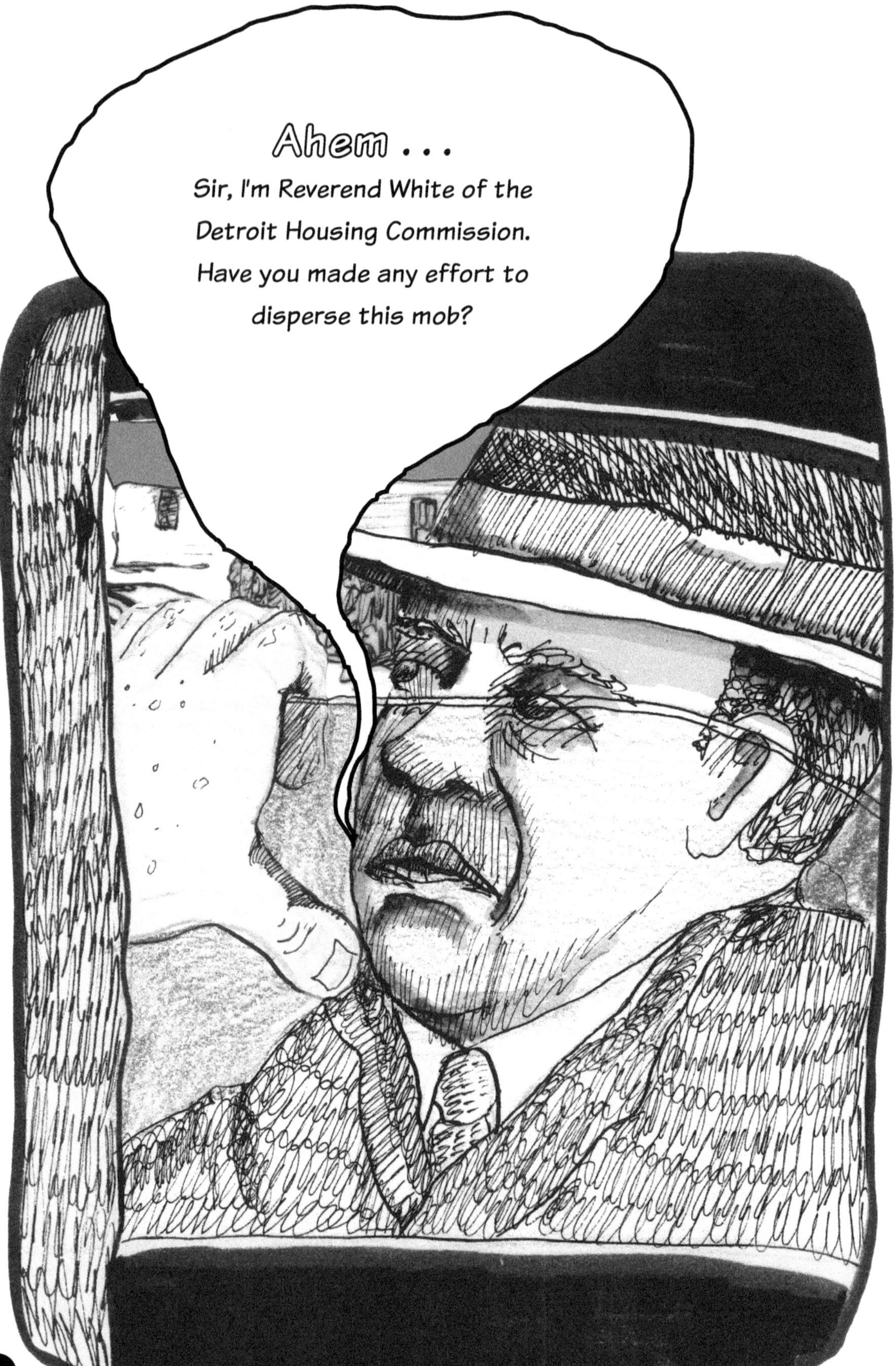
Ahem . . .
Sir, I'm Reverend White of the Detroit Housing Commission. Have you made any effort to disperse this mob?

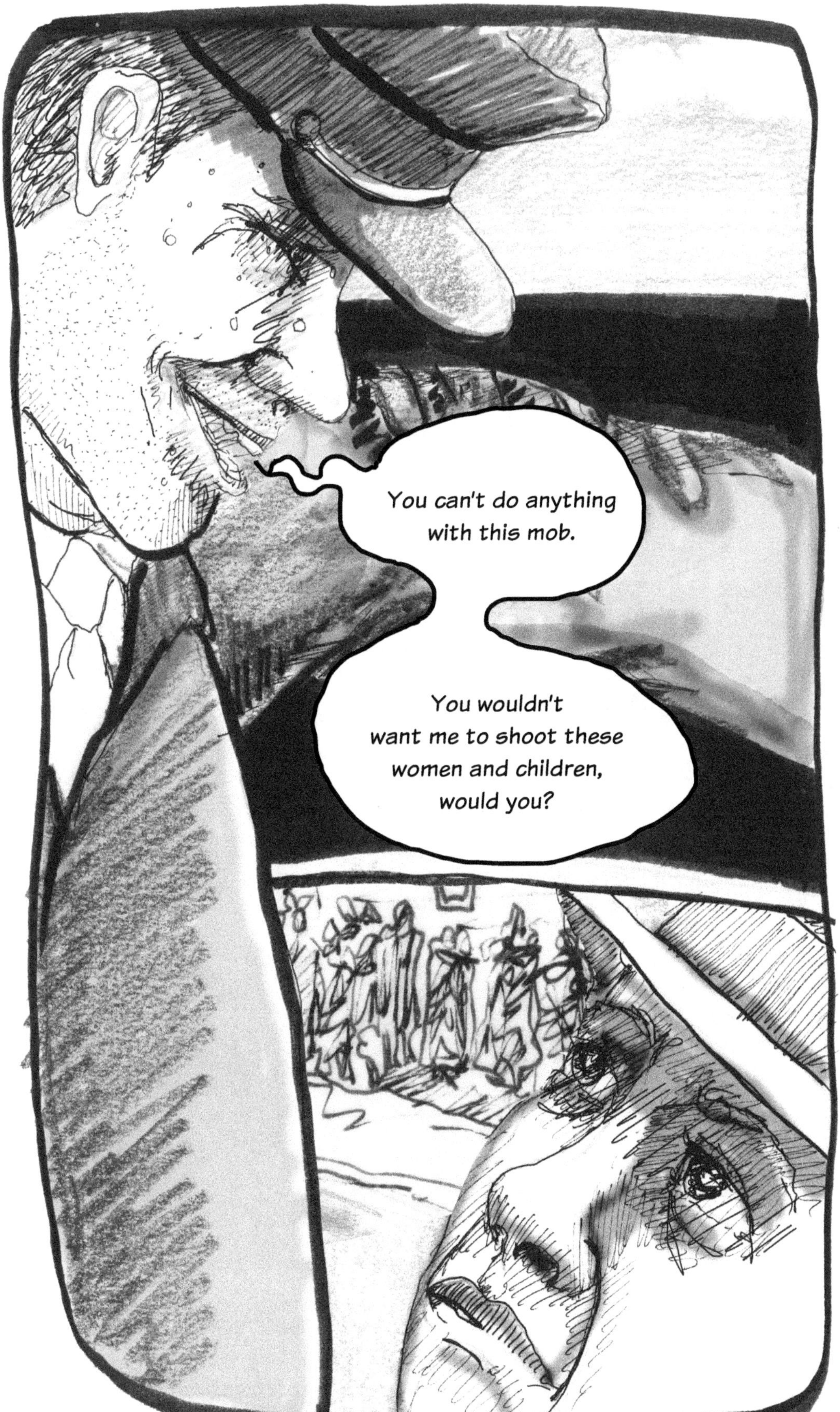
You can't do anything with this mob.
You wouldn't want me to shoot these women and children, would you?

The Reverend Horace White had come to encourage a peaceful moving day.

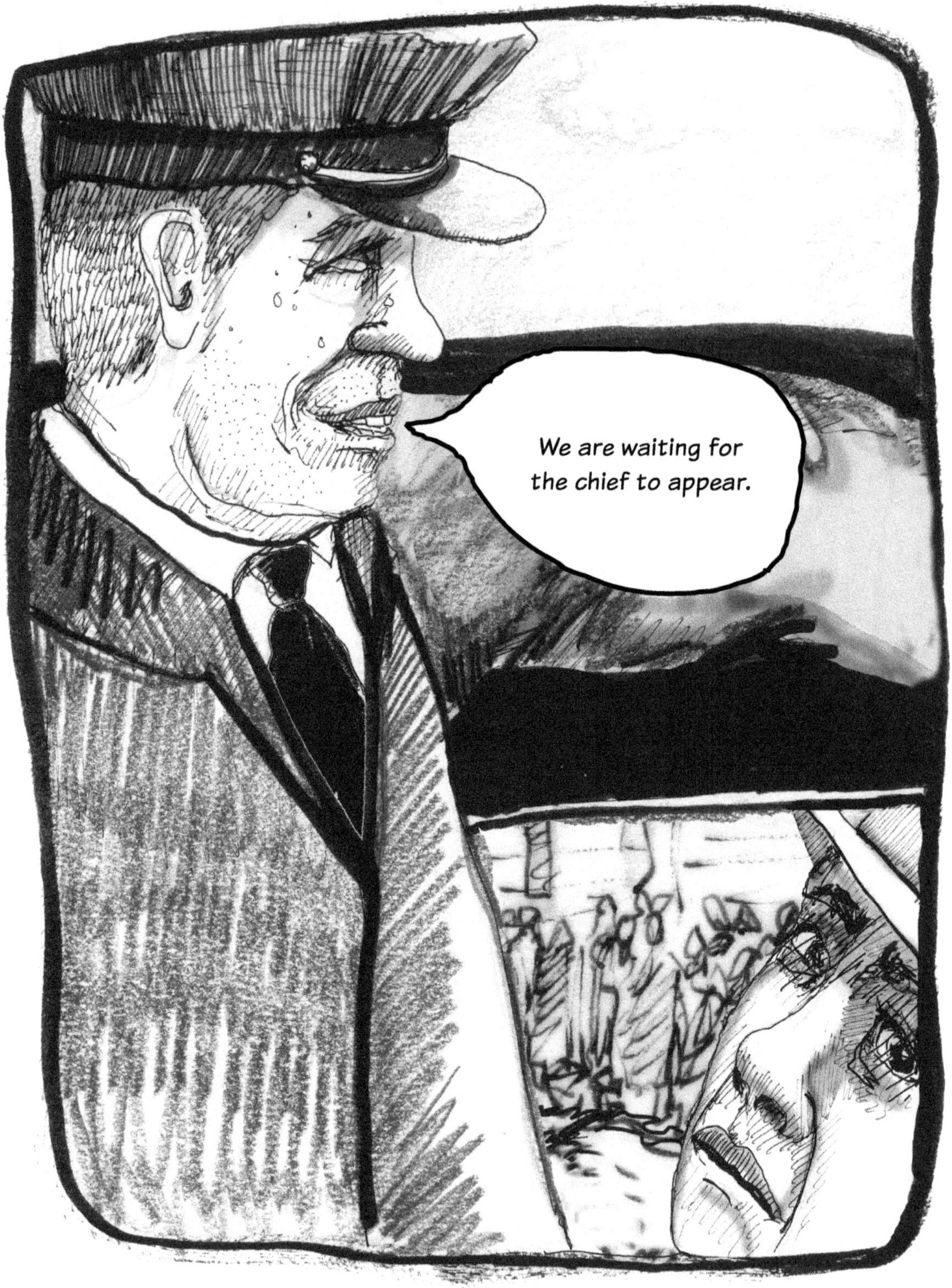
We are waiting for the chief to appear.

Clearly the police, who were white, were there because it was their duty, but in most cases it was obvious they were loyal to members of their race and shared their concerns about Black people gaining too many privileges.

Everyone watched as the first moving truck came into view. Along with picketers who itched for violence and people like Reverend White who hoped for peace, there were also 150 policemen, 21 mounted police on horses, 26 police vehicles, a gas squad of 10 men, 45 police shotguns, 2 police gas guns, and various gas bombs. There was not a single Black police officer.

The first moving truck came closer and closer. People grew tense with anticipation.

Here they come. Get ready, all hell's going to break loose . . .

Black supporters of the housing project lined one side of Ryan Street and white protesters lined the other.

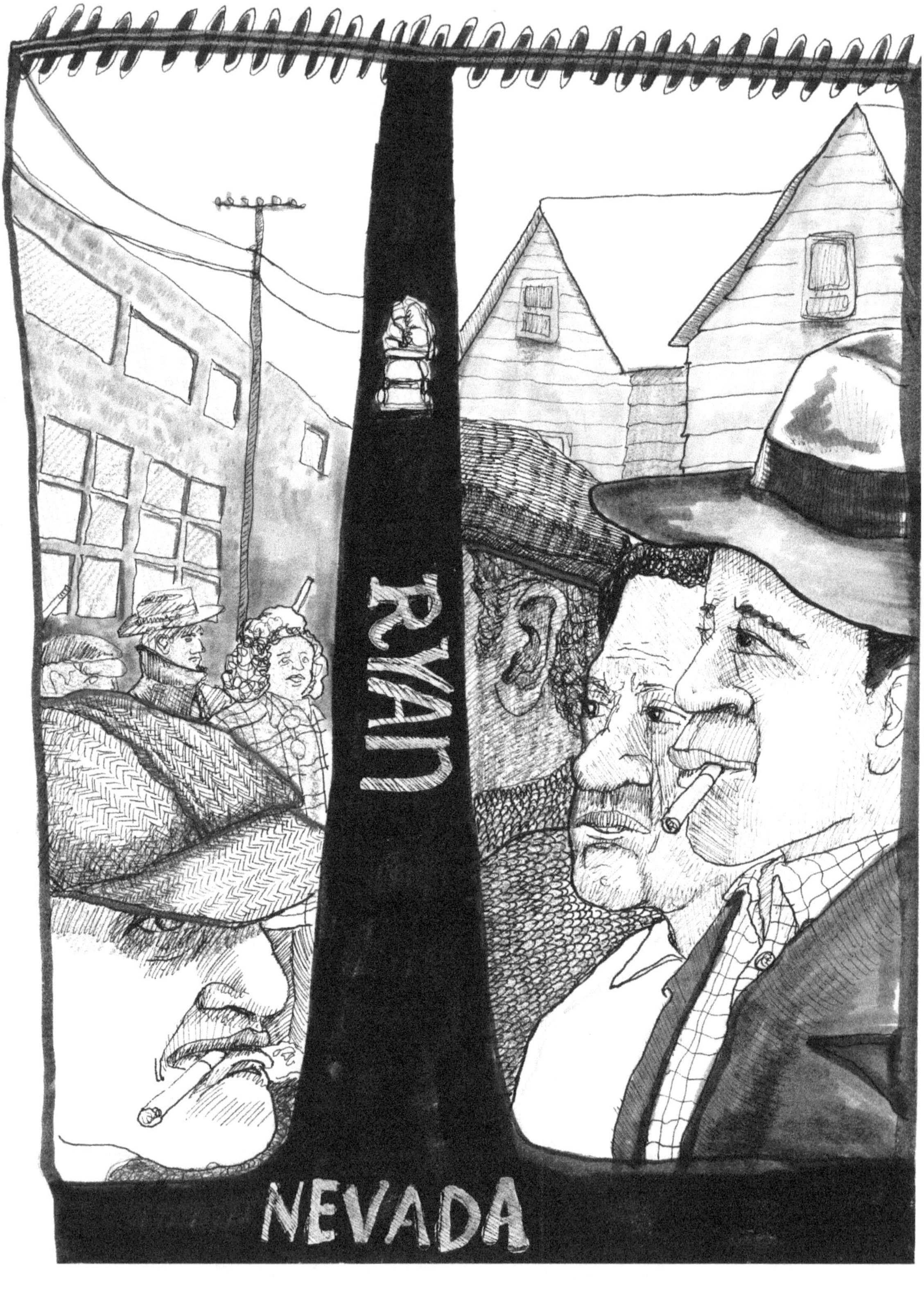
RYAN
NEVADA

What happened next was inevitable.

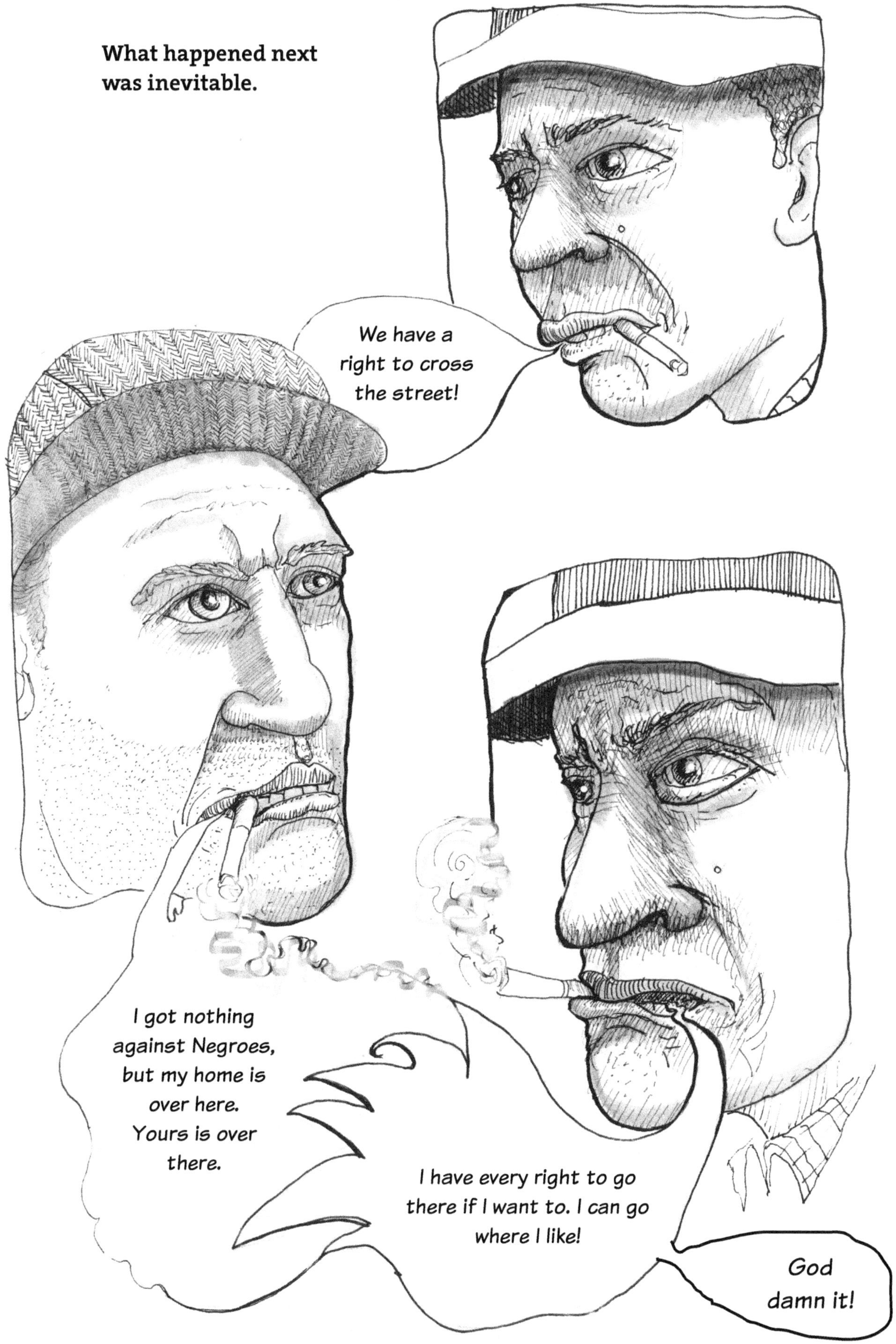
We have a right to cross the street!
I got nothing against Negroes, but my home is over here. Yours is over there.
I have every right to go there if I want to. I can go where I like!
God damn it!

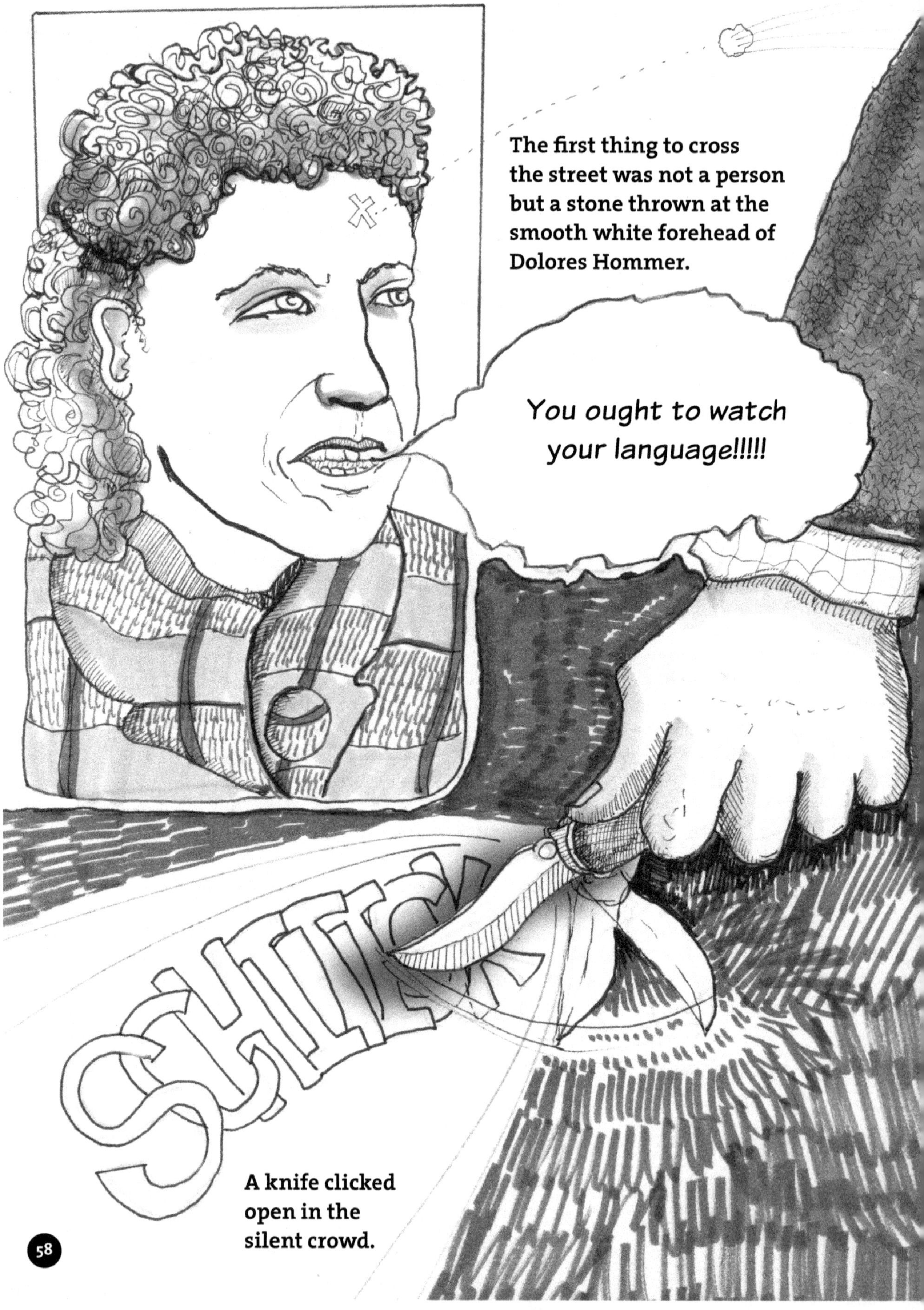
The first thing to cross the street was not a person but a stone thrown at the smooth white forehead of Dolores Hommer.
You ought to watch your language!!!!!
A knife clicked open in the silent crowd.

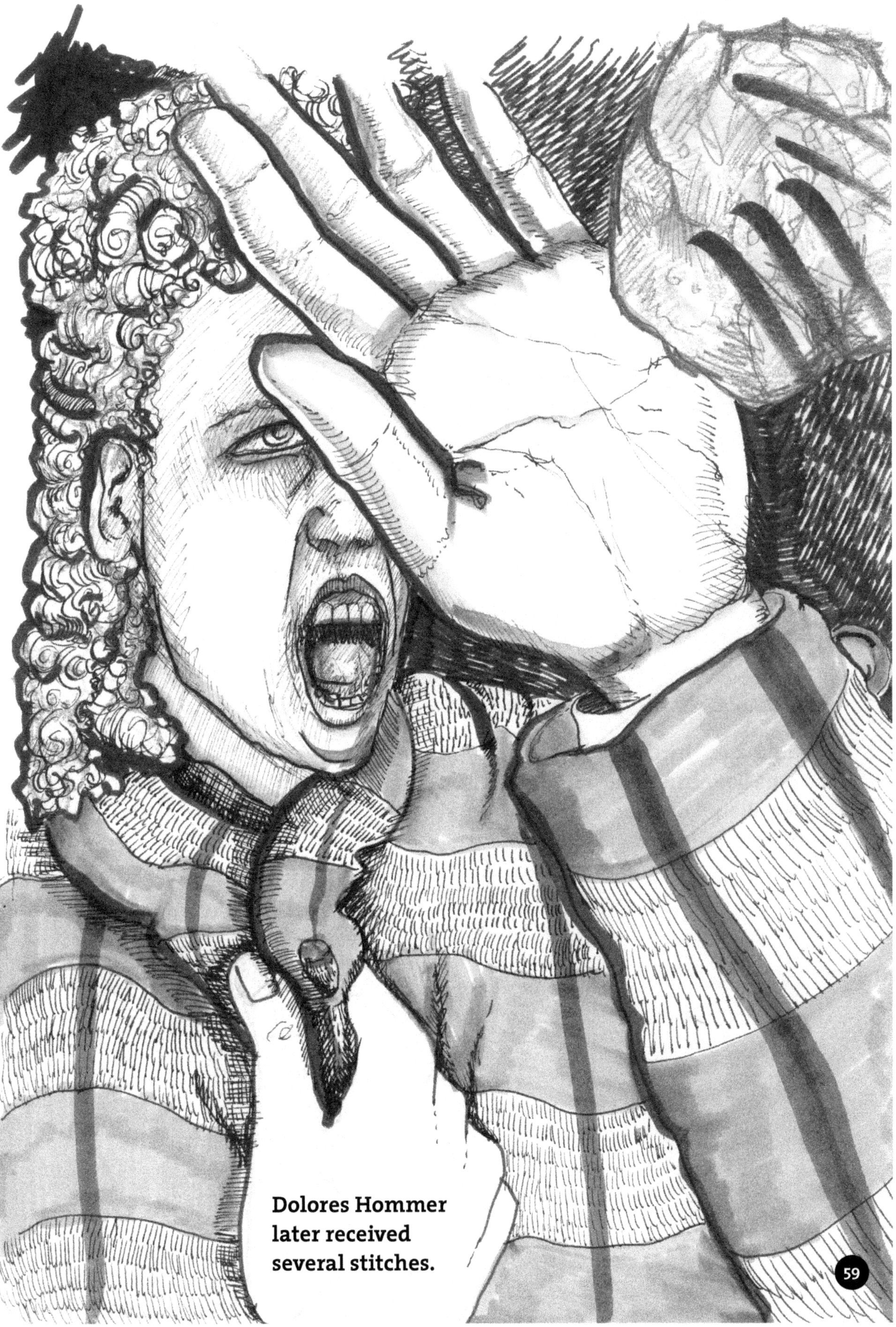

Dolores Hommer later received several stitches.

White police began to beat and arrest Black people who had come to support the new residents. Police on shiny dark horses drew blood with their batons and fists.

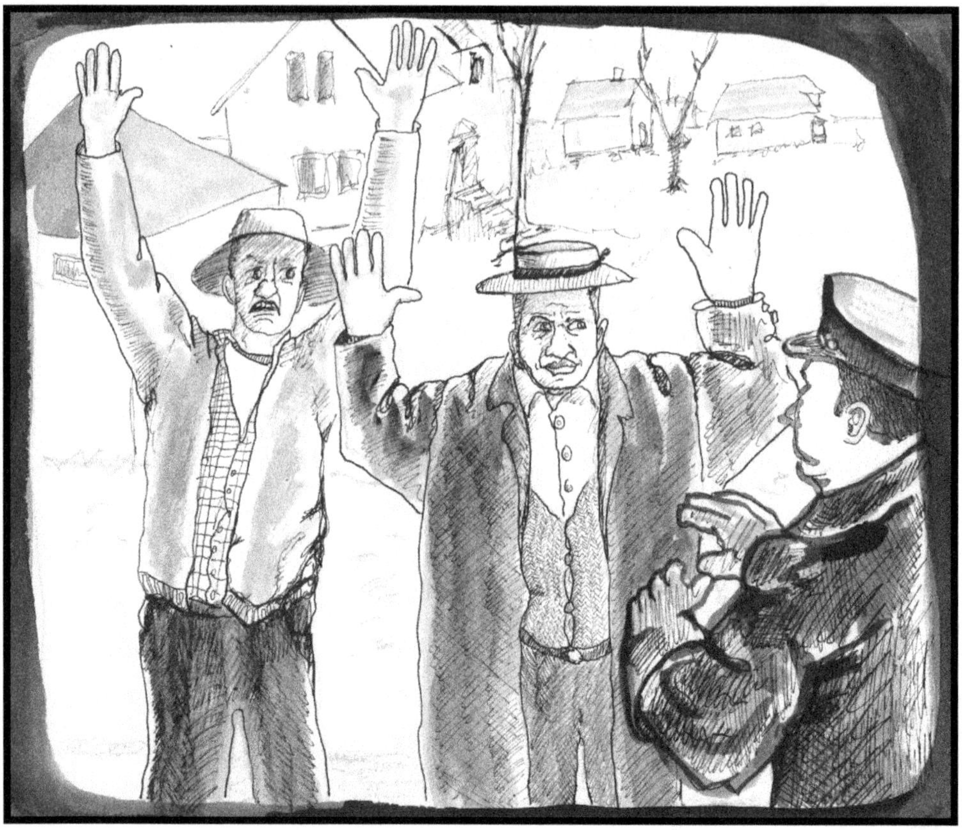

By 11:00 a.m. the mayor feared that the Sojourner Truth housing project would become a bloody chapter in the history of Detroit.

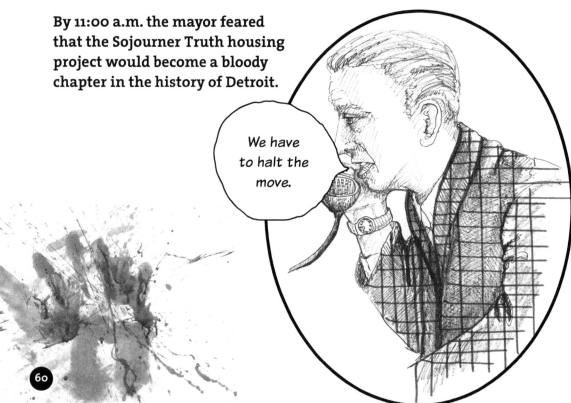

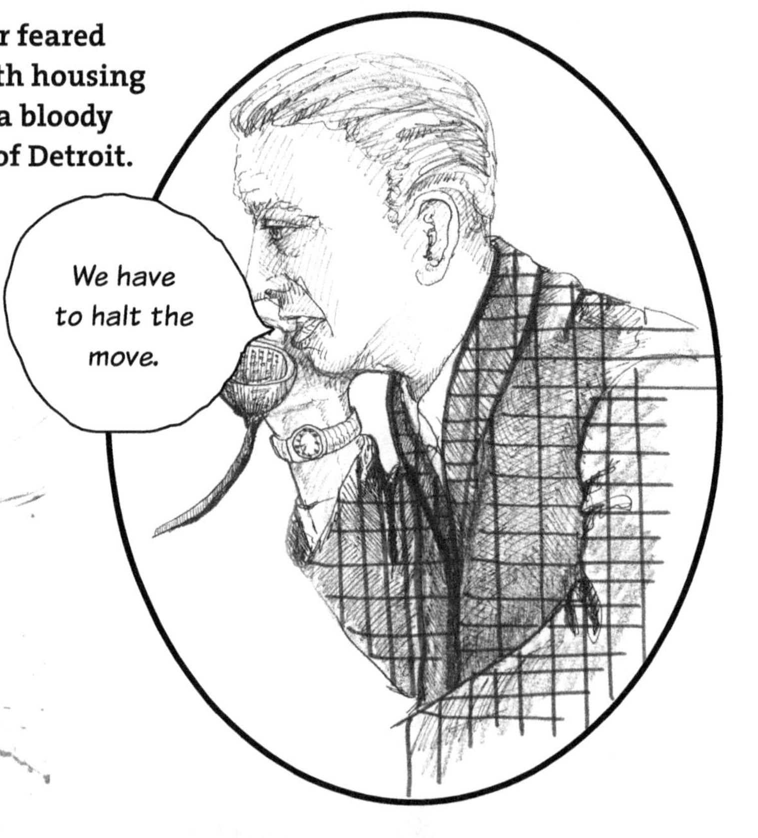
We have to halt the move.

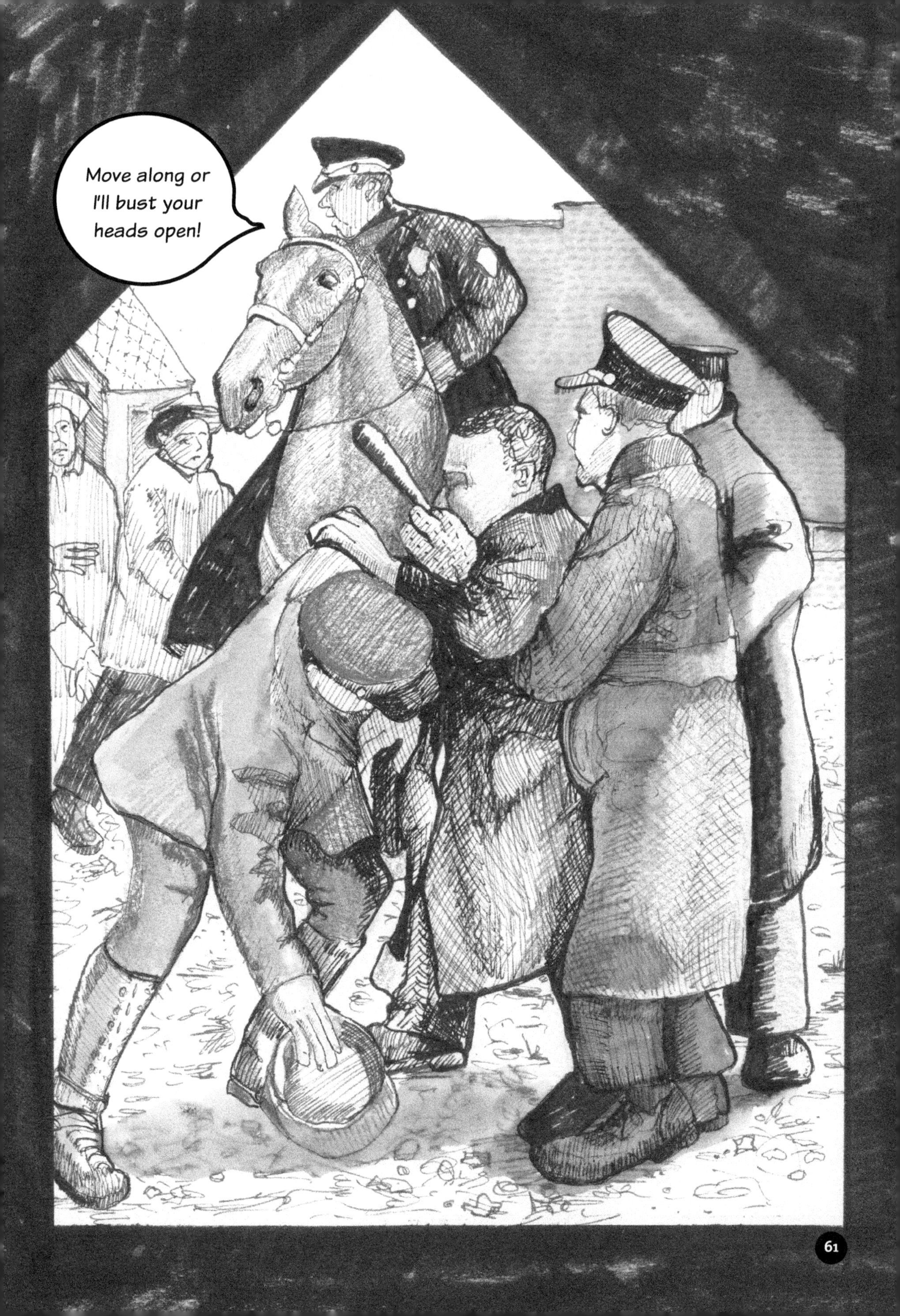
Move along or I'll bust your heads open!

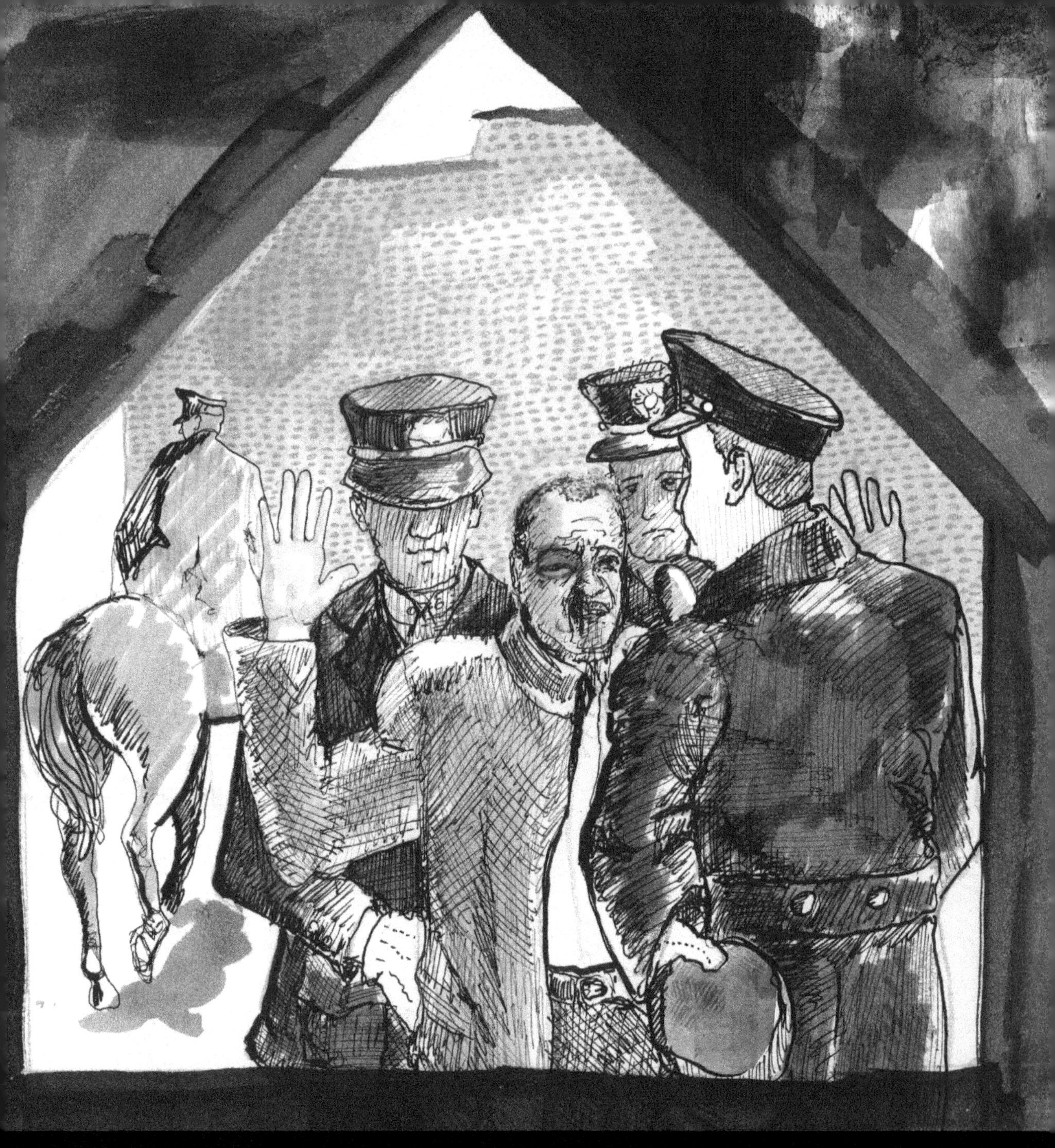

White police acted as though they were there to stop an armed rebellion rather than ensure Black families could move into their homes. Black onlookers were terrorized by police mounted on horses and savagely beaten by police on foot.

The Reverend Horace White witnessed the violence firsthand.

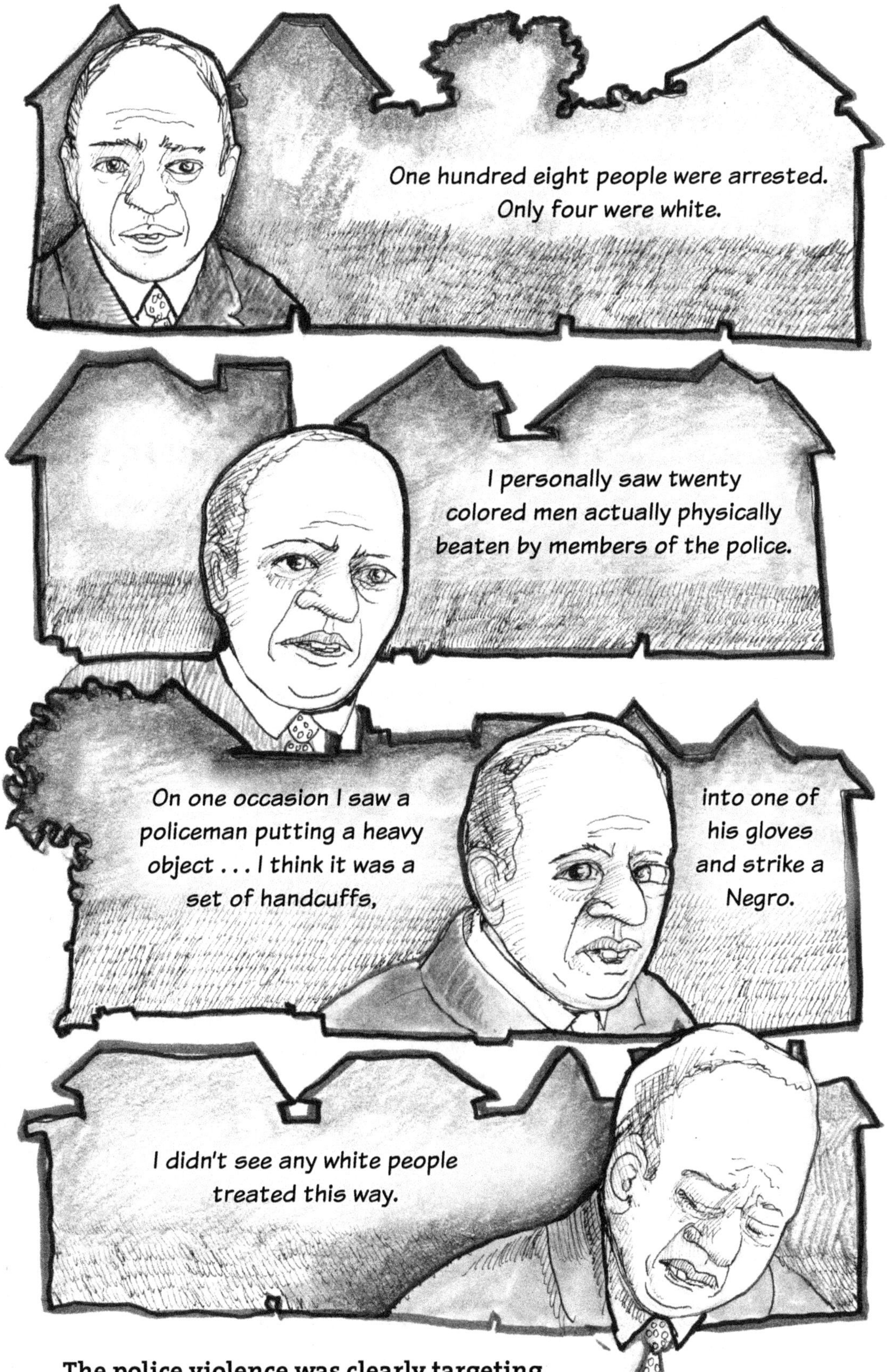
One hundred eight people were arrested. Only four were white.
I personally saw twenty colored men actually physically beaten by members of the police.
On one occasion I saw a policeman putting a heavy object . . . I think it was a set of handcuffs,
into one of his gloves and strike a Negro.
I didn't see any white people treated this way.

The police violence was clearly targeting African Americans.

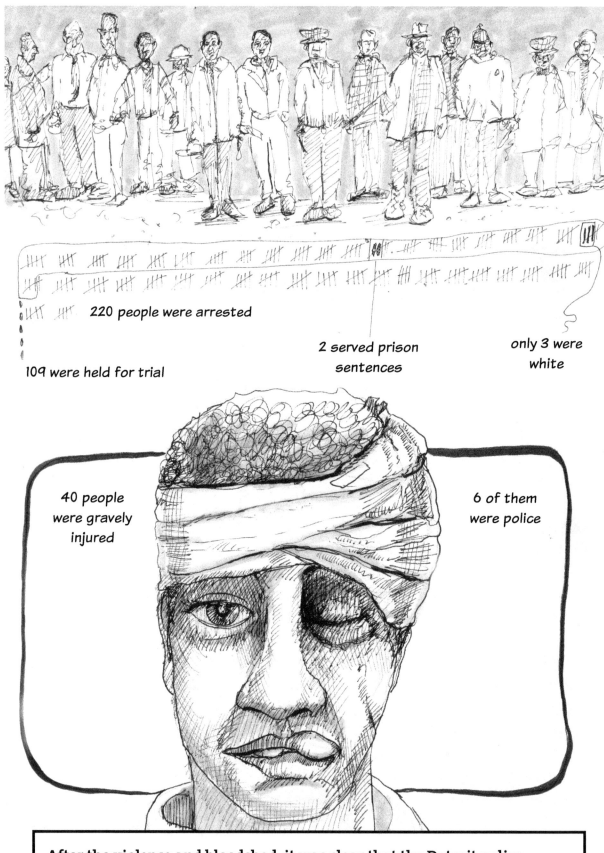

220 people were arrested

109 were held for trial

2 served prison sentences

only 3 were white

40 people were gravely injured

6 of them were police

After the violence and bloodshed, it was clear that the Detroit police were incapable of maintaining peace and order—and unwilling to do so—so that Black families could move into the Sojourner Truth houses.

People sought scapegoats to explain how the violence had begun. The police refused to accept any responsibility for their part in the disastrous day.

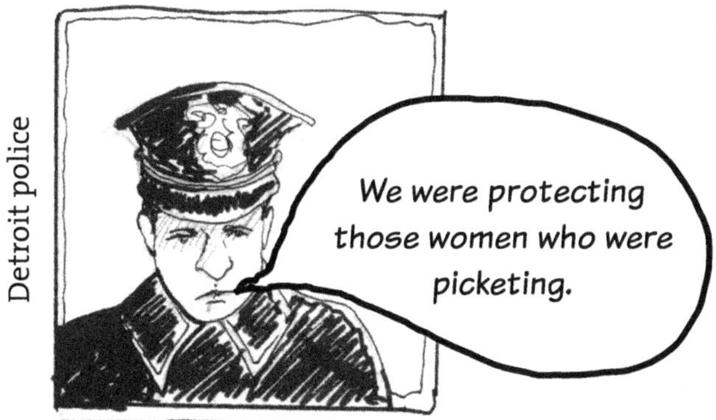
Detroit police
We were protecting those women who were picketing.

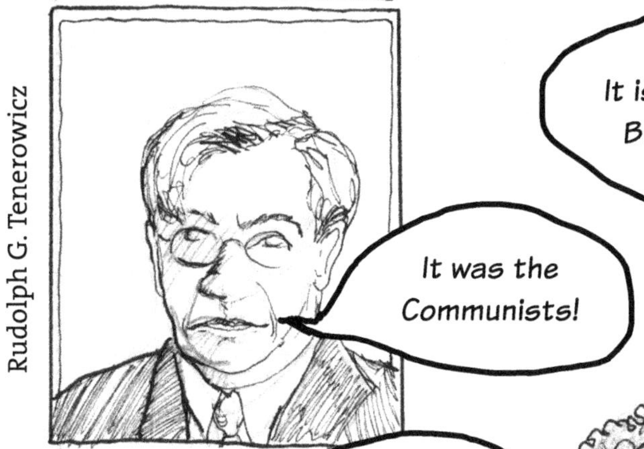
Rudolph G. Tenerowicz
It was the Communists!

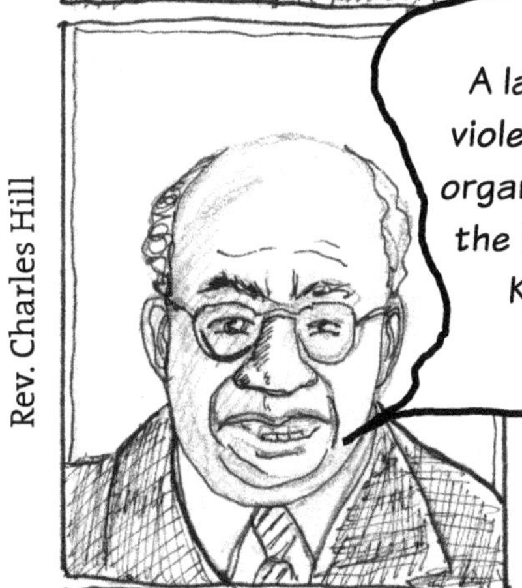
Rev. Charles Hill
A lawless violent mob organized by the Ku Klux Klan.

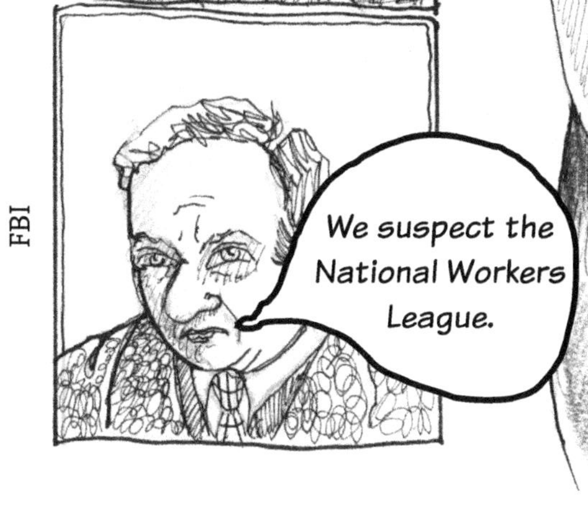
FBI
We suspect the National Workers League.

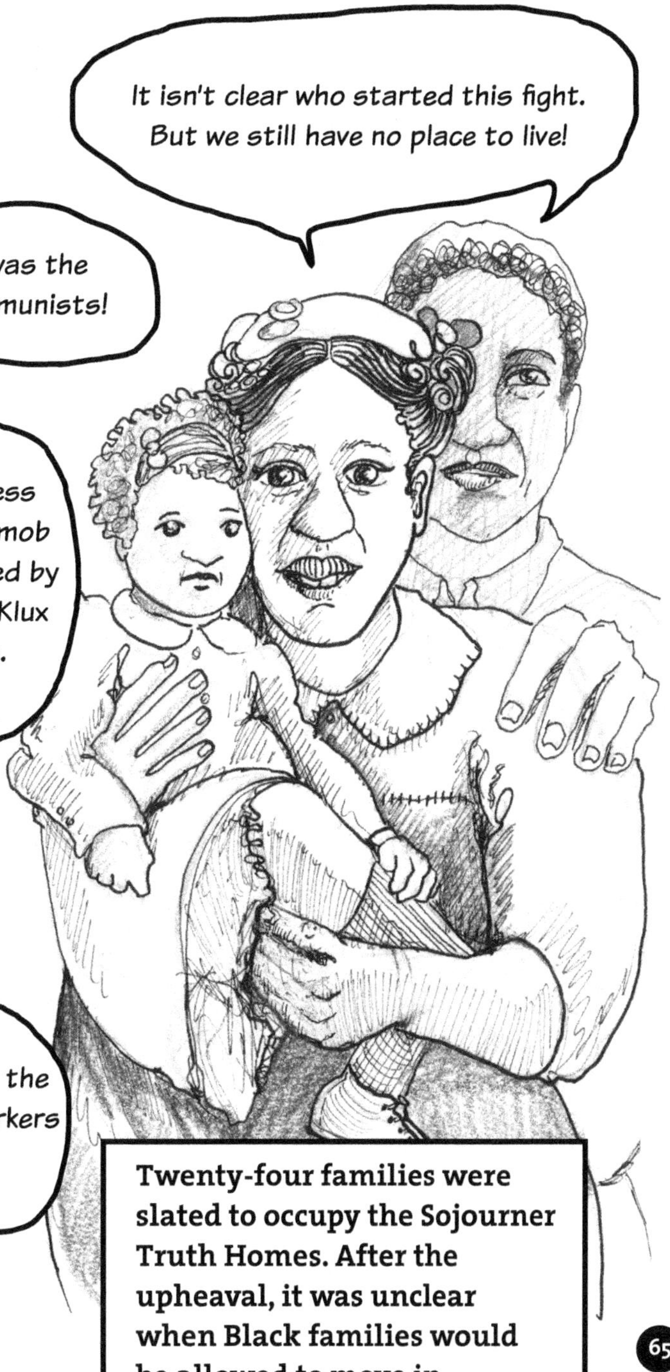
It isn't clear who started this fight. But we still have no place to live!

Twenty-four families were slated to occupy the Sojourner Truth Homes. After the upheaval, it was unclear when Black families would be allowed to move in.

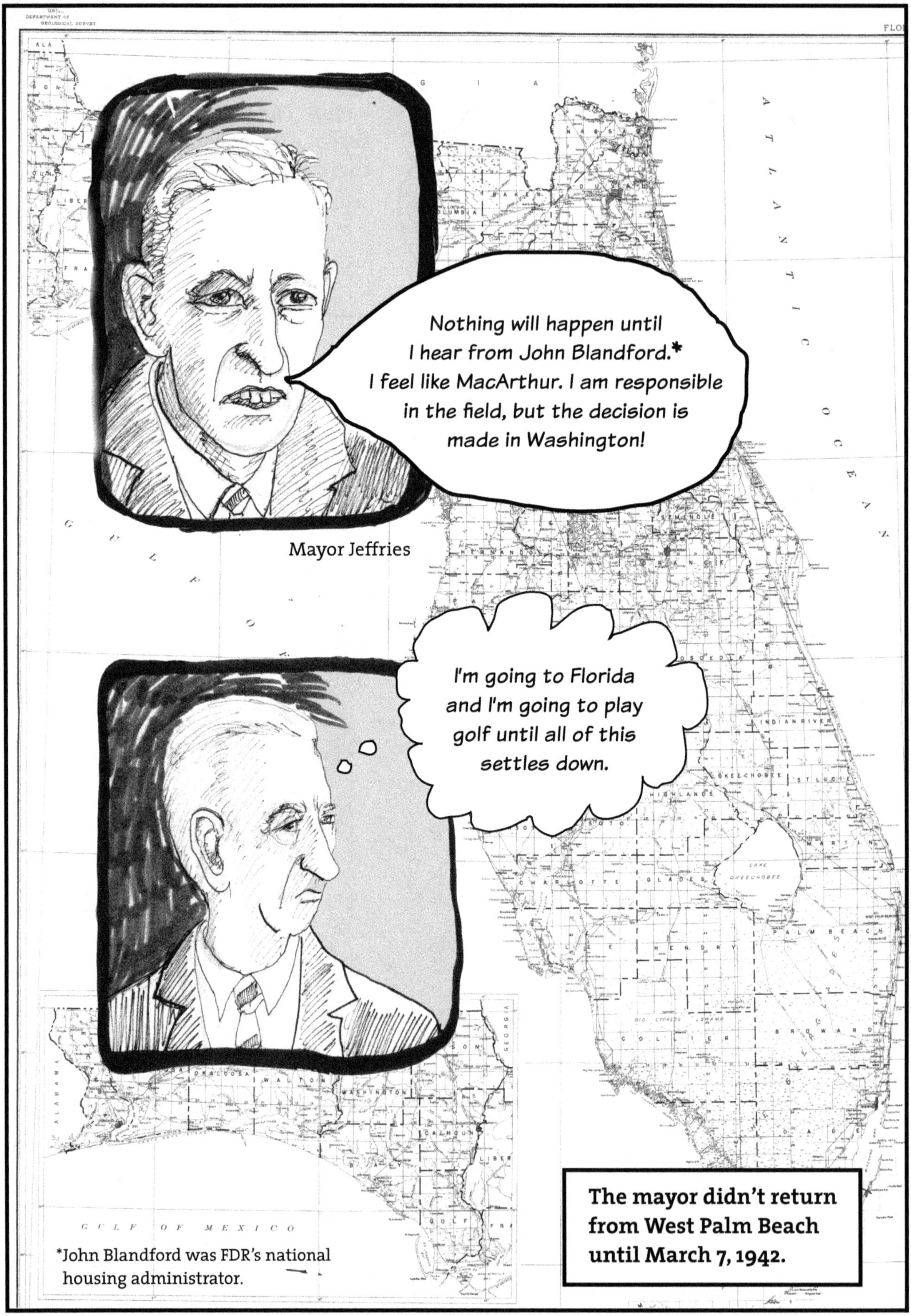
Nothing will happen until I hear from John Blandford.* I feel like MacArthur. I am responsible in the field, but the decision is made in Washington!
Mayor Jeffries
I'm going to Florida and I'm going to play golf until all of this settles down.
The mayor didn't return from West Palm Beach until March 7, 1942.

*John Blandford was FDR's national housing administrator.

March 10, 1942: Police finally forced white protesters near the Sojourner Truth Homes to disperse.

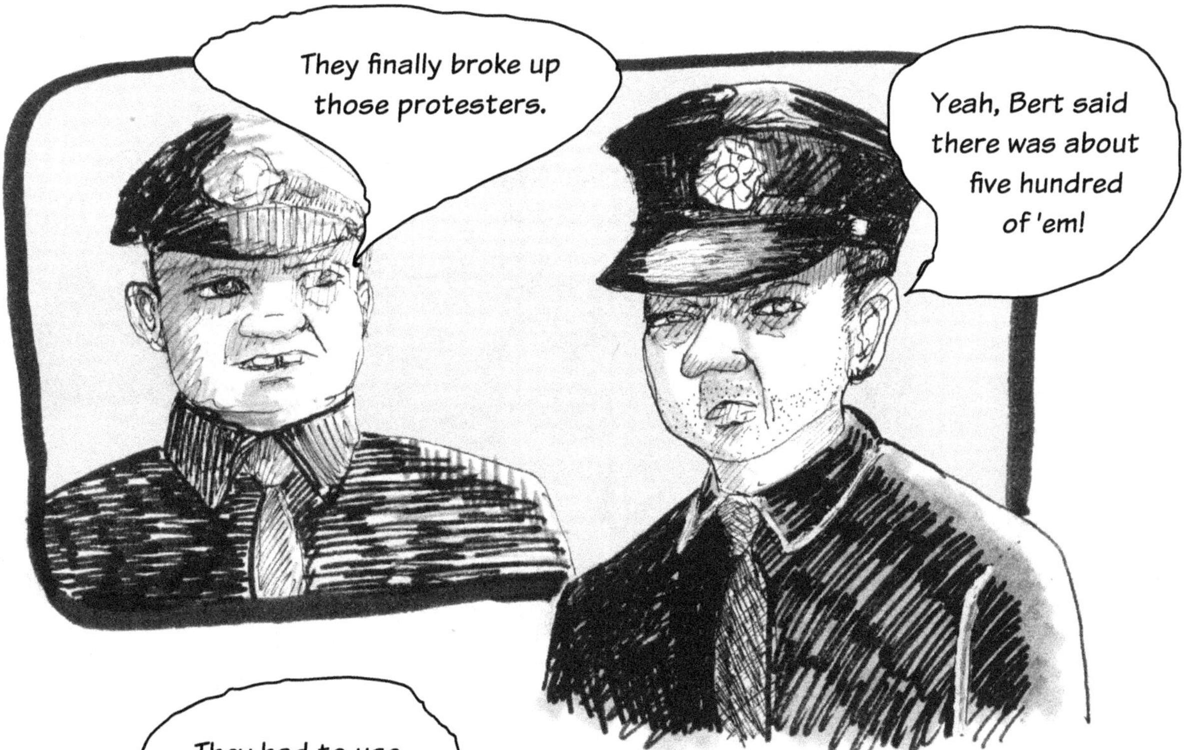
They finally broke up those protesters.
Yeah, Bert said there was about five hundred of 'em!

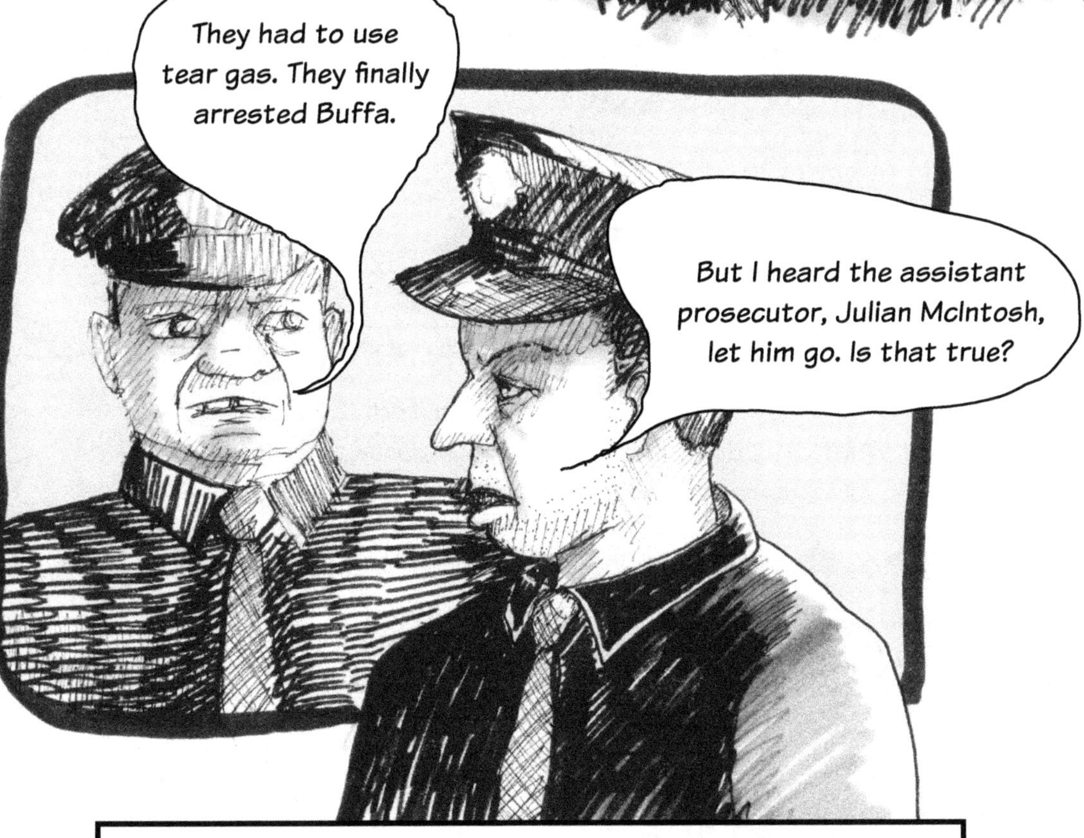
They had to use tear gas. They finally arrested Buffa.
But I heard the assistant prosecutor, Julian McIntosh, let him go. Is that true?

It took over a month for a decision to be made about the future occupants of the Sojourner Truth Homes.

April 15, 1942: Finally, John Blandford announced that Black families could move into the homes. Mayor Jeffries struggled with the decision, weighing the mandate against his resources for keeping peace and order and providing safety.

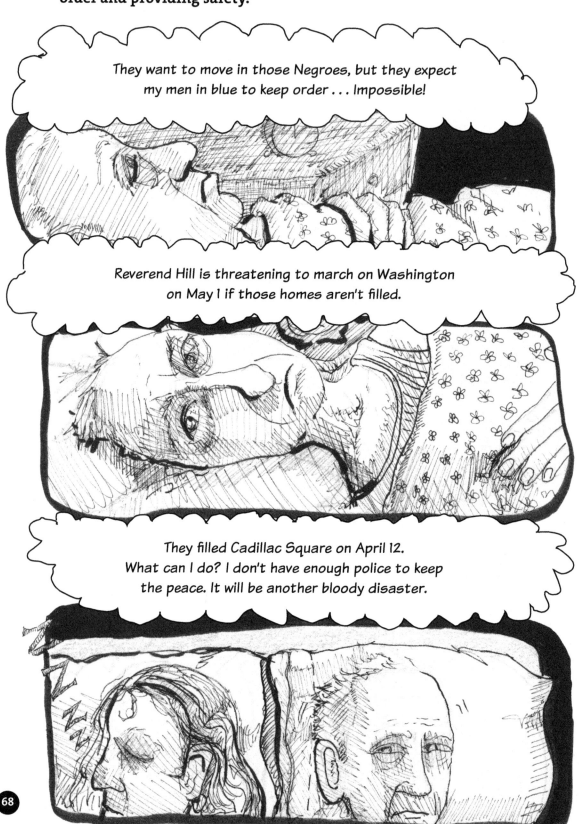

They want to move in those Negroes, but they expect my men in blue to keep order . . . Impossible!

Reverend Hill is threatening to march on Washington on May 1 if those homes aren't filled.

They filled Cadillac Square on April 12. What can I do? I don't have enough police to keep the peace. It will be another bloody disaster.

Maybe the governor will help me tomorrow . . .

On April 16, 1942, the mayor met with Governor Van Wagoner. He agreed to use state resources to help Black families in Detroit move into the Sojourner Truth housing project.

April 24, 1942

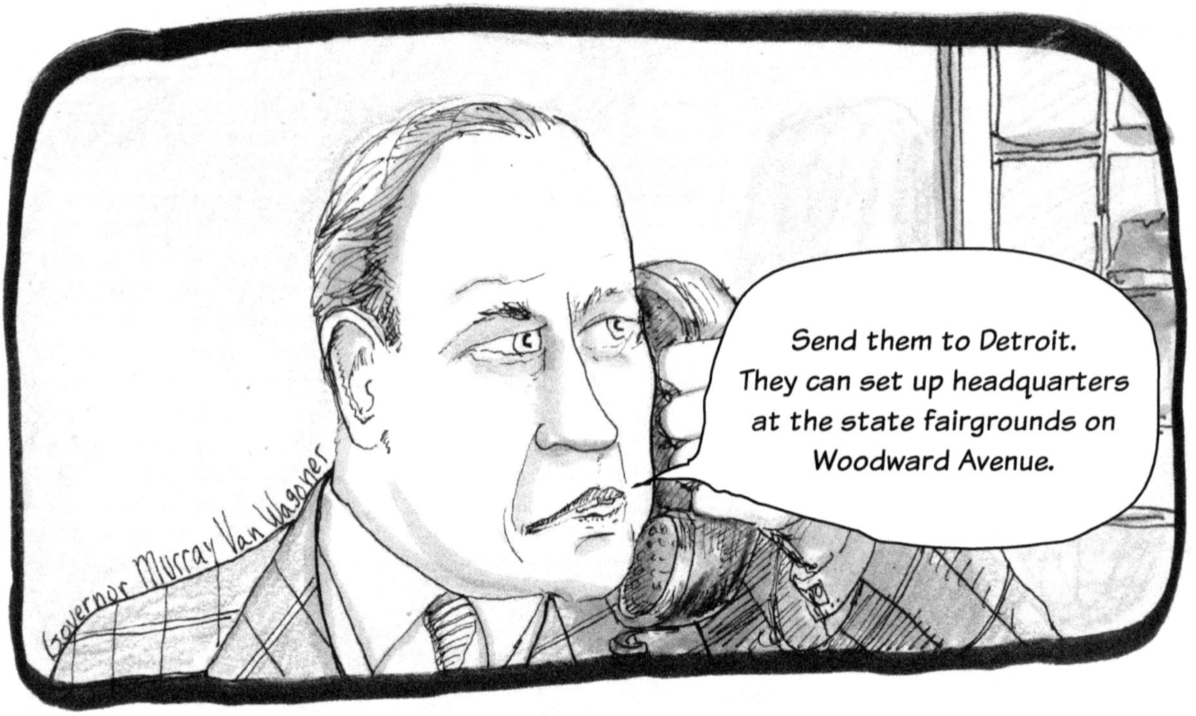
Governor Murray Van Wagoner
Send them to Detroit. They can set up headquarters at the state fairgrounds on Woodward Avenue.

Between April 27 and April 29, 24 companies of state troopers, 1,720 men with the Michigan Home Guard, and 1,400 city and state police officers were mobilized to keep the peace. On April 28, in the early-morning hours before dawn, troopers occupied the area around the project in order to keep the peace.

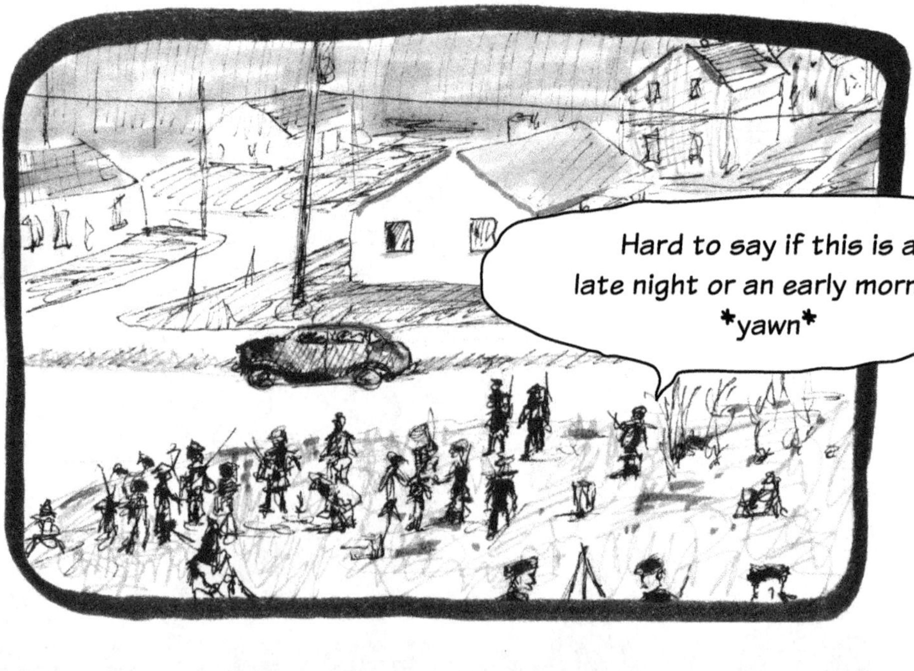
Hard to say if this is a late night or an early morning! *yawn*

There was only one incident of serious violence: a crowd of whites threw stones at a car driven by a Black man.

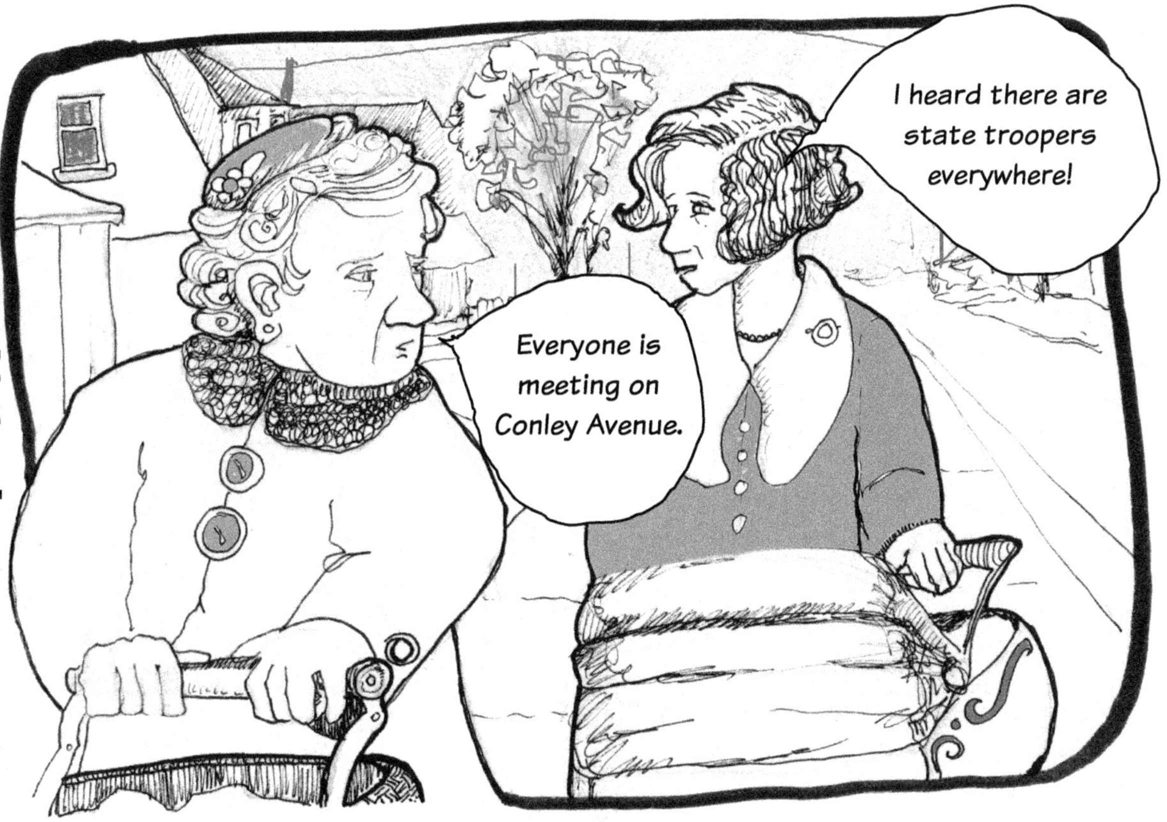
I heard there are state troopers everywhere!
Everyone is meeting on Conley Avenue.

April 29, 1942

After two days of tension and vigilance, fourteen families safely occupied the Sojourner Truth housing project.

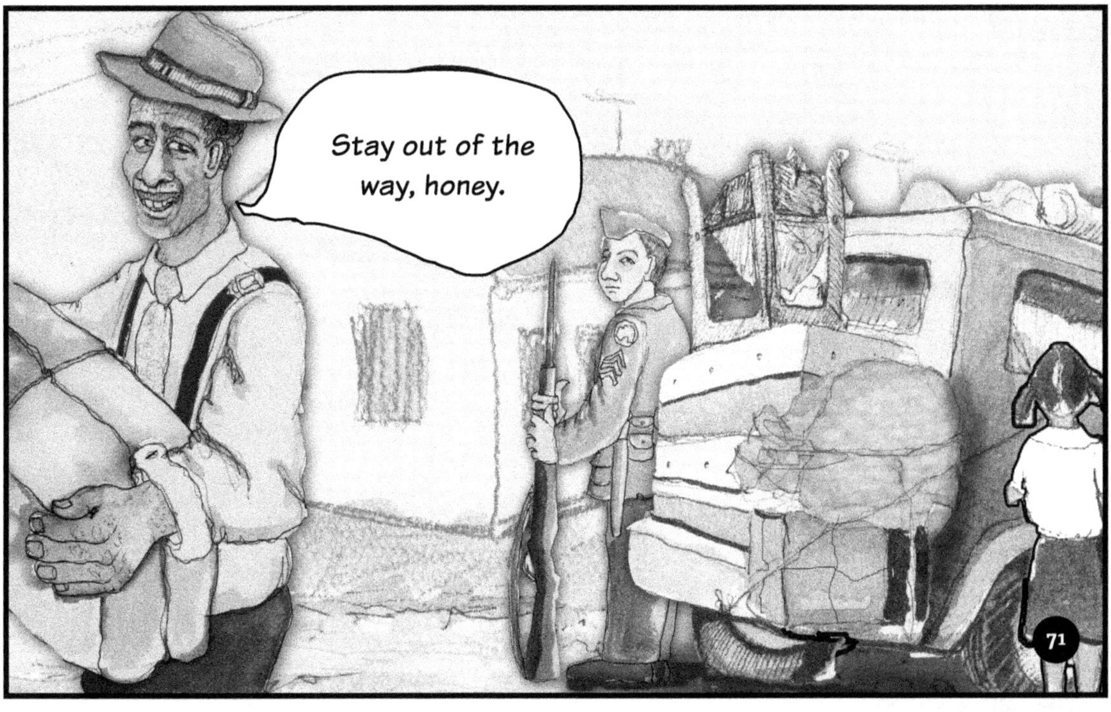
Stay out of the way, honey.

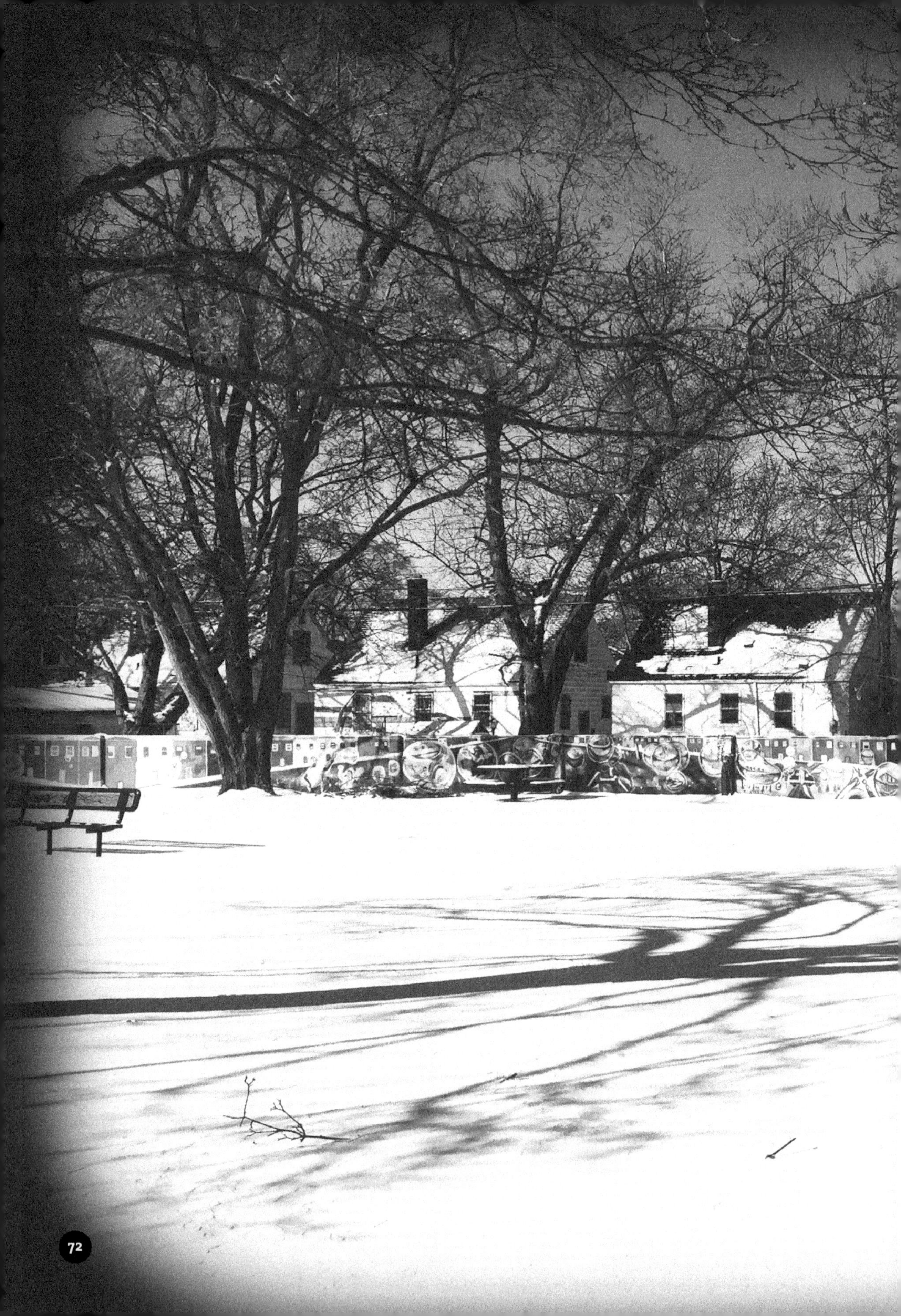

The violence around the occupation of the Sojourner Truth Homes was a small hint of the coming unrest in the city of Detroit. The bloodshed and disorder happened on a relatively small scale for six reasons:

1) The weather was cold.
2) The melee took place away from heavily populated African American communities in Detroit like Paradise Valley.
3) Local religious leaders were vocal in calling for peace.
4) The African American community took a united stance.
5) The picketers were mostly Polish American women who were afraid of bloodshed.
6) In the end, the extreme mobilization of state police and military forces prevented violence.

But the economic violence and police brutality against the Black population of Detroit continued to escalate. Small-scale skirmishes continued to flare up on streetcars and in schools, defense plants, and recreational areas of the city. Housing segregation would remain a constant issue in the city for years to come. Today, racial segregation is still visible in the neighborhoods of Detroit.

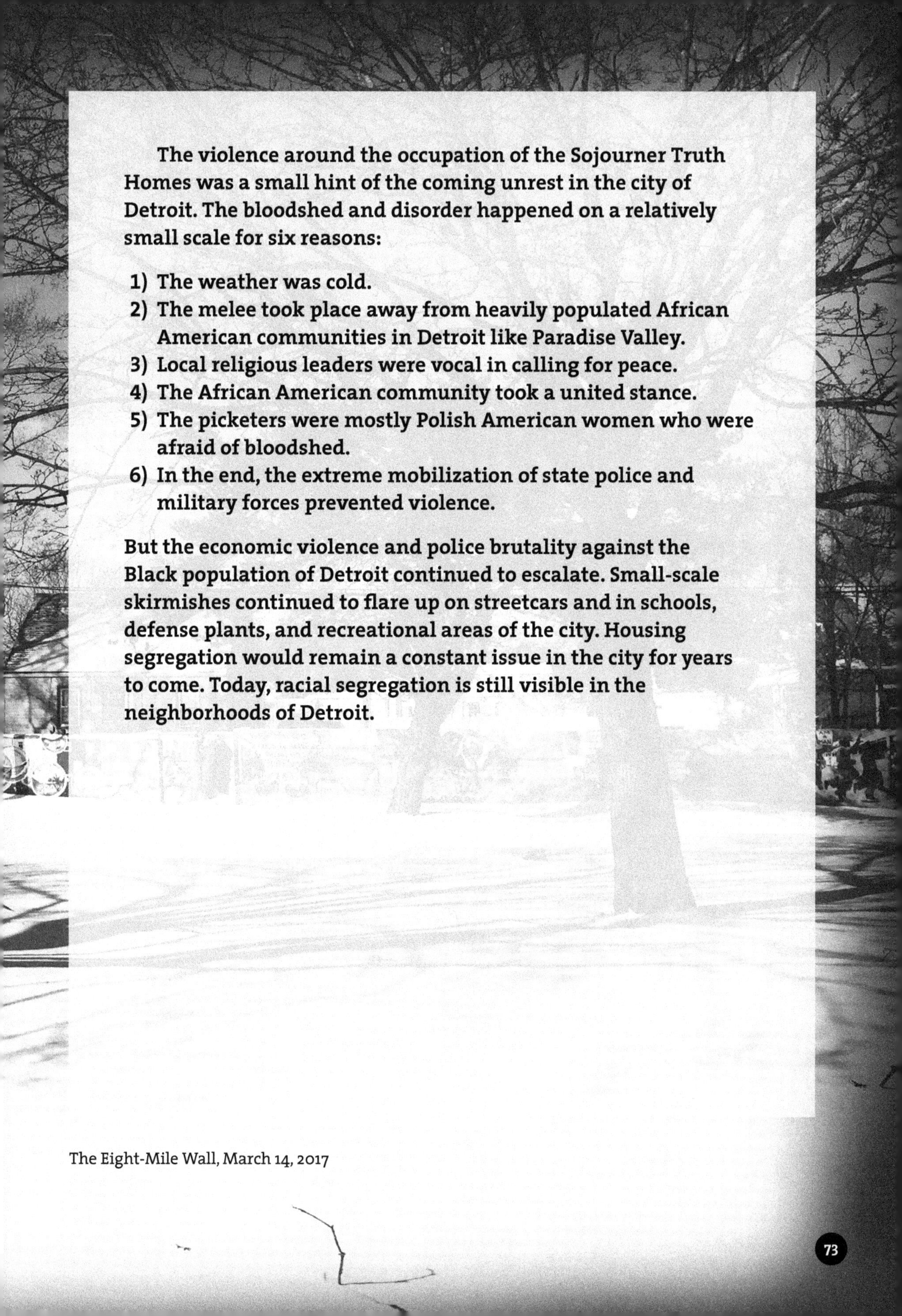

The Eight-Mile Wall, March 14, 2017

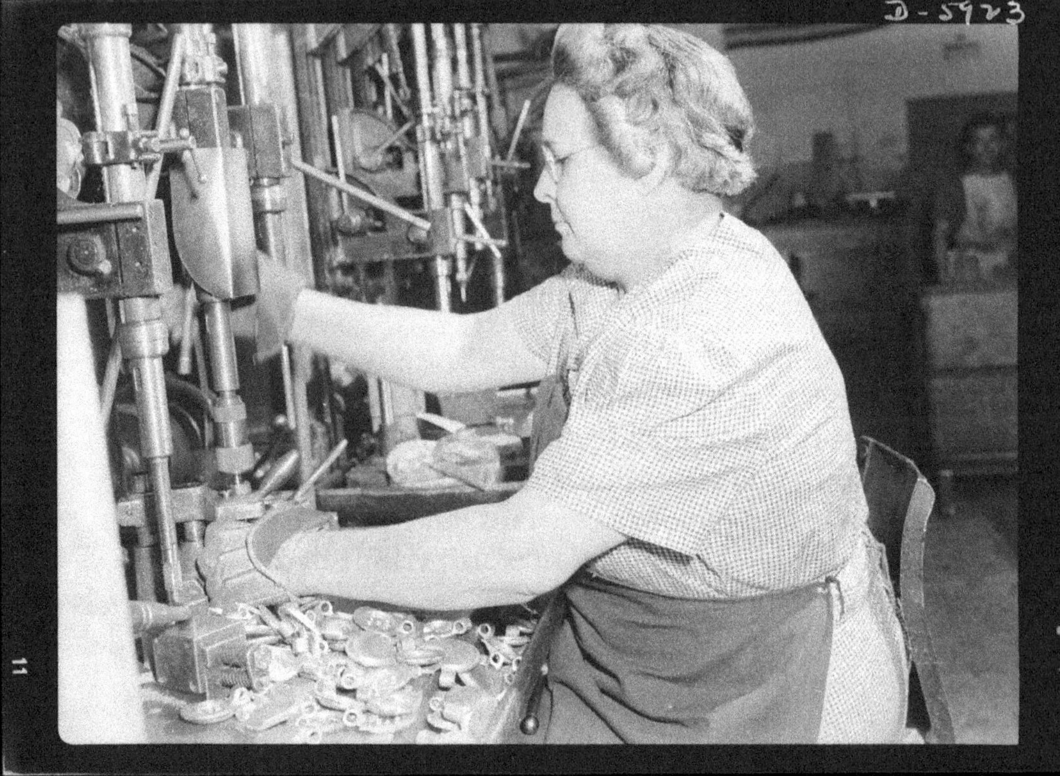
D-5923

Annette Caines, pictured here in July 1942, made flare guns at the Eureka plant in Detroit. "We women want to fight with our men folks. Maybe we can't shoot guns, but we sure can make the stuff for them to shoot with." Her son was serving in the United States Army.

Photograph by Ann Rosener, July 1942, Library of Congress, Prints & Photographs Division, LC-DIG-fsa-8b07366.

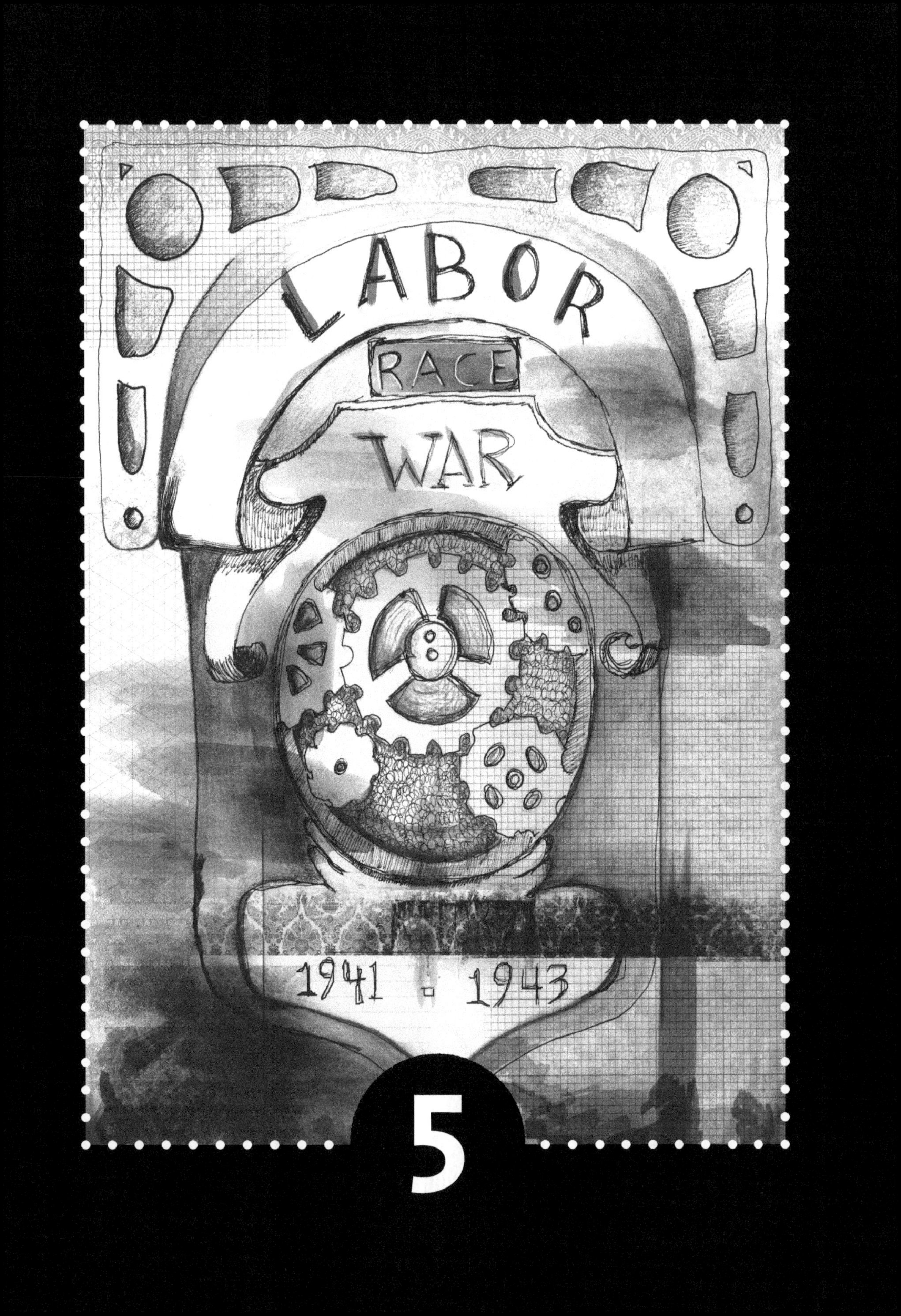
LABOR
RACE
WAR
1941 - 1943
5

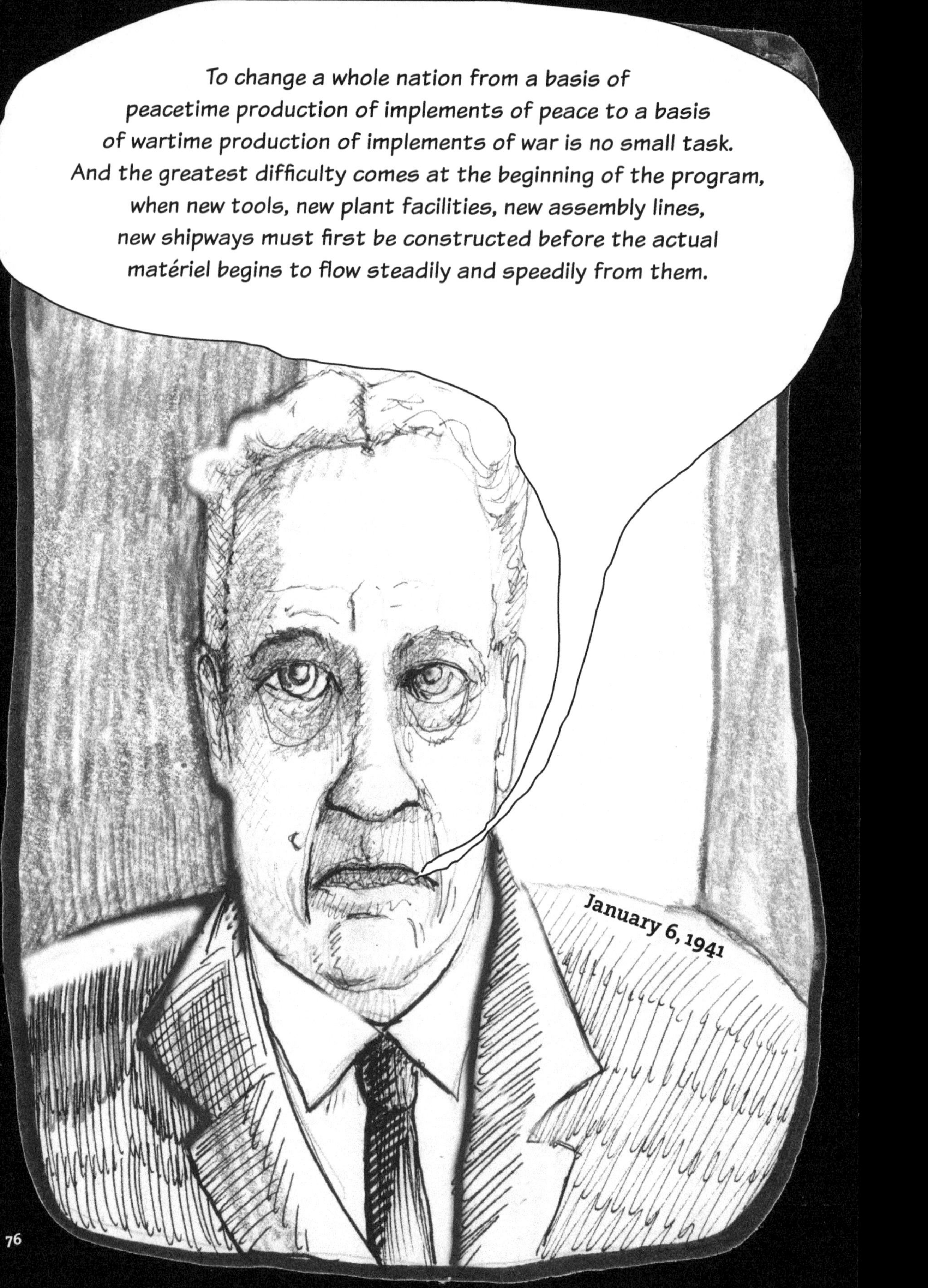
To change a whole nation from a basis of peacetime production of implements of peace to a basis of wartime production of implements of war is no small task. And the greatest difficulty comes at the beginning of the program, when new tools, new plant facilities, new assembly lines, new shipways must first be constructed before the actual matériel begins to flow steadily and speedily from them.
January 6, 1941

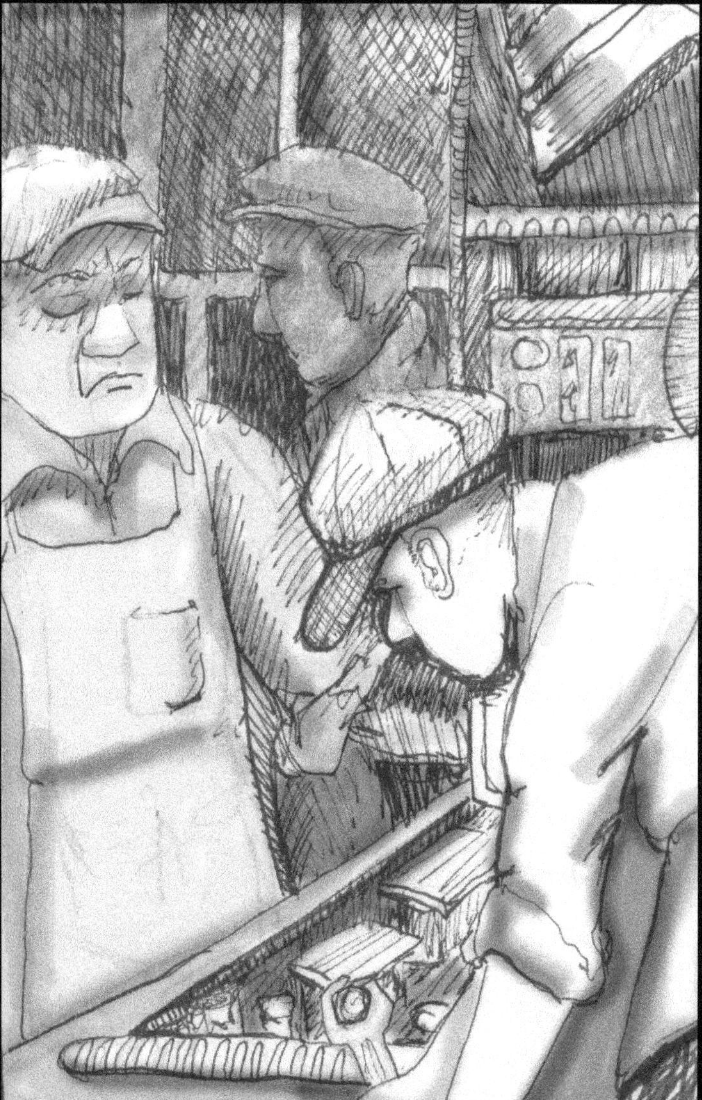

In 1941, in his famous Four Freedoms speech, FDR laid the groundwork for the Lend-Lease Act and for Detroit to become the "arsenal of democracy." The conversion from a city famous for automobiles to a city that was a linchpin of the U.S. defense manufacturing network brought with it fierce competition for jobs, an expansion of the labor union movement, and more opportunities for women and African Americans. The racial strife on factory floors in the early 1940s resulted in hate speech, wildcat strikes, and, as with the struggle over housing, violence.

On December 28, 1940, Walter Reuther, the director of the General Motors Department of the UAW-CIO, proposed a conversion plan on the NBC Red Network.

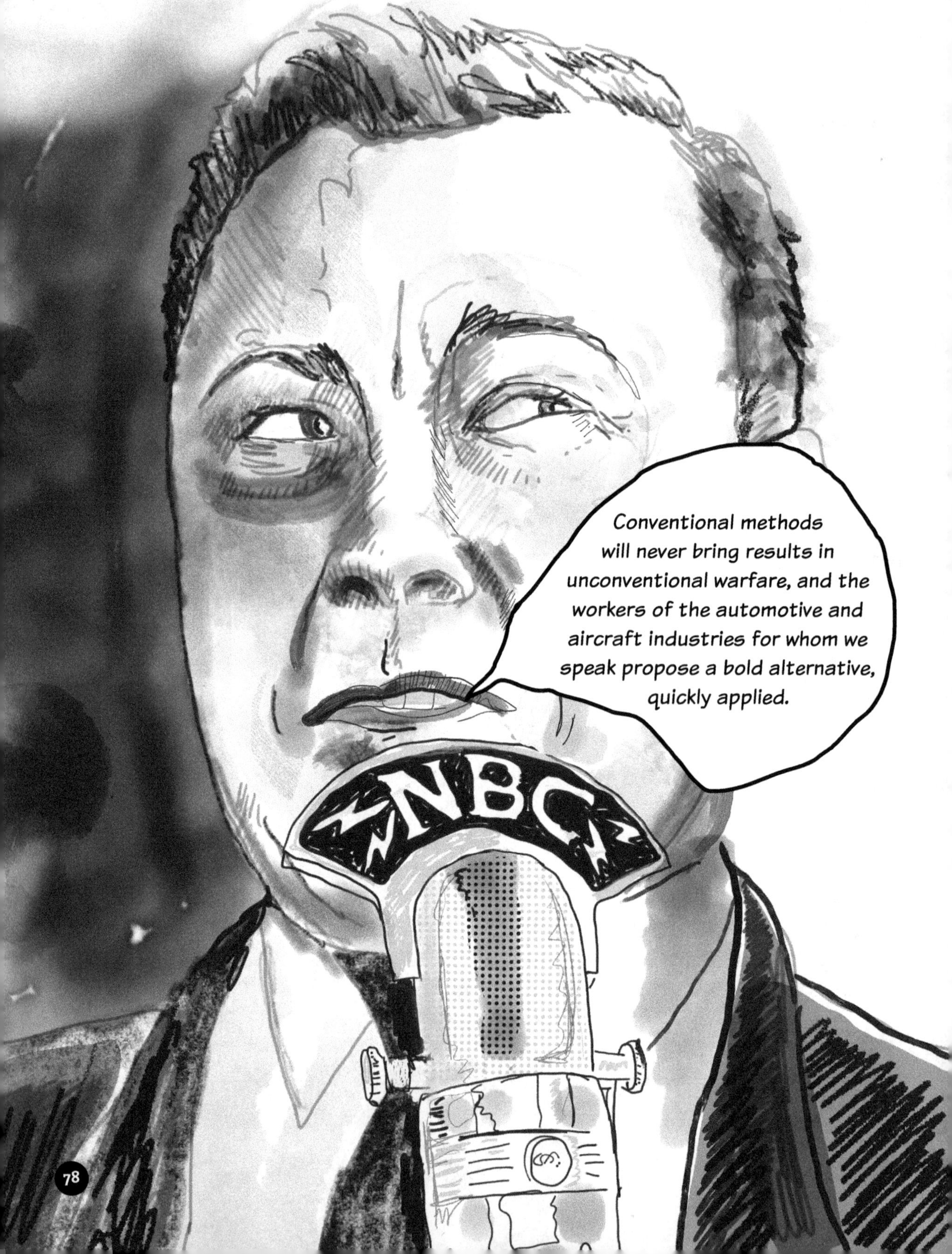
Conventional methods will never bring results in unconventional warfare, and the workers of the automotive and aircraft industries for whom we speak propose a bold alternative, quickly applied.
NBC

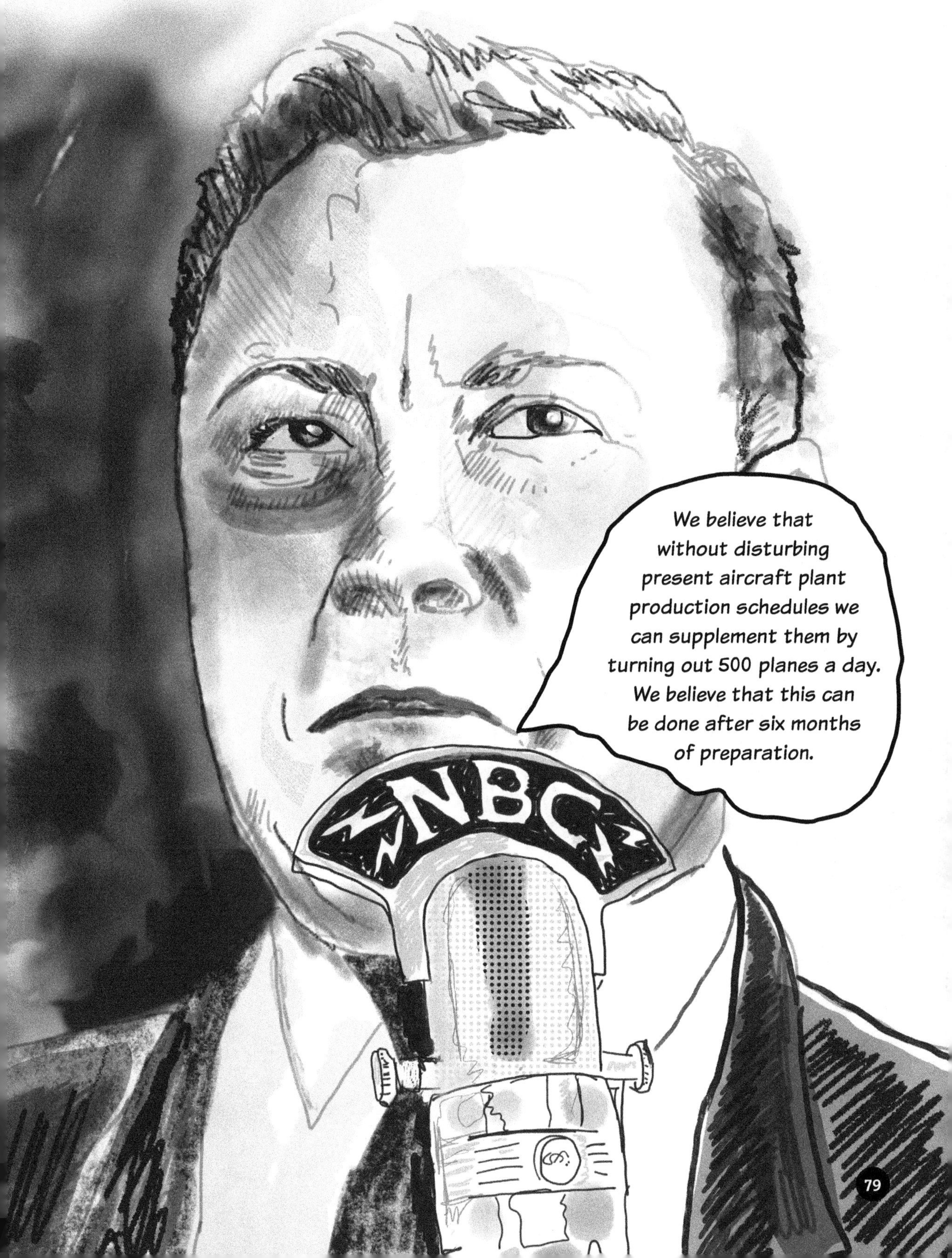
We believe that without disturbing present aircraft plant production schedules we can supplement them by turning out 500 planes a day. We believe that this can be done after six months of preparation.
NBC

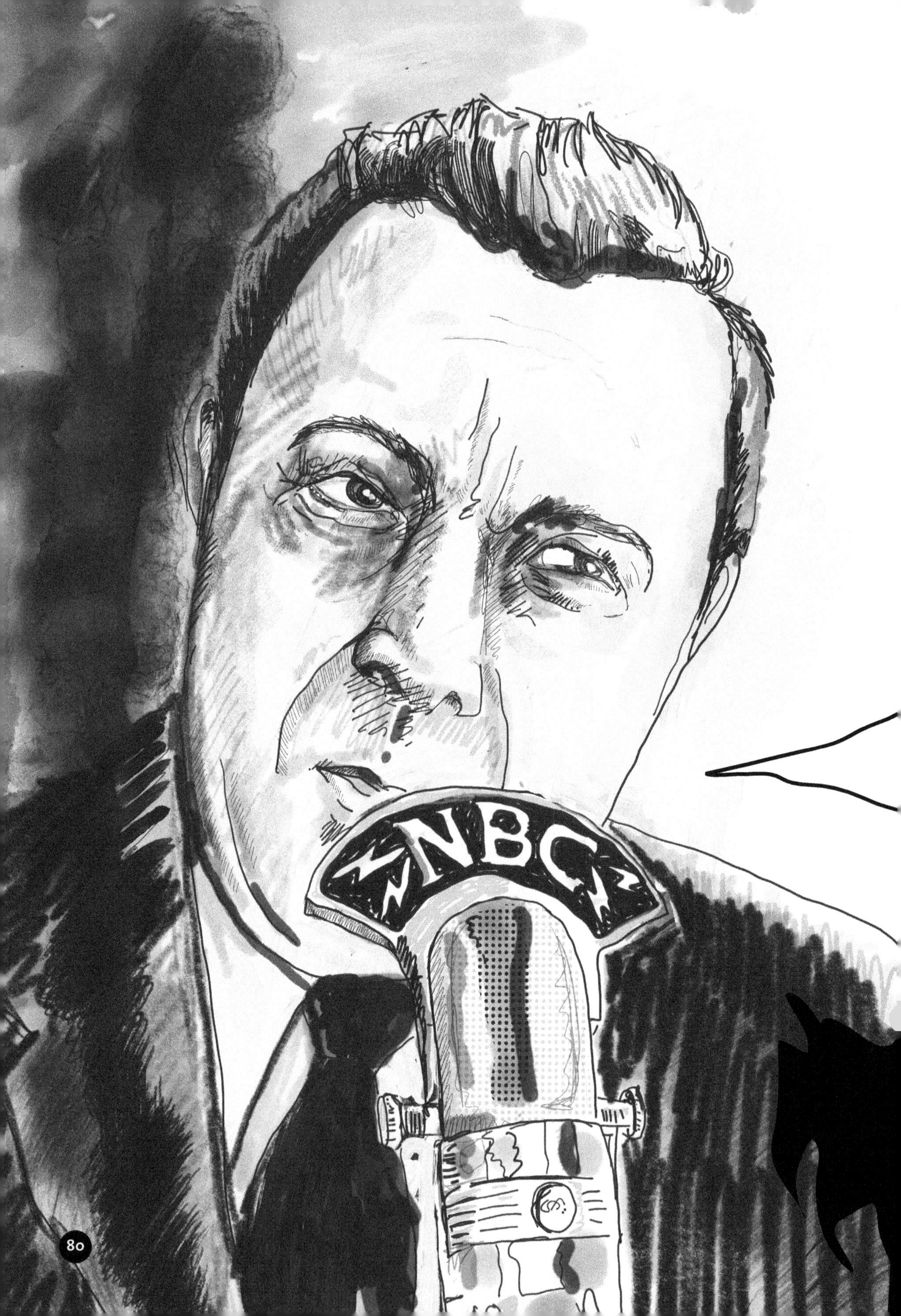
NBC

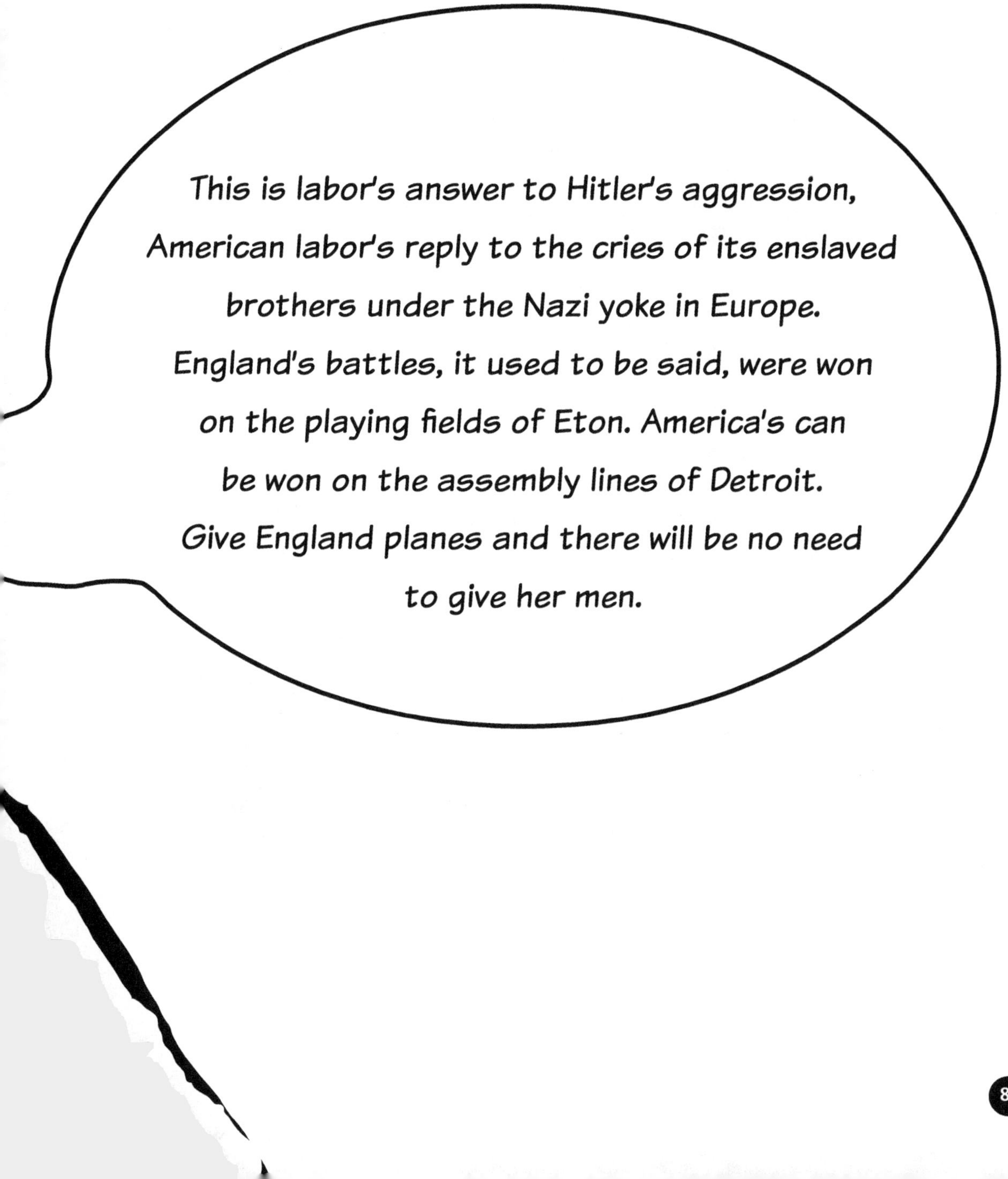
This is labor's answer to Hitler's aggression, American labor's reply to the cries of its enslaved brothers under the Nazi yoke in Europe. England's battles, it used to be said, were won on the playing fields of Eton. America's can be won on the assembly lines of Detroit. Give England planes and there will be no need to give her men.

As labor movement demands intensified during the war, the labor force began to shift. This affected a number of groups that had been traditionally marginalized. For example, Ford hired Black men to work in its plants but paid them less than most white workers and assigned them to jobs that were menial or risky. This was true of other auto manufacturing plants as well. In the late 1930s and early 1940s, when there were conflicts with union organizers, Ford routinely brought in Black workers as strike breakers. The loyalty of the African American community to Ford Motors—the biggest auto manufacturer in Detroit and a key player in the conversion—shifted over time as discrimination persisted and support for union politics grew more popular.

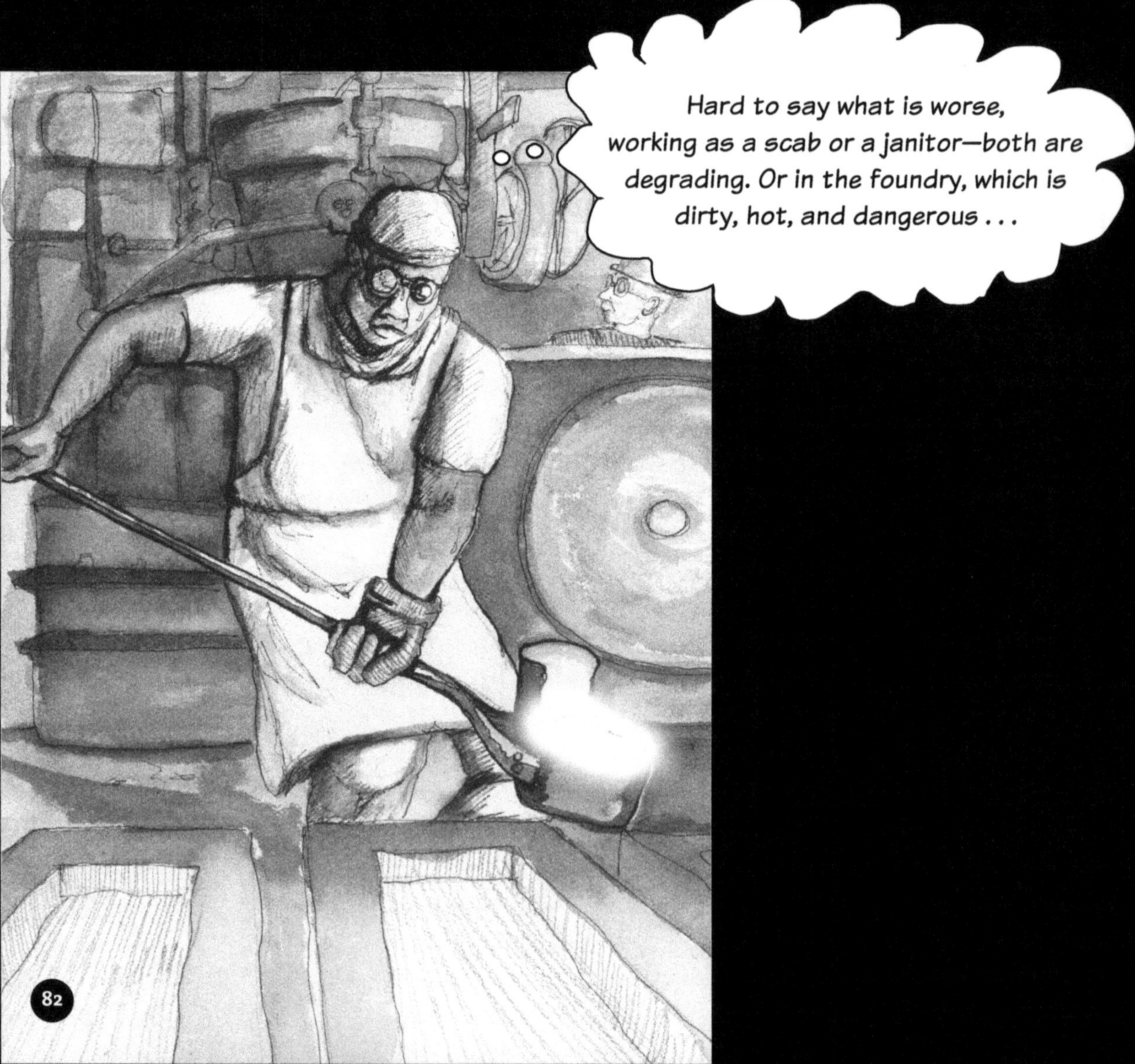
Hard to say what is worse, working as a scab or a janitor—both are degrading. Or in the foundry, which is dirty, hot, and dangerous . . .

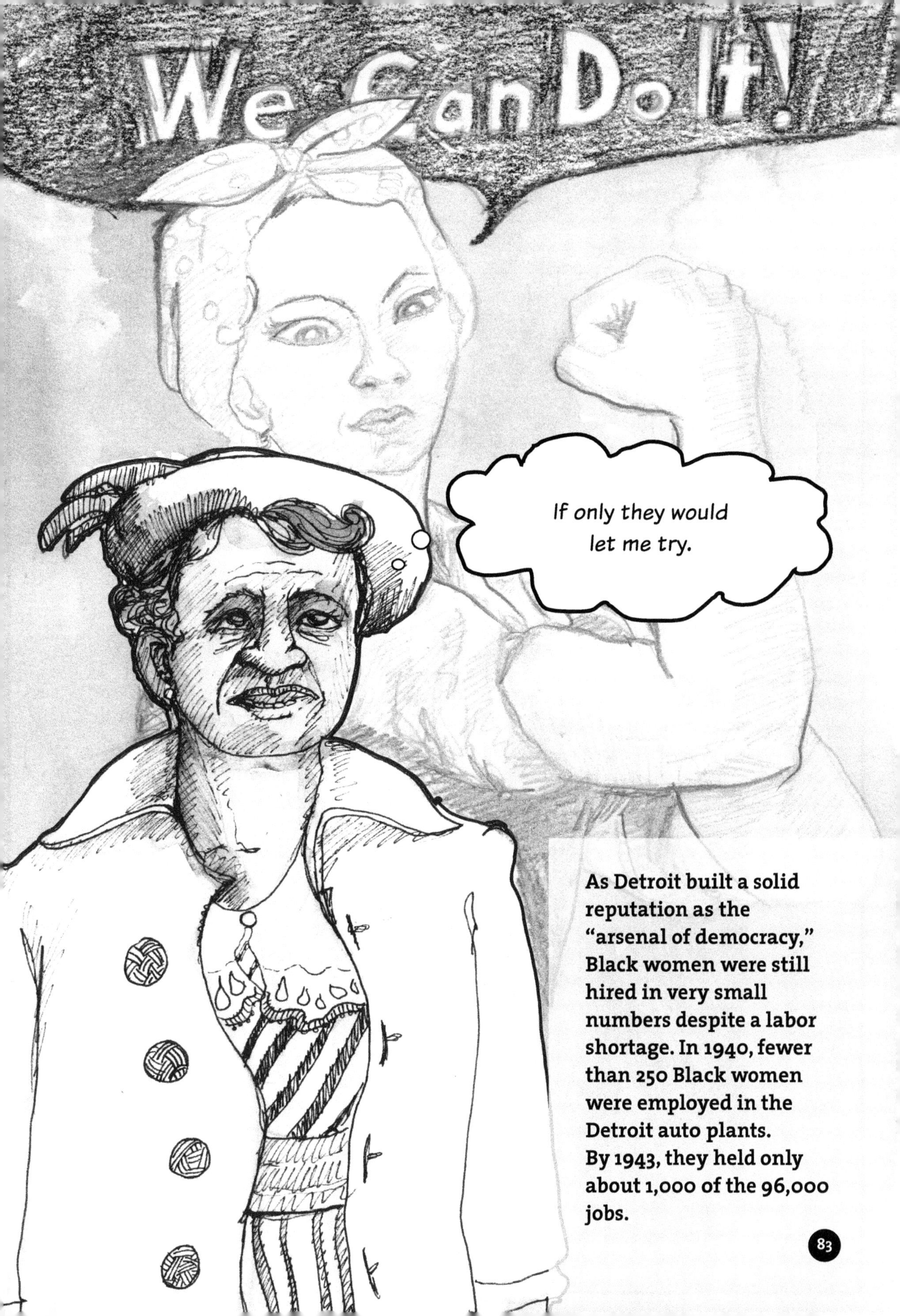
We Can Do It!
If only they would let me try.
As Detroit built a solid reputation as the "arsenal of democracy," Black women were still hired in very small numbers despite a labor shortage. In 1940, fewer than 250 Black women were employed in the Detroit auto plants. By 1943, they held only about 1,000 of the 96,000 jobs.

In 1941, 12 percent of Ford's employees were Black. Despite this, Ford's views on African Americans were not progressive; they were patronizing and racist. He felt that African Americans were naturally inferior to whites, who in his mind were the supreme race.

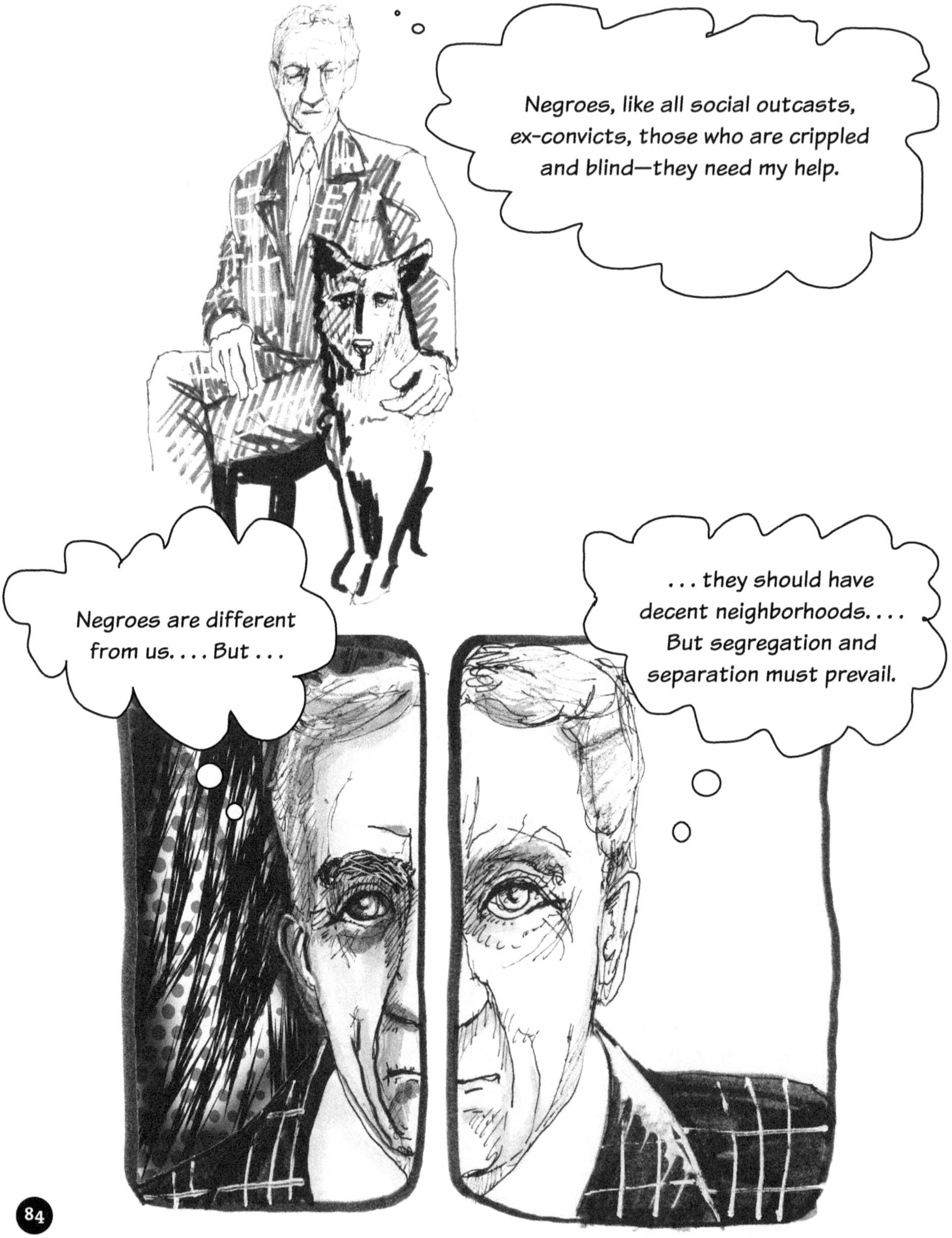
Negroes, like all social outcasts, ex-convicts, those who are crippled and blind—they need my help.
Negroes are different from us. . . . But . . .
. . . they should have decent neighborhoods. . . . But segregation and separation must prevail.

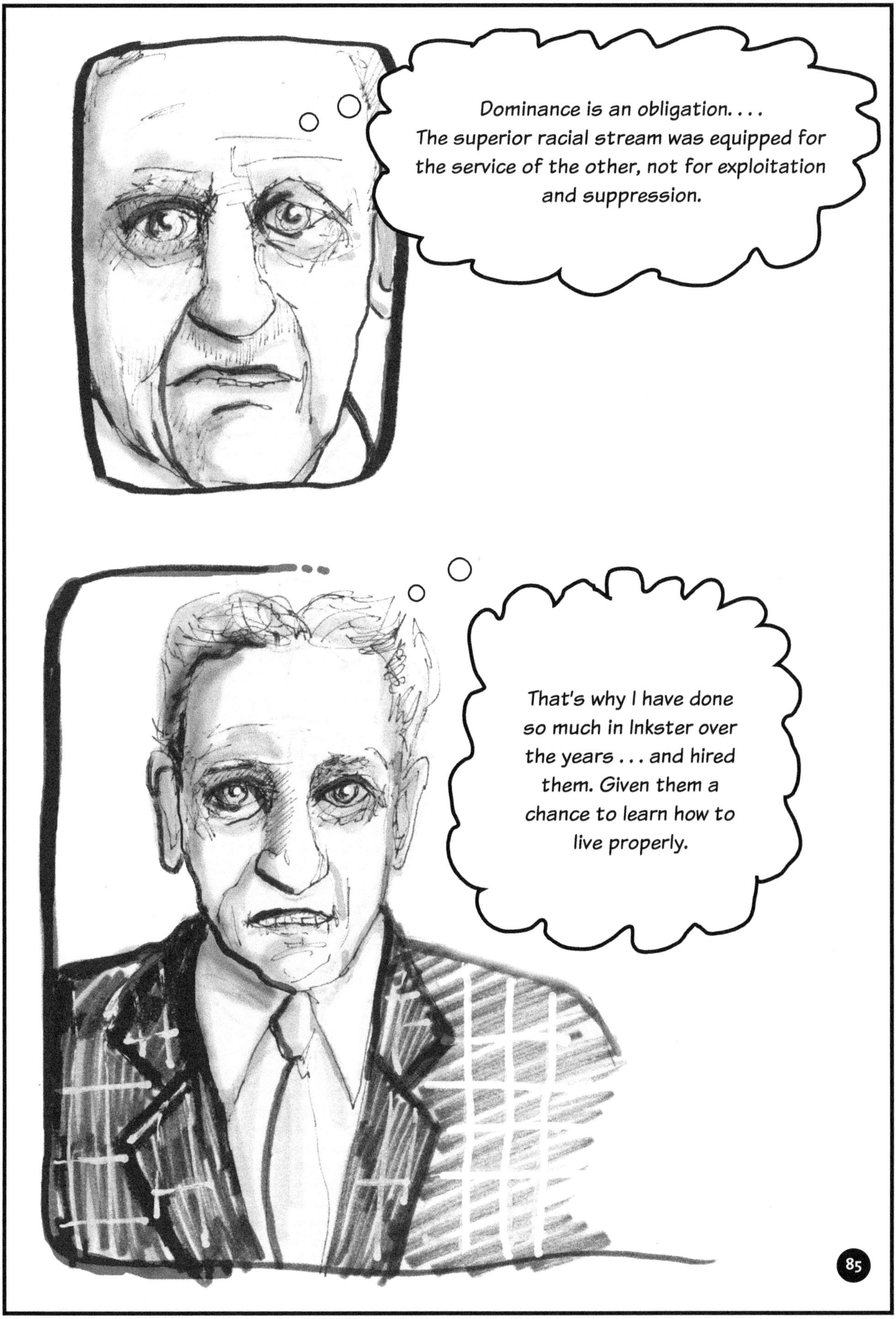
Dominance is an obligation. . . . The superior racial stream was equipped for the service of the other, not for exploitation and suppression.
That's why I have done so much in Inkster over the years . . . and hired them. Given them a chance to learn how to live properly.

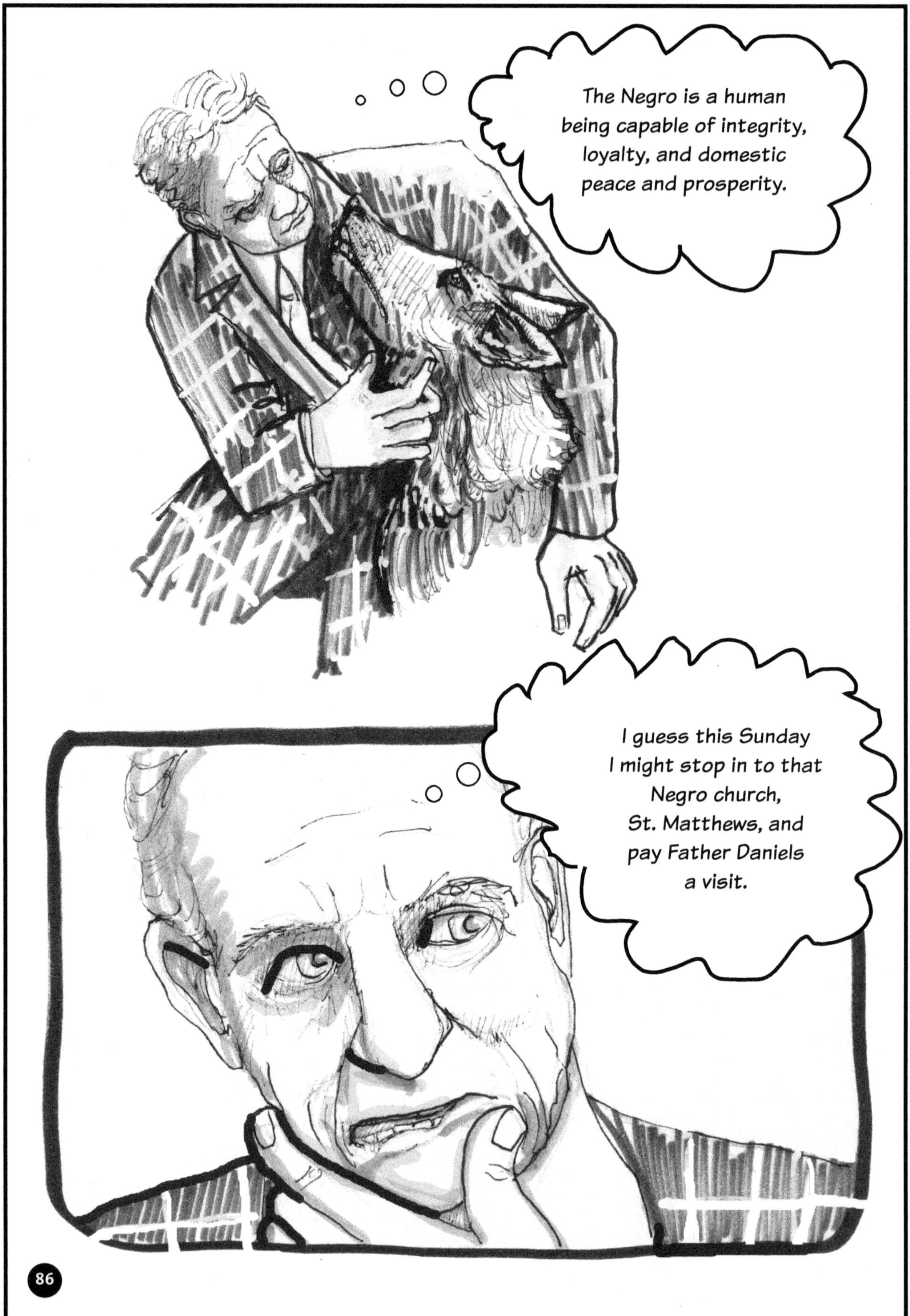
The Negro is a human being capable of integrity, loyalty, and domestic peace and prosperity.
I guess this Sunday I might stop in to that Negro church, St. Matthews, and pay Father Daniels a visit.

By the end of World War I approximately 8,000 African Americans were employed in the automobile manufacturing industry. Ford Motor Company was the largest employer of African Americans in Detroit.

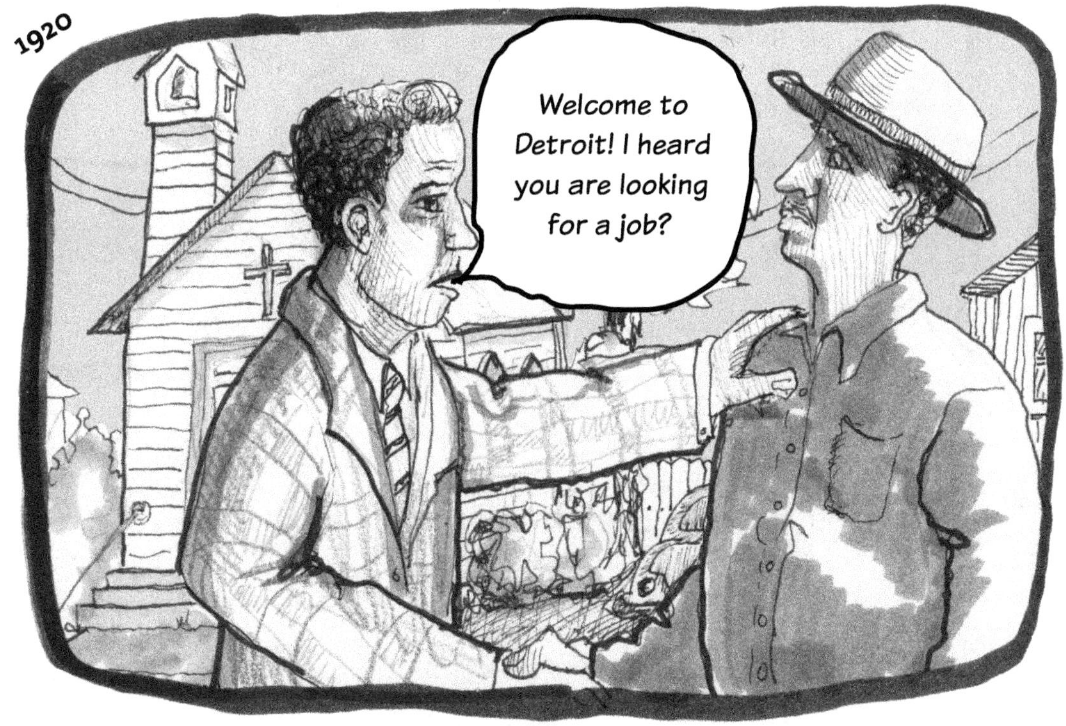
1920
Welcome to Detroit! I heard you are looking for a job?

Ford used a network of Black clergy members to find workers for his plants.

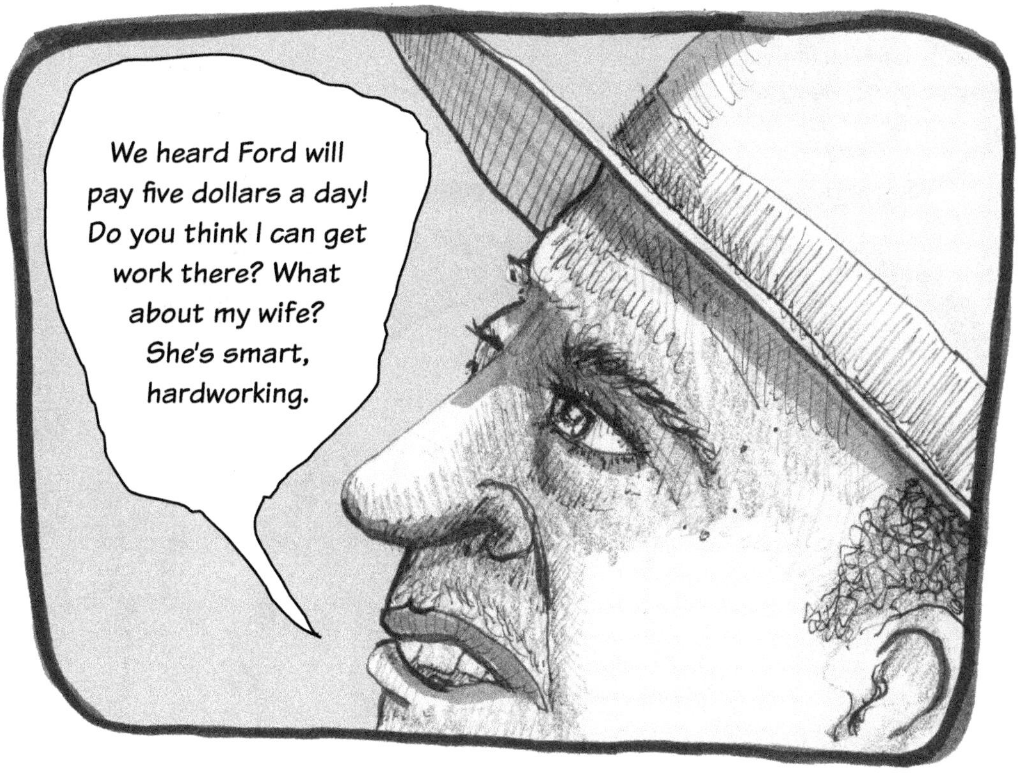
We heard Ford will pay five dollars a day! Do you think I can get work there? What about my wife? She's smart, hardworking.

African Americans proved to be a loyal workforce for Ford Motors.

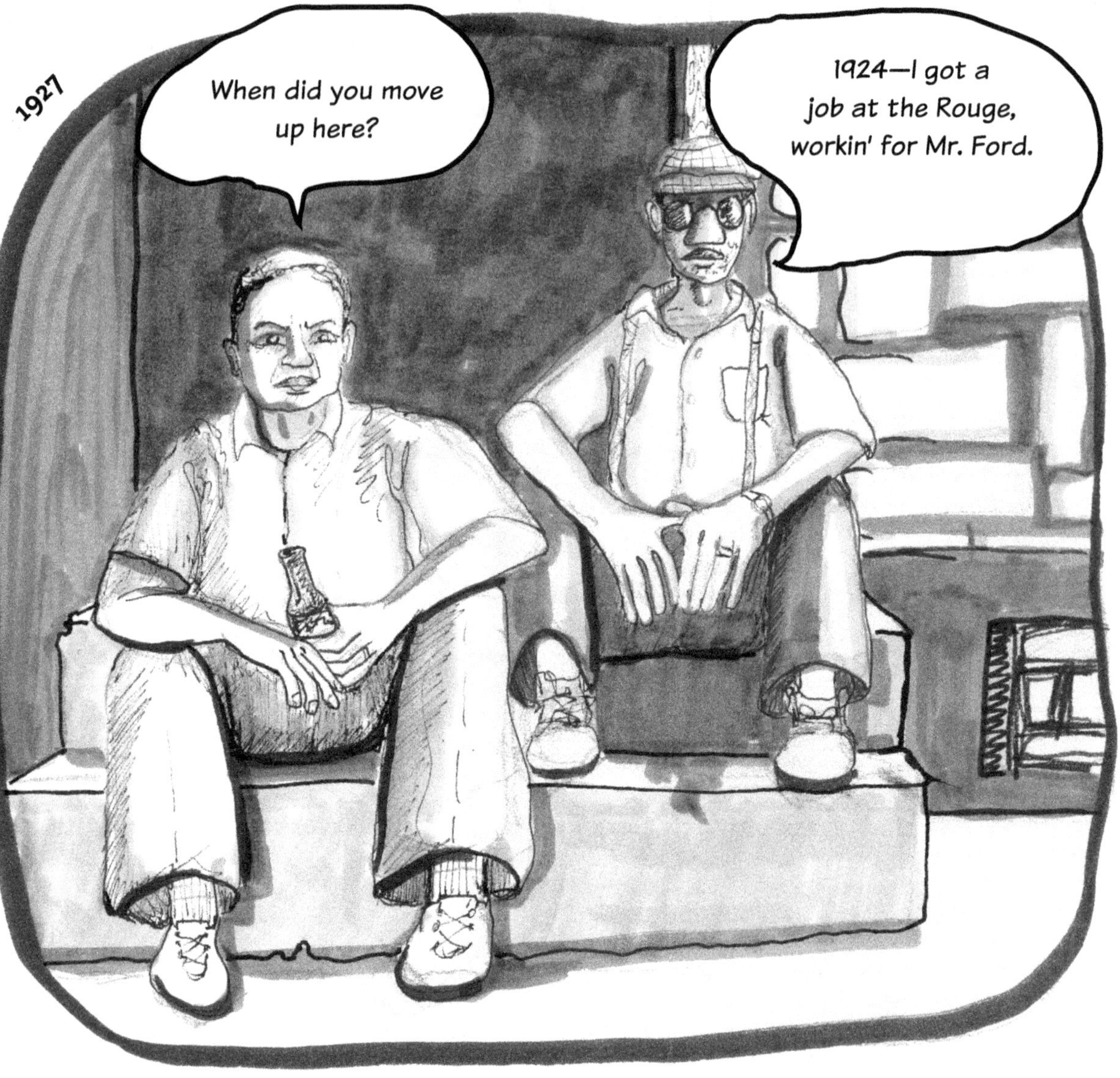
1927
When did you move up here?
1924—I got a job at the Rouge, workin' for Mr. Ford.

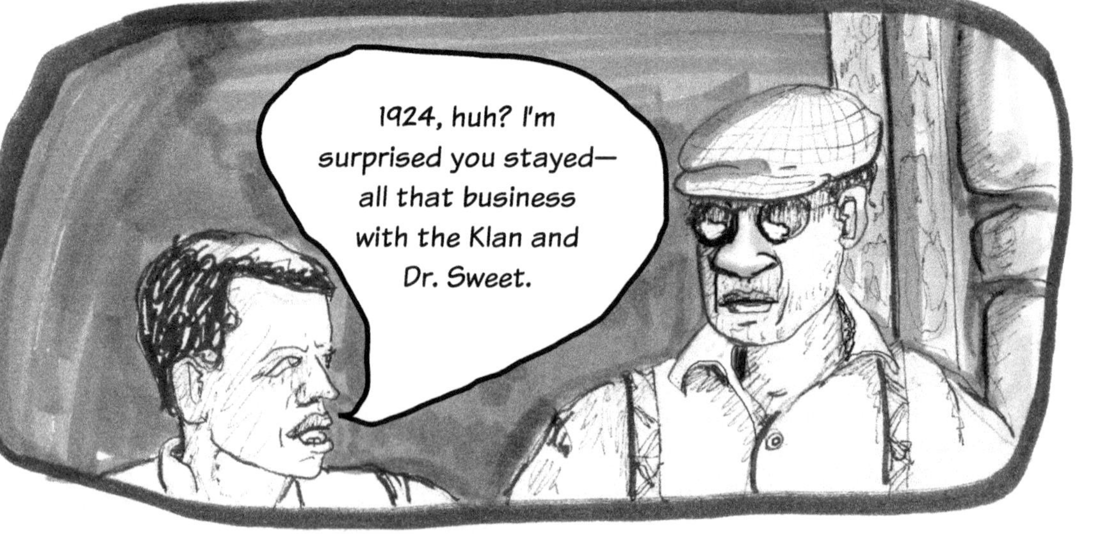
1924, huh? I'm surprised you stayed—all that business with the Klan and Dr. Sweet.

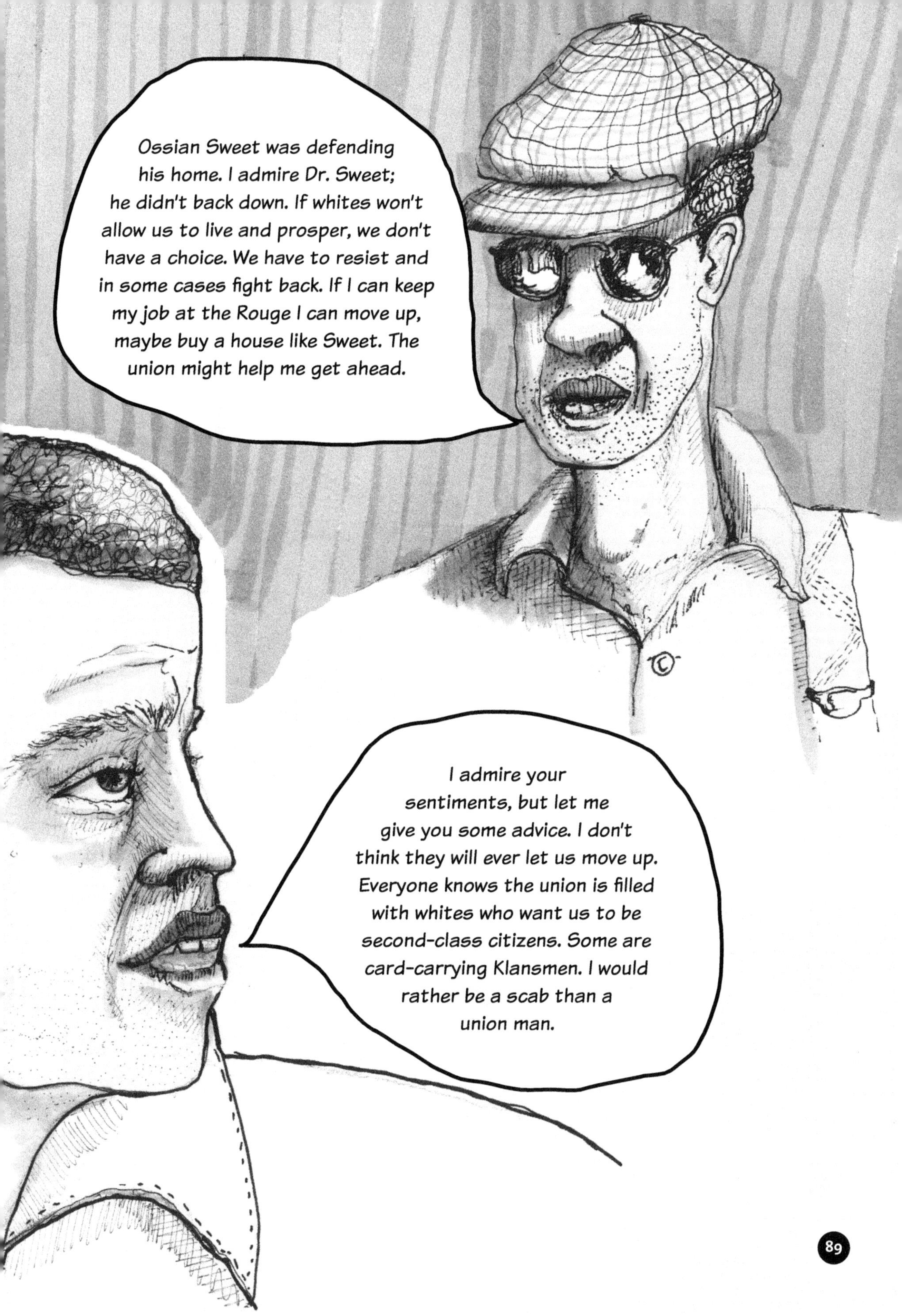
Ossian Sweet was defending his home. I admire Dr. Sweet; he didn't back down. If whites won't allow us to live and prosper, we don't have a choice. We have to resist and in some cases fight back. If I can keep my job at the Rouge I can move up, maybe buy a house like Sweet. The union might help me get ahead.
I admire your sentiments, but let me give you some advice. I don't think they will ever let us move up. Everyone knows the union is filled with whites who want us to be second-class citizens. Some are card-carrying Klansmen. I would rather be a scab than a union man.

Ford's reputation as a generous employer had evaporated by the late 1930s. African American workers struggled to obtain employment. In 1941, as the conversion from automotive manufacturing to defense took place, African American workers were still discriminated against and had difficulty finding jobs that required specialized skills and paid a living wage.

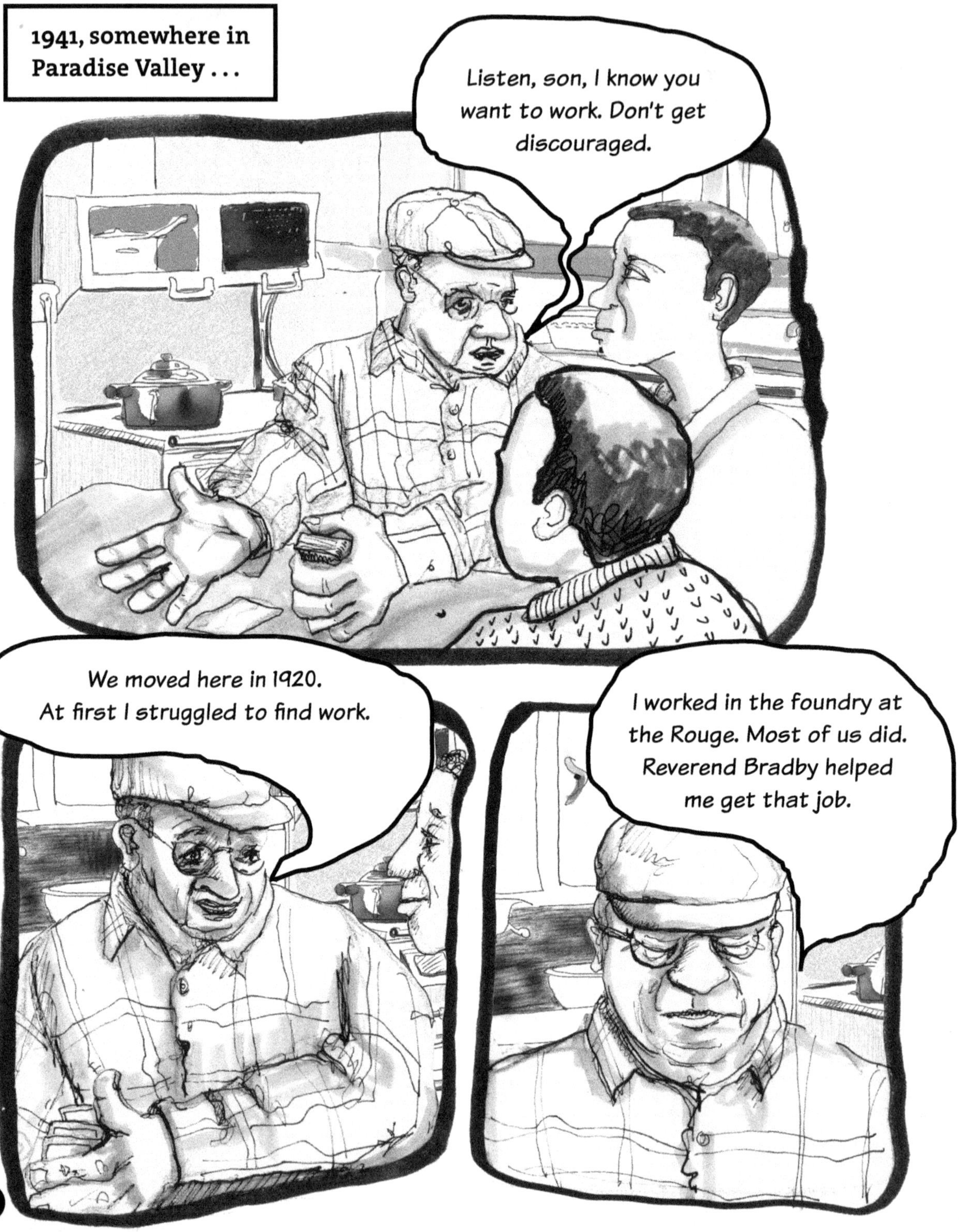
1941, somewhere in Paradise Valley . . .
Listen, son, I know you want to work. Don't get discouraged.
We moved here in 1920. At first I struggled to find work.
I worked in the foundry at the Rouge. Most of us did. Reverend Bradby helped me get that job.

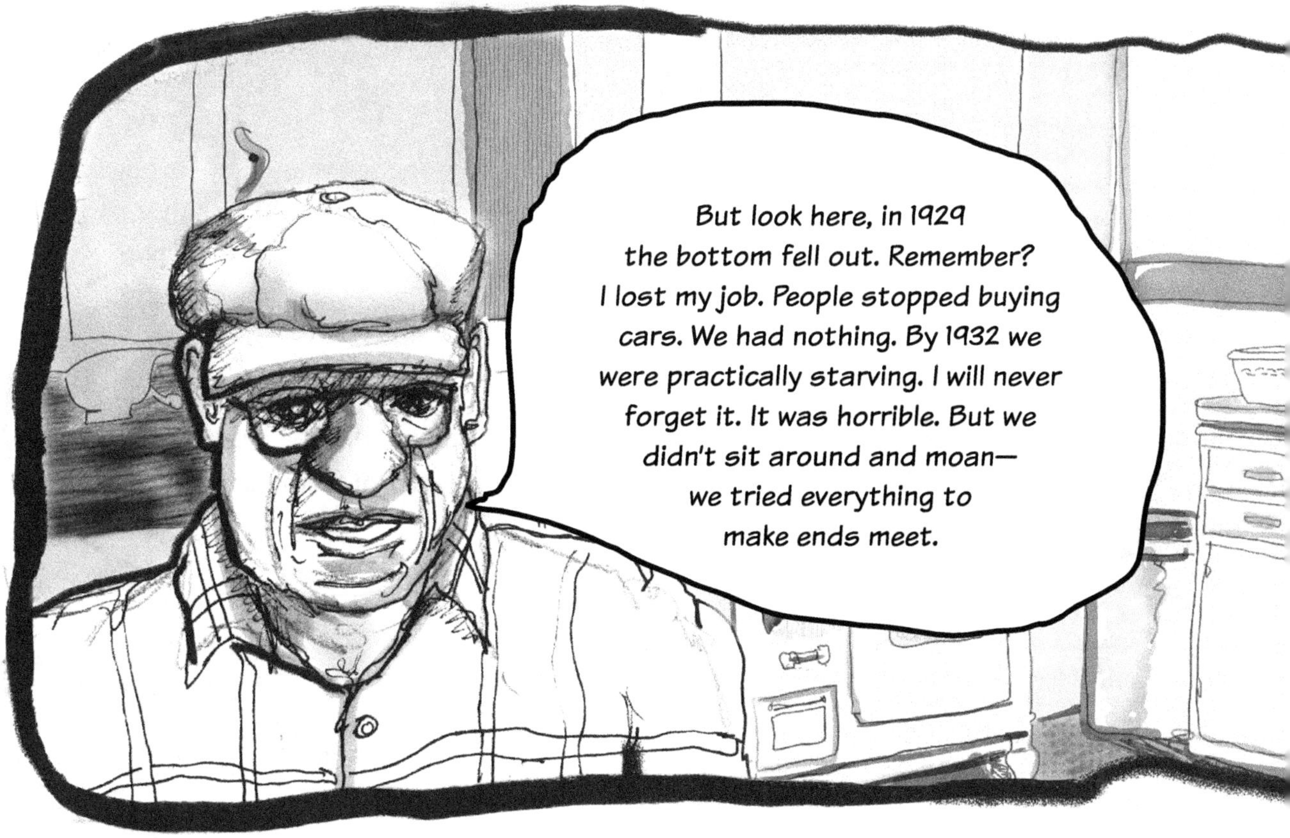
But look here, in 1929 the bottom fell out. Remember? I lost my job. People stopped buying cars. We had nothing. By 1932 we were practically starving. I will never forget it. It was horrible. But we didn't sit around and moan— we tried everything to make ends meet.

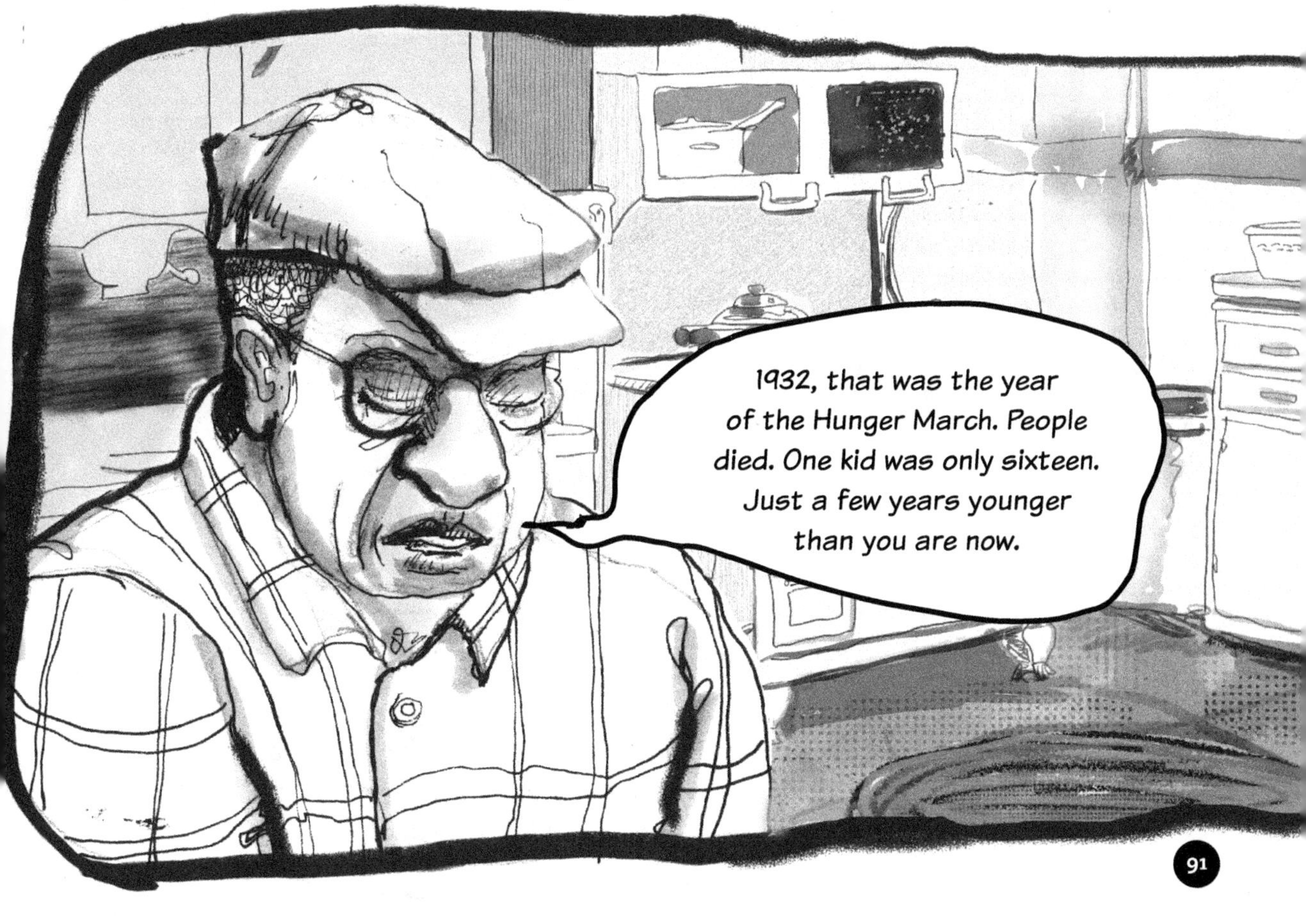
1932, that was the year of the Hunger March. People died. One kid was only sixteen. Just a few years younger than you are now.

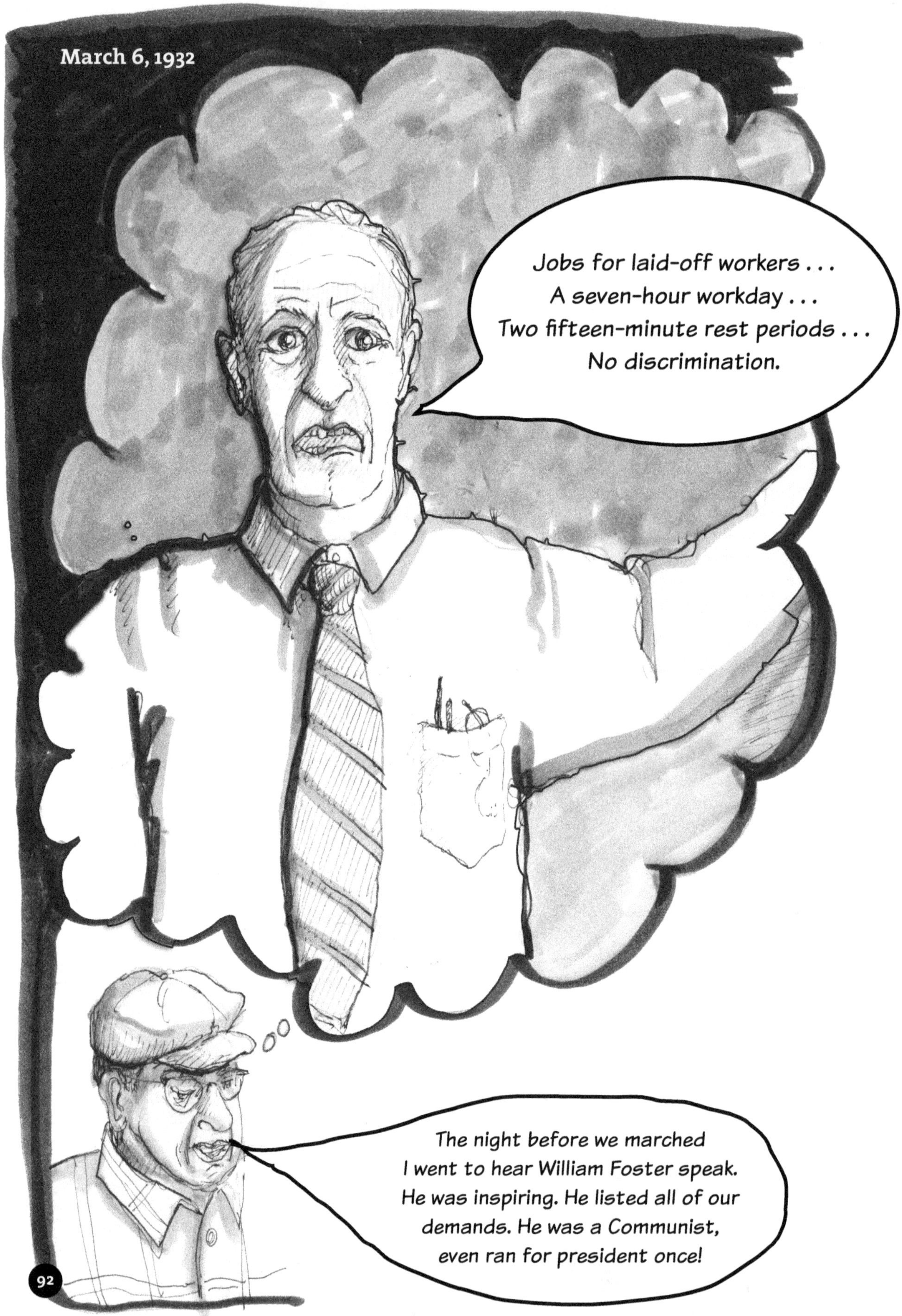
March 6, 1932
Jobs for laid-off workers . . . A seven-hour workday . . . Two fifteen-minute rest periods . . . No discrimination.
The night before we marched I went to hear William Foster speak. He was inspiring. He listed all of our demands. He was a Communist, even ran for president once!

March 7, 1932

We got up early in the morning. I put on the only pair of boots I owned. It was so cold. I drank a weak cup of coffee. I never could stomach Postum.

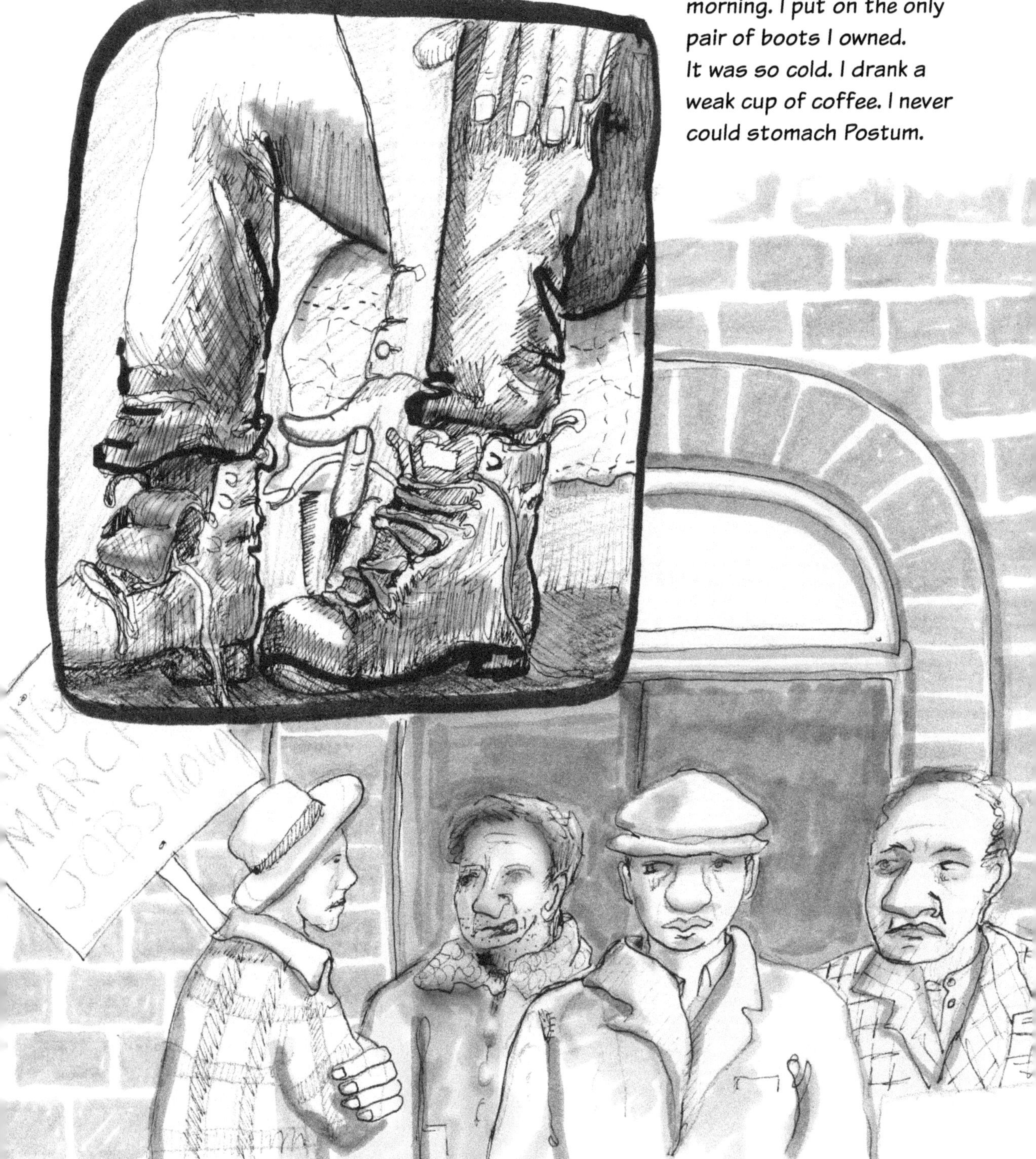
JOBS NOW

I met up with some other guys from the union. It was so cold we slapped our arms with our hands and ran in place just to stay warm. But we didn't care—we were fired up. We planned to march to the Rouge in Dearborn. It was going to be an exciting day. We had no idea what was in store for us.

Despite the cold, lots of folks joined in. There were people as far as I could see. I was so proud to be part of the march.

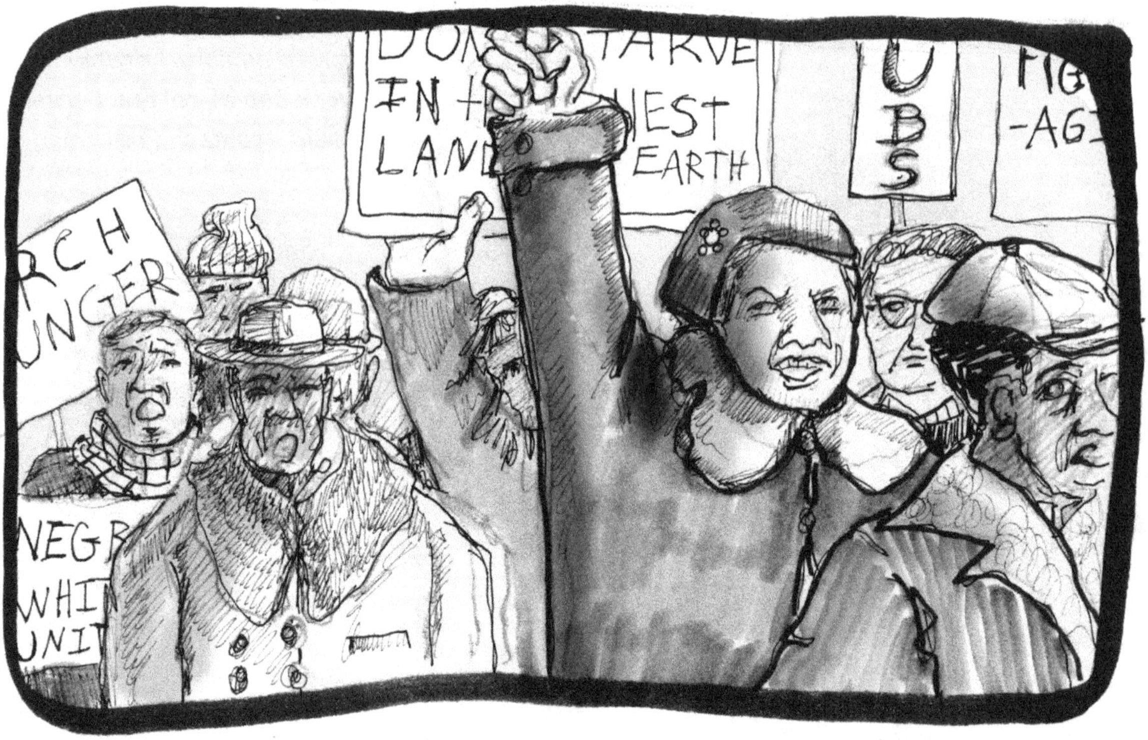
DON TARVE
IN TH EST
LAN EARTH
UBS
FIG
-AG
RCH
UNGER
NEGR
WHI
UNI

But things got ugly when we reached the gates.

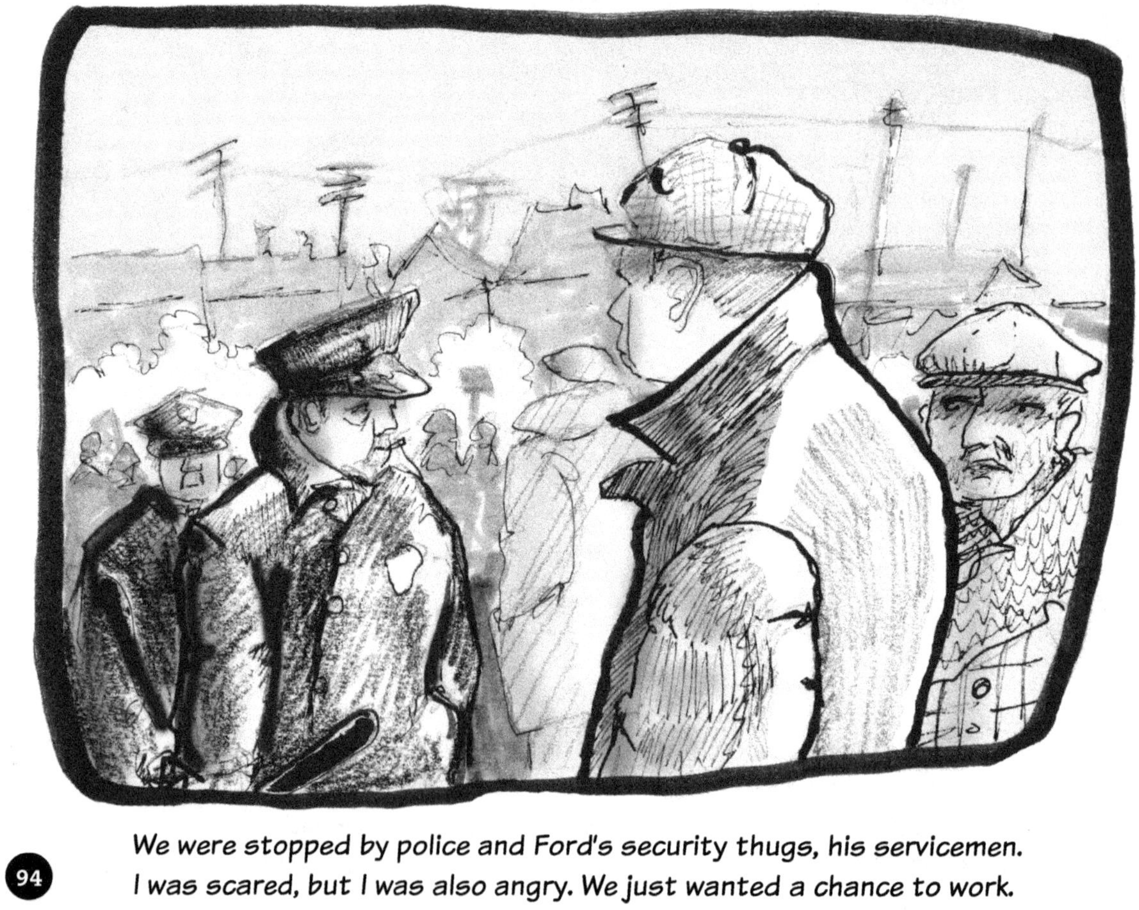

We were stopped by police and Ford's security thugs, his servicemen. I was scared, but I was also angry. We just wanted a chance to work.

Then the fire department from Dearborn, the police . . . They sprayed us with hoses and used tear gas. Some of our folks threw mud and stones, but when the gunshots started I lit out of there. I could hardly see because my eyes were watering so hard.

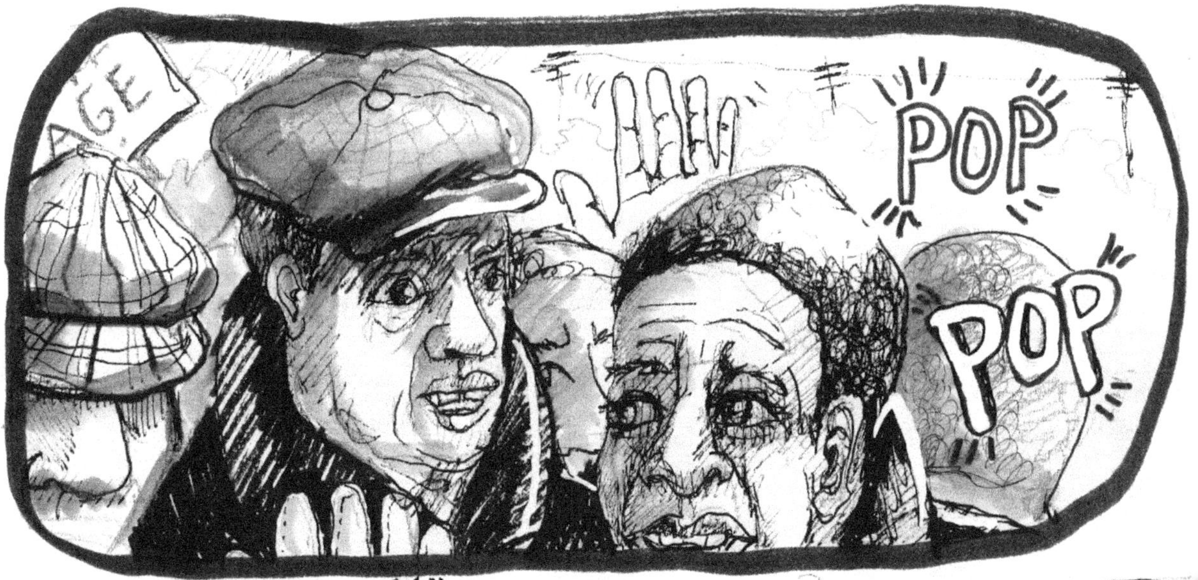

POP
POP

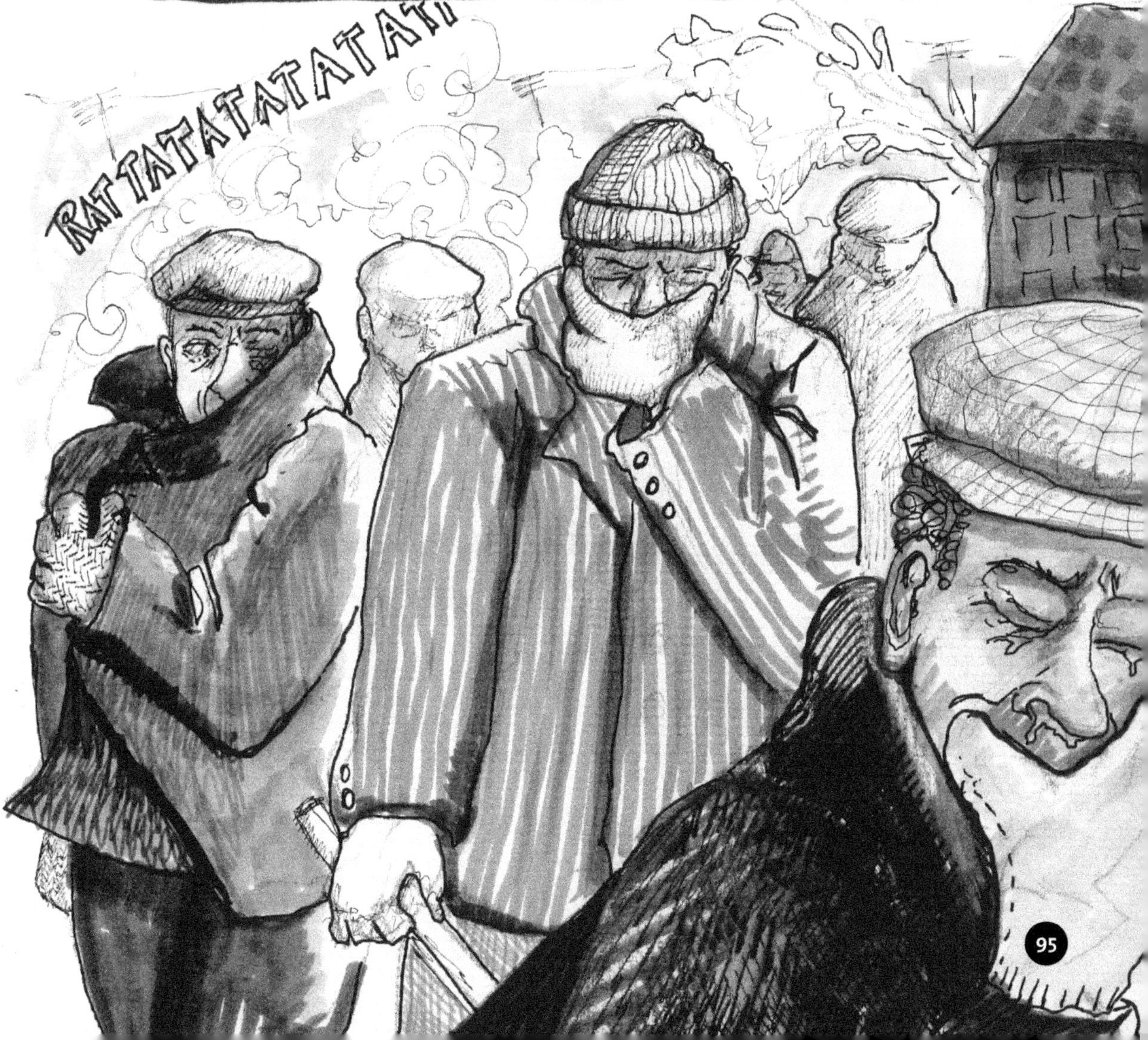

RATTATATATATAT!!

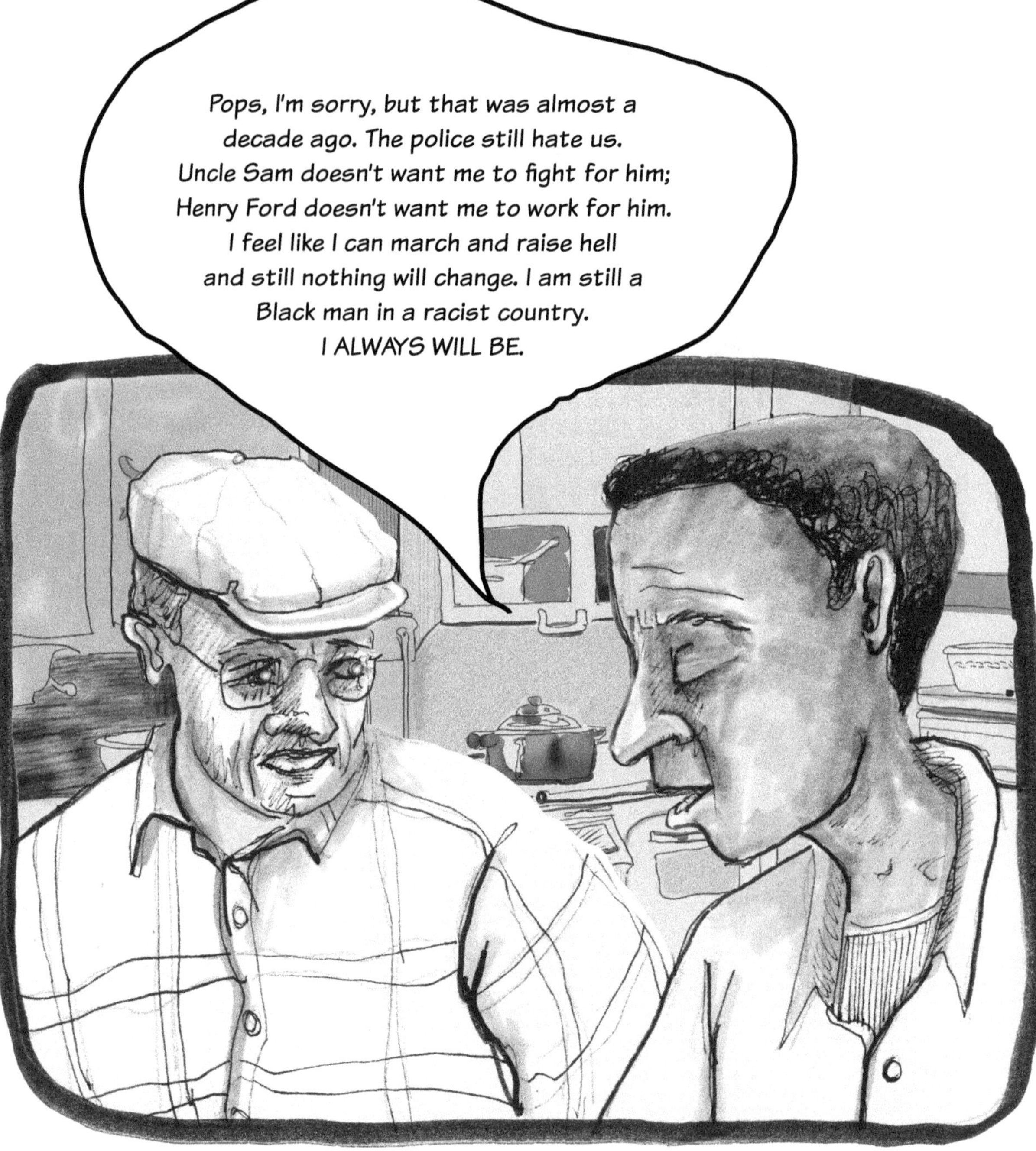
Pops, I'm sorry, but that was almost a decade ago. The police still hate us. Uncle Sam doesn't want me to fight for him; Henry Ford doesn't want me to work for him. I feel like I can march and raise hell and still nothing will change. I am still a Black man in a racist country. I ALWAYS WILL BE.

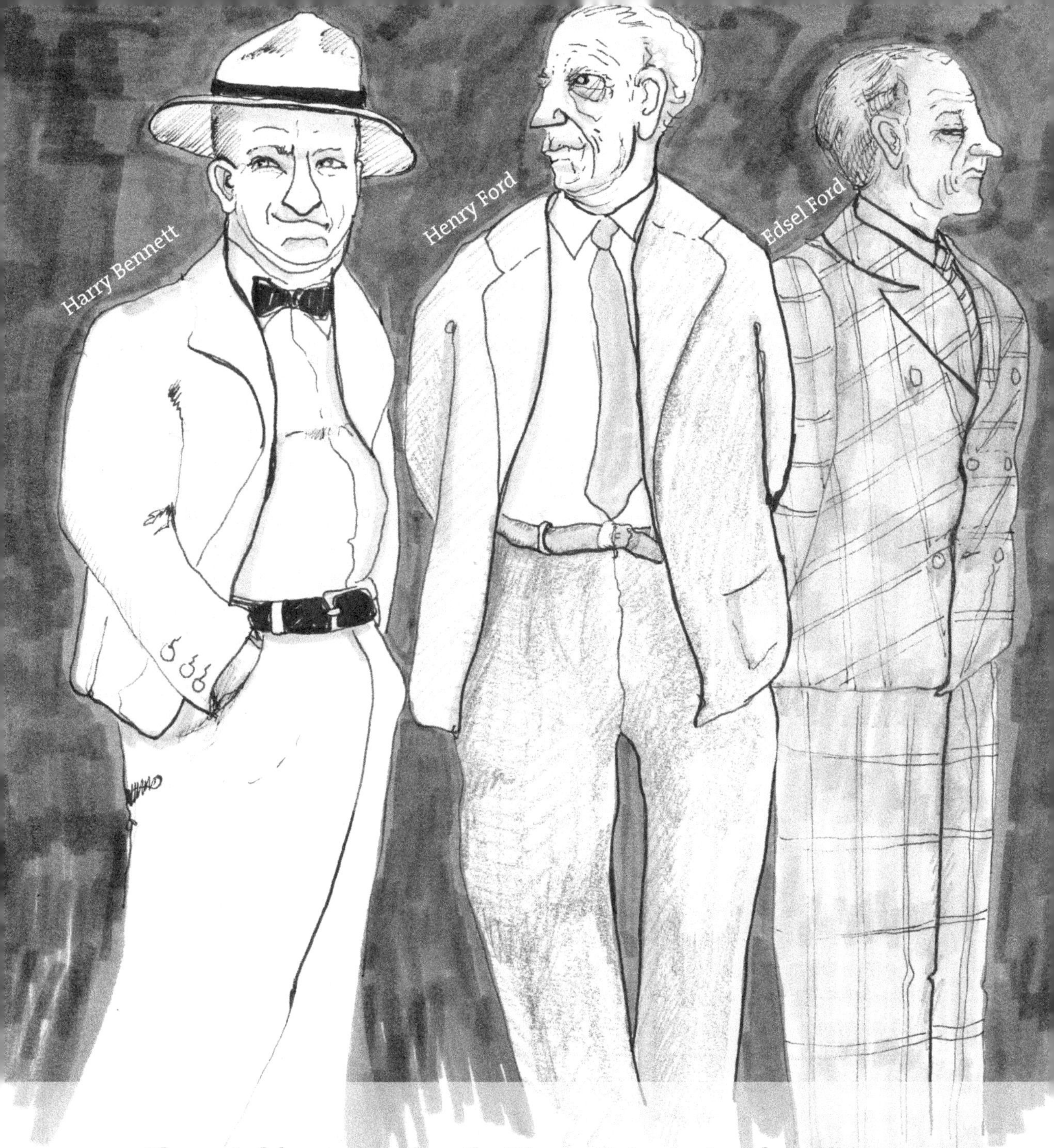
Harry Bennett
Henry Ford
Edsel Ford

The period from 1935, when the Wagner Act was signed, until 1941 was filled with strife and skirmishes between Ford and his workers. Even Ford's son, Edsel, tried to reason with him, but Ford was skeptical of the new ideas related to labor and production. He put his faith in the muscle of Harry Bennett and his service department instead. At the same time, labor organizations like the UAW-CIO worked hard to change their reputation among Black workers. Both white and Black workers organized against Ford to improve working conditions for everybody. Women played a key role in the effort.

The year 1937 marked a sharp turning point in labor relations and the African American community in Detroit. The unions were integrating and needed the support of the Black community more than ever.

1937, after a meeting at the Detroit Housewives' League . . .

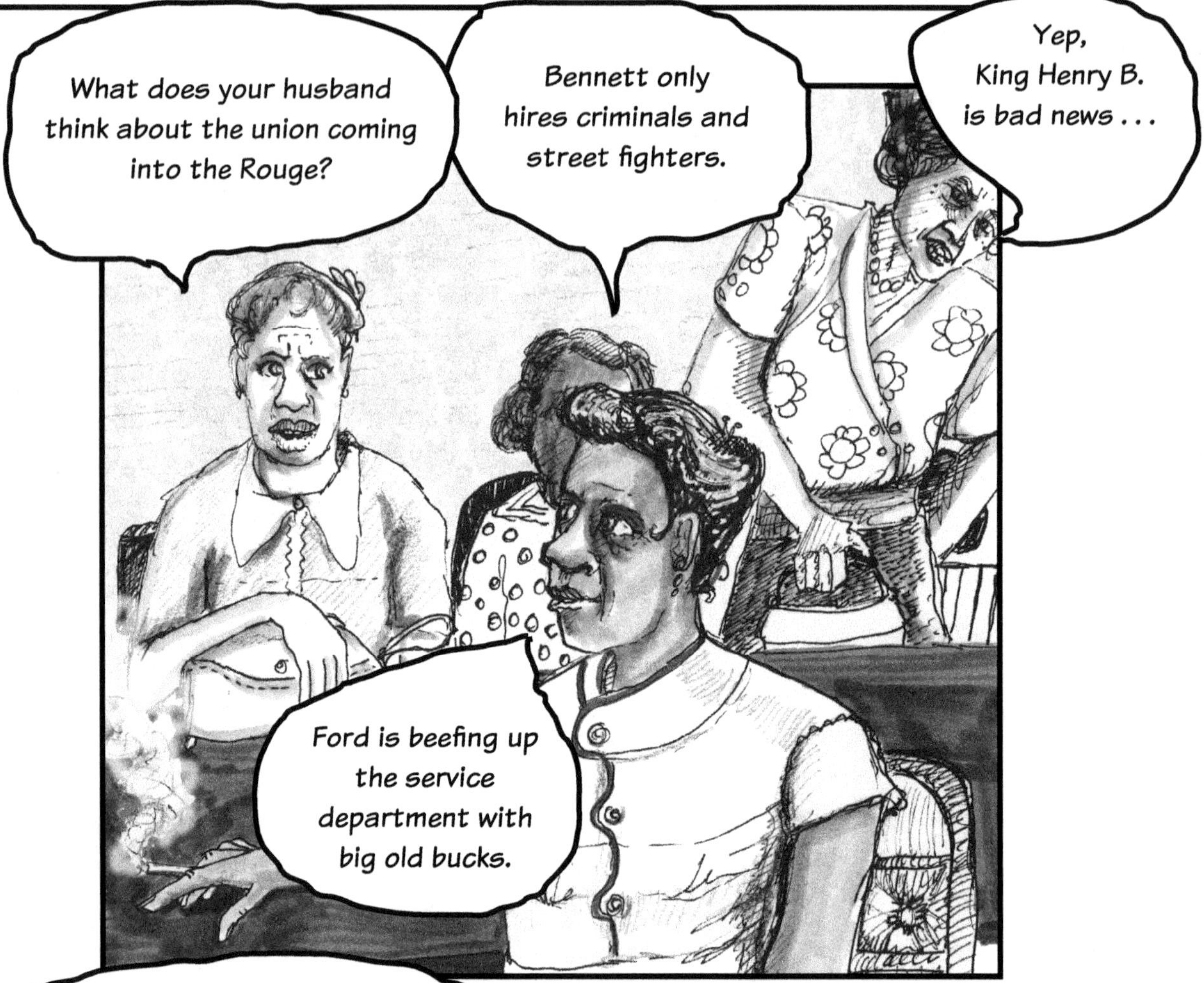
What does your husband think about the union coming into the Rouge?
Bennett only hires criminals and street fighters.
Yep, King Henry B. is bad news . . .
Ford is beefing up the service department with big old bucks.

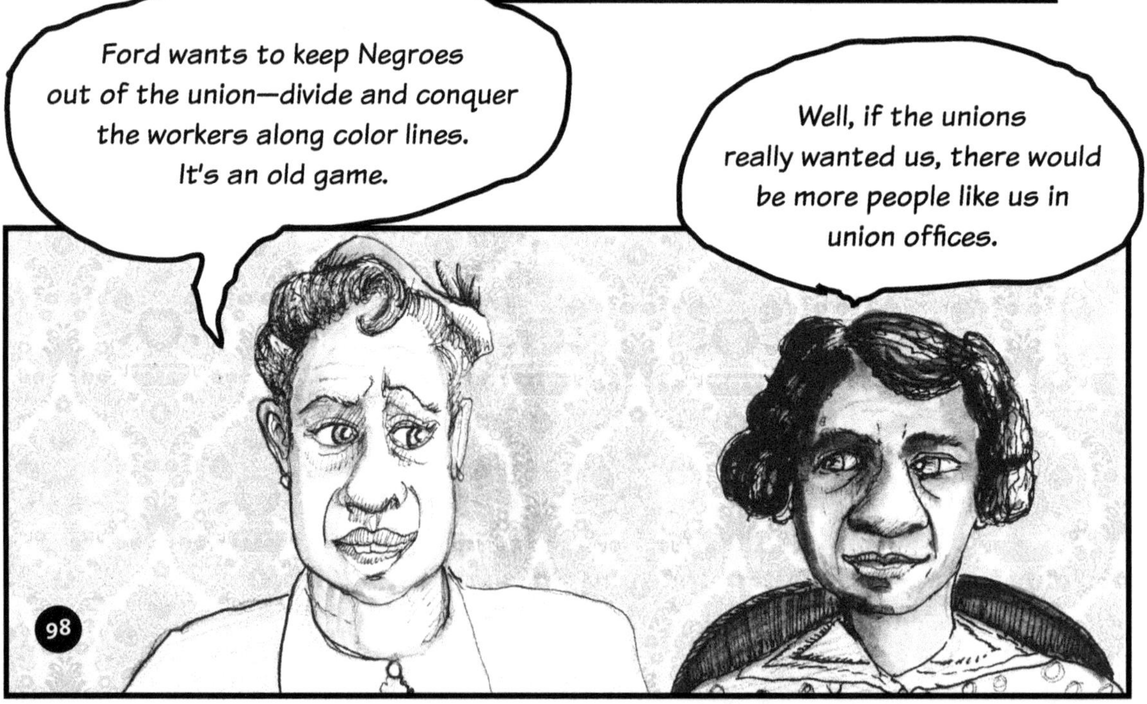
Ford wants to keep Negroes out of the union—divide and conquer the workers along color lines. It's an old game.
Well, if the unions really wanted us, there would be more people like us in union offices.

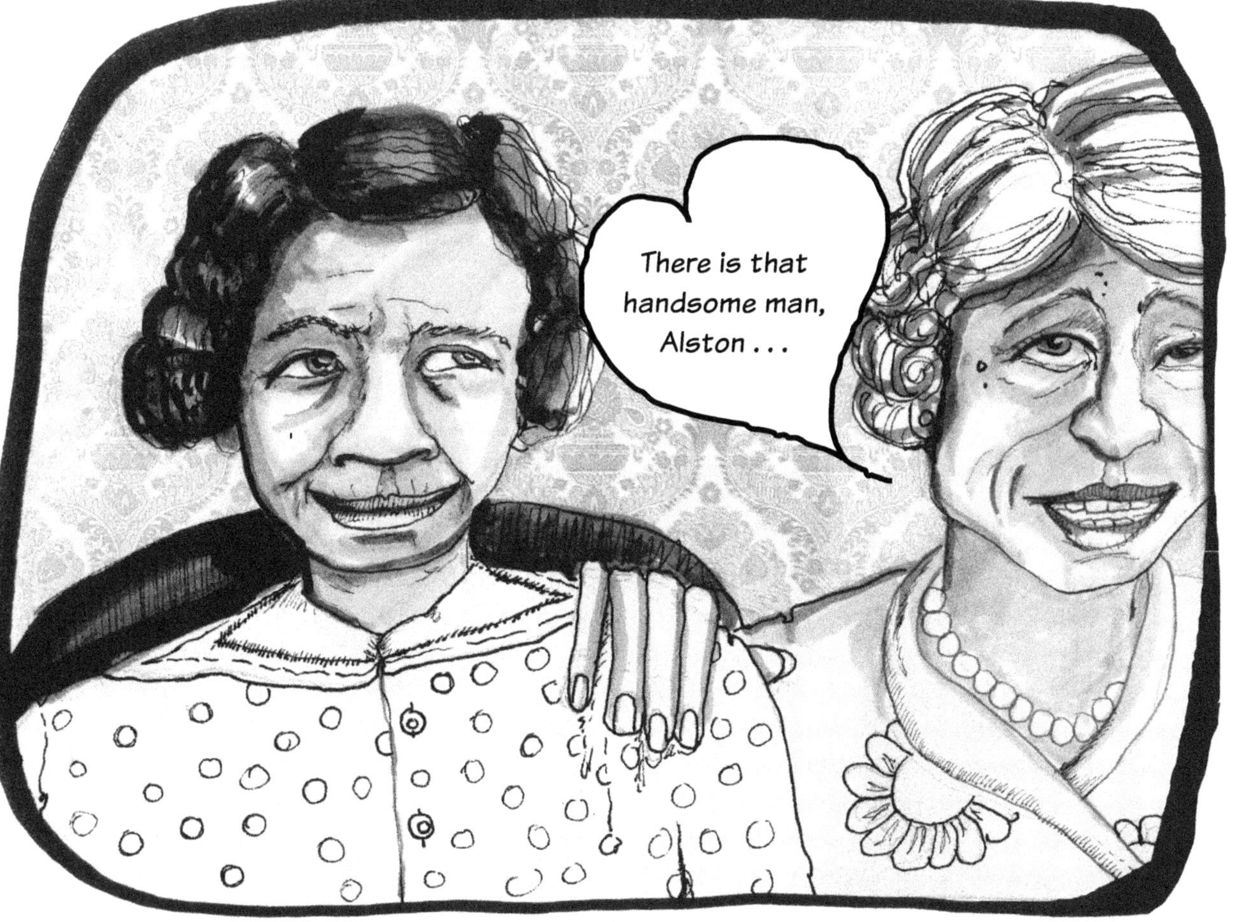
There is that handsome man, Alston . . .

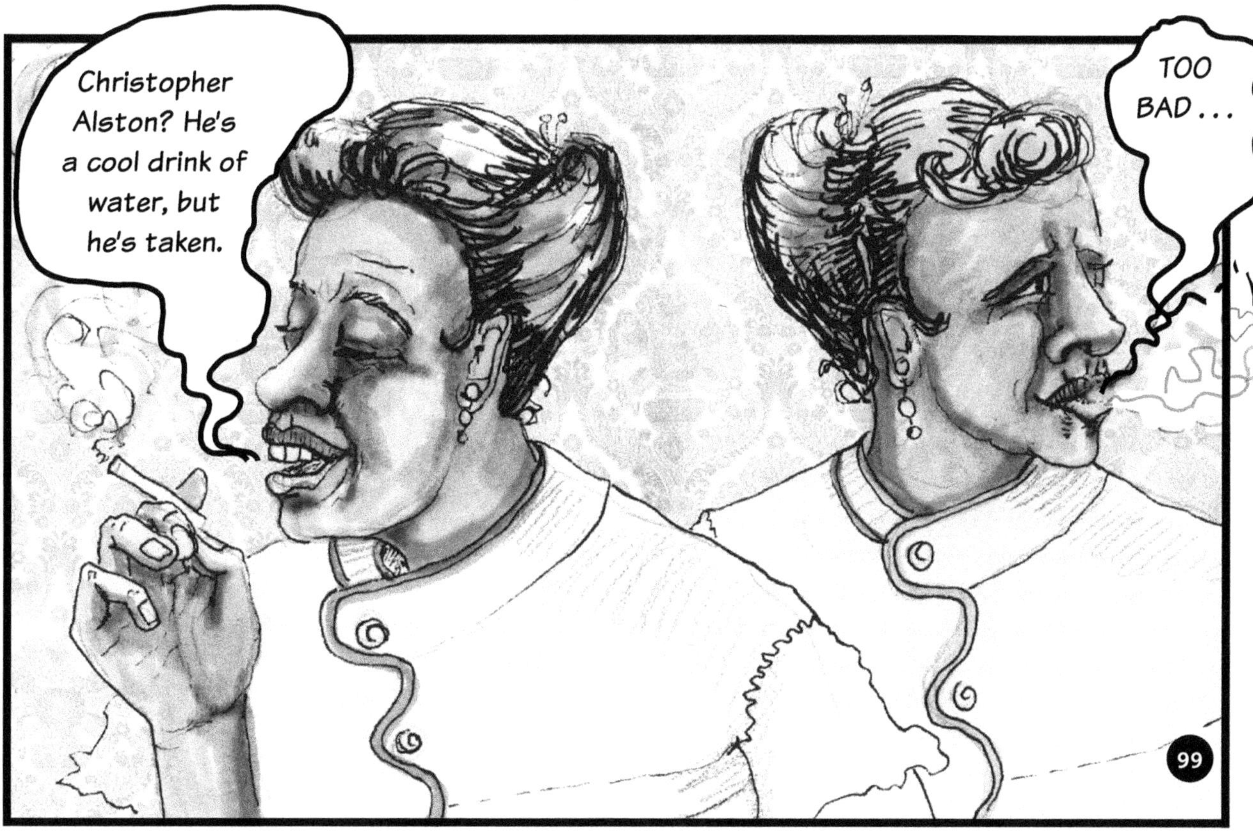
Christopher Alston? He's a cool drink of water, but he's taken.
TOO BAD . . .

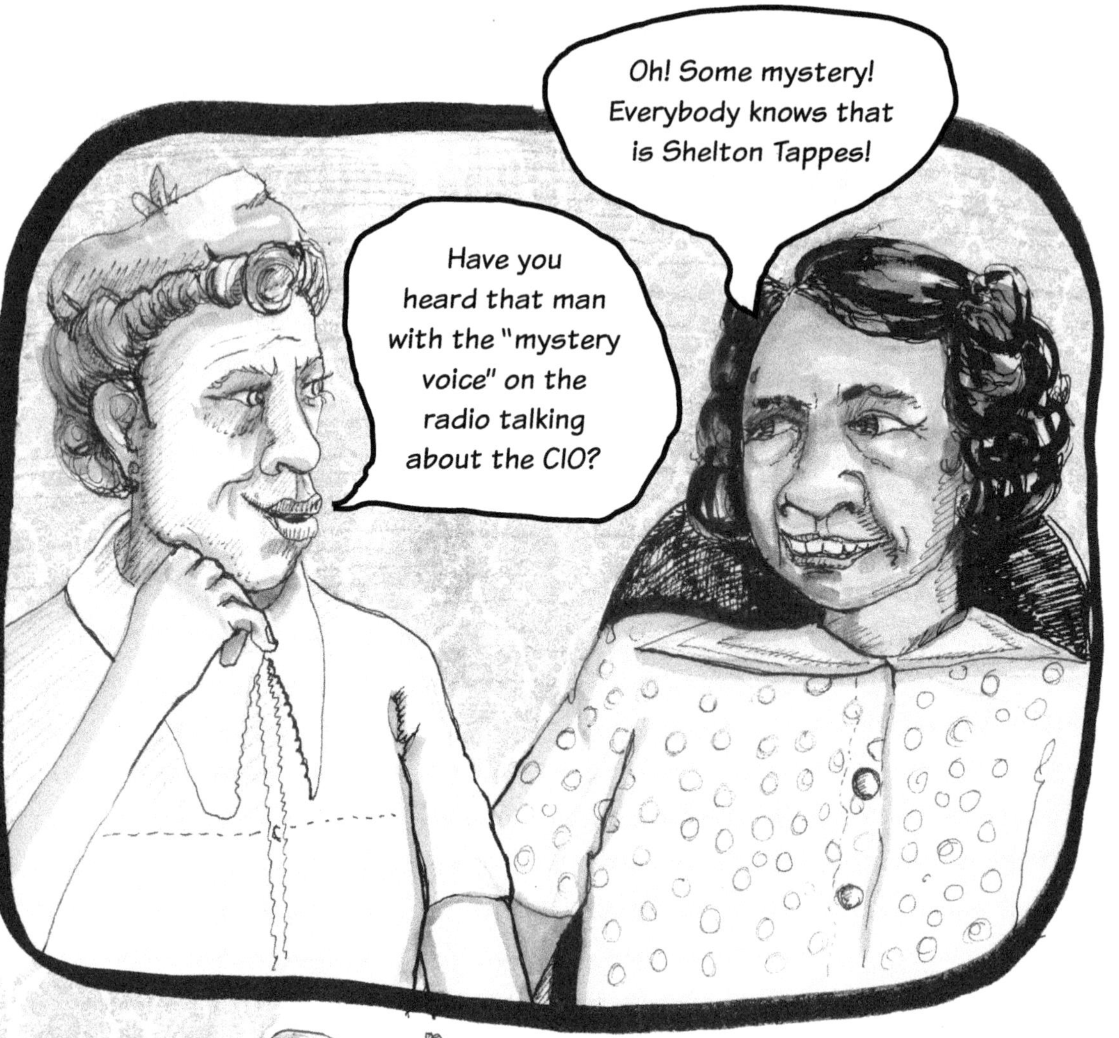
Have you heard that man with the "mystery voice" on the radio talking about the CIO?
Oh! Some mystery! Everybody knows that is Shelton Tappes!

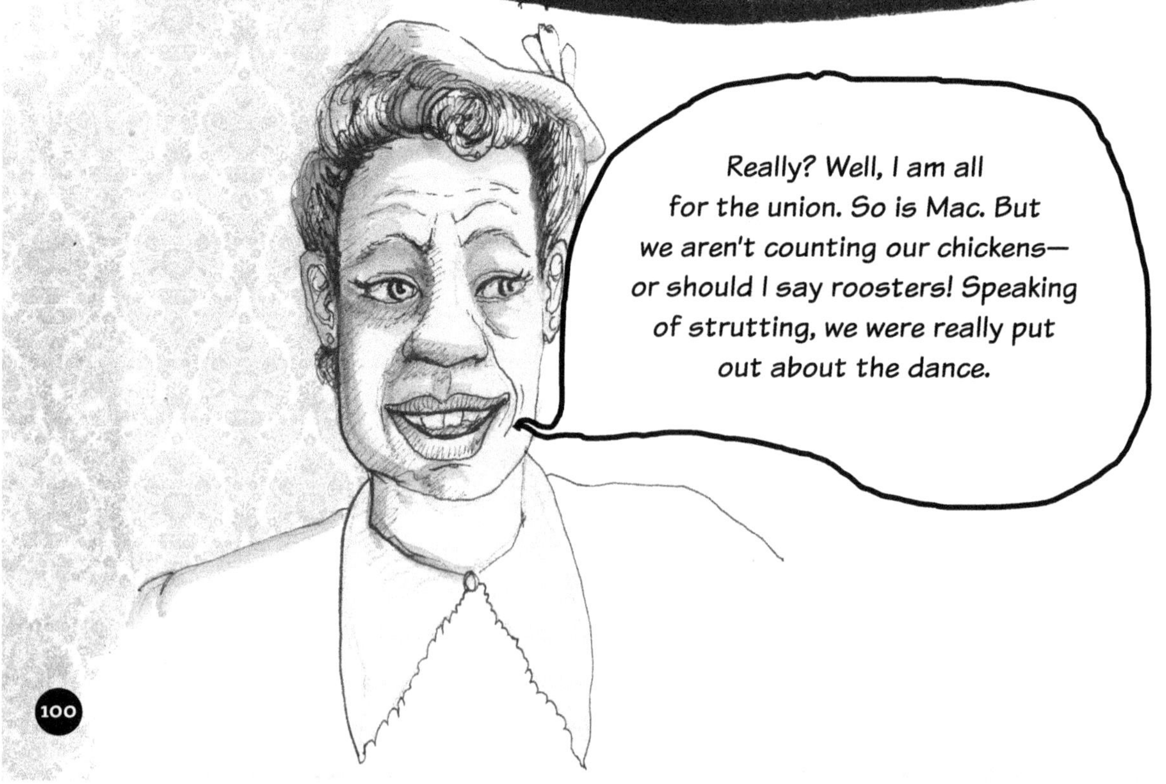
Really? Well, I am all for the union. So is Mac. But we aren't counting our chickens— or should I say roosters! Speaking of strutting, we were really put out about the dance.

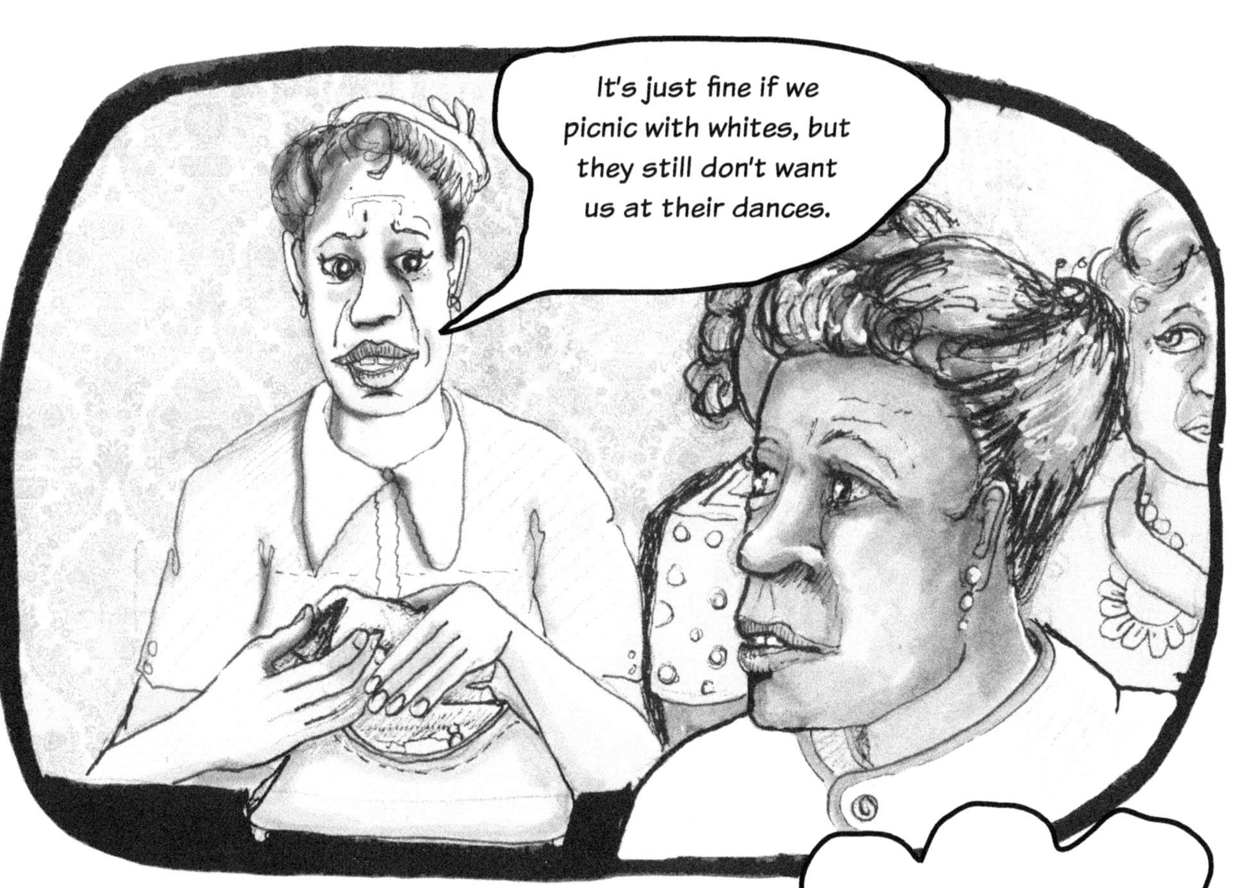
It's just fine if we picnic with whites, but they still don't want us at their dances.

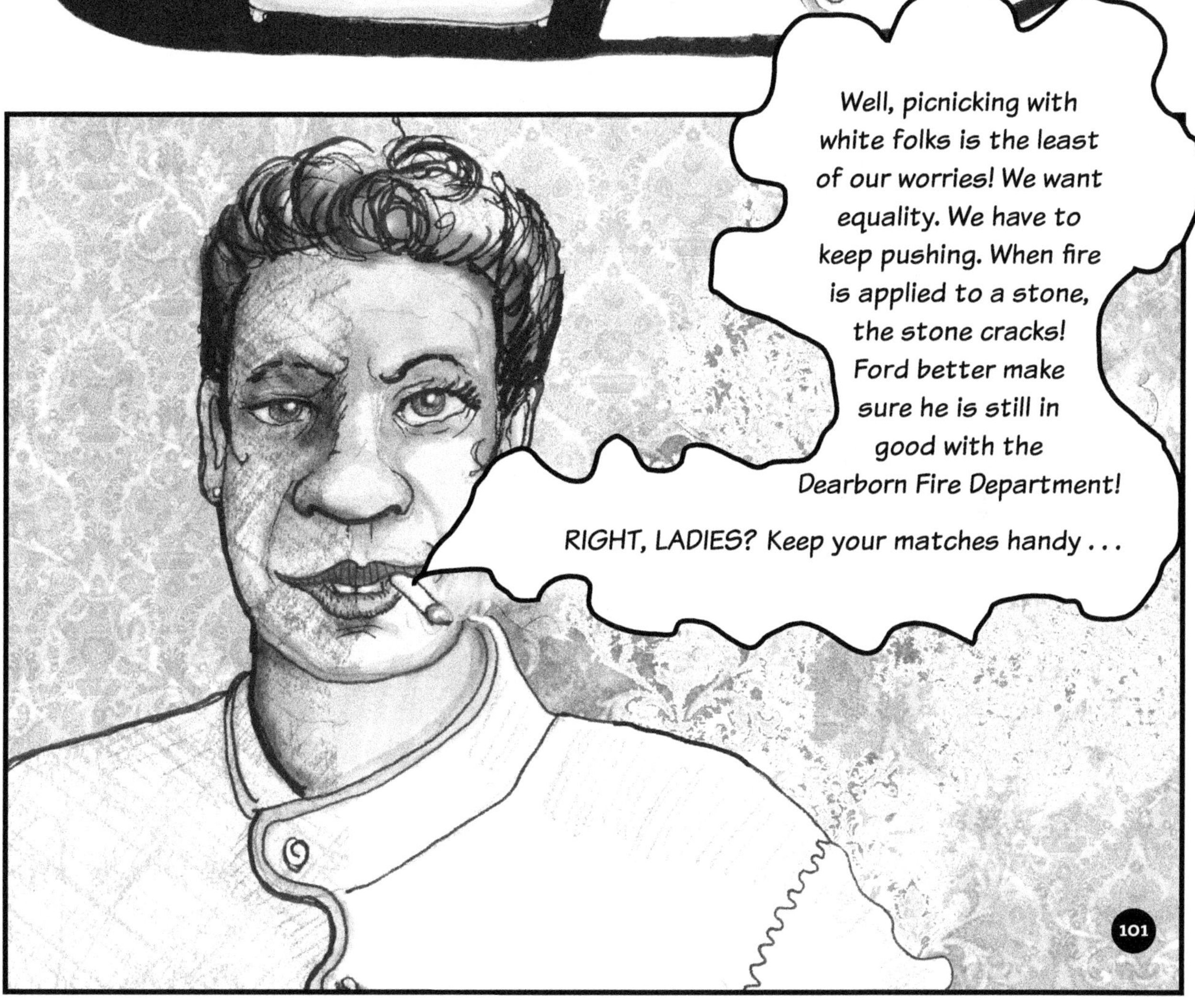
Well, picnicking with white folks is the least of our worries! We want equality. We have to keep pushing. When fire is applied to a stone, the stone cracks! Ford better make sure he is still in good with the Dearborn Fire Department!
RIGHT, LADIES? Keep your matches handy . . .

On May 25, 1937, somewhere on the west side of Detroit, a couple gets ready for bed . . .

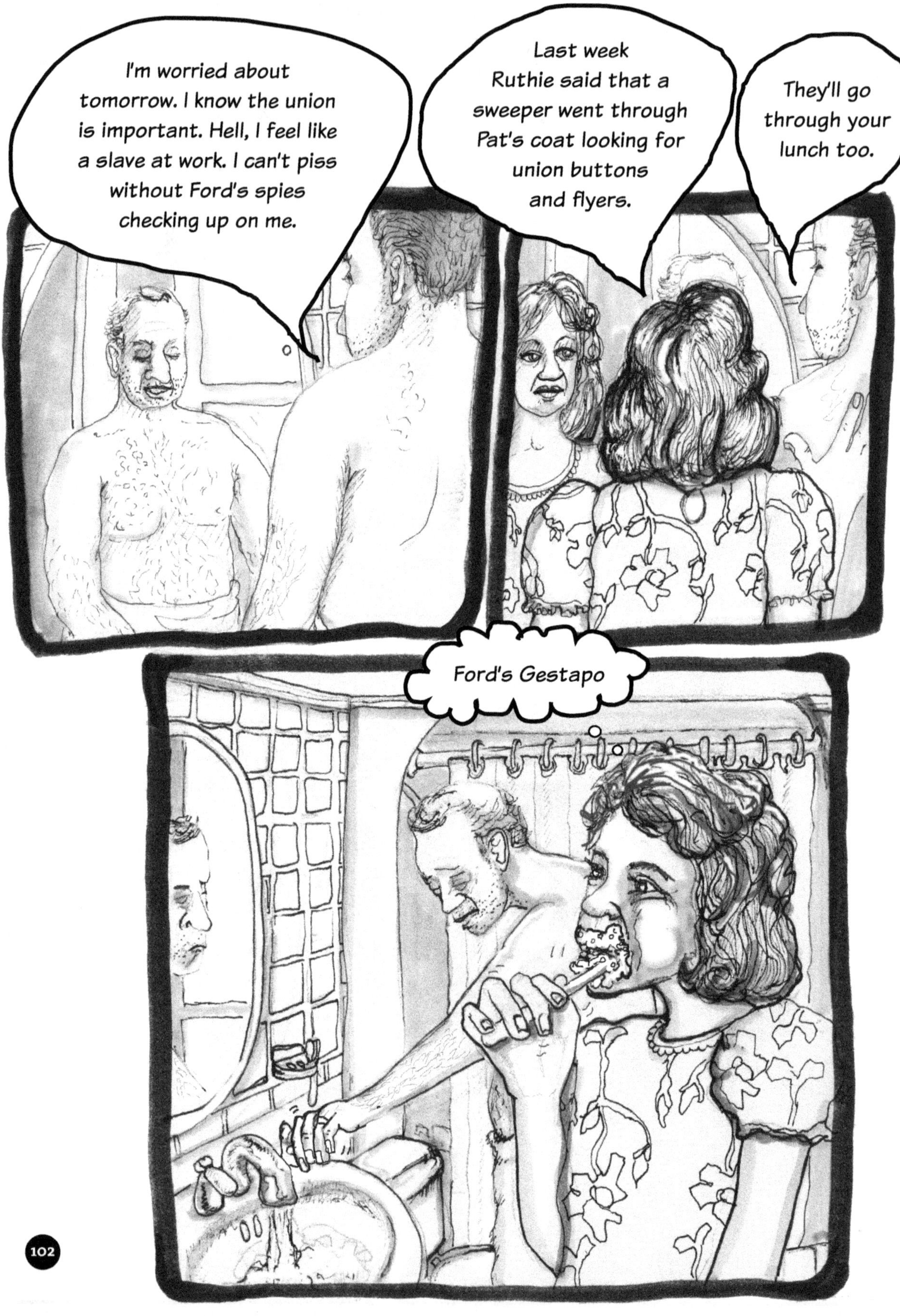
I'm worried about tomorrow. I know the union is important. Hell, I feel like a slave at work. I can't piss without Ford's spies checking up on me.
Last week Ruthie said that a sweeper went through Pat's coat looking for union buttons and flyers.
They'll go through your lunch too.
Ford's Gestapo

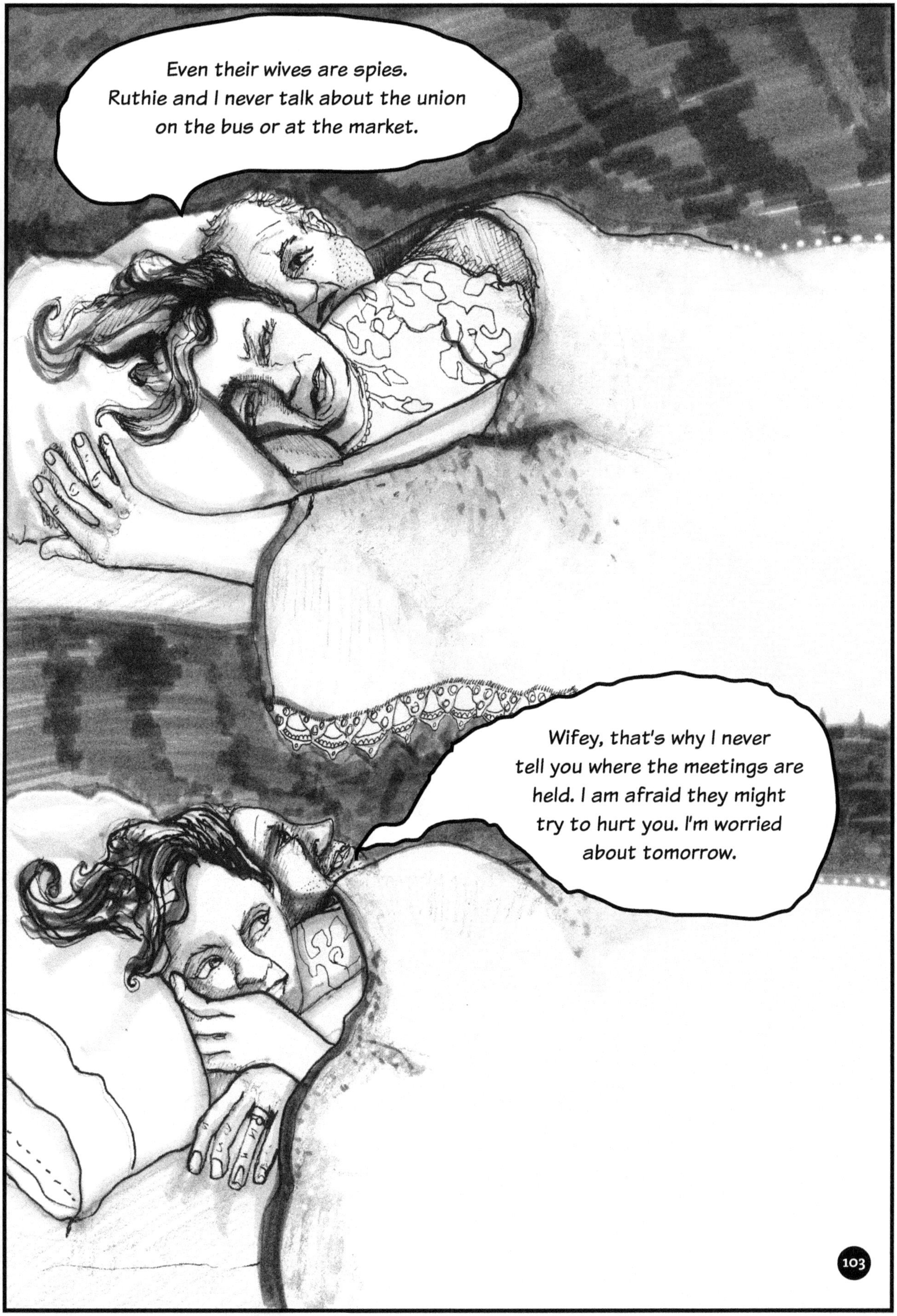
Even their wives are spies. Ruthie and I never talk about the union on the bus or at the market.
Wifey, that's why I never tell you where the meetings are held. I am afraid they might try to hurt you. I'm worried about tomorrow.

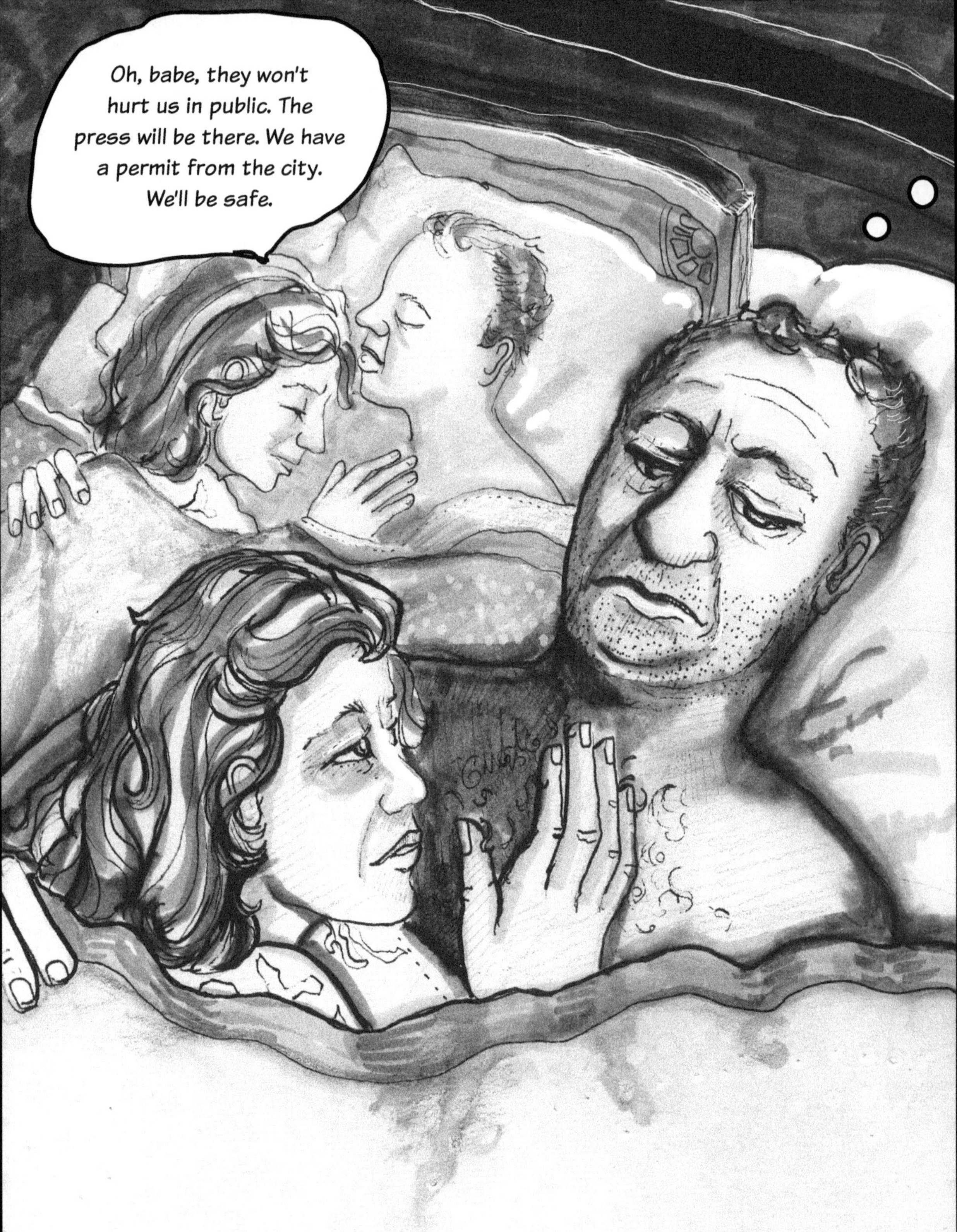
Oh, babe, they won't hurt us in public. The press will be there. We have a permit from the city. We'll be safe.

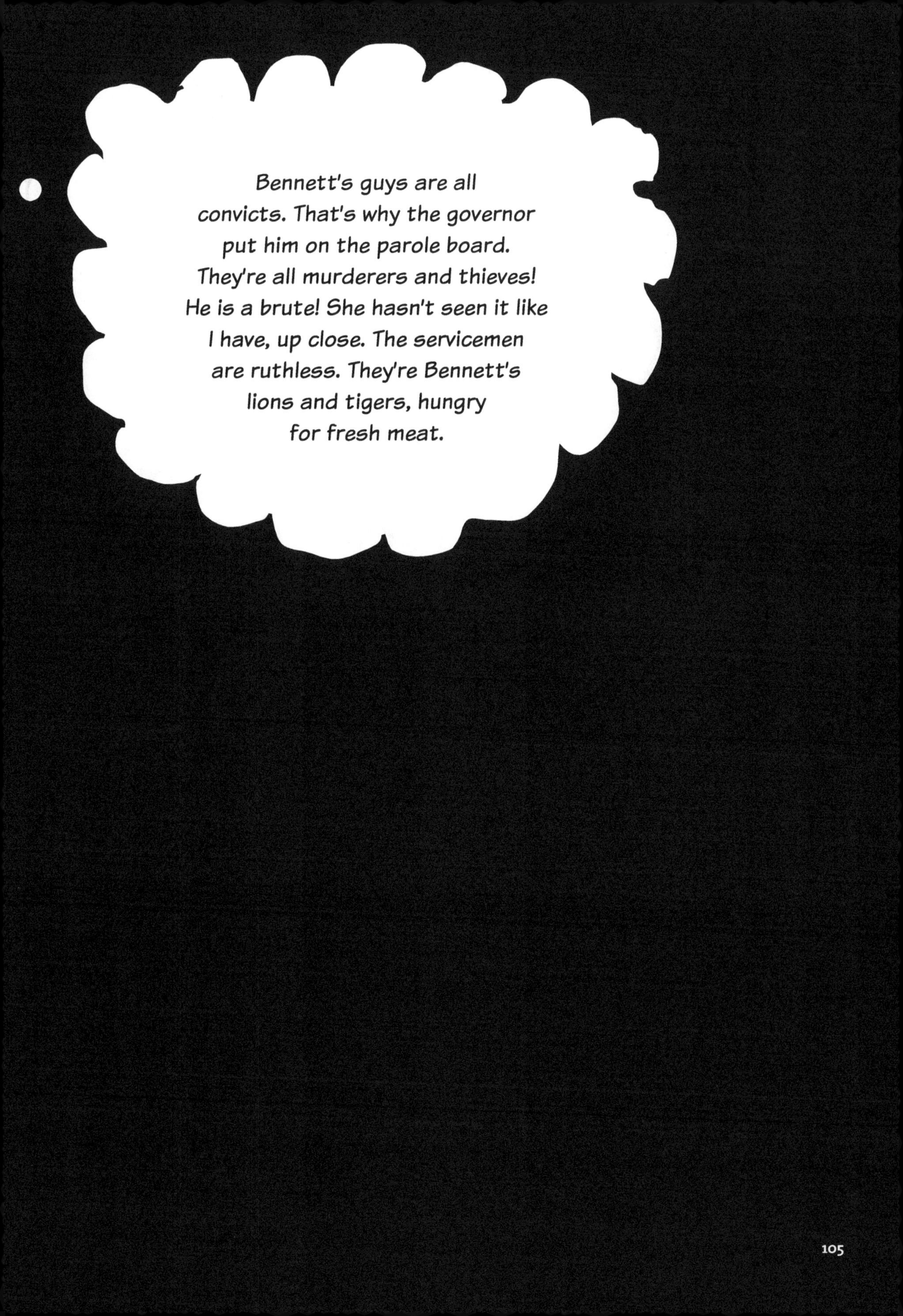
Bennett's guys are all convicts. That's why the governor put him on the parole board. They're all murderers and thieves! He is a brute! She hasn't seen it like I have, up close. The servicemen are ruthless. They're Bennett's lions and tigers, hungry for fresh meat.

May 26, 1937, the day of the Battle of the Overpass at River Rouge, was a turning point.

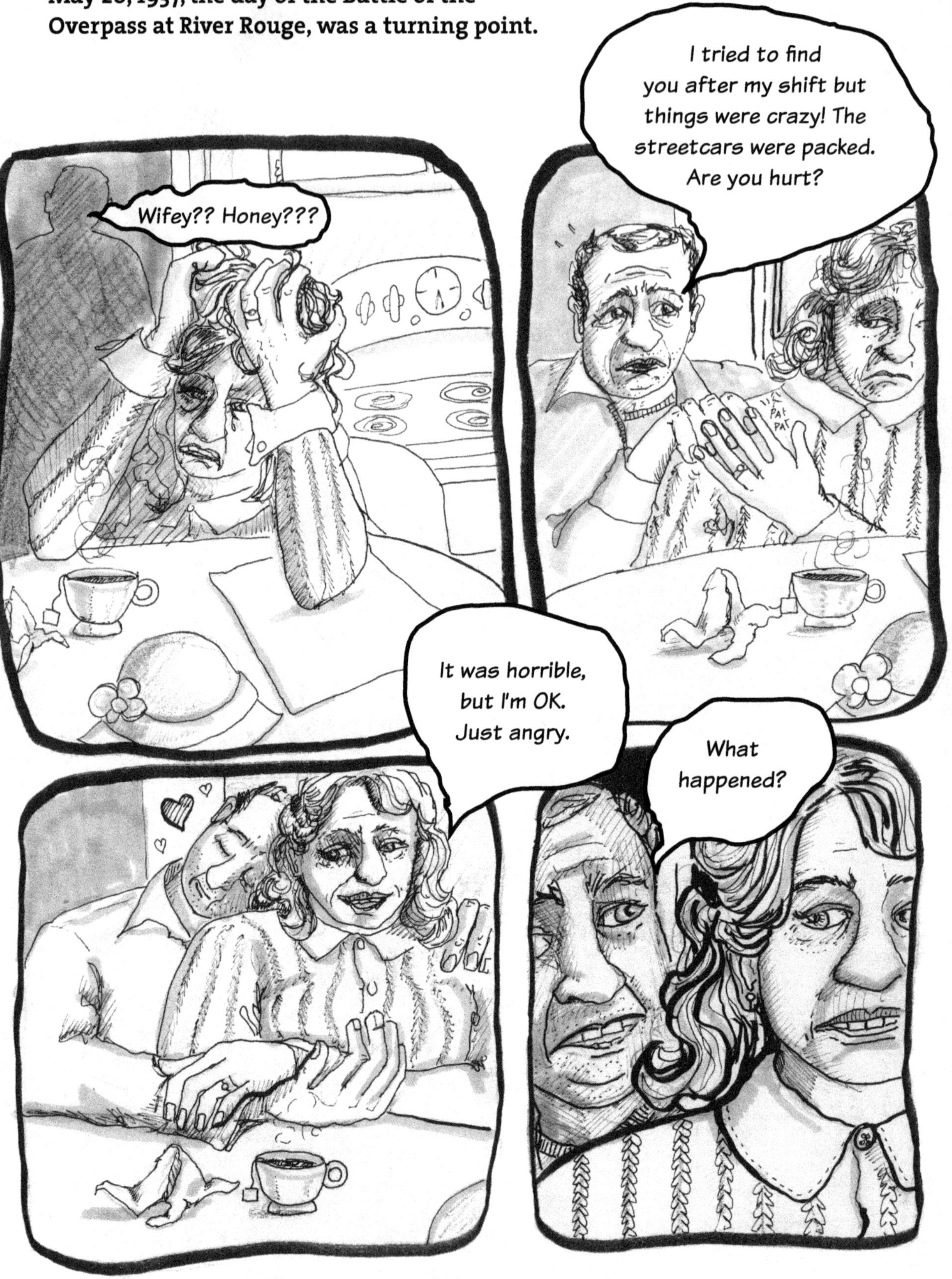
Wifey?? Honey???
I tried to find you after my shift but things were crazy! The streetcars were packed. Are you hurt?
PAT PAT
It was horrible, but I'm OK. Just angry.
What happened?

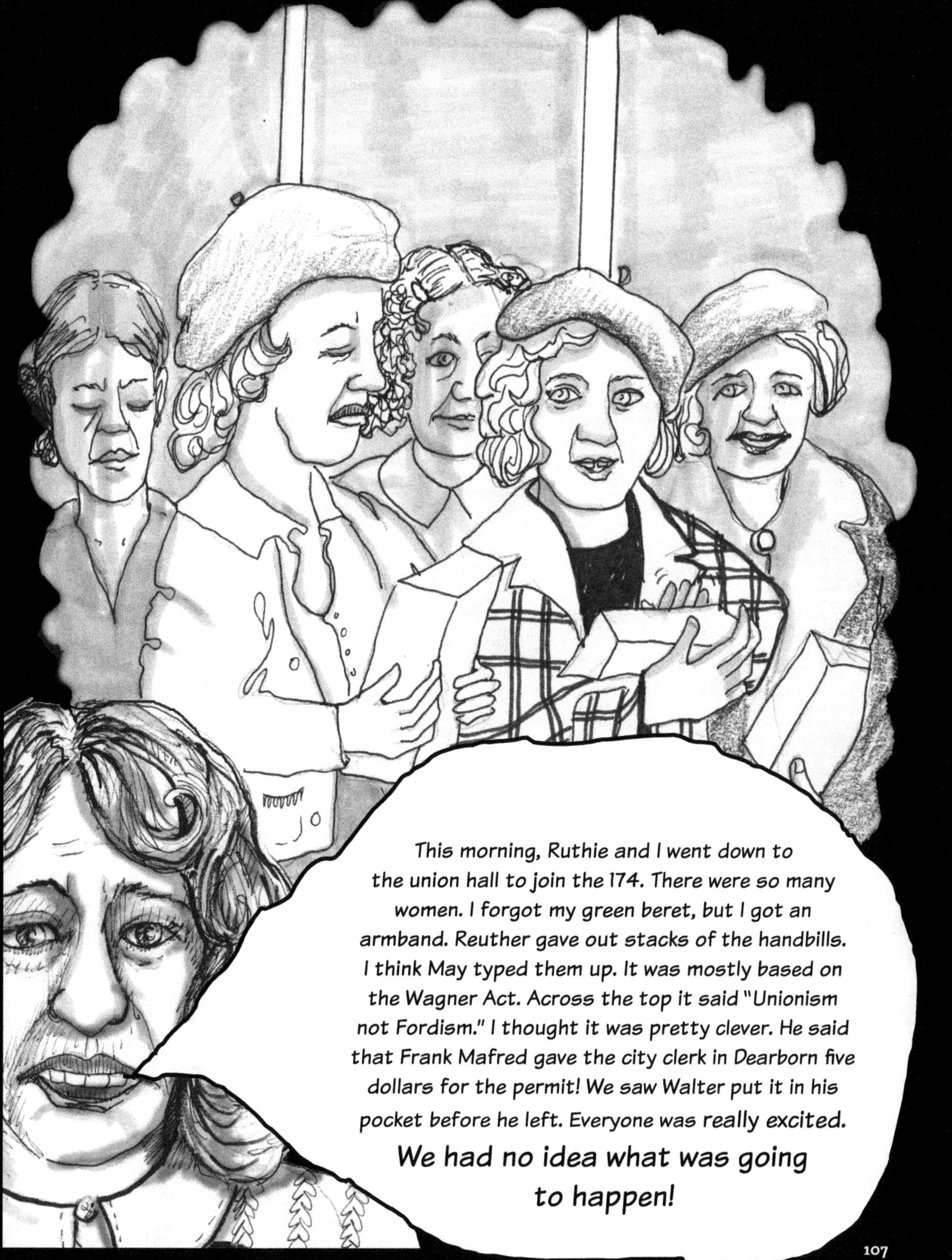
This morning, Ruthie and I went down to the union hall to join the 174. There were so many women. I forgot my green beret, but I got an armband. Reuther gave out stacks of the handbills. I think May typed them up. It was mostly based on the Wagner Act. Across the top it said "Unionism not Fordism." I thought it was pretty clever. He said that Frank Mafred gave the city clerk in Dearborn five dollars for the permit! We saw Walter put it in his pocket before he left. Everyone was really excited.
We had no idea what was going to happen!

I got on the streetcar and Ruthie and I sat next to each other. We had a map of Miller Road, so we knew what was public and what belonged to Mr. Ford. There was a lot of chatter and excitement until we pulled up at the platform. We could see that some of the 174 was already outside.

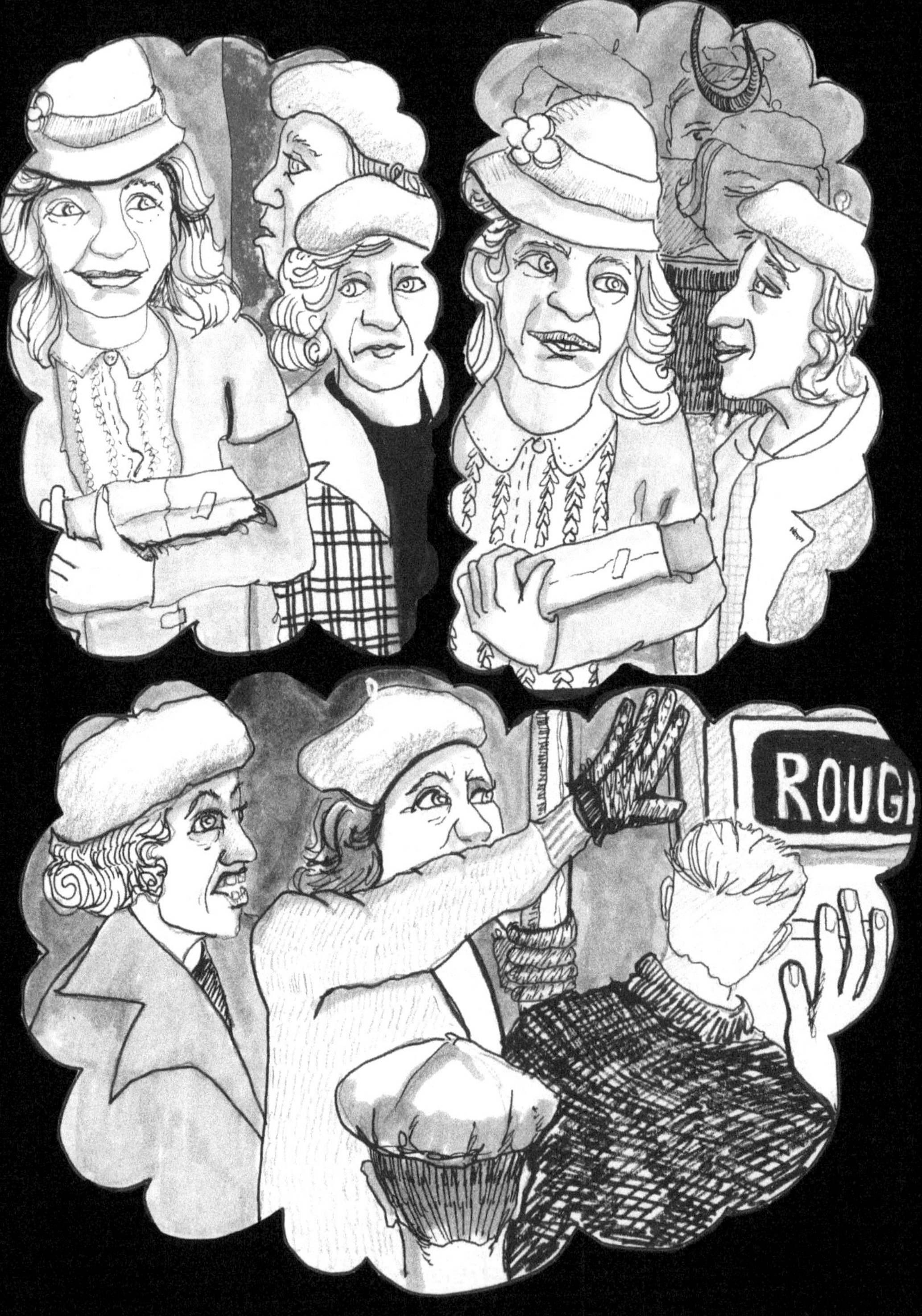
ROUG

Ford's servicemen were there too. When we tried to get off the streetcar, they pushed us back on! Ruthie and I were so scared at first.

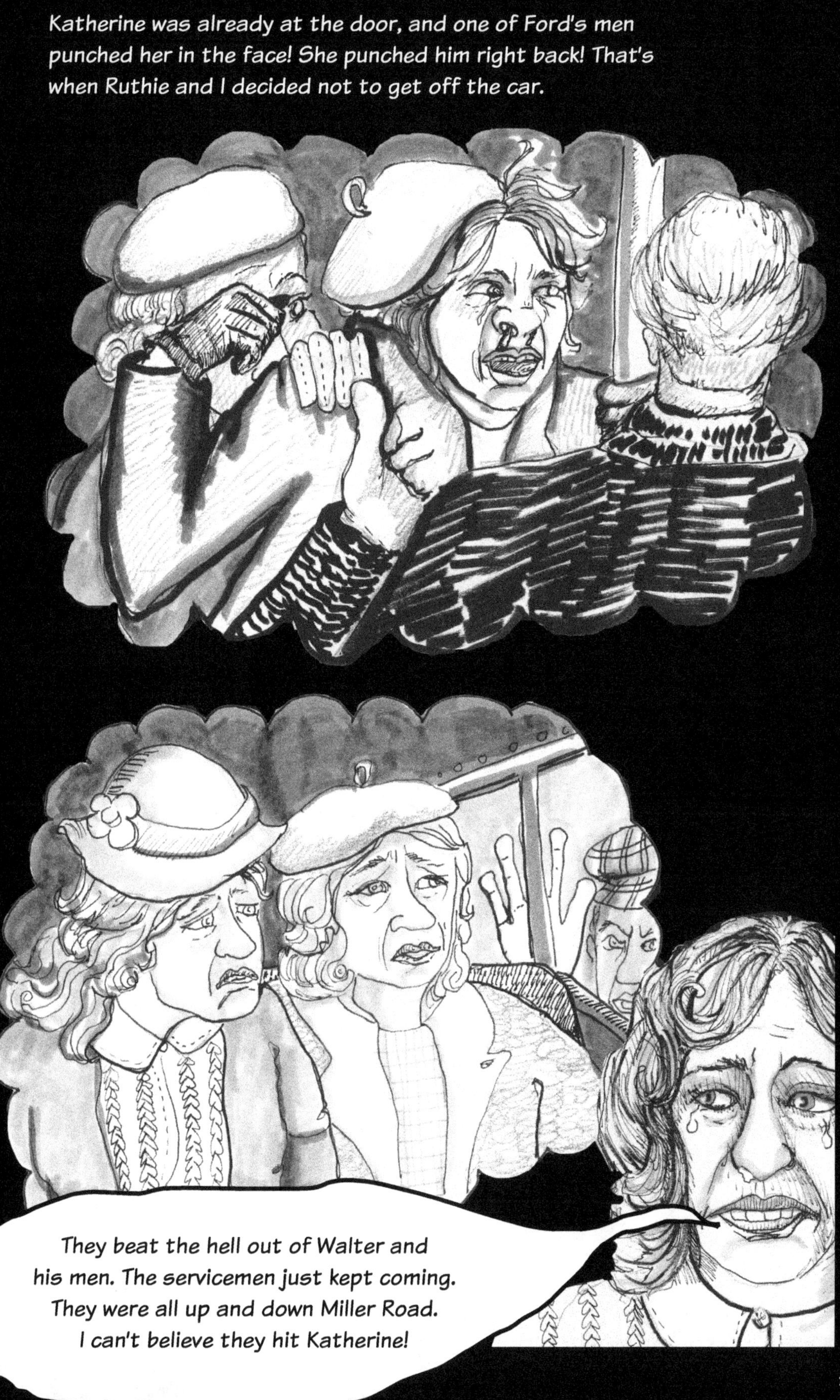
Katherine was already at the door, and one of Ford's men punched her in the face! She punched him right back! That's when Ruthie and I decided not to get off the car.
They beat the hell out of Walter and his men. The servicemen just kept coming. They were all up and down Miller Road. I can't believe they hit Katherine!

The Battle of the Overpass was a public relations disaster for the Ford Motor Company. Images of the melee were splashed across newspapers. But despite the bad press, things in the Ford plants grew worse and tension continued to escalate.

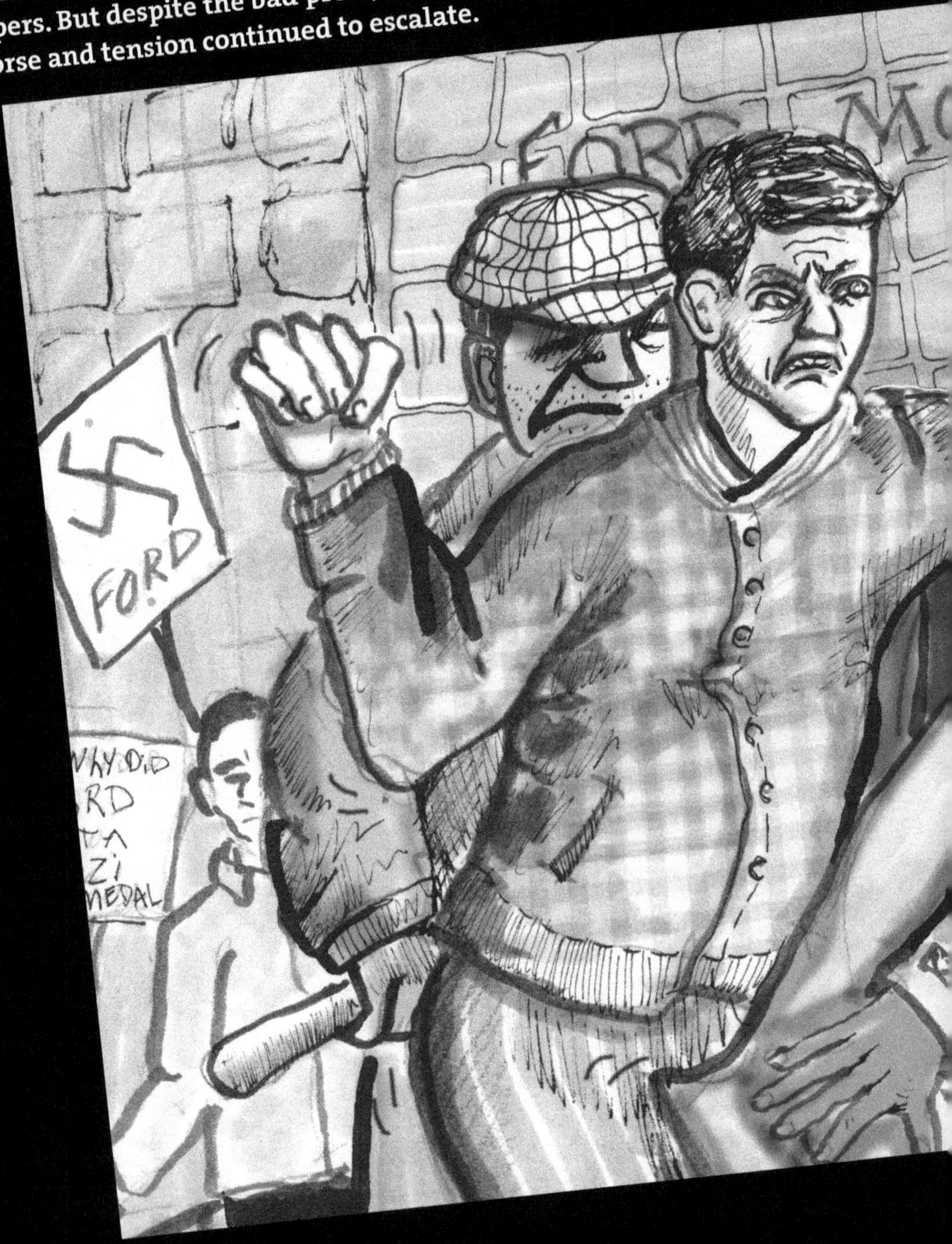
FORD

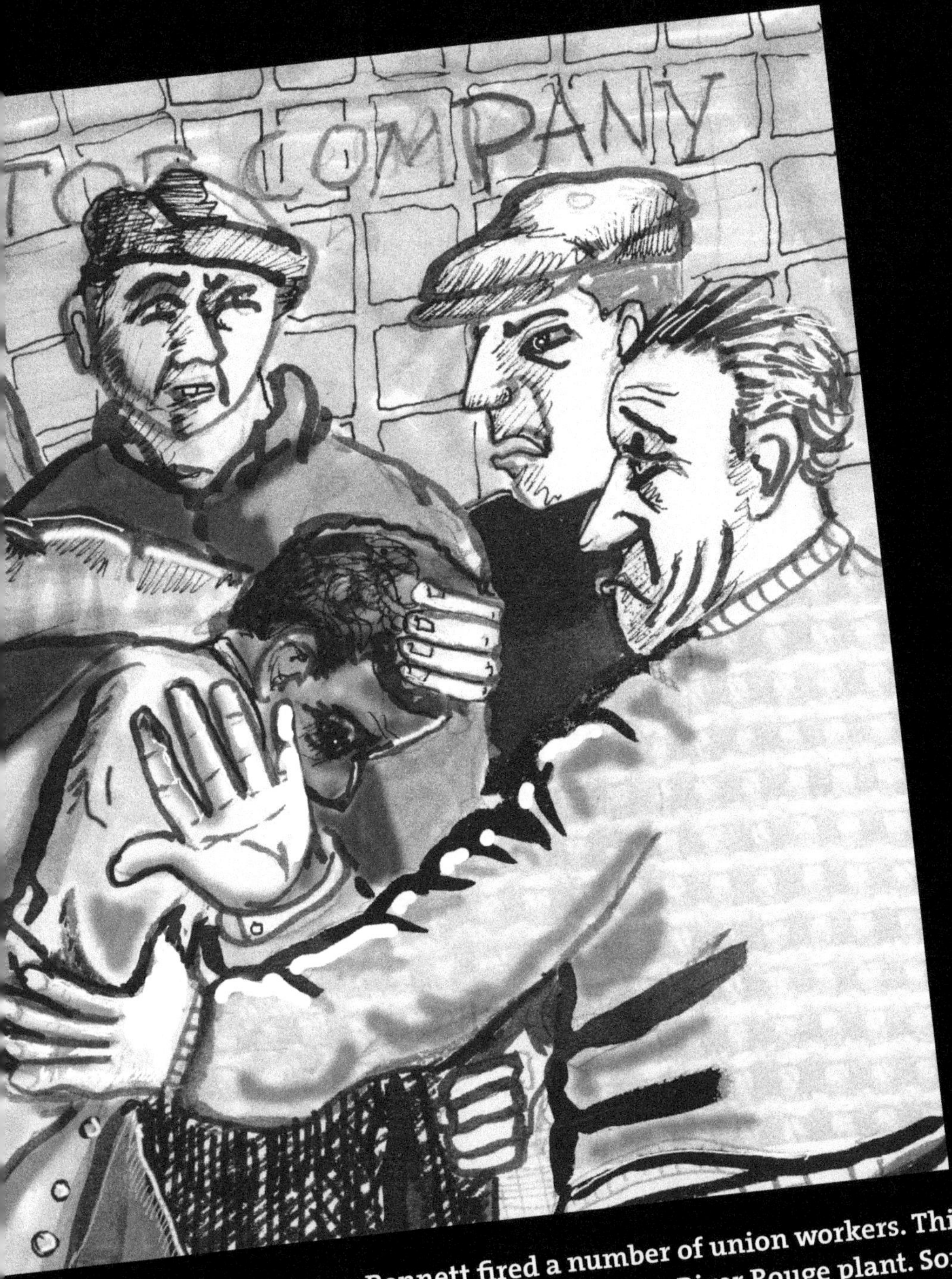
COMPANY

In April 1941, Harry Bennett fired a number of union workers. This resulted in a dramatic ten-day strike at the River Rouge plant. Some nonunion workers, the majority of whom were Black men, stayed inside the plant, and Ford paid them a dollar per hour not to strike. On April 2, some of the African American workers inside the plant charged the white picketers at Gate 4, and fights broke out.

The NAACP and pro-union Black ministers in Detroit worked with the UAW to convince Black workers to join the union. They argued that building a strong union would create better working conditions for all workers at Ford. Union membership soared by leaps and bounds that spring, and Ford was feeling intense pressure.

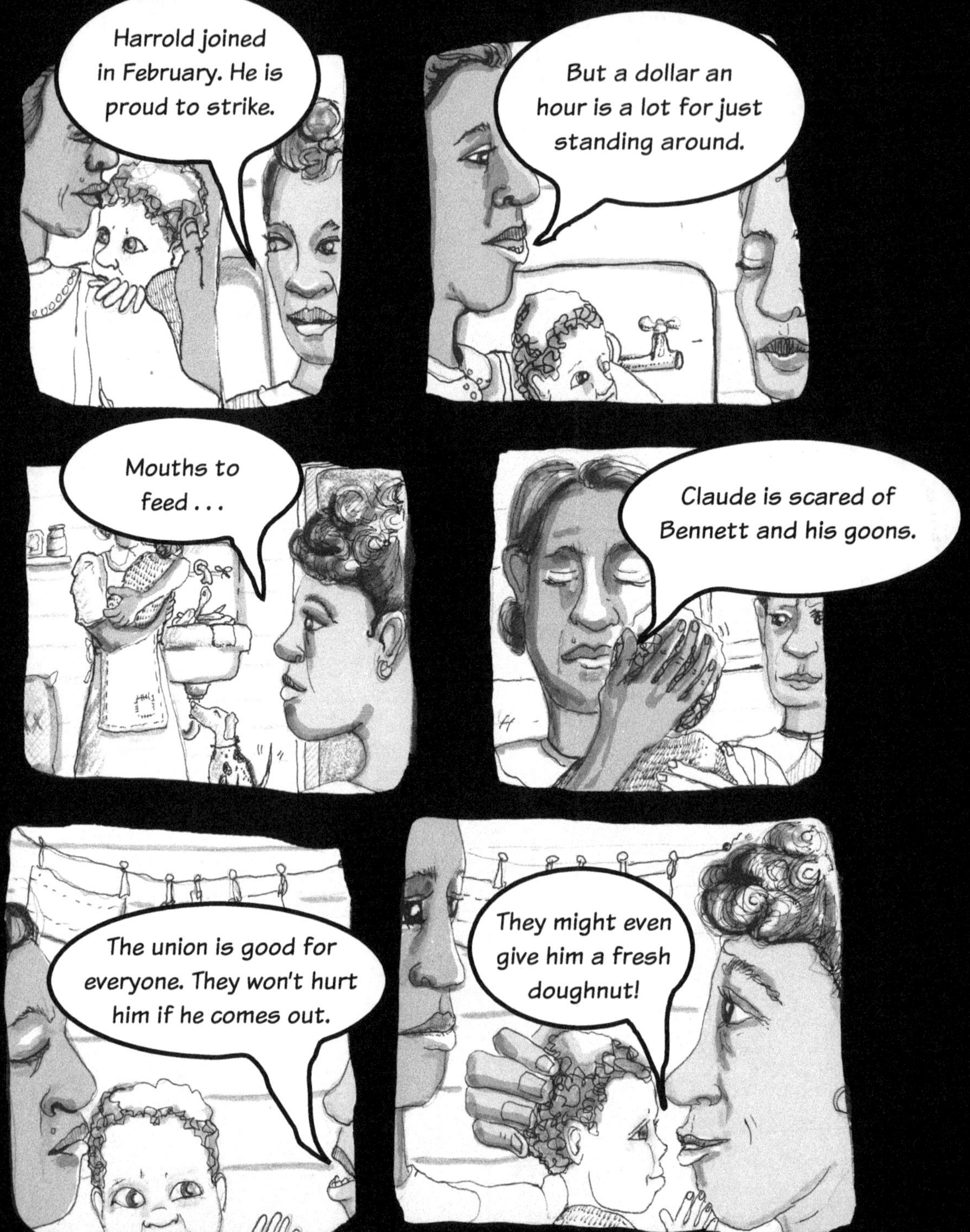
Harrold joined in February. He is proud to strike.
But a dollar an hour is a lot for just standing around.
Mouths to feed . . .
Claude is scared of Bennett and his goons.
The union is good for everyone. They won't hurt him if he comes out.
They might even give him a fresh doughnut!

Some Black workers were torn between their loyalty to Ford, economic constraints, and the promise of racial equality.

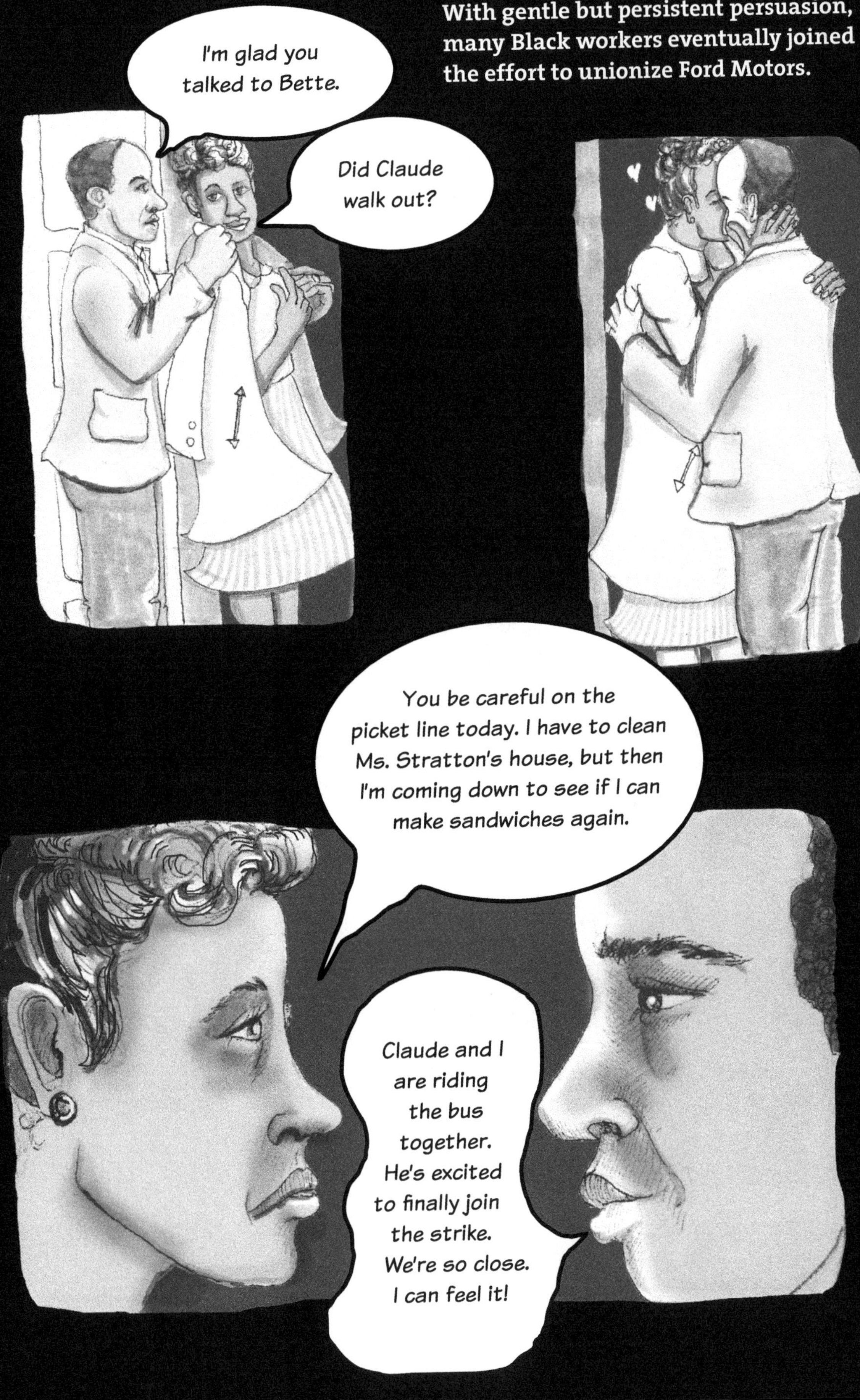

With gentle but persistent persuasion, many Black workers eventually joined the effort to unionize Ford Motors.
I'm glad you talked to Bette.
Did Claude walk out?
You be careful on the picket line today. I have to clean Ms. Stratton's house, but then I'm coming down to see if I can make sandwiches again.
Claude and I are riding the bus together. He's excited to finally join the strike. We're so close. I can feel it!

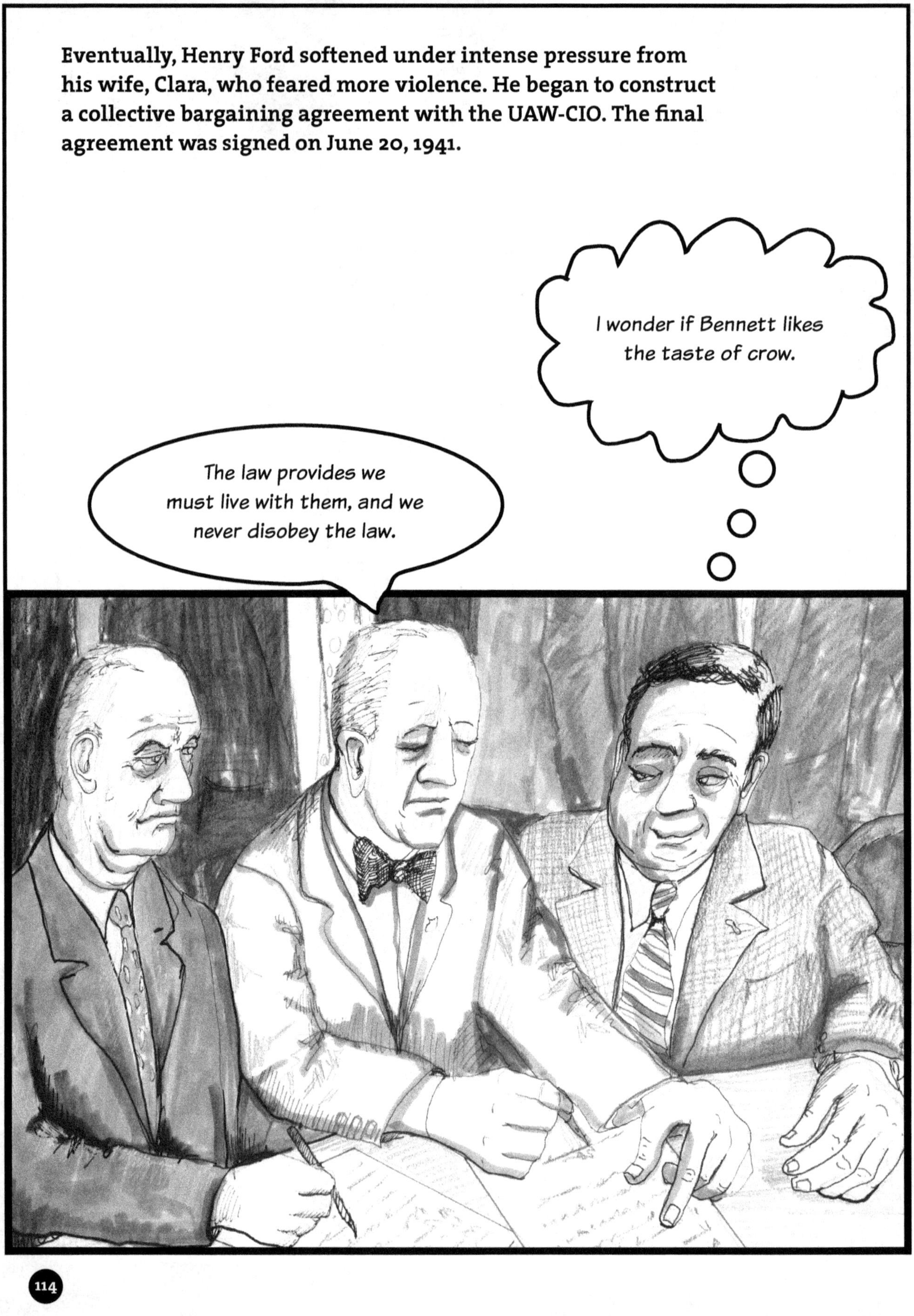
Eventually, Henry Ford softened under intense pressure from his wife, Clara, who feared more violence. He began to construct a collective bargaining agreement with the UAW-CIO. The final agreement was signed on June 20, 1941.
The law provides we must live with them, and we never disobey the law.
I wonder if Bennett likes the taste of crow.

Despite the labor agreement, little changed for Black workers.

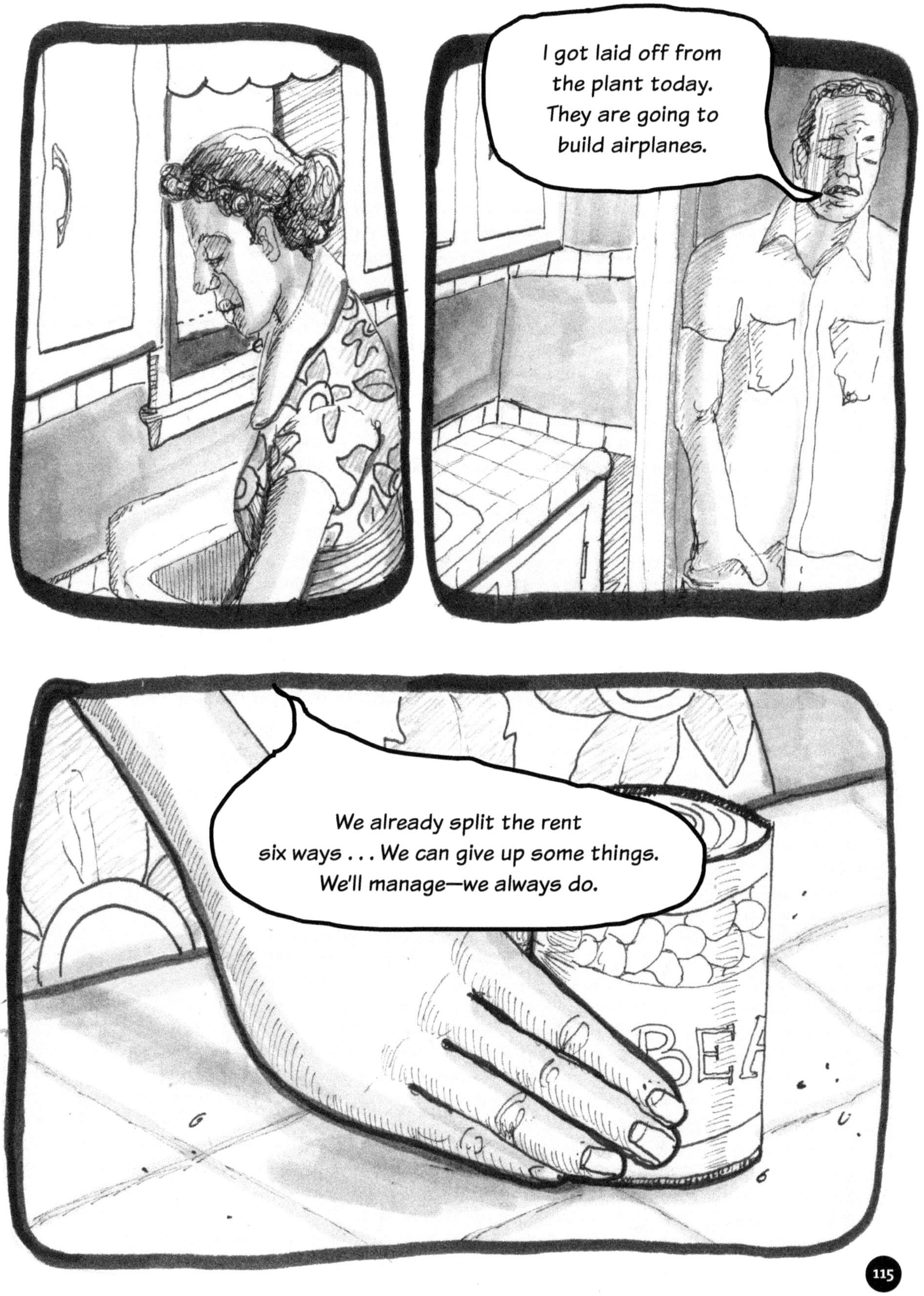
I got laid off from the plant today. They are going to build airplanes.
We already split the rent six ways . . . We can give up some things. We'll manage—we always do.
BEA

There was rampant unemployment in the African American community in 1941 and finding a job was difficult, especially for African American women. Many working-class African American families struggled to survive.

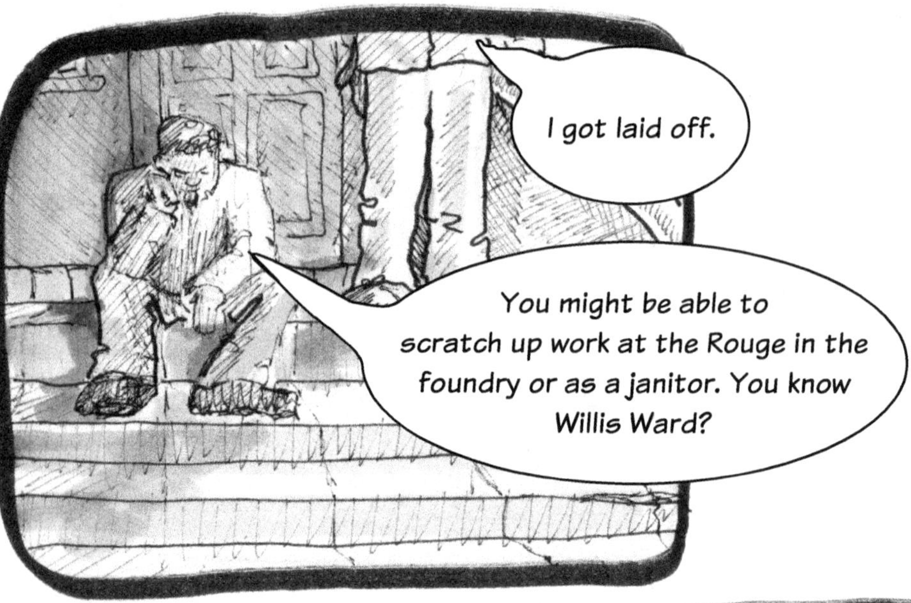
I got laid off.
You might be able to scratch up work at the Rouge in the foundry or as a janitor. You know Willis Ward?

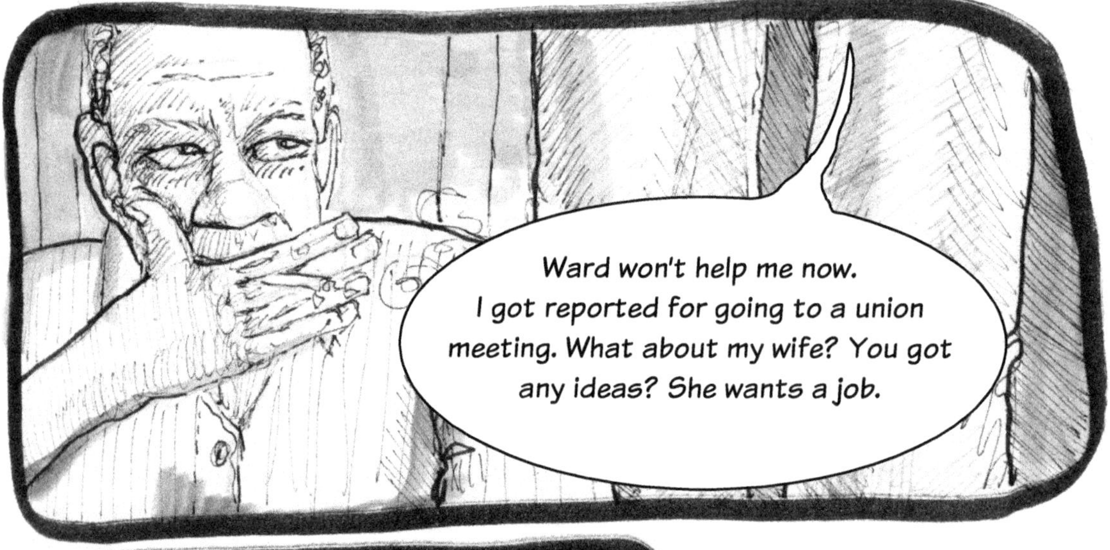
Ward won't help me now. I got reported for going to a union meeting. What about my wife? You got any ideas? She wants a job.

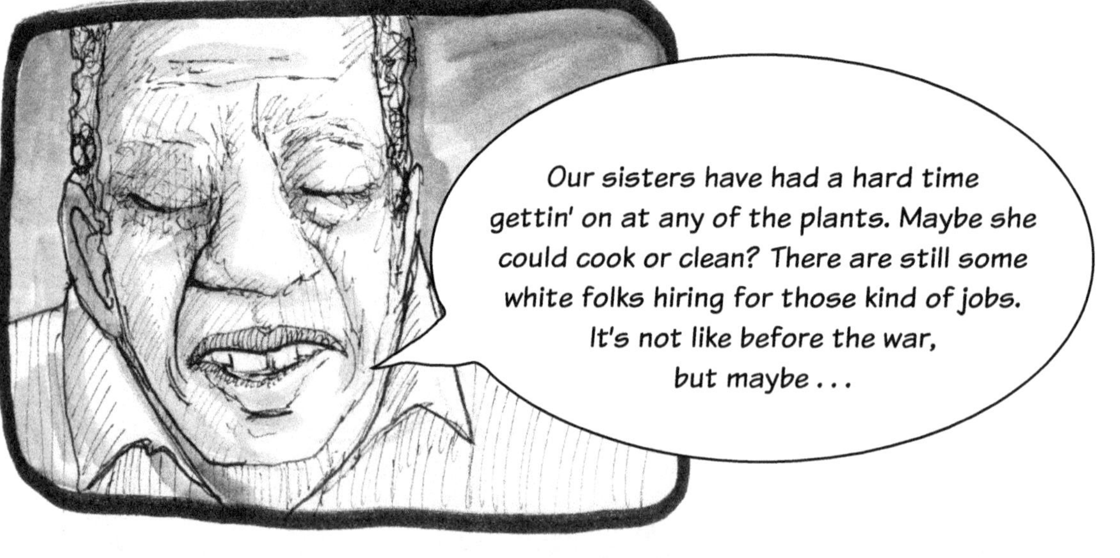
Our sisters have had a hard time gettin' on at any of the plants. Maybe she could cook or clean? There are still some white folks hiring for those kind of jobs. It's not like before the war, but maybe . . .

When plants began to hire people again to make implements of war, Black workers and activists in Detroit became firm about putting an end to discrimination. The union had not changed the landscape for Black workers on the scale they had expected. On January 16, 1942, activists and organizers met at the Lucy Thurman YWCA to make a plan.

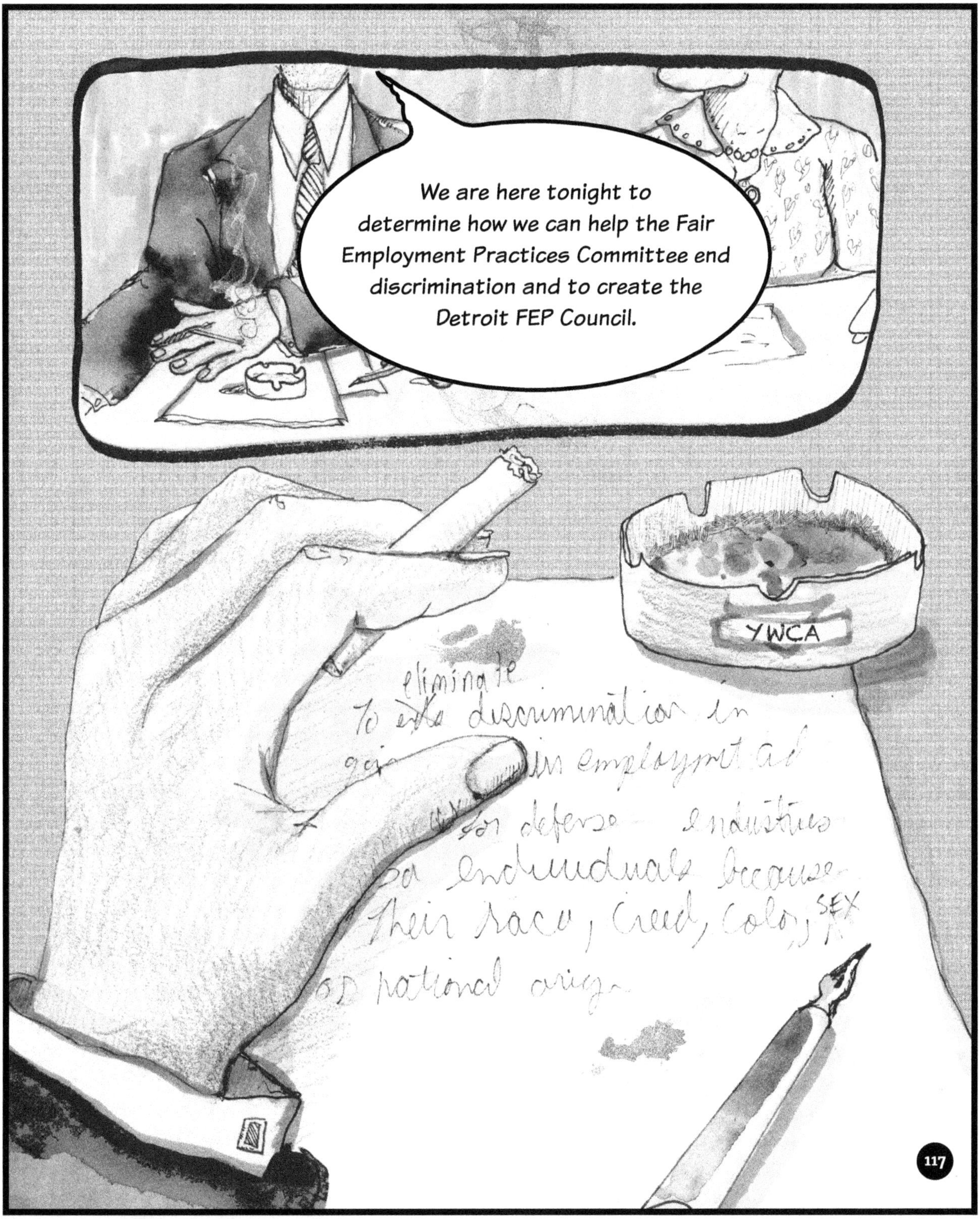
We are here tonight to determine how we can help the Fair Employment Practices Committee end discrimination and to create the Detroit FEP Council.
YWCA

They worked together to determine their purpose and create a bold plan of action. They drafted a statement condemning discrimination on the basis of race, creed, color, sex, or national origin in the defense industries and moved to improve the hiring of Black women.

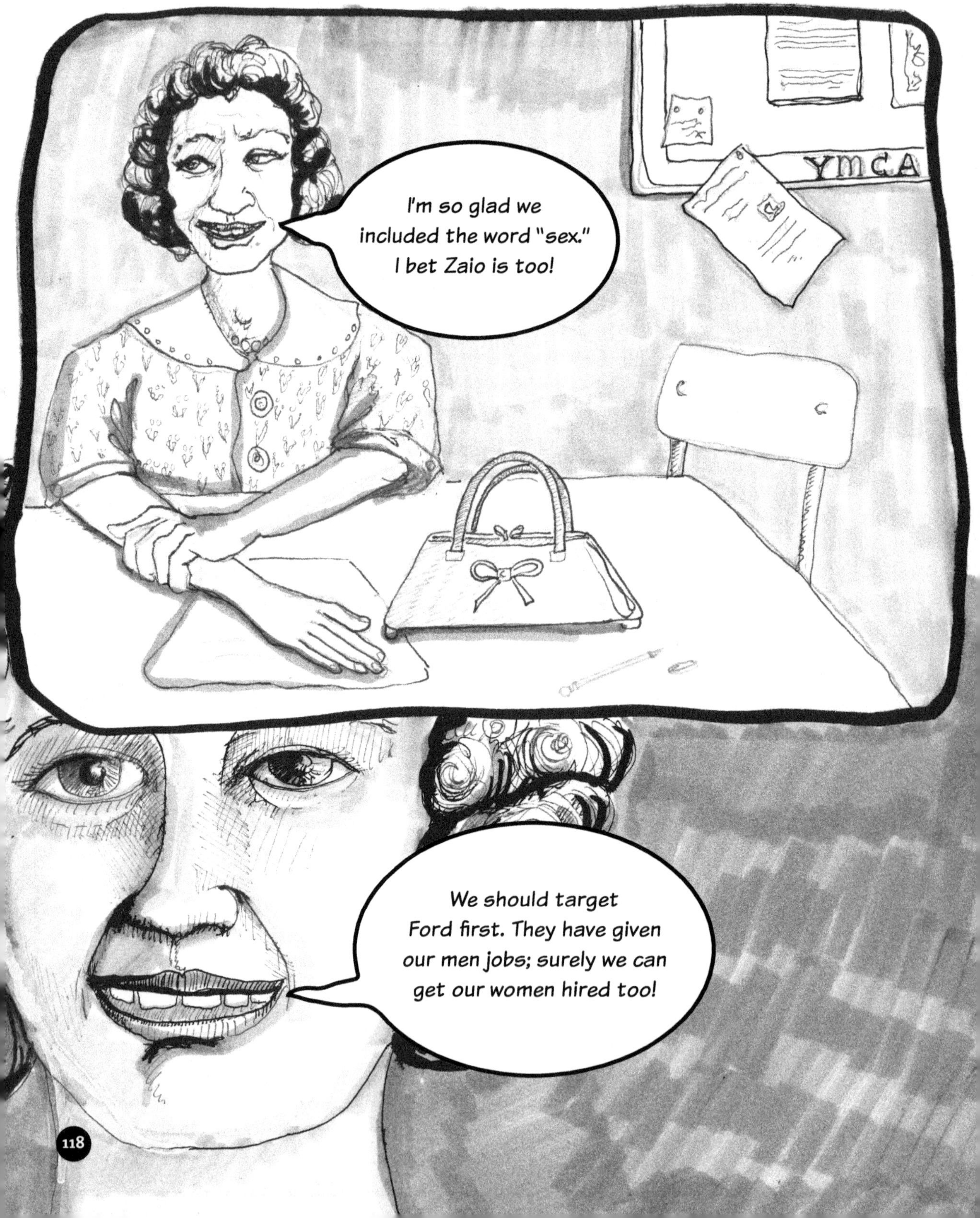
YMCA
I'm so glad we included the word "sex." I bet Zaio is too!
We should target Ford first. They have given our men jobs; surely we can get our women hired too!

On May 29, 1942, members of the council, led by Zaio Woodford, a feminist, met with Harry Bennett, the head of Ford's service department. After the 1937 Battle of the Overpass, many deemed him and his men to be pernicious.

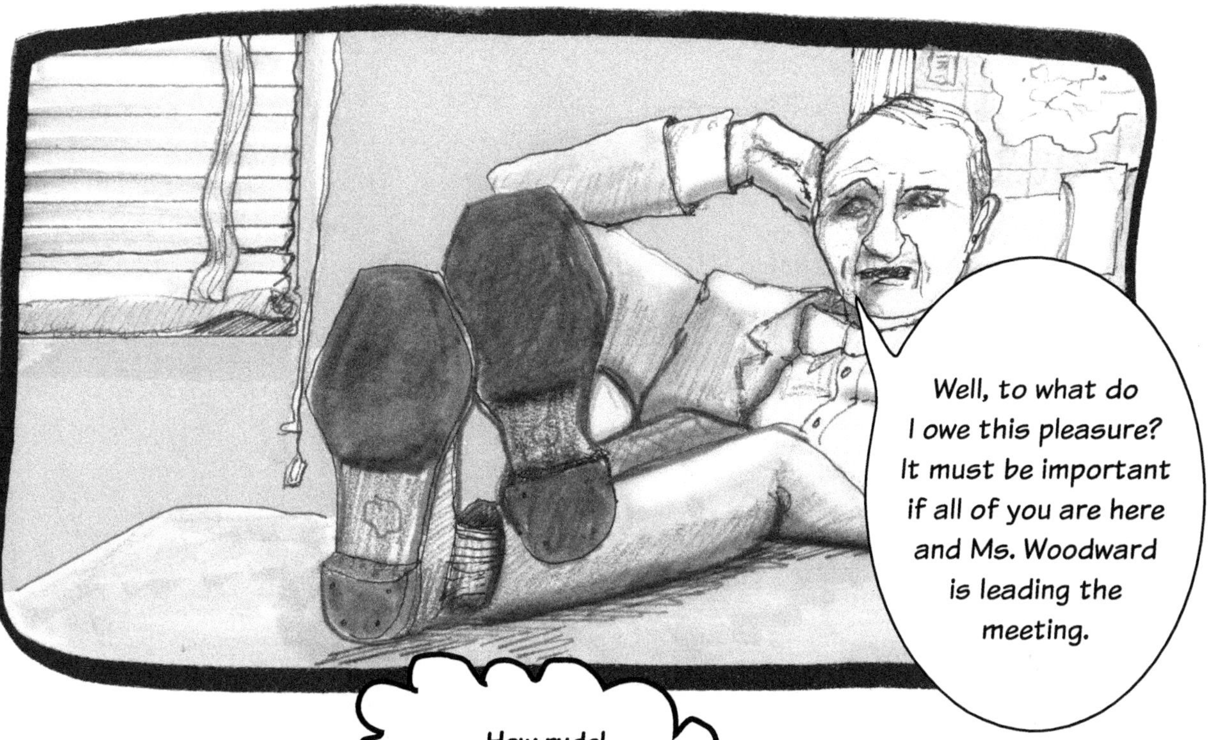
Well, to what do I owe this pleasure? It must be important if all of you are here and Ms. Woodward is leading the meeting.

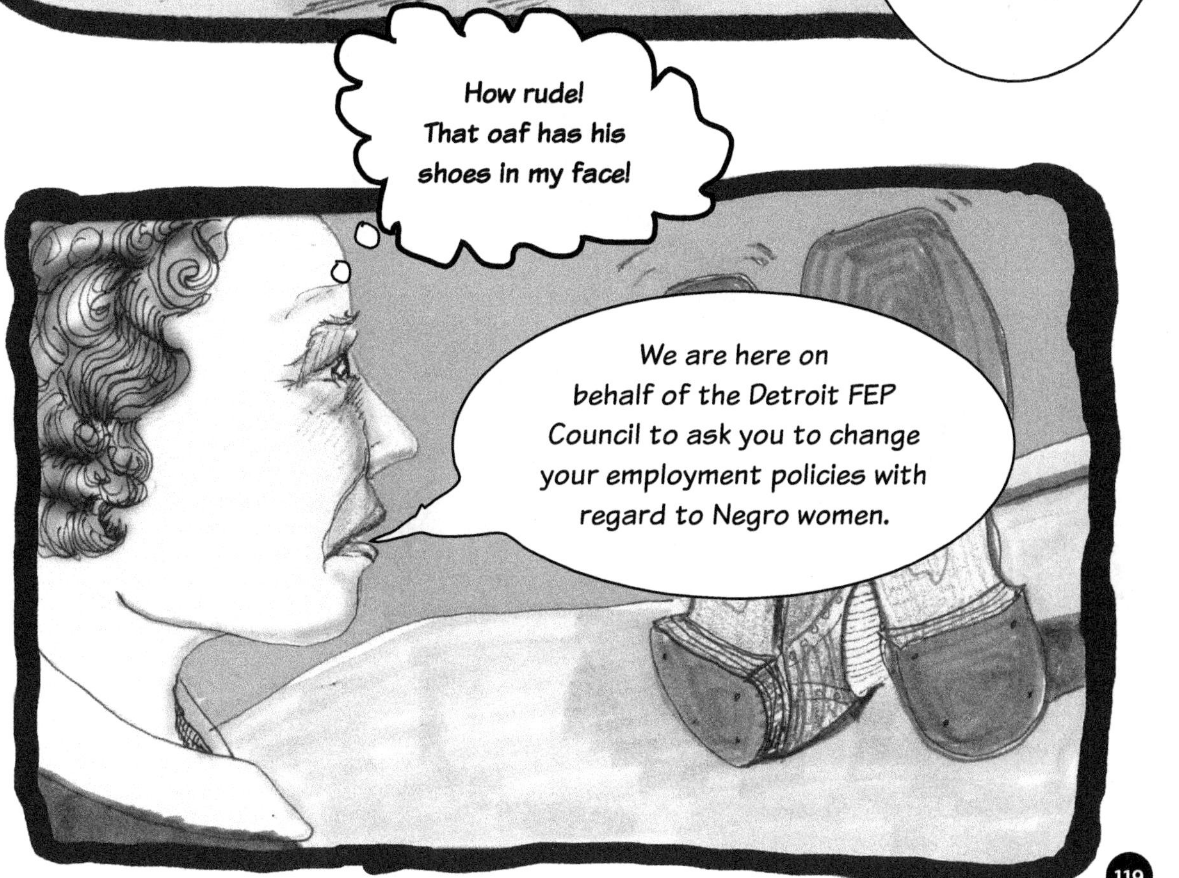
How rude! That oaf has his shoes in my face!
We are here on behalf of the Detroit FEP Council to ask you to change your employment policies with regard to Negro women.

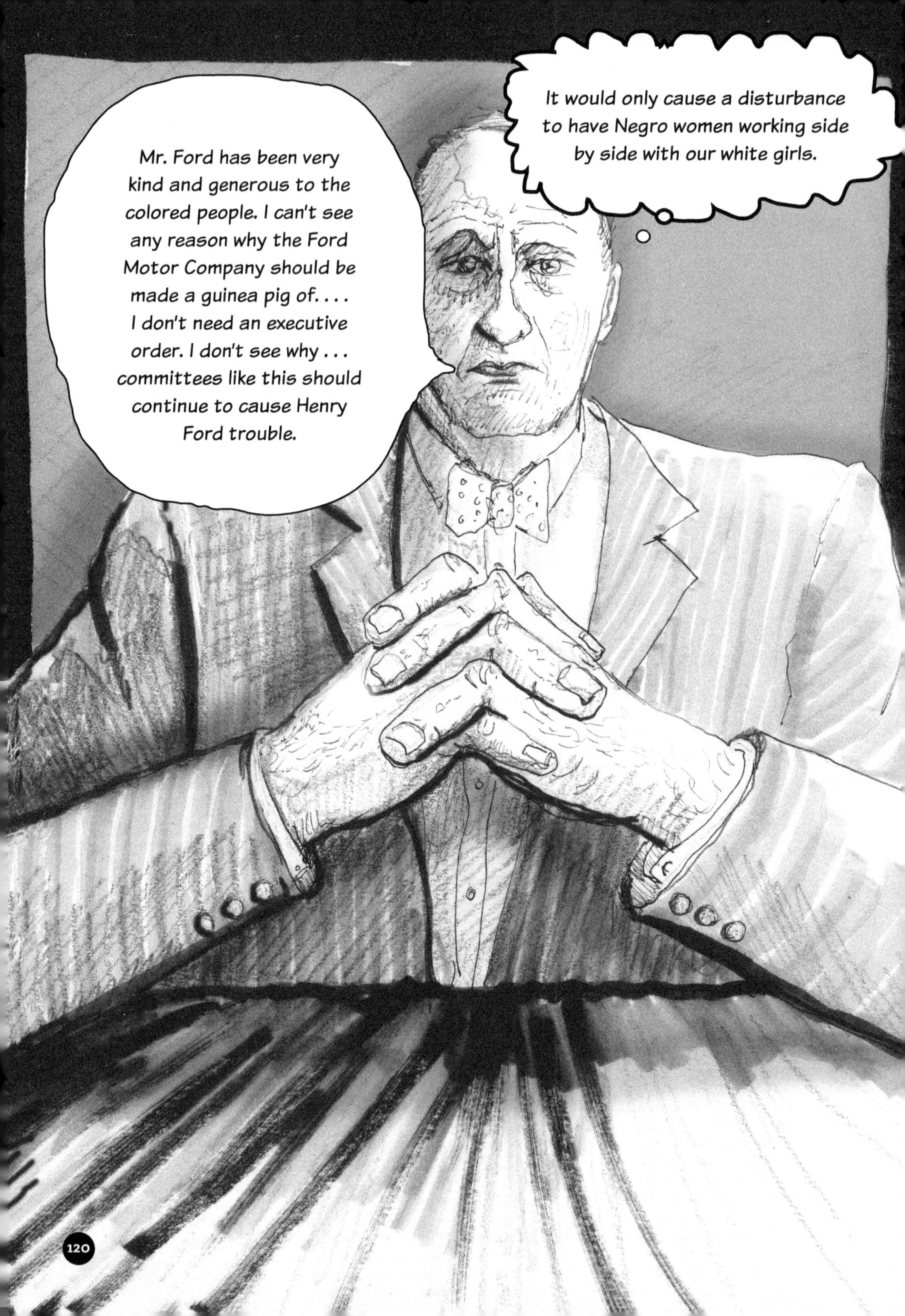
Mr. Ford has been very kind and generous to the colored people. I can't see any reason why the Ford Motor Company should be made a guinea pig of. . . . I don't need an executive order. I don't see why . . . committees like this should continue to cause Henry Ford trouble.
It would only cause a disturbance to have Negro women working side by side with our white girls.

After the meeting with Bennett, the council felt demoralized.

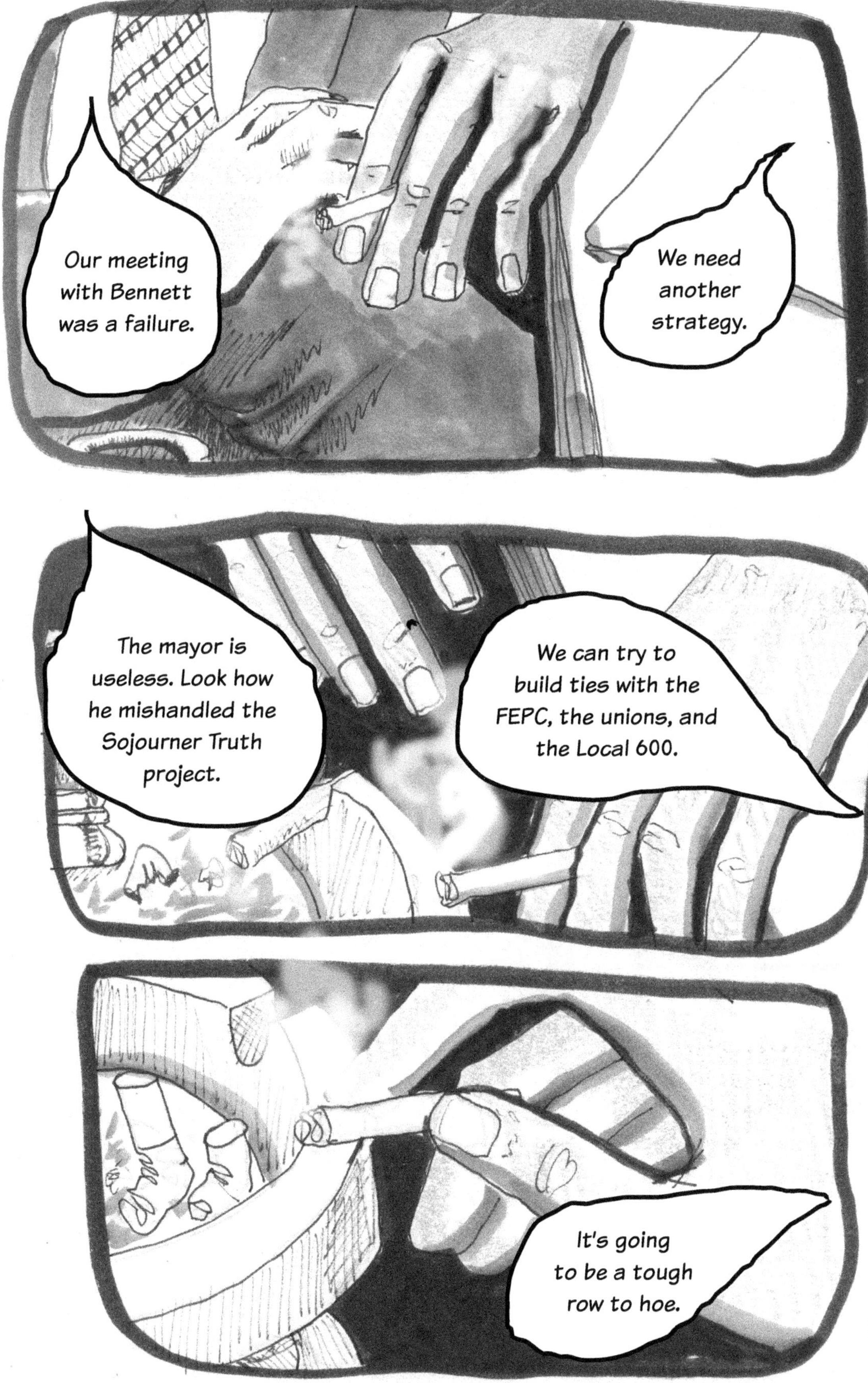
Our meeting with Bennett was a failure.
We need another strategy.
The mayor is useless. Look how he mishandled the Sojourner Truth project.
We can try to build ties with the FEPC, the unions, and the Local 600.
It's going to be a tough row to hoe.

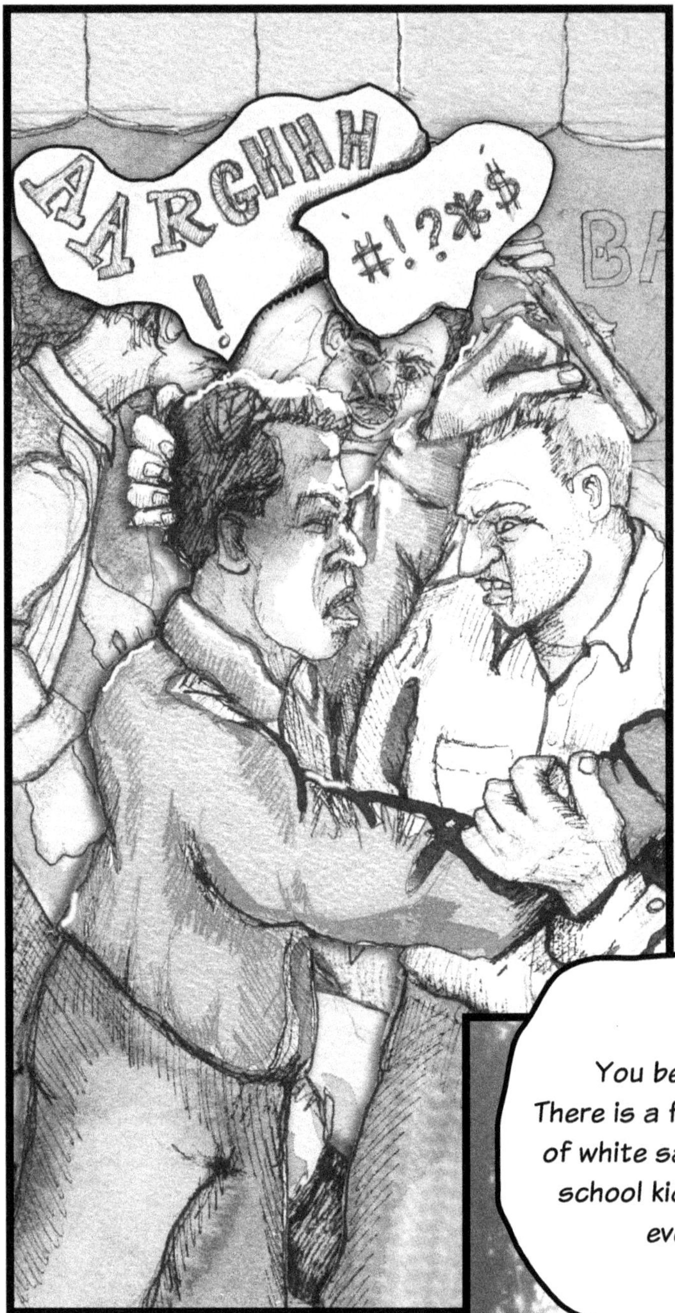
AARGHHH !
#!?*$

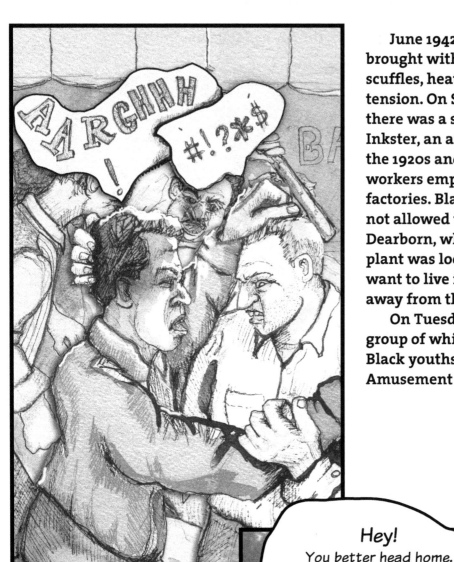

June 1942 in Detroit brought with it small street scuffles, heat, and growing tension. On Sunday, June 14, there was a street battle in Inkster, an area populated in the 1920s and 1930s by Black workers employed in Ford's factories. Black residents were not allowed to live in nearby Dearborn, where the Rouge plant was located, and did not want to live in Detroit, farther away from their work.

On Tuesday, June 16, a group of white soldiers chased Black youths from Eastwood Amusement Park.

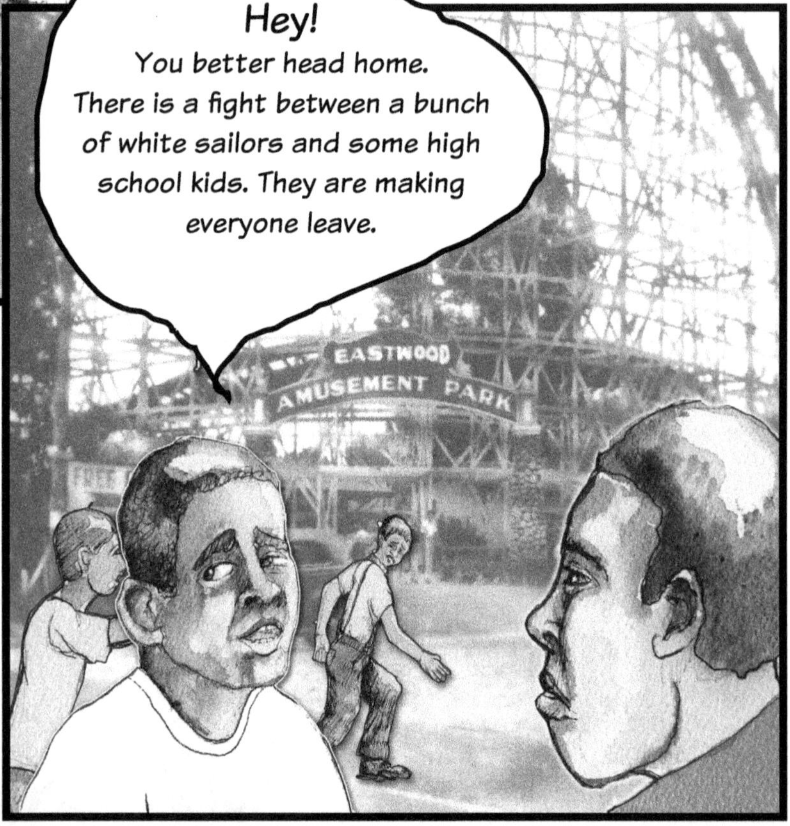
Hey!
You better head home. There is a fight between a bunch of white sailors and some high school kids. They are making everyone leave.
EASTWOOD AMUSEMENT PARK

Both of these incidents were harbingers of the violence that would erupt almost exactly one year later. Detroit was a tinderbox.

Even *Life* magazine wrote about the violence and volatility building between the Black and white populations in Detroit.

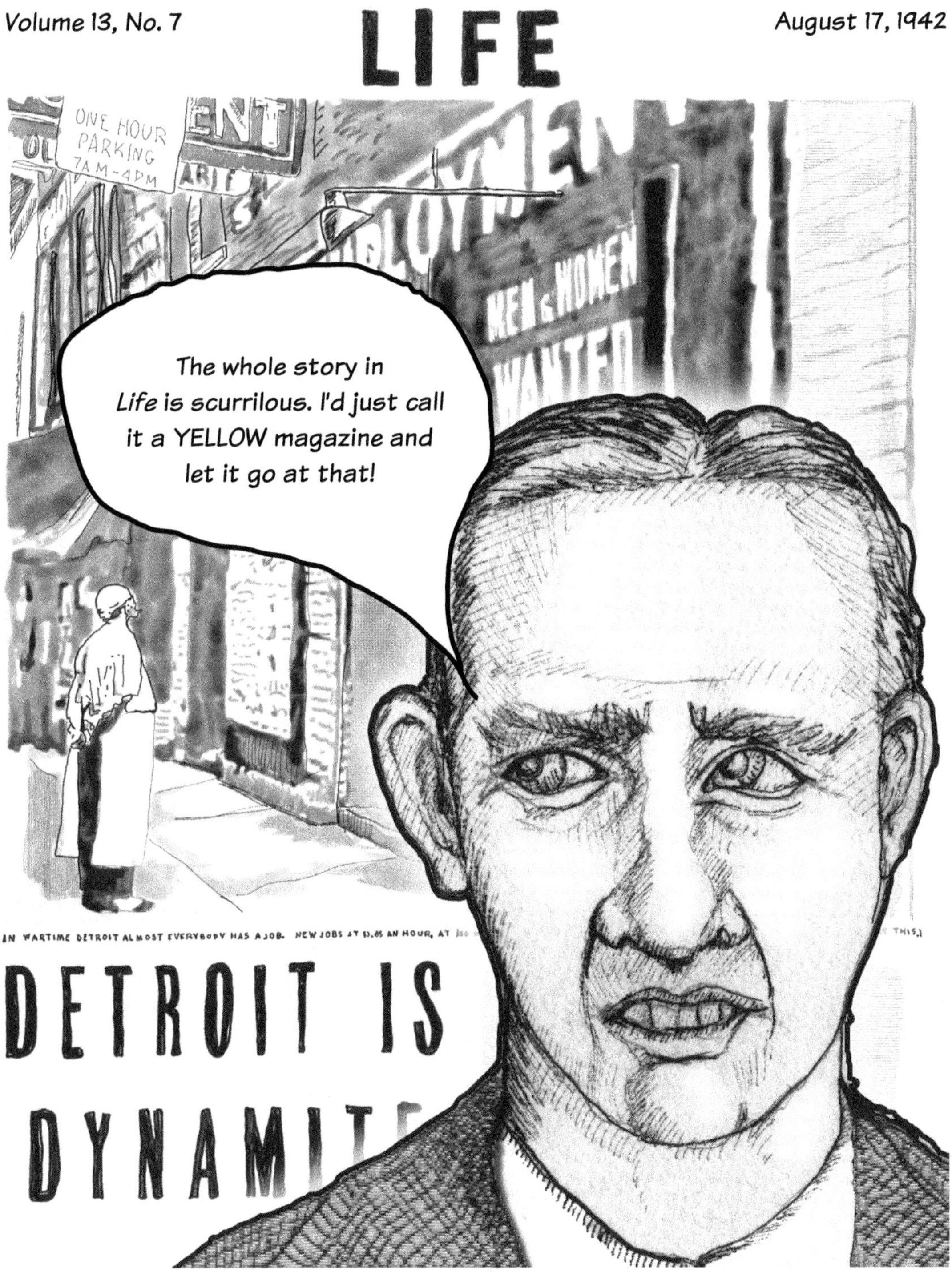

Volume 13, No. 7
LIFE
August 17, 1942
ONE HOUR PARKING 7AM-4PM
MEN & WOMEN WANTED
The whole story in *Life* is scurrilous. I'd just call it a YELLOW magazine and let it go at that!
IN WARTIME DETROIT ALMOST EVERYBODY HAS A JOB. NEW JOBS AT $1.05 AN HOUR, AT
DETROIT IS
DYNAMIT

Mayor Edward Jeffries kept his head buried in the sand and failed to acknowledge the real possibility of a large-scale clash between white and Black residents, between those who were prospering and those who were not.

Fair employment practices were a big issue. Ford, one of the largest employers in Detroit, had no intention of ending discriminatory hiring practices or hiring Black women.

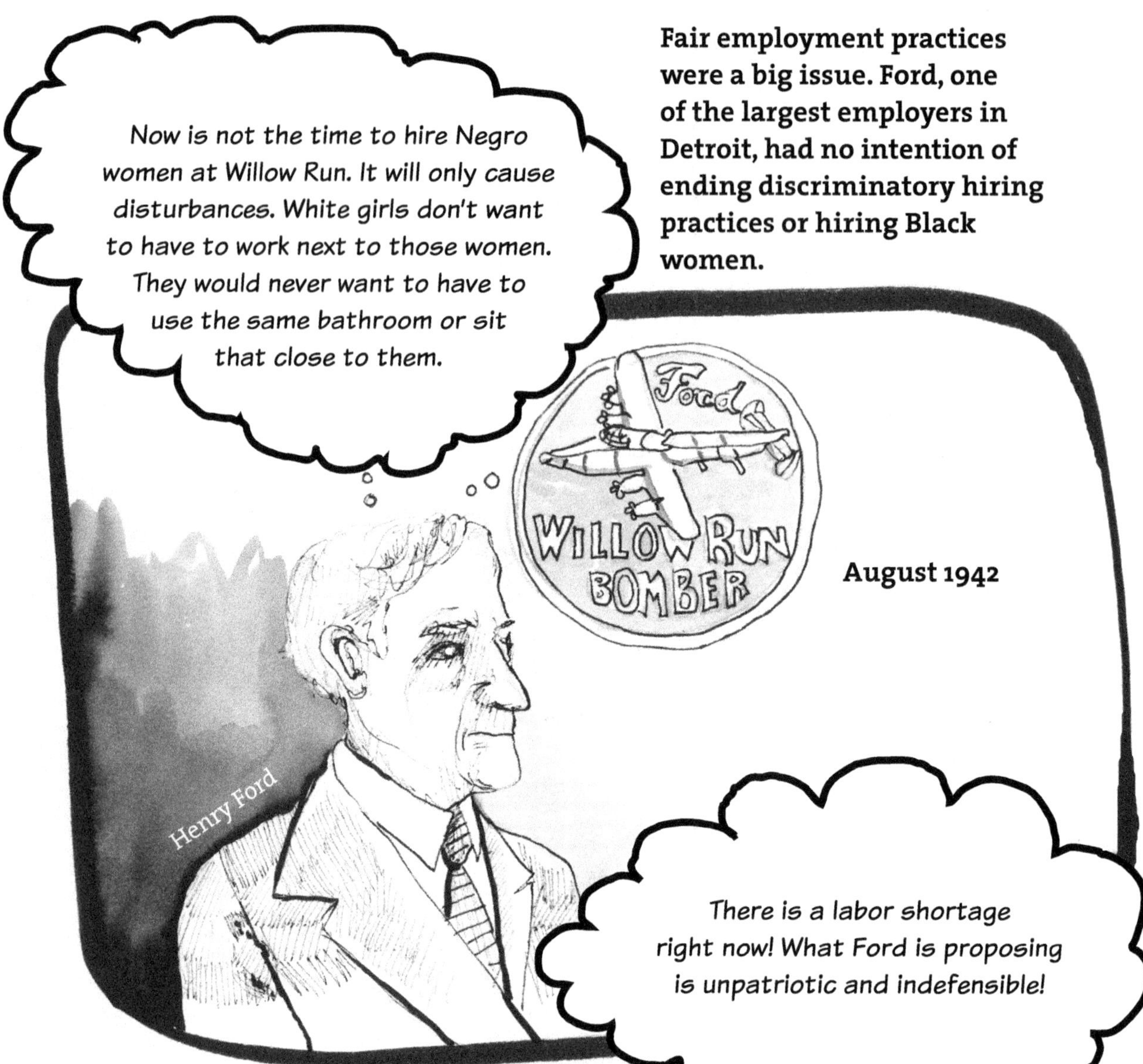
Now is not the time to hire Negro women at Willow Run. It will only cause disturbances. White girls don't want to have to work next to those women. They would never want to have to use the same bathroom or sit that close to them.
Ford
WILLOW RUN BOMBER
August 1942
Henry Ford

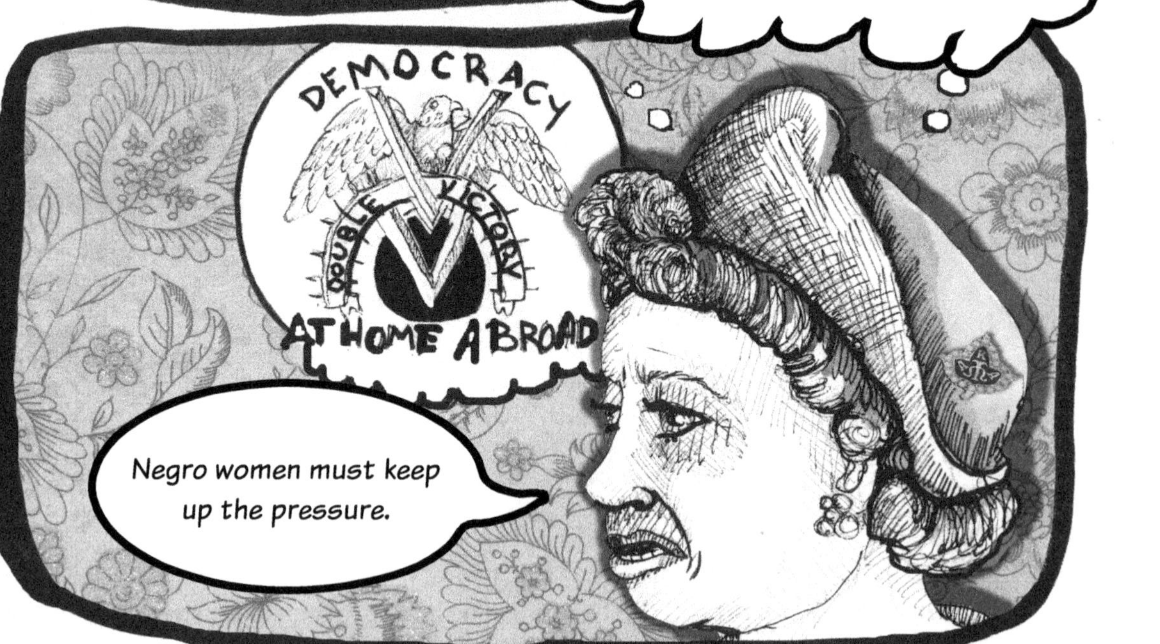
There is a labor shortage right now! What Ford is proposing is unpatriotic and indefensible!
DEMOCRACY
DOUBLE VICTORY
AT HOME ABROAD
Negro women must keep up the pressure.

Change was afoot.

On August 16, 1942, in a small kitchen in Paradise Valley, two women wash dishes after Sunday dinner.

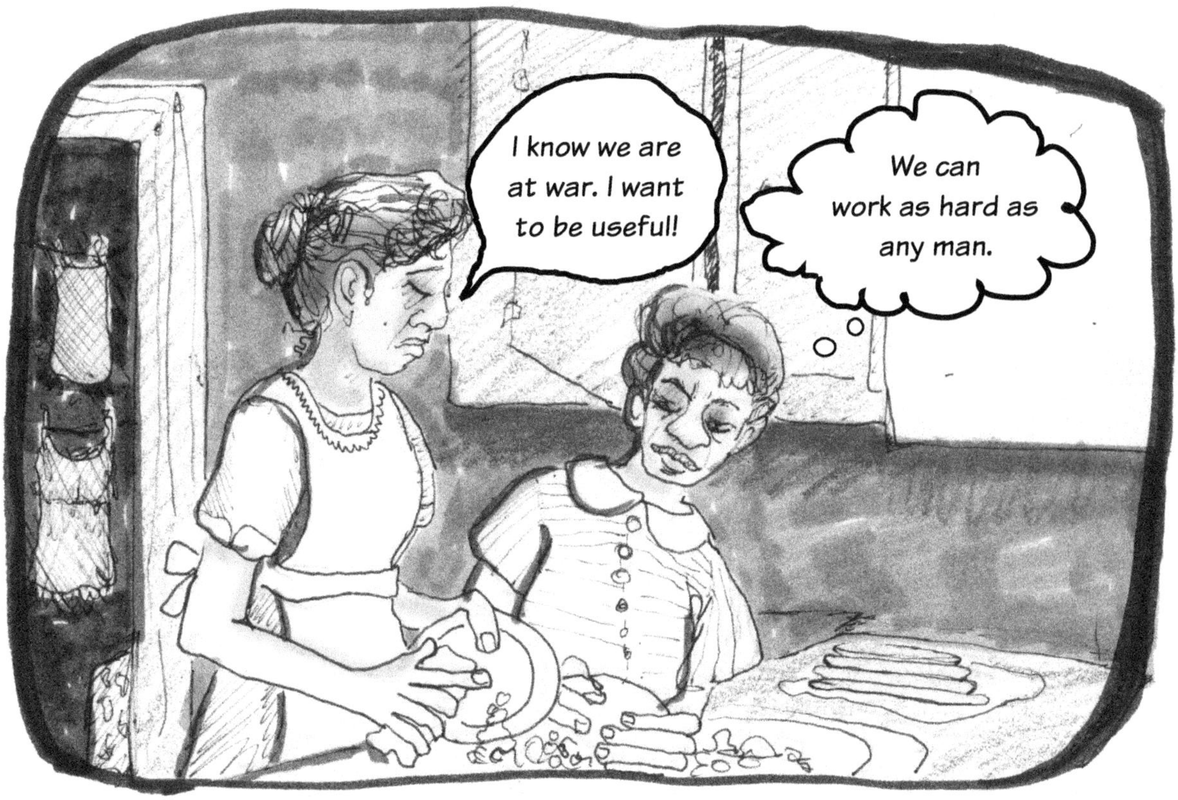
I know we are at war. I want to be useful!
We can work as hard as any man.

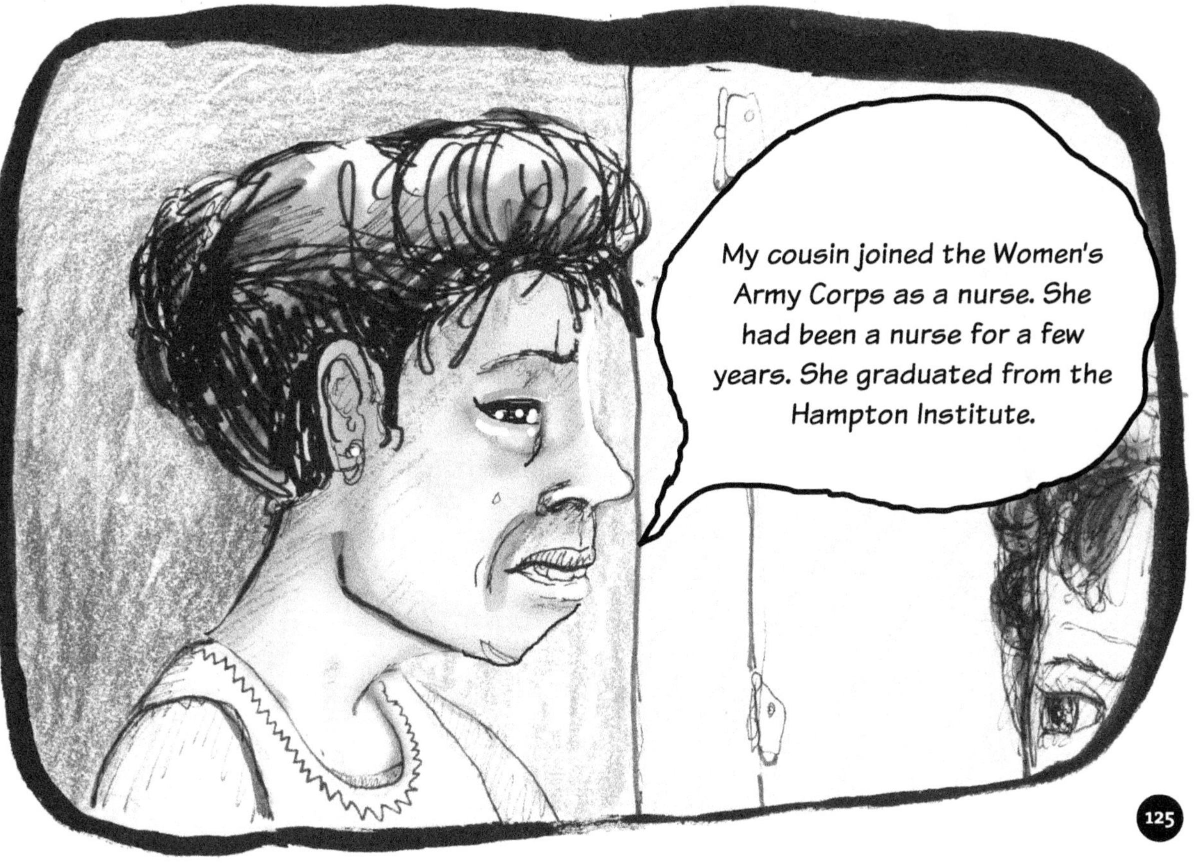
My cousin joined the Women's Army Corps as a nurse. She had been a nurse for a few years. She graduated from the Hampton Institute.

She said there were just a few folks like us. Less than fifty. She wrote to me when she was sent to Australia.

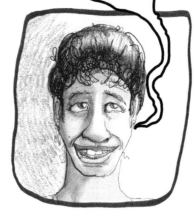

One of the soldiers there had heard we had tails. Can you believe that? Idiots . . .

Honestly, I am no nurse. I can't serve in the military. Heck, when John joined they put him to work as a stevadore. He just got upgraded to do construction in the Pacific.

The work is miserable, the barracks are segregated. He is still treated like a second-class citizen.

Sounds like Detroit . . .

MASS DEMONSTRATION AT FORD EMPLOYMENT OFFICE

Thursday, August 20, 1942 — 1 P. M. to 5 P. M.

GATE No. 2 — MILLER ROAD

Why? Because we want to share fully in the Defense Program, to do our part to win the war. We can no longer tolerate the Ford Motor Company's policy of discrimination against the Negro women. We resent Harry Bennett's assertion that the Ford Motor Company is the only company giving the Negro a chance. Studebaker Co., Murray Corp., Buick and Allen Industries, all have hired Negro women in the past and still are hiring them.

Willis Ward, "the Yes and No Man" of the Ford Motor Company relative to the Negro question, is a traitor to the cause of Better Labor and Race relations among the Ford Workers. The segregated employment office set-up (all Negroes channeled through Ward's office and all white workers sent elsewhere) is a great demoralizing factor. This demonstration is an irresistible, spontaneous mass movement on the part of all Ford workers and many civic organizations who desire full participation of _All The People_ in carrying out the war against Hitler. _We want the whole world to know that the Ford Motor Company is flagrantly violating the executive order of President Roosevelt, No. 8802, which declares that "there shall be no discrimination against Race, Creed, or Color in hiring in Defense Industries."_ We feel that this is every man's war regardless of race. We are fighting for Democracy abroad. We want Democracy at home as well. _Mr. Ford, Negro women and men will and must play their rightful part in helping win this war._

We Meet at the Employment Office Gate No. 2, Thursday, Aug. 20 — 1:00 P. M.

Upwards of 3,000 new women hired at the Bomber Plant — Not one Negro woman

THIS IS NOT A STRIKE

74

Mass demonstrations were staged in order to

In September 1942, in the Westside neighborhood, a woman greets her partner at the end of a long day.

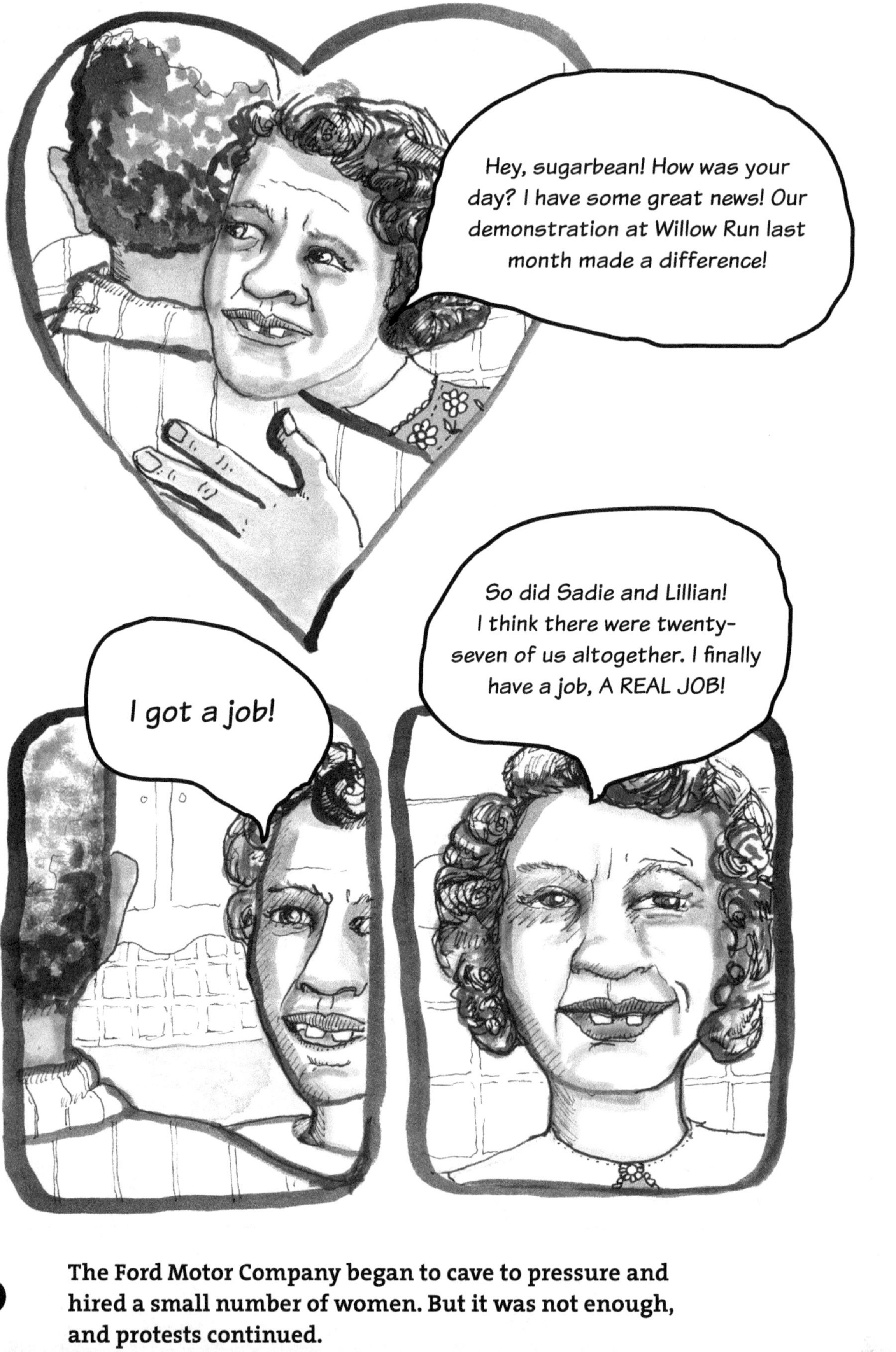
Hey, sugarbean! How was your day? I have some great news! Our demonstration at Willow Run last month made a difference!
I got a job!
So did Sadie and Lillian! I think there were twenty-seven of us altogether. I finally have a job, A REAL JOB!

The Ford Motor Company began to cave to pressure and hired a small number of women. But it was not enough, and protests continued.

Jim Crow must go in War Industries

MASS MEETING ★
OF CITIZENS COMMITTEE

||||

HEAR:

Earl B. Dickerson,
Member F. E. P. C.,
Chicago Alderman

CITIZENS—

Join in Mass Demonstration
for Jobs . . .

• AT FORD HIGHLAND PARK
PLANT, 4:00 to 6:00 P. M.

Sunday,
NOV. 15TH

1 9 4 2

|||

At 3:30 P. M.

°At Shiloh Baptist Church

BENTON STREET, NEAR ST. ANTOINE

★ ★ ★

Sponsored by: Citizens Committee for Jobs
In War Industry
446 E. Warren Ave., N.A.A.C.P. Office, TEmple 1-3609

1942

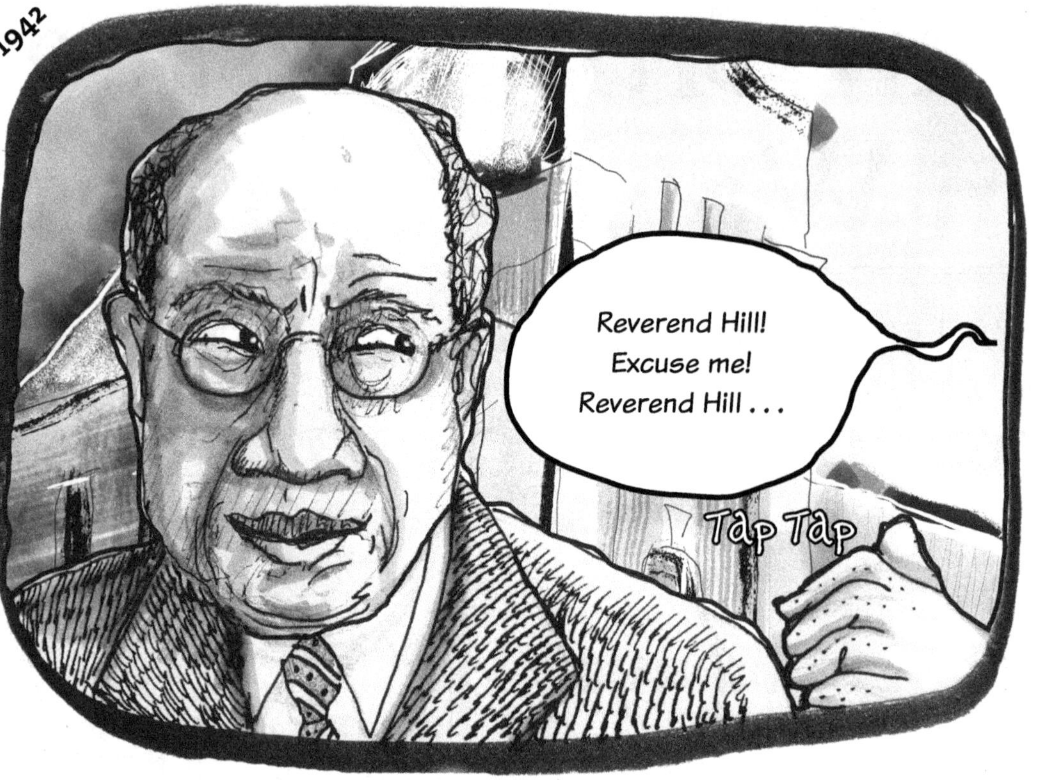
Reverend Hill! Excuse me! Reverend Hill . . .
Tap Tap

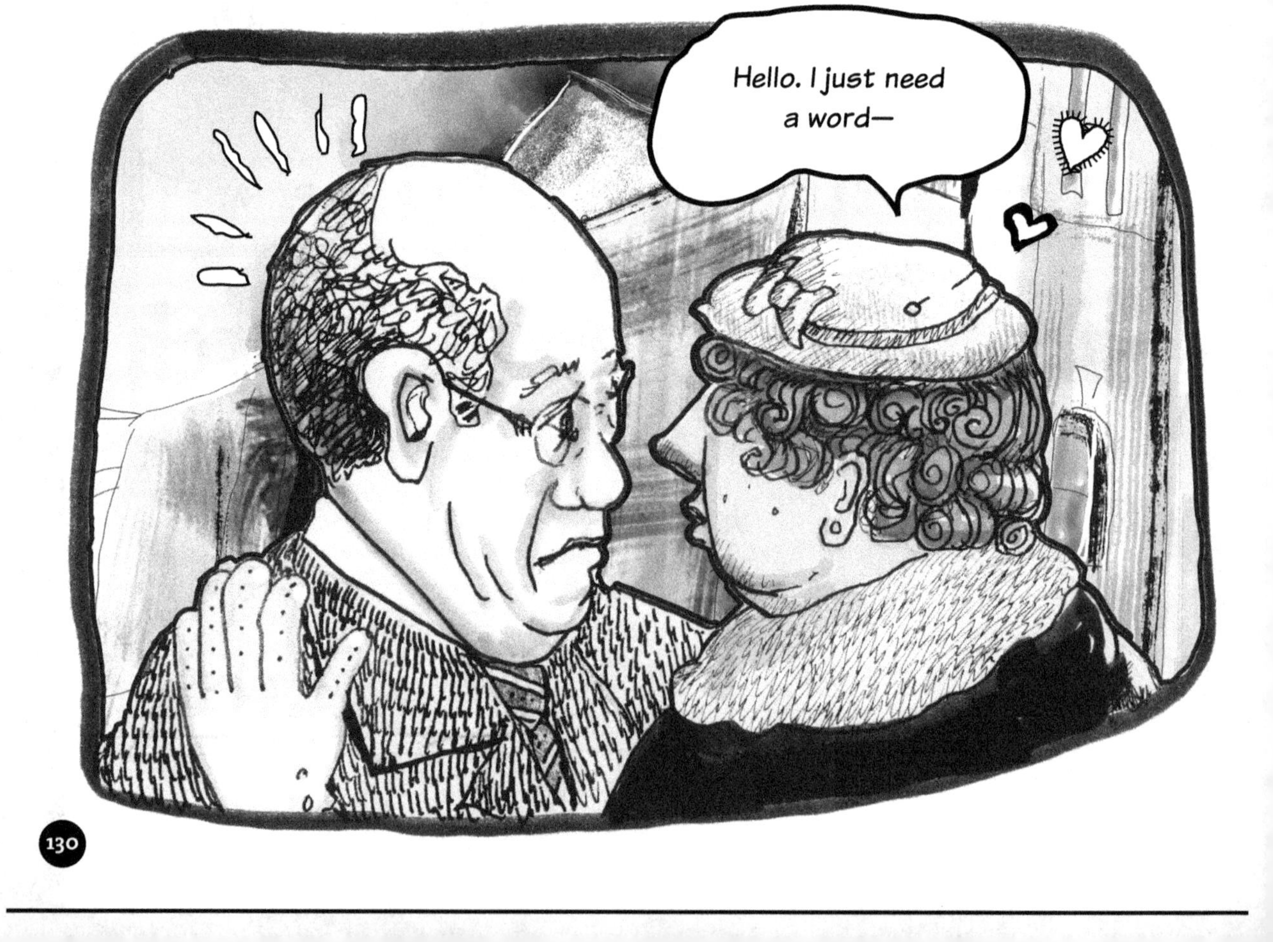
Hello. I just need a word—

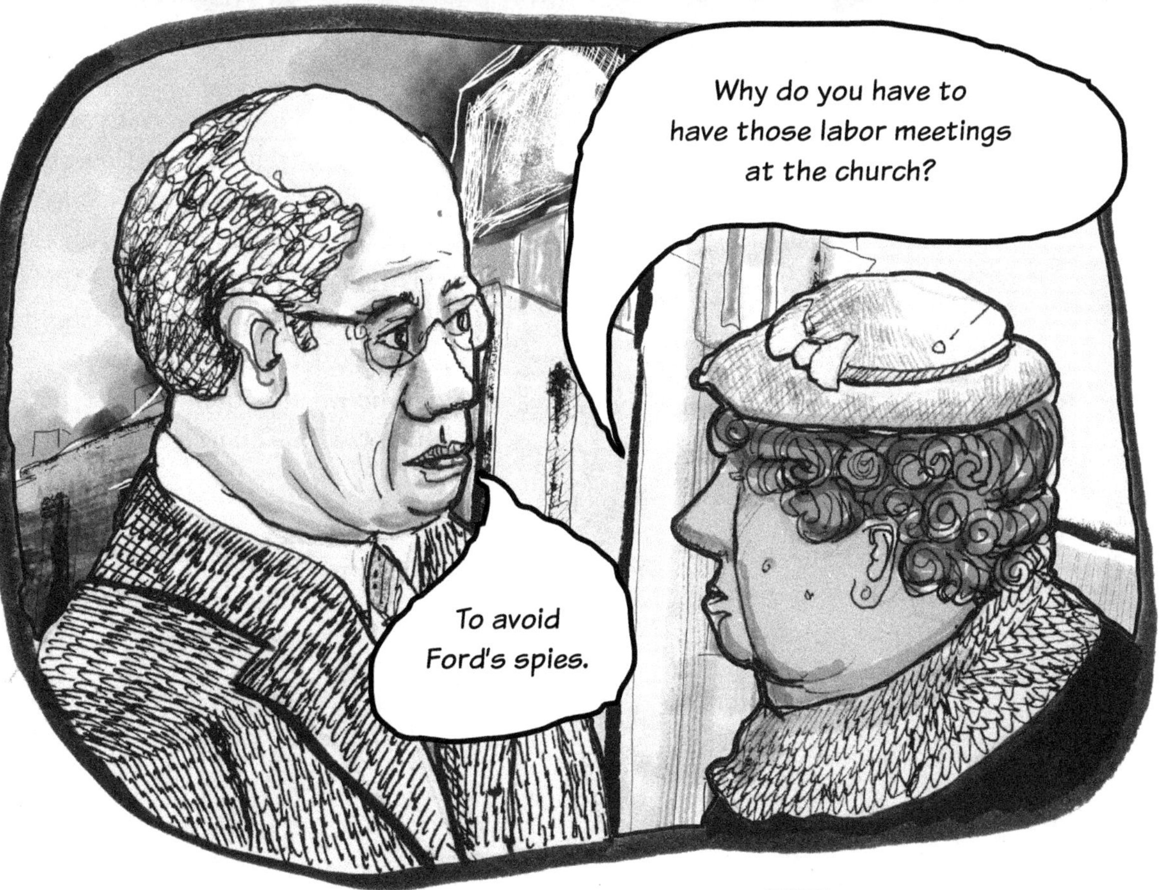
Why do you have to have those labor meetings at the church?
To avoid Ford's spies.

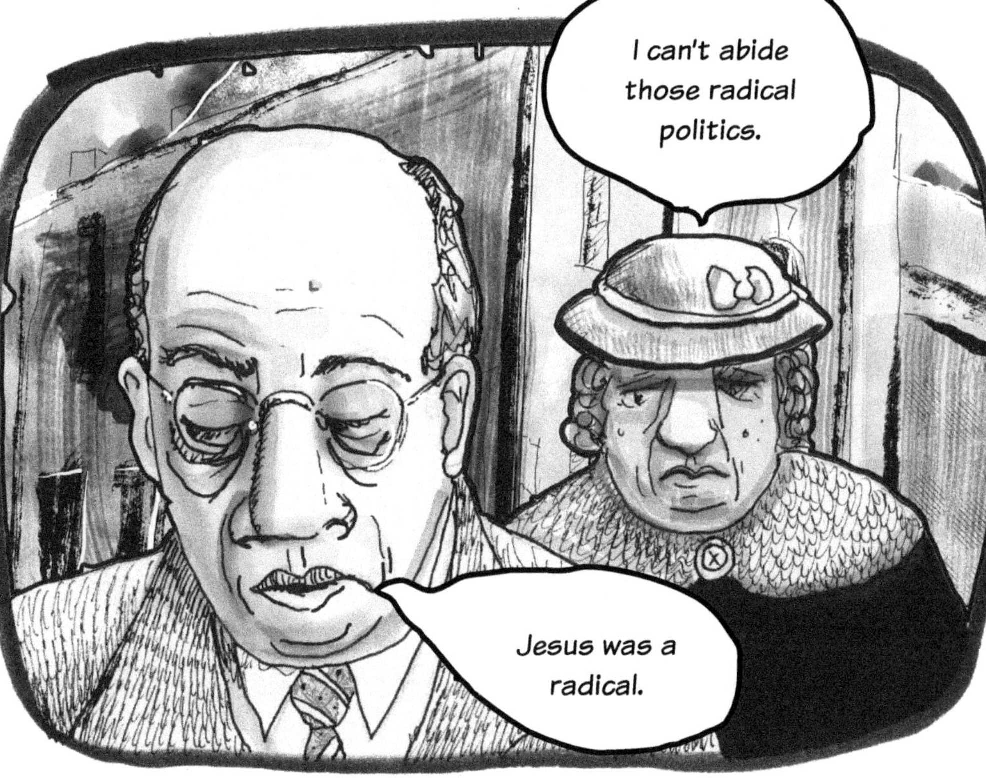
I can't abide those radical politics.
Jesus was a radical.

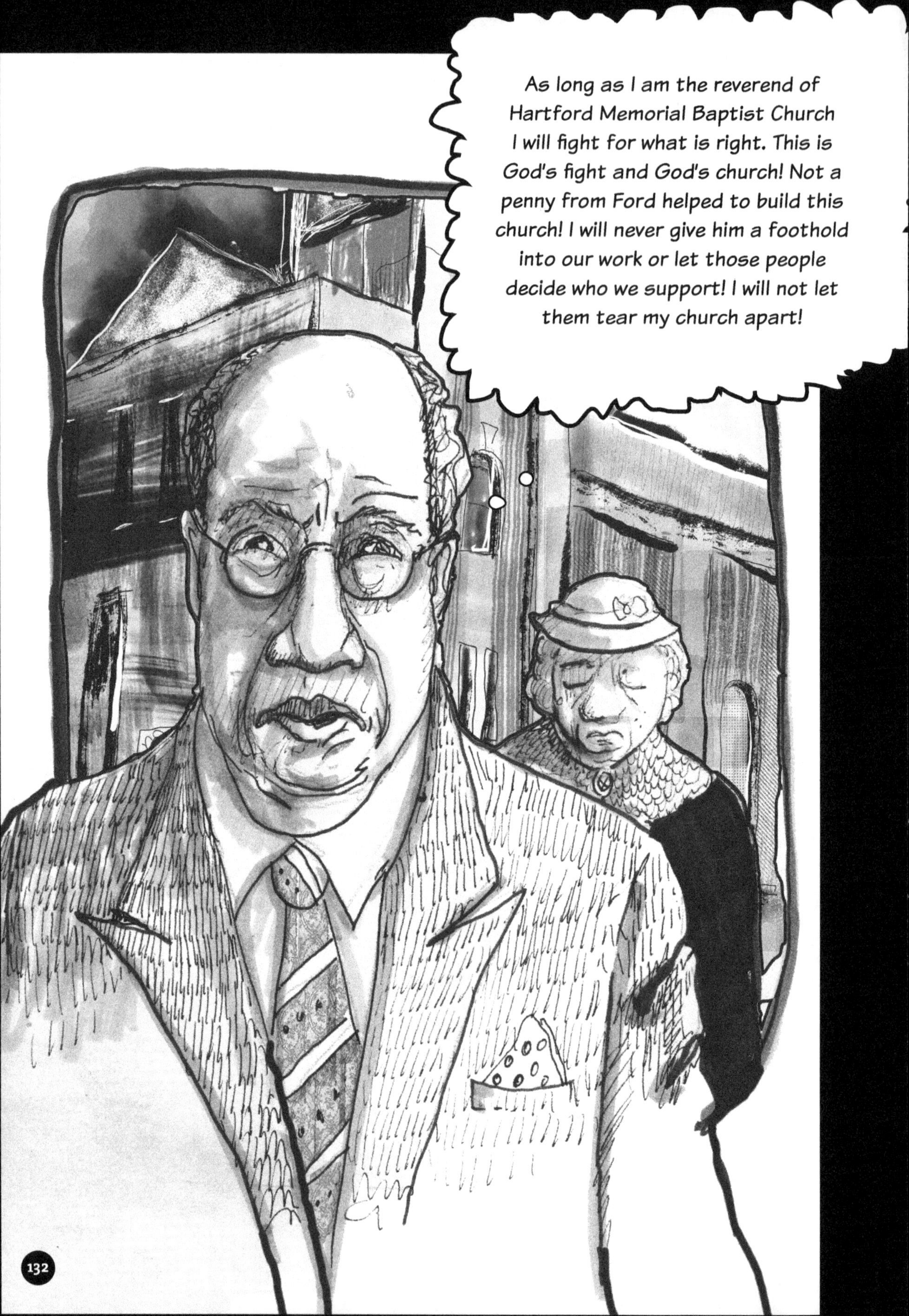
As long as I am the reverend of Hartford Memorial Baptist Church I will fight for what is right. This is God's fight and God's church! Not a penny from Ford helped to build this church! I will never give him a foothold into our work or let those people decide who we support! I will not let them tear my church apart!

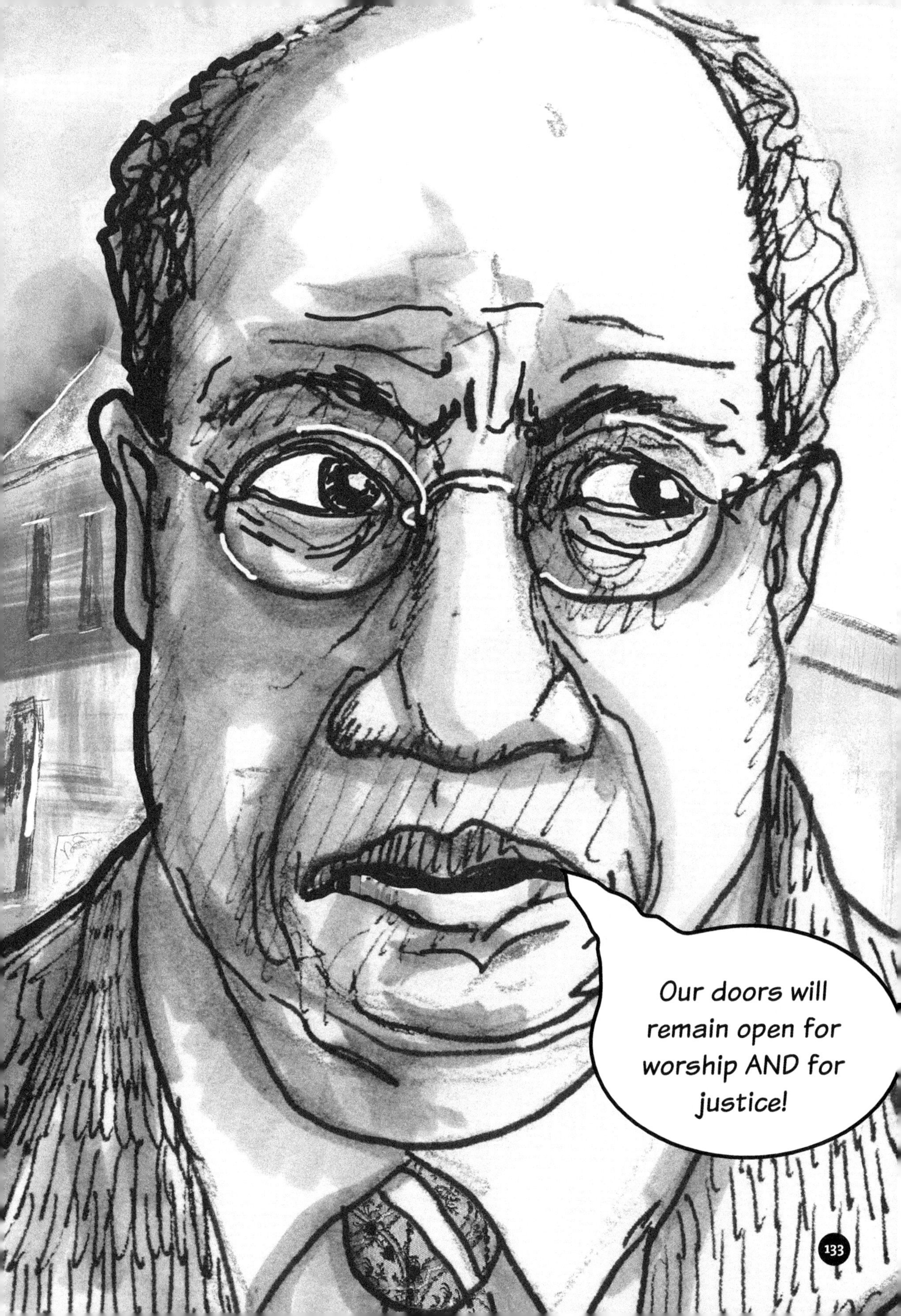
Our doors will remain open for worship AND for justice!

In November 1942 four Black women were hired for production line work at the River Rouge plant. This created a great deal of tension within the plant.

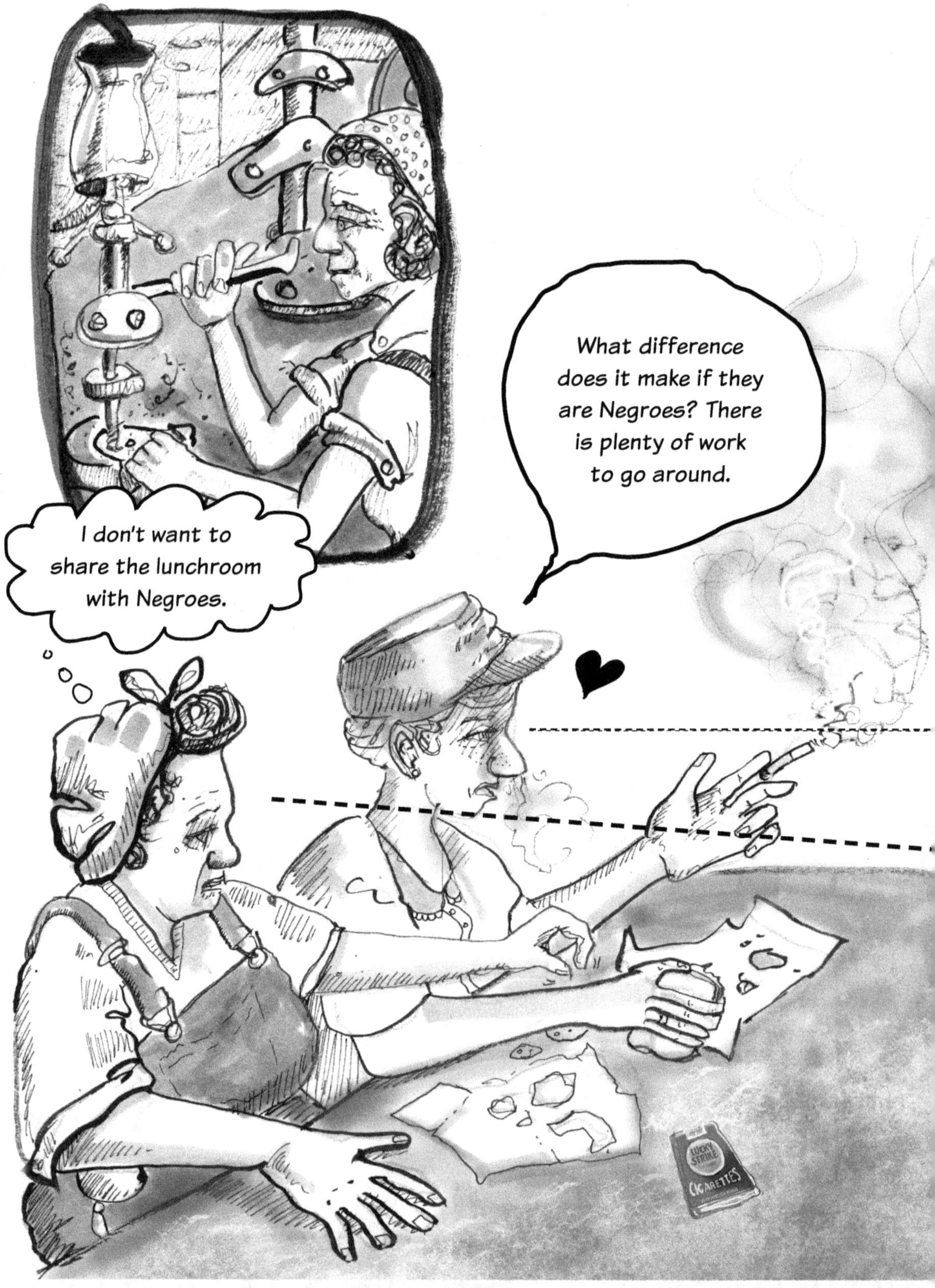
What difference does it make if they are Negroes? There is plenty of work to go around.
I don't want to share the lunchroom with Negroes.
LUCKY STRIKE
CIGARETTES

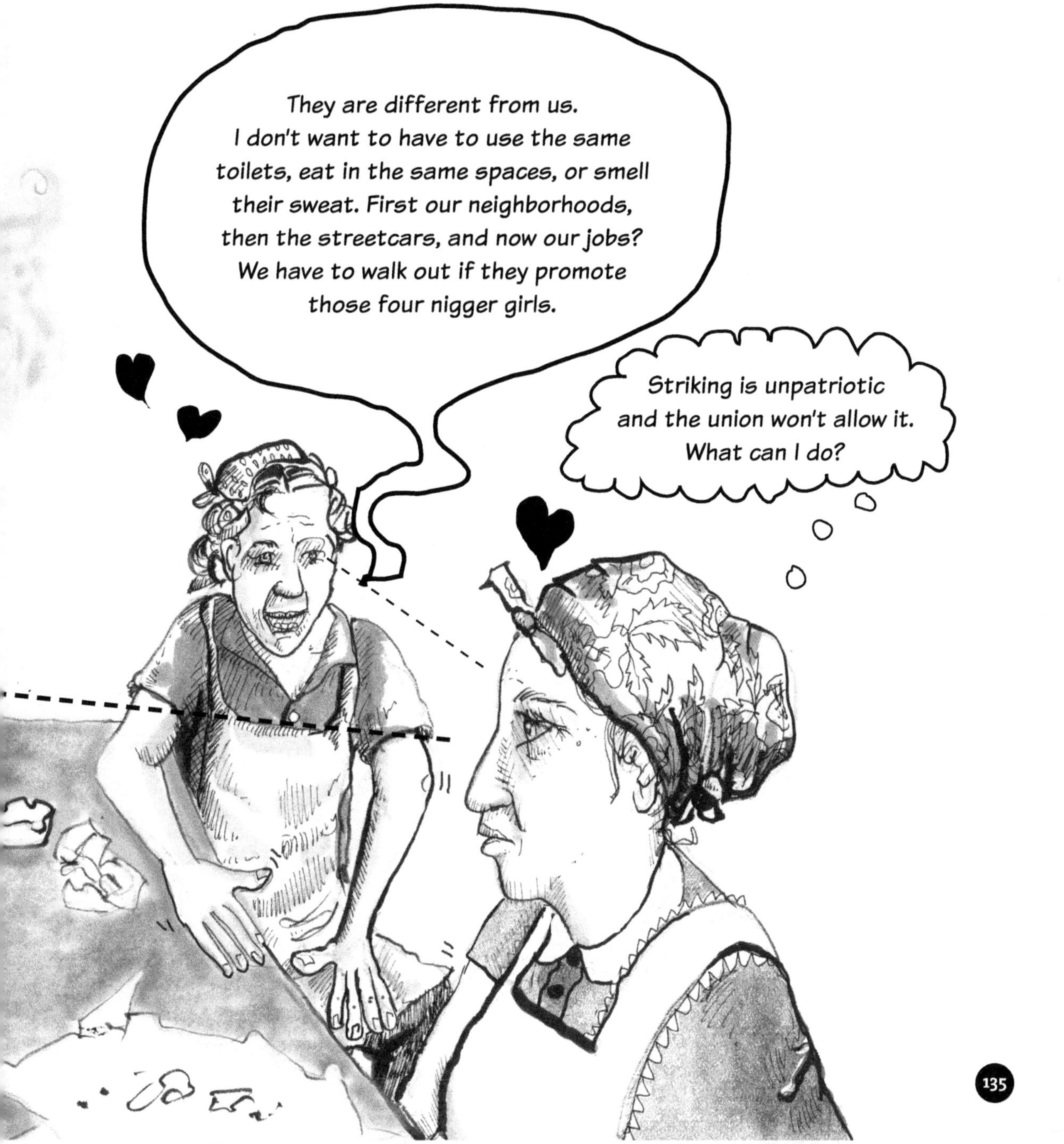
They are different from us. I don't want to have to use the same toilets, eat in the same spaces, or smell their sweat. First our neighborhoods, then the streetcars, and now our jobs? We have to walk out if they promote those four nigger girls.
Striking is unpatriotic and the union won't allow it. What can I do?

ALL OUT FOR....

Big Demonstration Against Discrimination

● APRIL 11th, 1943, at 2:30 P. M.

Starting from
Detroit Institute of Arts—Theodore at John R.

Marching—
THOUSANDS STRONG!! – Negro and White
TO CADILLAC SQUARE

WHY DEMONSTRATE?

Trained Negro women war workers are denied employment in most plants. In many where they are hired, they are relegated to jobs of an inferior status, or given work too difficult for men.

Negro men war workers are not being upgraded to more skilled jobs. Management practices discrimination by hiring in migrant workers for skilled jobs and refuse to upgrade trained, loyal Negro employees.

NEGROES SUPPORT THE WAR EFFORT!

Not only by working hard to produce the materiel of VICTORY, but by purchasing thousands of dollars worth of War Bonds and Stamps.

UNDEMOCRATIC WAR WORKERS ARE IGNORING THE NEGRO'S CONTRIBUTION TO THE WAR EFFORT BY HATE STRIKES.

Stirred on by the Klan and other subversive forces, workers at Vickers, Packard, U. S. Rubber, and many other plants have struck when Negroes were advanced to machines.

ALL OUT FOR THE DEMONSTRATION
SPONSORED BY THE
Labor Committee of the National Association for the Advancement of Colored People
WALTER HARDIN — PRINCE CLARK, Co-Chairmen
DR. JAMES McCLENDON, President, NAACP

For Information Call NAACP — 446 East Warren Avenue — TE. 1-3609

On April 11, 1943, approximately 10,000 protesters, Black and white, filled Cadillac Square to hear the Reverend Charles Hill; James McClendon, who was the president of the Detroit chapter of the NAACP; Walter Reuther, who would be elected president of the UAW in 1946; and U.S. Army colonel George Strong, who had been a key player in negotiations to end wildcat strikes. After the speeches, the crowd was presented with the Cadillac Charter, a document that stated that the war industry giants needed to fully observe Executive Order 8802 and end their ongoing practice of discrimination. This document was later sent to the president of the United States.

Despite the charter, tensions continued to build and workers continued to go on strike.

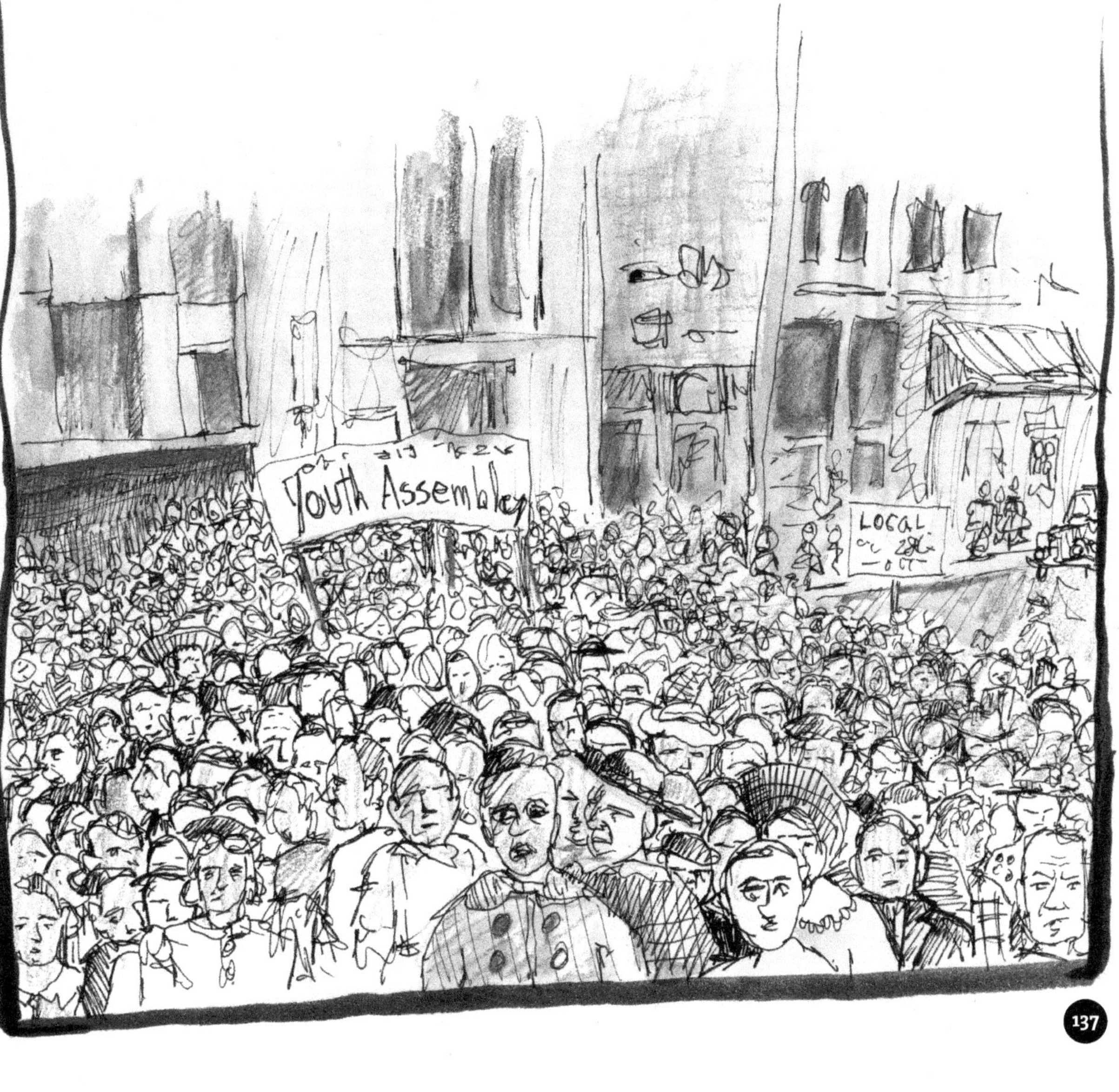
Youth Assembley
LOCAL

On May 24, 1943, at the Packard plant, two Klan members learn about the promotion of three Black men.

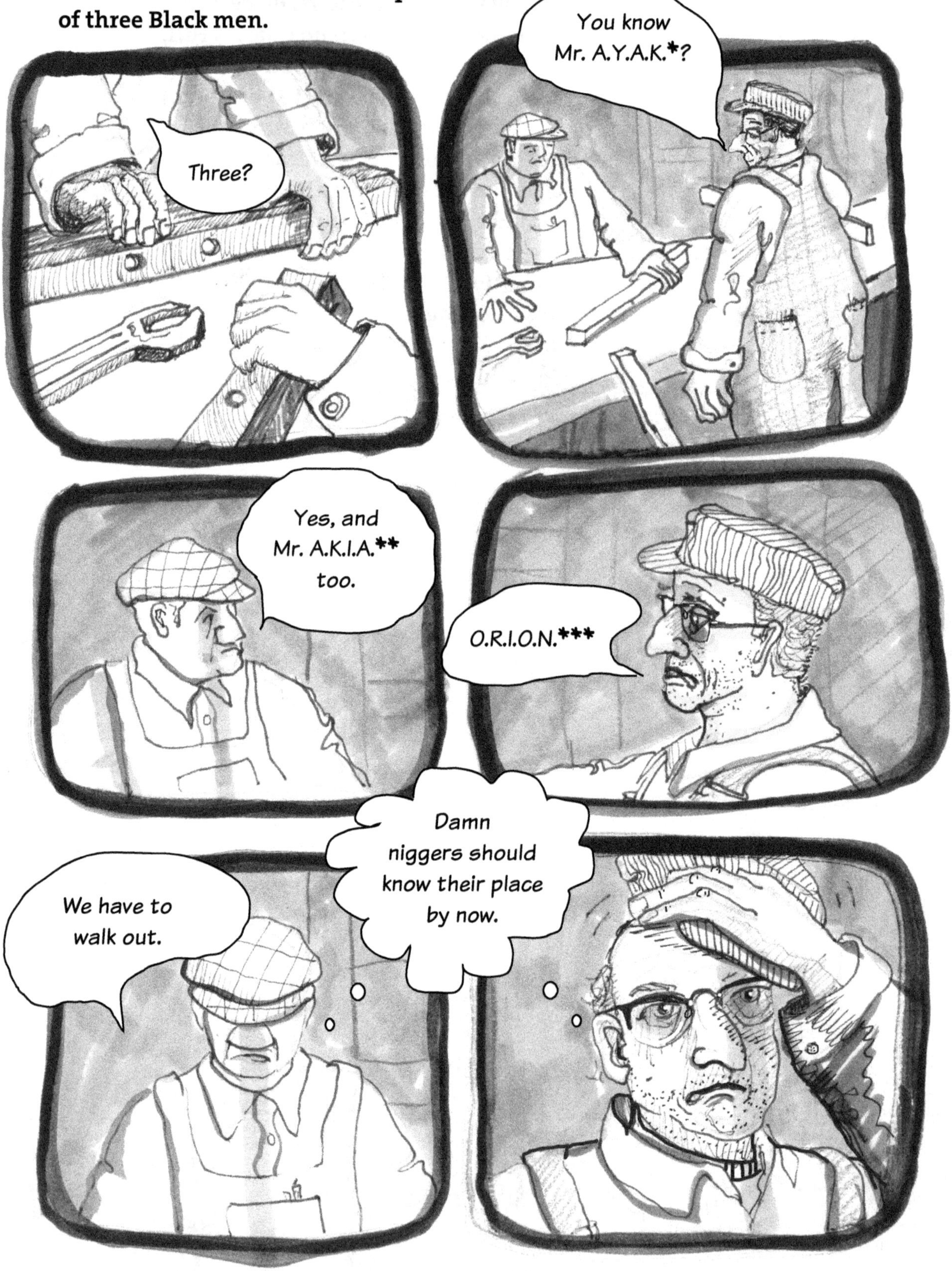
Three?
You know Mr. A.Y.A.K.*?
Yes, and Mr. A.K.I.A.** too.
O.R.I.O.N.***
We have to walk out.
Damn niggers should know their place by now.

Despite the executive order, racist white workers continued to strike when Black workers were hired or promoted.

*Are you a Klansman **A Klansman I am ***Our race is our nation

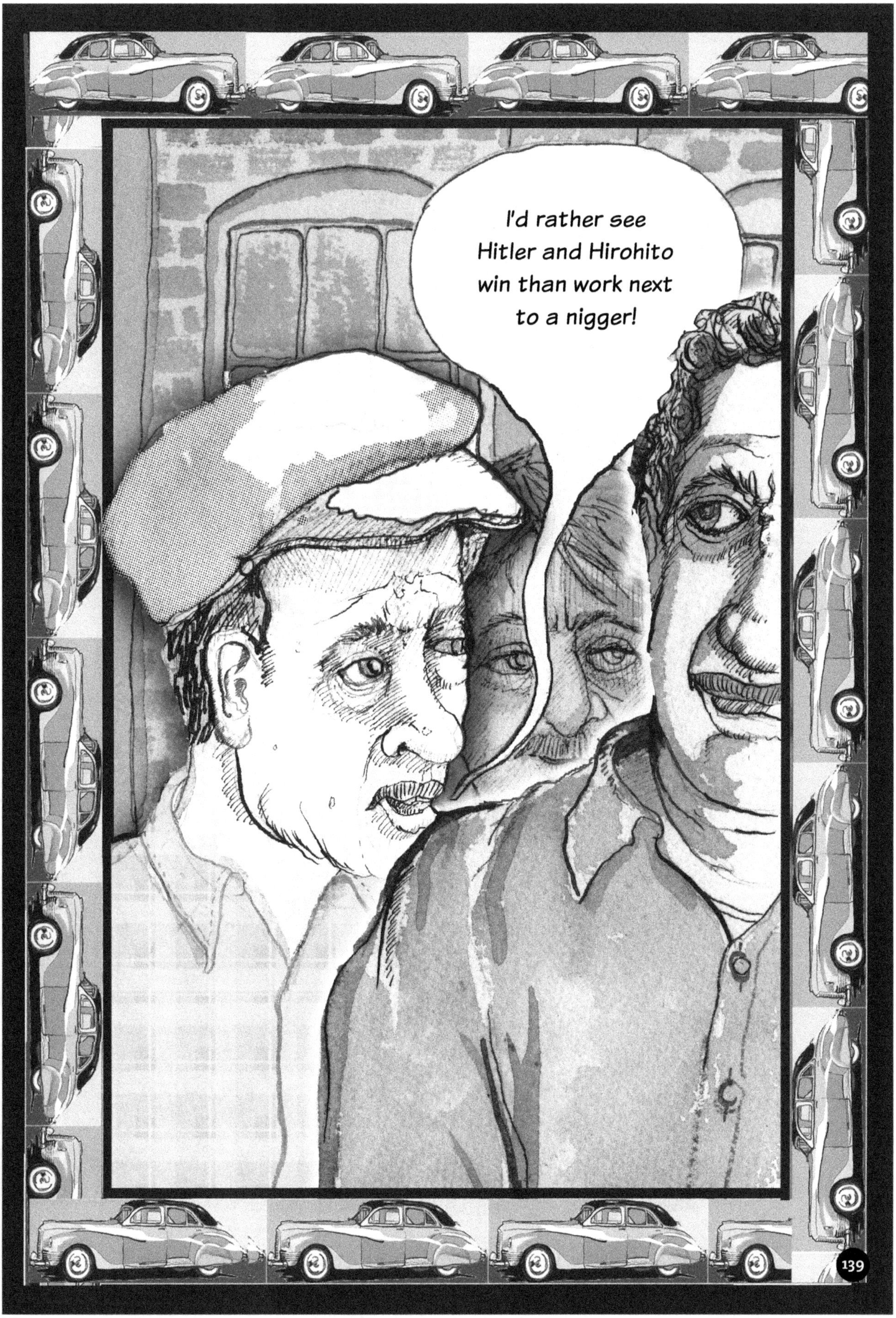
I'd rather see Hitler and Hirohito win than work next to a nigger!

Things were getting worse, not better.

During the Packard wildcat strike in June, 20,000 workers walked off the job because three African American men were promoted.

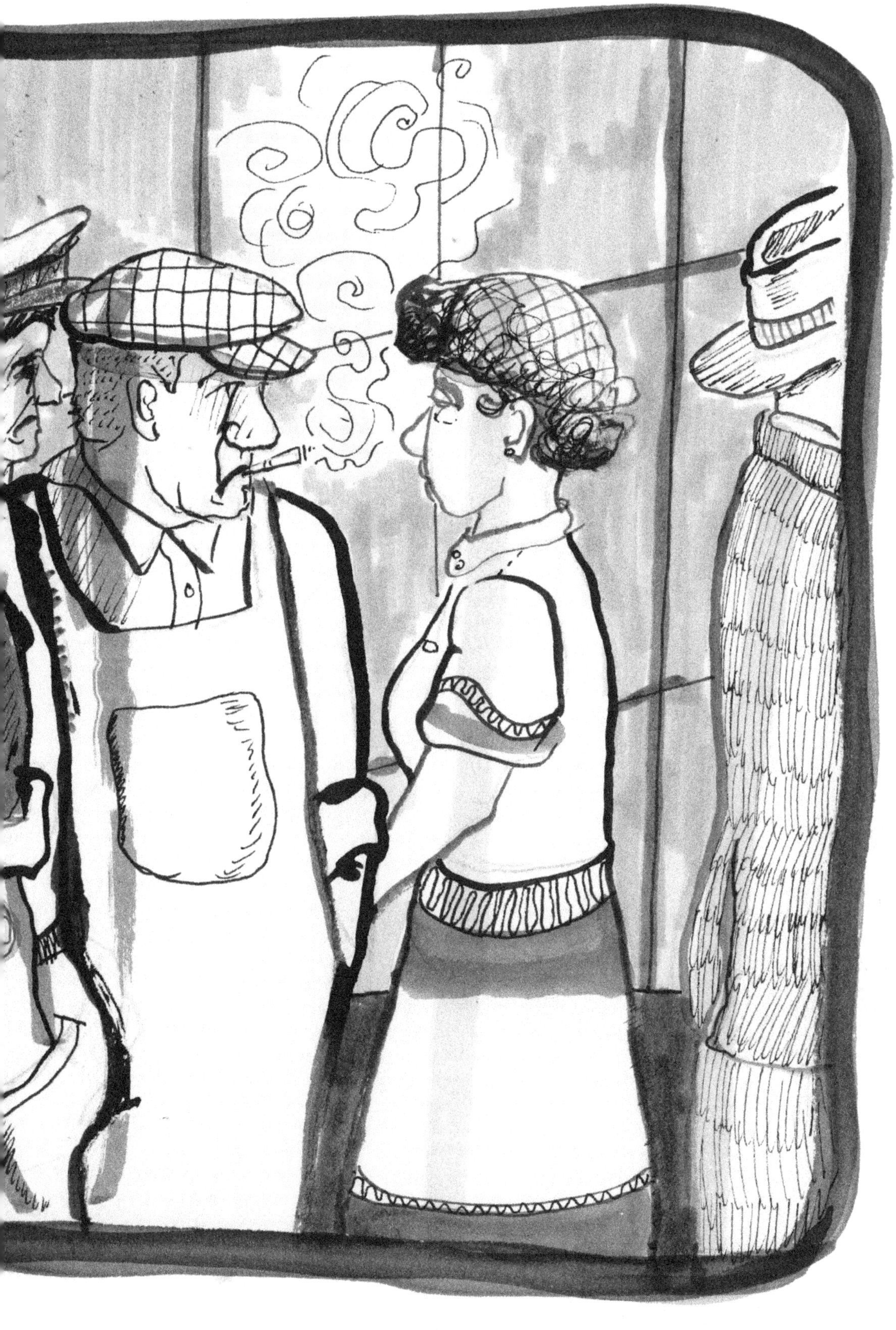

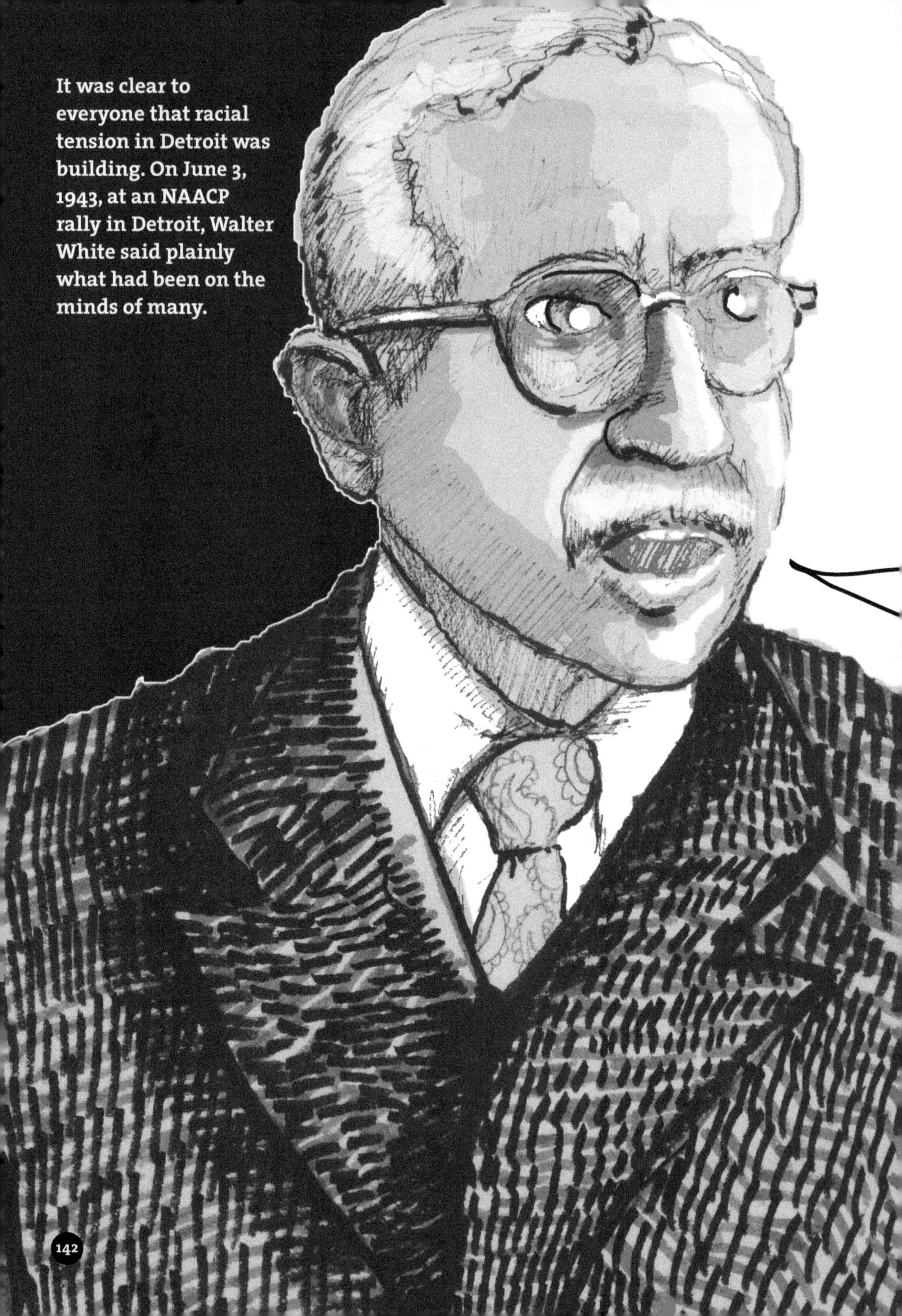
It was clear to everyone that racial tension in Detroit was building. On June 3, 1943, at an NAACP rally in Detroit, Walter White said plainly what had been on the minds of many.

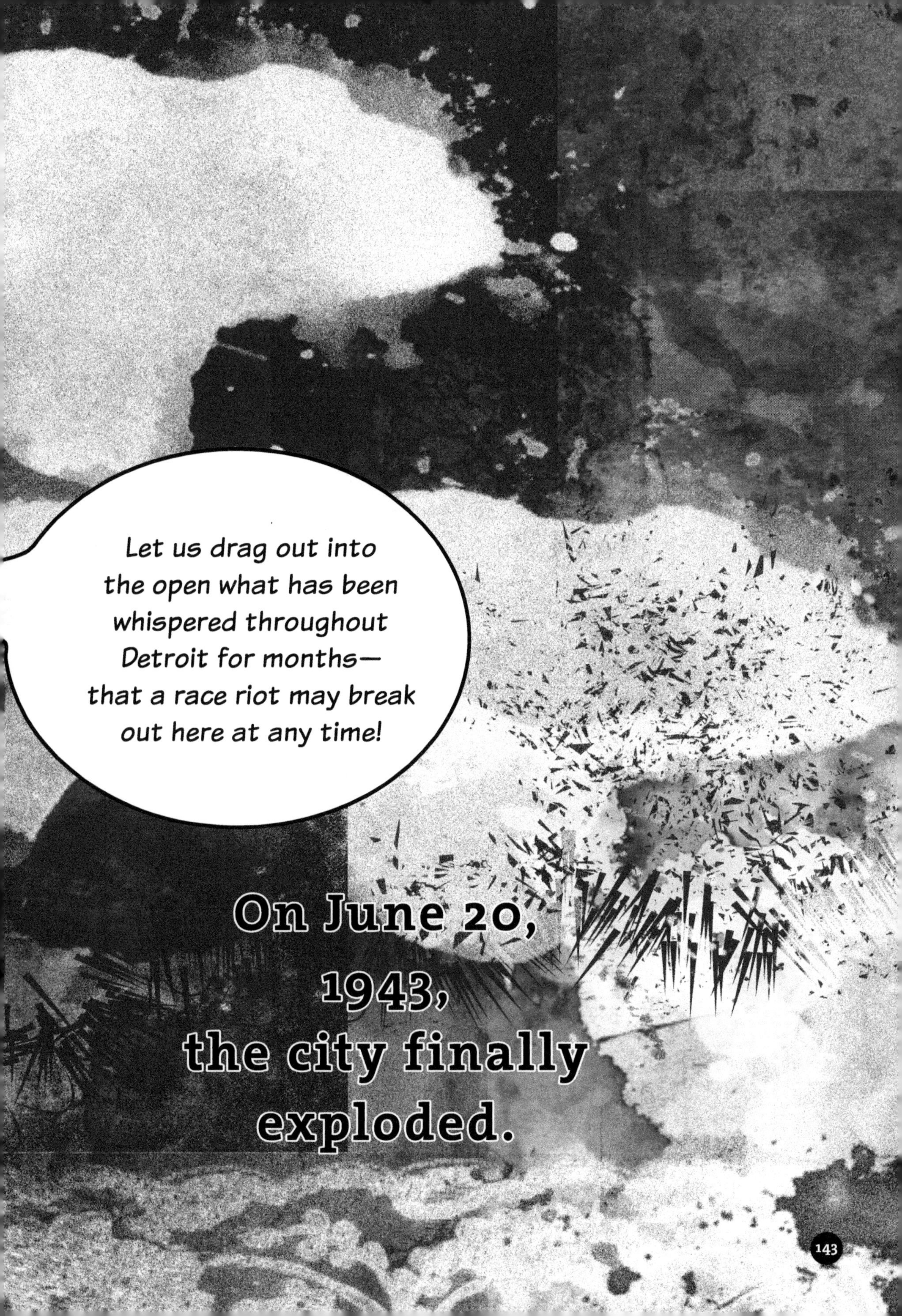
Let us drag out into the open what has been whispered throughout Detroit for months— that a race riot may break out here at any time!
On June 20, 1943, the city finally exploded.

6

Île aux Cochons
Hog Island
Belle Isle

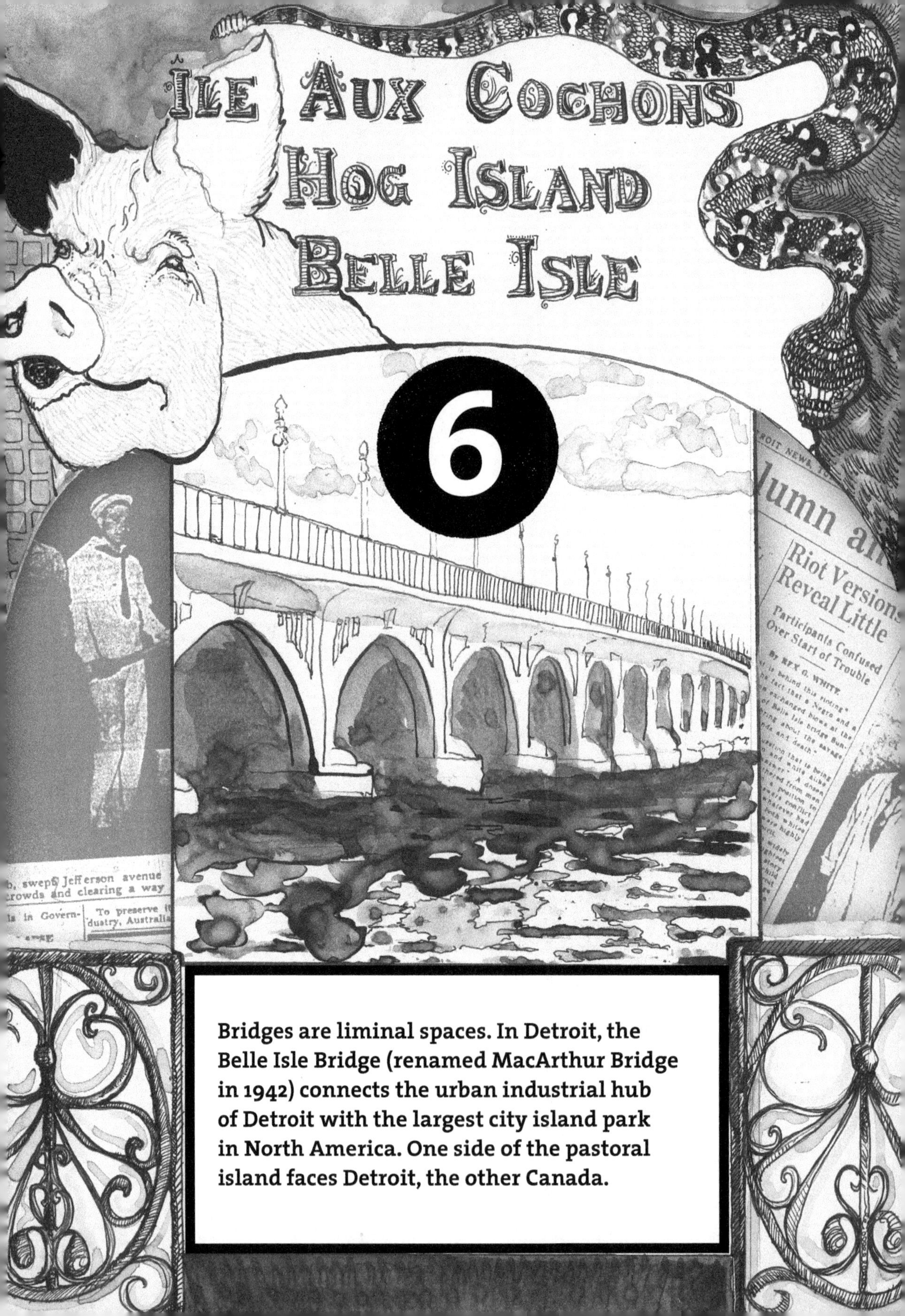
Riot Versions
Reveal Little
Participants Confused
Over Start of Trouble
swept Jefferson avenue
crowds and clearing a way

Bridges are liminal spaces. In Detroit, the Belle Isle Bridge (renamed MacArthur Bridge in 1942) connects the urban industrial hub of Detroit with the largest city island park in North America. One side of the pastoral island faces Detroit, the other Canada.

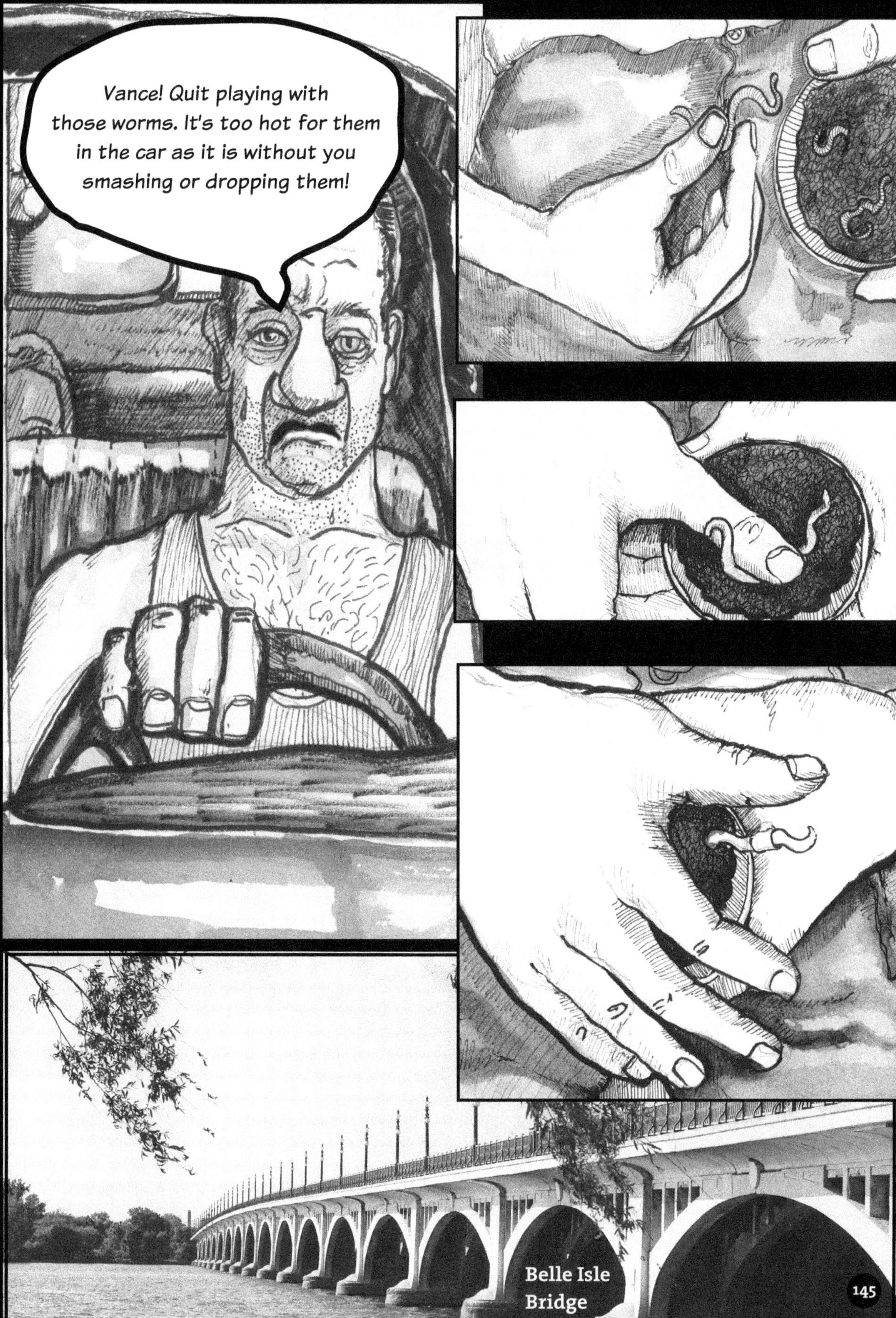
Vance! Quit playing with those worms. It's too hot for them in the car as it is without you smashing or dropping them!
Belle Isle Bridge

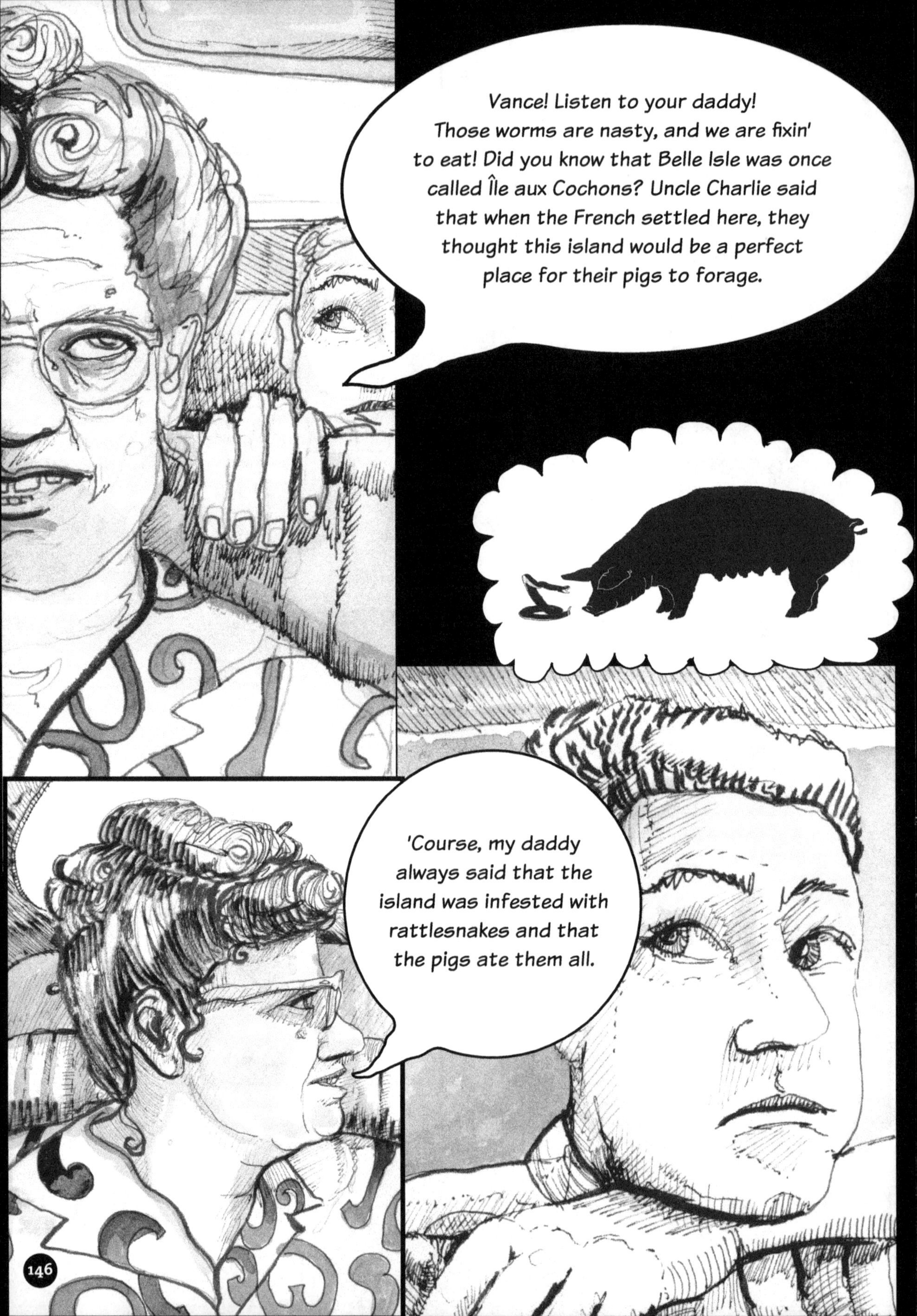
Vance! Listen to your daddy! Those worms are nasty, and we are fixin' to eat! Did you know that Belle Isle was once called Île aux Cochons? Uncle Charlie said that when the French settled here, they thought this island would be a perfect place for their pigs to forage.
'Course, my daddy always said that the island was infested with rattlesnakes and that the pigs ate them all.

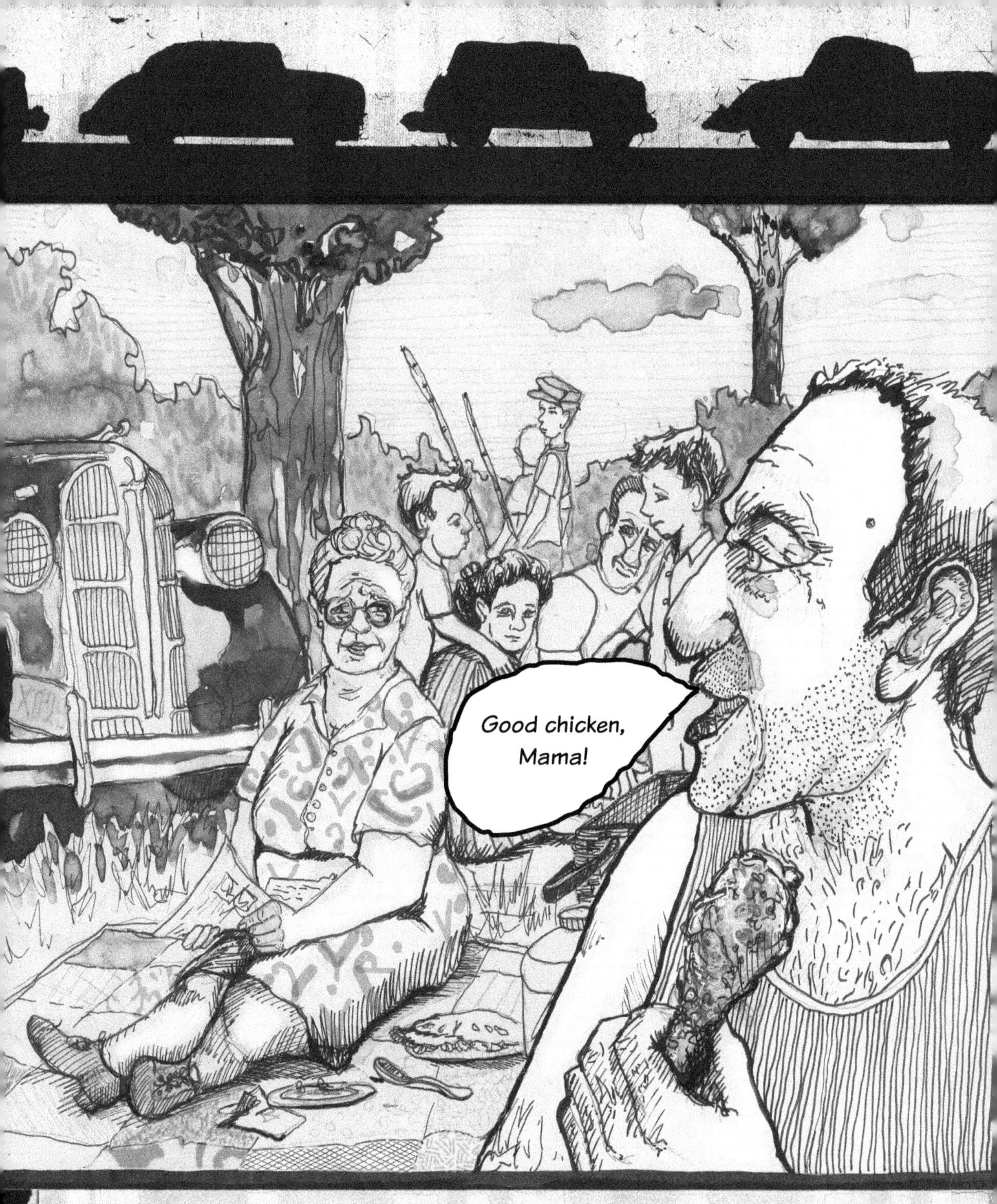
Good chicken, Mama!

On Sunday, June 20, 1943, Belle Isle gave roughly 100,000 people an escape from the ninety-degree weather. Racial and ethnic tension followed them like a long shadow as they crossed the bridge to enjoy an afternoon of cold chicken, deviled eggs, potato salad, and leisure time.

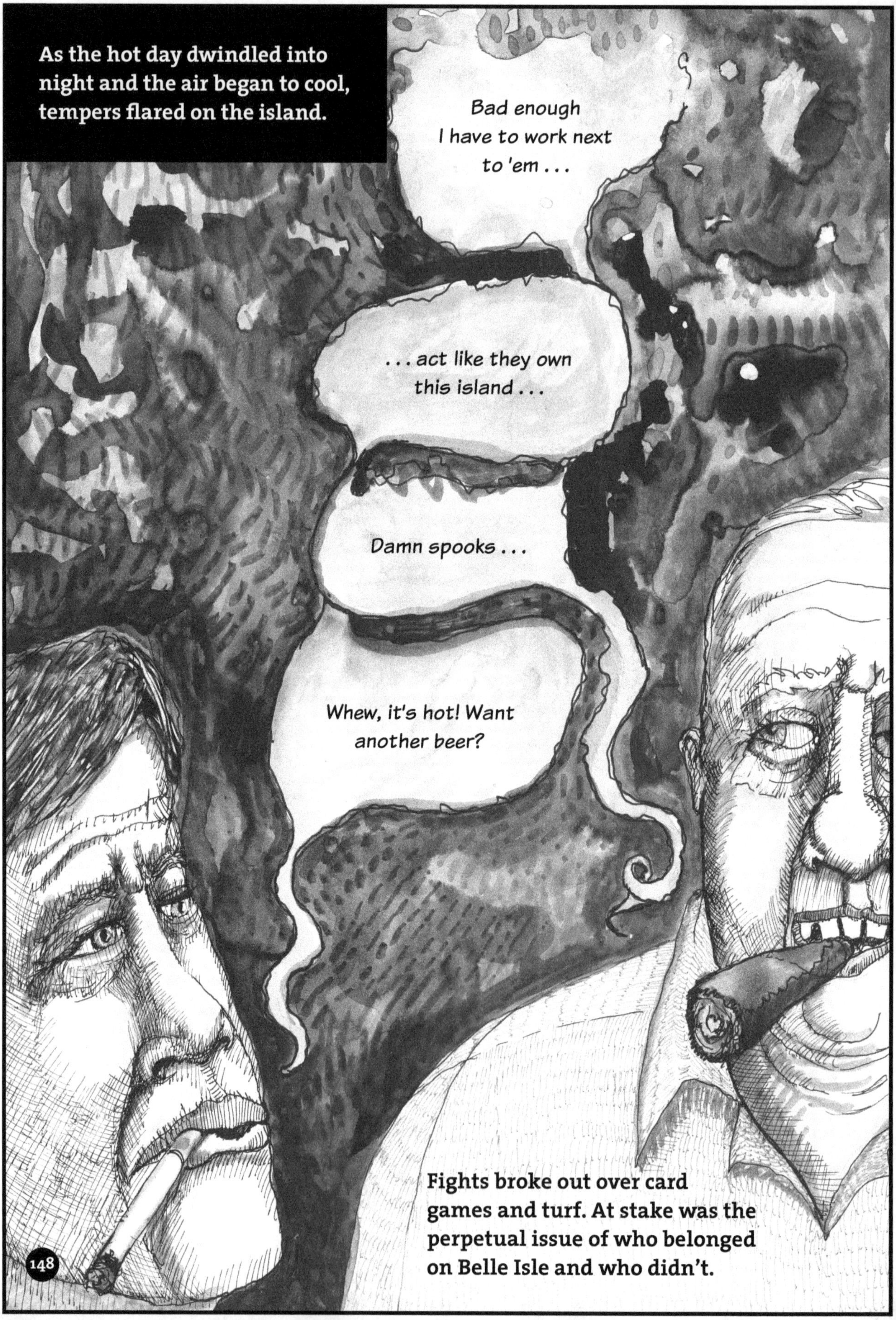
As the hot day dwindled into night and the air began to cool, tempers flared on the island.
Bad enough I have to work next to 'em . . .
. . . act like they own this island . . .
Damn spooks . . .
Whew, it's hot! Want another beer?
Fights broke out over card games and turf. At stake was the perpetual issue of who belonged on Belle Isle and who didn't.

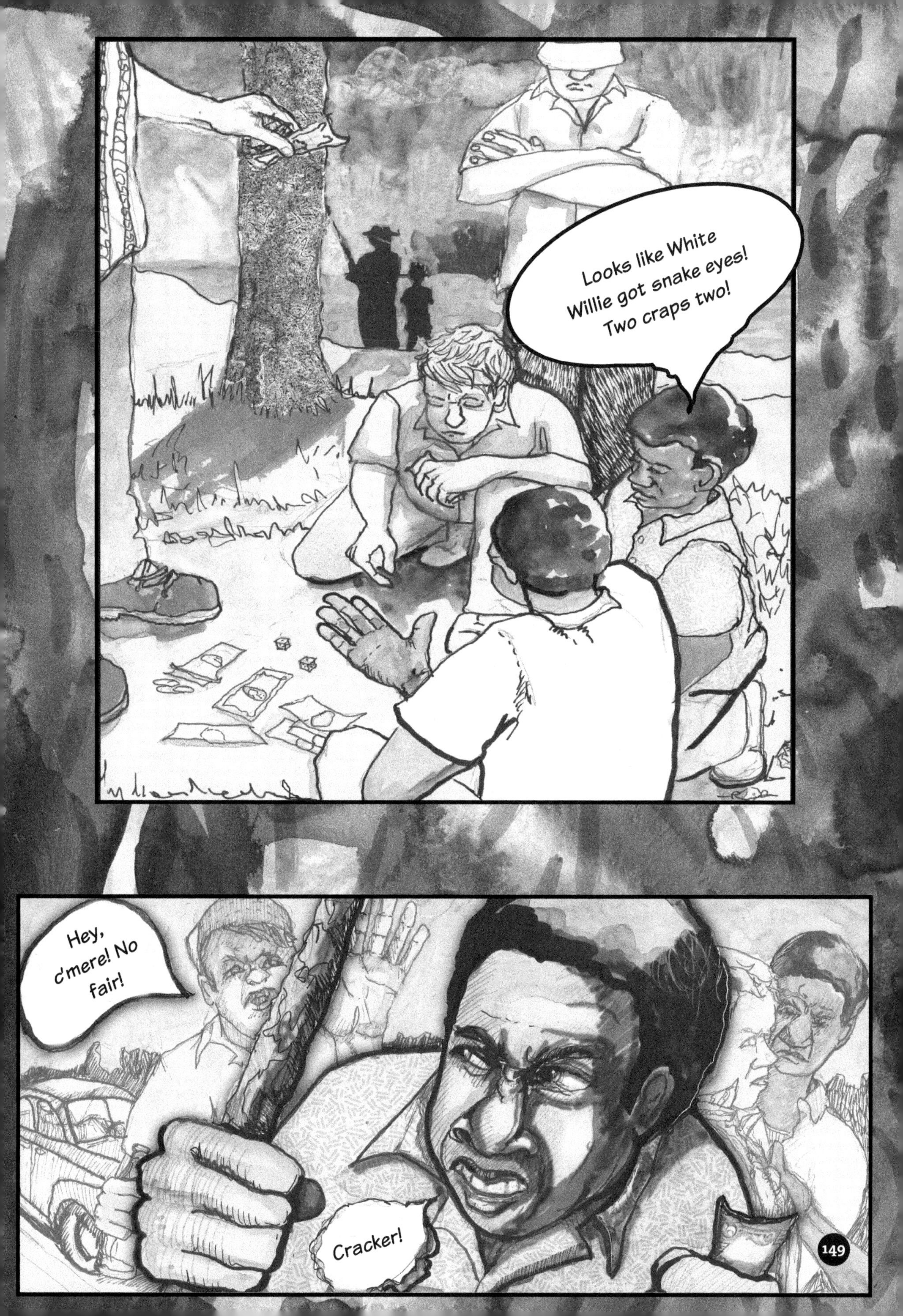
Looks like White Willie got snake eyes! Two craps two!
Hey, c'mere! No fair!
Cracker!

The tension that had been building in Detroit exploded on the bridge of Belle Isle sometime in the early evening. No one knows who threw the first punch.

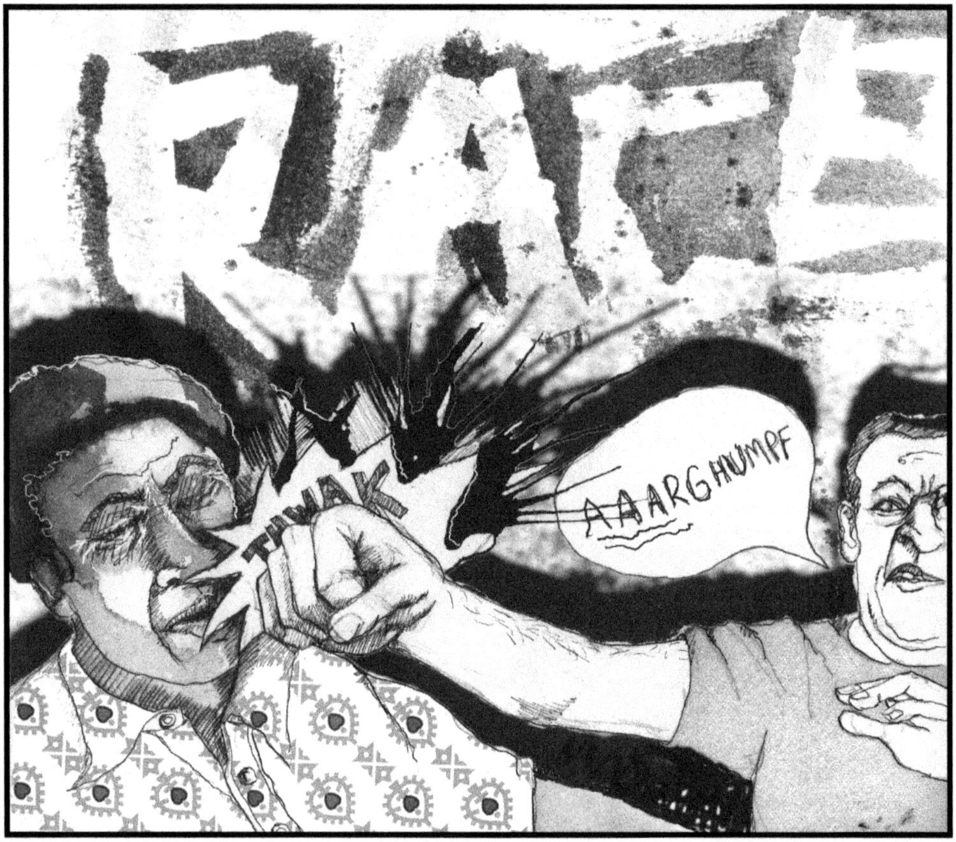
THWAK
AAARGHUMPF

On the island that day there were nearly 60,000 African Americans and 40,000 whites. By the time police arrived, there was a brawl that involved over 200 people who were identified as white sailors fighting with "Negroes" and white men. Eventually, nearly 5,000 people were swept up in the violence.

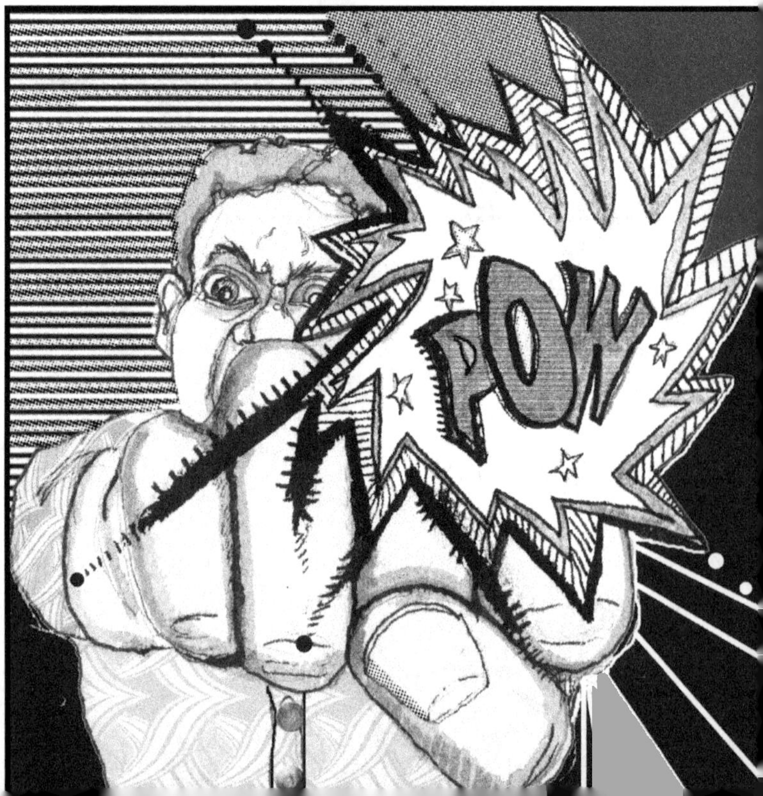
POW

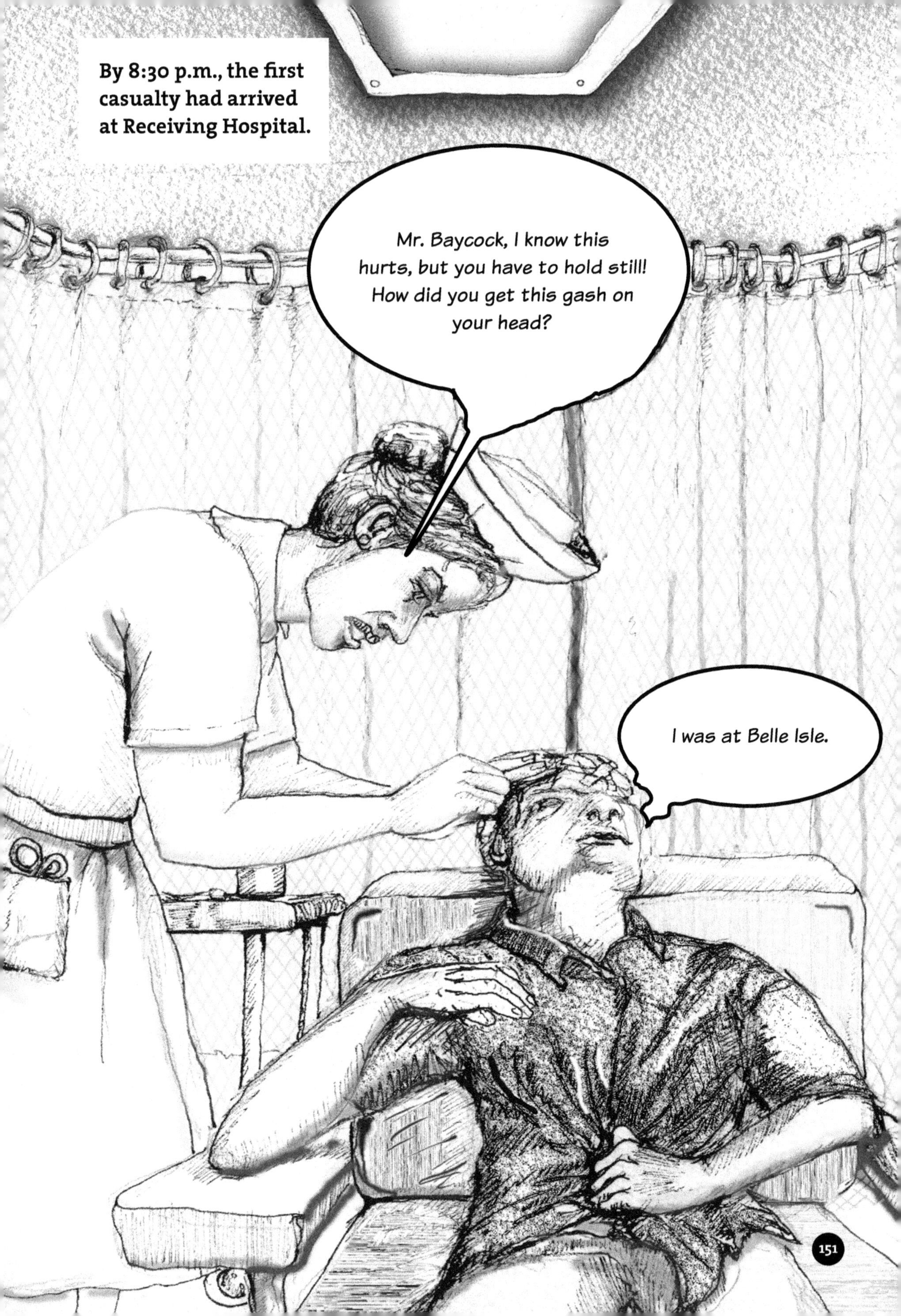
By 8:30 p.m., the first casualty had arrived at Receiving Hospital.
Mr. Baycock, I know this hurts, but you have to hold still! How did you get this gash on your head?
I was at Belle Isle.

For many people caught up in the violence on Belle Isle, it was a matter of being Black and being in the wrong place at the wrong time.

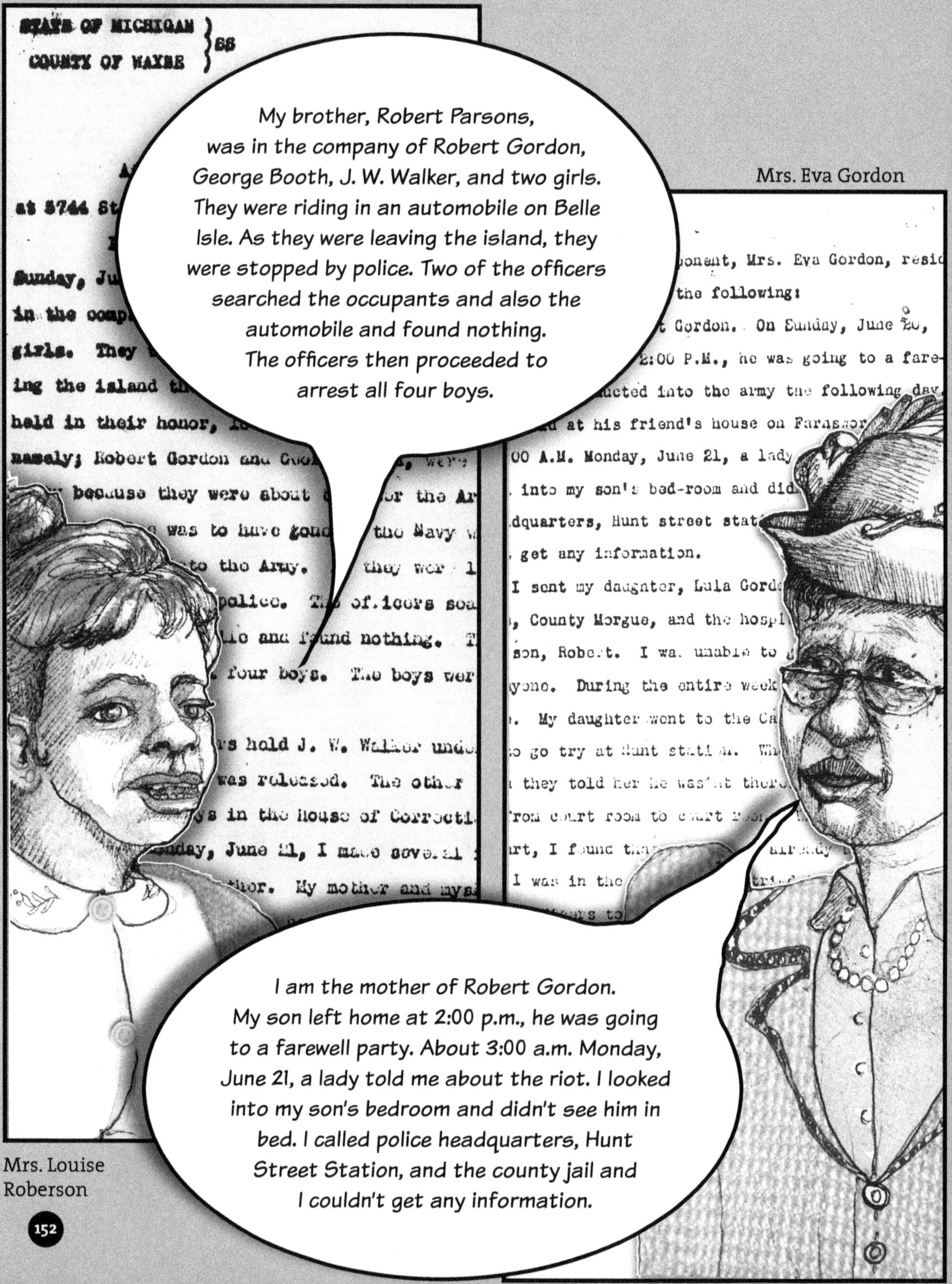
My brother, Robert Parsons, was in the company of Robert Gordon, George Booth, J. W. Walker, and two girls. They were riding in an automobile on Belle Isle. As they were leaving the island, they were stopped by police. Two of the officers searched the occupants and also the automobile and found nothing. The officers then proceeded to arrest all four boys.
Mrs. Eva Gordon
I am the mother of Robert Gordon. My son left home at 2:00 p.m., he was going to a farewell party. About 3:00 a.m. Monday, June 21, a lady told me about the riot. I looked into my son's bedroom and didn't see him in bed. I called police headquarters, Hunt Street Station, and the county jail and I couldn't get any information.
Mrs. Louise Roberson

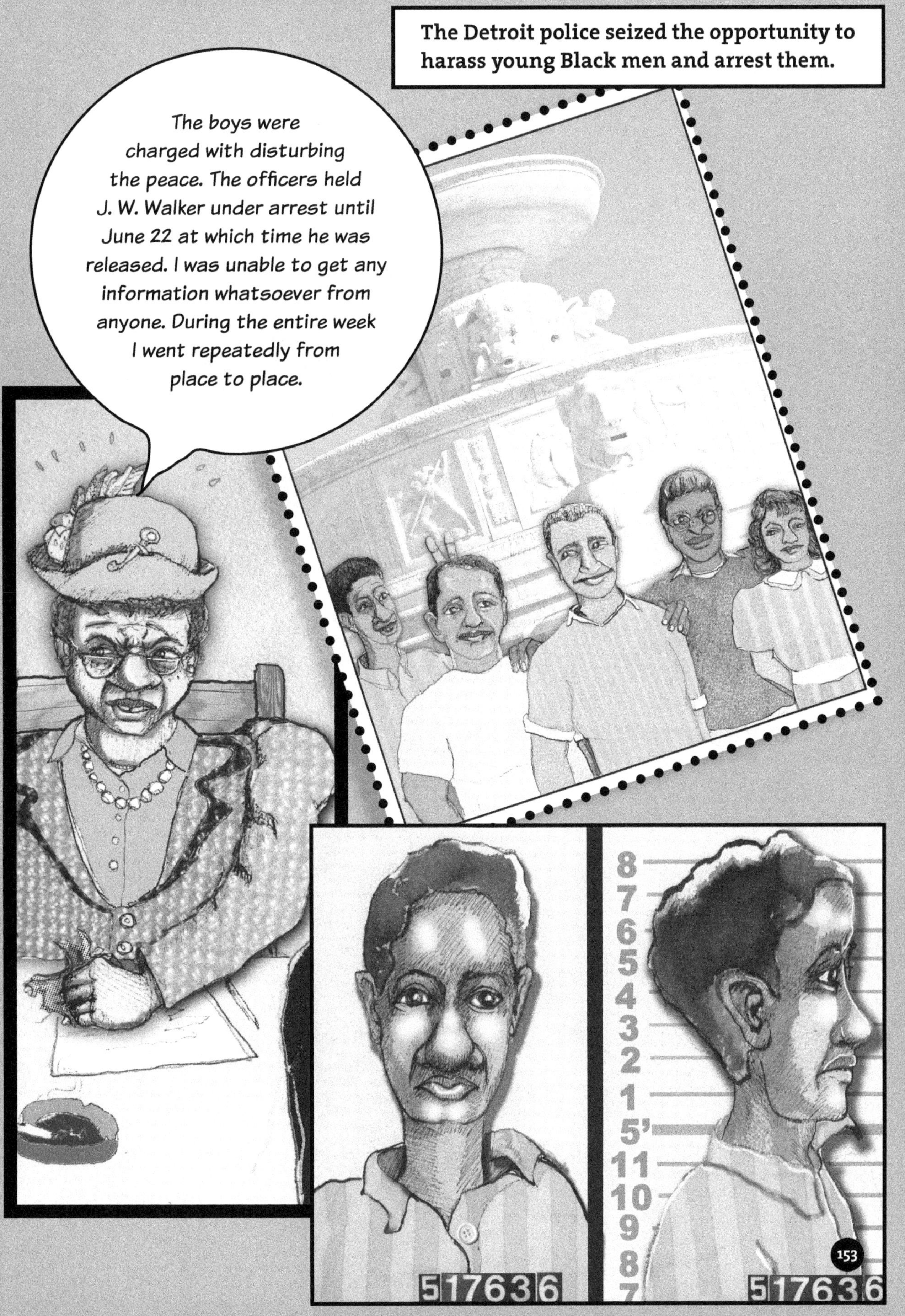

The Detroit police seized the opportunity to harass young Black men and arrest them.
The boys were charged with disturbing the peace. The officers held J. W. Walker under arrest until June 22 at which time he was released. I was unable to get any information whatsoever from anyone. During the entire week I went repeatedly from place to place.
517636
517636

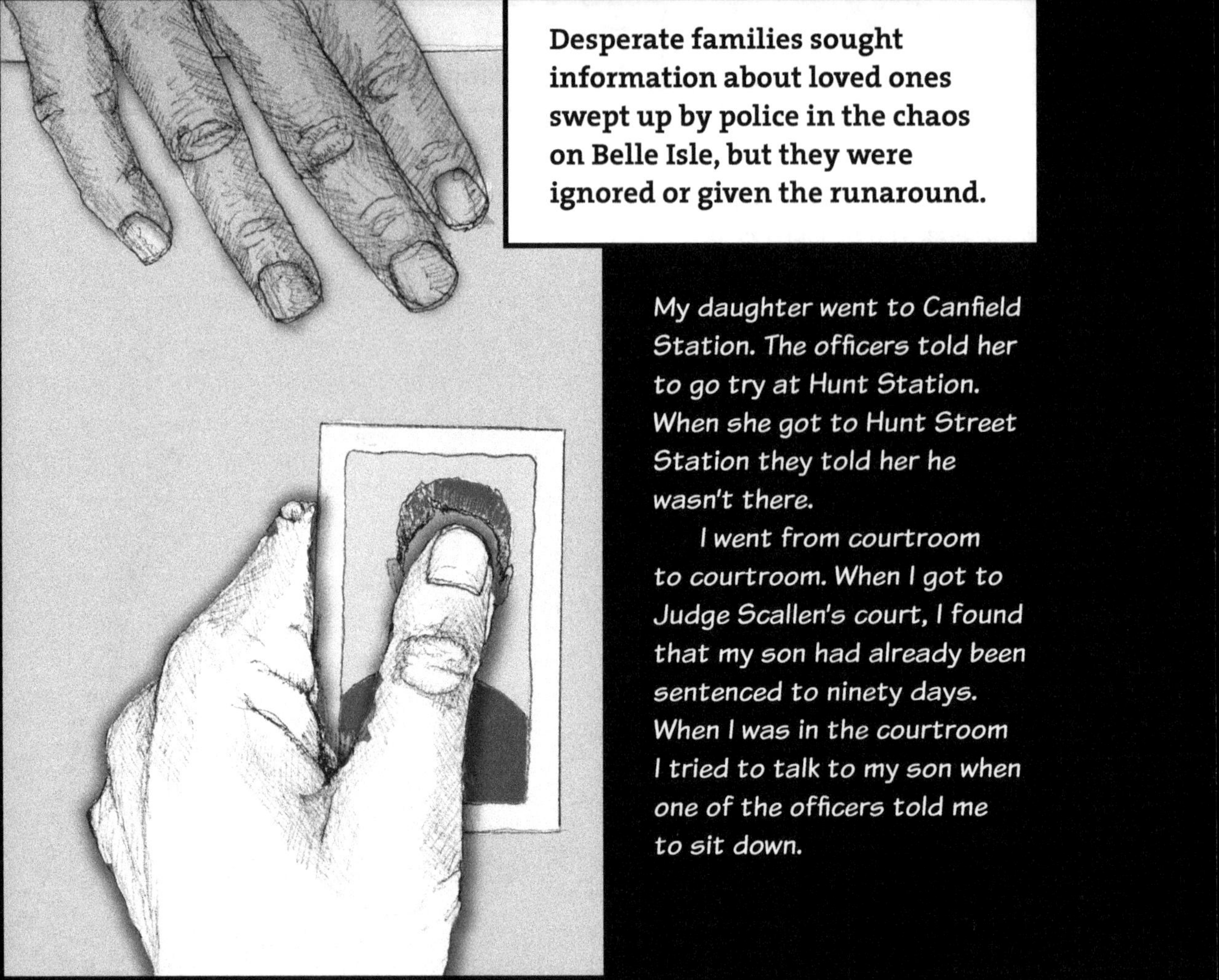
Desperate families sought information about loved ones swept up by police in the chaos on Belle Isle, but they were ignored or given the runaround.
My daughter went to Canfield Station. The officers told her to go try at Hunt Station. When she got to Hunt Street Station they told her he wasn't there.
I went from courtroom to courtroom. When I got to Judge Scallen's court, I found that my son had already been sentenced to ninety days. When I was in the courtroom I tried to talk to my son when one of the officers told me to sit down.

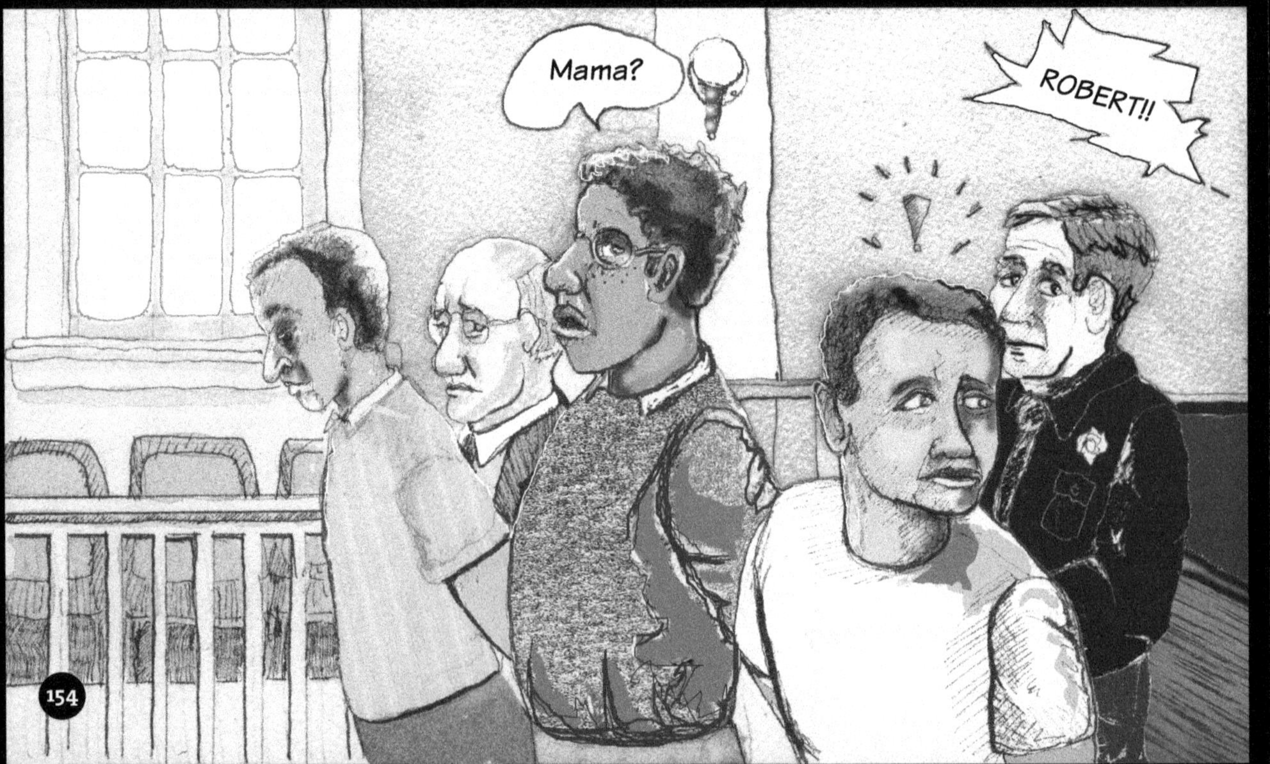
Mama?
ROBERT!!

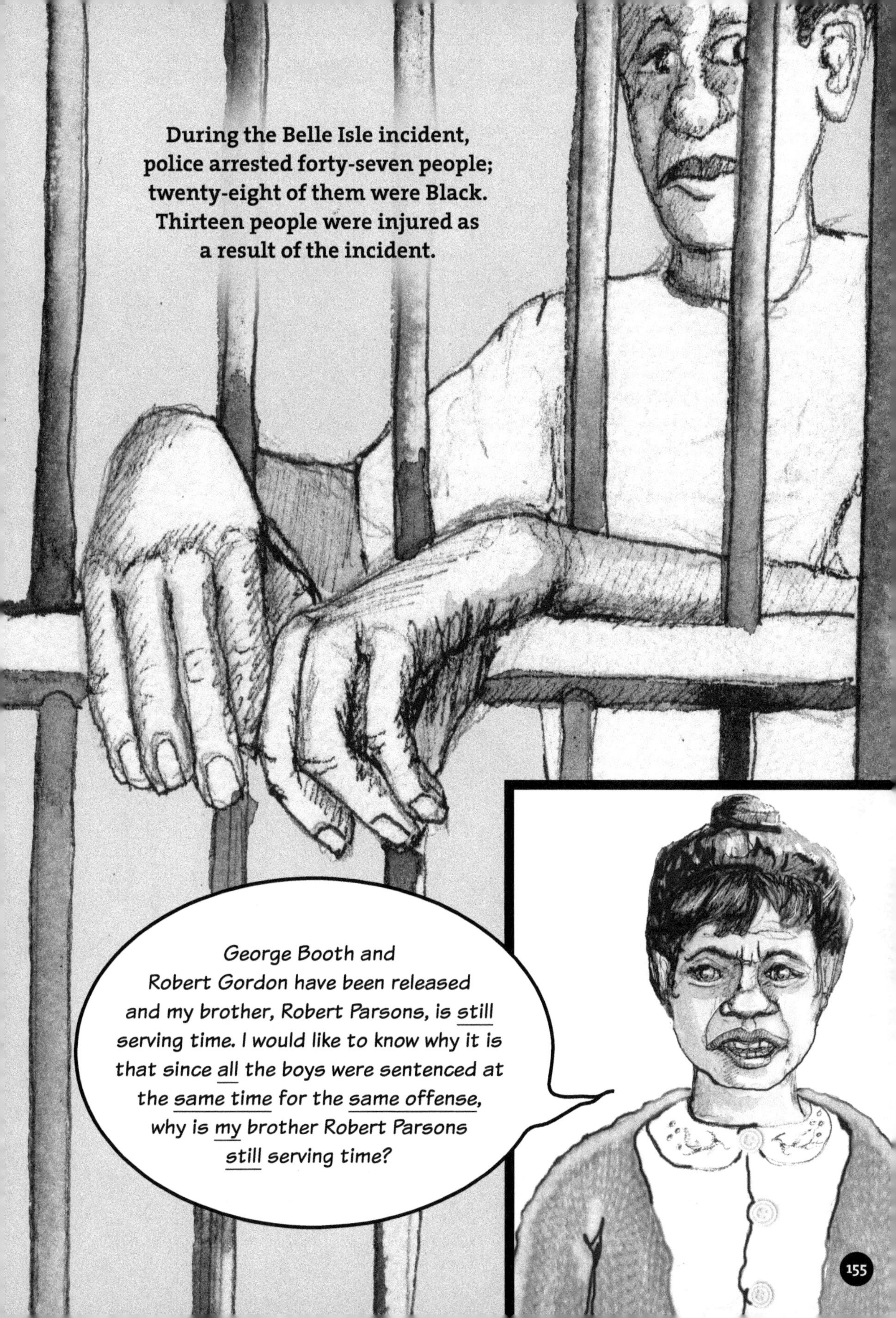
During the Belle Isle incident, police arrested forty-seven people; twenty-eight of them were Black. Thirteen people were injured as a result of the incident.
George Booth and Robert Gordon have been released and my brother, Robert Parsons, is still serving time. I would like to know why it is that since all the boys were sentenced at the same time for the same offense, why is my brother Robert Parsons still serving time?

Dawn came. The police thought they had quelled the violence.

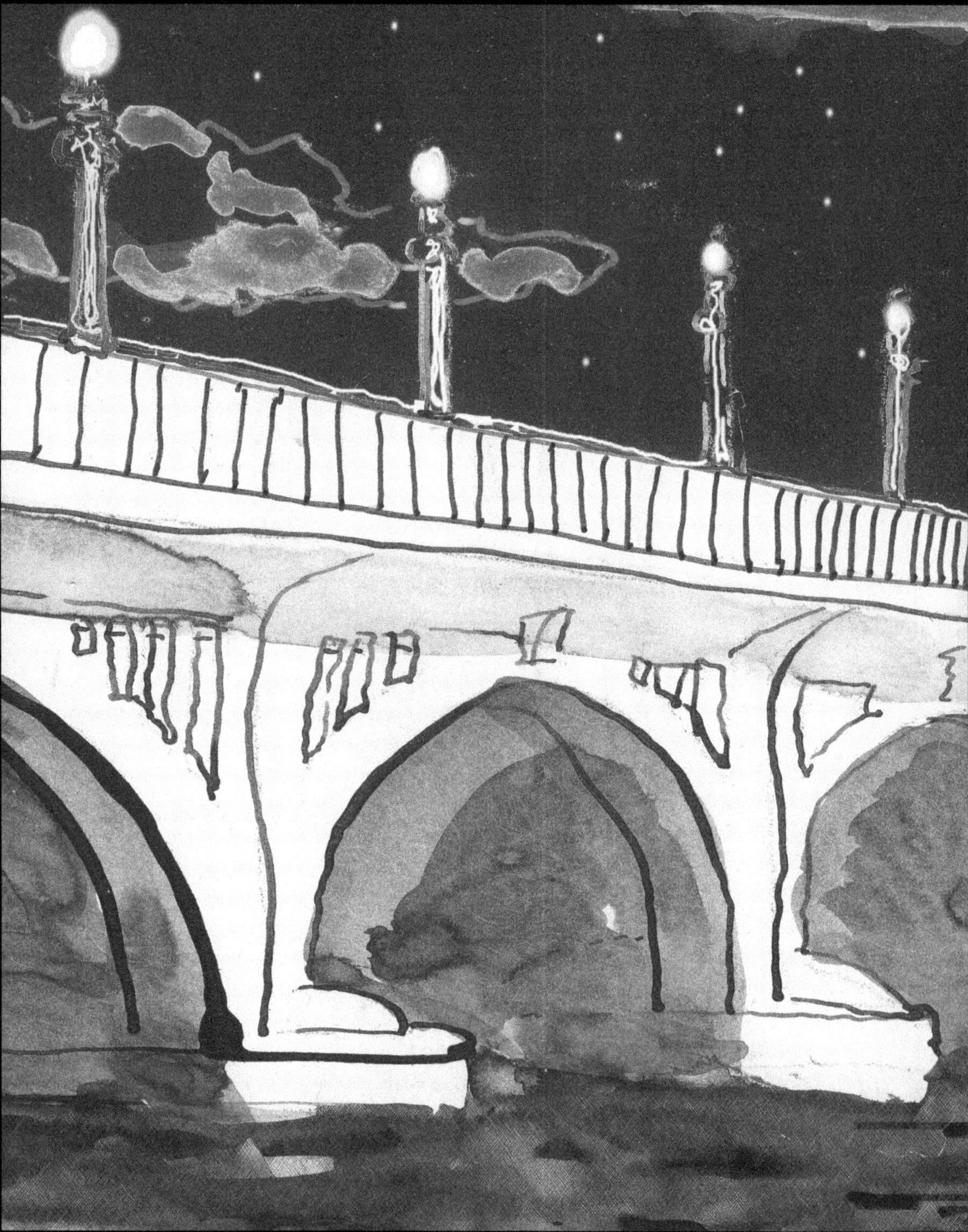

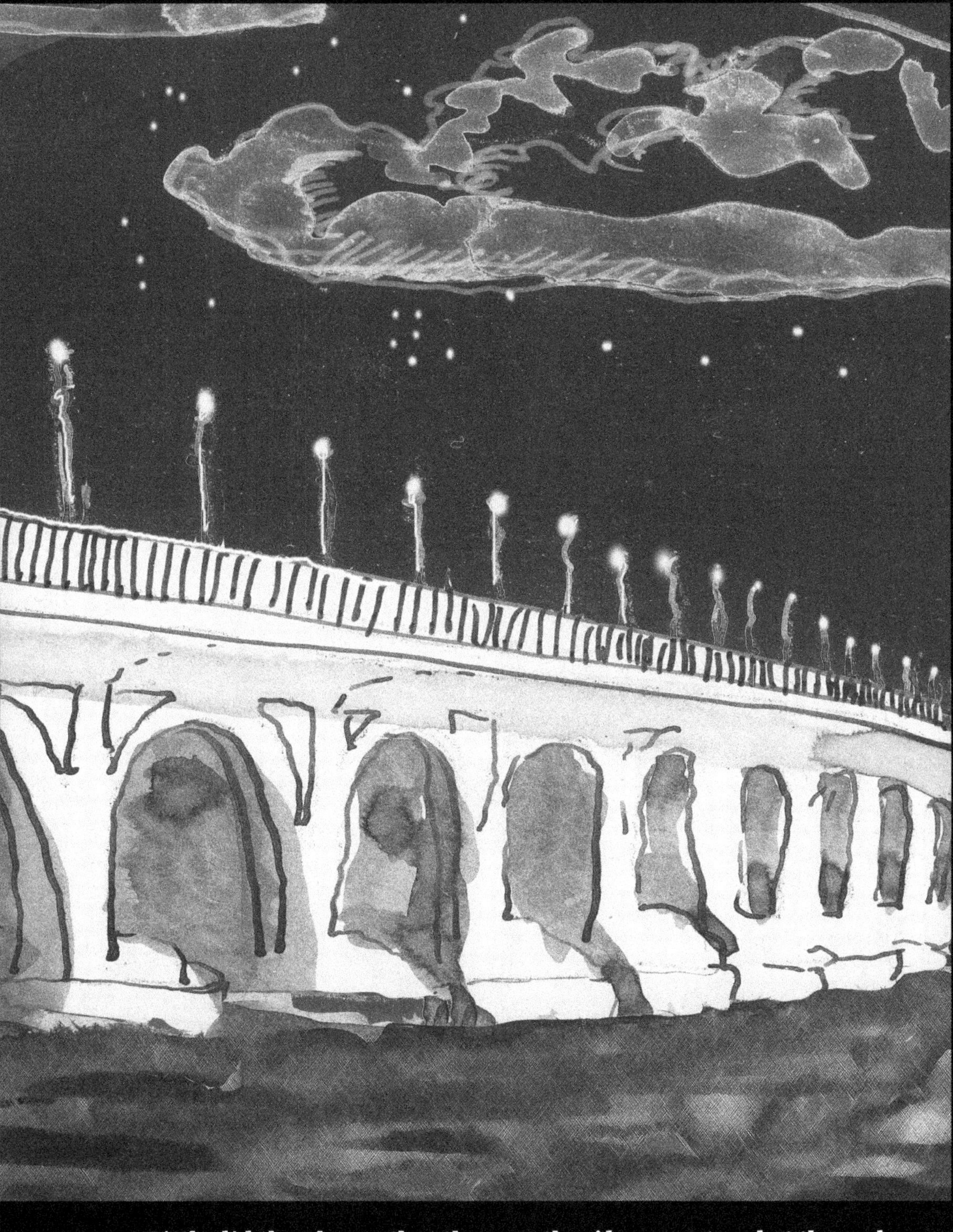

Little did they know that the rage they'd encountered at the end of the bridge leading to Belle Isle had spread through Paradise Valley like wildfire on a dry summer prairie.

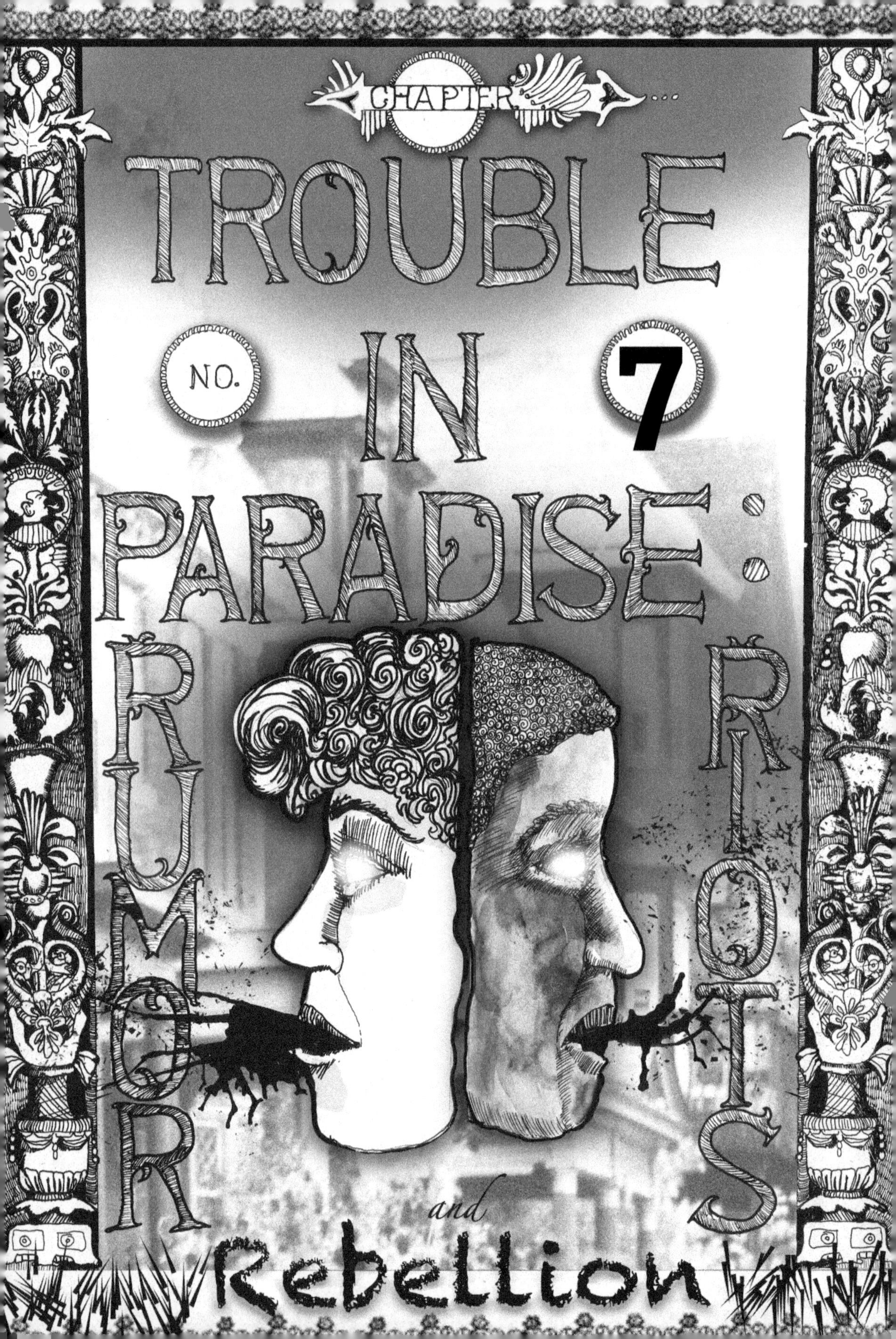
CHAPTER
NO. 7
TROUBLE IN PARADISE:
RUMOR
RIOTS
and
Rebellion

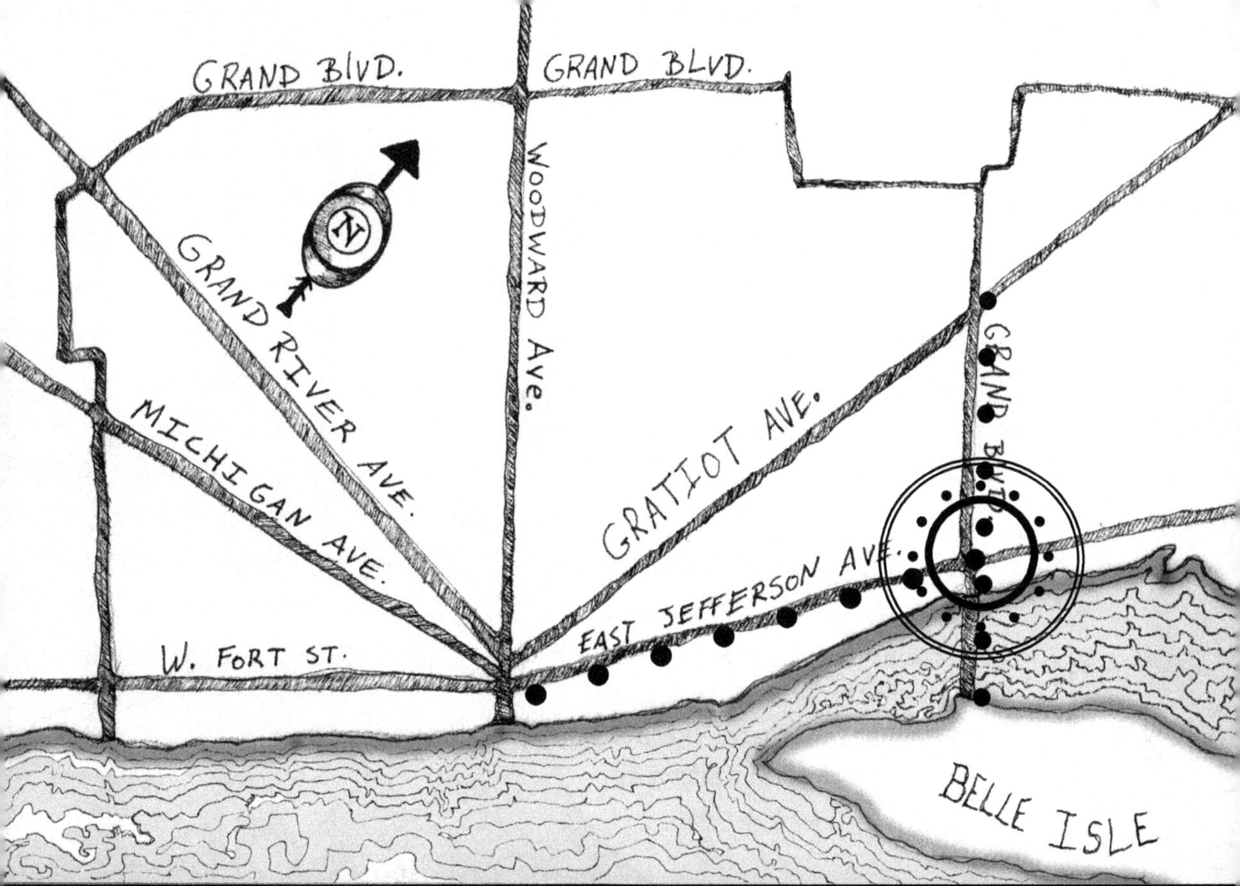
GRAND BLVD.
GRAND BLVD.
N
WOODWARD Ave.
GRAND RIVER AVE.
MICHIGAN AVE.
GRATIOT AVE.
GRAND BLVD.
EAST JEFFERSON AVE.
W. FORT ST.
BELLE ISLE

The fierce fighting spread north from the Belle Isle Bridge to Grand Boulevard and along Jefferson Avenue.

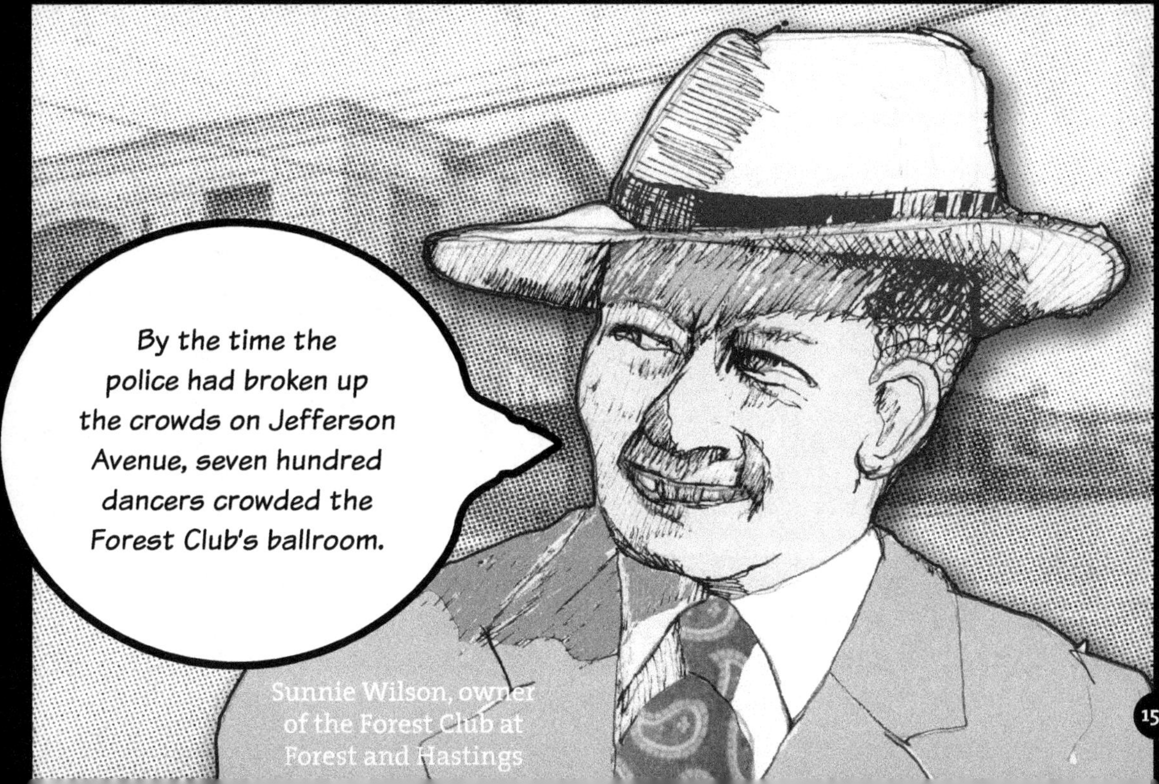
By the time the police had broken up the crowds on Jefferson Avenue, seven hundred dancers crowded the Forest Club's ballroom.

Sunnie Wilson, owner of the Forest Club at Forest and Hastings

The Forest Club was the largest nightclub in the country under Black ownership. It was swanky, larger than Madison Square Garden, and it featured a bowling alley, a bar that was over a hundred feet long, a banquet hall, and a roller rink. On most nights it was packed to the roof.

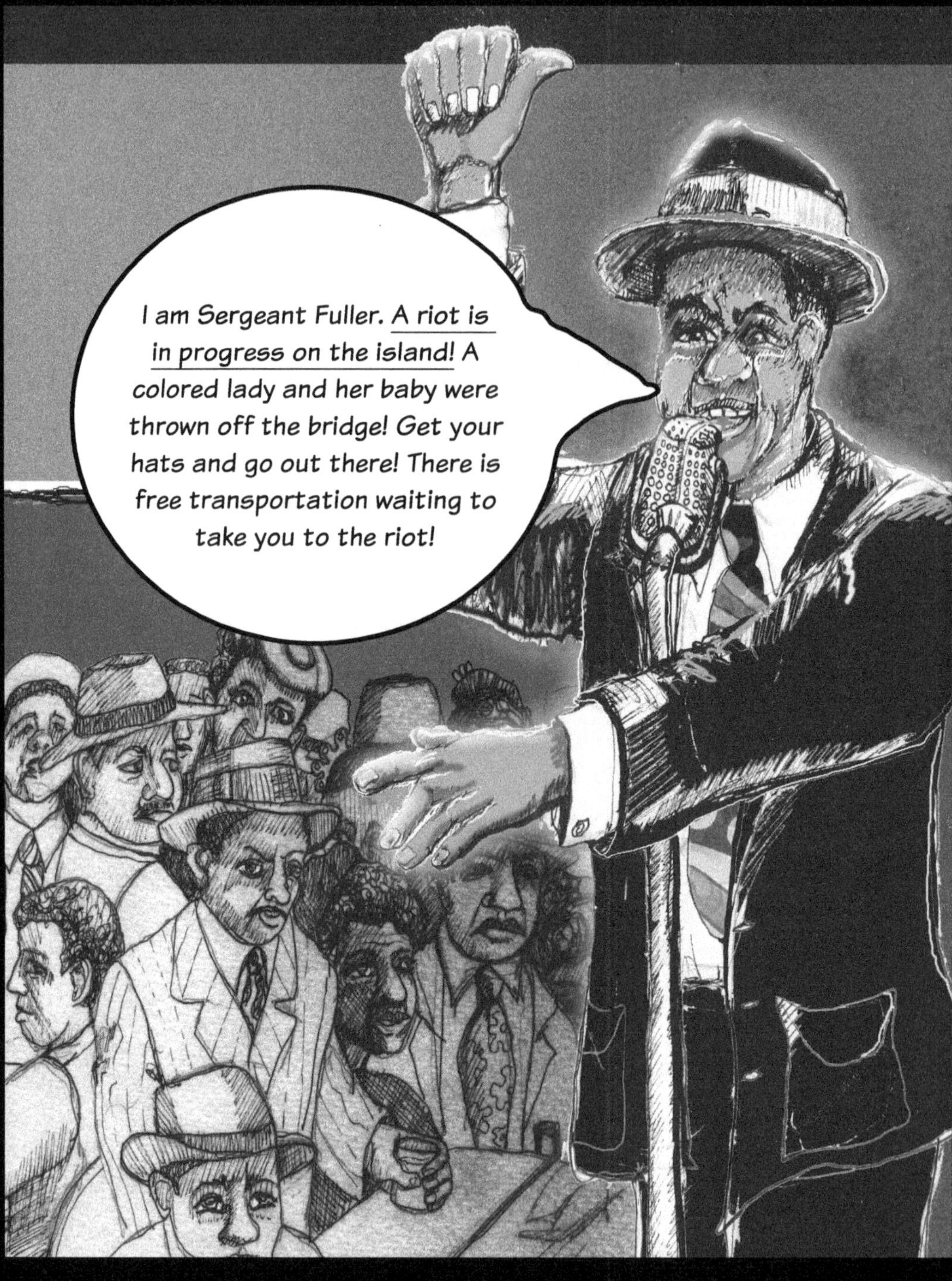
I am Sergeant Fuller. A riot is in progress on the island! A colored lady and her baby were thrown off the bridge! Get your hats and go out there! There is free transportation waiting to take you to the riot!

At approximately 12:30 a.m. Leo Tipton grabbed a microphone and, pretending to be a police sergeant, mesmerized the crowd of 500 to 700 Black patrons with rumors and false promises.

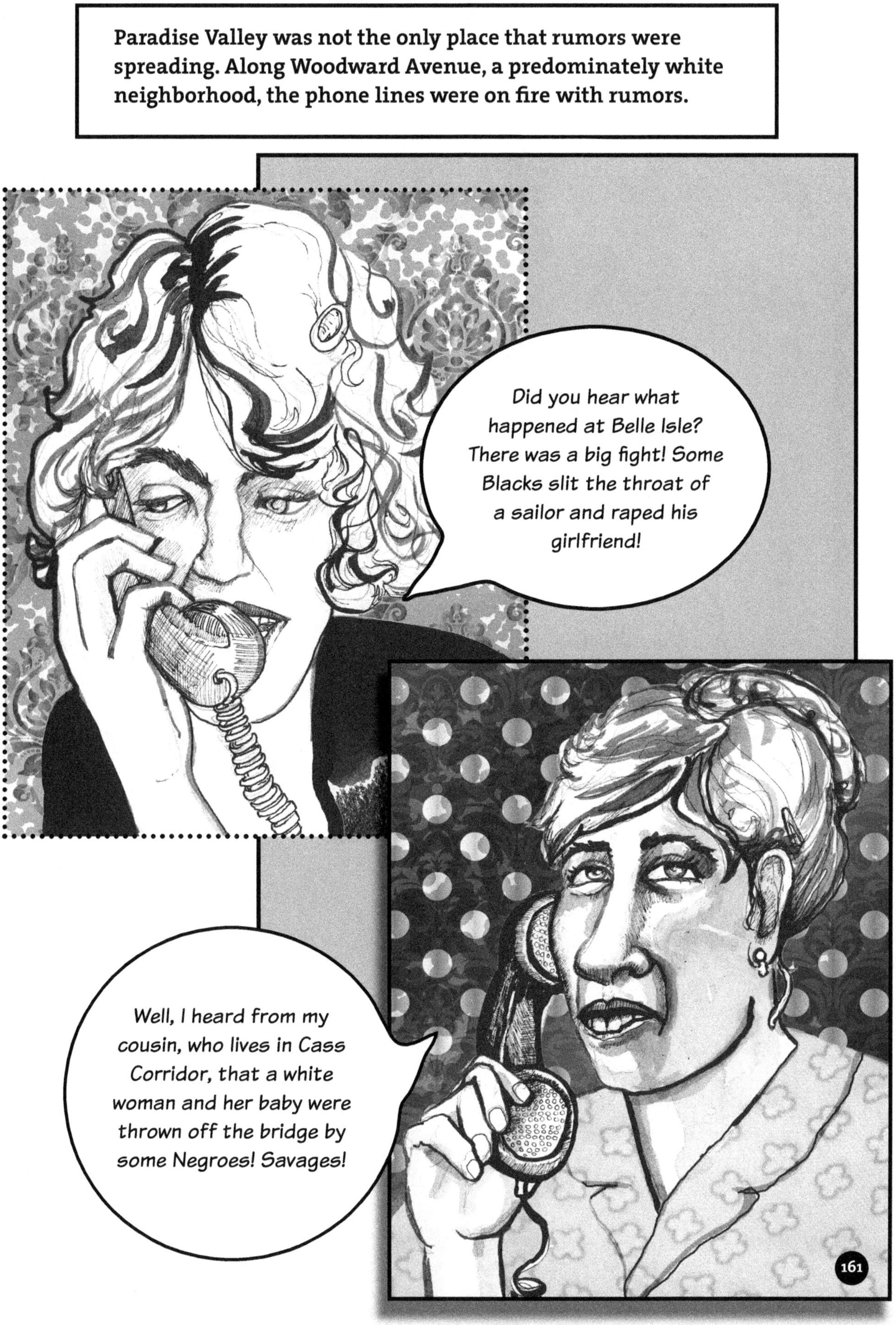
Paradise Valley was not the only place that rumors were spreading. Along Woodward Avenue, a predominately white neighborhood, the phone lines were on fire with rumors.
Did you hear what happened at Belle Isle? There was a big fight! Some Blacks slit the throat of a sailor and raped his girlfriend!
Well, I heard from my cousin, who lives in Cass Corridor, that a white woman and her baby were thrown off the bridge by some Negroes! Savages!

Rumors spread quickly through the white and Black communities of urban Detroit. The Black community was tired of discrimination, police brutality, deprivation, and systemic racism. The white community felt they had to keep the status quo in place and maintain their privilege through any means necessary.

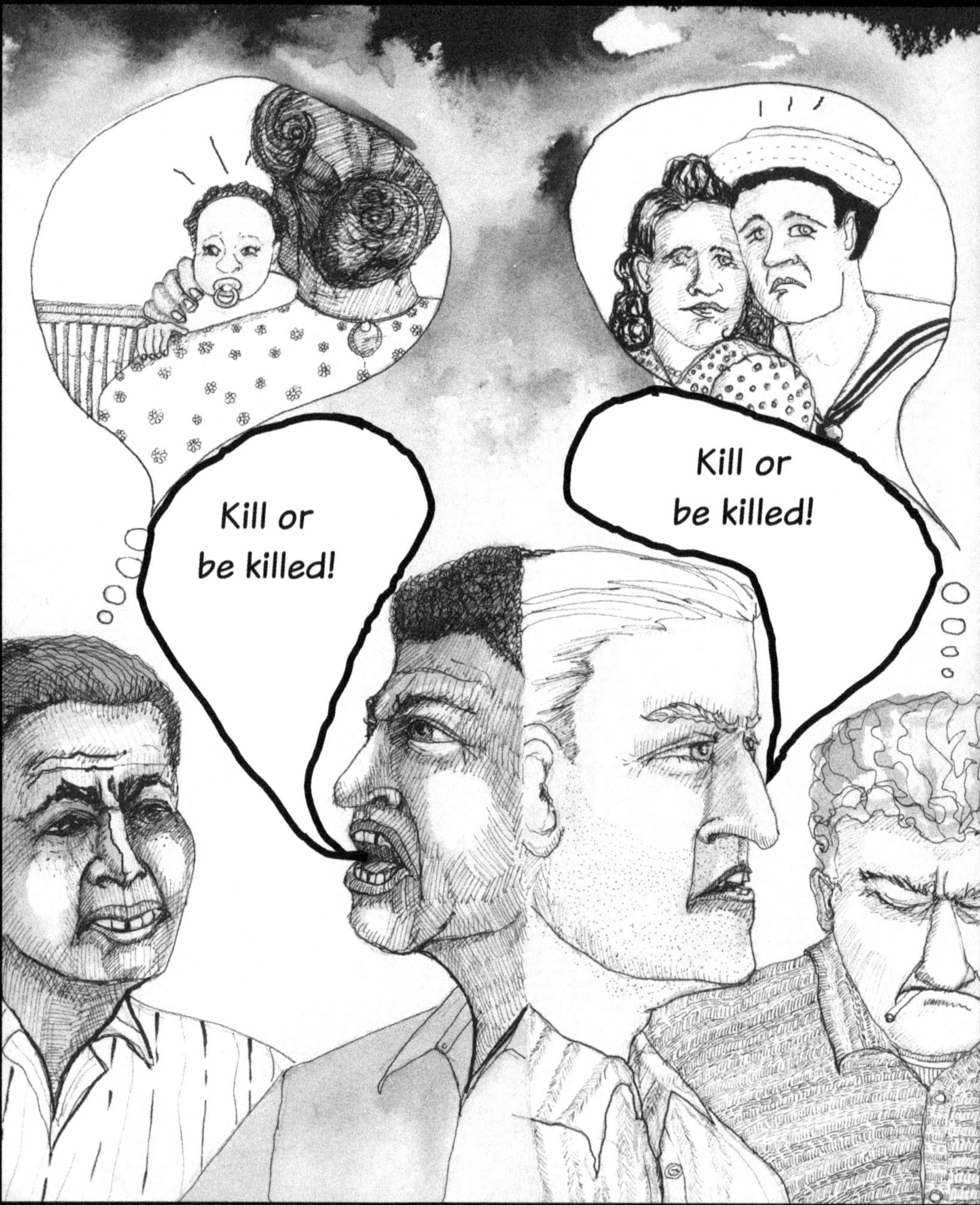

Kill or be killed!
Kill or be killed!

African Americans rebelled against the social injustices, insults, violence, and inequities that they had long encountered in Detroit. Their political reality had become untenable. Whites fought back out of fear and a belief that they were superior and deserved to be favored. They fought against change.

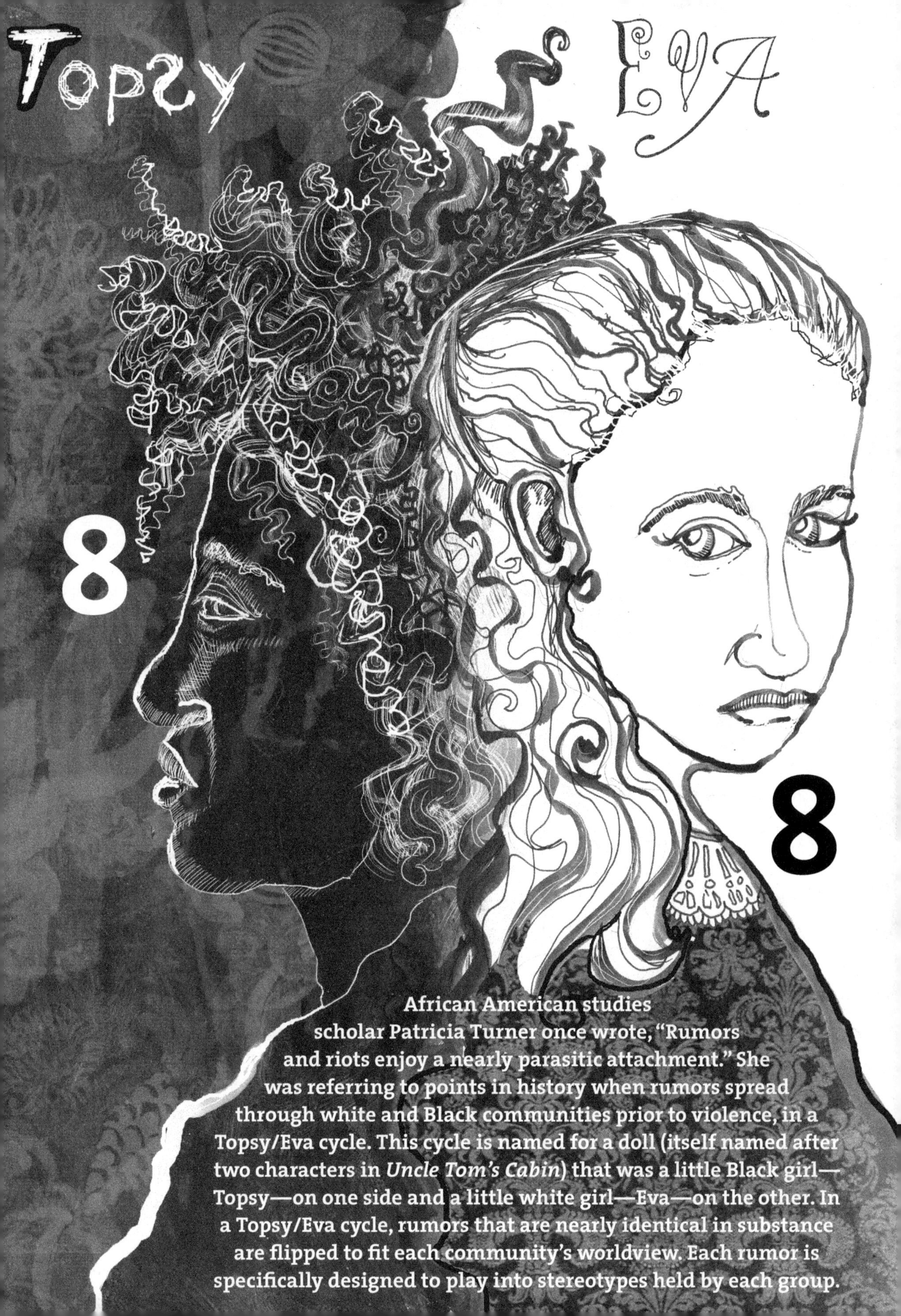

Topsy
Eva
8
8

African American studies scholar Patricia Turner once wrote, "Rumors and riots enjoy a nearly parasitic attachment." She was referring to points in history when rumors spread through white and Black communities prior to violence, in a Topsy/Eva cycle. This cycle is named for a doll (itself named after two characters in *Uncle Tom's Cabin*) that was a little Black girl—Topsy—on one side and a little white girl—Eva—on the other. In a Topsy/Eva cycle, rumors that are nearly identical in substance are flipped to fit each community's worldview. Each rumor is specifically designed to play into stereotypes held by each group.

Typology of Race Rumors

The "folkways of self-defense"

Sociologist Howard Odum coined this term to describe the way that whites believed violence against Black communities was justifiable if they caught wind of ensuing violence in advance.

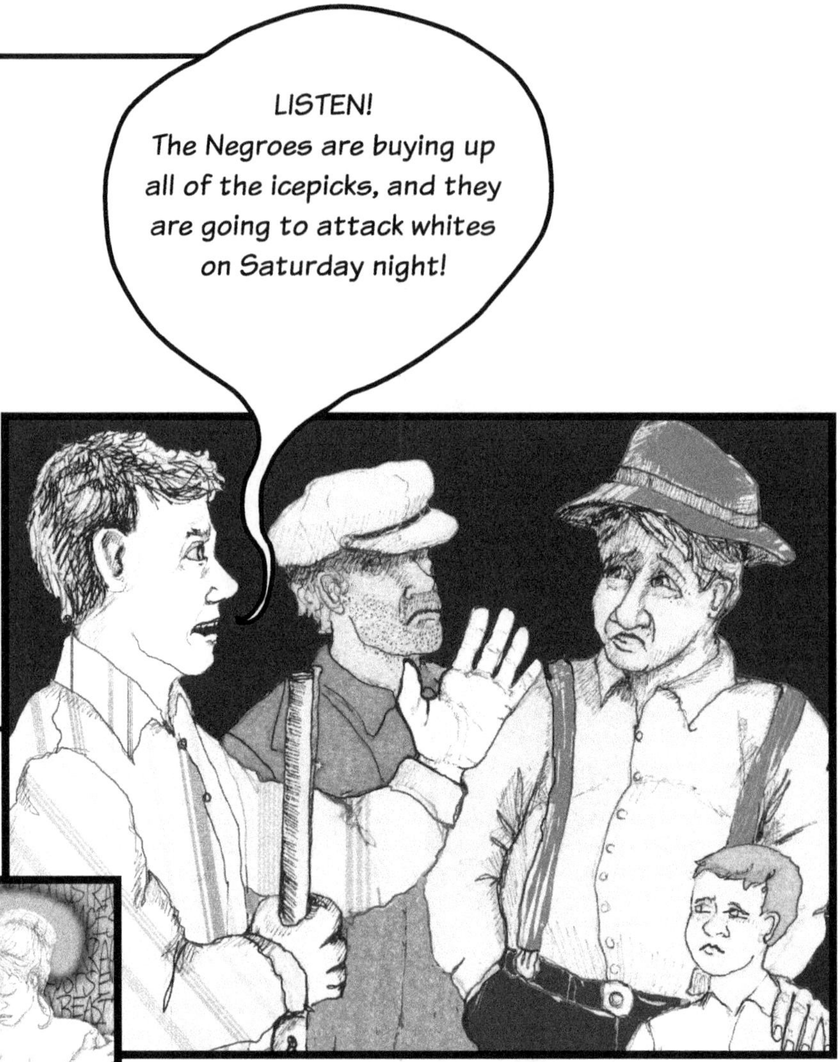
LISTEN!
The Negroes are buying up all of the icepicks, and they are going to attack whites on Saturday night!

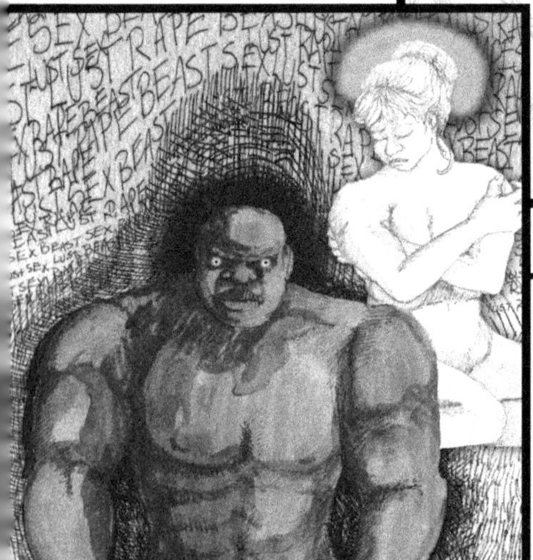
LUST RAPE BEAST
SEX

Black men are rapists; white women must be protected at all costs

Sociologist Barbara Omolade referred to the rumor of ravenous Black brutes hell-bent on raping and ruining young, virginal white women as the "folk pornography of the Bible Belt." This common rumor was used to justify lynchings of Black men and other forms of white violence against Black communities.

The revolt of Black soldiers

Rumors and myths about cowardly Black soldiers who were lazy, dangerous, and disobedient plagued the United States from the Civil War to the mid-twentieth century. Historically, the U.S. military was hesitant to train Black men. Some whites believed that when Black soldiers returned home they would be even more dangerous because they had been trained to fight and kill. They also felt that they would use their military skills to upend the inscribed discriminatory social order, which had always been advantageous to whites.

Good enough to die for our country but not to be treated like an equal citizen . . .

Come on, baby, I just want to have me a little fun!

NOOOOO!

White soldiers are rapists; Black women must be protected at all costs

From before the Civil War to the mid-twentieth century, there was much truth in the rumor that white soldiers regularly raped Black women with little or no punishment. During World War II Black women living close to military bases, especially in the Jim Crow South, lived in constant fear that they might be victimized by white soldiers.

Up and Down the Street

9

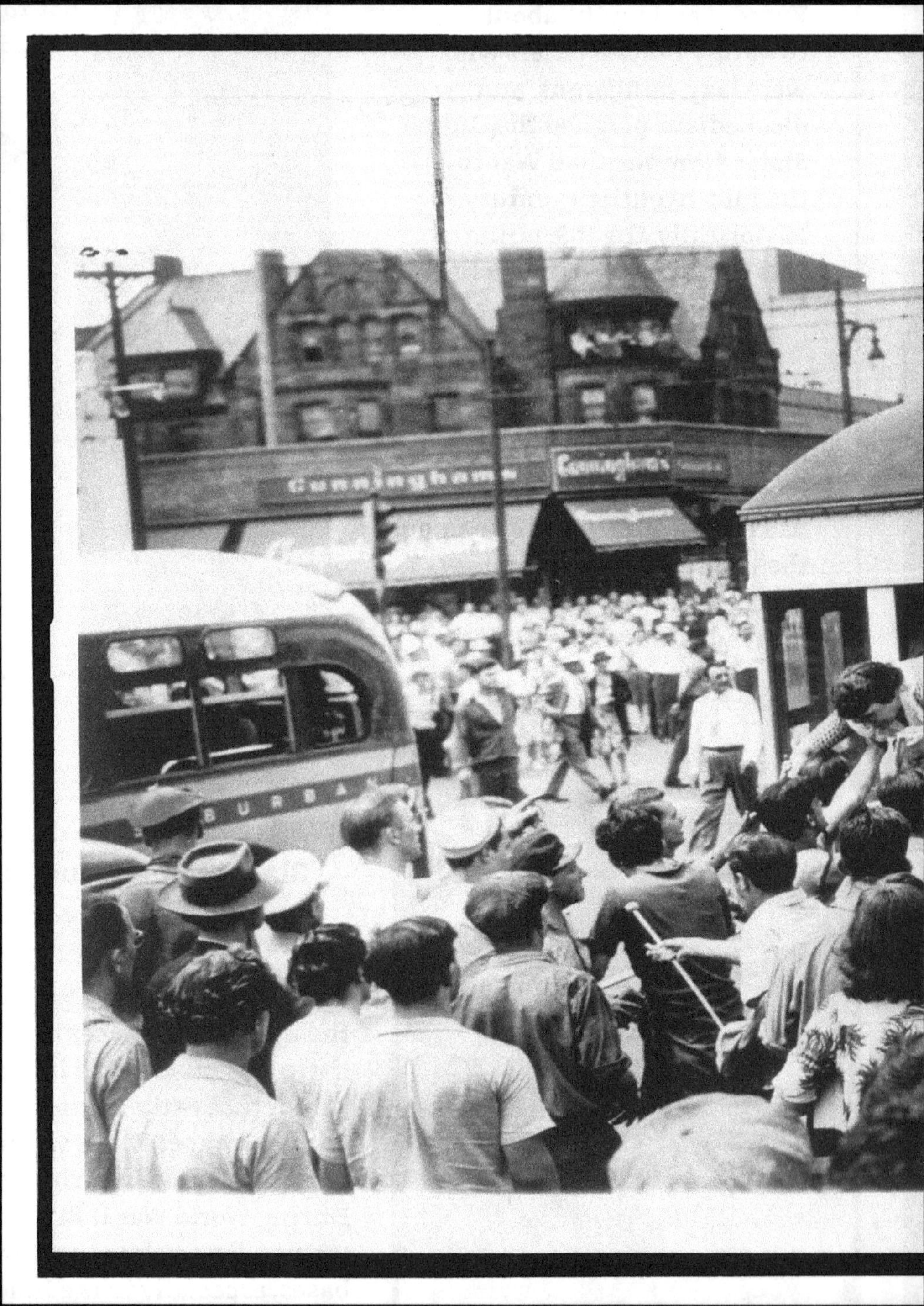
Cunninghams

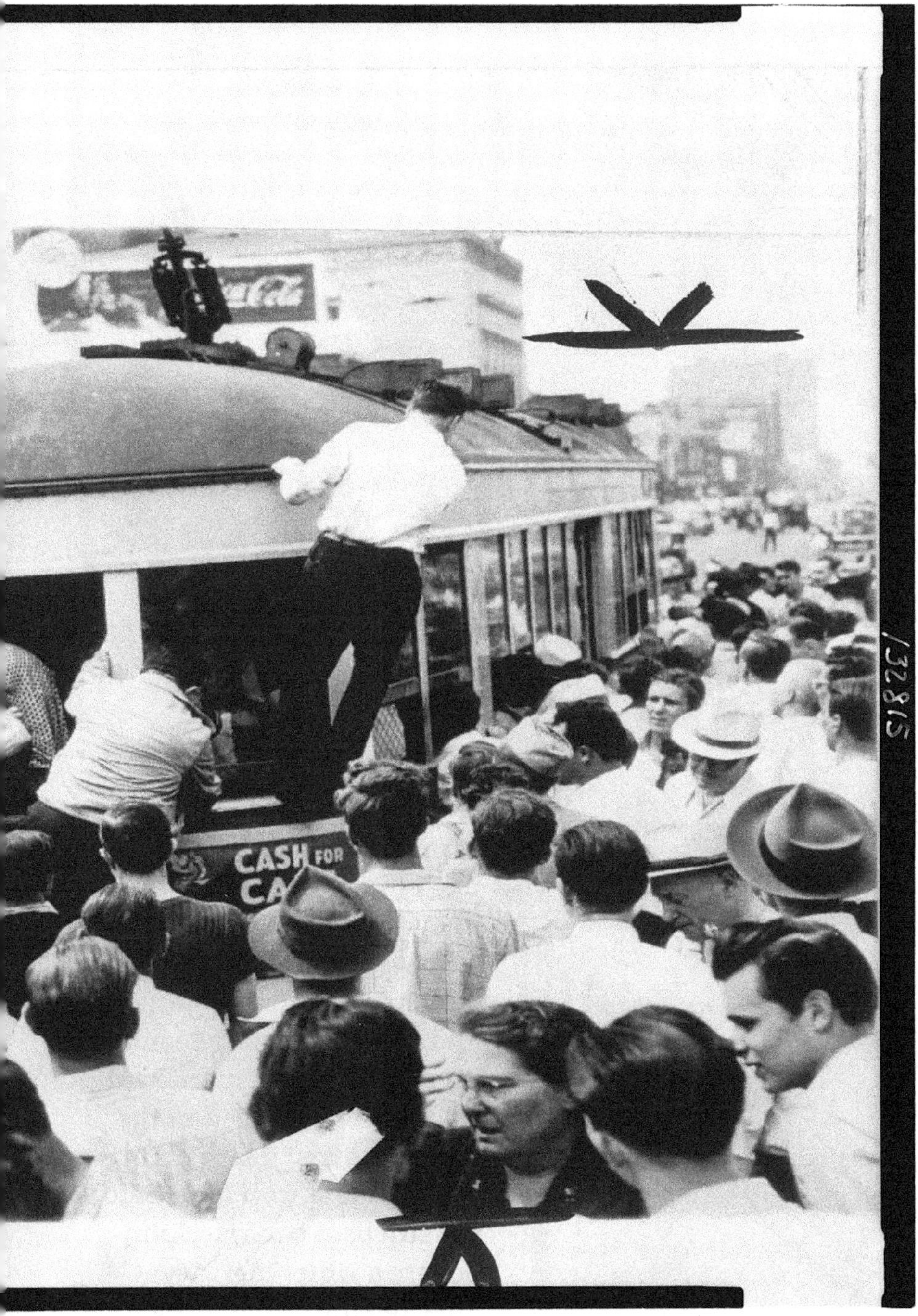
CASH FOR
132815

Frightened passengers try to escape an angry white mob by climbing through the rear of a streetcar during the Detroit uprising.

Library of Congress, Prints & Photographs Division, Washington, D.C., LC-USZ62-132815

After Black patrons poured out of the Forest Club, they were dismayed to learn that there was no transportation available to Belle Isle. They felt their community was under siege, and some began to vent their fear and frustrations on whites up and down Hastings Street.

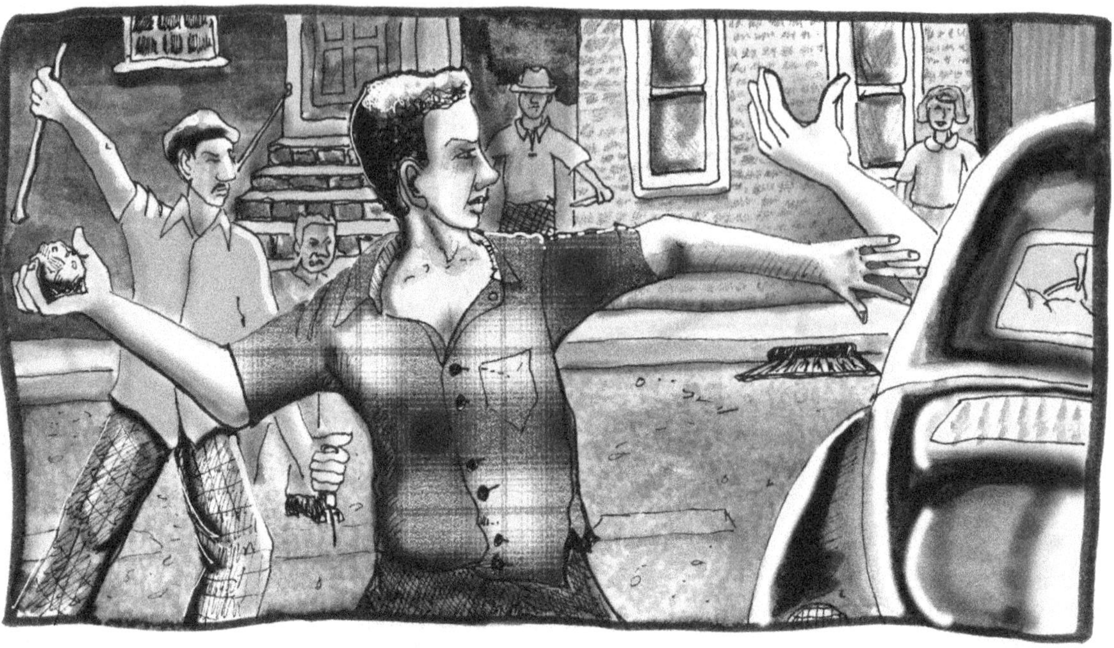

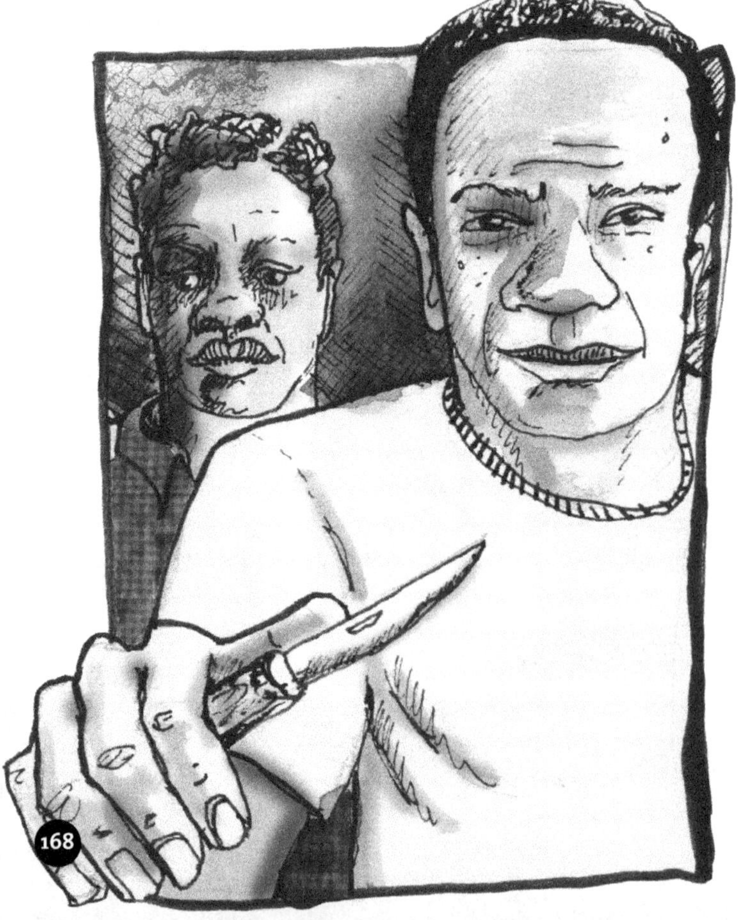

Black citizens of Detroit stopped trolleys to violently assault unsuspecting white passengers and conductors. They threw rocks at policemen who were called to stop the violence, which was growing and moving toward Beaubien Street. One white man, Paul Haaker, was stabbed in the chest. The first death occurred approximately an hour before the sun began to rise. John Bogan, a white man, was knocked unconscious by a Black rioter on Brush Street. He was left in the street and run over by a passing taxicab.

Many Black rioters vented their frustrations not on people but on property. By the time the sun rose in Paradise Valley, every store window lining Hastings Street was busted. At first there was no interest in looting, but by lunchtime people were filling their arms with food, clothing, and liquor. Nearly all of the stores were owned by white merchants who lived outside of Paradise Valley.

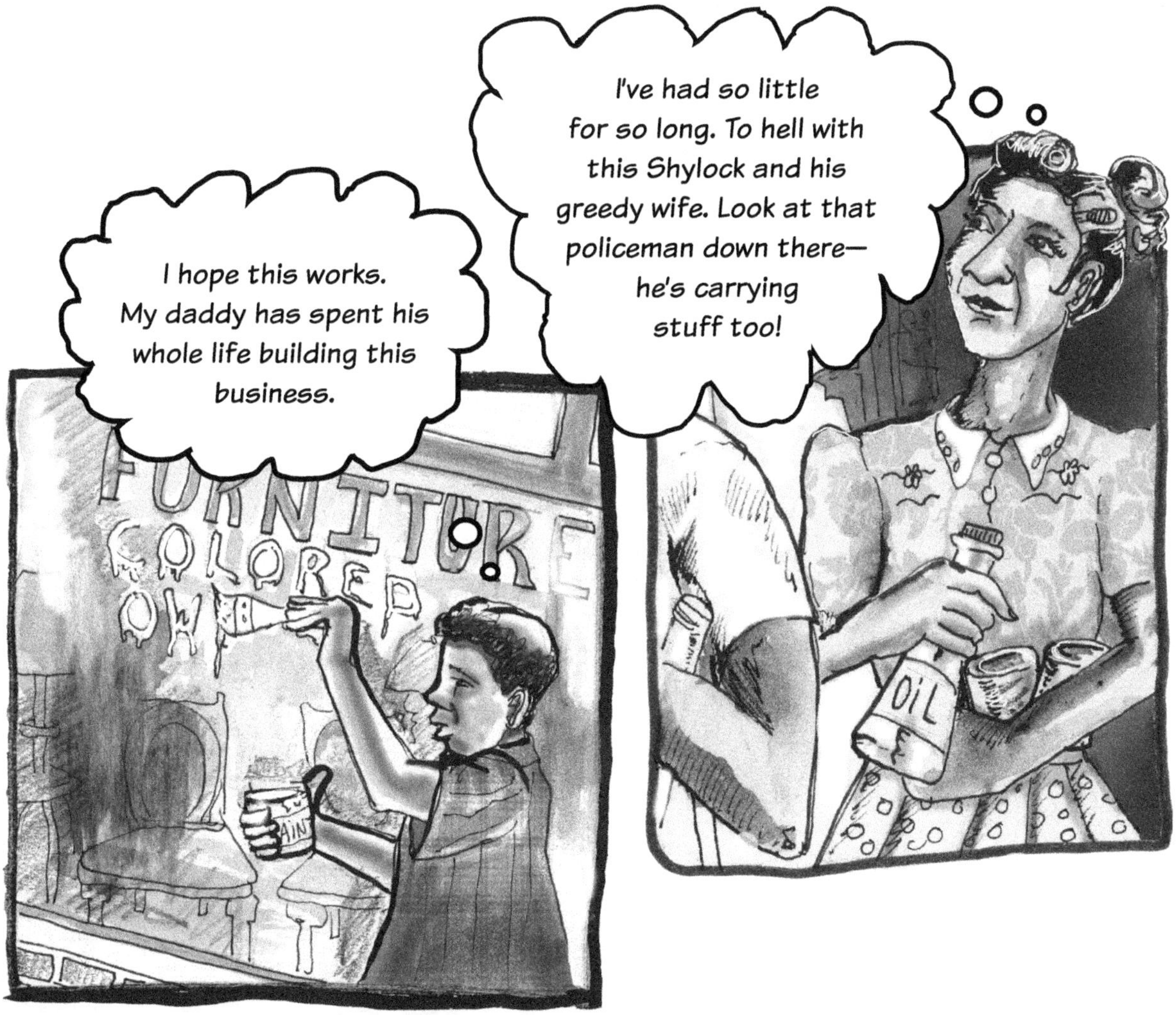
I hope this works. My daddy has spent his whole life building this business.
FURNITURE
COLORED
I've had so little for so long. To hell with this Shylock and his greedy wife. Look at that policeman down there—he's carrying stuff too!
OIL

Between the time the fighting broke out and the time that the city began to wake up, the police had shot several rioters—some in the back, most unarmed—trying to steal merchandise from vandalized shops. The Receiving Hospital had become overrun with people who were injured in the melee, and Detroit was entering into the full throes of a citywide emergency. Black people came to the chaos with knives and rocks; white police answered with guns. Paradise Valley was a war zone.

At 10 a.m., police who were patrolling Paradise Valley tried to divert traffic from Hastings Avenue. Dr. Joseph De Horatiis, a physician, was on his way to make a house call. He ignored their warnings.

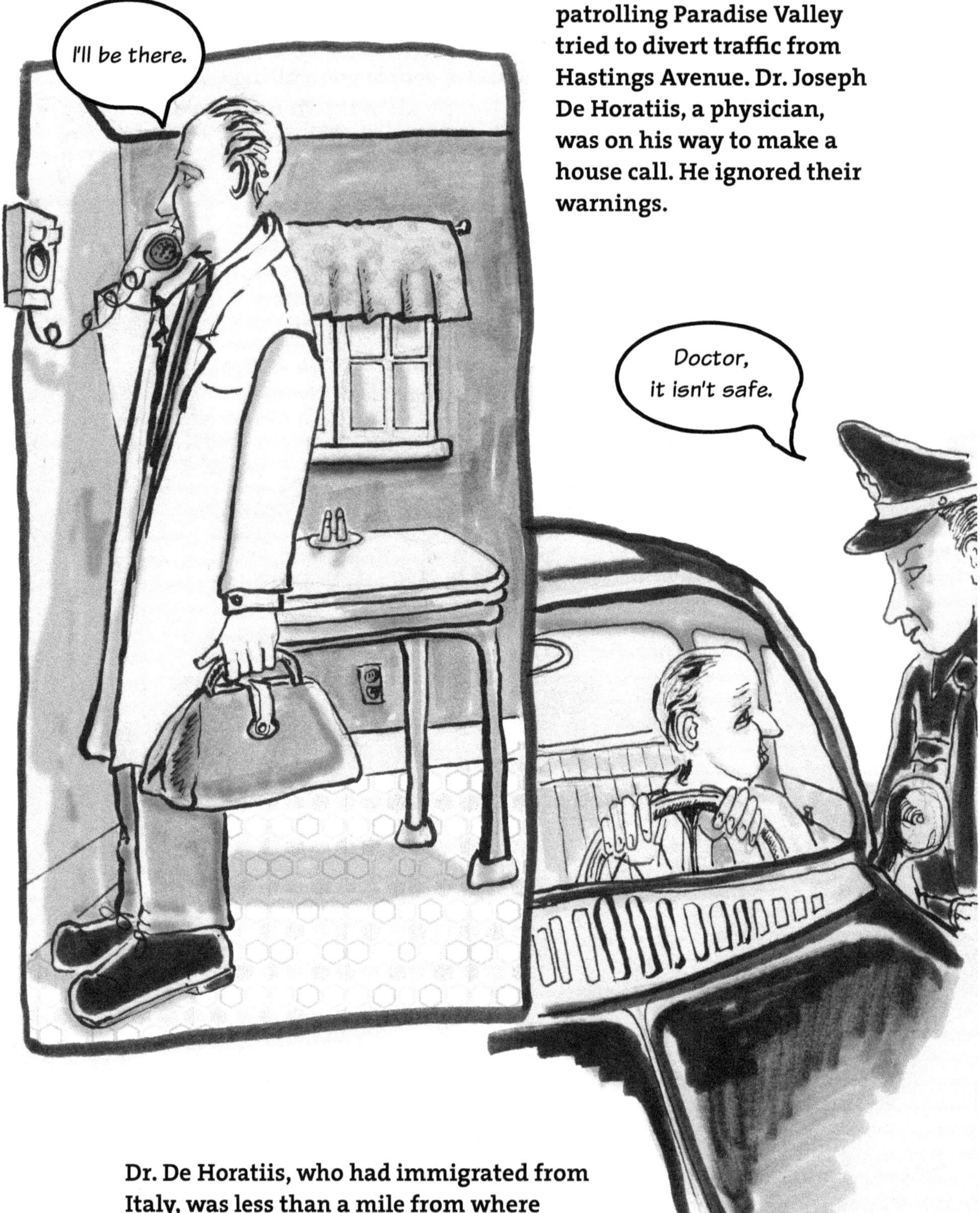
I'll be there.
Doctor, it isn't safe.

Dr. De Horatiis, who had immigrated from Italy, was less than a mile from where police had stopped him when he was fatally attacked. He was one of nine white people to die because of the violence.

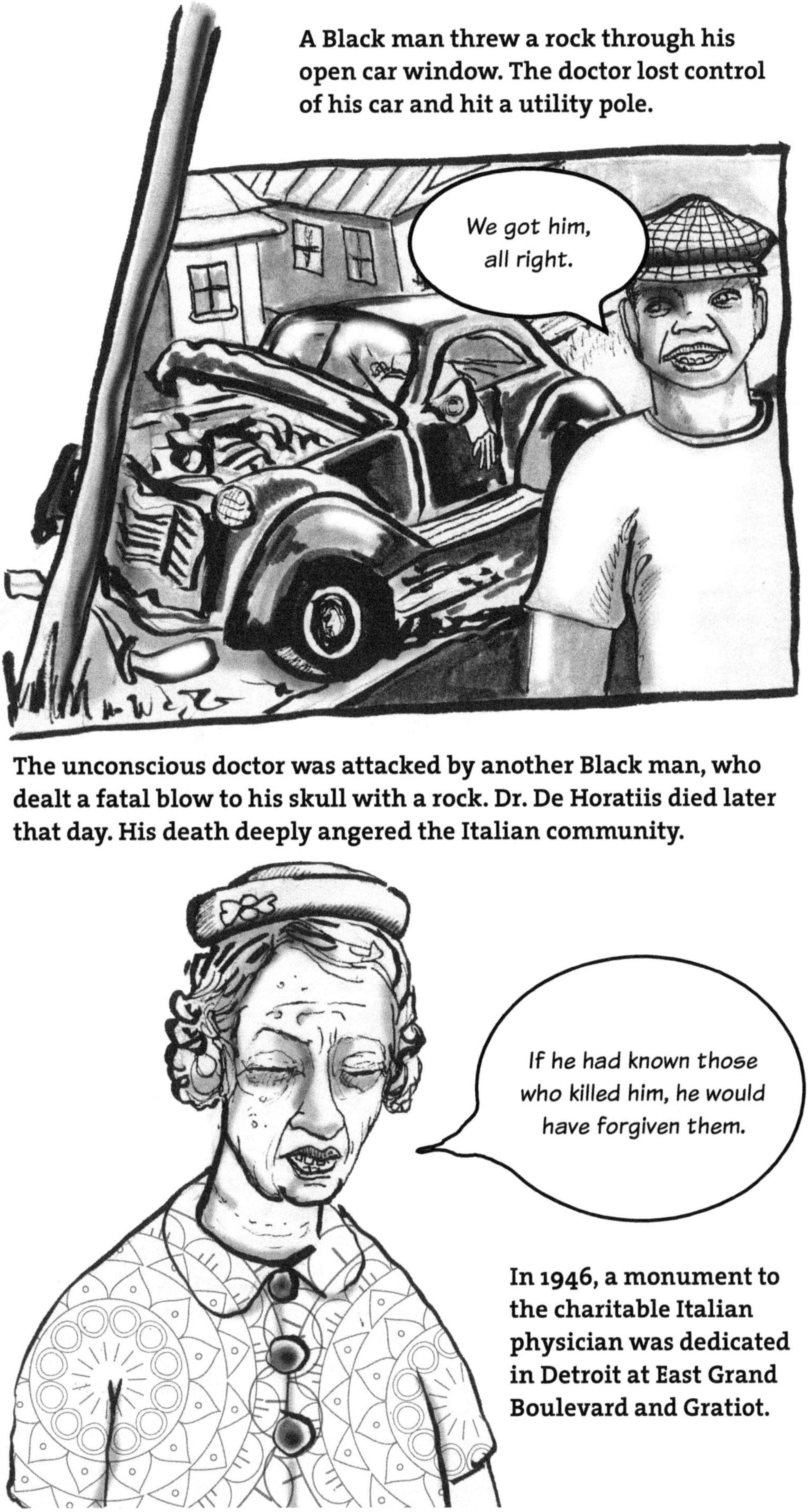
A Black man threw a rock through his open car window. The doctor lost control of his car and hit a utility pole.
We got him, all right.
The unconscious doctor was attacked by another Black man, who dealt a fatal blow to his skull with a rock. Dr. De Horatiis died later that day. His death deeply angered the Italian community.
If he had known those who killed him, he would have forgiven them.
In 1946, a monument to the charitable Italian physician was dedicated in Detroit at East Grand Boulevard and Gratiot.

Monday, June 21, 1943: Rumors fueled rage among different groups in the city; violence and unrest mounted. Many residents of the city, like Samuel Mitchell, had no idea that violence had erupted overnight. For them, it was another Monday morning. Like Dr. De Horatiis, they had a job to do.

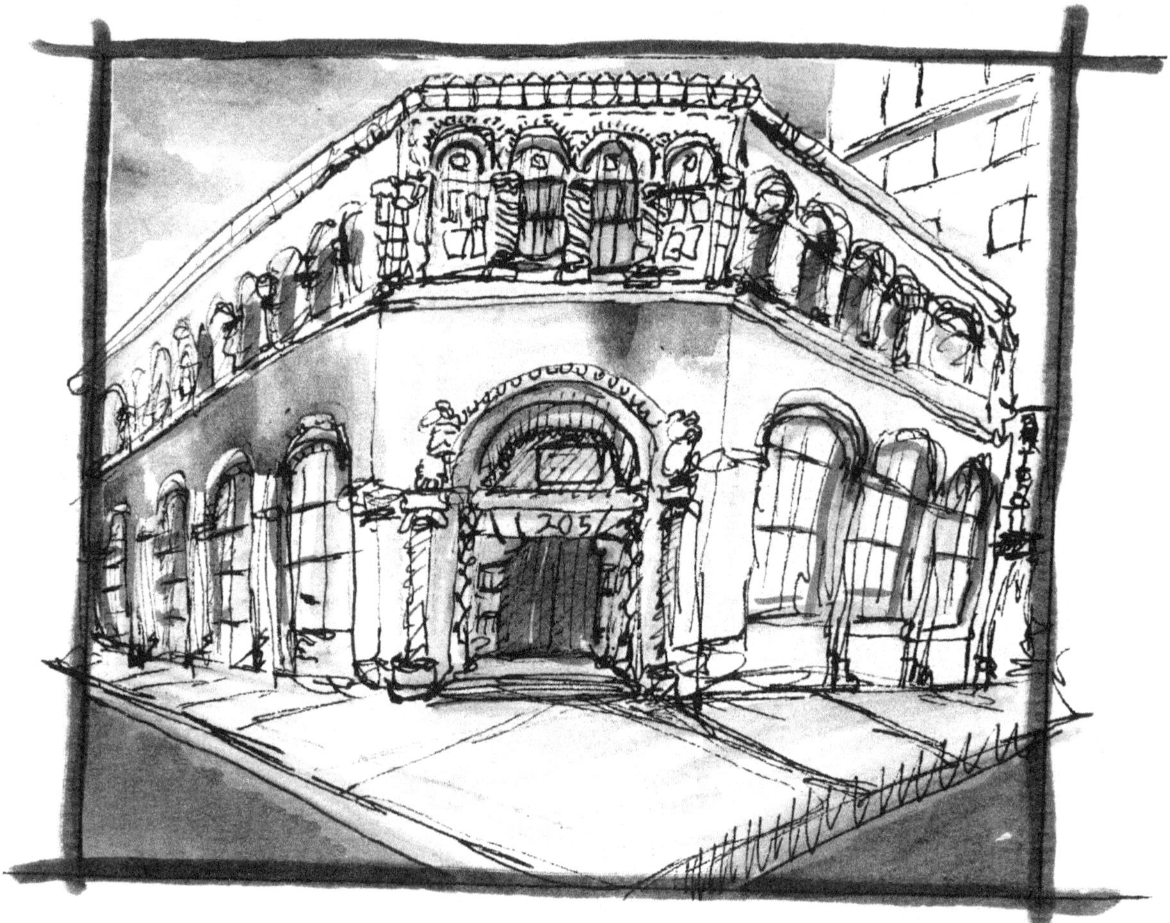
205

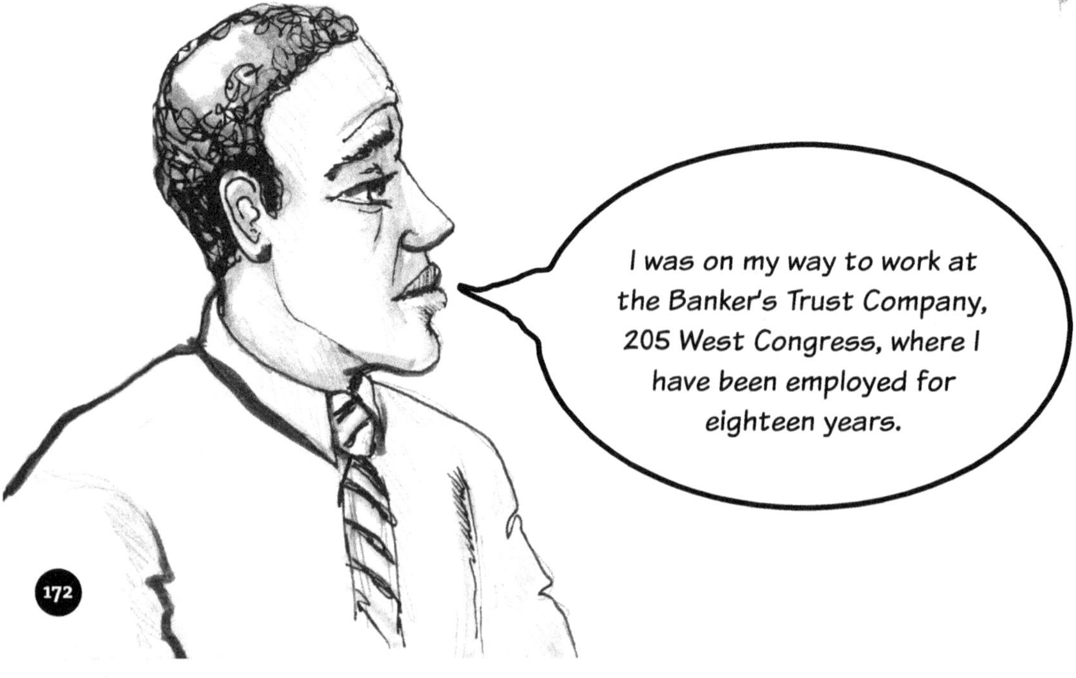
I was on my way to work at the Banker's Trust Company, 205 West Congress, where I have been employed for eighteen years.

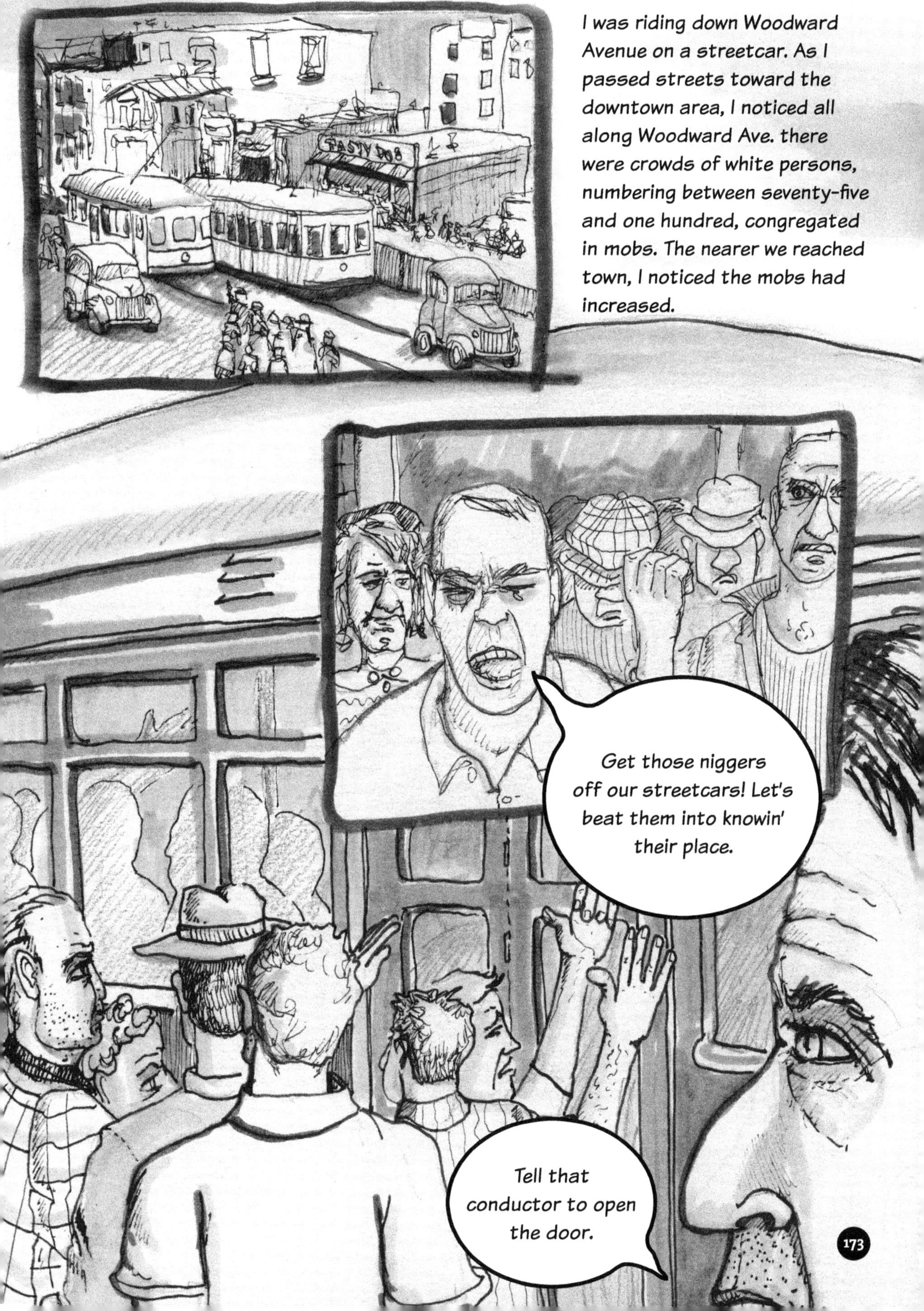
I was riding down Woodward Avenue on a streetcar. As I passed streets toward the downtown area, I noticed all along Woodward Ave. there were crowds of white persons, numbering between seventy-five and one hundred, congregated in mobs. The nearer we reached town, I noticed the mobs had increased.
TASTY DOG
Get those niggers off our streetcars! Let's beat them into knowin' their place.
Tell that conductor to open the door.

South of Eliot Street, the streetcar was forced to a complete standstill by a large mob of people in the street. The mob surrounded the car. Passengers began to move from their seats to the door of the streetcar.

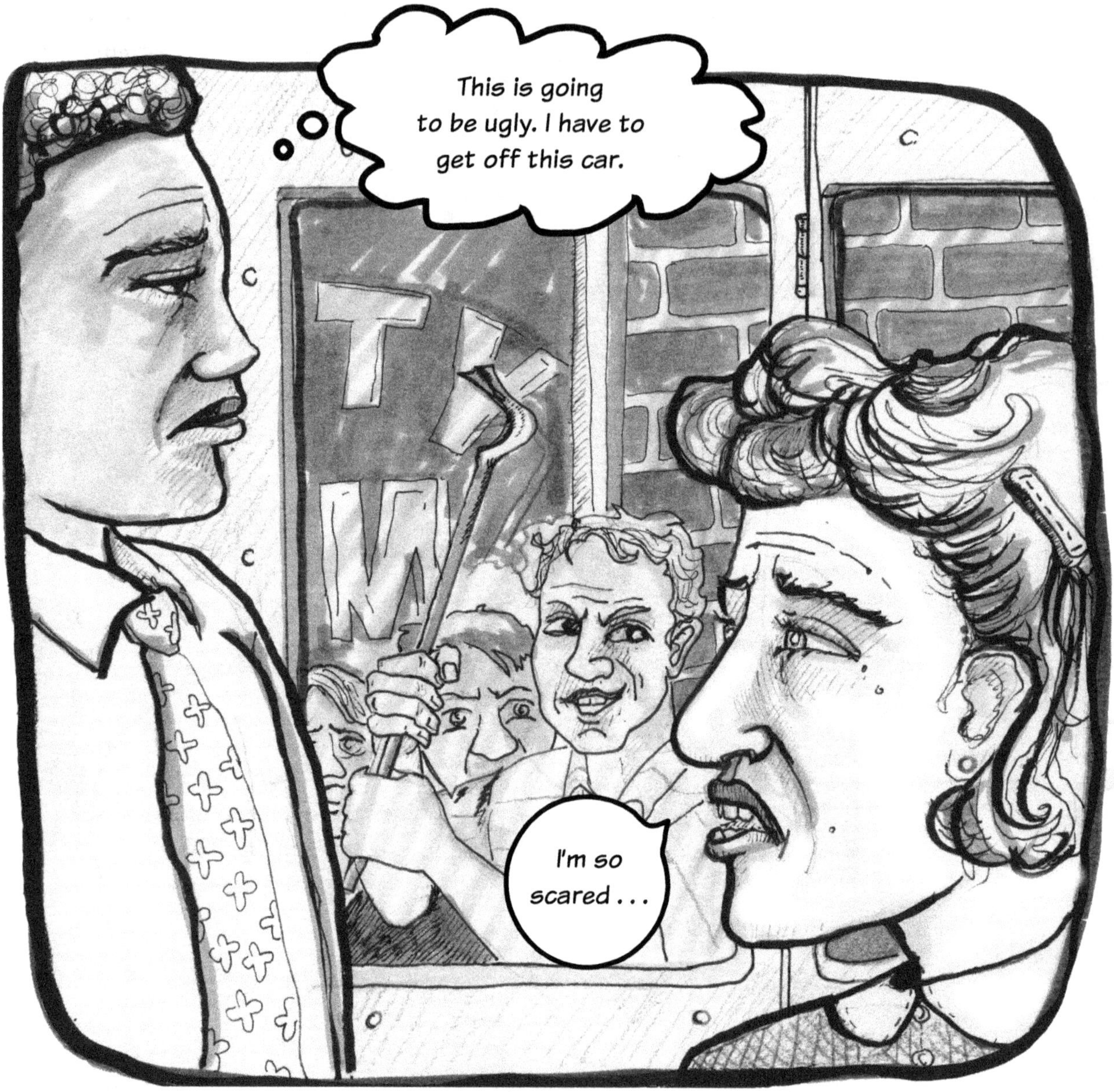
This is going to be ugly. I have to get off this car.
I'm so scared . . .

One man in the street had a crowbar. He smashed the front door of the car, and the mob began to surge into the car. The conductor, who is in the center of the streetcar, was asked by several members of the mob to open his door, but he refused.

I forced my way to the front of the crowd, to the front of the car, and managed to squeeze through the door to get to the street.

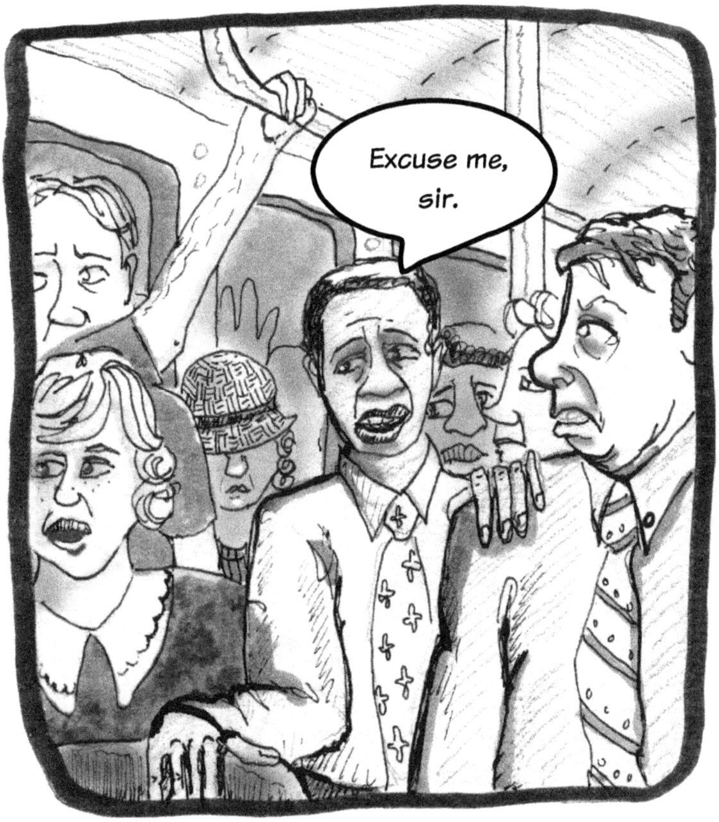
Excuse me, sir.

As I alighted from the streetcar, three gunshots were fired in the presence of several policemen who were at the scene. At this point someone hit the side of my body.

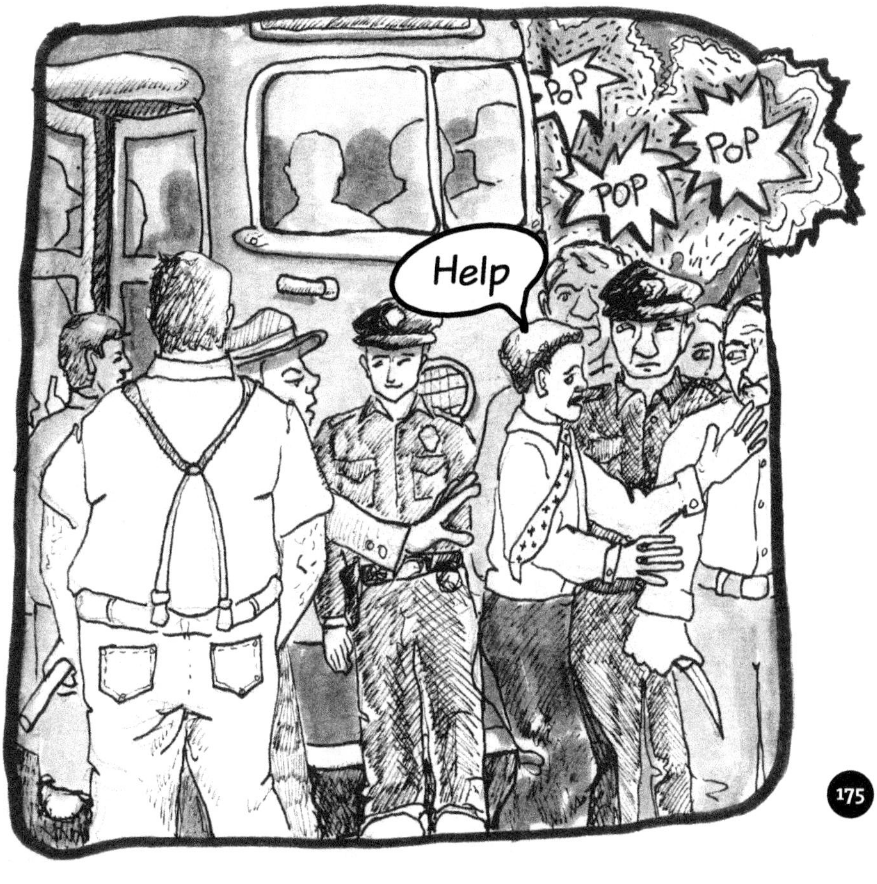
POP
POP
POP
Help

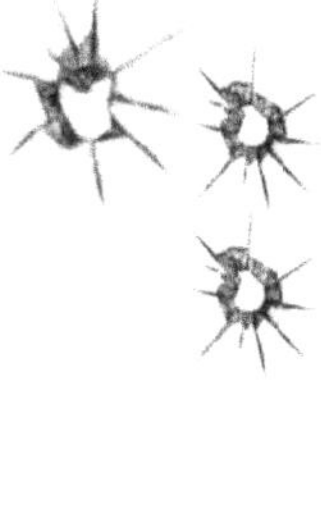

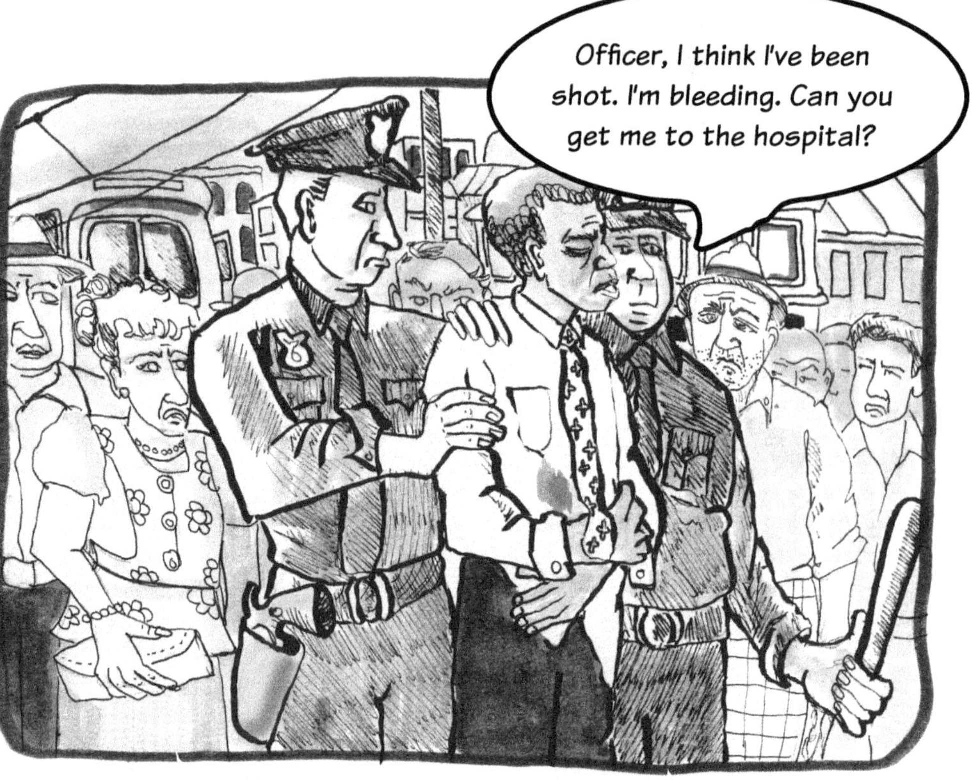
Officer, I think I've been shot. I'm bleeding. Can you get me to the hospital?

There were two mounted policemen at the scene of the beating. These officers saw men in the mob with pistols, but they made no attempt to disarm them. Two other officers walked up to the scene. Both of them grabbed me by the arms and held me up because I was so weak. About ten persons from the mob took turns beating me while officers held me by the arm.

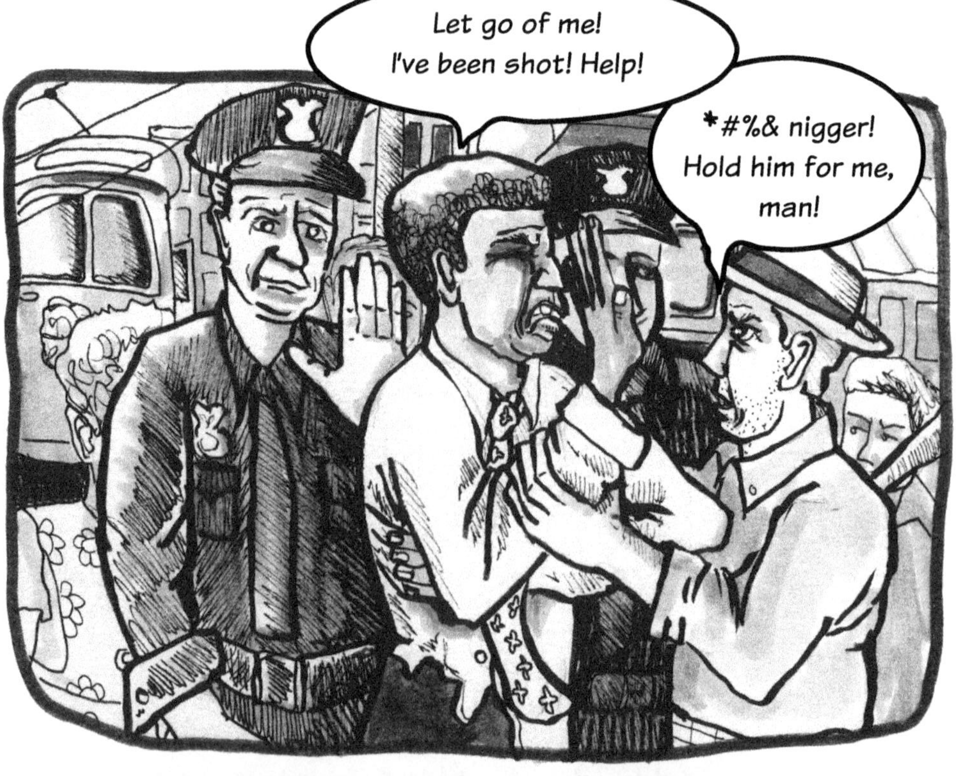
Let go of me! I've been shot! Help!
*#%& nigger! Hold him for me, man!

At this point, seeing that the policemen were not protecting me, I managed to free myself from their hold. I spied a scout car not far from where I was standing. I ran to the scout car.

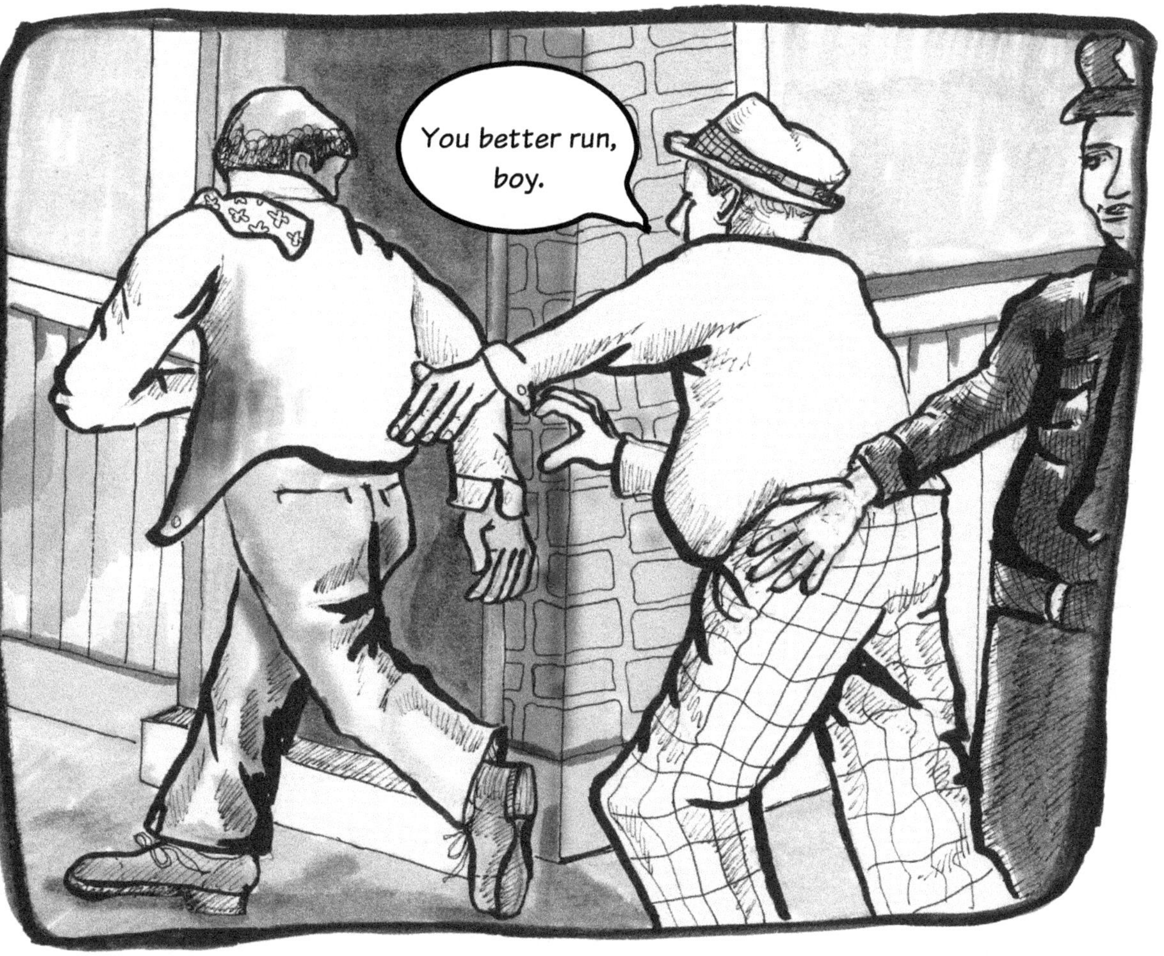
You better run, boy.

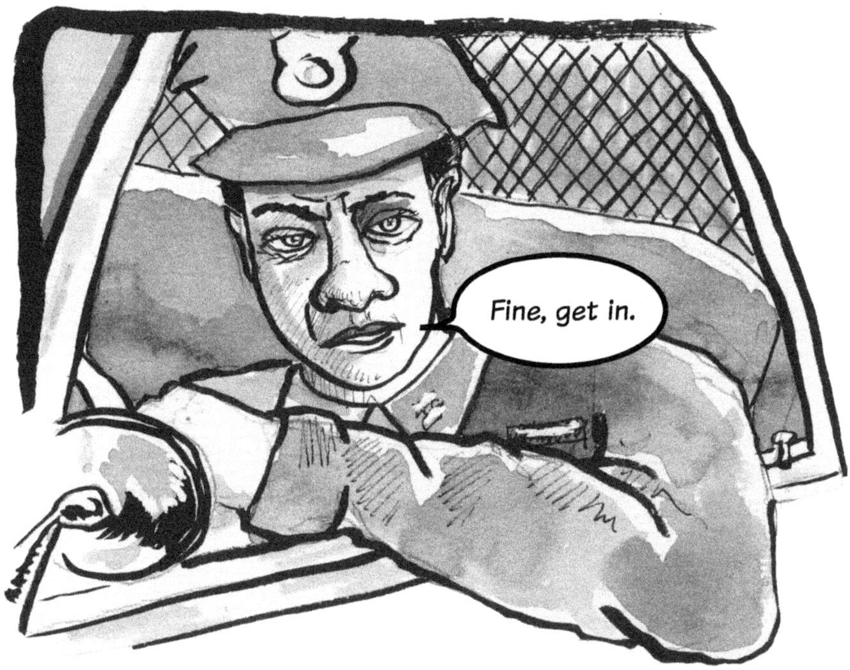
Fine, get in.

I ran to the scout car not far from where I was standing. I asked the officer behind the wheel to take me to the hospital because I had been injured. This officer drove me to the Receiving Hospital. The officer did not ask my name or other particulars.

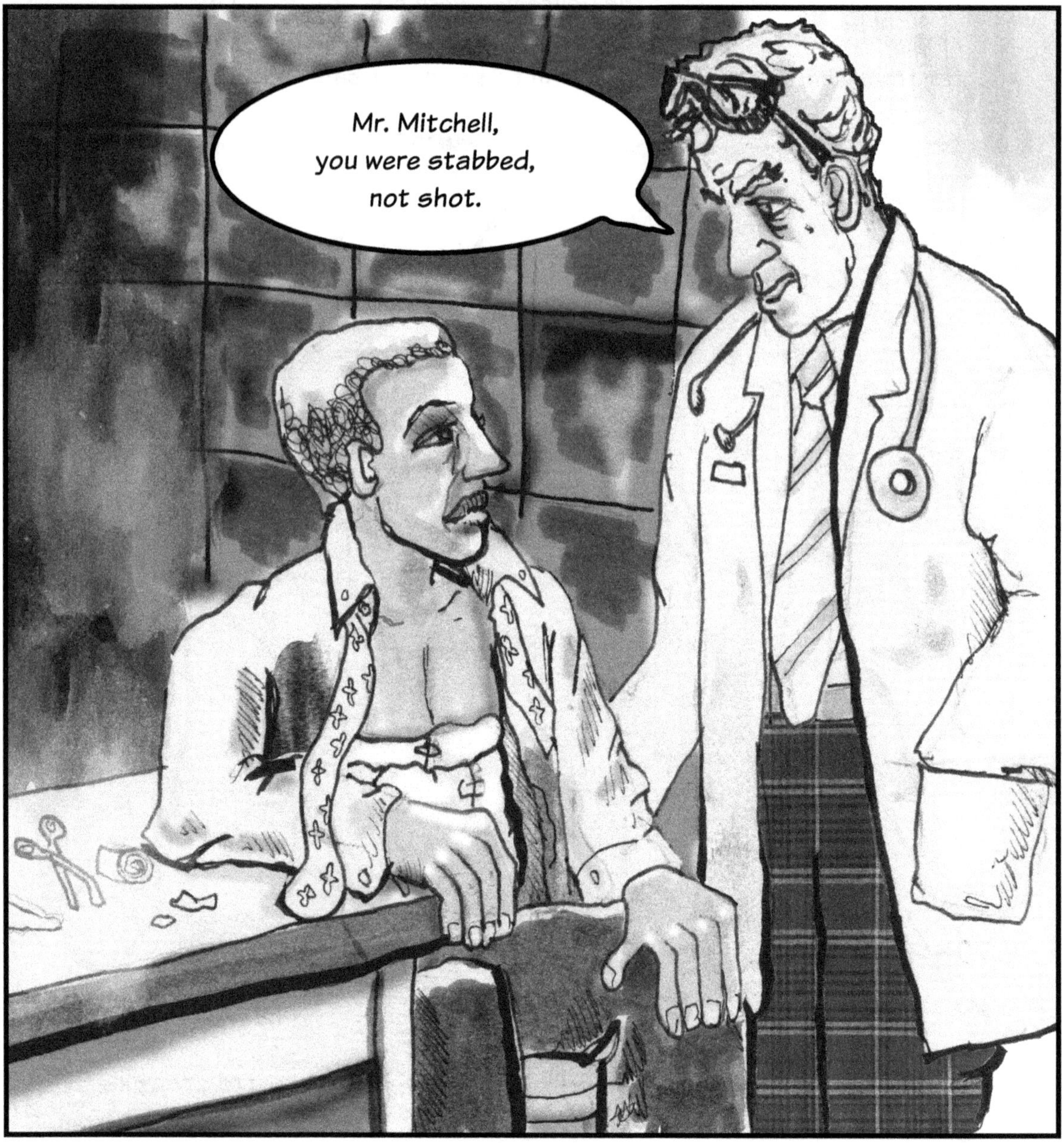
Mr. Mitchell, you were stabbed, not shot.

At the Receiving Hospital I was examined thoroughly.

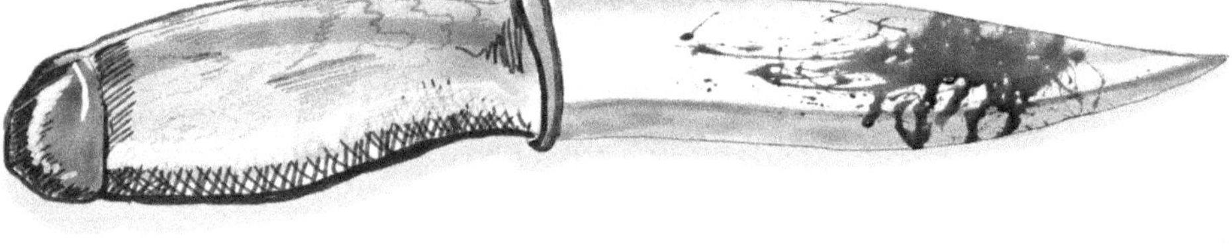

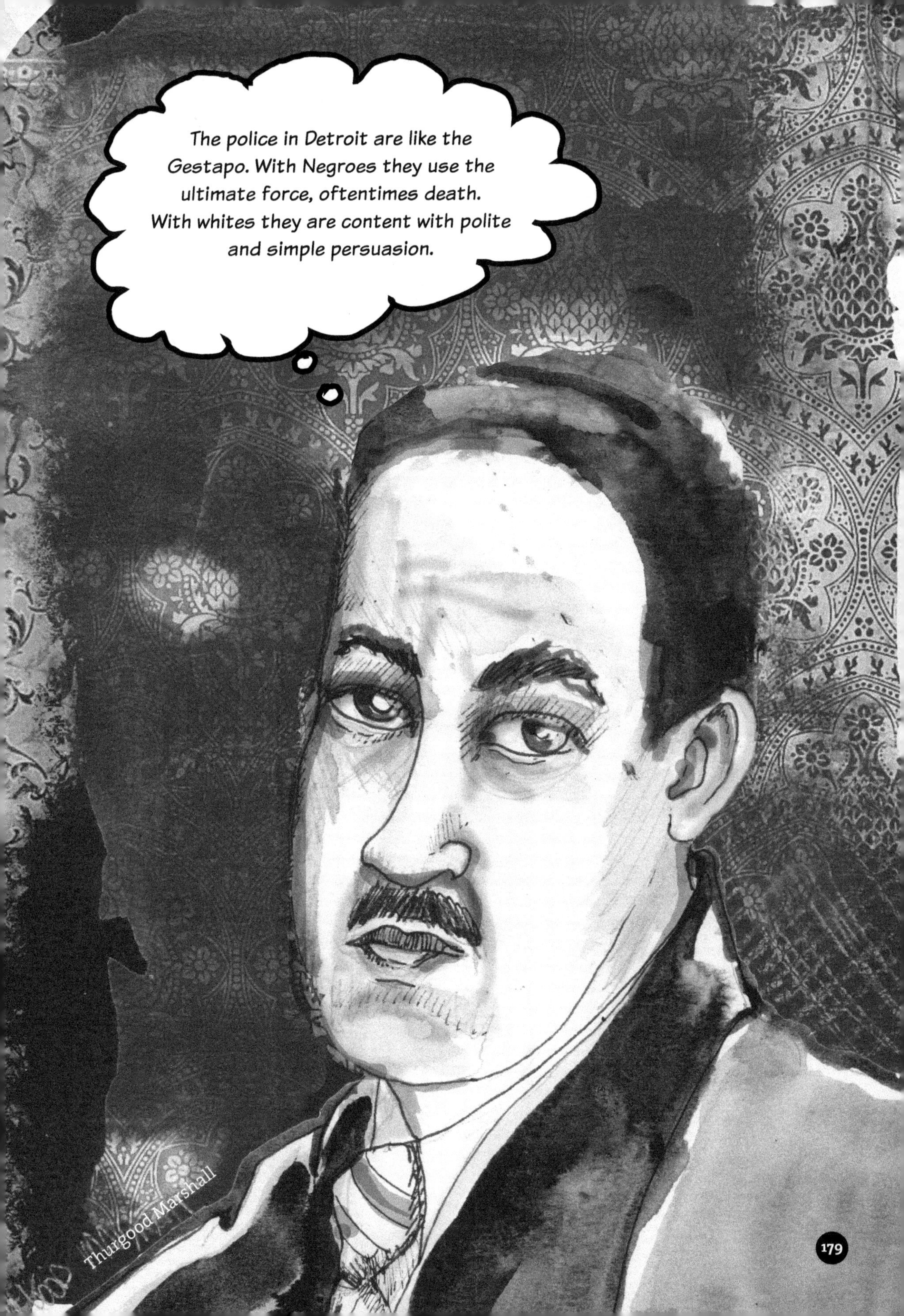
The police in Detroit are like the Gestapo. With Negroes they use the ultimate force, oftentimes death. With whites they are content with polite and simple persuasion.
Thurgood Marshall

Violence broke out in pockets throughout the city as the summer heat began to simmer. John Lewis, a soldier, and Susie Mae Ransom, a homemaker, became victims of police brutality.

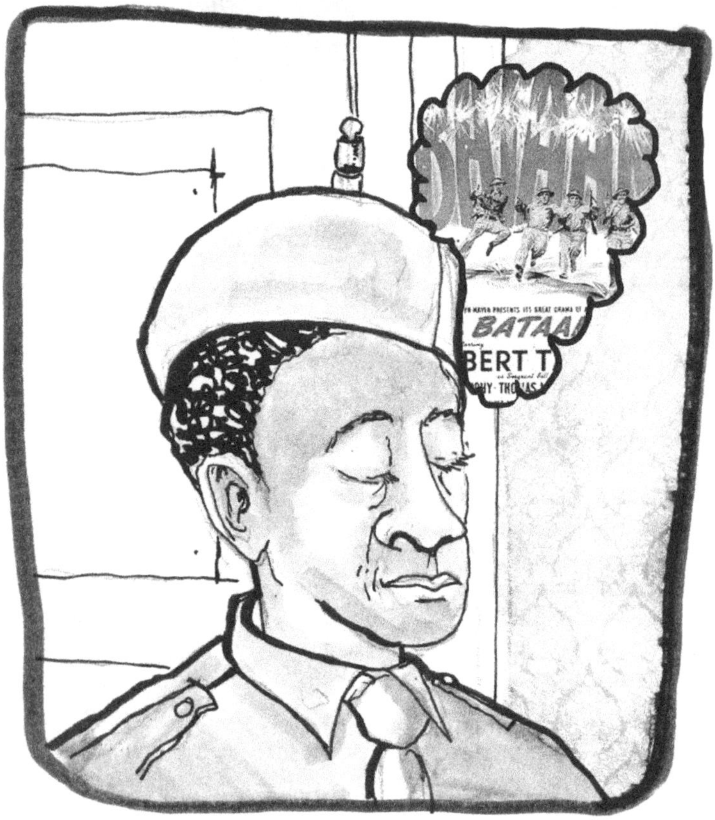

On Monday morning, June 21, I left my home at eleven a.m. to go to a theatre. I was fully dressed in my army uniform.

As I walked through Brush Street to the corner of Brewster, I saw a number of officers dispersing a crowd of people. I kept right on walking.

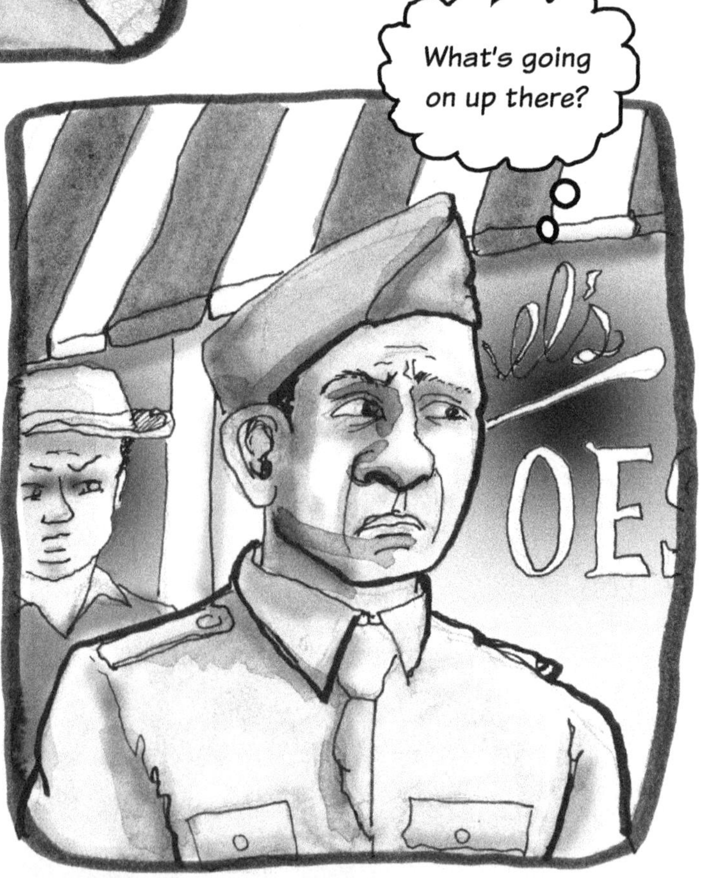
What's going on up there?

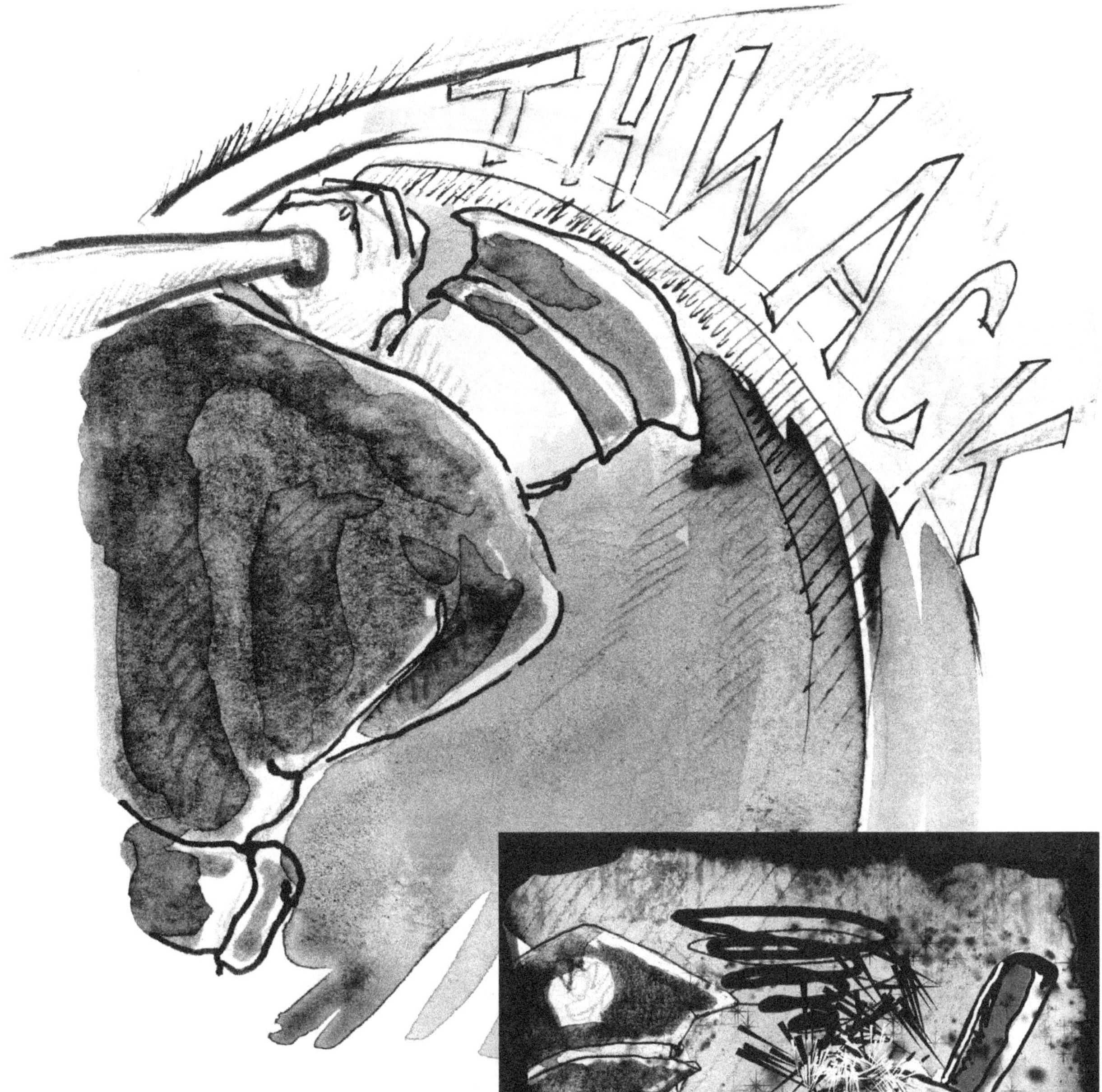
THWACK

As I reached the corner, I was grabbed from behind by an officer. I was struck over the head with a blunt instrument of some kind. My head was split, and I was dazed and fell to the street.

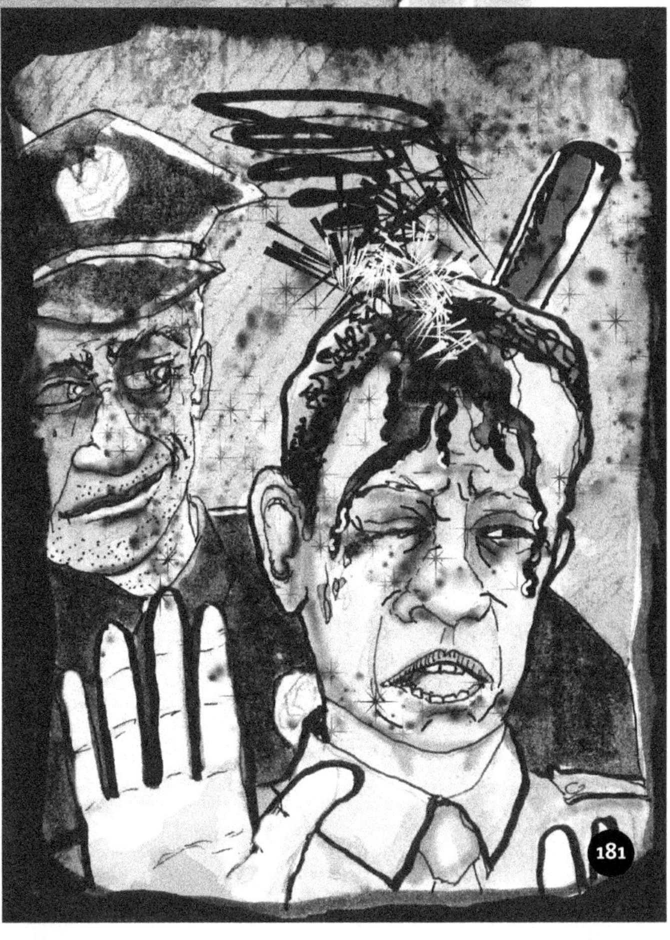

Susie Mae Ransom lived with her family at 2930 Brush Street, Apartment 18. She saw what happened to John Lewis when she stepped outside to watch her eleven-year-old daughter play.

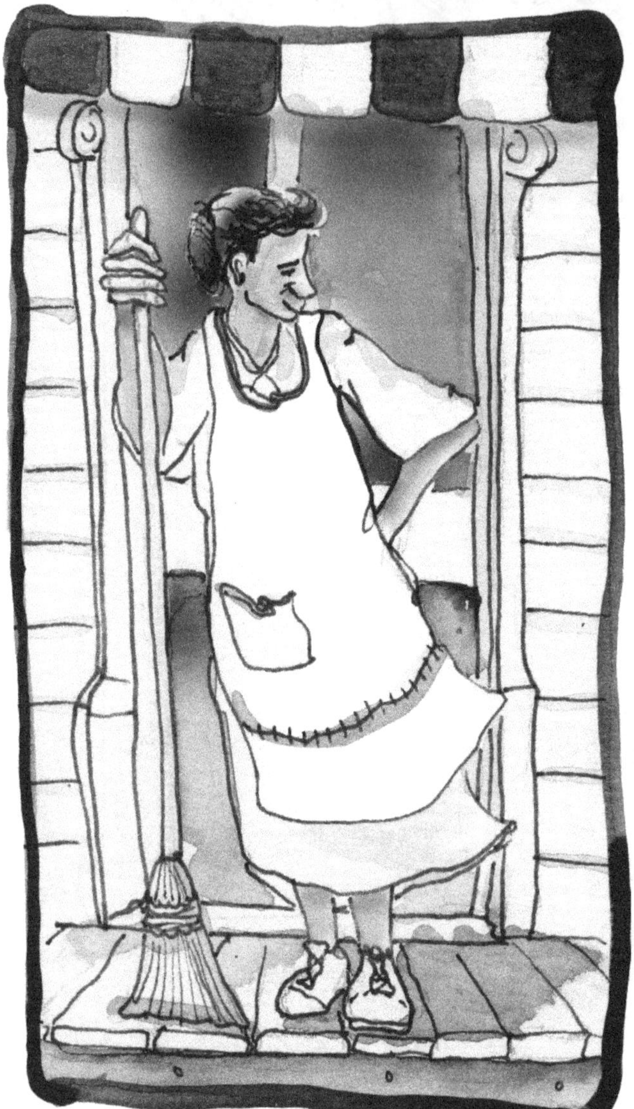

I saw a crowd collected at Brewster, Edmund and Alfred Streets which [was] comprised of both white and colored people. They were gathered on the corners with battles raging from time to time between the two masses of people.

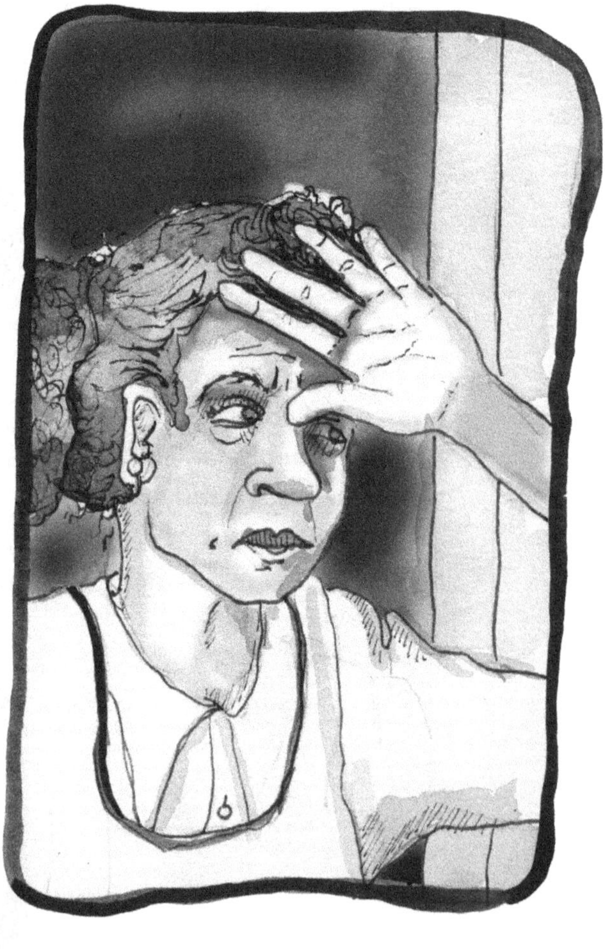

After the police had cleared the corner of these people [they] were standing around to see that nothing happened. I saw from my stoop a colored soldier walking up the street in full uniform attending his own business . . .

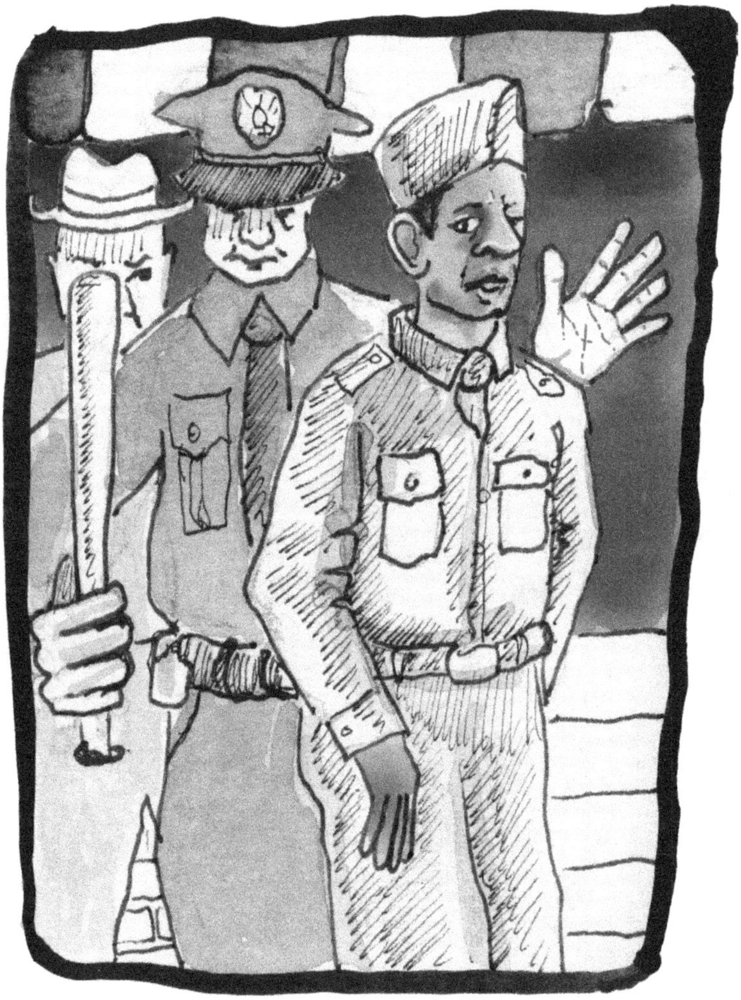

... when suddenly a police officer grabbed him from behind and struck him in the head with something, leaving this man bleeding profusely in the street. The officers made no attempt to see how badly this man was wounded or to give any aid. They passed on about their business.

I returned to my apartment, secured some cold towels, and rushed down the street ...

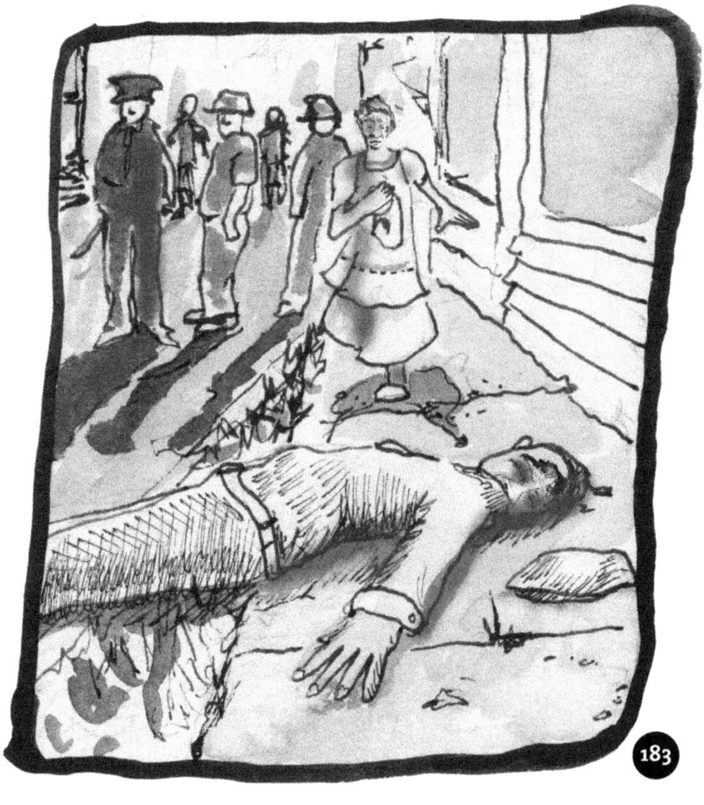

Despite the real possibility of more violence by police, Susie Mae Ransom bravely intervened.

. . . where I bound this man's head and tried to stop the blood. The man seemingly so badly wounded, I felt it advisable to get him to the hospital as quickly as possible and stood with him trying to wave some automobiles as they passed to get someone to take him to the hospital.

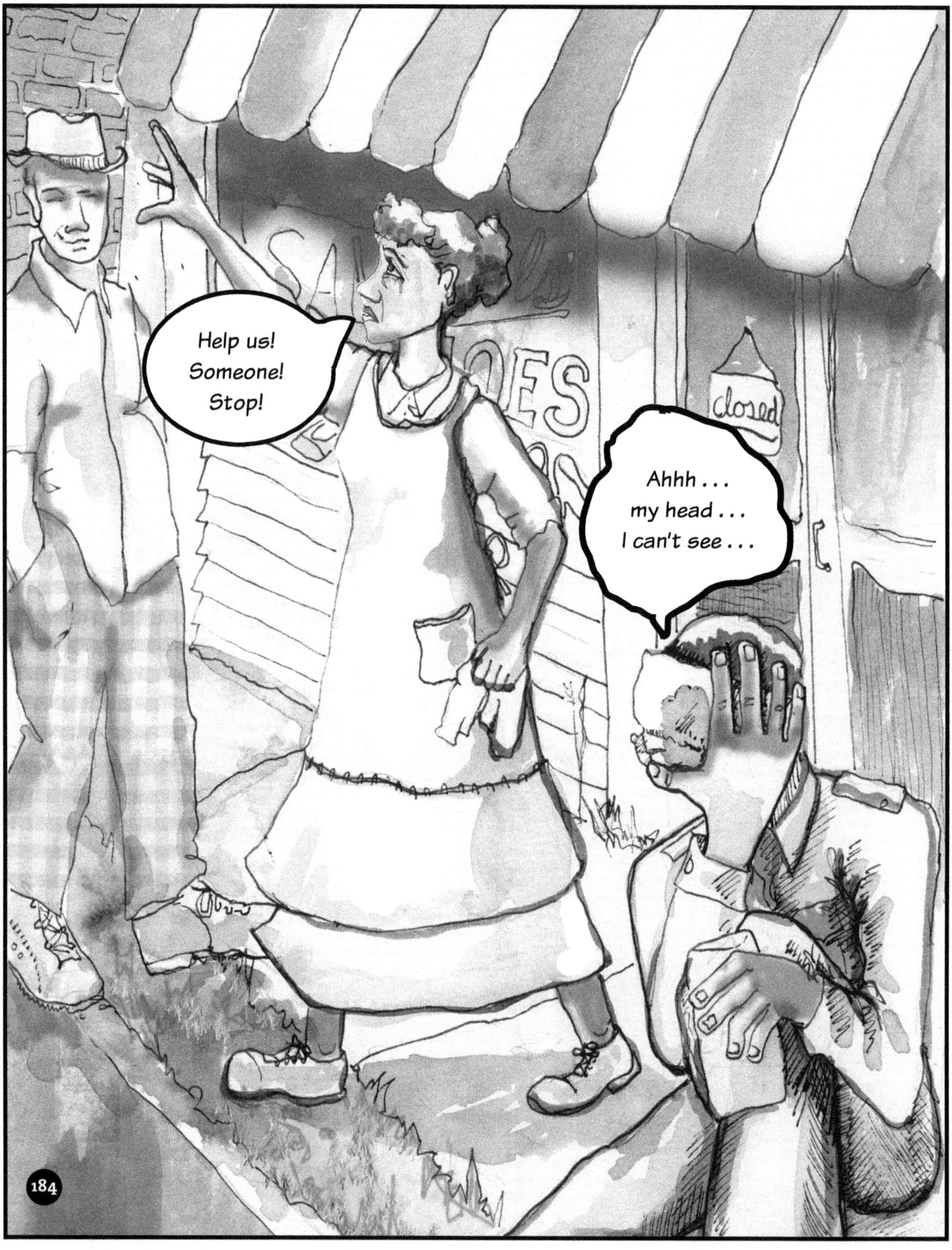
Help us! Someone! Stop!
Ahhh . . . my head . . . I can't see . . .
closed

Later, two letter carriers driving in a private car came along, and at my solicitations assisted this man into a car and took him to the hospital. Afterward, I learned that they had carried him to the Parkside Hospital.

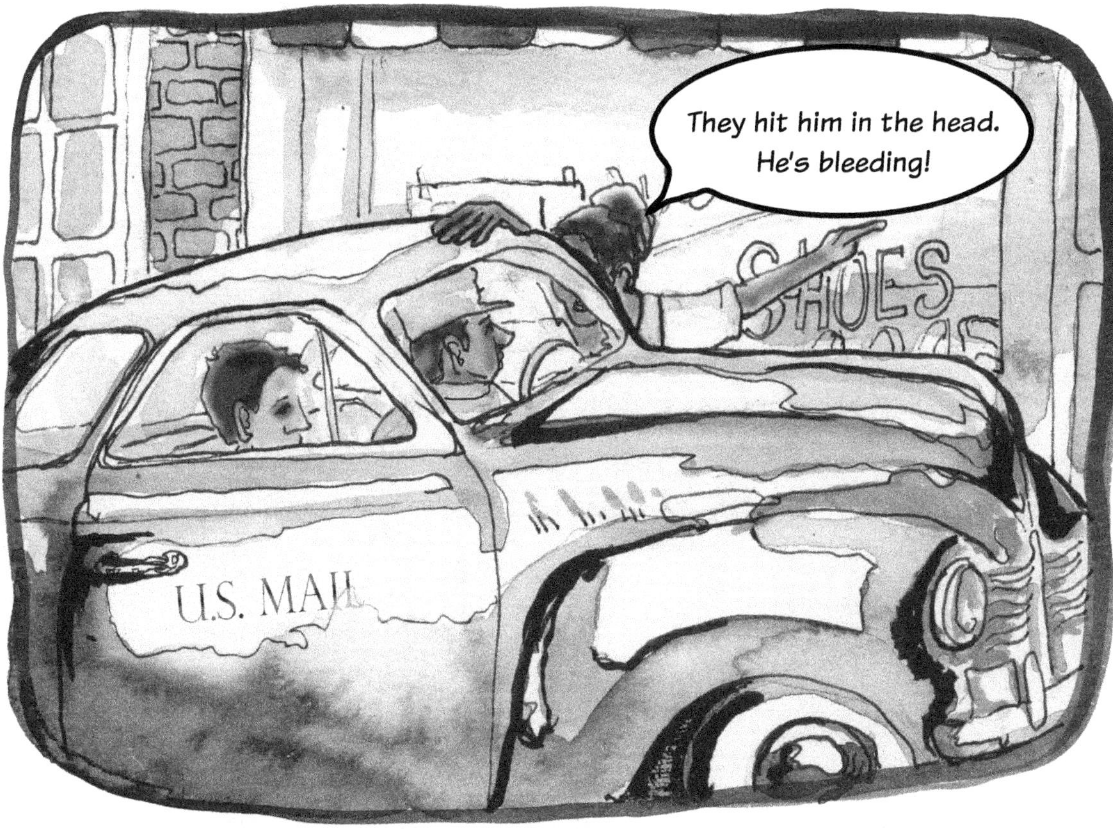
They hit him in the head. He's bleeding!
SHOES
U.S. MAIL

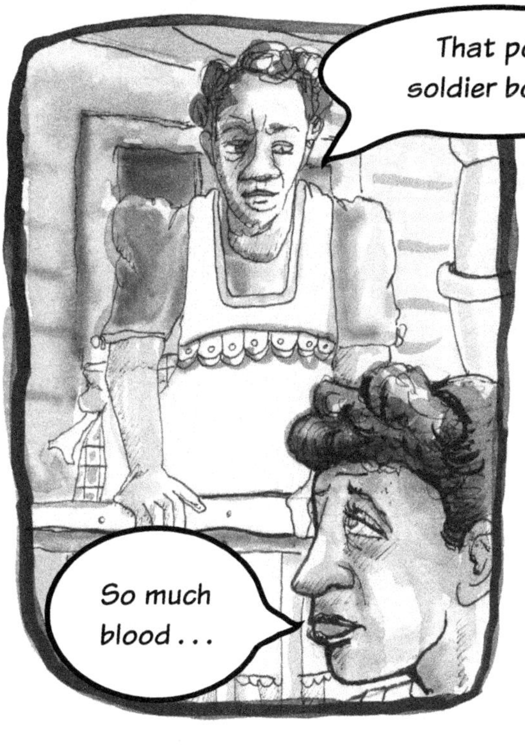
That poor soldier boy . . .
So much blood . . .

I returned to my apartment, where the neighbors and I sat around discussing the affair, when suddenly. . . .

. . . a number of policemen came up the street in automobiles, stopped the car, and began to shoot at the house where we were sitting from across the street.

We hurried into the building . . .

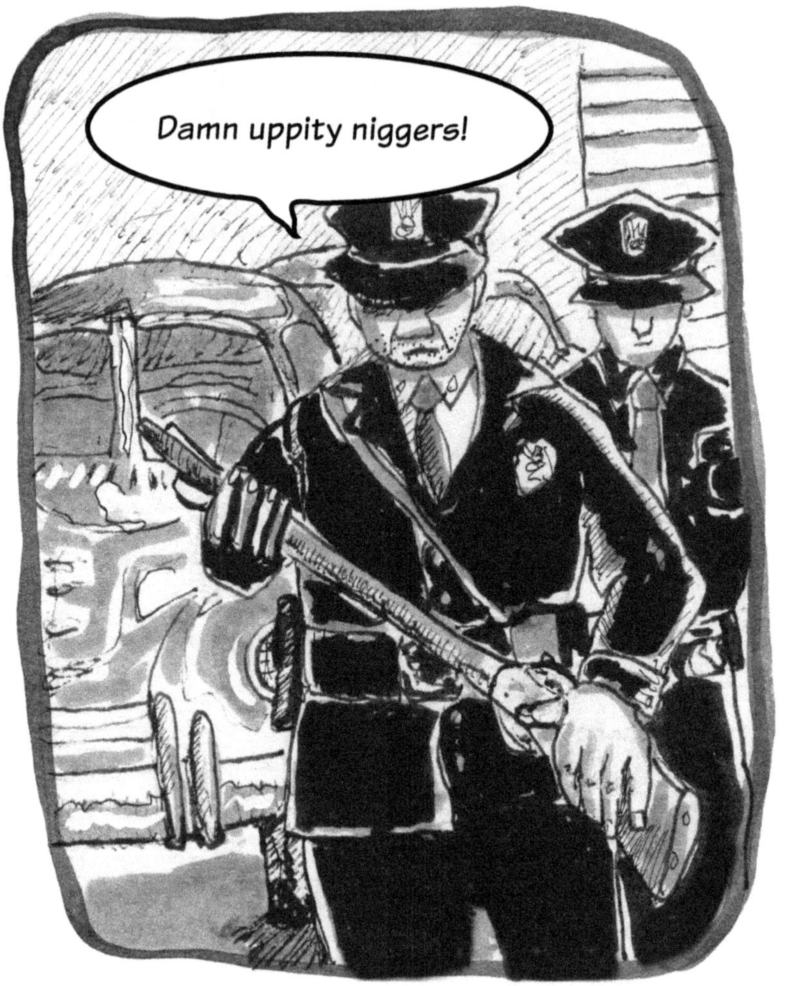
Damn uppity niggers!

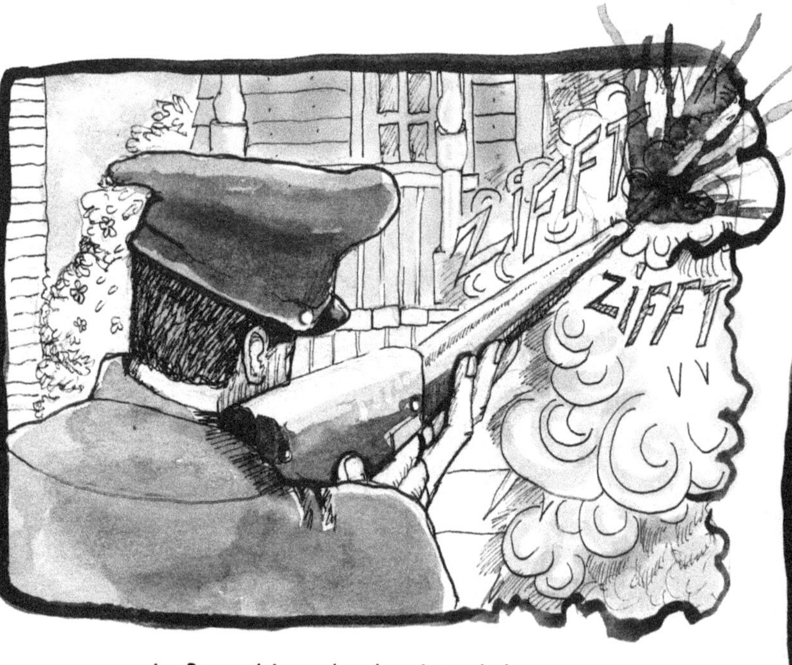
ZIFFT
ZIFFT

. . . and fortunately no one was hit, but the bullets spatted the front of the house . . .

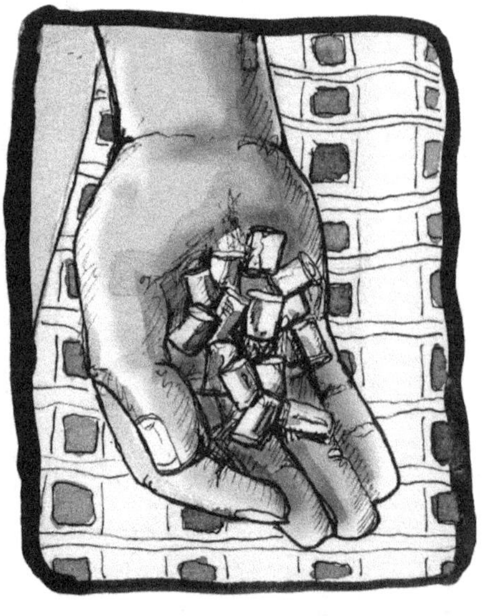

. . . and after things had quieted down we were able to pick up the shells.

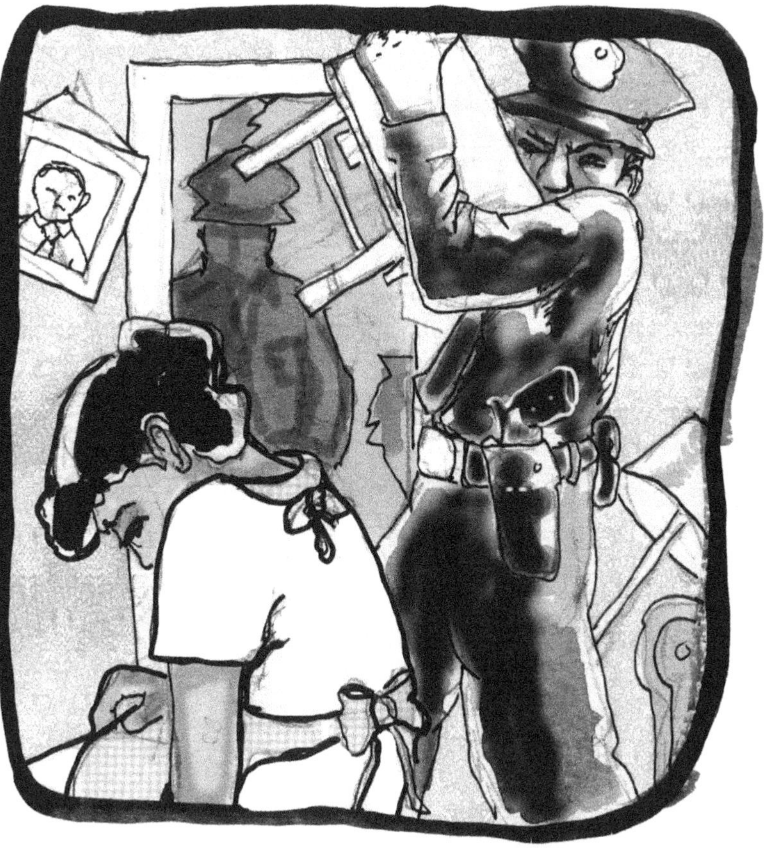

Everything was quiet at our house from then on, until Sunday, June 27, about 3 p.m. two city policemen with rifles and three plainclothes men came into my apartment without making any announcement and began to search the place and break up my furniture. They threw things into a general disorder.

My husband, who is a cripple, was lying on the bed while they turned the bed over. They pulled out the springs and broke the bottom of the bed. After searching the place thoroughly they saw a box of cigars and some chewing tobacco which belonged to my husband. They also took some chewing gum with them which was on the shelf.

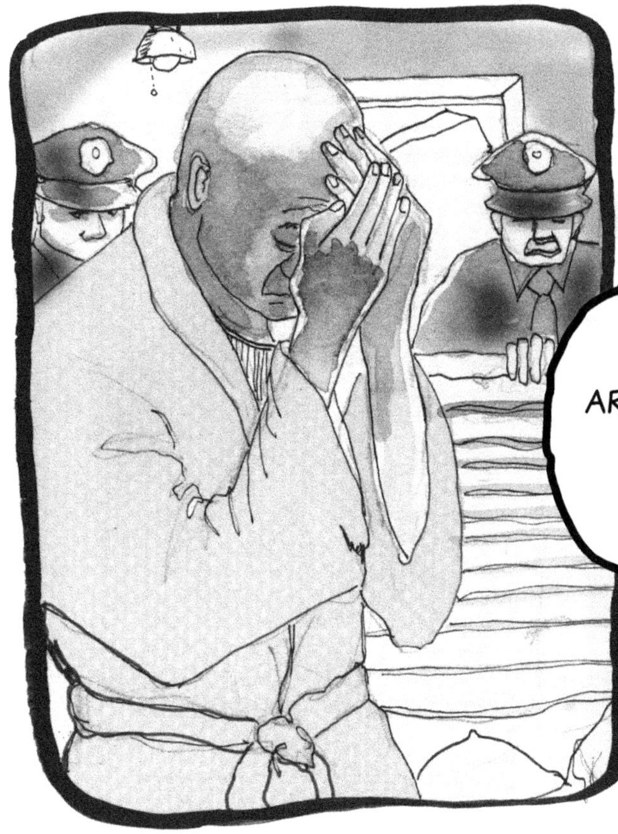

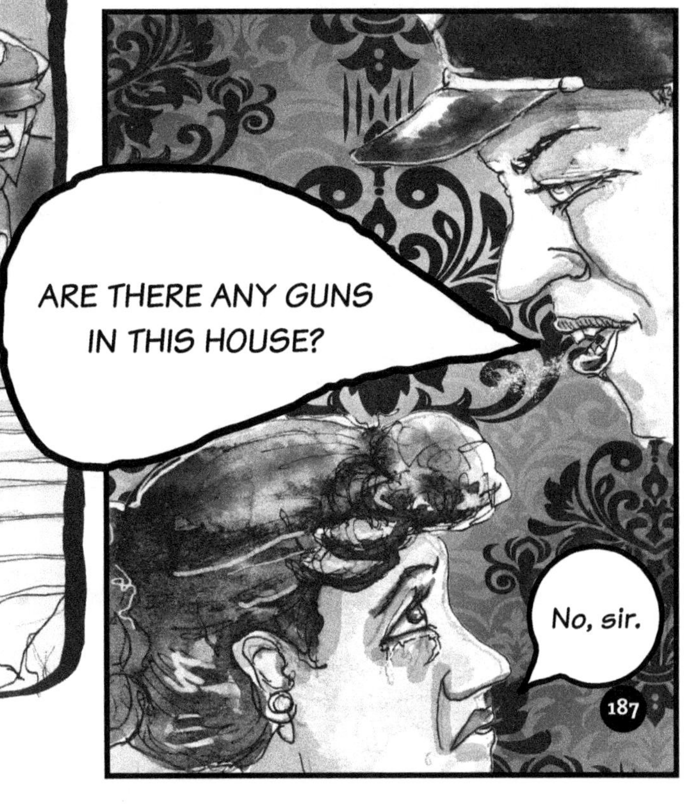
ARE THERE ANY GUNS IN THIS HOUSE?
No, sir.

All day on June 21, violence continued to spread throughout the city. Many residents tried to avoid the chaos, but like Ransom and Lewis, Mrs. Mateel Forniss was swept up in it because she was Black.

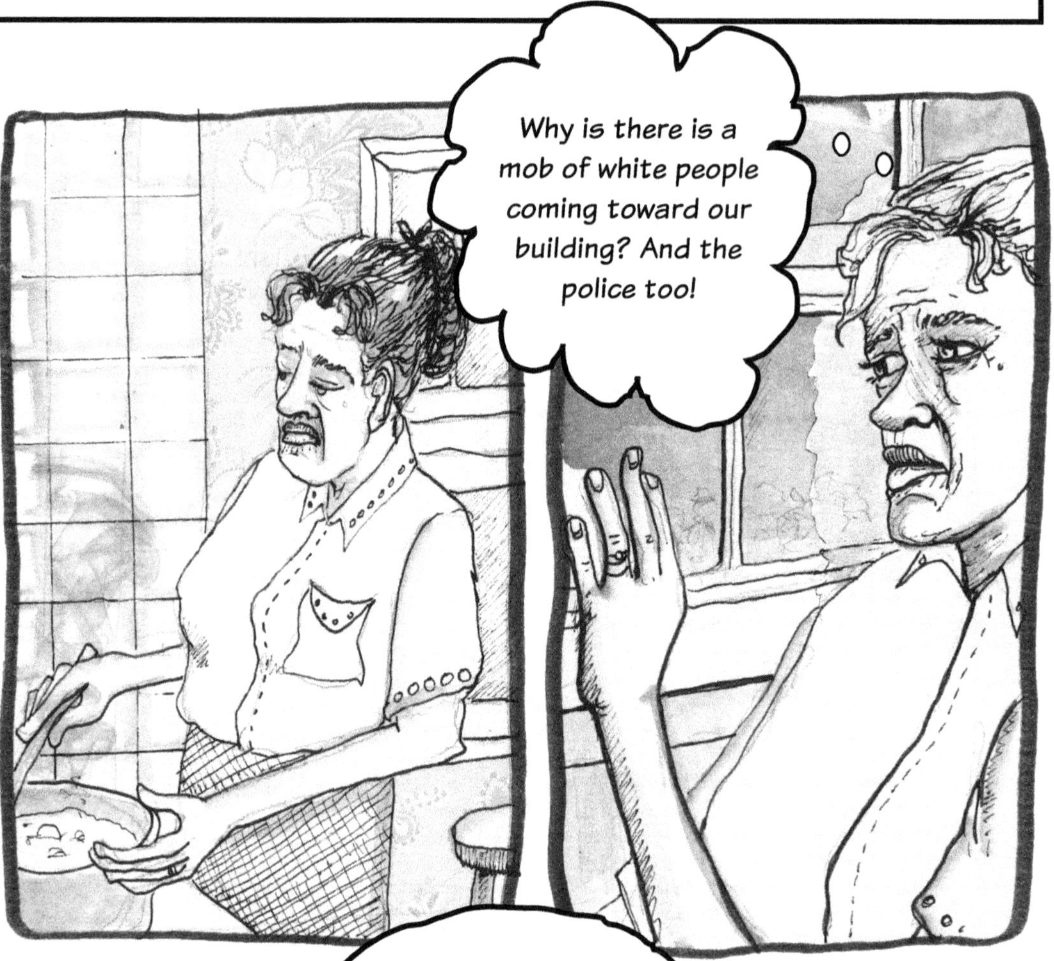
Why is there is a mob of white people coming toward our building? And the police too!

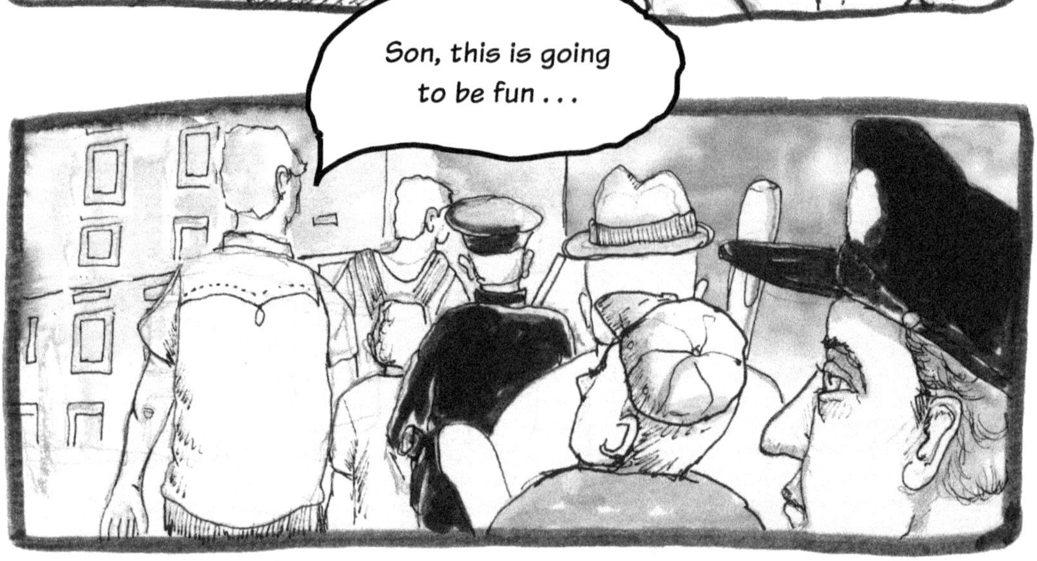
Son, this is going to be fun . . .

On Monday, June 21, I was cooking dinner for my husband during which time I heard some noise outside my window.

Officers passed through the white mob and came toward the Vernor Apartments. About this time I saw a policeman fall to the ground.

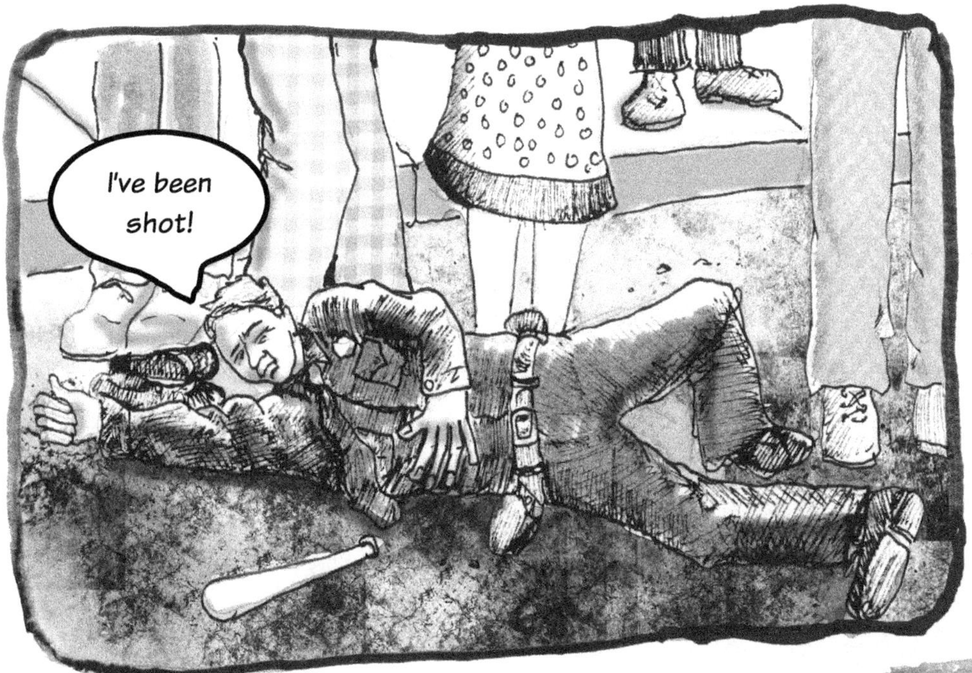
I've been shot!

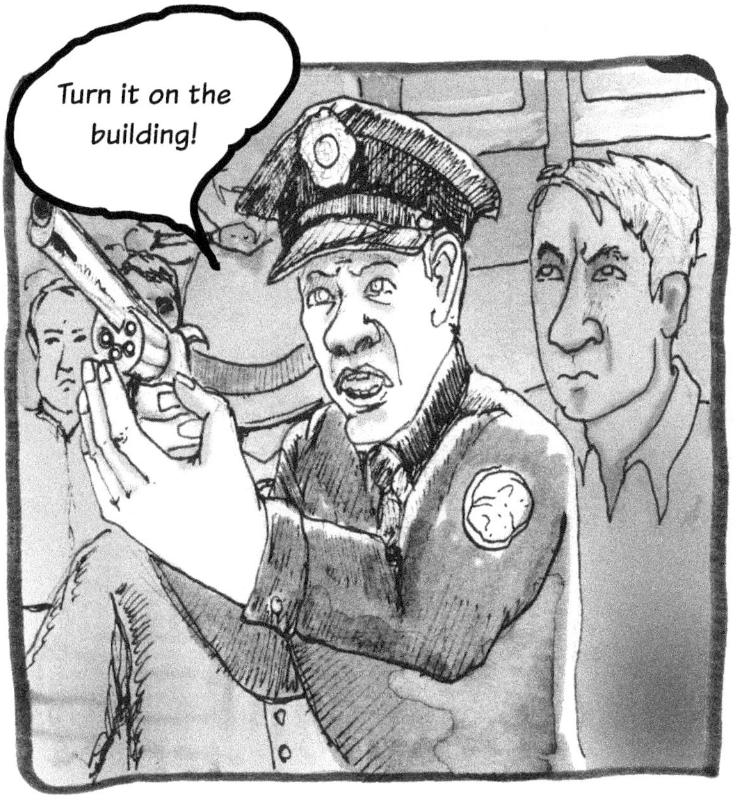
Turn it on the building!

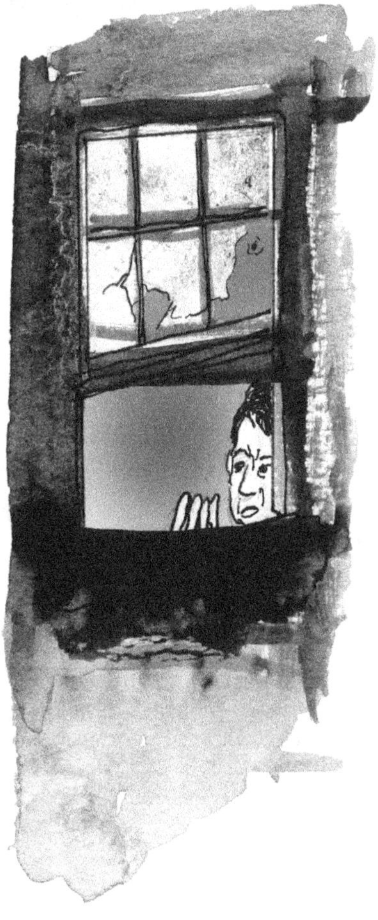

At this time bullets began to ring out through the Vernor Apartment windows.

I became frightened and rushed out of my apartment, locking my door, [and] ran into the hall to seek safety. At this point the police began coming into the building, yelling as they came, "Come out, you damn niggers, with your hands in the air."

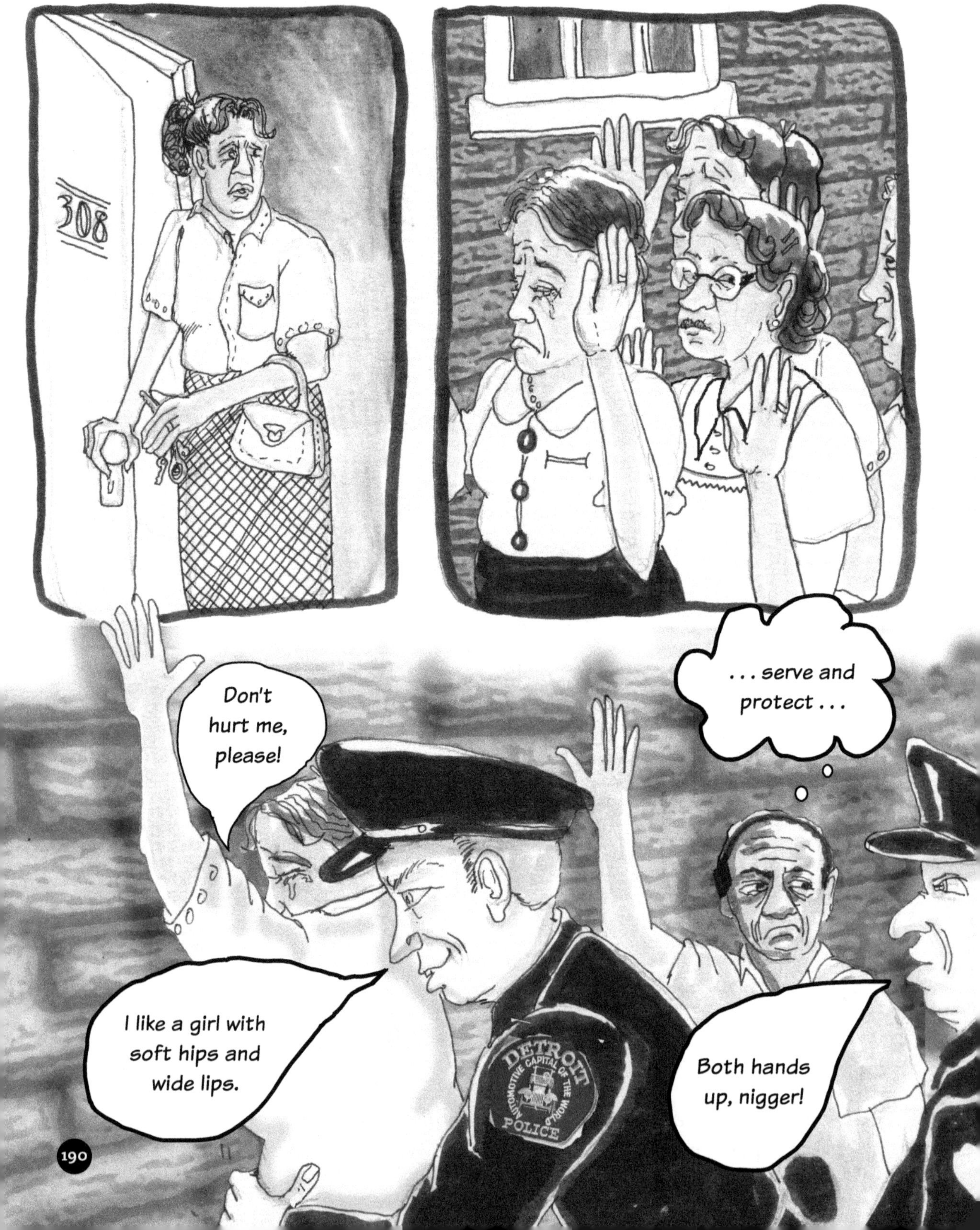
308
Don't hurt me, please!
. . . serve and protect . . .
I like a girl with soft hips and wide lips.
DETROIT
AUTOMOTIVE CAPITAL OF THE WORLD
POLICE
Both hands up, nigger!

When I reached my apartment I found that my door had been bust open. The lock was broken and the drawers of the dresser had been ransacked. After I looked around I discovered that everything I had . . . in the house of any value, what was in the order of jewelry, had been taken. No one entered my apartment before I did except the policemen. These officers were city police and state troopers.

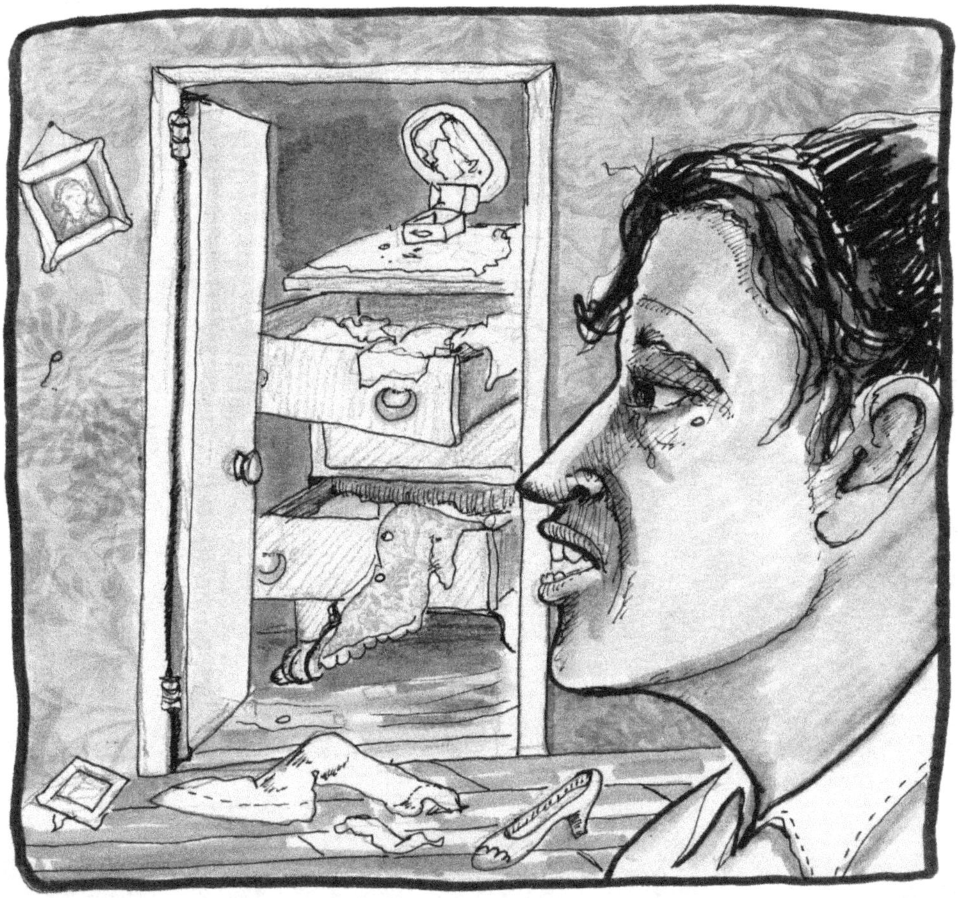

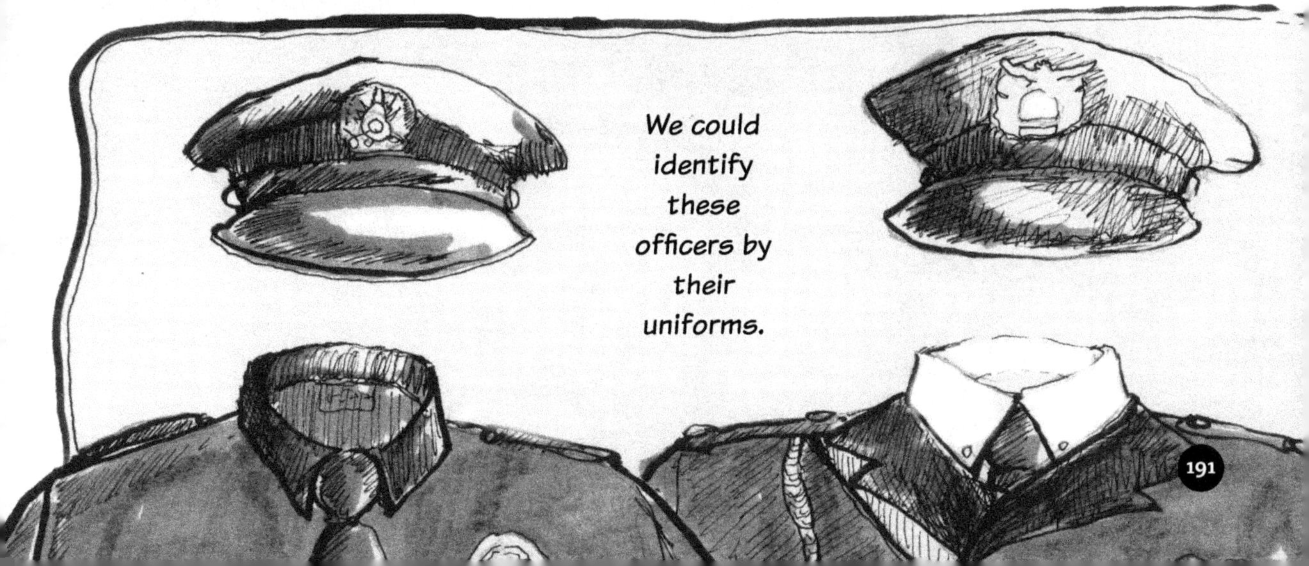
We could identify these officers by their uniforms.

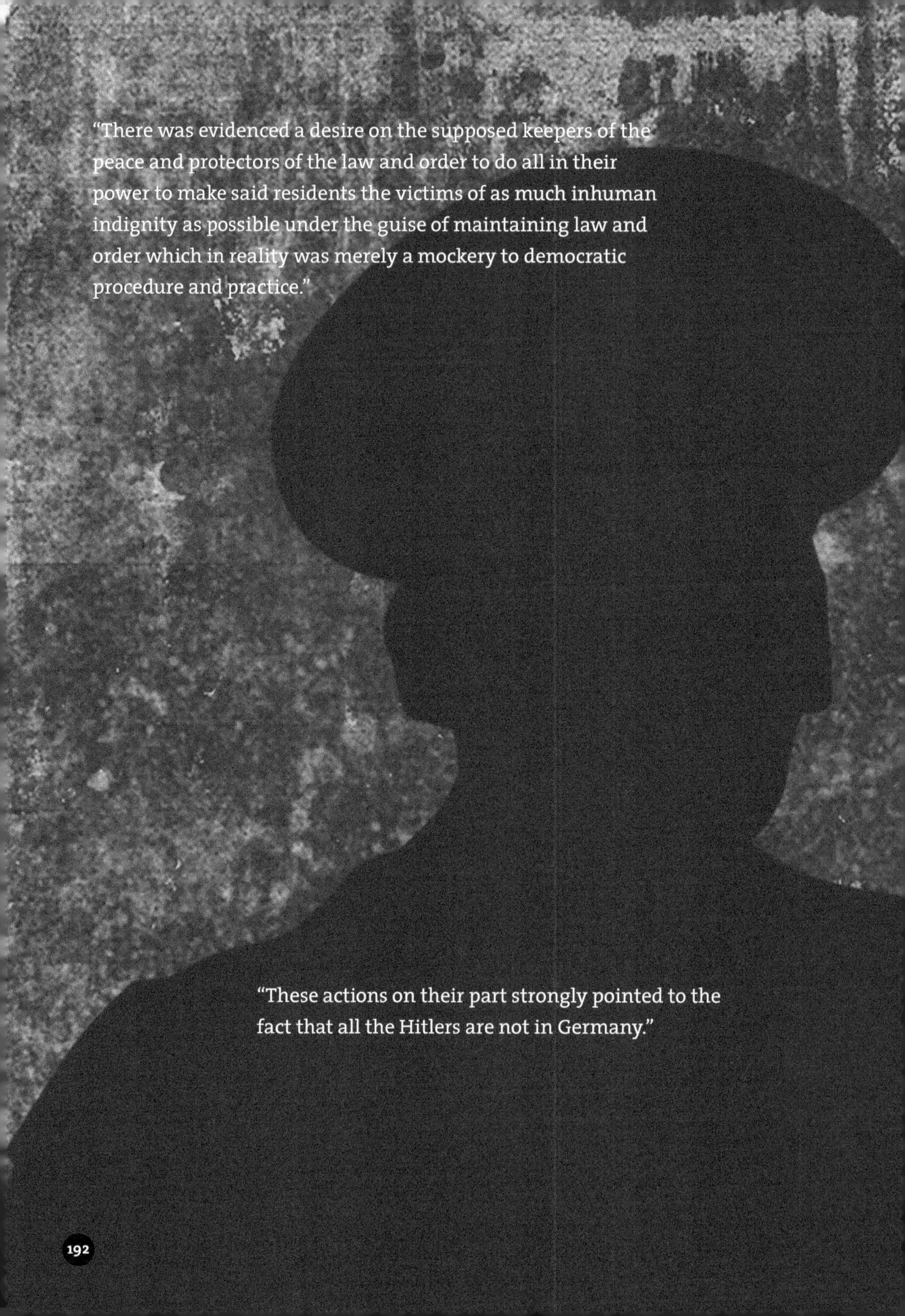

“There was evidenced a desire on the supposed keepers of the peace and protectors of the law and order to do all in their power to make said residents the victims of as much inhuman indignity as possible under the guise of maintaining law and order which in reality was merely a mockery to democratic procedure and practice.”

“These actions on their part strongly pointed to the fact that all the Hitlers are not in Germany.”

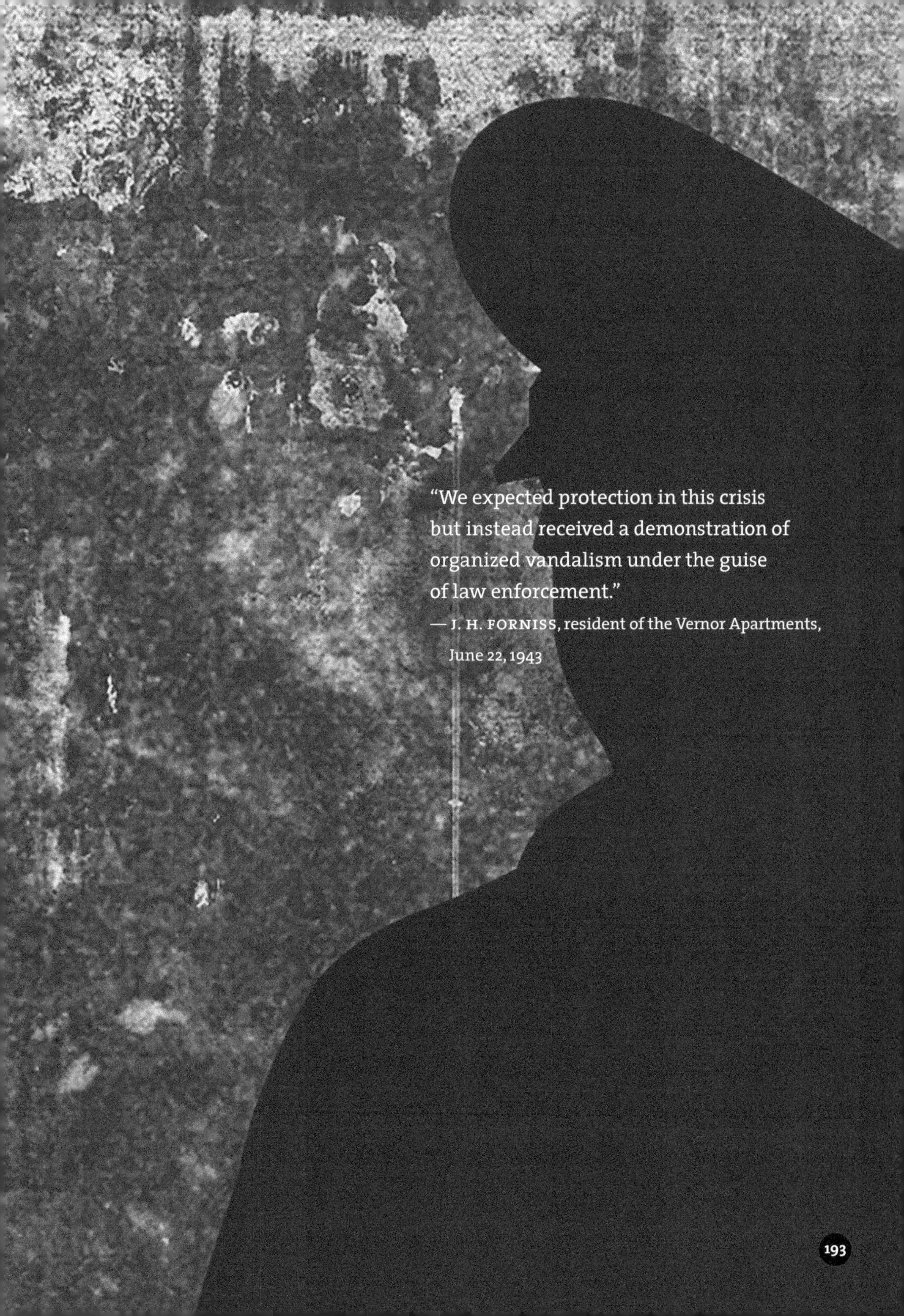

"We expected protection in this crisis but instead received a demonstration of organized vandalism under the guise of law enforcement."

—J. H. FORNISS, resident of the Vernor Apartments, June 22, 1943

On Tuesday, June 22, at 10:05 p.m. James Reid, who lived in room 213 of the St. Antoine Branch YMCA, was coming home from the Lucy Thurman YWCA when he witnessed a police officer shoot Julian Witherspoon, an innocent bystander.

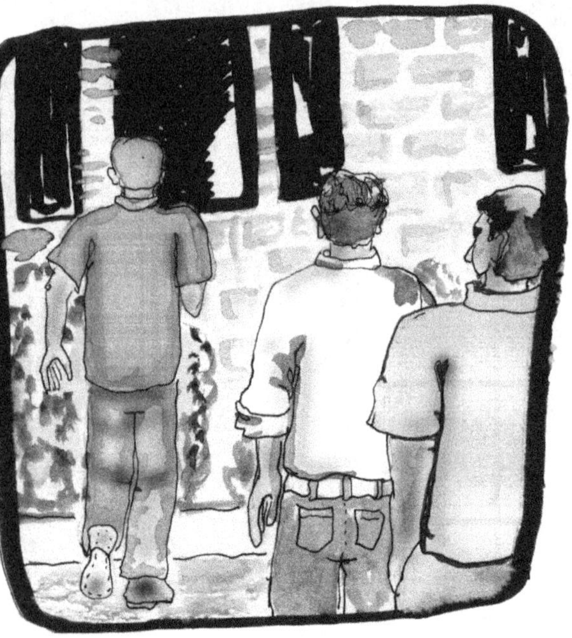

As I crossed the street to enter the YMCA building, I was stopped by a state policeman. Two other occupants of the building were with me at the time.

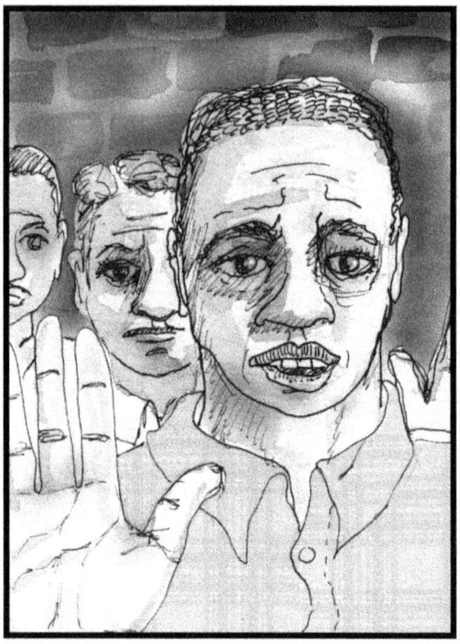

The officer demanded us to stop, pointing his gun in our faces. After having searched us, the officer found us harmless, told us to "get off the street." I was the last to be searched. The other two proceeded into the building.

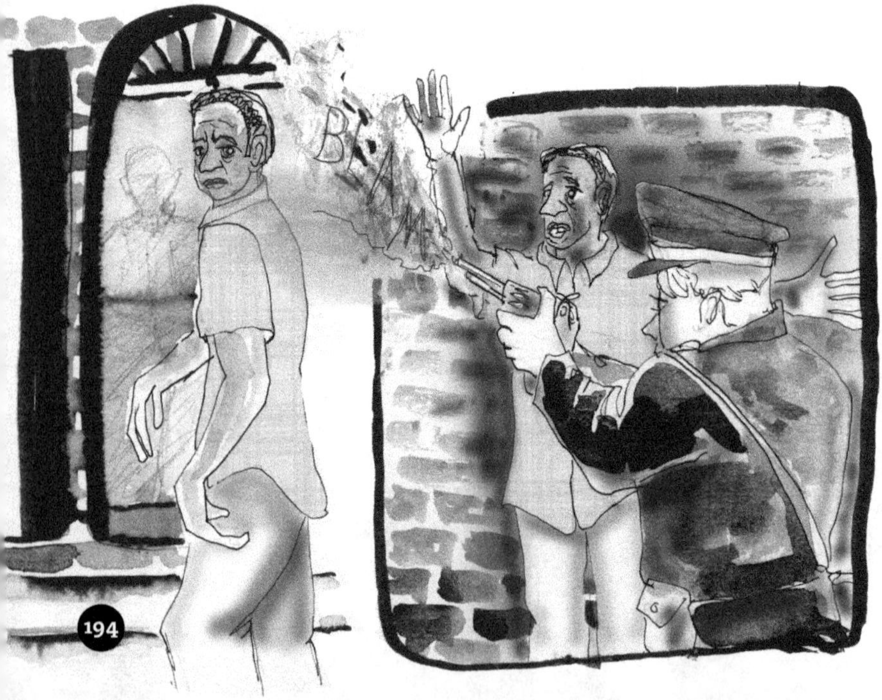
BLAM

An officer jumped from a scout car and ran toward the entrance of the building. . . . I glanced at this officer who had a gun in his hand and I stepped back. As this officer got to the door, he took one step and fired through the glass, not giving warning of any kind.

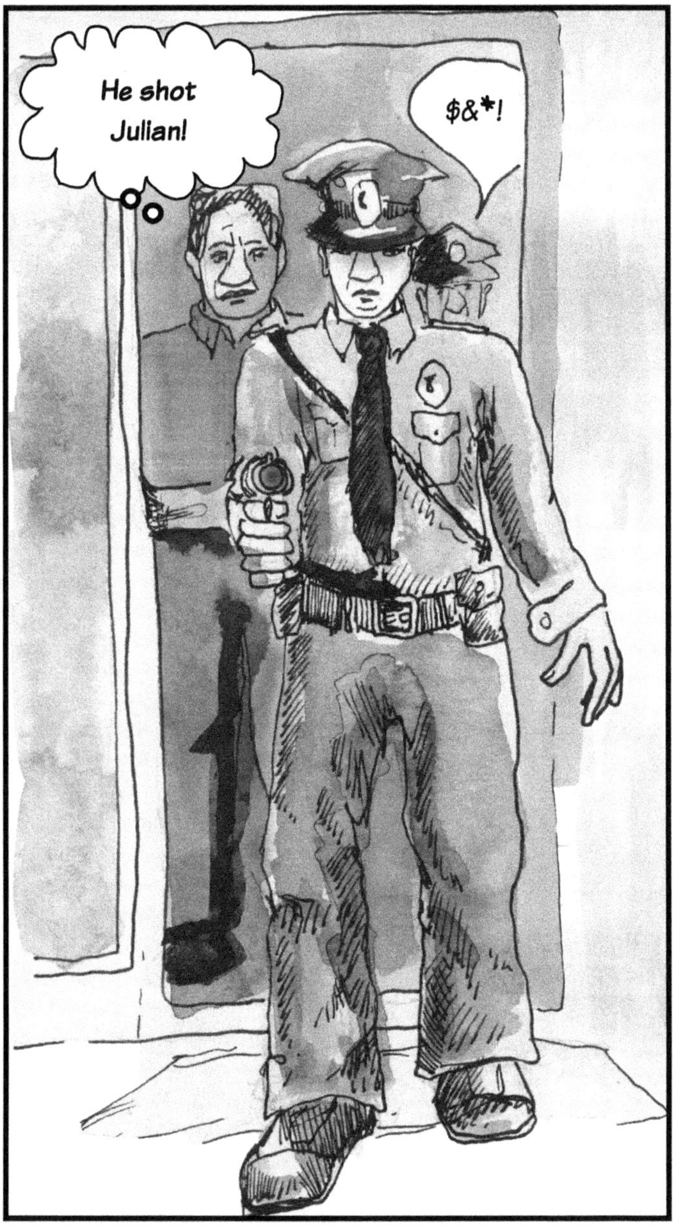
He shot Julian!
$&*!

Immediately after firing the shot the officer entered the building. After having been cursed by the officers, I was told to get off the street.

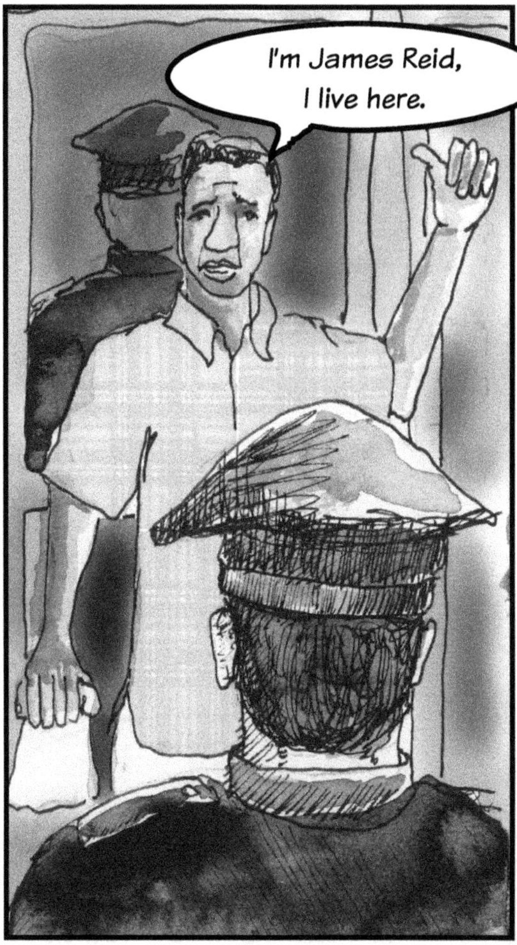
I'm James Reid, I live here.

As I entered the building I was told to get over by the wall and raise my hands in the air. Along with a group of other boys, I was told to face the wall with my hands in the air.

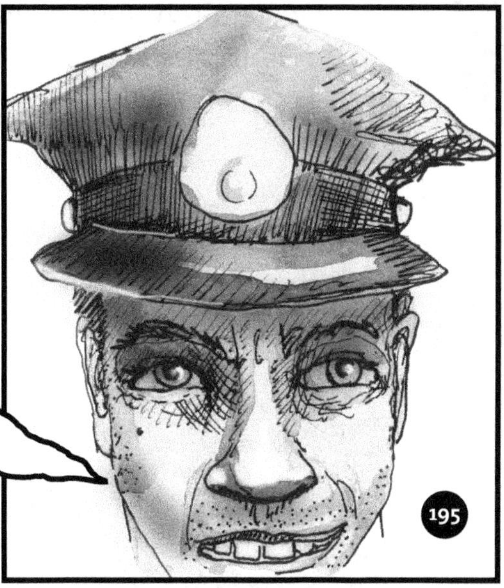
Black bastard.

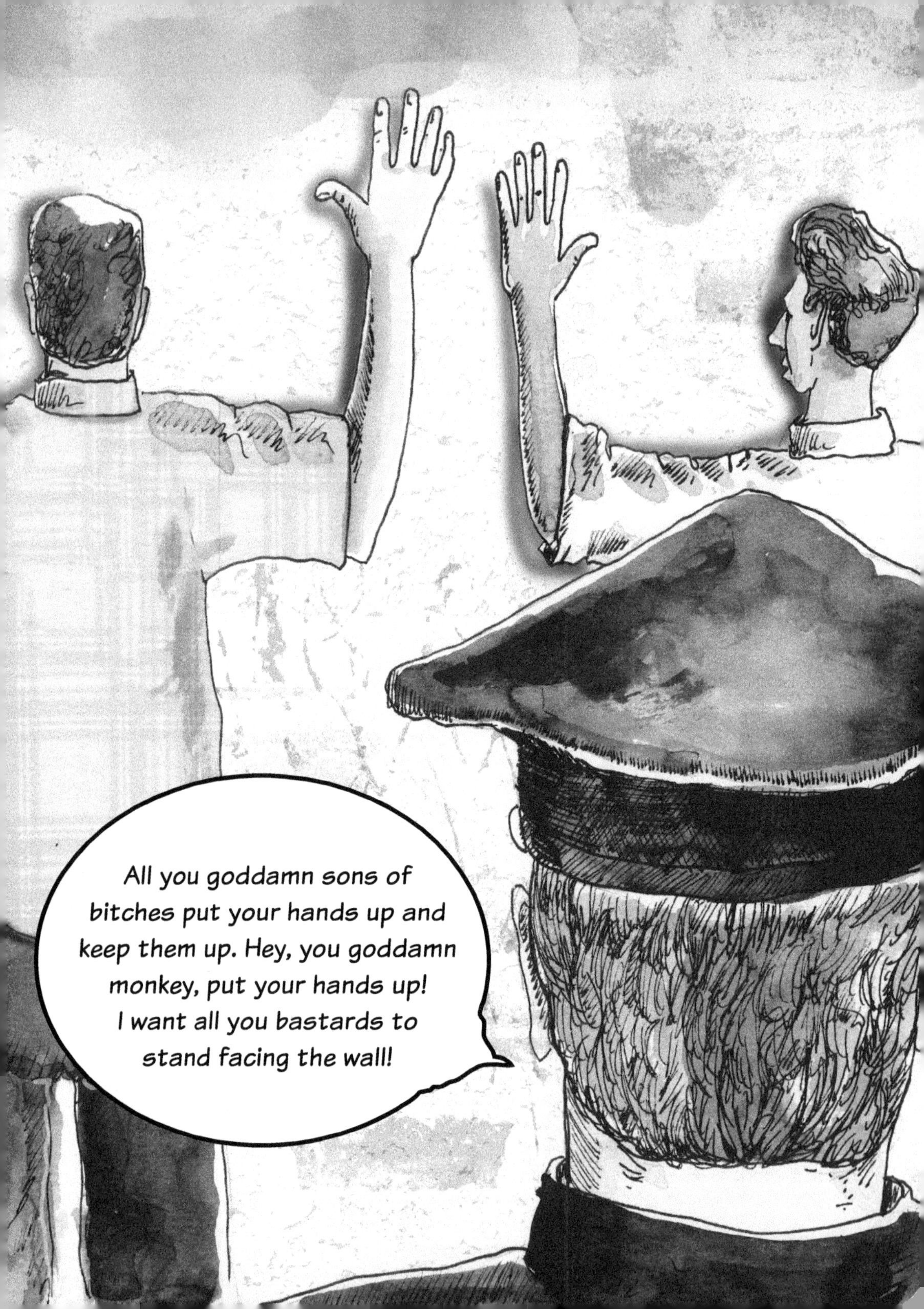
All you goddamn sons of bitches put your hands up and keep them up. Hey, you goddamn monkey, put your hands up! I want all you bastards to stand facing the wall!

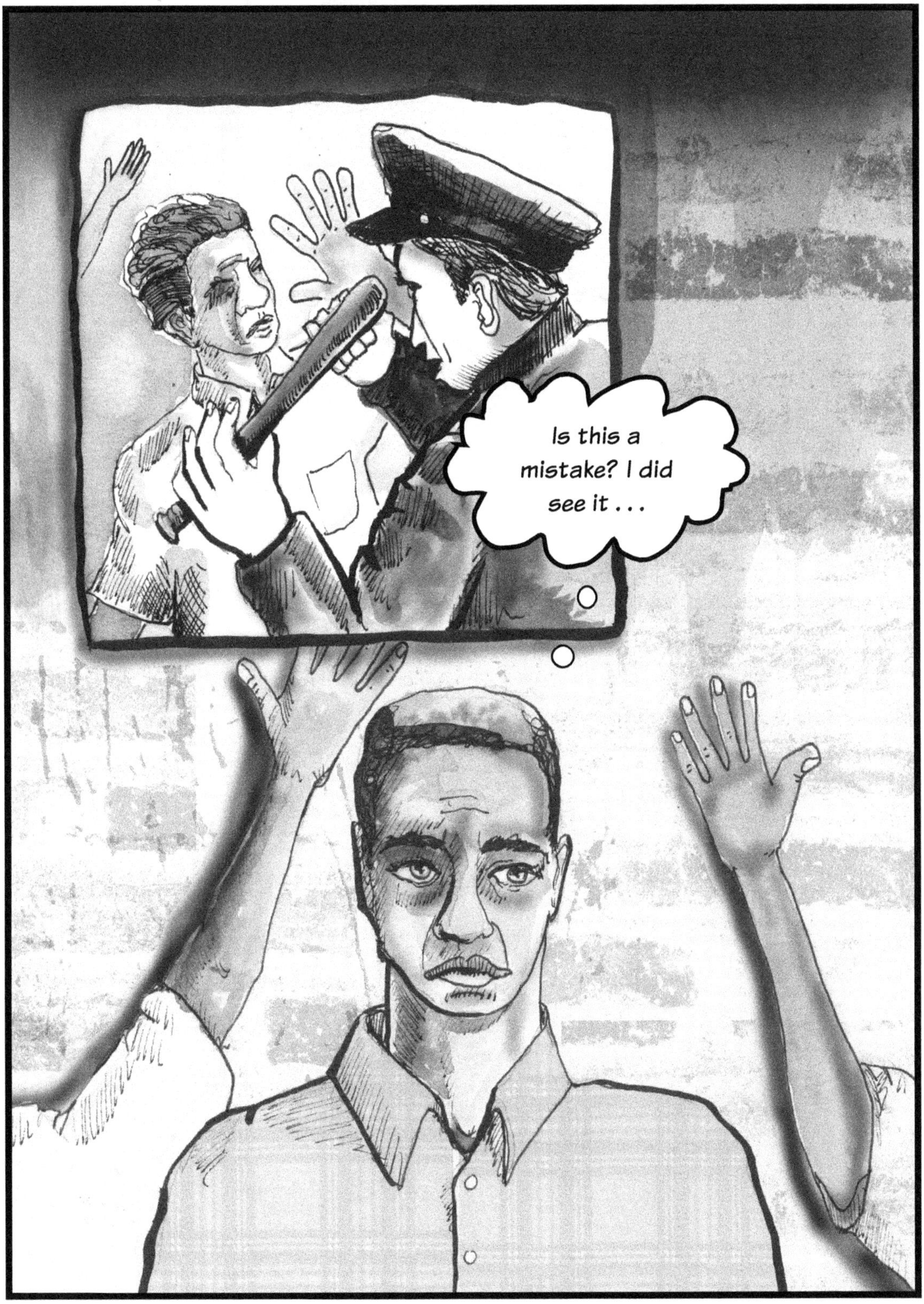
Is this a mistake? I did see it . . .

While we were turned, facing the wall, a man from the dormitory came into the lounge and was struck several times by an officer. At this point, one of the officers asked for a witness of the shooting. After a bit of hesitation, I volunteered as a witness. I was told to step out of [the] line.

I was taken outside to the street by a police lieutenant. I was told to go back into the building to get my bag of food. While in the building I was told by an officer to stand over by the desk. . . . During all of this time Witherspoon was still lying on the floor with a bullet wound in his side. I was then taken outside again to the police car to be taken to the homicide squad for a statement. While we were outside, a patrol wagon arrived and the policemen asked for a stretcher to be brought to the building. This was about forty minutes after the shooting occurred.

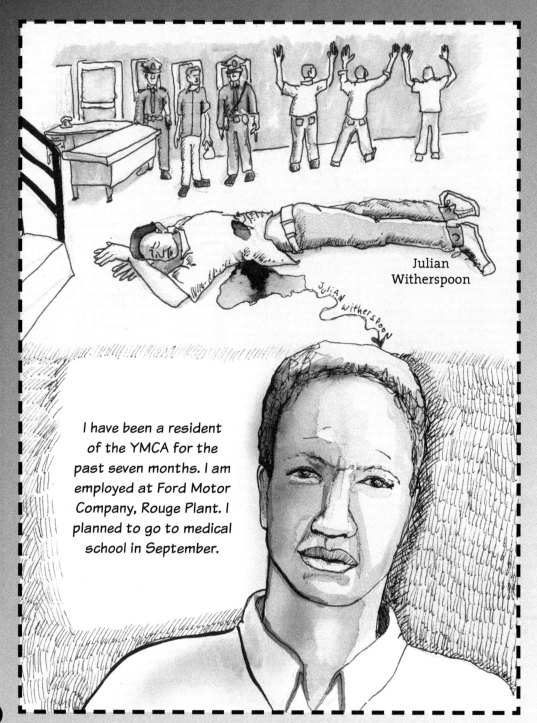

Julian
Witherspoon

I have been a resident of the YMCA for the past seven months. I am employed at Ford Motor Company, Rouge Plant. I planned to go to medical school in September.

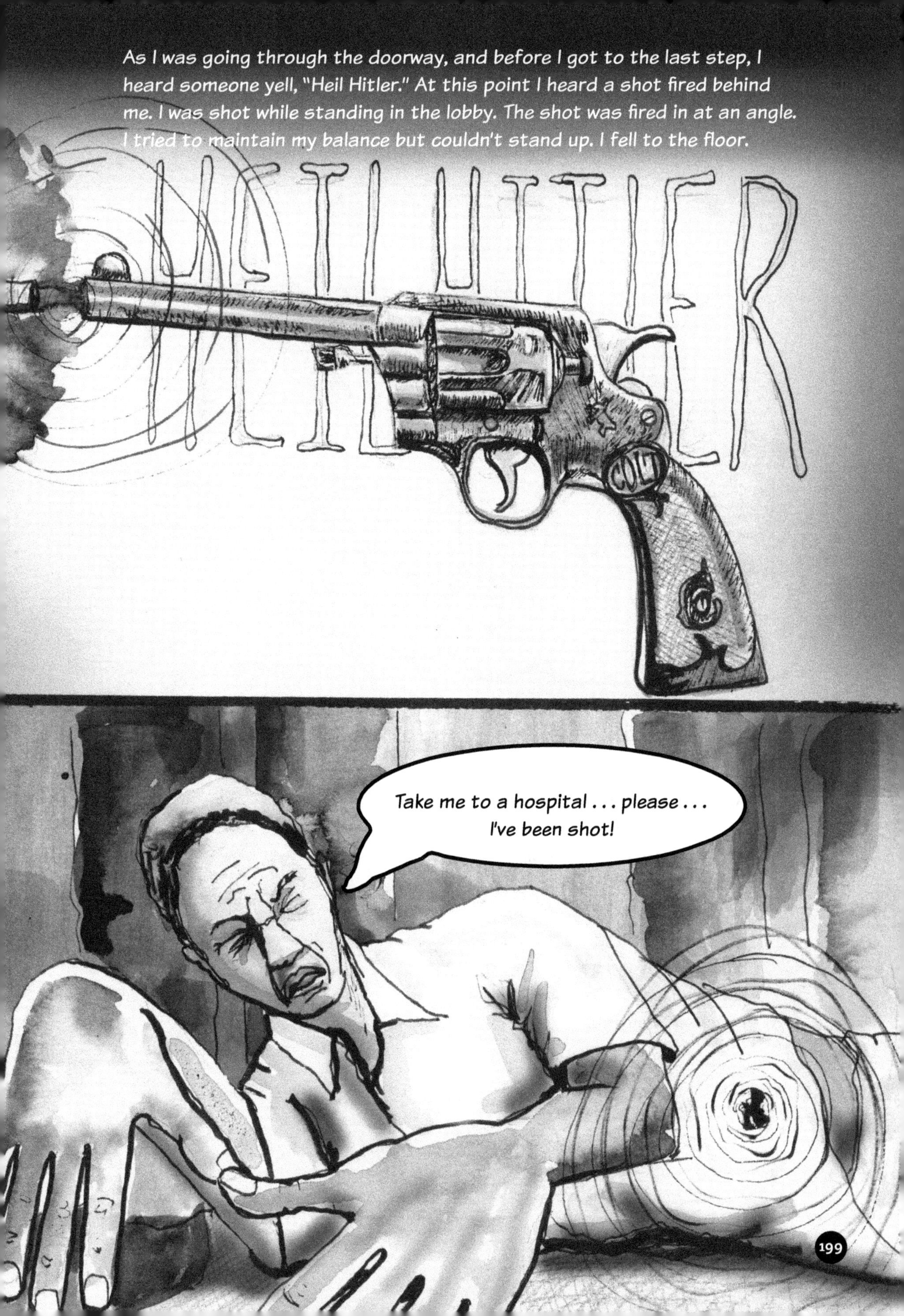
As I was going through the doorway, and before I got to the last step, I heard someone yell, "Heil Hitler." At this point I heard a shot fired behind me. I was shot while standing in the lobby. The shot was fired in at an angle. I tried to maintain my balance but couldn't stand up. I fell to the floor.
HEIL HITLER
COLT
Take me to a hospital . . . please . . . I've been shot!

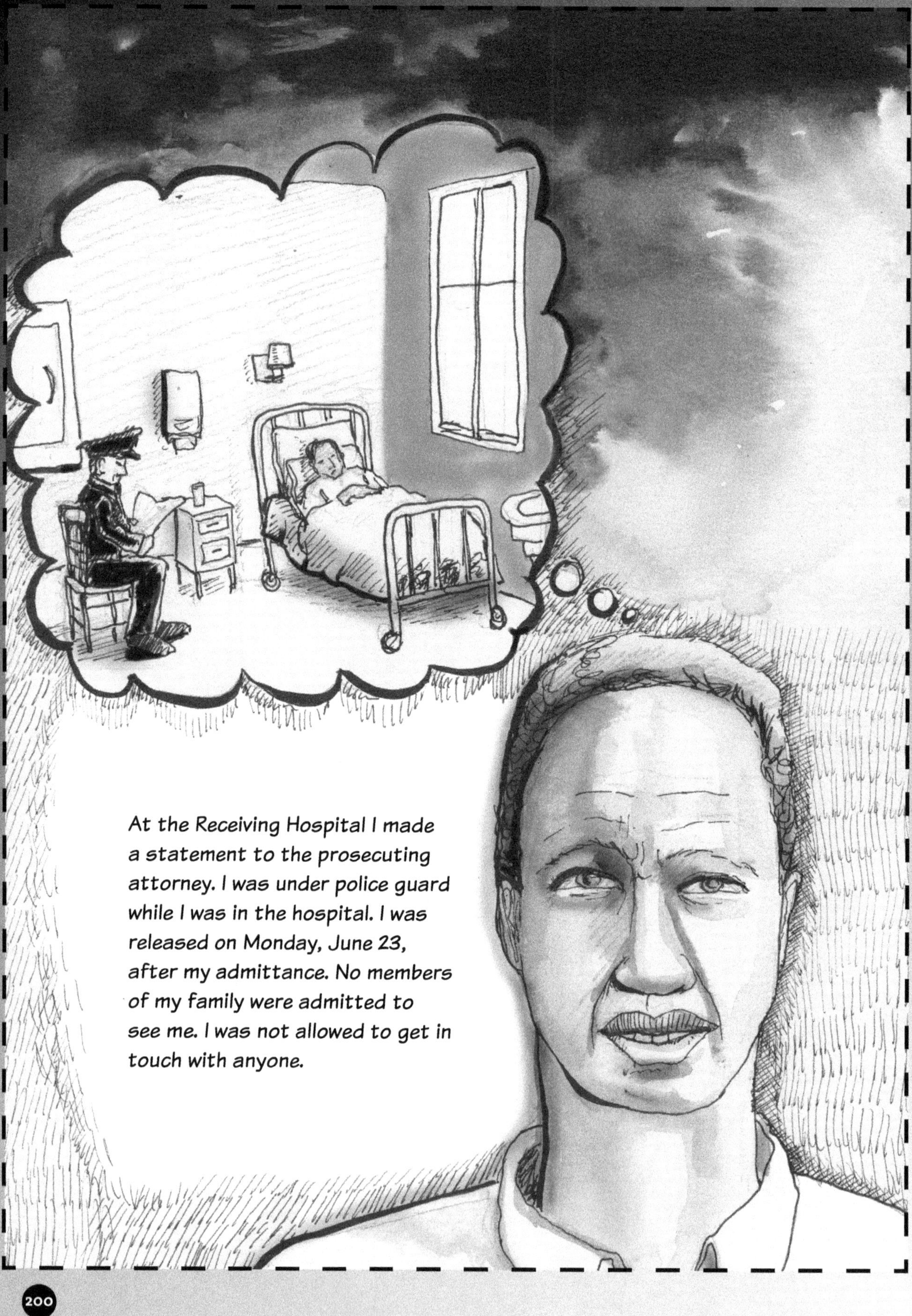
At the Receiving Hospital I made a statement to the prosecuting attorney. I was under police guard while I was in the hospital. I was released on Monday, June 23, after my admittance. No members of my family were admitted to see me. I was not allowed to get in touch with anyone.

The violence raged on for so long because city officials wavered. The first indication that things were out of control came in the form of a 3 a.m. phone call to Police Commissioner John H. Witherspoon from one of his officers. For hours it was unclear if the Detroit police could contain the violence.

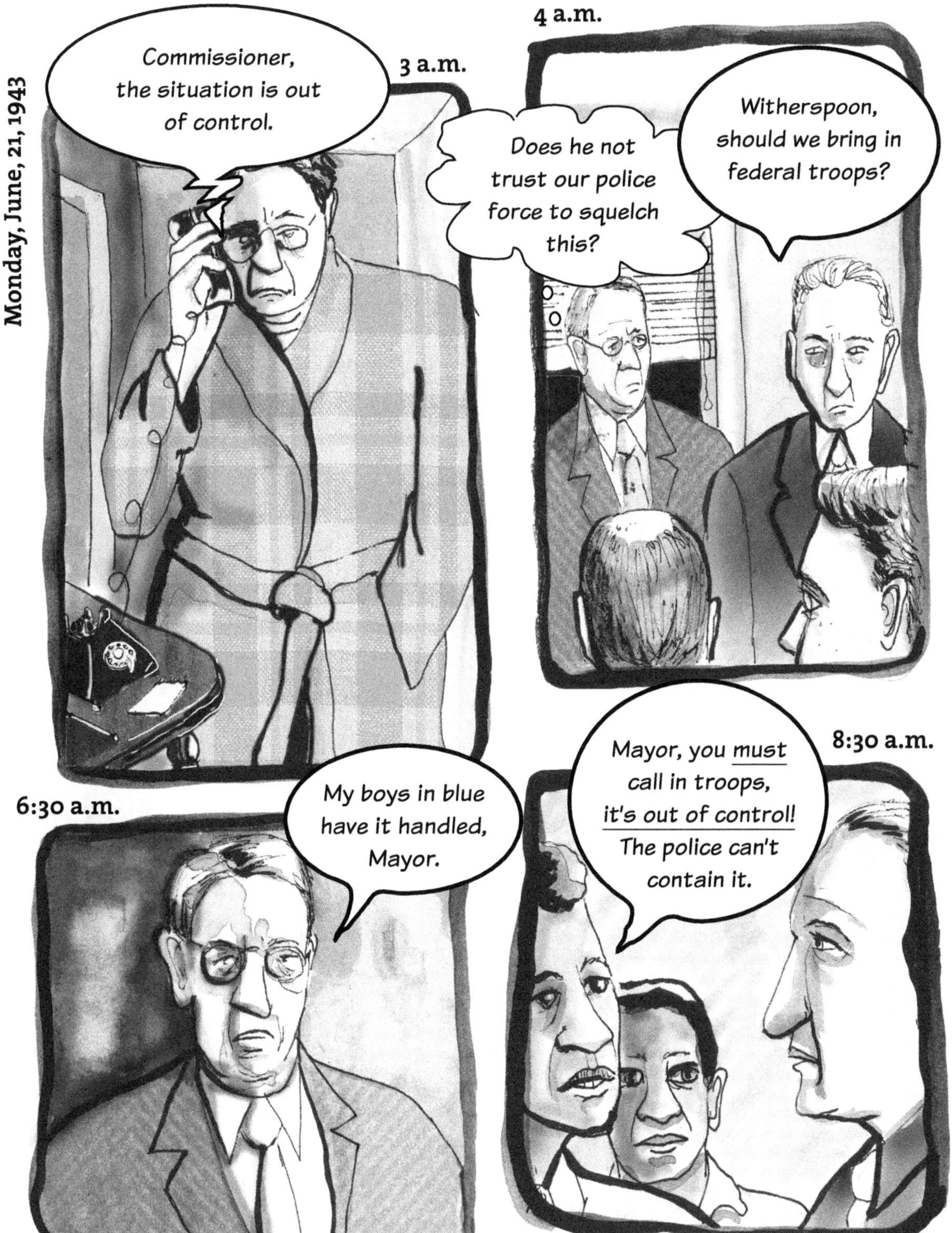
Monday, June, 21, 1943
3 a.m.
Commissioner, the situation is out of control.
4 a.m.
Witherspoon, should we bring in federal troops?
Does he not trust our police force to squelch this?
6:30 a.m.
My boys in blue have it handled, Mayor.
8:30 a.m.
Mayor, you must call in troops, it's out of control! The police can't contain it.

The mayor finally called the governor, who was at the Governor's Conference in Columbus, Ohio.

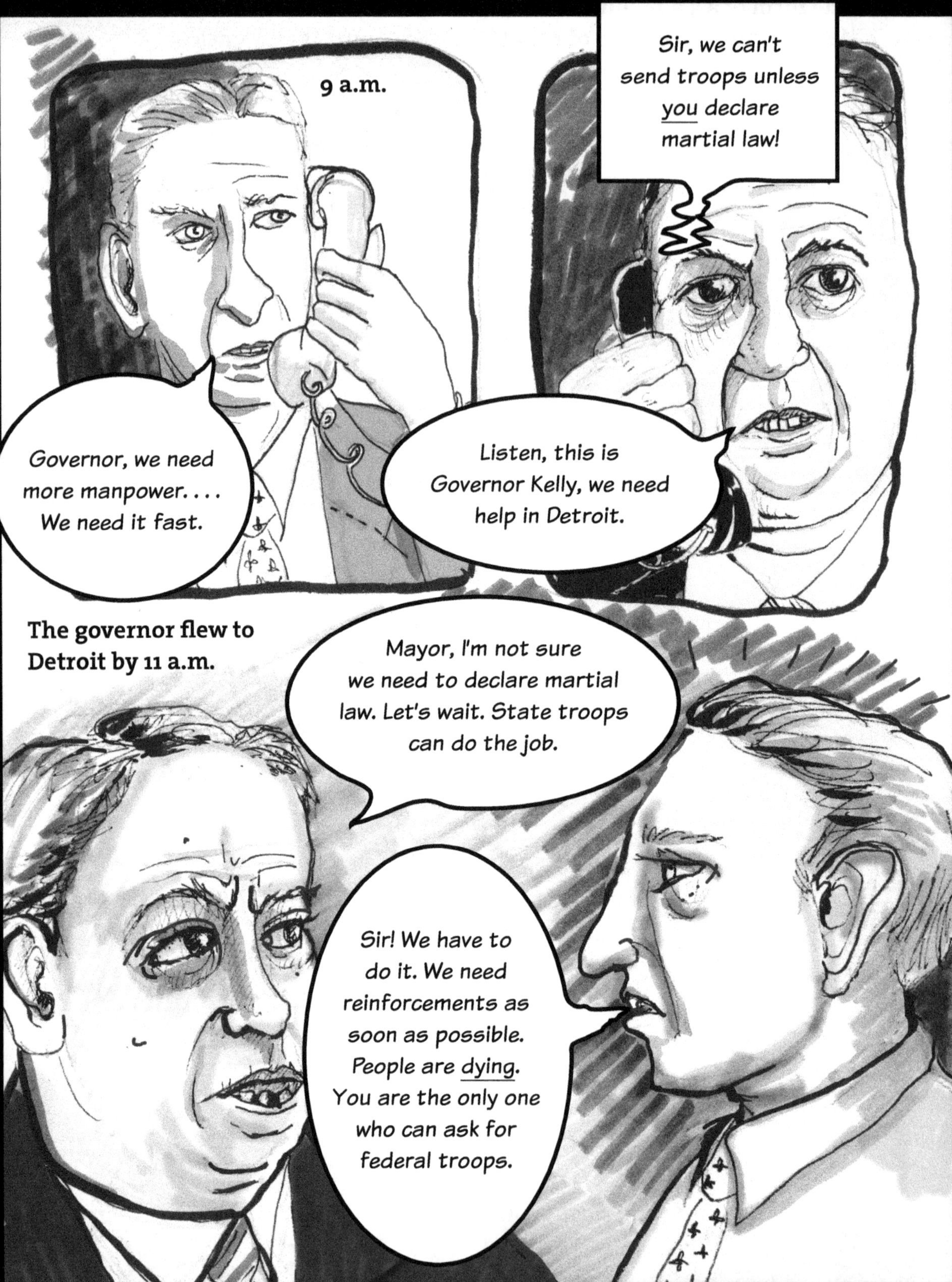

9 a.m.
Governor, we need more manpower. . . . We need it fast.
Listen, this is Governor Kelly, we need help in Detroit.
Sir, we can't send troops unless you declare martial law!
The governor flew to Detroit by 11 a.m.
Mayor, I'm not sure we need to declare martial law. Let's wait. State troops can do the job.
Sir! We have to do it. We need reinforcements as soon as possible. People are dying. You are the only one who can ask for federal troops.

It would be twelve hours before federal

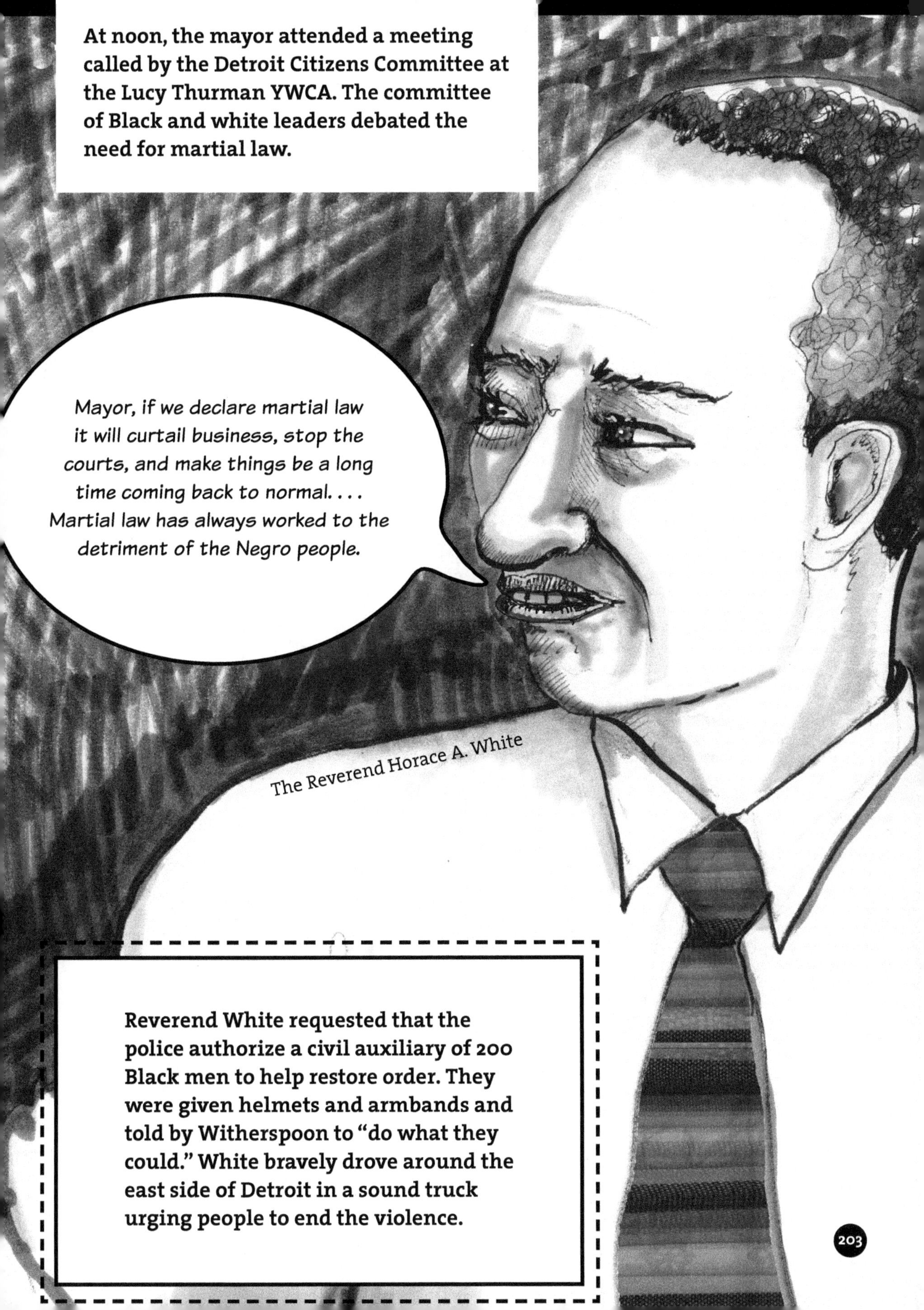
At noon, the mayor attended a meeting called by the Detroit Citizens Committee at the Lucy Thurman YWCA. The committee of Black and white leaders debated the need for martial law.
Mayor, if we declare martial law it will curtail business, stop the courts, and make things be a long time coming back to normal. . . . Martial law has always worked to the detriment of the Negro people.
The Reverend Horace A. White
Reverend White requested that the police authorize a civil auxiliary of 200 Black men to help restore order. They were given helmets and armbands and told by Witherspoon to "do what they could." White bravely drove around the east side of Detroit in a sound truck urging people to end the violence.

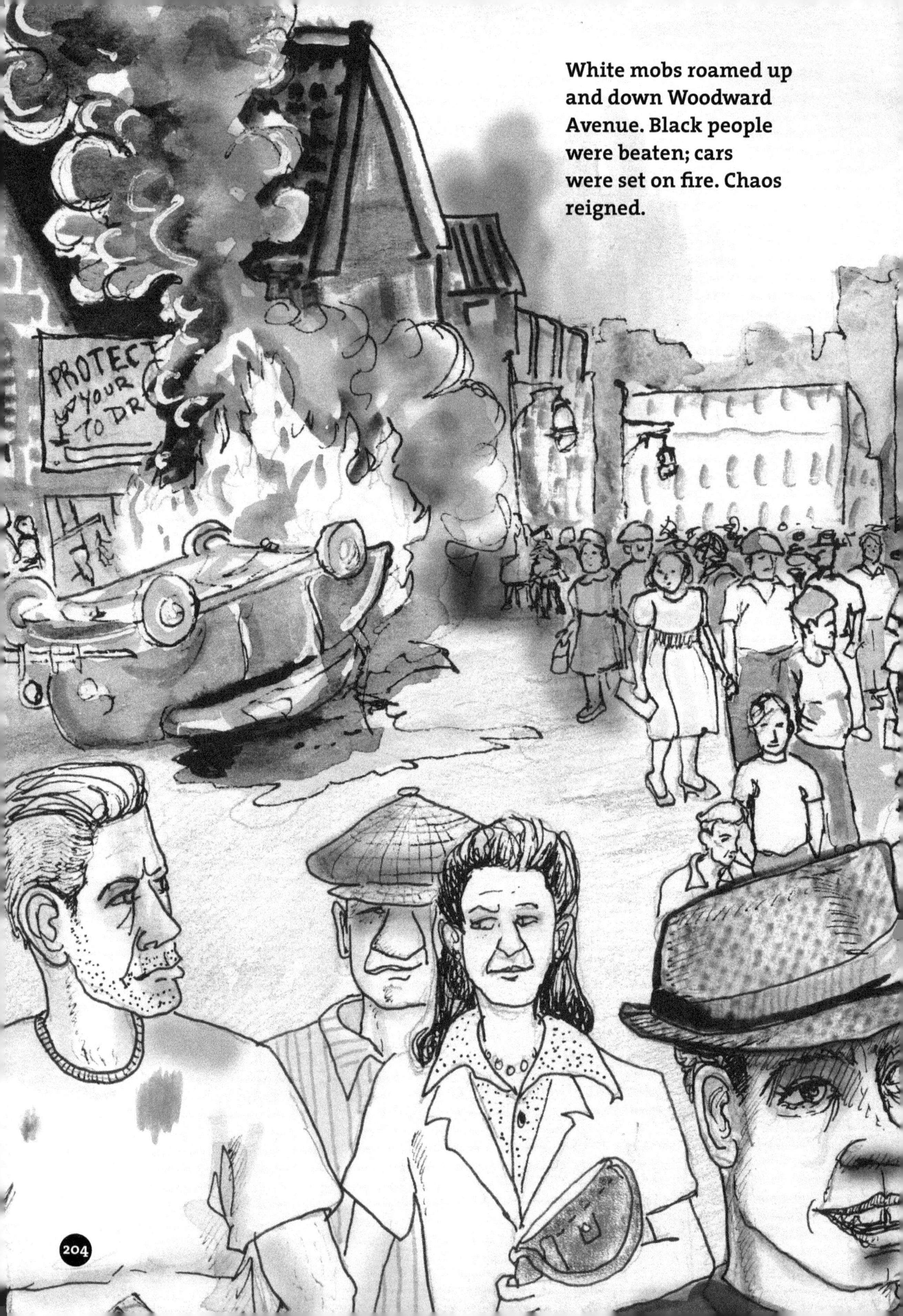
White mobs roamed up and down Woodward Avenue. Black people were beaten; cars were set on fire. Chaos reigned.
PROTECT YOUR

June 21, 1943, would come to be known as

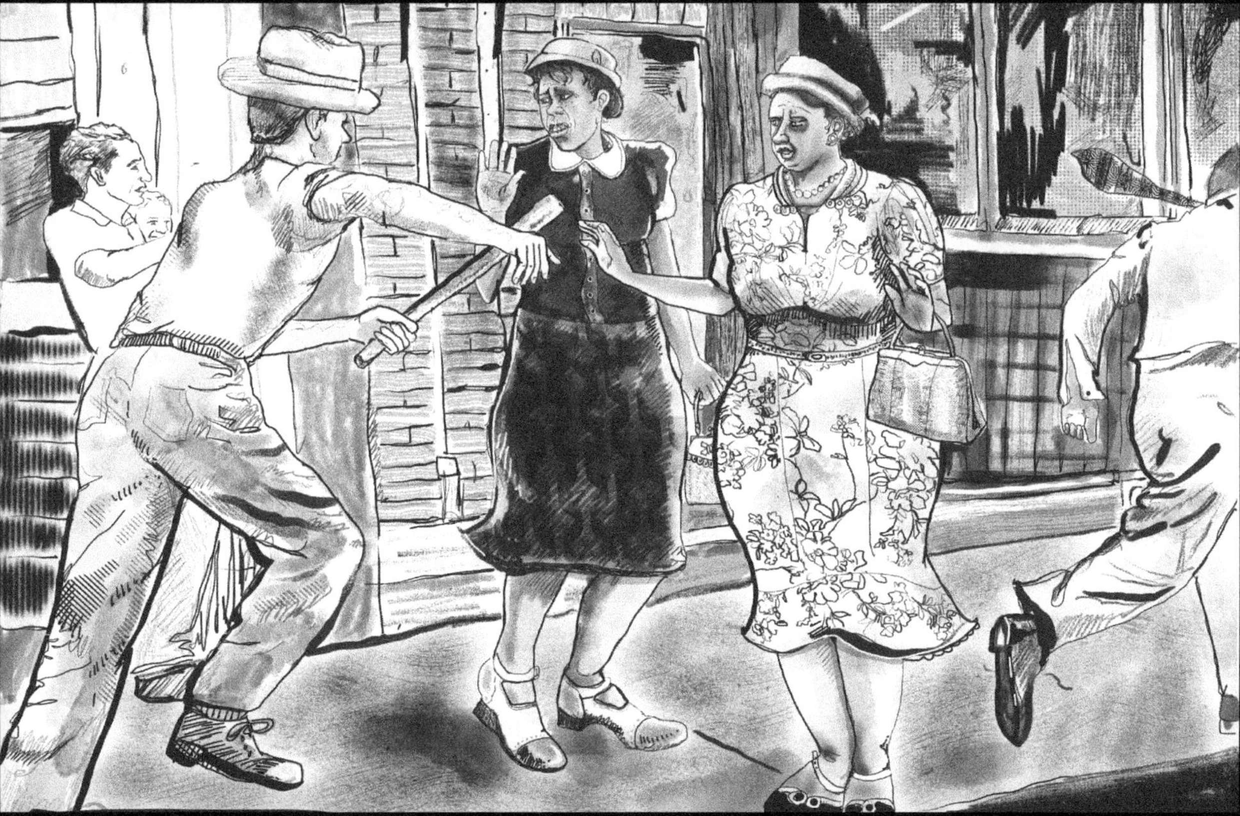

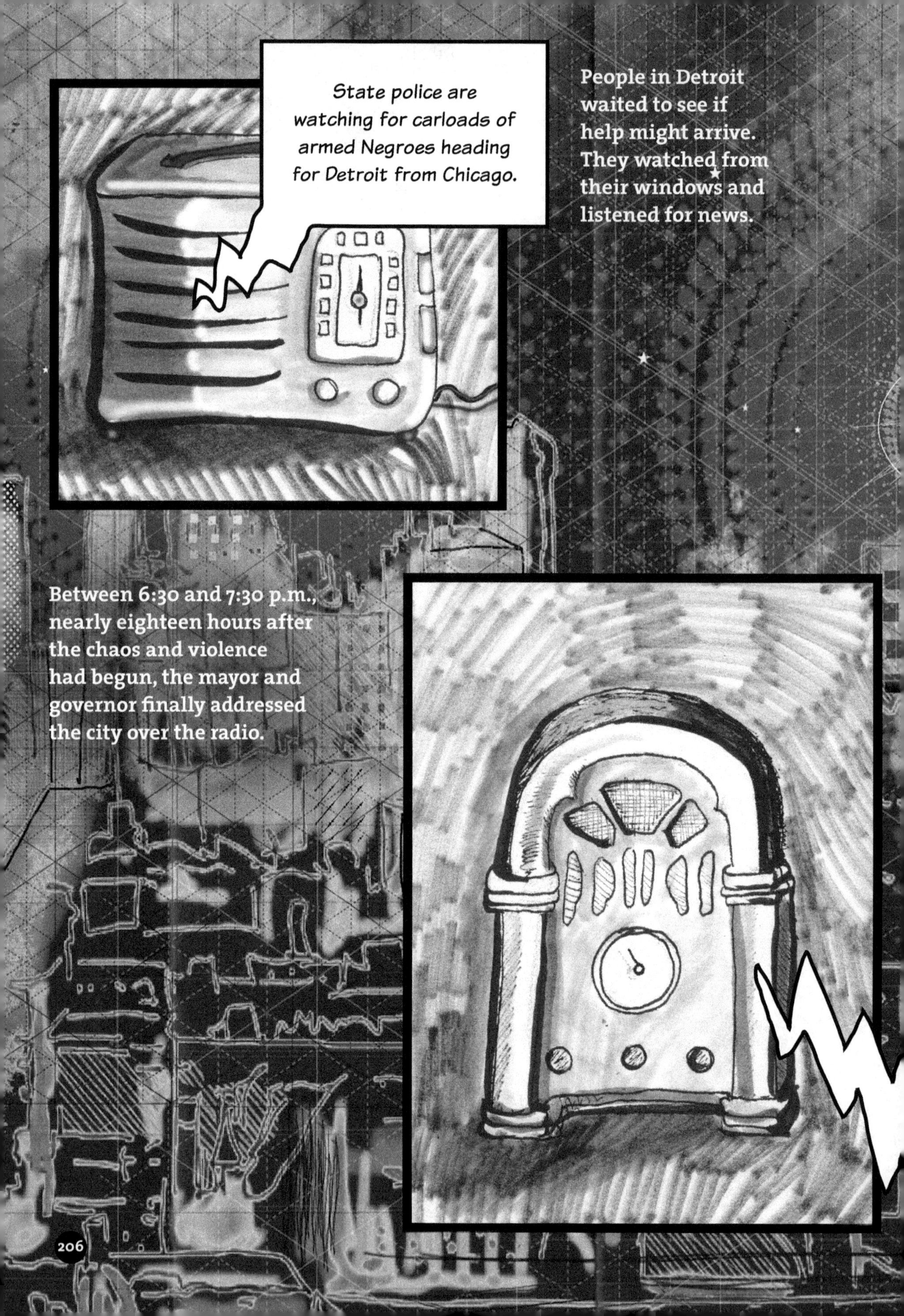
State police are watching for carloads of armed Negroes heading for Detroit from Chicago.
People in Detroit waited to see if help might arrive. They watched from their windows and listened for news.
Between 6:30 and 7:30 p.m., nearly eighteen hours after the chaos and violence had begun, the mayor and governor finally addressed the city over the radio.

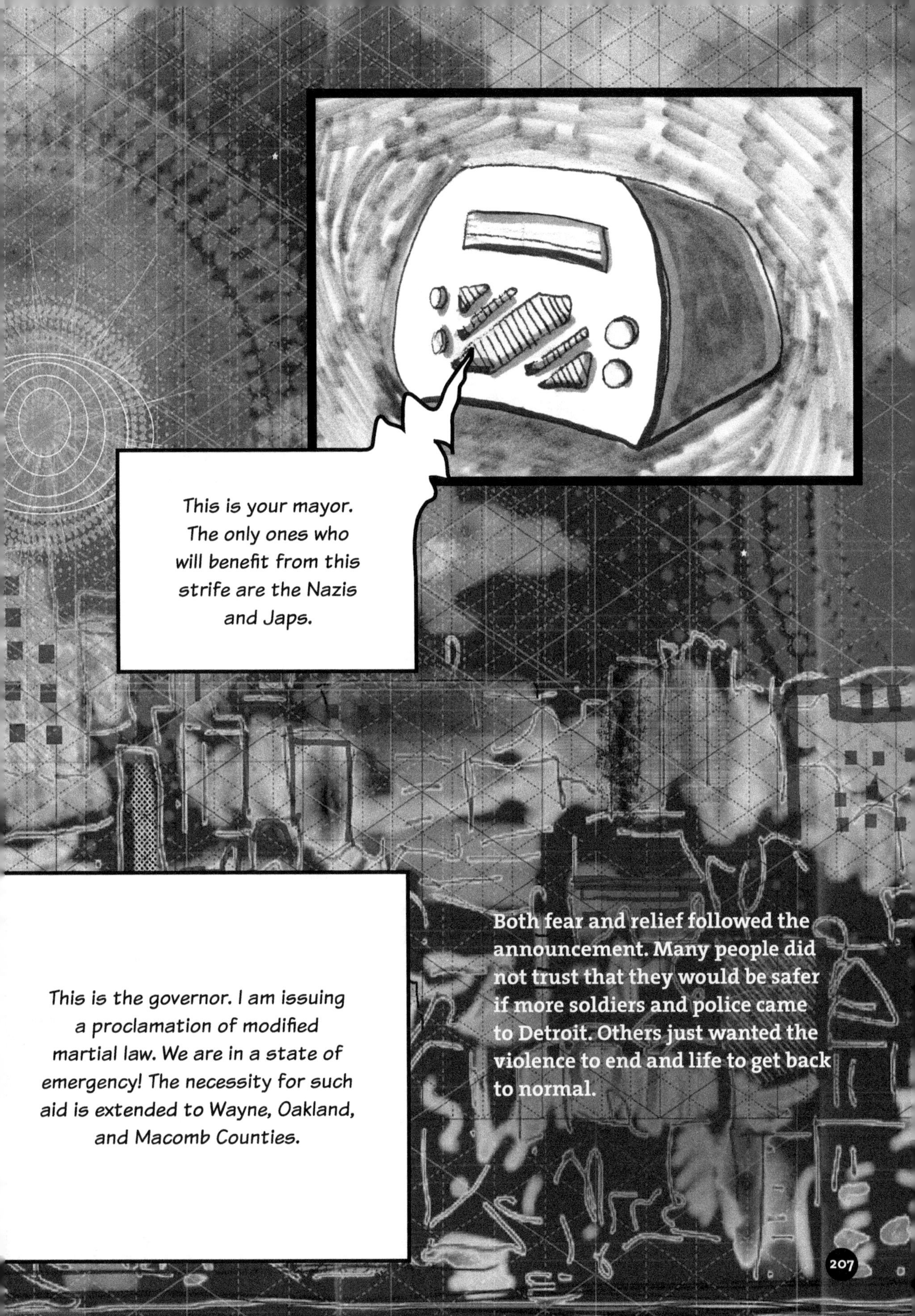
This is your mayor. The only ones who will benefit from this strife are the Nazis and Japs.
This is the governor. I am issuing a proclamation of modified martial law. We are in a state of emergency! The necessity for such aid is extended to Wayne, Oakland, and Macomb Counties.
Both fear and relief followed the announcement. Many people did not trust that they would be safer if more soldiers and police came to Detroit. Others just wanted the violence to end and life to get back to normal.

At 9:25 p.m. martial law was imposed on Detroit and help was on the way.

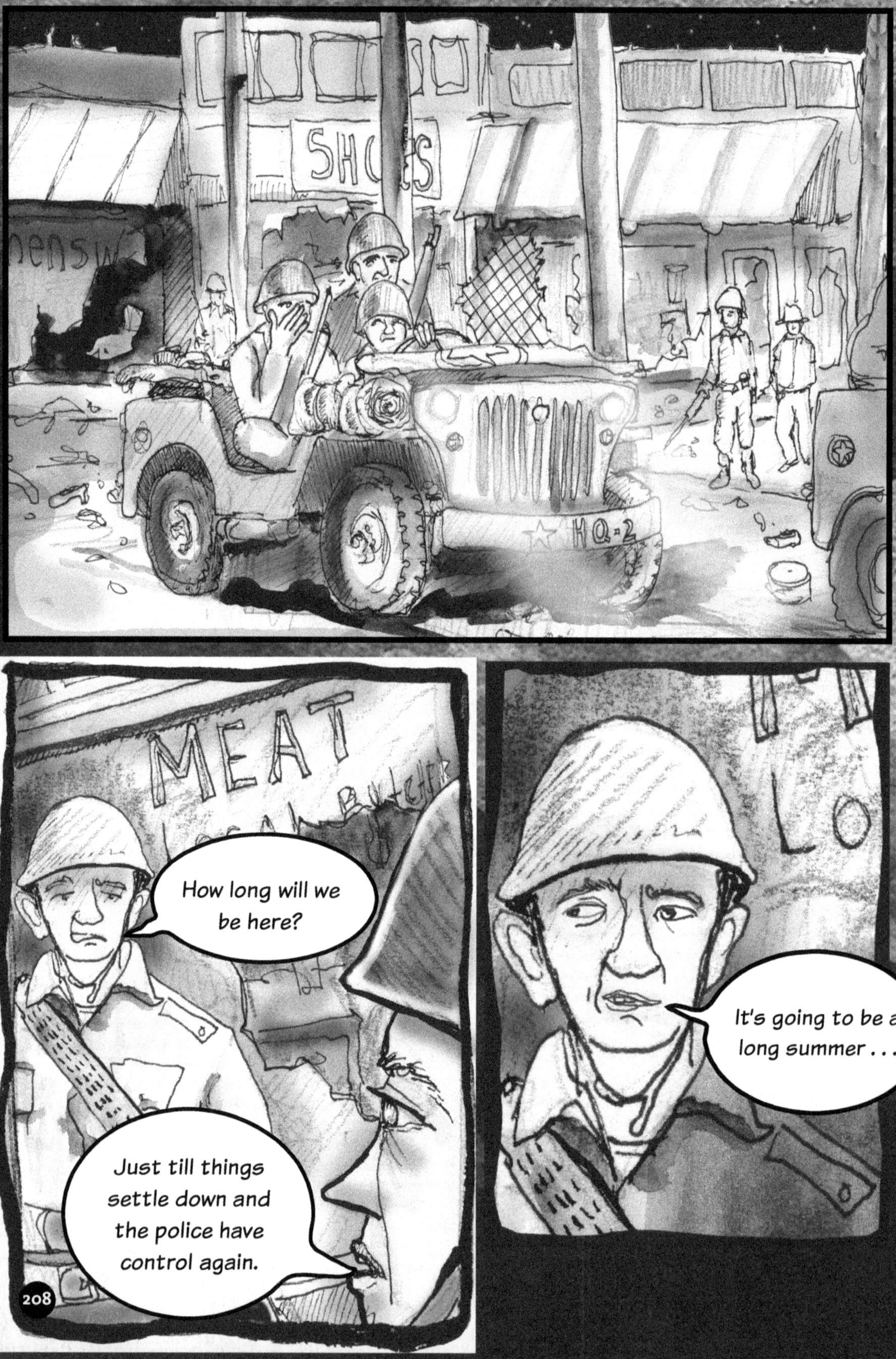
HQ-2
MEAT
How long will we be here?
Just till things settle down and the police have control again.
It's going to be a long summer . . .

Soldiers remained in the city in dwindling
numbers until after July 4, 1943.

In the aftermath of the uprising,
residents of the city of Detroit repaired the
damage, buried their dead, and tried to
sort out what had happened.

Thirty-four people had been killed,
twenty-five Black and nine white. Seventeen
Black people had been killed by police.

More than 750 people had sought help at
local hospitals for their injuries.

The police had arrested nearly 2,000 people,
most of whom were African American.

There was $2 million in property damage.

Industry in the "arsenal of democracy"
had lost 1 million hours of labor.

white

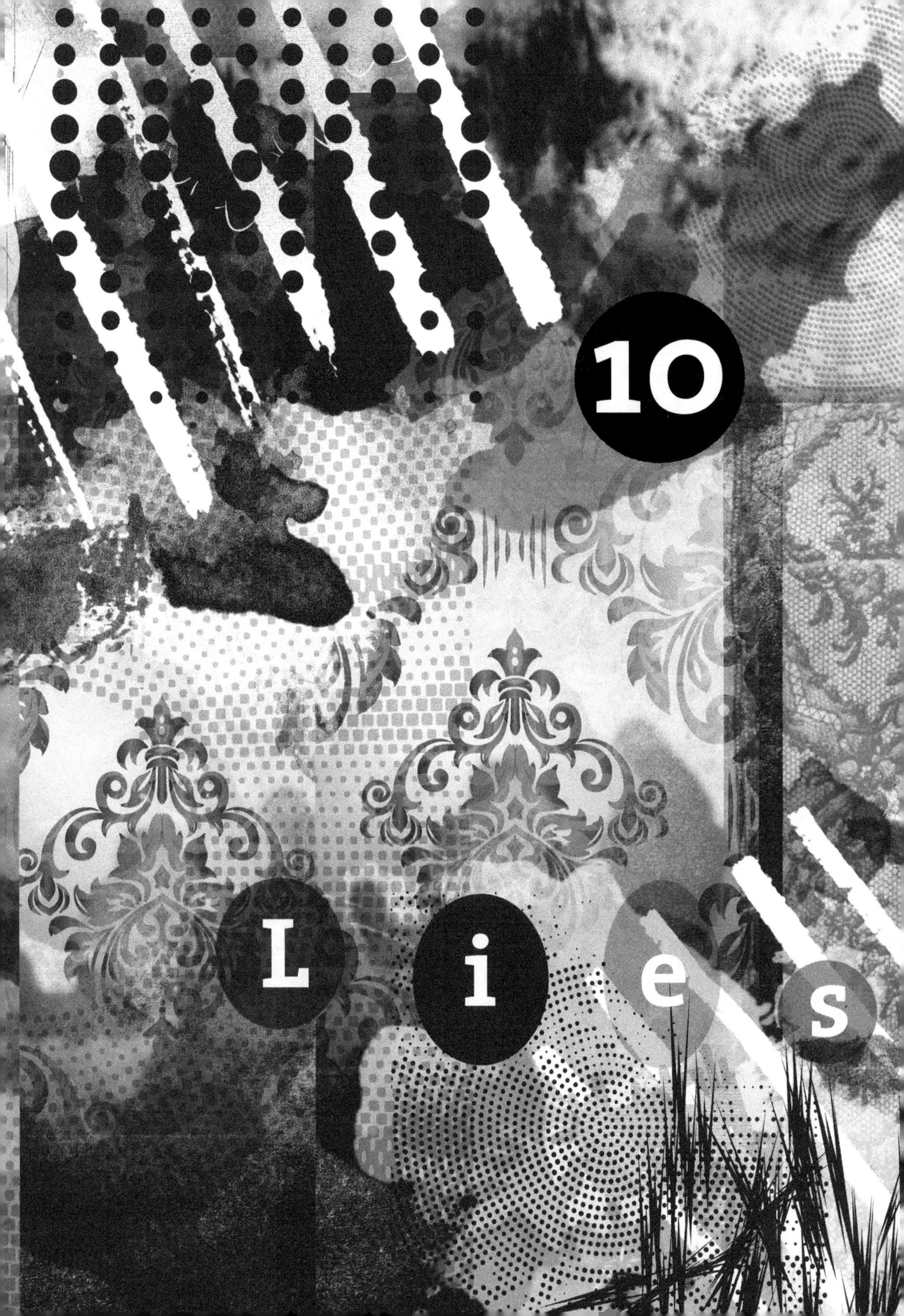
10
Lies

"*It is blood on your hands, Mrs. Roosevelt. . . .* In Detroit, a city noted for the growing impudence and insolence of its Negro population, an attempt was made to put your preachements [*sic*] into practice Mrs. Roosevelt.

What followed is now history."

—*Jackson (Miss.) Daily News*, June 22, 1943

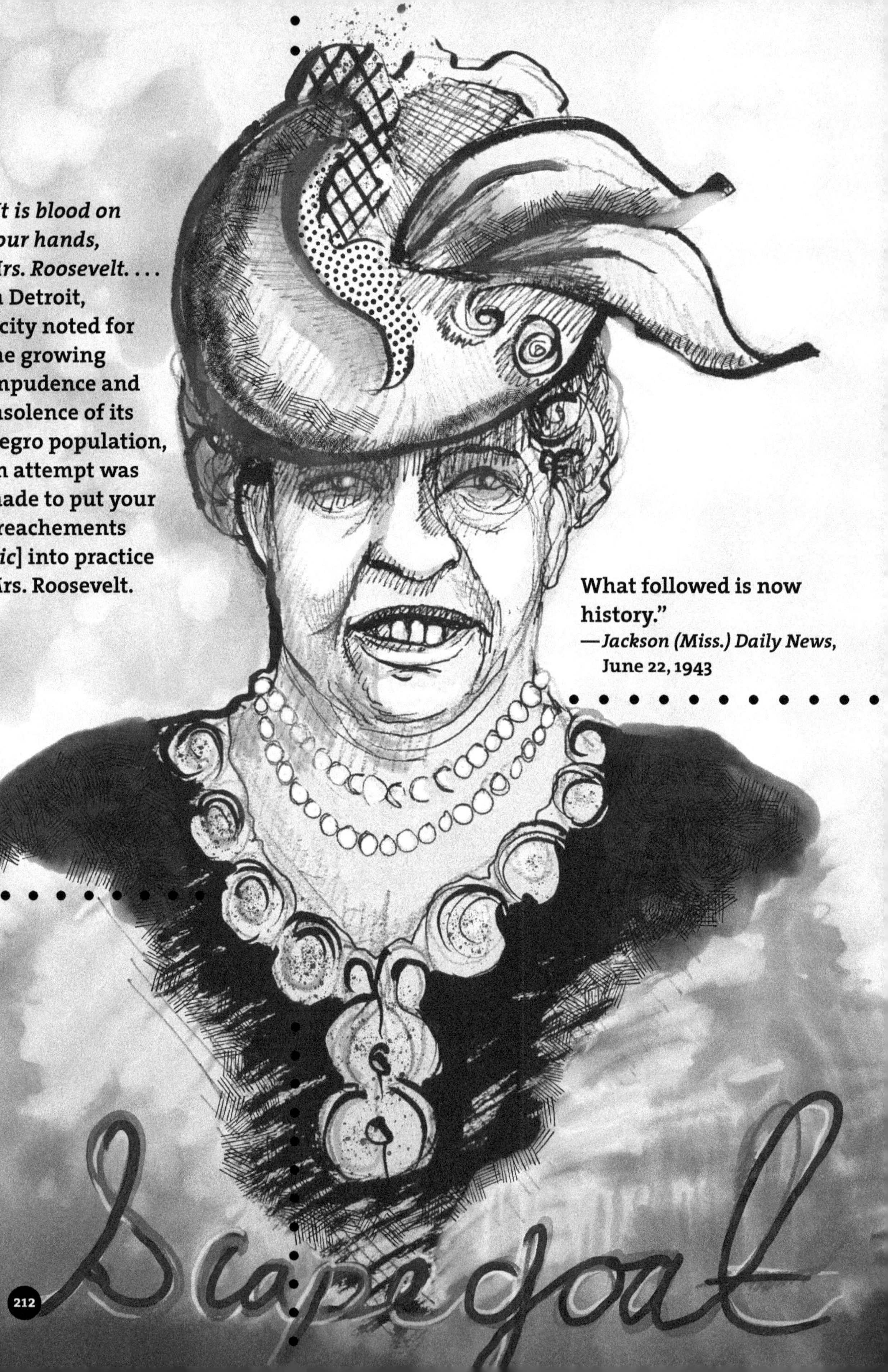
Scapegoat

People sought someone to blame for the death and destruction; politicians looked for a scapegoat. In Washington, lawmakers were debating what to do about the uprising and whom to blame.

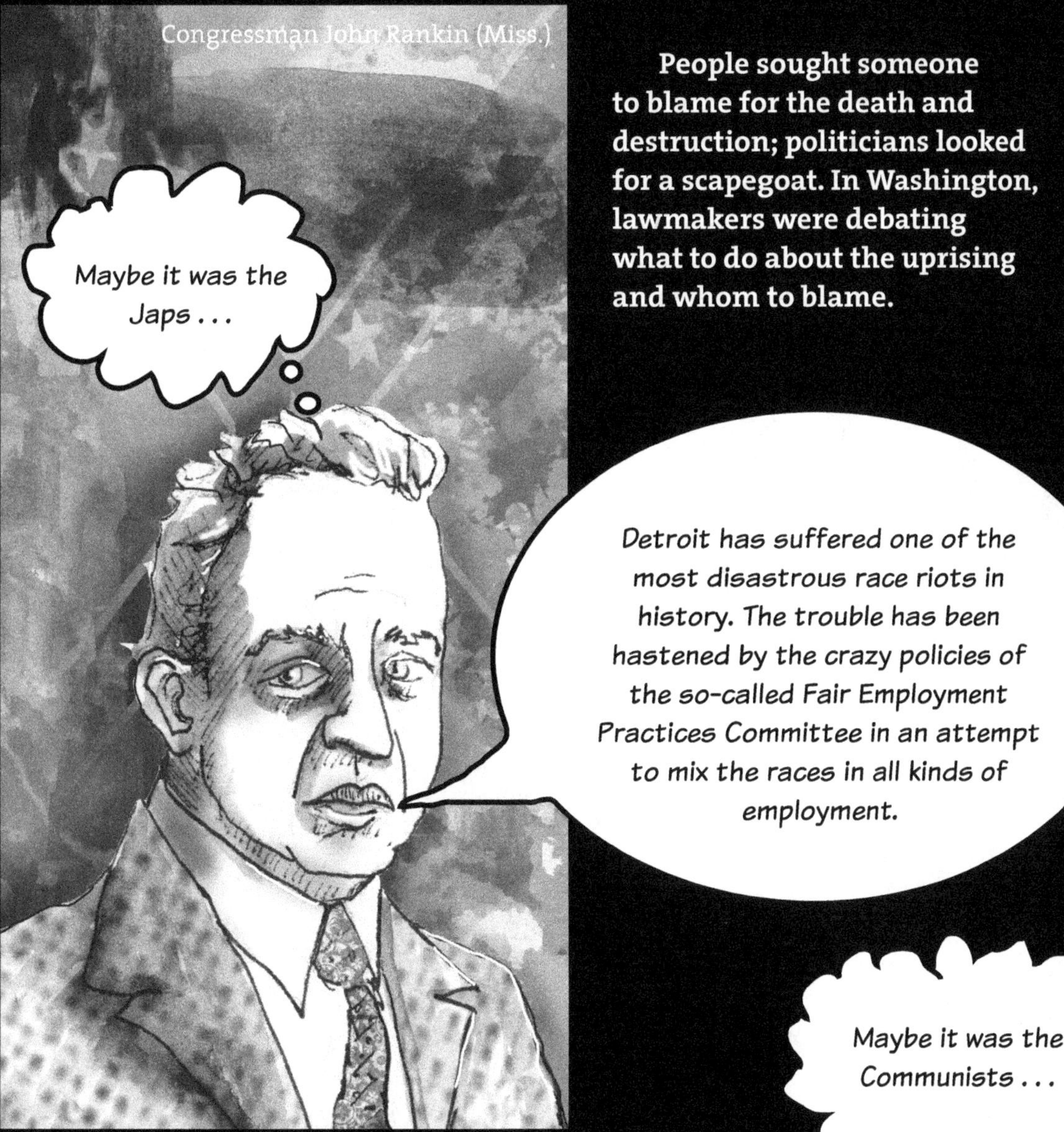
Congressman John Rankin (Miss.)
Maybe it was the Japs . . .
Detroit has suffered one of the most disastrous race riots in history. The trouble has been hastened by the crazy policies of the so-called Fair Employment Practices Committee in an attempt to mix the races in all kinds of employment.

World War II was a time of internal paranoia and panic. Some white Americans still defended bigotry and sought any reason to defend their views with punitive measures and hateful rhetoric.

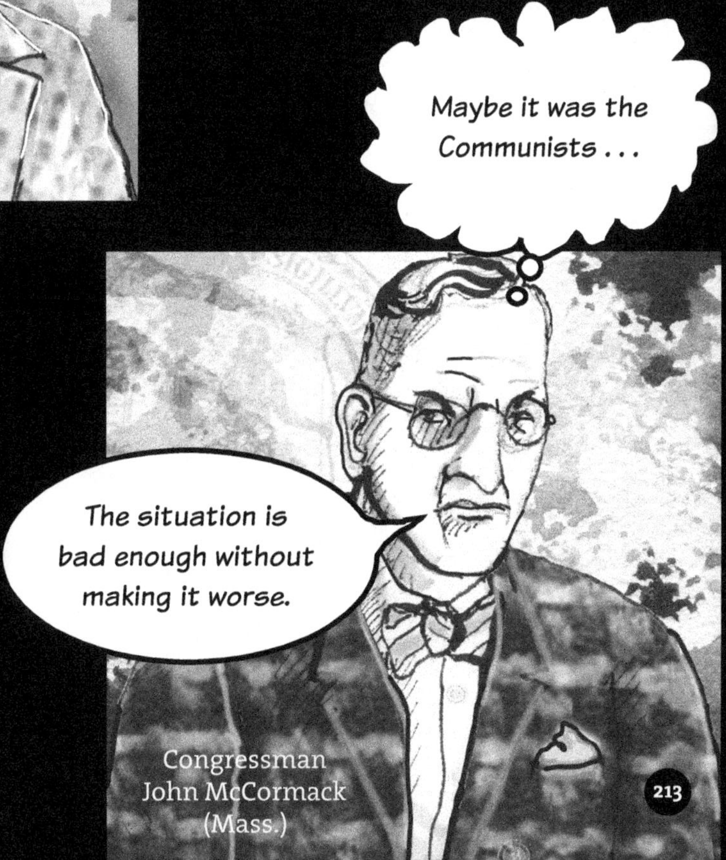
Maybe it was the Communists . . .
The situation is bad enough without making it worse.
Congressman John McCormack (Mass.)

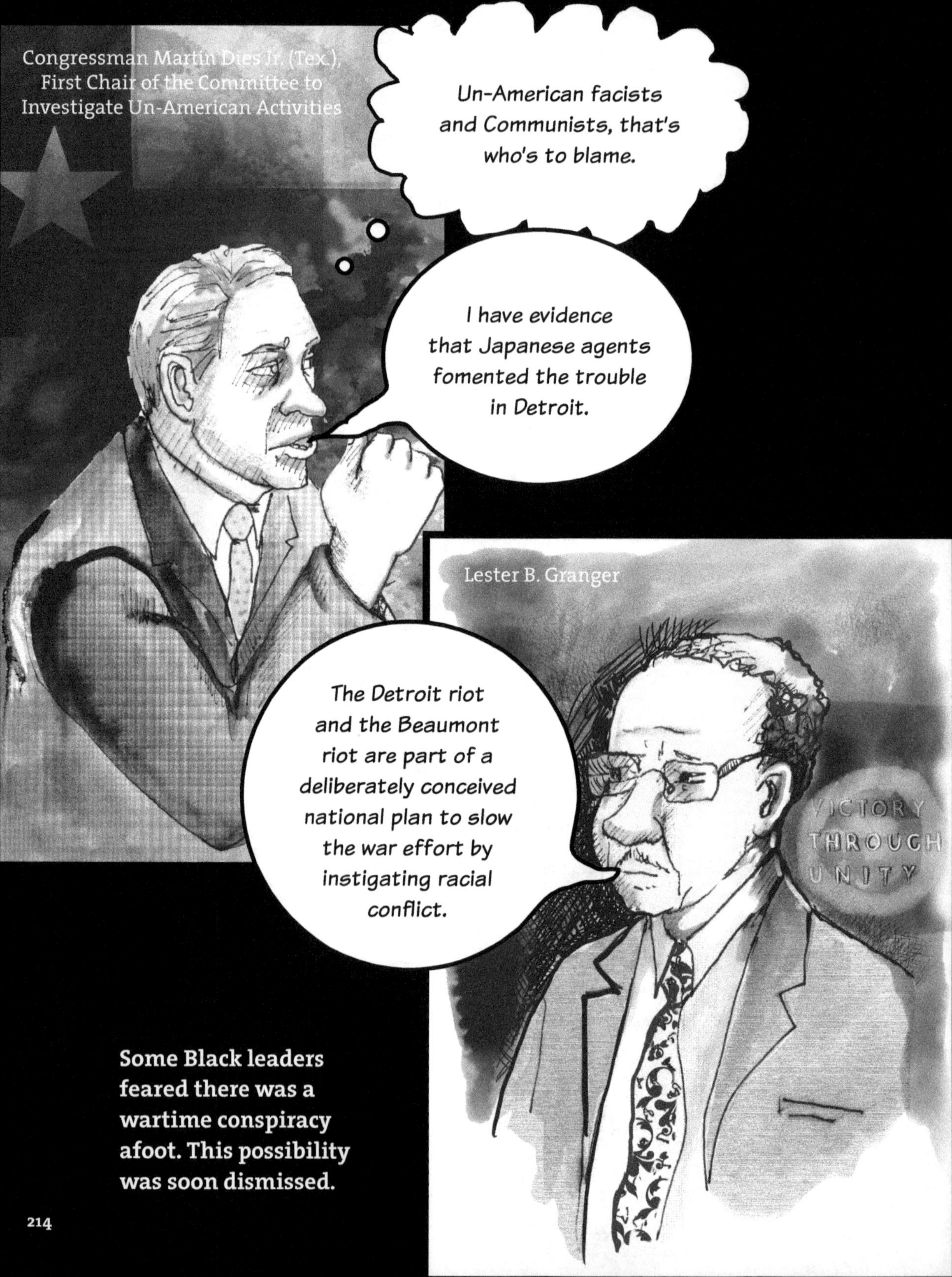
Congressman Martin Dies Jr. (Tex.), First Chair of the Committee to Investigate Un-American Activities
Un-American facists and Communists, that's who's to blame.
I have evidence that Japanese agents fomented the trouble in Detroit.
Lester B. Granger
The Detroit riot and the Beaumont riot are part of a deliberately conceived national plan to slow the war effort by instigating racial conflict.
VICTORY THROUGH UNITY
Some Black leaders feared there was a wartime conspiracy afoot. This possibility was soon dismissed.

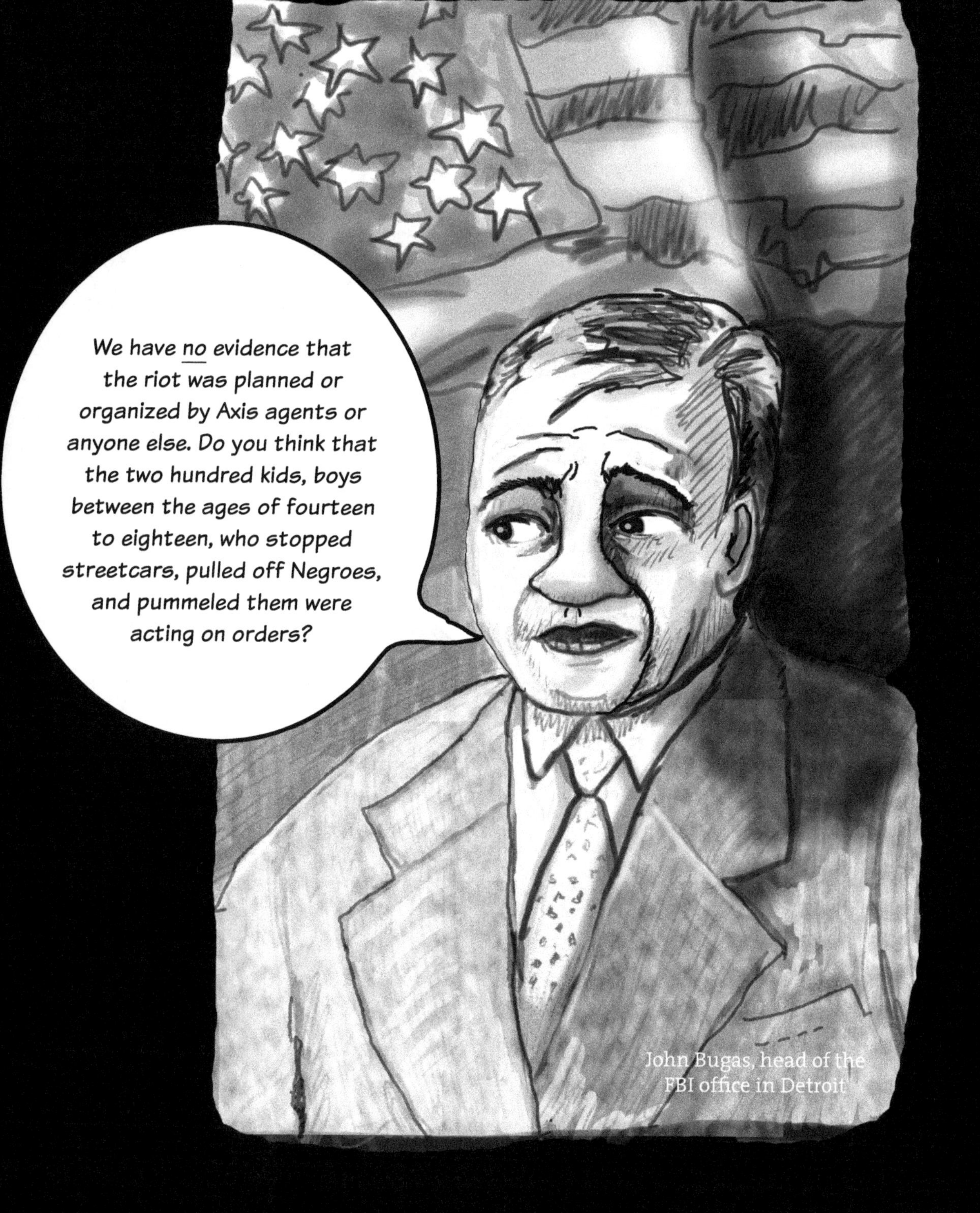
We have no evidence that the riot was planned or organized by Axis agents or anyone else. Do you think that the two hundred kids, boys between the ages of fourteen to eighteen, who stopped streetcars, pulled off Negroes, and pummeled them were acting on orders?
John Bugas, head of the FBI office in Detroit

People were desperate to find out who started the fighting and why there had been so much looting and violence.

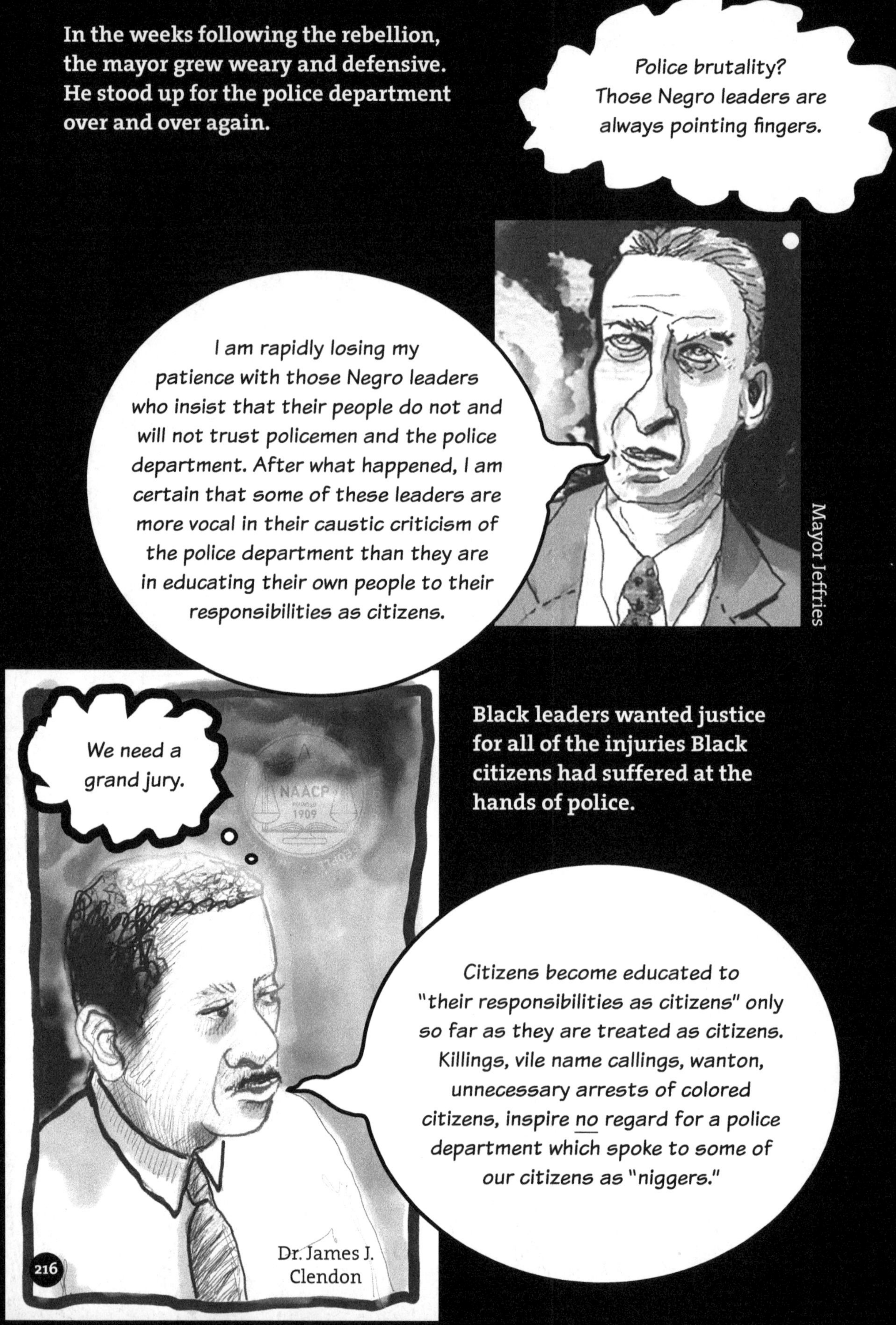
In the weeks following the rebellion, the mayor grew weary and defensive. He stood up for the police department over and over again.
Police brutality? Those Negro leaders are always pointing fingers.
I am rapidly losing my patience with those Negro leaders who insist that their people do not and will not trust policemen and the police department. After what happened, I am certain that some of these leaders are more vocal in their caustic criticism of the police department than they are in educating their own people to their responsibilities as citizens.
Mayor Jeffries
Black leaders wanted justice for all of the injuries Black citizens had suffered at the hands of police.
We need a grand jury.
NAACP
1909
Citizens become educated to "their responsibilities as citizens" only so far as they are treated as citizens. Killings, vile name callings, wanton, unnecessary arrests of colored citizens, inspire no regard for a police department which spoke to some of our citizens as "niggers."
Dr. James J. Clendon

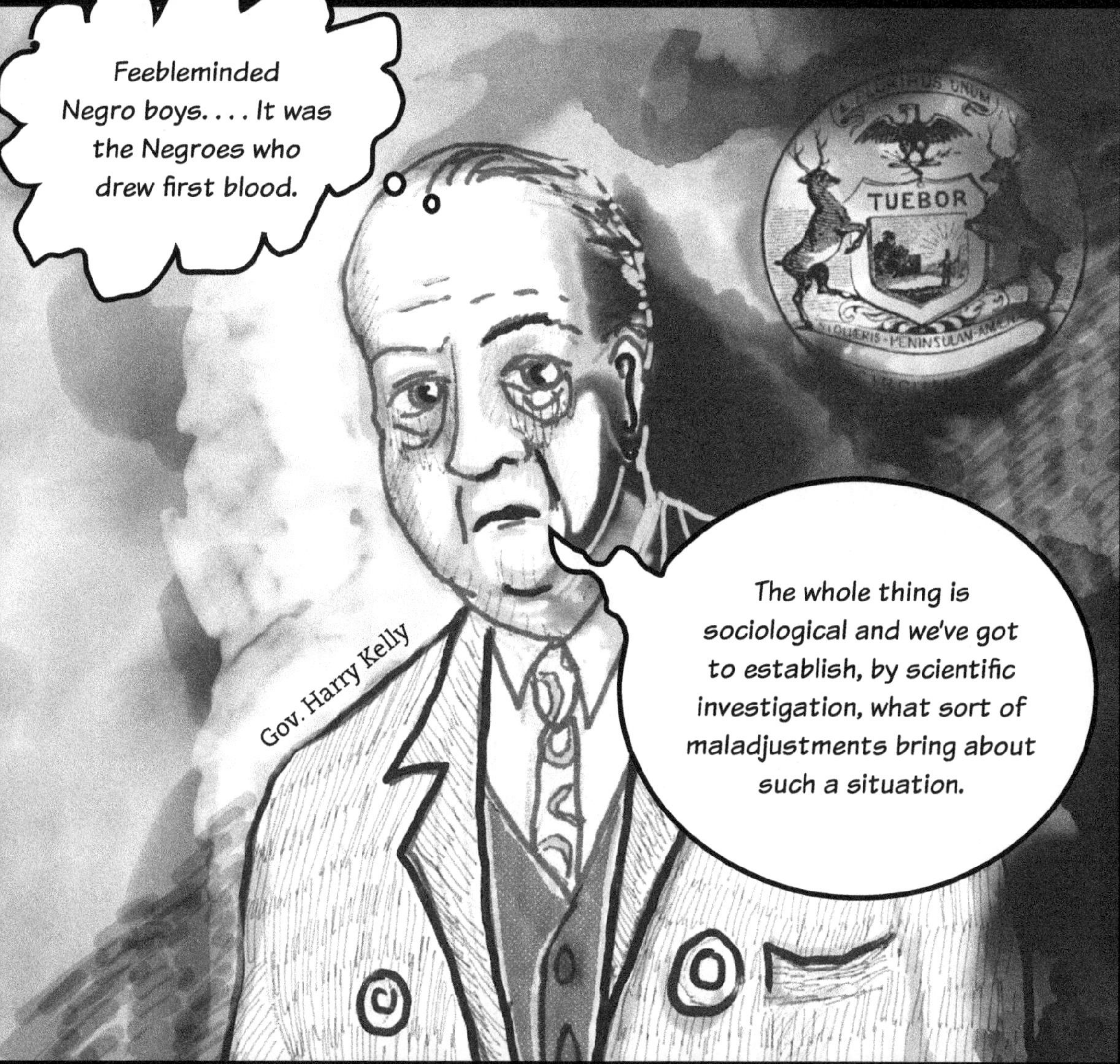
Feebleminded Negro boys. . . . It was the Negroes who drew first blood.
TUEBOR
Gov. Harry Kelly
The whole thing is sociological and we've got to establish, by scientific investigation, what sort of maladjustments bring about such a situation.

The unrest in Detroit was studied and investigated by activists and advocates from the NAACP, including Walter White and Thurgood Marshall; sociologists like Alfred McClung Lee; journalists like John Wood, W. K. Kelsey, Edward McCall, and Earl Brown; psychiatrist Lowell Selling; and high-ranking employees of the state and local government, like attorney William E. Dowling, Commissioner Witherspoon, and C. F. Ramsey, supervisor of the State Bureau of Child Welfare. Conclusions included that the instigators were African American men and boys, hillbillies, and "feebleminded" immigrants from the South. Some reports stated that inept responses from the mayor, racism, and overzealous, violent police were large contributing factors. Calls for an independent grand jury to investigate were ignored.

11

AFTERMATH

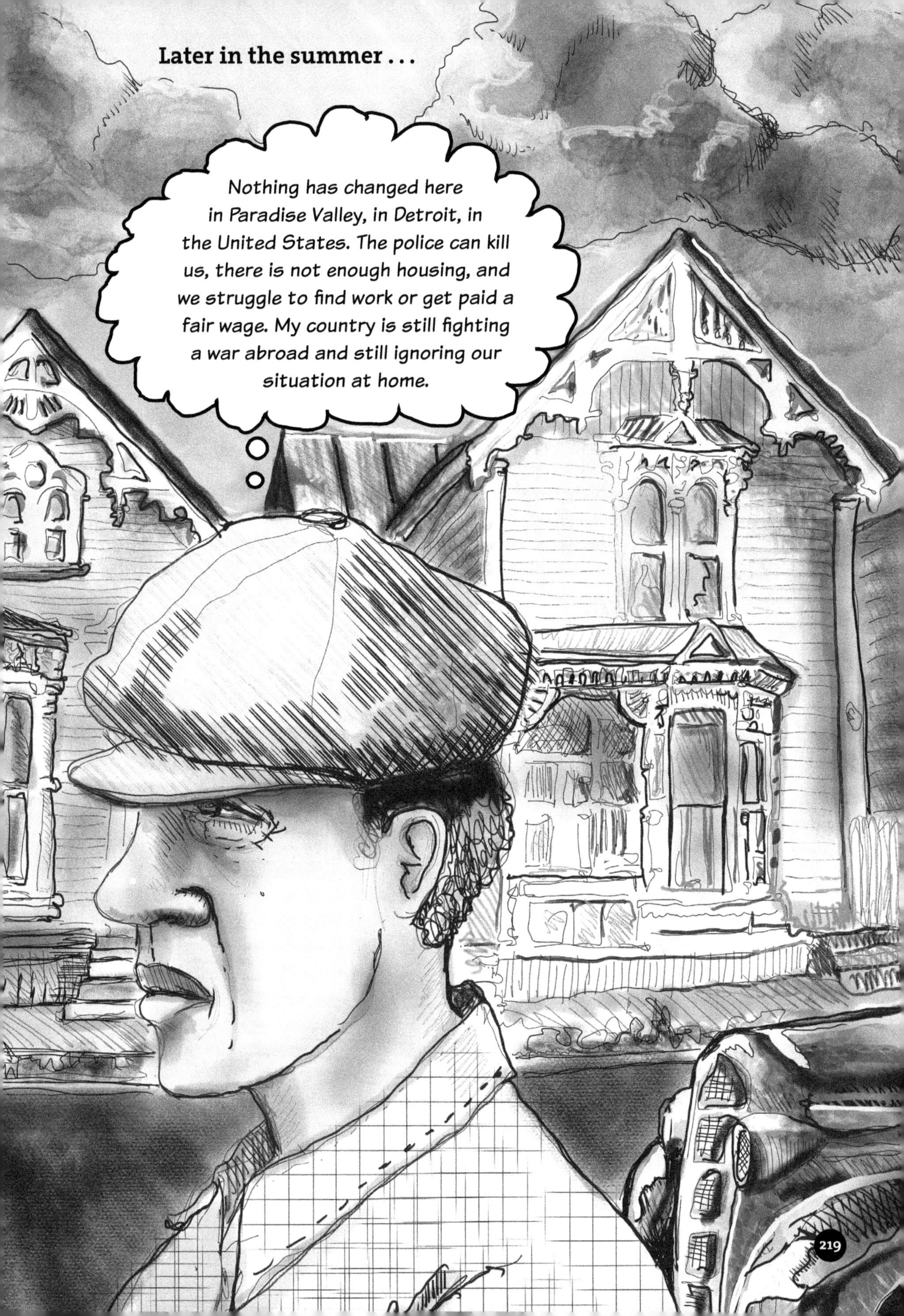
Later in the summer . . .
Nothing has changed here in Paradise Valley, in Detroit, in the United States. The police can kill us, there is not enough housing, and we struggle to find work or get paid a fair wage. My country is still fighting a war abroad and still ignoring our situation at home.

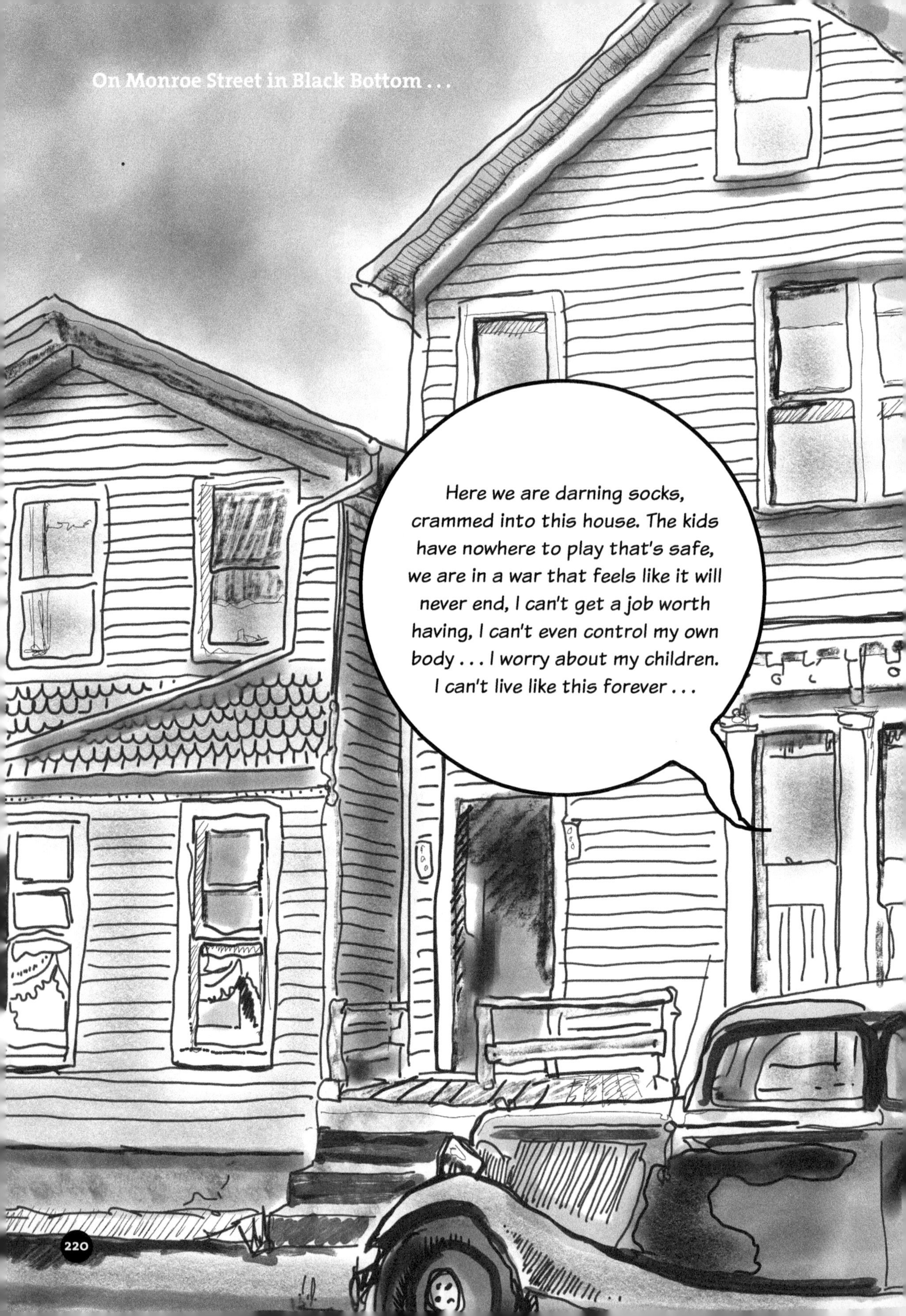
On Monroe Street in Black Bottom . . .
Here we are darning socks, crammed into this house. The kids have nowhere to play that's safe, we are in a war that feels like it will never end, I can't get a job worth having, I can't even control my own body . . . I worry about my children. I can't live like this forever . . .

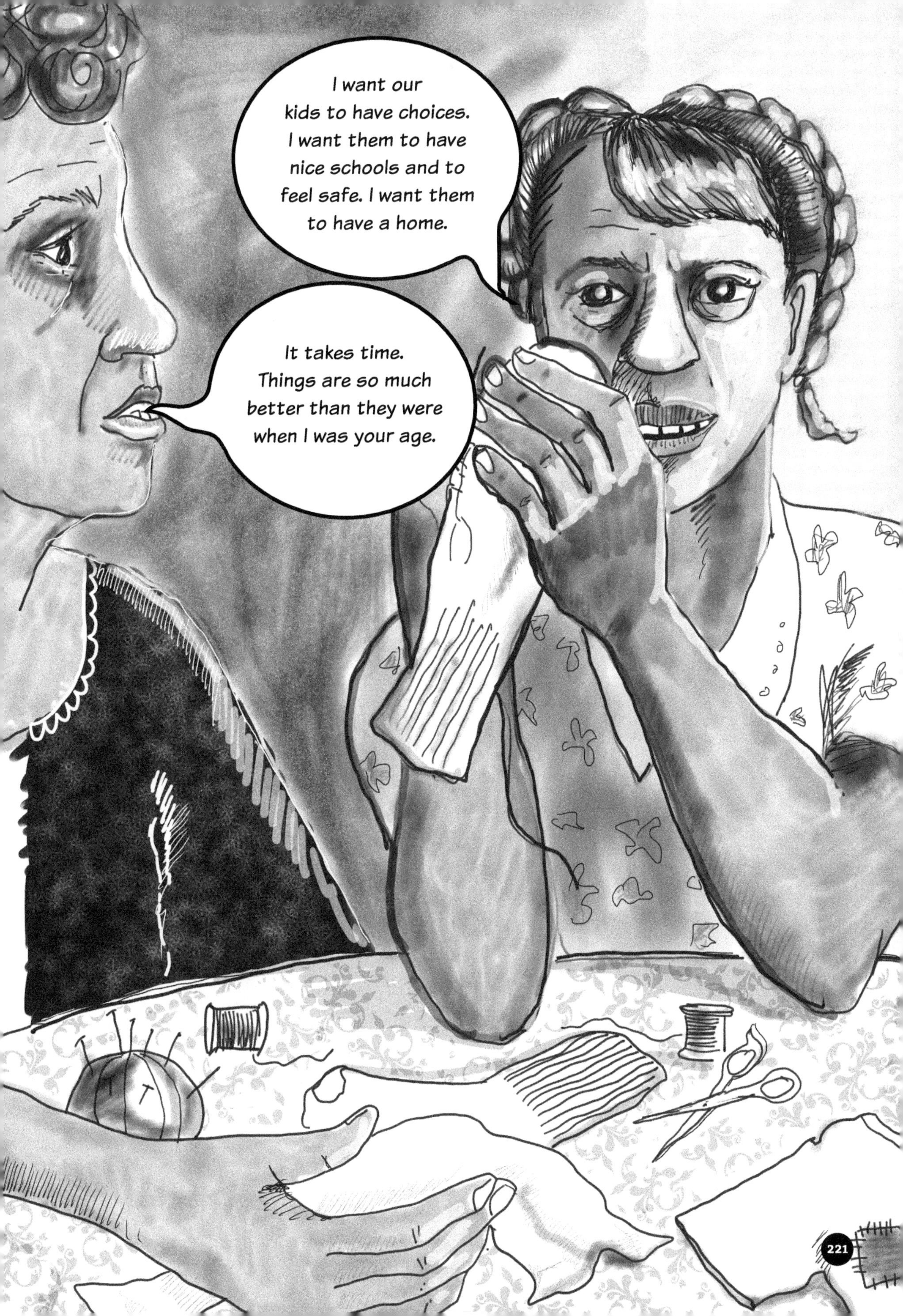
I want our kids to have choices. I want them to have nice schools and to feel safe. I want them to have a home.
It takes time. Things are so much better than they were when I was your age.

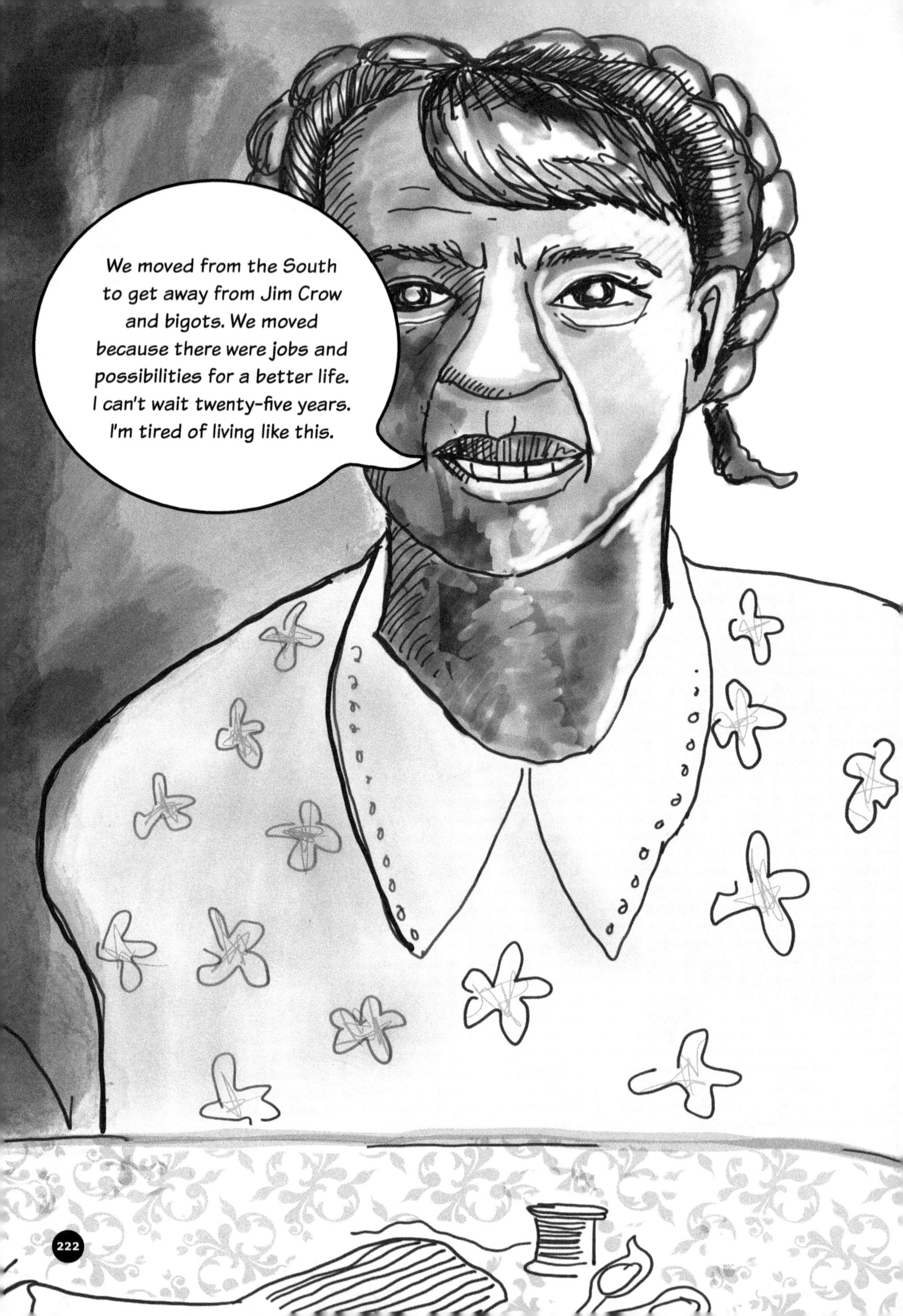
We moved from the South to get away from Jim Crow and bigots. We moved because there were jobs and possibilities for a better life. I can't wait twenty-five years. I'm tired of living like this.

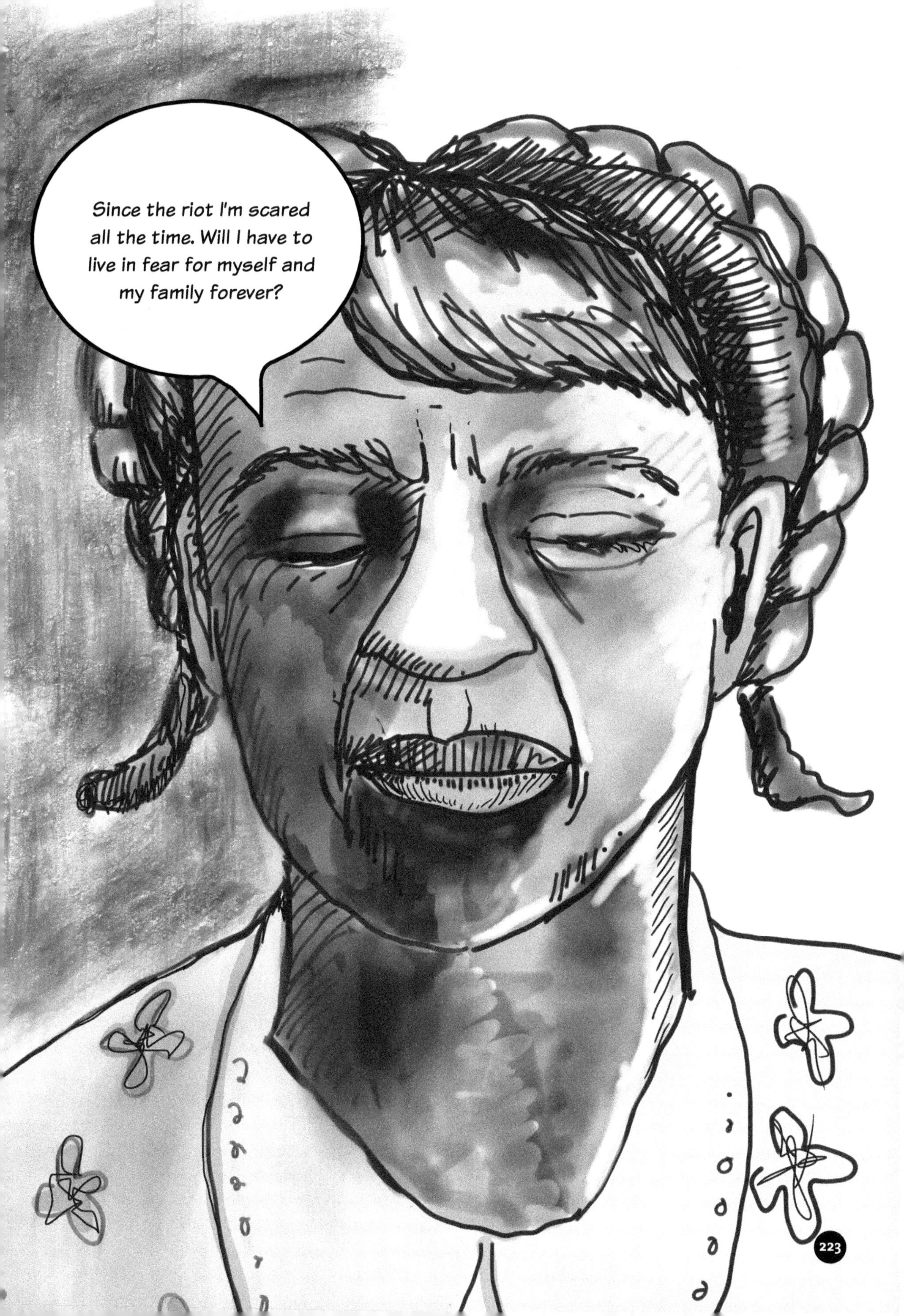
Since the riot I'm scared all the time. Will I have to live in fear for myself and my family forever?

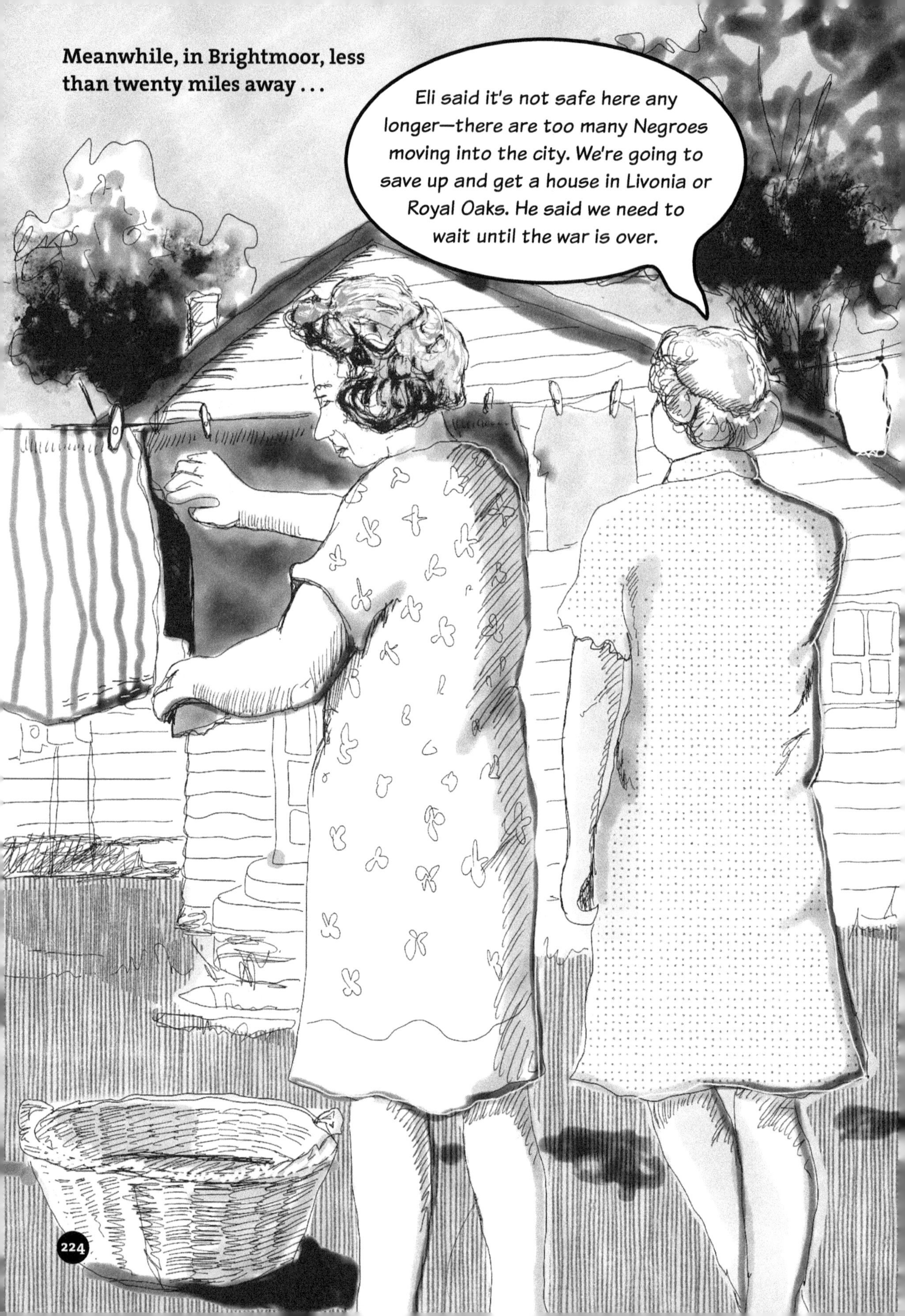
Meanwhile, in Brightmoor, less than twenty miles away . . .
Eli said it's not safe here any longer—there are too many Negroes moving into the city. We're going to save up and get a house in Livonia or Royal Oaks. He said we need to wait until the war is over.

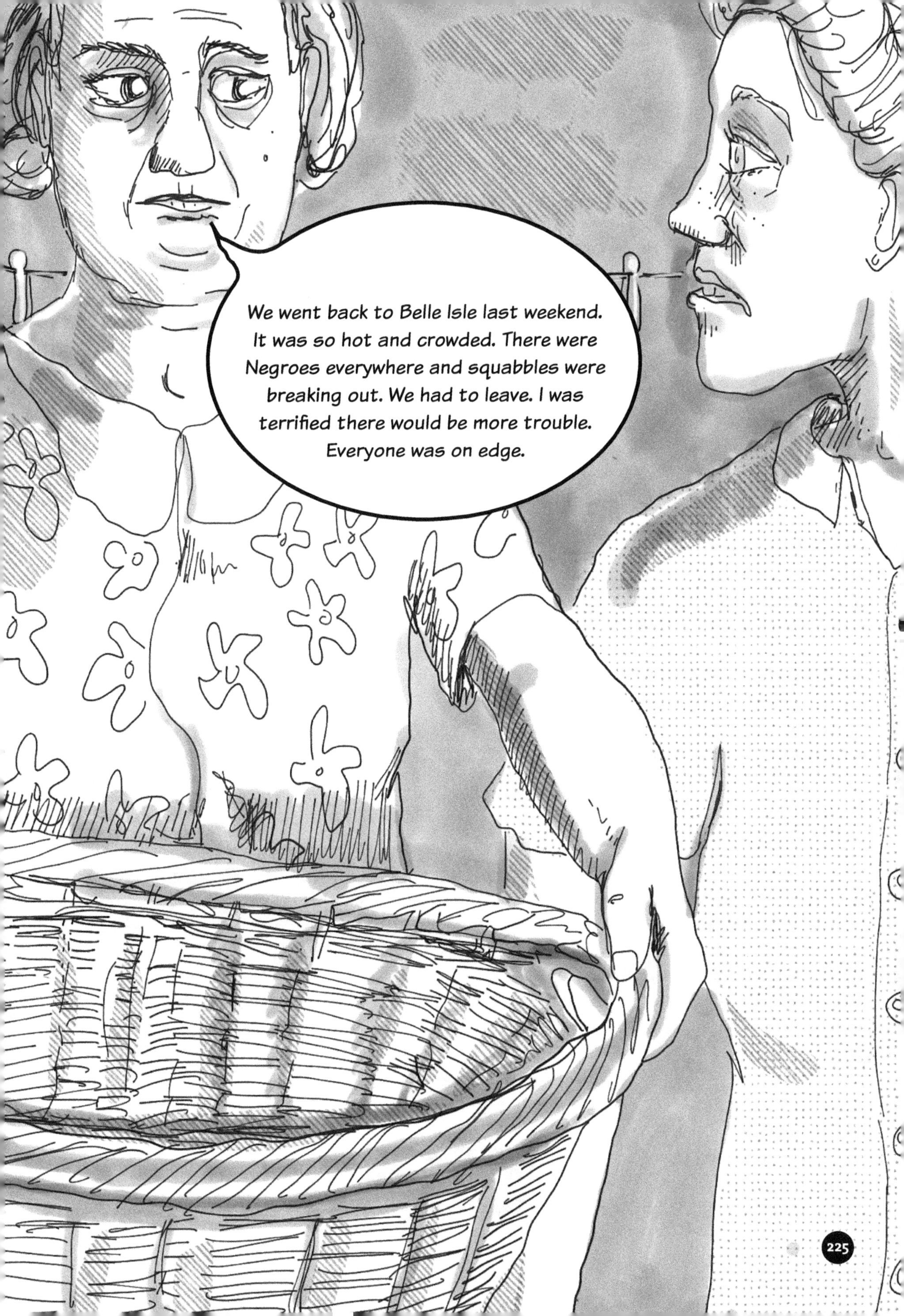
We went back to Belle Isle last weekend. It was so hot and crowded. There were Negroes everywhere and squabbles were breaking out. We had to leave. I was terrified there would be more trouble. Everyone was on edge.

12

Eden

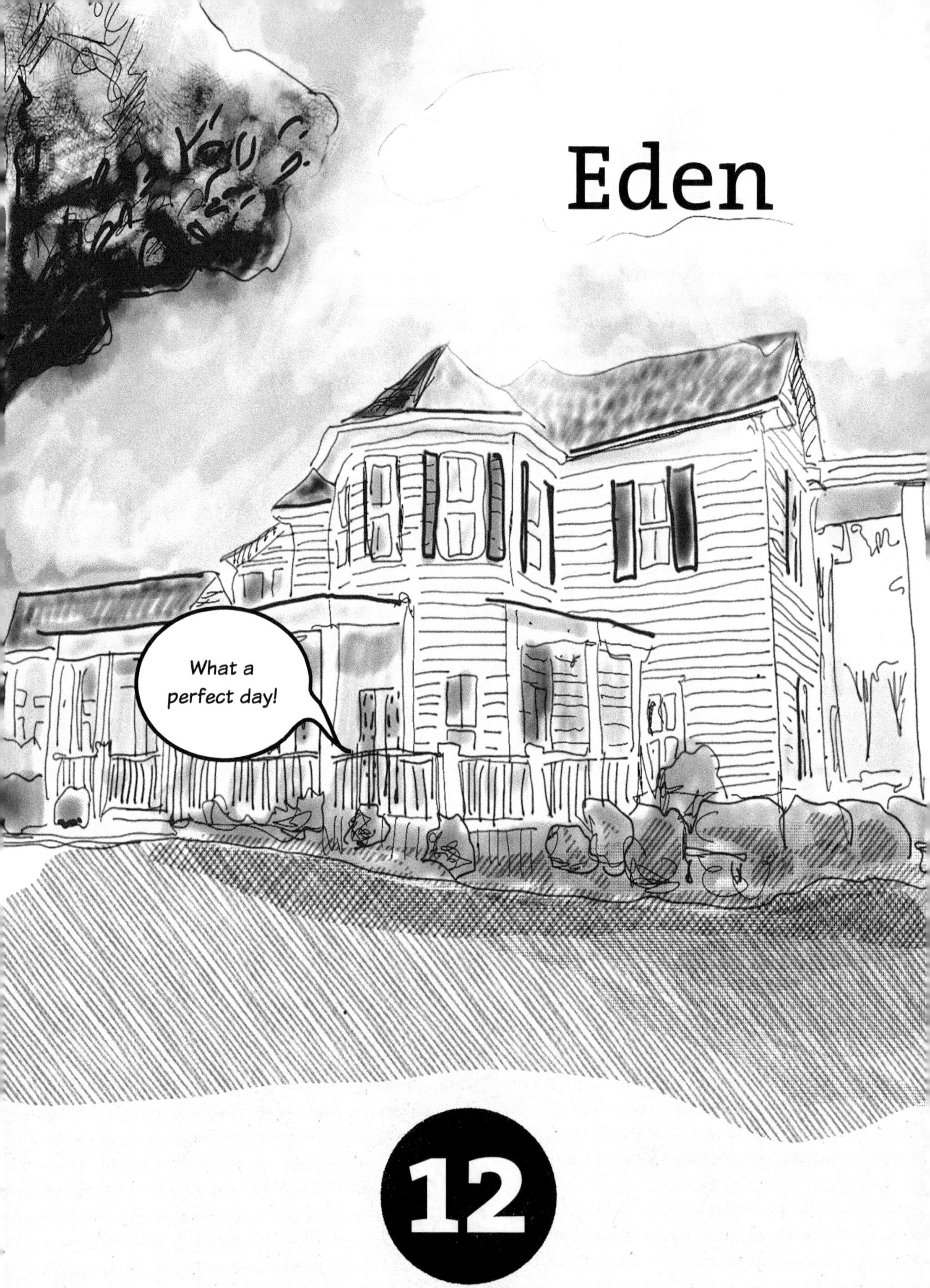
What a perfect day!

Late May 1968, somewhere near Idlewild, Michigan . . .

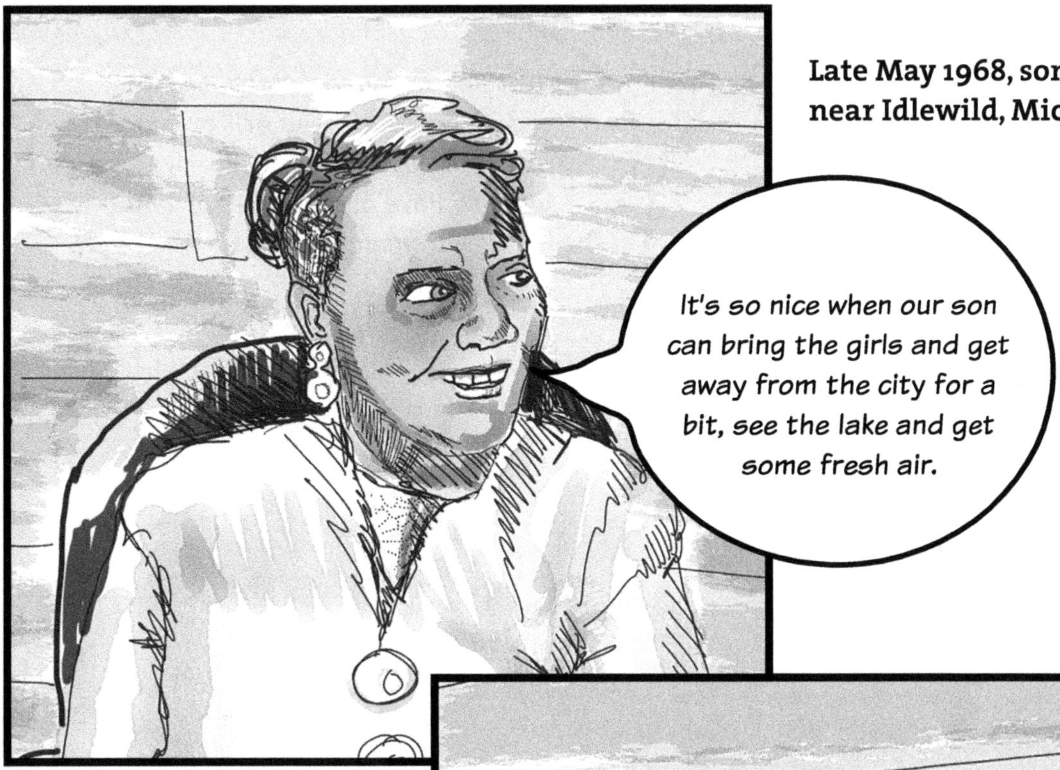
It's so nice when our son can bring the girls and get away from the city for a bit, see the lake and get some fresh air.

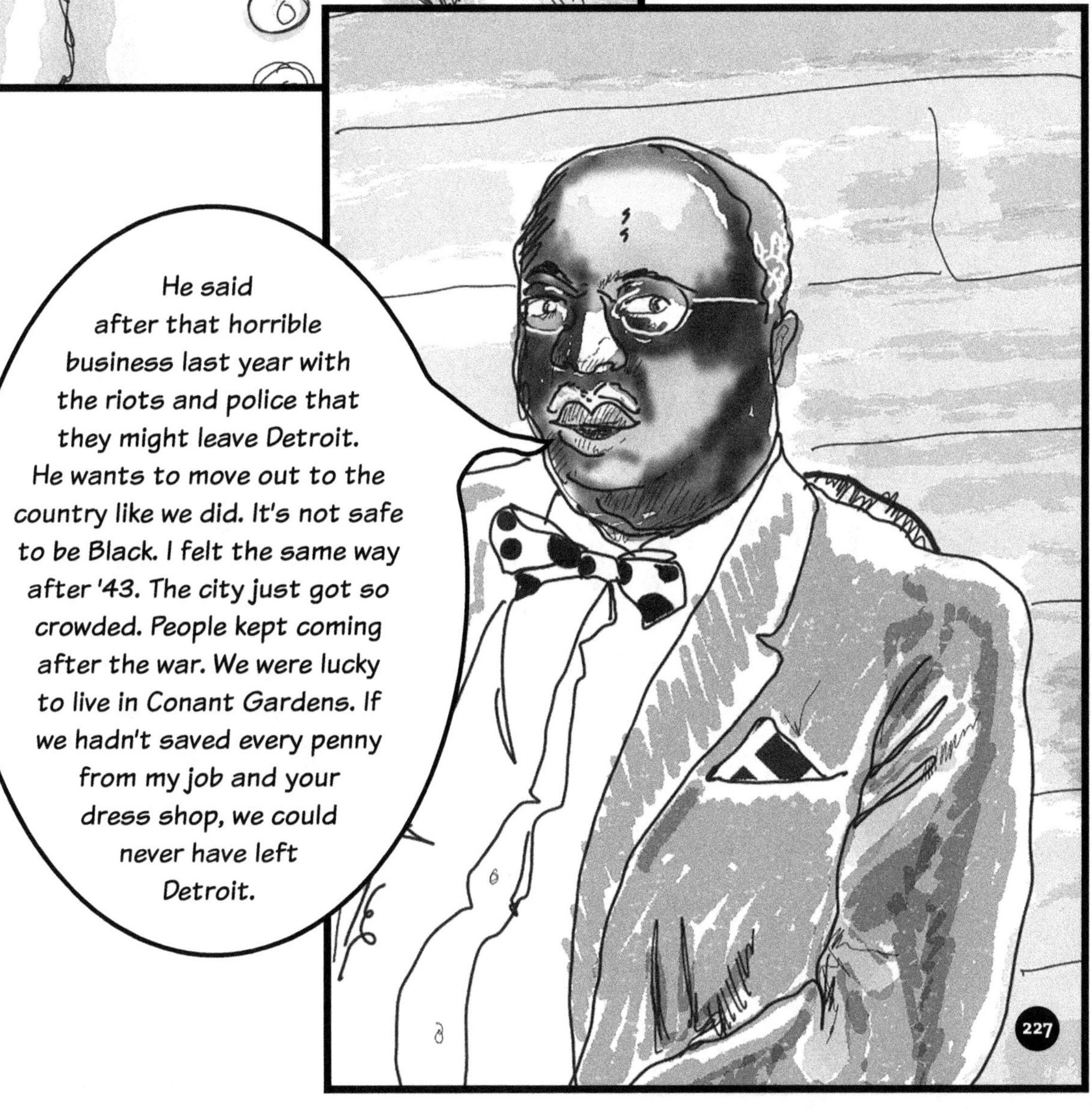
He said after that horrible business last year with the riots and police that they might leave Detroit. He wants to move out to the country like we did. It's not safe to be Black. I felt the same way after '43. The city just got so crowded. People kept coming after the war. We were lucky to live in Conant Gardens. If we hadn't saved every penny from my job and your dress shop, we could never have left Detroit.

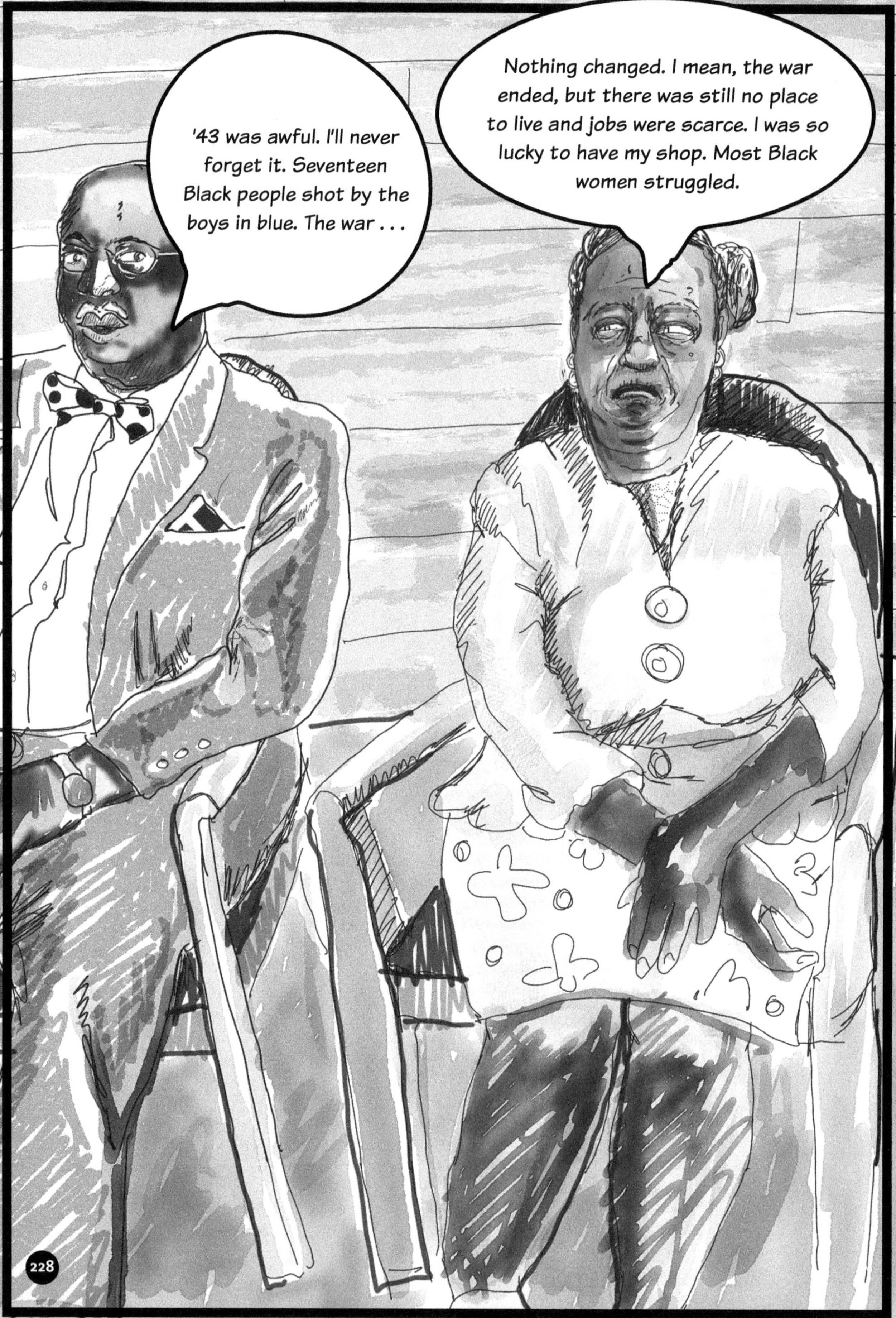
'43 was awful. I'll never forget it. Seventeen Black people shot by the boys in blue. The war . . .
Nothing changed. I mean, the war ended, but there was still no place to live and jobs were scarce. I was so lucky to have my shop. Most Black women struggled.

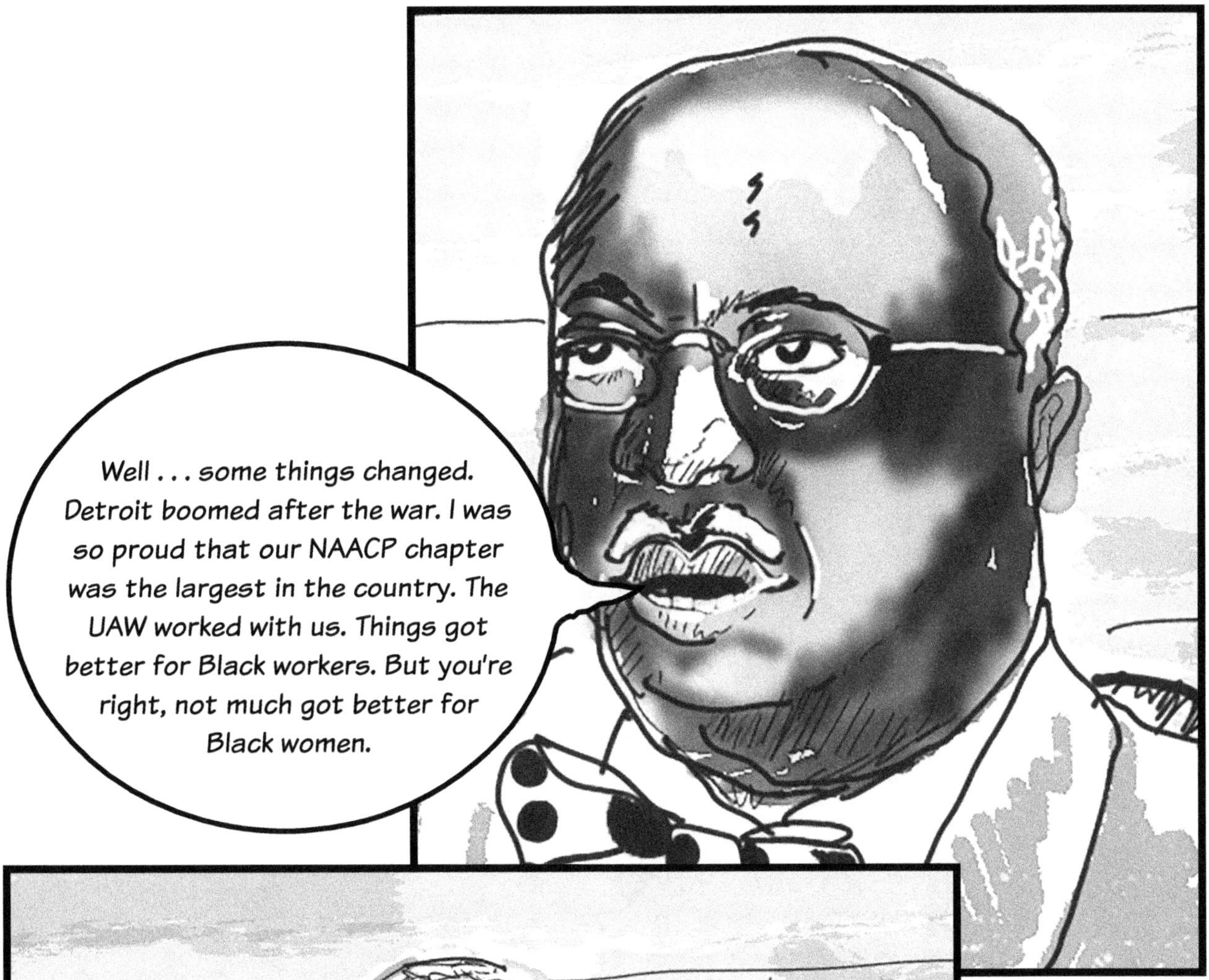
Well . . . some things changed. Detroit boomed after the war. I was so proud that our NAACP chapter was the largest in the country. The UAW worked with us. Things got better for Black workers. But you're right, not much got better for Black women.

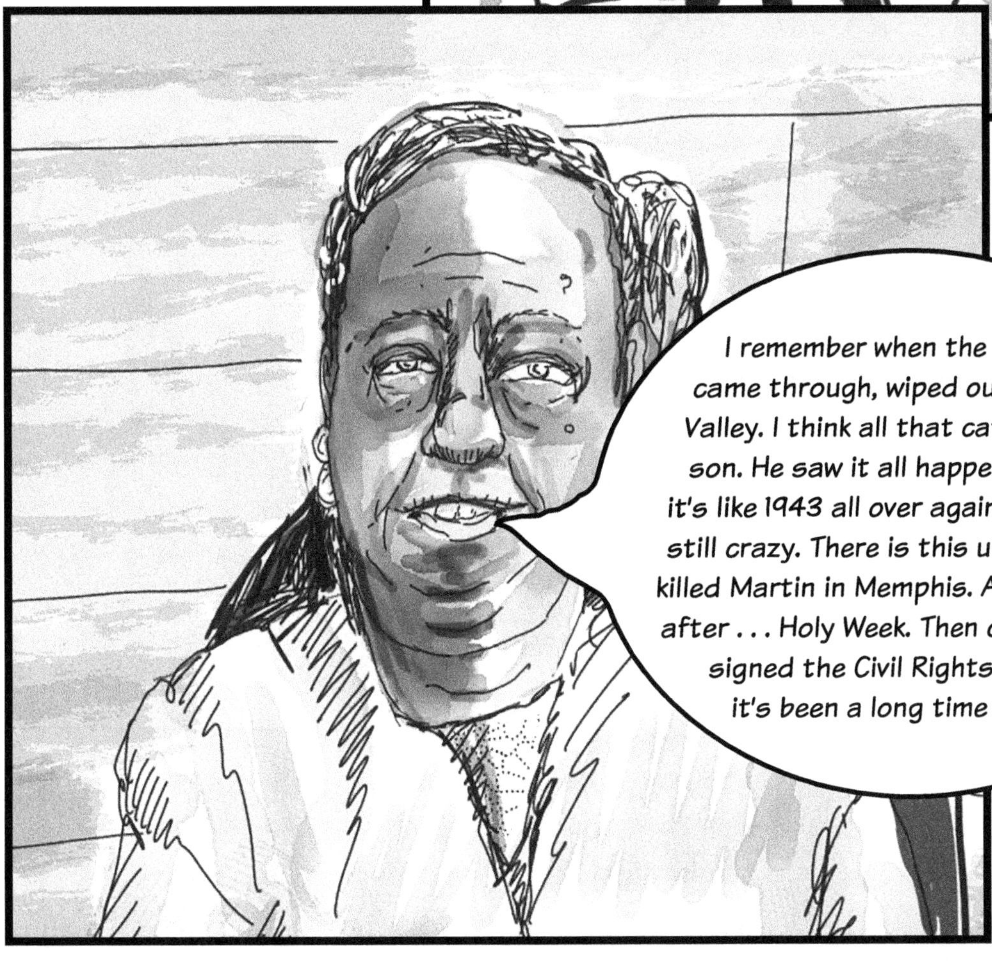
I remember when the highway came through, wiped out Paradise Valley. I think all that catalyzed our son. He saw it all happen. But now, it's like 1943 all over again—things are still crazy. There is this ugly war. They killed Martin in Memphis. All those riots after . . . Holy Week. Then our president signed the Civil Rights Act—but it's been a long time coming.

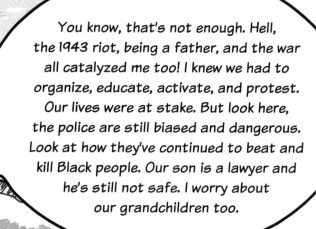

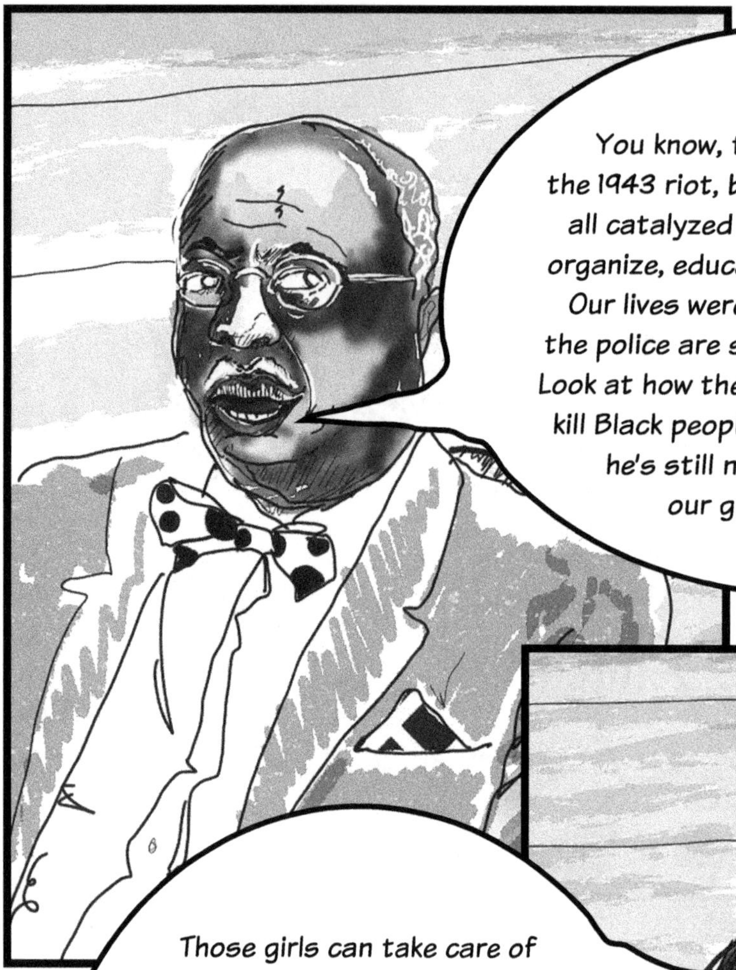
You know, that's not enough. Hell, the 1943 riot, being a father, and the war all catalyzed me too! I knew we had to organize, educate, activate, and protest. Our lives were at stake. But look here, the police are still biased and dangerous. Look at how they've continued to beat and kill Black people. Our son is a lawyer and he's still not safe. I worry about our grandchildren too.

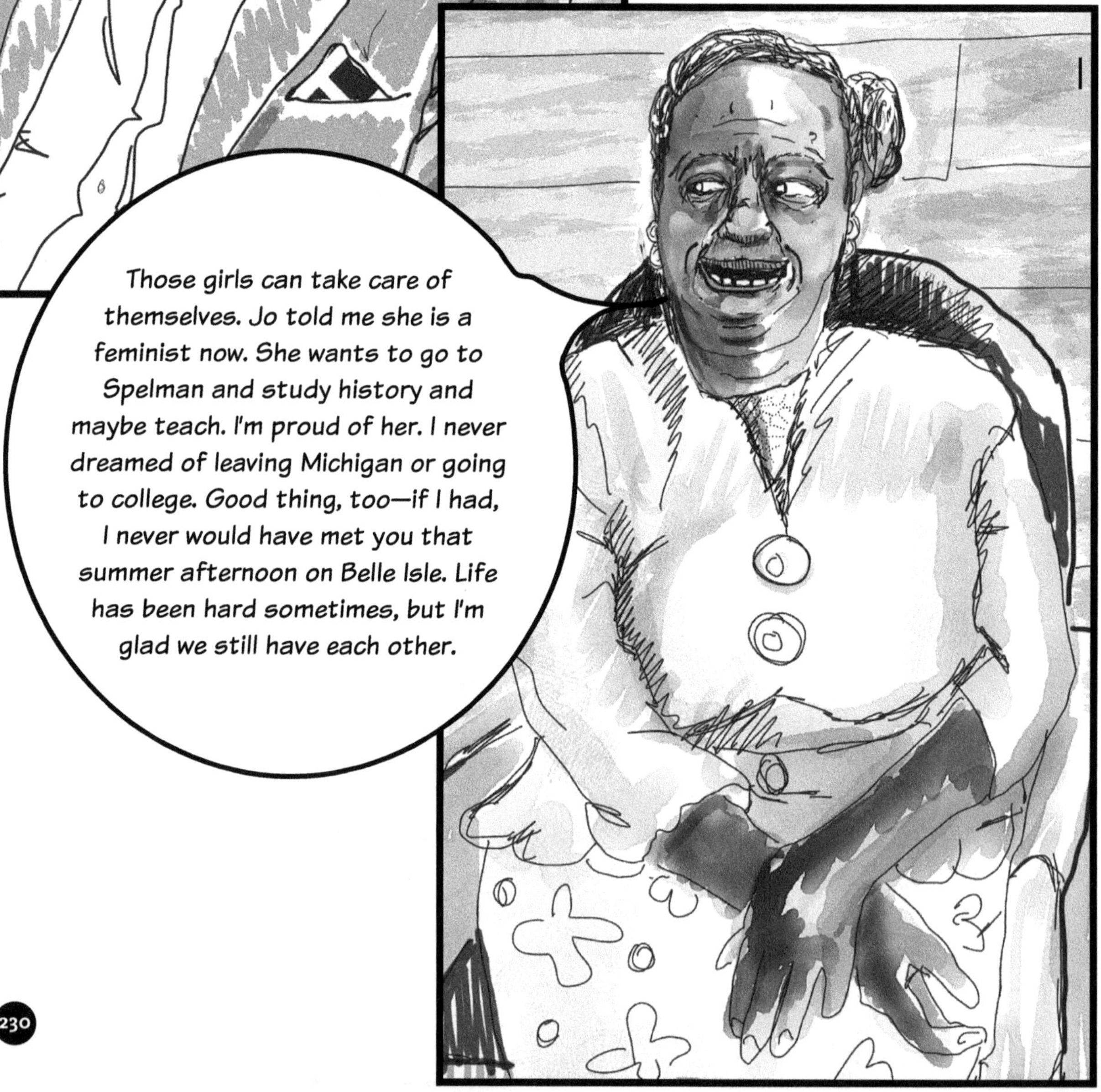
Those girls can take care of themselves. Jo told me she is a feminist now. She wants to go to Spelman and study history and maybe teach. I'm proud of her. I never dreamed of leaving Michigan or going to college. Good thing, too—if I had, I never would have met you that summer afternoon on Belle Isle. Life has been hard sometimes, but I'm glad we still have each other.

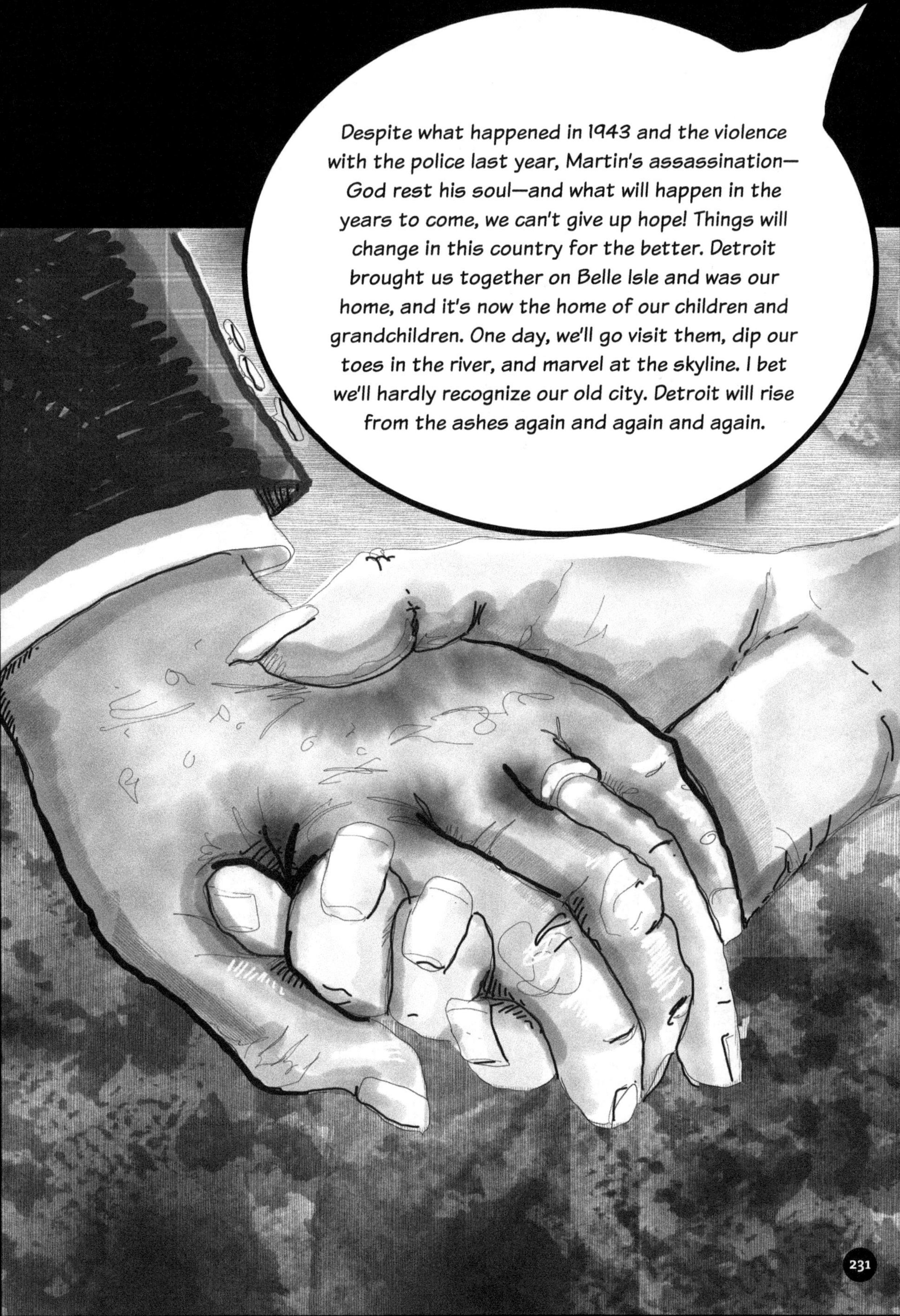
Despite what happened in 1943 and the violence with the police last year, Martin's assassination—God rest his soul—and what will happen in the years to come, we can't give up hope! Things will change in this country for the better. Detroit brought us together on Belle Isle and was our home, and it's now the home of our children and grandchildren. One day, we'll go visit them, dip our toes in the river, and marvel at the skyline. I bet we'll hardly recognize our old city. Detroit will rise from the ashes again and again and again.

CODA

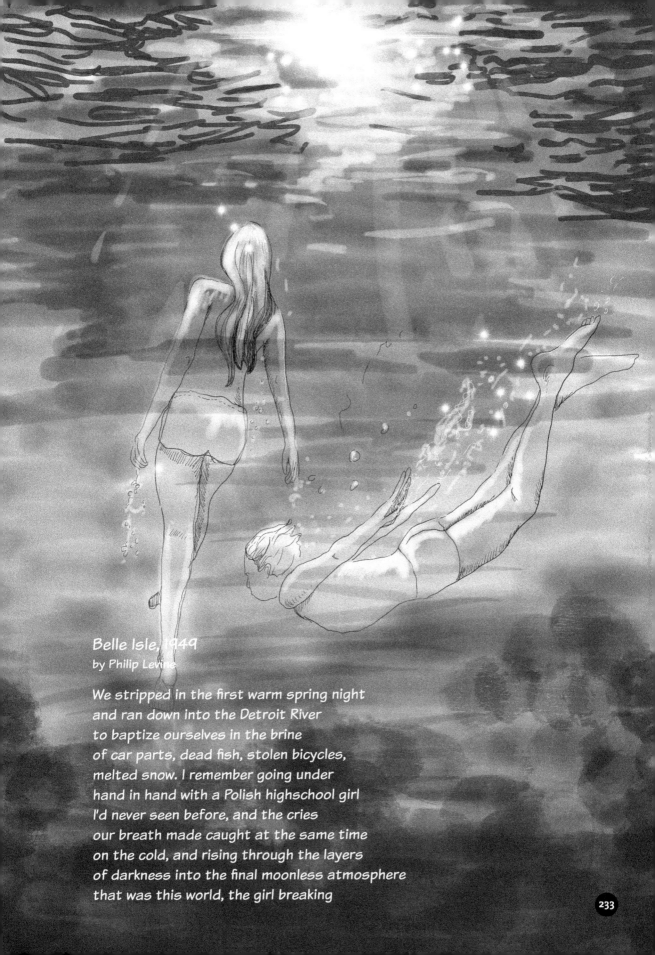

Belle Isle, 1949
by Philip Levine

We stripped in the first warm spring night
and ran down into the Detroit River
to baptize ourselves in the brine
of car parts, dead fish, stolen bicycles,
melted snow. I remember going under
hand in hand with a Polish highschool girl
I'd never seen before, and the cries
our breath made caught at the same time
on the cold, and rising through the layers
of darkness into the final moonless atmosphere
that was this world, the girl breaking

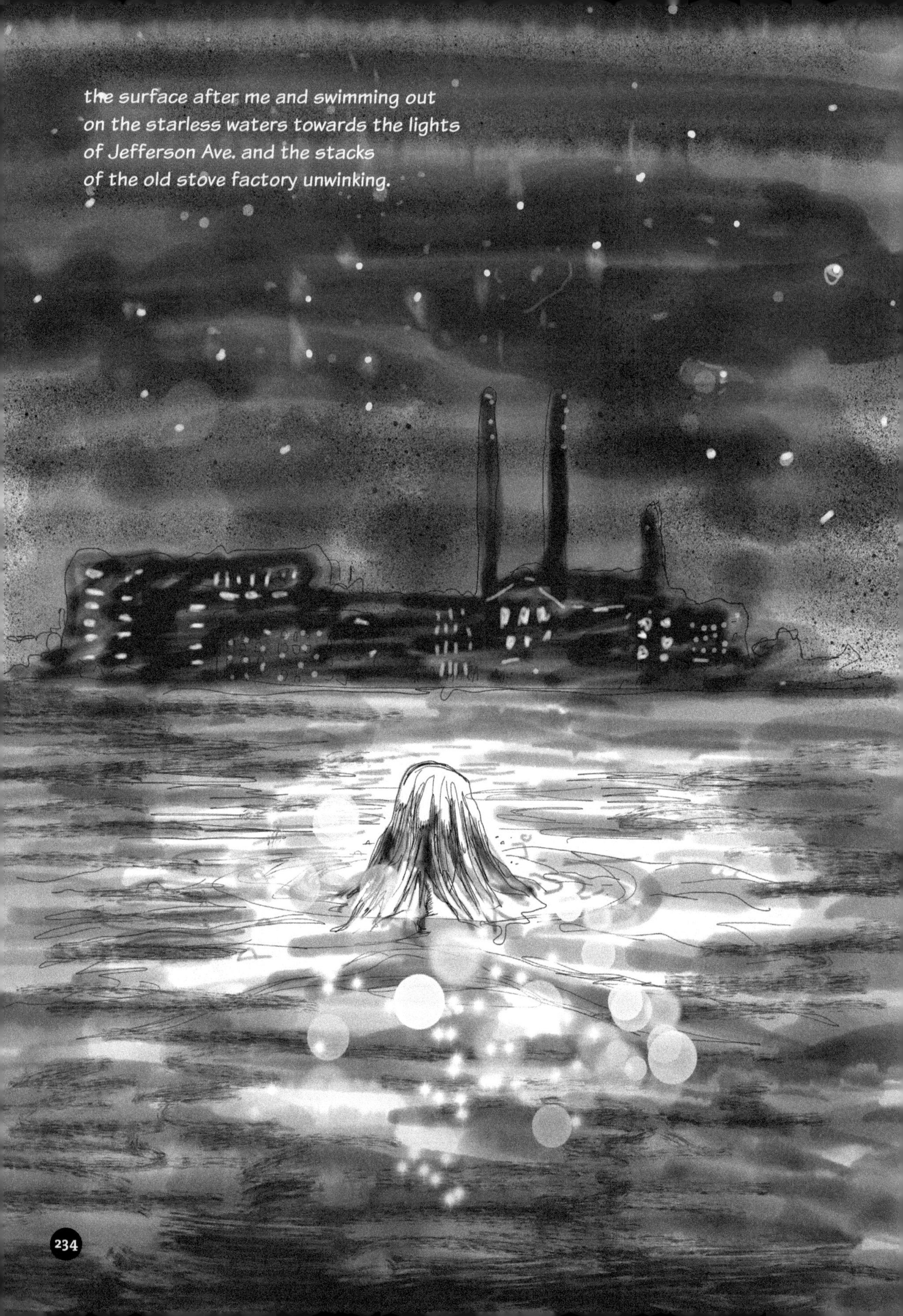
the surface after me and swimming out
on the starless waters towards the lights
of Jefferson Ave. and the stacks
of the old stove factory unwinking.

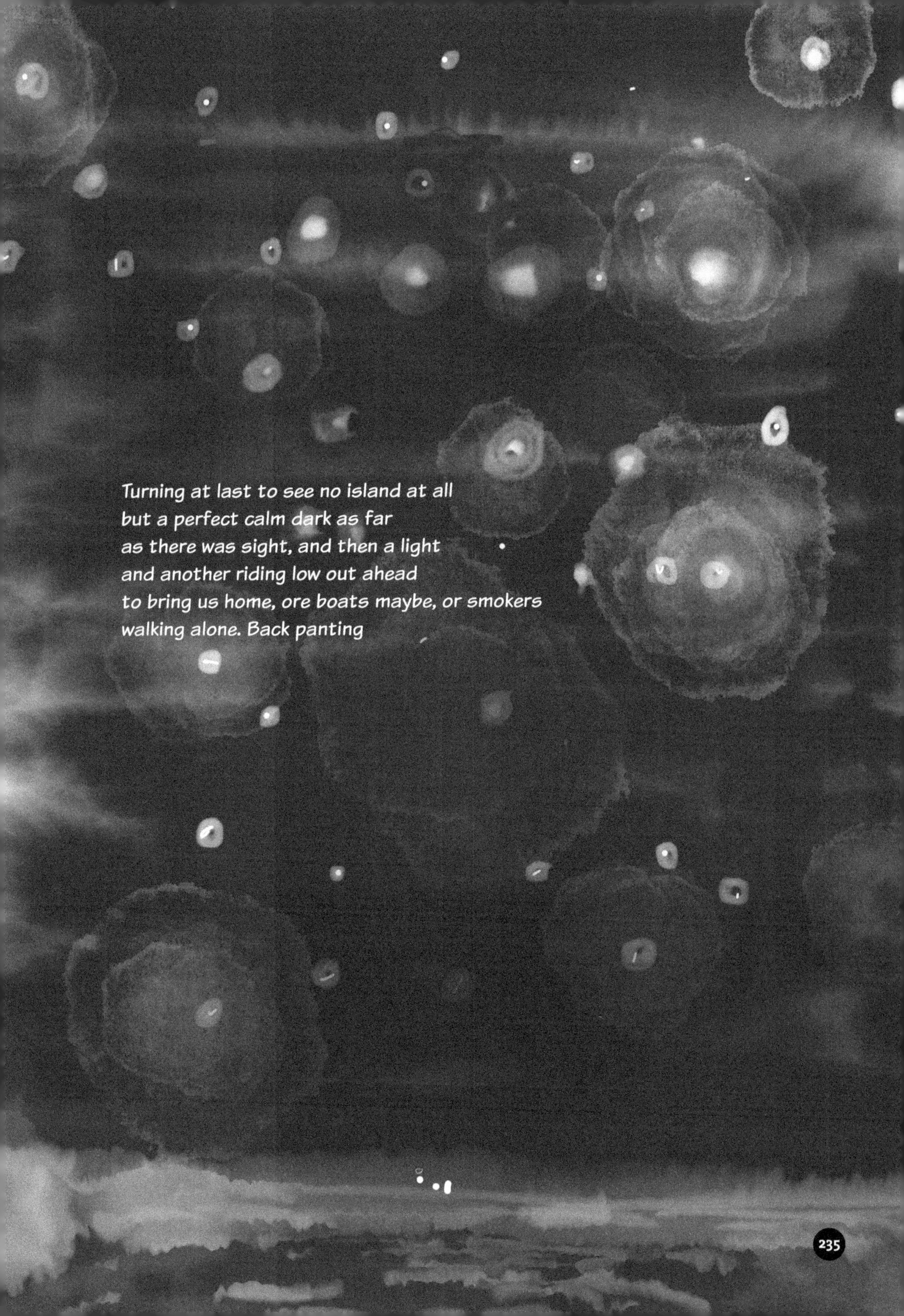

Turning at last to see no island at all
but a perfect calm dark as far
as there was sight, and then a light
and another riding low out ahead
to bring us home, ore boats maybe, or smokers
walking alone. Back panting

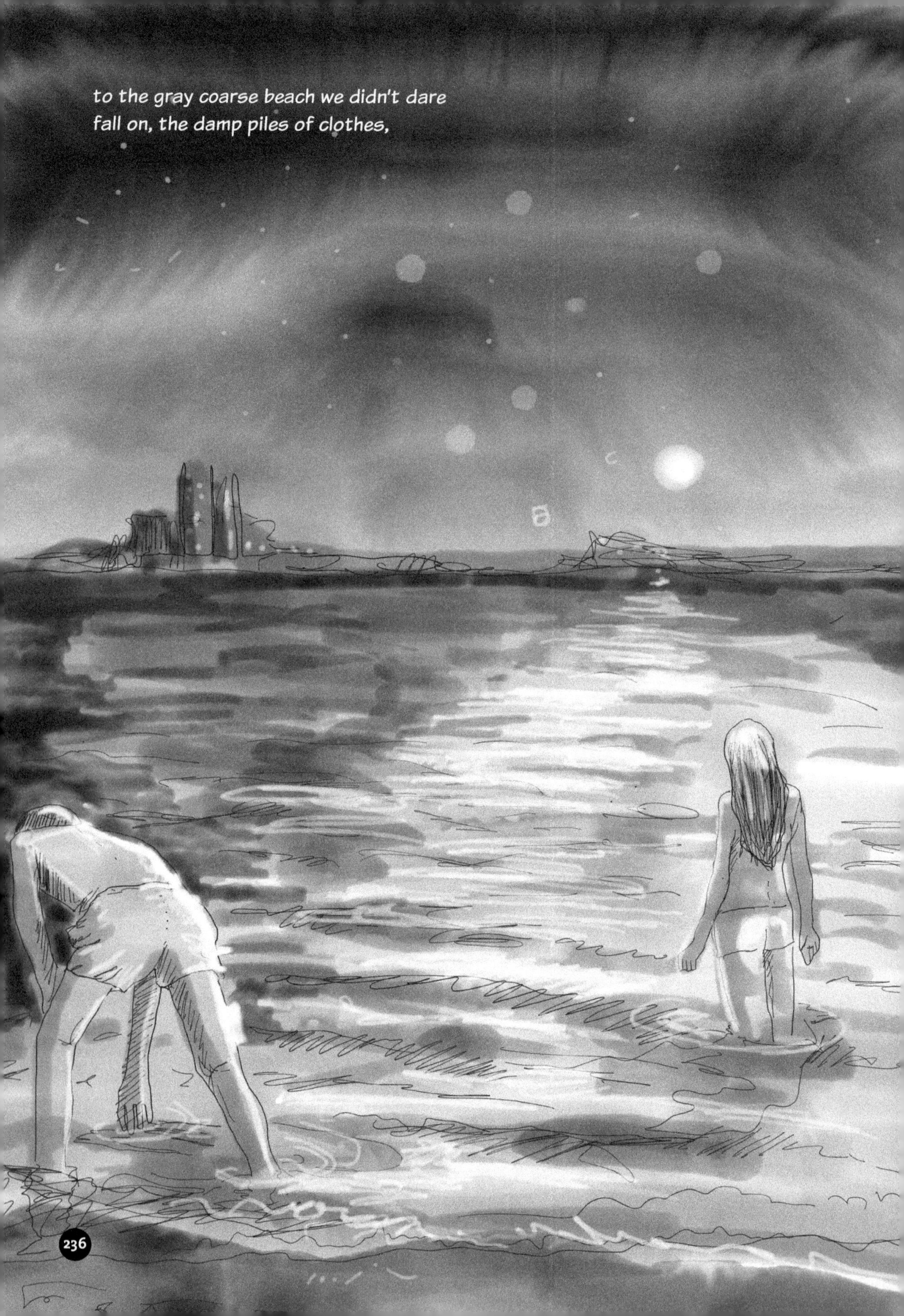
to the gray coarse beach we didn't dare
fall on, the damp piles of clothes,

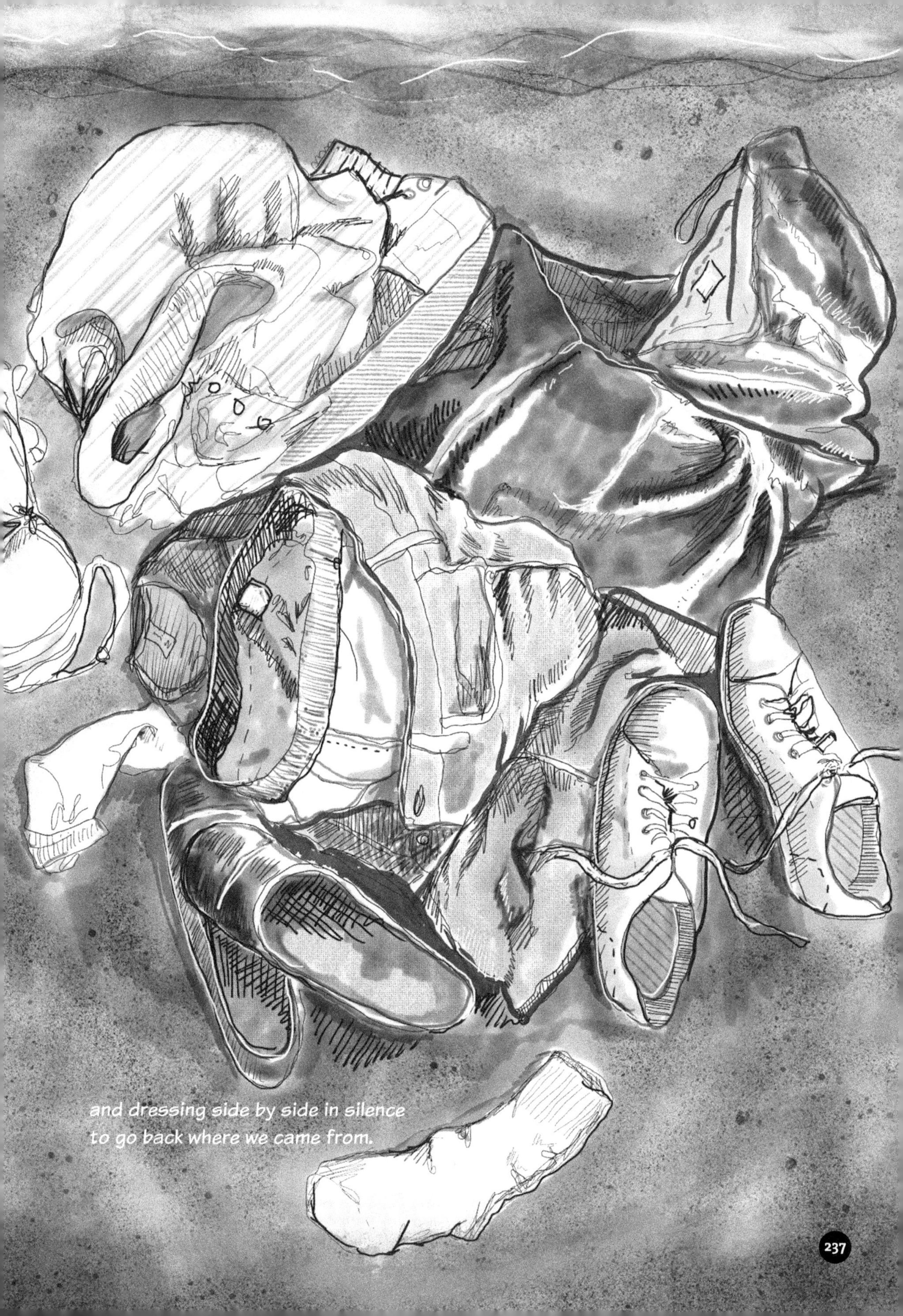
and dressing side by side in silence
to go back where we came from.

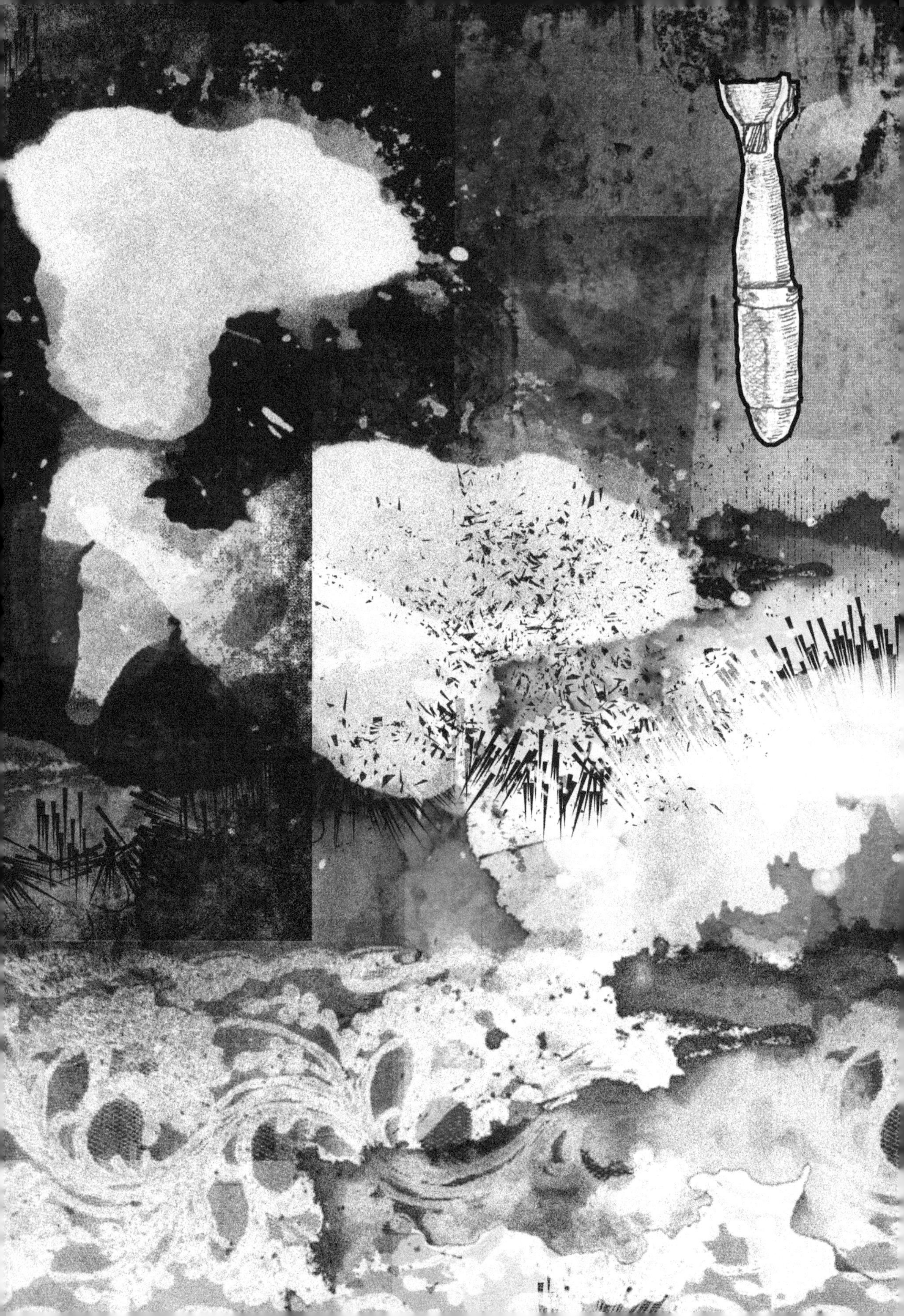

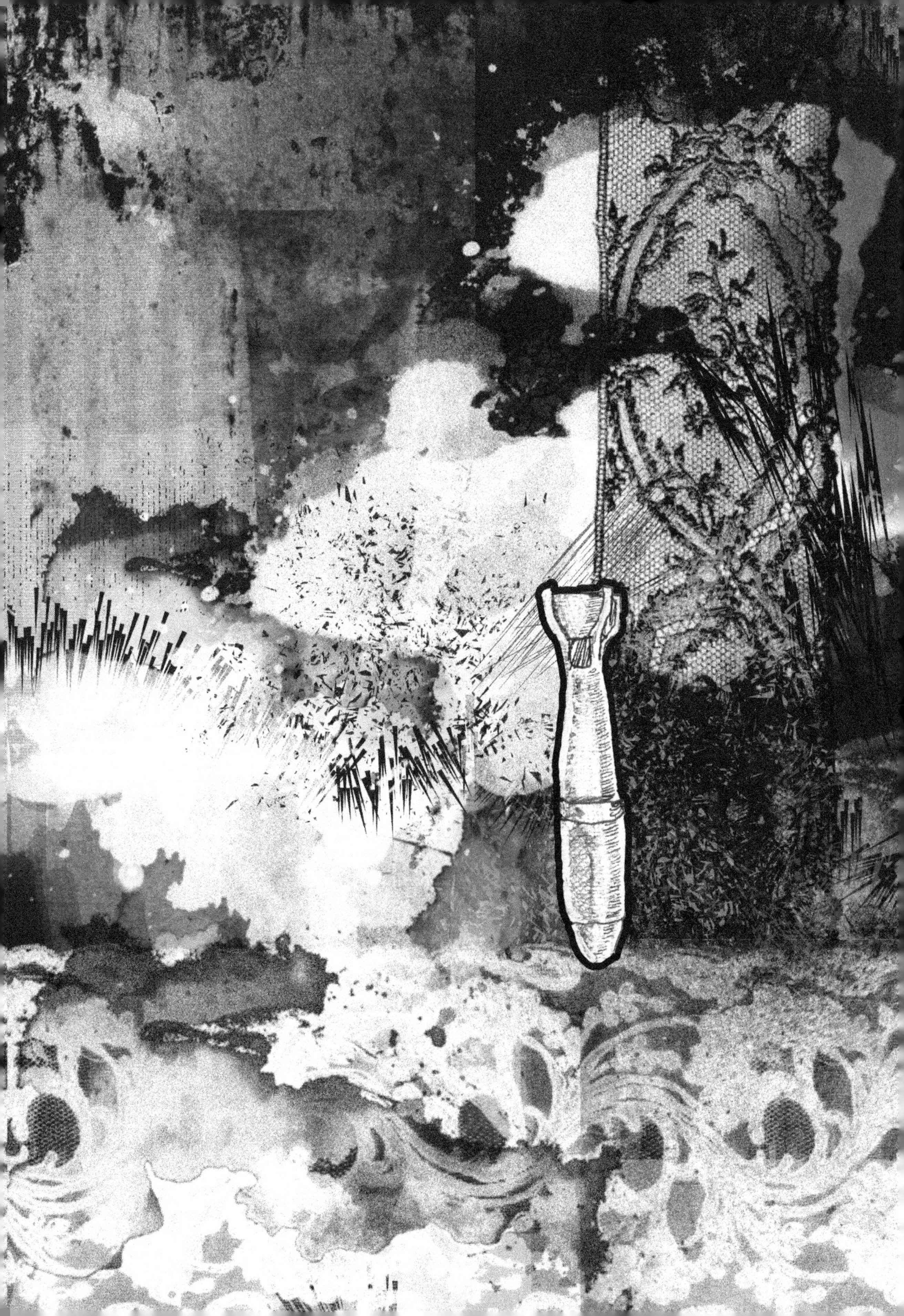

AUTHOR'S NOTE

Any act of visualization—drawing in this case—
comes with an unavoidable measure of refraction.

—JOE SACCO, *Footnotes in Gaza*

Many things in my life have changed over the course of a meal. This book was hatched over lunch with my friend Joe Parsons, a history buff. I was in the middle of doing research for a graphic narrative about the white supremacist coup in Wilmington, North Carolina, in 1898. That project was inspired by my work with public historian Tim Tyson and was my first foray into long-form comics about history. Joe and I ordered our food and talked about Joe Sacco's work and how comics paired perfectly with ethnography, journalism, and history. I was throwing out ideas for the next thing I wanted to tackle, and Joe commented, "If you really want to sink your teeth into something, you should look at the 1943 riot in Detroit." At the time I knew there was a rebellion in Detroit in 1967, but I had no idea there was one in 1943.

In most popular depictions of the World War II era, the overt racism, economic competition between Blacks and whites, and the ways that our country shifted as a result of urban opportunities and capitalism are largely invisible. Rarely do we see the redlining, the roots of women's liberation, the rise of the labor movement, the ongoing violence of Jim Crow laws, and the civil unrest represented in images, despite the fact that the repercussions of these issues are still present in our lives today. We often see shiny images of patriotism and a united front in the United States. Mainstream wartime America was flooded with whitewashed pictures of the home front filled with flags, apron-clad women in pin curls tending victory gardens, and well-scrubbed white kids collecting cans. There was a purposeful propaganda campaign carried out by commercial artists, designers, journalists, writers, and photographers. Those employed in the media industry were pressured by the government to create and deploy uplifting images of the home front that would inspire patriotism and raise morale. This seemed especially important at a time when images that came through from the war were gruesome and frightening. These domestic images have created an archive that has in some ways blotted out less-dominant voices and images of our country during this time. But despite the propaganda campaign, social, economic, and cultural pressures—compounded by the hypocrisy of the country's fighting against oppression abroad while still maintaining a racist system of apartheid at home—led to violent uprisings all across the country. These signaled the beginning of an organized racial sea change.

The 1943 Detroit uprising was the largest and most violent one that took place in America during World War II. It came on after the Red Summer of 1919, Dr. Ossian Sweet's struggle over discriminatory housing practices in 1925, and the Phoenix Thanksgiving clash and the Sojourner Truth housing project debacle in 1942, and prior to uprisings in Harlem and Los Angeles in 1942 and the 12th Street Rebellion in 1967. In Detroit, the lack of decent housing, racist rhetoric, police brutality, patriarchy, and lack of organization for newly arriving workers created a firestorm of violence fueled by resentment and hostility. By the time the violence started, the entire country had been watching the powder keg of Detroit, the nation's fourth largest city at the time, for over a year. Everyone knew that sooner or later there would be a major racial disturbance, yet nothing was done to prevent it. Even after the murderous destruction began, the municipal government did not declare martial law or call in the National Guard until hours of terror had passed. In the wake of the unrest, the official report (coauthored by the Detroit police commissioner) blamed only African Americans for the disturbance. Other sources blamed poor white southerners and African Americans who had migrated to Detroit.

After reading Dominic Capeci and Martha Wilkerson's book *Layered Violence: The Detroit Rioters of 1943*, I realized the story of Detroit in the early 1940s was perfect for a graphic narrative. I did further research and discovered that what captivated me most were the affidavits gathered by the NAACP in the wake of the violence: they were perfect for a graphic retelling, partly because within the interviews are numerous descriptive images. Nearly all of them relayed stories of police brutality and indifference. In the preface to his graphic novel *Nat Turner*, Kyle Baker wrote, "Comic books/graphic novels are a visual medium, so it's most important for an artist to choose a subject with opportunities for compelling graphics." I could not get the images from the affidavits out of my head.

The interviews with women who were affected by the violence also offered a series of untold stories. Researchers have noted that most of the people who were arrested identified as men. Black men were arrested more than white men, and Black women were arrested as well, while white women were not targeted by police for their participation. (It is important to note that though the police force in Detroit consisted of 3,400 male officers, only 43 were Black.) There was a women's division in the police department, but they were tasked with cases involving children, sexual assaults, and juvenile delinquency. They were not allowed to work on cases deemed criminal unless they were accompanied by a policeman. This was the practice for fifty-two years. Most women affected by the brutality and violence of the uprising did not participate but were victims of police brutality, or they were witnesses. Their voices have been nearly erased in the literature about the rebellion, although photographs of the events reveal that a number of women were present. White patriarchy prevailed. In much of the literature, Black women are presented as looters and white women are generally invisible, with the exceptions of the Polish women like Dolores Hommer who picketed the Sojourner Truth Homes, defense industry workers, the women of the UAW Women's Auxiliary, and women involved in the Detroit Council on Fair Employment Practices. The uprising was caused in part by rumors related to violence against women and a sense of vigilante justice fueled by patriarchy.

Women were an important part of the story I wanted to retell. Black women have always been extensively involved in the civil rights movement and in shaping the future of our country. This fact has been made even more visible in contemporary history texts by the work of several feminist scholars, whose research contributed greatly to my interpretation of events. In Detroit, prior to the end of the Second World War and after, Black women were key participants in the development of fair labor and housing practices and resource allocation for schools and recreation. Like most people who experienced the violence firsthand, they were deeply affected by what was happening in the streets and the ways police were complicit in the harm that Black people experienced at the hands of whites and white police. While the events of the Detroit uprising disrupted their families and neighborhoods, it also spurred more conversations around change and a deeper examination of societal inequities. In late 1943 Detroit mayor Edward Jeffries created an interracial committee tasked with making recommendations to improve interactions between the local government and the community, address discrimination, and produce programs where people could learn more about the issues that affected Detroit.

When I think of 1943, it is impossible not to see a long, bloody thread of white violence, oppression, and police brutality drawn through the events of the past that connects our present moment with the rest of history. The issues present in the uprising of 1943 were the same ones present even before the Red Summer of 1919, the Tulsa massacre of 1921, the Watts rebellion in 1965, and the unrest in Los Angeles in 1992, in Ferguson in 2015, and in Minneapolis in 2020. This list does not even begin to be exhaustive in scope. Communities of color suffer from state-sanctioned brutality, there is little to no accountability when harm is caused, and believers in white supremacy continue to exert their deadly influence and dominion. This is a pattern repeated not only in Black communities but on Indigenous lands and in Latinx and Asian communities across the United States. It is a broader project of power and oppression woven into social services, education, medicine, law, and our ever-growing carceral landscape. This story is just one of hundreds that have taken place in the past century. I hope that in the future we are able to say, "There was a time in our history . . . but that time has passed."

In the present, Detroit is a city filled with possibility. I fell in love with Detroit on my first research trip. I divided my time between archives, neighborhoods, and museums. Belle Isle, where the uprising began, is a magical place. So are the Detroit Institute of Arts, the Museum of Contemporary Art Detroit, and the Charles H. Wright Museum. A glimmering jewel within the city is the Detroit Public Library.

Much of what was in Detroit in 1943 is now gone because of urban renewal, urban flight, gentrification, and the construction of a giant highway. But I easily found the bridge to Belle Isle, the site of the Sojourner Truth Homes, the Ford River Rouge plant, Woodward Avenue, and the Eight Mile Wall, a monument to white supremacy. There are beautiful old houses and amazing examples of architecture. You can still find the bones of old factories like the Packard Automotive Plant. If you stand in front of these places and squint really hard, you can imagine them in their heyday in the 1940s. Since my first trip to Detroit, I have returned several more times. I even took my students at the University of Iowa there to learn about the history of Detroit and enjoy sites like the Heidelberg Project and the Motown Museum that mark Detroit as a rich center of art, music, food, and culture.

In spite of the hundreds of photographs and drawings that I produced as part of my fieldwork for this book, trying to reconstruct the world of Detroit in the 1940s in drawings was no easy task. I have never been good at drawing cars, which gave me pause when I decided to do this project. I apologize to readers who love cars and who find my renderings subpar. What I do love to draw is people, and I found inspiration for depicting them in surprising places. My grandmother was a young mother and wife in the 1940s. Her mother's patchwork quilts, made from her father's work shirts and her mother's housedresses, as well as photographs and finds from eBay and thrift stores, made it easy and exciting to rebuild the domestic lives of people in that time.

I had more difficulty finding images of historical figures who were part of the 1943 story. It was easy to locate images of some of the more notable people: their legacies are preserved in libraries and news clippings. Others, like the people who were interviewed by Gloster B. Current at the NAACP, did not leave an easy-to-find photographic footprint. I sifted through obituaries and scoured the internet, but in the end, much of what I drew had to be conjured. Many of the depictions of people are based on real accounts, but because I couldn't find any photographs, I had to take the liberty of inventing their physical appearance. This is the downside of creating comics about history: sometimes you have to imagine things and try to make them believable.

In an article in the *Journal of Aesthetic Education,* psychologist Jerome Bruner stated, "Narrative accounts must have at least two characteristics. They should center upon people and their intentional states: their desires, beliefs, and so on; and they should focus on how these intentional states led to certain kinds of activities. Such an account should also be or appear to be order preserving, in the sense of preserving or appearing to preserve sequence—the sequential properties of which life itself consists or is supposed to consist." In telling the story of the events in Detroit, I wanted very much to depict people in their intentional states and use sequence to show how those states shifted in the face of violence. In photographs, the uprising looks like masses of people wandering the streets, but it was really composed of intentional individual acts. One person hit another. Others joined in. One person broke a window; others decided to do the same thing or to walk away. A person saw another suffering and decided to intervene—or not. On the whole, the uprising was a large event composed of smaller individual decisions, many of which caused harm, some of which showed deep compassion and bravery. The people who participated were not aimless nihilists. They were responding to years of simmering oppression and fear of scarcity. Whites were afraid of losing privileges and property, and Blacks were afraid of losing their lives. Black people were pushing back against the state-sanctioned economic, physical, and psychological violence and oppression that was woven into their lives. Whites were afraid of the status quo shifting; poor whites were afraid they might lose any progress toward upward mobility if they had to compete with Black people in any meaningful way for status, housing, jobs, and social/recreational spaces. It is impossible not to acknowledge that some people joined the uprising because they felt there was a space for violent action without accountability. In spite of the outcomes, most people who witnessed what was happening probably felt fear and disdain for the actions of those in the streets who were turning over cars, beating innocent bystanders, or pulling people who were on their way to work off streetcars. On the whole, most people in Detroit did not participate in the violence, nor were they victims.

There are many scholarly books and articles that mention the events in Detroit in 1943, like Earl Brown's (1944) *Why Race Riots? Lessons from Detroit* (1944) and Thomas Sugrue's *The Origins of the Urban Crisis: Race and Inequality in Postwar Detroit* (1996), though only a handful explore it as a subject worthy of lengthy scholarly analysis. Numerous articles focus on various subjects tied to the uprising, including rumor, gender, police violence, and the typology of riots. Some works, like *Layered Violence: The Detroit Rioters* by Dominic J. Capeci Jr. and Martha Wilkerson (1991), relied on records kept by police and the courts. While these all offer a worthwhile insight into participants who were targeted and arrested by police, I wanted to take a different approach. So I relied most heavily on the work of the NAACP, which maintained an emergency office at the St. Antoine YMCA from June 24 to July 9, 1943. During that time, they spoke with numerous people about the violence, investigated their stories, and analyzed the situation in Detroit.

The word "riot" is used in all of these sources. I've chosen not to use this word, though it does occasionally appear in quoted material. In our current lexicon, "riot" is a racially coded word that stands for aimless mass violence perpetrated mostly by Black people in Black communities; during the events in Detroit, violence was widely perpetrated by white participants, especially police. Riots typically are characterized as random outbreaks of meaningless violence by large groups of people; what happened in Detroit had meaning. White participants sought to assert their dominance through violence, intimidation, and fear. Black participants, reacting to decades of police brutality, scarcity, and oppression, sought a way to have their voices heard and to gain recognition, power, and access that was impossible under the stifling cloak of white supremacy. Yet after the events in Detroit, the word "riot" was employed, and the Black community was blamed and suffered the consequences of arrests, imprisonment, and demonization.

For the subtitle for this book, "rebellion" did not seem fitting because in many instances there was little room for even small acts of rebellion and resistance without dire consequences: the rights and agency of Black people were stripped away by police brutality. This is evidenced in the pages and pages of NAACP affidavits. In the end it seemed that "uprising" was a better fit. What happened in Detroit is not easy to describe, nor does it easily fit into any category. It could be described as having characteristics of both communal and commodity "rioting." But people in the streets had a collective purpose.

I tried to employ a lens that alternated between the extreme violence and destruction on the streets, on streetcars, and on factory floors, and the day-to-day life that continued behind closed doors. I wanted to put marginalized Black communities front and center. In spite of the violence, people were still living their lives—making dinner, tending to babies, looking for lost umbrellas, trying to make ends meet. Most people in the city of Detroit did not seek to actively participate in the violence. What I did not write and draw was the aftermath of the uprising for Detroit. So many people were injured, arrested, or killed. The saga in the courts after the uprising could fill a whole volume and would illustrate how our justice system is biased and harmful in many instances, especially to communities of color. There are a myriad of ways this story could be told; I hope others will take it up and create their own accounts of these events based on primary sources.

One of the challenges I faced was my own shifting aesthetic sensibilities and interests. I drew this book over the course of eleven years. My drawings reflect my evolving experience, changing preferences for ways of working, and the use of different materials. The end result is like a tapestry of approaches. I did try to stay consistent in the materials I used in each chapter, but some chapters took years. There were periods of time when I worked on a large board where I taped paper and stored bottles of ink and pens in a small plastic storage tub. I kept my studio under my bed and set it up on the kitchen table or bedroom floor at night when my young children had gone to sleep. At other times my studio was a table in Prairie Lights bookstore or my tray table on an airplane. I scanned every drawing and tinkered with it in Photoshop. I rendered the final bits on my iPad. It took a decade for technology to evolve to the point that drawing with a stylus instead of a pen somewhat satisfied my tactical sensibilities as a painter. Some of my drawings were labored over; others came easily and seemed to draw themselves. I usually started by writing out what happened, breaking it down into dialogue, and then making thumbnails. I really like some drawings; I really hate others. I wish I could draw like Joe Sacco, my hero, but I have to be happy to draw like me.

I always had historians as imaginary over-the-shoulder readers. Leslie Schwalm and Timothy Tyson encouraged me not to put words in the mouths of real people, so I worked hard to use quotes that I found in the works of other scholars and primary sources like newspapers and documents. In some quoted material, spelling and punctuation have been updated and standardized. Sometimes the narrative required that I paraphrase or invent dialogue. In these cases, I made sure that the words I gave characters represented their own beliefs and practices as expressed in primary sources. When I first began, my approach was more like text and illustration. Corey Creekmur said, "It's a comic! Let the characters tell the story." This freed me up to invent scenarios and characters that could fill in the blanks in the story, making it more cohesive. For many of these characters I dipped back into my high school yearbooks for faces and expressions; I also watched people in restaurants and coffeehouses, and made a note of the way they moved, how their teeth were fitted in their head, and if their earlobes were connected. Newspapers from 1943 were also a rich source of imagery. In total I made almost 200 nine-by-twelve-inch drawings. When these are assembled into a stack, it is taller than my father's hardbound *Webster's Encyclopedic Dictionary*.

I learned so much from making this book. It led me to the story of Mary Turner, which spawned another book. I fell in love with an amazing city. And I have a new appreciation for the role and work of historians, comics creators, activists, and archivists. I wanted this book to be a testimony, to center voices that made it only to the margins of other works, and to show connections between acts in the past and our present day. Making this book would have been impossible if I hadn't had the chance to pore through piles and piles of primary sources with the assistance of archivists who were patient and extremely helpful. I had to see things for myself firsthand, and visiting archives is enchanting. I could spend hours sifting through boxes, smelling old paper, and finding bits and pieces of history that are like small puzzle pieces. One of the most rewarding archive experiences I have ever had was looking thought the filing cabinets in the *Detroit Free Press* office. It was a gray day and there was a single person there in charge of the archives. She was amazing and gave me access to everything from 1943. I found original unpublished photographs of the uprising, complete with crop marks and touch-ups. I've also passed hours of my life at tables in the Walter P. Reuther Library, the

Bentley Historical Library in Ann Arbor, and the Library of Congress, sifting through folders, holding letters and leaflets, staring at dog-eared photographs and delicate newspaper clippings.

I want to thank all of the historians, archivists, librarians, curators, cartoonists, and other kind people who helped me on this journey. I was not trained as a historian, and working in archives is a relatively new part of my research. Without help from people far more knowledgeable than I am, I would never have found even half of what I needed. In Washington, D.C., a patient librarian helped me photograph microfiche. After a few hours I turned to her and said, "You are a goddess and the world's best librarian. They need to build temples in your honor." She laughed and said, "They already have—they are called libraries."

I also want to thank all of the people at UNC Press, who were infinitely patient and waited over a decade for me to finish this. Especially important were the encouragement of Lucas Church; the eagle eyes and brilliant minds of Mary Caviness and especially Erin Granville; the assurance of Andrew Winters that everything would be OK; the marketing genius of Dino Battista and Elizabeth Orange, who were patient enough to read my rambling author's questionnaire; and of course the amazing work of the designers directed by Kim Bryant. There is a reason that I was kicked out of design school, and I'm sure that without them this book would be a painterly mess.

Finally, I think the most important people are the readers. Without you I would be lost and aimless.

—RACHEL MARIE-CRANE WILLIAMS, April 2020

GLOSSARY OF PEOPLE, ORGANIZATIONS, AND LAWS

Christopher Alston

Christopher Alston was a Black member of the Communist Party who was instrumental in organizing labor at Ford's River Rouge plant. (See page 99.)

Harry Bennett

Harry Bennett, a white Michigan native, has been called America's most famous corporate thug. He was in charge of Ford's service department, which employed 8,000 men. Bennett's role was mainly to engage in the dirty work required to undermine organized labor at Ford Motor Company. This included bodily violence, spying, coercion, and intimidation. Eventually he was ousted by Henry Ford's grandson, Henry Ford II. (See pages 97–98, 105, 112, 114, and 119–21.)

Mary McLeod Bethune

Mary McLeod Bethune was a Black educator and activist. She cofounded Bethune-Cookman College, which issued its first degrees in 1943, and was the director of Negro affairs for the National Youth Administration during FDR's presidency. She also held the post of vice president at the NAACP from 1940 until her death in 1955. She was a friend of Eleanor Roosevelt, and she attended the founding of the United Nations in 1945, where she was the only Black woman present. (See page 27.)

John Blandford

John Blandford, a white man, was the national housing administrator in 1942. He announced that the Sojourner Truth Homes would be filled by African American families. (See pages 66 and 68.)

Joseph Buffa

Joseph Buffa (in some sources cited as "Bulla") was a powerful white real estate developer and builder in Detroit who spoke for white protesters during the Sojourner Truth housing controversy. He was arrested for trying to incite a riot but later released. (See pages 47 and 67.)

John Bugas

John "Jack" Bugas, a white native of Wyoming, was the head of Detroit's FBI office in 1943. The next year he quit to join the Ford Motor Company. In 1945 he was tasked with firing Bennett under the direction of Henry Ford II. Legend has it that when Bugas delivered the news, Bennett went for his .45-caliber pistol, but Bugas drew his .38 revolver first, trained it on Bennett, and calmly told him to leave. Bugas was known to be an excellent marksman. (See page 215.)

Everard W. Daniels

The Reverend Everard Daniels was a Black Episcopal priest and rector of St. Matthew's Episcopal Church in Detroit. He worked closely with Ford to help Black workers find jobs in Ford factories. (See page 86.)

Detroit Council on Fair Employment Practices

The Detroit FEP Council was founded in January of 1942 by an interracial, interdenominational group of community leaders. Like other local FEP councils around the country, it was formed to enforce Executive Order 8802, which outlawed discrimination in the defense industries and government based on race, creed, color, sex, or national origin. Detroit's was the only FEP council to address discrimination on the basis of sex in its constitution. The council, in collaboration with the NAACP, the FEPC, and the UAW-CIO, was responsible for changing hiring practices in the defense industry to include more African American women. For more information, see Kersten, *Race, Jobs, and the War.* (See pages 117–21, 243, and 263.)

Detroit Housewives' League

The Detroit Housewives' League was founded in 1930 and had 10,000 members by 1934. Its mission was to keep money in the African American community during the Great Depression by patronizing Black businesses. The idea gained national attention, and the National Housewives' League was founded in 1933. In 1935 the Detroit branch set fire to a warehouse full of meat to protest high meat prices. Polish housewives engaged in similarly militant protests in Detroit. (See pages 98 and 268n.)

Martin Dies Jr.

Martin Dies Jr., a white Texan, followed in his father's footsteps as a U.S. congressman, serving from 1931 to 1945 and again from 1953 to 1959. He was the chairman of the House Committee to Investigate Un-American Activities and opposed desegregation. (See page 214.)

Constantine Dzink

The Reverend Constantine Dzink was a white Roman Catholic priest who led parishioners, most of whom were Polish immigrants, at the St. Louis the King Catholic Church in Detroit. According to Angela Dillard's *Faith in the City*, Dzink held strong views against people who were Jewish and people who were Black. She explains Dzink believed his views against race mixing were divine dictates of God. He held firm to the belief that the Sojourner Truth Homes should be for white tenants only. (See page 45.)

Frank D. Eaman

Frank D. Eaman was a white lawyer and Detroit police commissioner during the Sojourner Truth housing controversy, which led to his resignation. (See page 49.)

Executive Order 8802

In response to pressure by African American leaders, President Franklin D. Roosevelt signed Executive Order 8802 on June 25, 1941, to eliminate racial and ethnic discrimination in the defense industry. It also resulted in the establishment of the Fair Employment Practices Committee. (See pages 27–28, 30, and 137.)

Fair Employment Practices Committee (FEPC)

The FEPC was founded in 1941 as a result of FDR's Executive Order 8802. The local Detroit FEP council, like other FEP councils around the country, was founded to further the goals of the FEPC. They pressured state employment offices and local companies and also gathered evidence of discrimination for the FEPC. (See pages 117 and 121.)

Henry Ford

Henry Ford was a white industrialist who founded the Ford Motor Company and implemented the modern assembly line. He was well known for his antisemitic, racist, and anti-union beliefs, but he also was one of the first owners to offer workers high wages, profit sharing, and a forty-hour workweek. (See pages 84–86, 96, 97, 114, 120, and 124.)

William Z. Foster

William Z. Foster was a radical white labor organizer and Communist Party leader. He ran three times for president and was chairman of the Communist Party USA for twenty years. (See page 92.)

Lester B. Granger

Lester B. Granger was a Black civil rights activist who led the National Urban League from 1941 to 1961. He also served as the first African American president of the National Conference on Social Work. (See page 214.)

Charles Hill

The Reverend Charles Hill was an African American minister who led Hartford Memorial Baptist Church, one of the largest and most influential Black churches in Detroit. He was an active member of the NAACP, the National Negro Congress, and the Civil Rights Federation, and he worked closely with several community organizations, particularly labor and civil rights groups. He was a major part of the civil rights movement in Detroit and was later labeled a Communist and closely monitored by the Criminal Intelligence Bureau. (See pages 45, 65, 68, 130–33, and 137.)

T. Arnold Hill

T. Arnold Hill, a Black activist, worked with the National Urban League from 1914 to 1940 and was the executive secretary of the Chicago division during the 1919 riot. He championed equality in housing, education, and employment and was heralded as a leader in the field of social work. (See pages 10 and 17.)

Sidney Hillman

Sidney Hillman was a white cofounder of the labor union the Amalgamated Clothing Workers of America. He worked closely with Jane Addams and other progressives on labor reforms in the early 1900s and was involved in drafting legislation for better working conditions in factories. Hillman was later a leader in the CIO and helped grow and strengthen the labor union during World War II. (See pages 19–20.)

Wilbert Holloway

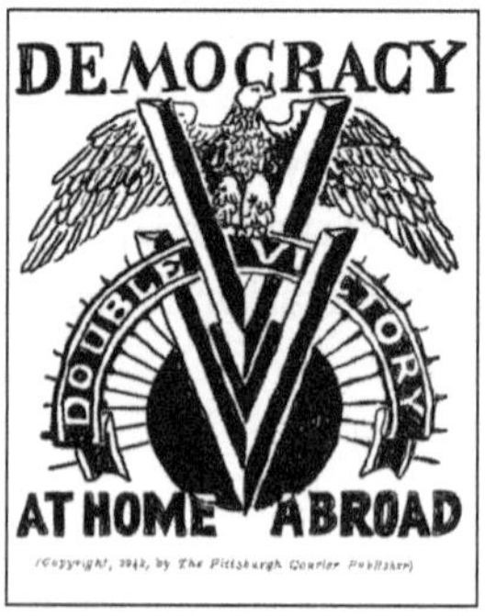
DEMOCRACY
DOUBLE VICTORY
AT HOME
ABROAD

Wilbert Holloway was a famous African American cartoonist best known for his long-running comic strip *Sunny Boy Sam*. He created the logo for the Double V for Victory campaign at the *Pittsburgh Courier*. (See page 29.)

Edward J. Jeffries

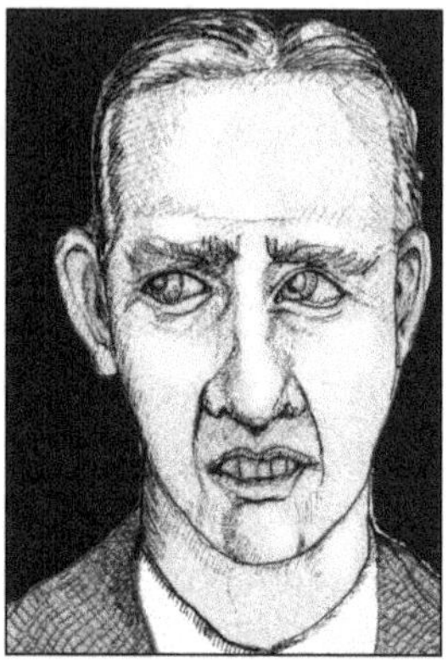

Edward Jeffries was the white mayor of Detroit from 1940 to 1948. He considered himself a moderate progressive and aimed to reduce conflict over race and labor, but he moved to the right after the uprising of 1943. He died at the age of fifty while on vacation in Florida. (See pages 48, 60, 66, 68–70, 121, 123, 201–3, 206-7, 216, 217, and 243.)

Harry F. Kelly

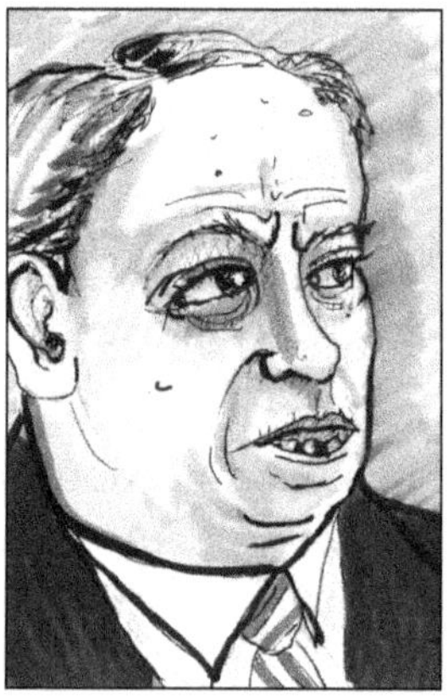

Harry Kelly, a white native of Illinois, was governor of Michigan from 1943 to 1947. He later served on the Michigan Supreme Court. He was a devout Irish Catholic and a war hero from World War I, where he lost a leg. He was a long-standing member of the Republican Party who sought to root out corruption and was a strong supporter of veterans when they returned from World War II. (See pages 105, 202, 206–7, and 217.)

Martin Luther King Jr.

Martin Luther King Jr. was one of the best-known civil rights activists in the United States. In 1963 he debuted his famous "I Have a Dream" speech in Detroit as part of a practice run for the March on Washington three months later. Three weeks before his assassination in 1968, he visited Grosse Pointe, a white suburb near Detroit, and gave a speech known as "The Other America." (See pages 229 and 231.)

Frank Knox

Frank Knox served in the army during the Spanish-American War and went on to become secretary of the navy during World War II. He was a journalist and politician and owned several newspapers during his career. He opposed the New Deal and was in favor of the Japanese internment during World War. Knox felt that integration would do nothing to further his goal of winning the war and that Black agitators were taking advantage of the vulnerability of the United States during wartime to gain a foothold. He believed that Black people were inferior to whites and that interracial disturbances like those seen in Detroit, New York, and Texas hindered the war effort. (See pages 10–12.)

Fiorello La Guardia

Fiorello La Guardia served three terms as the mayor of New York, from 1934 to 1945, and several terms in Congress. He was a white progressive Republican who supported and celebrated the diverse populations of New York, including immigrants and minorities, through collaboration, social reform, and political inclusion. He despised corruption and worked tirelessly to root out sources in the city. He also was instrumental in redesigning infrastructure throughout New York City. He was a supporter of FDR and worked closely with his administration. (See pages 21–22.)

Layle Lane

Layle Lane was a Black high school teacher and civil rights activist in New York City who held degrees from Howard and Columbia. She helped organize the 1941 March on Washington and ran for public office as a Socialist a number of times. She was an active member of the American Federation of Teachers. (See pages 17 and 18.)

Local 600

Local 600 was a UAW union whose charter was approved in 1938. Located in Dearborn, Michigan, it was closely associated with the Ford River Rouge plant. The Local 600 paid for the first visit Rosa Parks made to Detroit, in the late 1950s. (See page 121.)

Julian G. McIntosh

Julian G. McIntosh was a white prosecuting attorney for Wayne County, Michigan. In that role, he helped determine who was arrested and prosecuted for participating in the 1943 Detroit uprising. (See page 67.)

Thurgood Marshall

Thurgood Marshall, an African American native of Baltimore, Maryland, was a lawyer and the first African American to serve on the U.S. Supreme Court. In the 1940s he was the executive director of the NAACP Legal Defense and Educational Fund. (See pages 179 and 217.)

James McClendon

Dr. James McClendon was an African American physician in Detroit and the branch president of the NAACP from 1938 to 1945. During that time the Detroit branch grew to become the largest in the country. (See pages 47 and 137.)

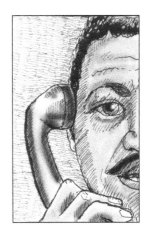

John McCormack

John McCormack was a white member of the U.S. House of Representatives from 1928 until 1971. He was born in Boston and represented Massachusetts during his time in Congress. He served as Speaker of the House from 1962 until 1971. He supported laws to expand civil rights in the United States. (See page 213.)

E. Pauline Myers

E. Pauline Myers was a Black social activist who was instrumental in the Brotherhood of Sleeping Car Porters and the NAACP. She was an organizer for the March on Washington Movement and worked for the integration of the armed forces and other government organizations. She promoted nonviolent direct action and in later years worked at the Department of Housing and Urban Development. (See pages 13 and 17.)

NAACP

The National Association for the Advancement of Colored People was founded in 1908 and is one of the largest civil rights organization in the United States. (See pages xiii–xiv, xv, 10, 18–20, 112, 137, 142, 217, 229, 242, 244, 245, and 246.)

Charles F. Palmer

Charles F. Palmer was a white real estate developer who created the United States' first public housing project. FDR appointed him defense housing coordinator at the Office for Emergency Management in 1940. (See pages 42 and 48.)

Robert Patterson

Robert Patterson was a white federal judge who became under secretary of war under FDR and secretary of war under Truman. He supported segregation, but he also supported the inclusion of African Americans in the military and was instrumental in the creation of the Tuskegee Airmen, a group of Black fighter pilots in World War II. He died in a plane crash in 1952. (See pages 10–11.)

A. Philip Randolph

A. Philip Randolph was a Black civil rights icon in the United States who is now best known for his organization and leadership of the Brotherhood of Sleeping Car Porters. He was instrumental in the labor movement during the 1930s and 1940s and helped pressure FDR to issue Executive Order 8802. He also helped to end discrimination in the armed services by persuading Harry S. Truman to issue Executive Order 9981. In 1960 he became the first president of the Negro American Labor Council, which was formed within the AFL-CIO. (See pages 10–12, 17, 19–20, 21, and 26.)

John Rankin

John Rankin, a white Democrat, served sixteen terms in Congress representing the state of Mississippi. He was known to be a white supremacist who supported segregation. (See page 213.)

Walter Reuther

Walter Reuther, a white man, was president of the United Auto Workers from 1946 to 1970. He was active in the civil rights movement and supported activism for the environment, public housing, labor, and national and international issues related to human rights and equity. The Walter P. Reuther Library at Wayne State University in Detroit is named in his honor. (See pages 78–81, 107, and 137.)

Eleanor Roosevelt

Eleanor Roosevelt was a white feminist, activist, and diplomat. Married to Franklin D. Roosevelt, she was first lady from 1933 to 1945. Throughout her life she was committed to improving the welfare of children and fighting for the rights of women and racial minorities. In 1945, President Harry S. Truman appointed her a delegate to the United Nations. (See pages 21 and 212.)

Franklin Delano Roosevelt

Franklin Delano Roosevelt was the thirty-second president of the United States. He served four terms, from 1933 to 1945, and steered the United States through the Great Depression and World War II. He is known for the New Deal and his unconventional but powerful political partnership with his wife (and fifth cousin), the well-known human rights advocate Eleanor Roosevelt. (See pages 10–12, 15–16, 20–21, 22–26, 27, and 77.)

Ossian Sweet

Ossian Sweet, an African American physician, moved to Detroit in 1925 and bought a home in a middle-class white neighborhood. Sweet anticipated trouble when he moved in and asked his brothers and several friends to help defend his home against a mob that had gathered and began throwing stones at his home. He and his companions were put on trial for murder when a shot fired from his house killed one participant in the mob and wounded another. (See pages 88–89 and 242.)

Shelton Tappes

Shelton Tappes was a Black labor activist who was instrumental in organizing the Ford River Rouge plant. He was very active in the labor and civil rights movements and was the recording secretary of the Local 600 in the 1940s. (See page 100.)

Rudolph G. Tenerowicz

Rudolph Tenerowicz was a white physician born in Budapest, Hungary, who immigrated to the United States as a child. He served as mayor of Hamtramck, Michigan, in the 1930s and was a congressman for the state of Michigan from 1938 to 1943. He supported making the Sojourner Truth housing project white-only. (See pages 43 and 65.)

James G. Thompson

James G. Thompson was a twenty-six-year-old African American cafeteria worker living in Wichita, Kansas, when he authored a letter to the *Pittsburgh Courier* that sparked the now-famous Double V for Victory campaign during World War II. The campaign, which highlighted discrimination toward Black soldiers and supported victory over oppression both abroad and at home, was so contentious among white people that some leaders in the American military banned African American newspapers from their libraries and J. Edgar Hoover tried to indict the publishers of the *Pittsburgh Courier* for treason. (See pages 6 and 29.)

UAW-CIO

UAW-CIO stands for United Auto Workers and Congress of Industrial Organizations. It was a labor union that organized workers in the auto industry. (See pages 78, 97, 100, 112–14, 137, 229, and 243.)

Wagner Act

The Wagner Act, another name for the National Labor Relations Act, was signed in 1935. It was designed to allow workers to join organized labor unions without retribution and to engage in collective bargaining with employers. It was sponsored by Senator Robert F. Wagner, a Democrat from New York. (See pages 97 and 107.)

Murray Van Wagoner

Murray Van Wagoner, a white native of Michigan and a Democrat, was the governor of Michigan from 1941 to 1943. (See pages 69 and 70.)

Horace A. White

The Reverend Horace A. White was a Black Congregationalist and the leader of Plymouth United Church of Christ from 1936 to 1958. He was a strong supporter of labor rights and the UAW. He was the head of the Detroit Housing Commission and the NAACP Legal Redress Committee in Detroit. He eventually won a seat in the Michigan State House of Representatives. (See pages 43, 45, 54–55, 63, and 203.)

Walter White

Walter White was a prolific writer and a prominent African American civil rights activist. He began his career investigating lynching in the South—his blue eyes and blond hair made it easy for him to infiltrate white culture and gain access to information regarding lynching. He led the NAACP as executive secretary from 1931 to 1955. Along with A. Philip Randolph and other civil rights leaders, White was instrumental in ending discriminatory labor practices in the defense industries and the armed forces. (See pages 10, 17, 18, 20, 22, 26, 142–43, and 217.)

Aubrey Willis Williams

Aubrey Willis Williams was a white social activist who was an important administrator of government programs in the New Deal. He grew up in poverty in Alabama and went on to play a vital role in the Federal Emergency Relief Administration, Civil Works Administration, Works Progress Administration, and National Youth Administration. He spent the last part of his life leading the Southern Conference Educational Fund and working to end racial segregation. (See page 21.)

Sunnie Wilson

William Nathaniel "Sunnie" Wilson was the owner of the Forest Club, the country's largest Black-owned nightclub, in 1943. Wilson was a patron of the arts and in 1930 was elected by community members as the unofficial mayor of Paradise Valley. (See page 159.)

John H. Witherspoon

John Witherspoon, a white Detroit native, was the police commissioner in Detroit from June 1942 until January 1944. During the 1943 uprising, he refused to issue shoot-to-kill orders to the police but primarily blamed African Americans for the violence. (See pages 201, 203, and 217.)

Zaio Woodford

Zaio Woodford (later Zaio Schroeder) was a white Michigan native, an outspoken feminist, and an attorney. She was part of the Detroit FEP Council and the vice president of the Detroit Federation of Women's Clubs, which was influential in the suffrage movement, started the first women's division in the Detroit Police Department, influenced child labor laws, and lobbied for the Sheppard-Towner Infancy and Maternity Protection Bill. While the federation was made up of mostly wealthy white women, Black women were also members. (See pages 118 and 119.)

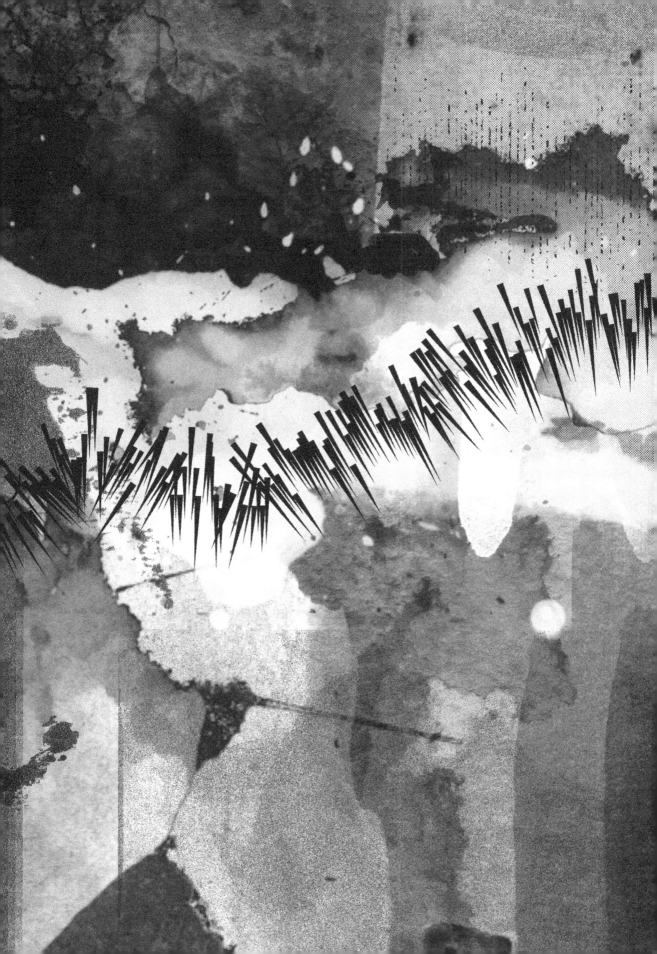

NOTES

Chapter 1: No Forgotten Men, No Forgotten Races

9   **"No forgotten men, no forgotten races"**: Franklin Roosevelt, speech at Howard University, October 26, 1936, quoted in "Roosevelt at Howard," *New York Times*, October 27, 1936. This phrase appeared in a speech FDR gave at Howard University in 1936, when he dedicated a chemistry building there. While he was referring to educational opportunities, the quote is a reminder that Black people also generally had few opportunities with regard to housing and employment. In addition, by excluding women, it reminds us that women, especially Black women, were basically forgotten altogether.

10   **"We want complete integration . . ."**: The conversation that took place at the White House regarding the March on Washington Movement is pieced together from quotes in Lucander, "It Is a New Kind of Militancy."

13   **"The old methods of conferences"**: E. Pauline Myers said this in 1943 and is quoted in Lucander, "It Is a New Kind of Militancy."

Chapter 2: The Four Freedoms

15   **"Just as our national policy"**: Roosevelt's reading copy of his Four Freedoms speech is housed at the Franklin D. Roosevelt Presidential Library and Museum in Hyde Park, New York, and can be viewed at https://www.fdrlibrary.org/four-freedoms.

17   **"demand the right to work and fight"**: A. Philip Randolph, "'Defense Rotten'—Randolph: Let's March on Capital 10,000 Strong, Urges Leader of Porters," *Pittsburgh Courier*, January 15, 1941. Quoted in Saldin, *War, the American State, and Politics*, 111.

17   **"nothing counts but pressure"**: Randolph, "Call to Negro America."

18   **"To this end, we propose"**: Randolph, "Call to Negro America."

18   **"stopped talking at the big gate"**: Walter White to A. Philip Randolph, March 28, 1941. Quoted in Kersten, *Race, Jobs, and the War*, 15.

18   **"hammer away"**: Quoted in Mullenbach, *Double Victory*, 47.

22   **"Mr. President, time . . .":** The meeting at the White House on June 18, 1941, is described in detail in Bates, *Pullman Porters*, 158. Quotes from the book were used to create these panels.

27   **"second Emancipation Proclamation":** Both Randolph and White compared Executive Order 8802 to the Emancipation Proclamation. See Kersten, *Race, Jobs, and the War*, 18.

27   **"refreshing shower in a thirsty land":** Quoted in Kersten, *Race, Jobs, and the War*, 18. Mary McLeod Bethune wrote this in a letter to FDR about Executive Order 8802.

29   **letter to the editor:** James G. Thompson, letter to the editor, *Pittsburgh Courier*, February 7, 1942. The newspaper page with the letter is available on microfiche in the Library of Congress: https://www.loc .gov/item/2003257260/. See also the Double "V" for Victory Campaign folder, box II, A239, NAACP Records, Library of Congress.

Chapter 4: The Sojourner Truth Housing Conflict

For a detailed description of the Sojourner Truth housing controversy, see Dominic Capeci's *Race Relations in Wartime Detroit: The Sojourner Truth Housing Controversy of 1942*, written in 1984. Capeci did a great deal of meticulous research with primary sources and detailed the involvement of the Polish community, Joseph Buffa, and the back-and-forth between Mayor Jeffries and Charles Palmer. The NAACP also did a great deal of extensive research on the series of events around the housing conflict; see Box II A316, NAACP Records, Library of Congress.

45   **"Mr. Palmer . . . ":** The quotes shown here as a letter from Reverend Constantine Dzink to Charles Palmer actually are from two sources, an August 1941 letter from Dzink to Palmer and a September 1943 interview with Dzink, both quoted in Capeci, *Race Relations in Wartime Detroit*, 78. The language Dzink used in the interview reflected his deep, ugly, racist views, while the language in his letter underscored the ways in which he sought a record of respectability. Constantine Dzink to C. F. Palmer, March 28, 1942, box 1, Charles A. Hill Papers, Walter P. Reuther Library, Wayne State University; "Interview with Djuik [*sic*]," "Survey of Racial and Religious Conflict Forces in Detroit," September 10–30, 1943, box 71, Civil Rights Congress of Michigan Collection, Walter P. Reuther Library, Wayne State University.

53   **"You wouldn't want me to shoot":** This quote is taken from an FBI report on an interview with Horace A. White, April 2, 1942. See Capeci, *Race Relations in Wartime Detroit*, 102.

63   **"One hundred eight people were arrested . . . treated this way":**
This quote is taken from an FBI report on an interview with Horace A.
White, April 2, 1942. In *Race Relations in Wartime Detroit*, Capeci goes
into great detail about the violence that ensued when Black families
tried to move into the Sojourner Truth Homes.

66   **"decision is made in Washington":** Nelson Foote, "Special Report on
Negro Housing Situation in Detroit," *Detroit Free Press*, March 7, 1942,
box 116, Maurice Sugar Papers, Walter P. Reuther Library, Wayne State
University. Quoted in Capeci, *Race Relations in Wartime Detroit*, 123.

Chapter 5: Labor, Race, War: 1941–1943

76   **"To change a whole nation":** This passage is taken from FDR's Four
Freedoms speech, January 6, 1941.

78   **"Conventional methods . . . give her men":** Walter Reuther, "More
Airplanes for Defense," radio address, December 28, 1940, Walter P.
Reuther Library, Wayne State University, http://reuther100.wayne
.edu/pdf/500_Planes_Speech.pdf. The Walter P. Reuther Library at
Wayne State University has collected extensive documents related
to the UAW, Reuther, and Detroit. Their archivists contributed a great
deal to my research on the Detroit rebellion and on the involvement
of the UAW in labor affairs prior to and during 1943.

84   **"Negroes, like all social outcasts . . . must prevail":** These comments
are not direct quotes from Ford but are adapted from Meier and
Rudwick, *Black Detroit and the Rise of the UAW*, 11–13.

85   **"Dominance . . . suppression":** Henry Ford, Ford's Page, *Dearborn
Independent*, June 17, 1922. Quoted in Meier and Rudwick, 12.

85   **"That's why I have done so much":** Adapted from Meier and Rudwick,
11–13.

86   **"The Negro is a human being":** Henry Ford, Ford's Page, *Dearborn
Independent*, October 21, 1922. Quoted in Meier and Rudwick, 14.

86   **"I guess this Sunday":** While this dialogue is invented, it's based on
the fact that Ford worked with pastors in various Black churches to
create an informal network of employment.

98   **after a meeting at the Detroit Housewives' League:** To learn more about the Detroit Housewives' League, see Wolcott, *Remaking Respectability*, and Barnes, "Buying, Boosting, and Building." In my research, I found the league's work and the ways they intervened in social crises so compelling. They worked with Polish housewives in Detroit to bring about change.

106   **May 26, 1937:** The Battle of the Overpass is chronicled in several places. In particular, see Lichtenstein, *Walter Reuther*, 84–87. The Walter P. Reuther Library at Wayne State University has an amazing collection of photographs taken during the Battle of the Overpass. These were crucial to my research.

114   **"The law provides":** *Life*, Life on the News Fronts of the World, June 2, 1941. Bennett did not say this on June 20, 1941, but it seemed appropriate in terms of his attitude toward African Americans.

120   **"Mr. Ford has been":** FEPC file memo regarding Ford Motor Company, May 29, 1942. Quoted in Kersten, *Race, Jobs, and the War*, 100.

123   **"yellow magazine":** "Jeffries Scathes Life Magazine for 'Scurrilous' Criticism of City," *Detroit Free Press*, August 17, 1942.

125   **"joined the Women's Army Corps as a nurse":** For more information about Black army nurses, see Gregory, "Forgotten War Nurses."

130   **"Reverend Hill! Excuse me!":** To learn more about the Reverend Charles Hill and the Hartford Memorial Baptist Church's involvement in the fight for civil rights, see Dillard, *Faith in the City*. The Charles A. Hill Family Papers are also available to researchers at the Bentley Historical Library at the University of Michigan.

134   **four Black women were hired:** See Shockley, *We, Too, Are Americans*, to learn more about the experiences of African American women in Detroit between 1940 and 1954.

139   **"rather see Hitler and Hirohito":** This was reportedly said by a worker during the Packard strike in the summer of 1943: Zieger, *For Jobs and Freedom*, 133.

143   **"a race riot may break out":** Walter White, speech at NAACP rally, Detroit, Michigan, June 3, 1943. Quoted in Thomas, *Life for Us*, 167.

Chapter 6: Île aux Cochons, Hog Island, Belle Isle

148   **tempers flared on the island:** The depiction of the beginning of the
violence on Belle Isle is drawn mostly from the following sources:
Lee and Humphrey, *Race Riot*; Shogan and Craig, *The Detroit Race Riot*;
Sitkoff, "The Detroit Race Riots of 1943"; Capeci and Wilkerson, *Layered
Violence*.

152   **wrong place at the wrong time:** The stories of Robert Parsons and
Robert Gordon are drawn directly from sworn accounts given to
Gloster Current at the NAACP by Eva Gordon and Louise Roberson.
Civil Rights Complaints and Affidavits, Detroit Race Riot 1943, box 70,
part I, series I, NAACP Detroit Branch Records, Walter P. Reuther
Library, Wayne State University.

Chapter 7: Trouble in Paradise

159   **"seven hundred dancers":** Wilson and Cohassey, *Toast of the Town*, 113.
In this fabulous book Wilson details the events on June 20, including
Leo Tipton's announcement to the crowd at the Forest Club about a
Black woman and her baby on the Belle Isle Bridge. Wilson verified
that "the riot wasn't about troublesome crowds on Belle Isle or the
rumors spread by Leo Tipton; it was about the brutality of the Detroit
Police Department. Traditionally, the police had always been cruel in
their treatment of Detroit's black folks" (114).

Chapter 9: Up and Down the Street

170   **Dr. Joseph De Horatiis:** The story of Dr. De Horatiis's death is told in
Don Lochbiler, "Puzzled Victims Crowd Corridors at Receiving," *Detroit
News*, June 21, 1943, and in Capeci and Wilkerson, *Layered Violence*,
92–93. De Horatiis was not identified by name in Lochbiler's article,
but it contains details of the attack.

172   **"I was on my way to work":** Samuel Mitchell's story is taken directly
from his account of the events shared with the NAACP: Civil Rights
Complaints and Affidavits, Detroit Race Riot 1943, box 70, part I, series
I, NAACP Detroit Branch Records, Walter P. Reuther Library, Wayne
State University (hereafter cited as CRCA).

179   **"like the Gestapo":** This is not an actual quote; I adapted it from
Thurgood Marshall, "The Gestapo in Detroit," in Marshall, *Supreme
Justice*, 9–16. Originally this essay appeared in *The Crisis*, August 1943.

180   **John Lewis, a soldier, and Susie Mae Ransom, a homemaker:**
This story is taken directly from accounts given by John Lewis and
Susie Mae Ransom to Gloster Current of the NAACP, CRCA.

189   **"came toward the Vernor Apartments":** The Vernor Apartments were
a site of violence perpetrated mostly by police. This story is taken
directly from an account given by Mateel Forniss to Gloster Current of
the NAACP, CRCA.

192   **"There was evidenced . . . guise of law enforcement":** J. H. Forniss,
sworn affidavit signed by Gloster Current, CRCA. Forniss was Mateel
Forniss's husband and a witness of the violence and police brutality
at the Vernor Apartments.

194   **shooting of Julian Witherspoon:** This story is chronicled in
Witherspoon's own account as well as that of his friend James Reid,
which were collected by Gloster Current of the NAACP in the wake
of the uprising. CRCA.

203   **"Mayor, if we declare":** CRCA. This quote is from a detailed transcript
of the emergency meeting of the Detroit Citizens Committee. During
the meeting, which became heated, Mayor Jeffries repeatedly tried to
leave.

206   **"State police are watching":** Harold True, as reported in Widick,
Detroit, 108. True was the announcer for the *Lone Ranger* radio show
and worked for stations WXYZ and WWJ in Detroit. See also Lee and
Humphrey, *Race Riot*, 38.

207   **"This is your mayor":** Edward Jeffries, radio address, June 21, 1943.
Quoted in Lee and Humphrey, *Race Riot*, 38.

207   **"proclamation of modified martial law":** Harry Kelly, radio address,
June 21, 1943. Quoted in Lee and Humphrey, *Race Riot*, 38. All day
authorities had gone back and forth about declaring martial law
and asking for help from the federal government. Many thought
the decision to declare martial law was reached much too late. The
Detroit Free Press chronicled the reactions of several leaders in its June
22, 1943, edition, under the headline "Leaders Join Appeal for Peace;
Citizens Exhorted Not to Take Law into Own Hands."

Chapter 10: White Lies

213 **"Detroit has suffered":** Grantham, *The South in Modern America*, 188–89; Shogan and Craig, *The Detroit Race Riot*, 98. These exchanges occurred during a meeting of the House Committee to Investigate Un-American Activities in June 1943.

213 **"The situation is bad enough":** Shogan and Craig, *The Detroit Race Riot*, 99.

214 **"Japanese agents":** Shogan and Craig, 99.

214 **"instigating racial conflict":** Shogan and Craig, 99.

215 **"We have no evidence":** Shogan and Craig, 99.

216 **"I am rapidly losing":** "Jeffries Warns of Danger of More Race Riots," *Detroit Free Press*, July 1, 1943. Quoted in Shogan and Craig, 103.

216 **"Citizens become educated":** "Negro Leader Assails Criticism by Mayor," *Detroit Free Press*, July 1, 1943. Quoted in Shogan and Craig, 104.

217 **"The whole thing is sociological":** "Michigan Inquiry Seeks Riot Causes," *New York Times*, June 25, 1943. Quoted in Shogan and Craig, 100. Dominic Capeci and Martha Wilkerson in *Layered Violence* go into great detail about the various investigations and committee reports in the chapter titled "Of Hoodlums and Hillbillies," 32–53. They also write about them extensively in their 1990 article "The Detroit Rioters of 1943: A Reinterpretation." See also Herbert J. Rushton, William E. Dowling, Oscar Olander, and John Witherspoon, *Factual Report of the Committee to Investigate the Riot Occurring in Detroit on June 21, 1943*, August 11, 1943, Burton Historical Collection, Detroit Public Library.

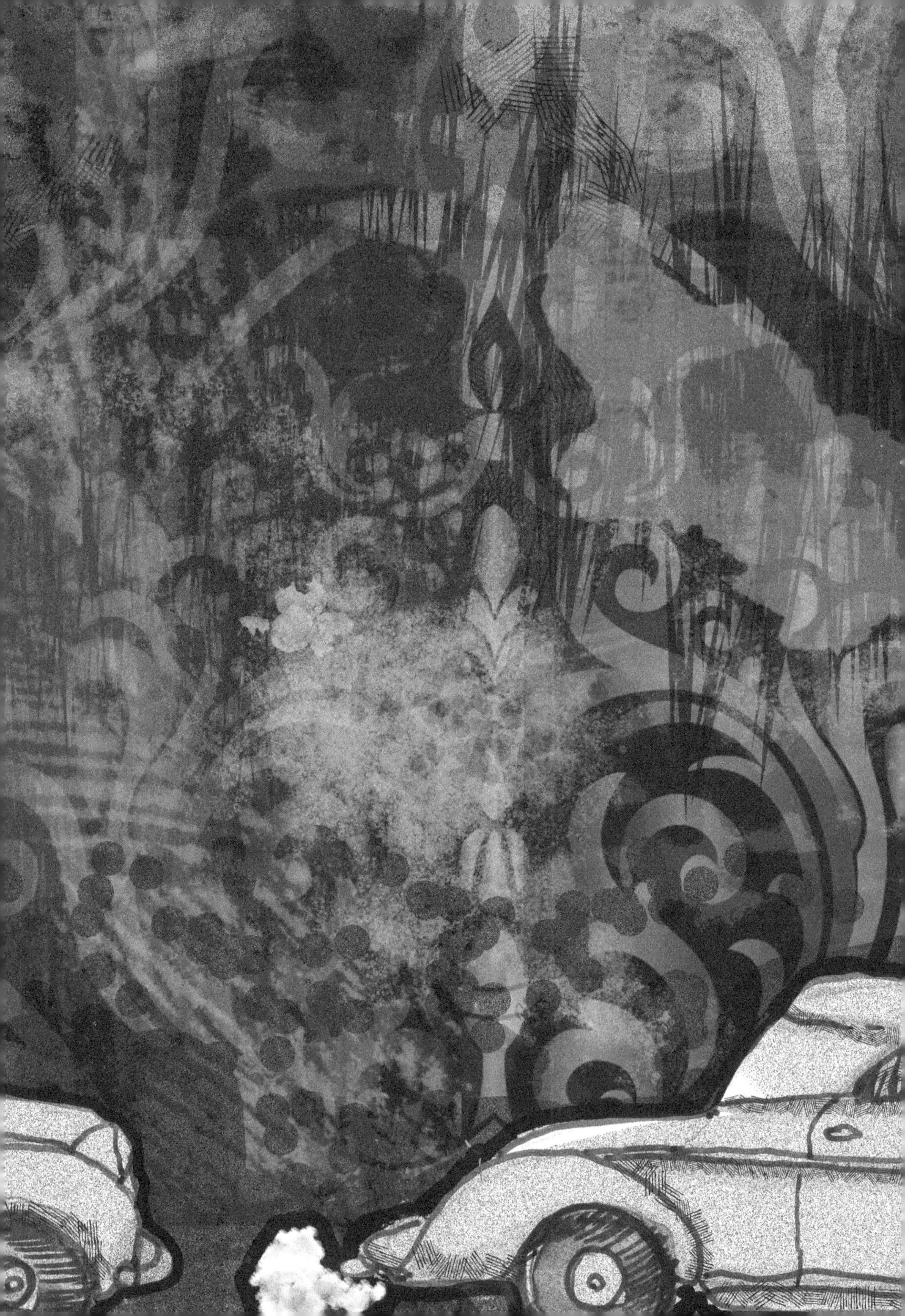

BIBLIOGRAPHY

Archives and Exhibitions

Bentley Historical Library, University of Michigan, Ann Arbor
    Charles A. Hill Family Papers: 1917–1981
    Detroit Urban League Records
Black Bottom Street View, Emily Kutil, exhibition at Detroit Public Library,
    January 2019
Burton Historical Collection, Detroit Public Library
Charles H. Wright Museum of African American History Reading Room,
    Detroit
Detroit Historical Museum
Detroit Industry Murals, Diego Rivera, Detroit Institute of Arts Museum
Library of Congress, Washington, D.C.
    The NAACP Records
    National Urban League Records
Mayor's Papers: Edward J. Jeffries Jr., Detroit Public Library
Walter P. Reuther Library, Wayne State University, Detroit
    Charles A. Hill Papers
    Civil Rights Congress of Michigan Collection
    Detroit Commission on Community Relations / Human Rights
        Department Records
    Maurice Sugar Papers
    NAACP Detroit Branch Records
    UAW Local 600 Records
    UAW President's Office: Walter P. Reuther Records

Newspapers

Chicago Tribune
Detroit Free Press
New York Times
Pittsburgh Courier

Books and Articles

Bailey, Beth, and David Farber. "The 'Double-V' Campaign in World War II
    Hawaii: African Americans, Racial Ideology, and Federal Power." *Journal
    of Social History* 26, no. 4 (Summer 1993): 817–43.

Barnes, Tamara. "Buying, Boosting, and Building with the National Housewives League." *Michigan History*, March/April 2013.

Baskin, Alex. "The Ford Hunger March—1932." *Labor History* 13, no. 3 (1972): 331–60.

Bates, Beth Tompkins. *The Making of Black Detroit in the Age of Henry Ford.* Chapel Hill: University of North Carolina Press, 2012.

———. *Pullman Porters and the Rise of Protest Politics in Black America, 1925–1945.* Chapel Hill: University of North Carolina Press, 2003.

Bjorn, Lars, with Jim Gallert. *Before Motown: A History of Jazz in Detroit, 1920–1960.* Ann Arbor: University of Michigan Press, 2001.

Boyd, Herb. *Black Detroit: A People's History of Self-Determination.* New York: HarperCollins, 2017.

Boyle, Kevin. *Arc of Justice: A Saga of Race, Civil Rights, and Murder in the Jazz Age.* New York: Henry Holt, 2004.

Brown, Earl. "The Truth about the Detroit Riot." *Harper's Magazine*, November 1943.

———. *Why Race Riots? Lessons from Detroit.* Public Affairs Pamphlets 87. New York: Public Affairs Committee, 1944.

Bruner, Jerome. "Self-Making and World-Making." In "More Ways of Worldmaking," special issue, *Journal of Aesthetic Education* 25, no. 1 (Spring 1991): 67–78.

Capeci, Dominic J., Jr. *Race Relations in Wartime Detroit: The Sojourner Truth Housing Controversy of 1942.* Philadelphia, Pa.: Temple University Press, 1984.

———, ed. *Detroit and the "Good War": The World War II Letters of Mayor Edward Jeffries and Friends.* Lexington: University Press of Kentucky, 1996.

Capeci, Dominic J., Jr., and Martha Wilkerson. "The Detroit Rioters of 1943: A Reinterpretation." *Michigan Historical Review* 16, no. 1 (Spring 1990): 49–72.

———. *Layered Violence: The Detroit Rioters of 1943.* Jackson: University Press of Mississippi, 1991.

Clive, Alan. *State of War: Michigan in World War II.* Ann Arbor: University of Michigan Press, 1979.

Daniels, Jim Ray. *Detroit Tales.* East Lansing: Michigan State University Press, 2003.

———. *Eight Mile High.* East Lansing: Michigan State University Press, 2014.

Davis, Michael. *Detroit's Wartime Industry: Arsenal of Democracy.* Charleston, S.C.: Arcadia Publishing, 2007.

Denby, Charles. *Indignant Heart: A Black Worker's Journal.* Detroit, Mich.: Wayne State University Press, 1989.

Dillard, Angela. *Faith in the City: Preaching Radical Social Change in Detroit.* Ann Arbor: University of Michigan Press, 2007.

Eugenides, Jeffery. *Middlesex*. London: Bloomsbury, 2002.

Fine, Gary Alan, and Patricia Turner. *Whispers on the Color Line: Rumor and Race in America*. Berkeley: University of California Press, 2004.

Franklin, John Hope, and Alfred A. Moss Jr. *From Slavery to Freedom*. 6th ed. New York: Alfred A. Knopf, 1988.

Gabin, Nancy. *Feminism in the Labor Movement: Women and the United Auto Workers, 1935–1975*. Ithaca, N.Y.: Cornell University Press, 1990.

Grantham, Dewey W. *The South in Modern America: A Region at Odds*. Fayetteville: University of Arkansas Press, 2001.

Gregory, Ted. "Forgotten War Nurses Keep Their Story Alive." *Chicago Tribune*, May 28, 2001. https://www.chicagotribune.com/news/ct-xpm-2001-05 -28-0105280153-story.html.

Henrickson, Wilma Wood. *Detroit Perspectives: Crossroads and Turning Points*. Detroit, Mich.: Wayne State University Press, 1991.

Huck, Karen. "The Arsenal on Fire: The Reader in the Riot, 1943." *Critical Studies in Mass Communication* 10, no. 1 (March 1993): 23–48.

Johnson, Marilynn. "Gender, Race, and Rumors: Re-examining the 1943 Race Riots." *Gender and History* 10, no. 2 (August 1998): 252–77.

Kersten, Andrew. "African Americans and World War II." *OAH Magazine of History* 16, no. 3 (Spring 2002): 13–17.

———. *A. Philip Randolph: A Life in the Vanguard*. Lanham, Md,: Rowman and Littlefield, 2007.

———. "Jobs and Justice: Detroit, Fair Employment, and Federal Activism during the Second World War." *Michigan Historical Review* 25, no. 1 (Spring 1999): 76–101.

———. *Race, Jobs, and the War: The FEPC in the Midwest, 1941–46*. Chicago: University of Illinois Press, 2000.

Knopf, Terry Ann. *Rumors, Race, and Riots*. New Brunswick, N.J.: Transaction Books, 1975.

Kowalski, Greg. *Hamtramck: The World War II Years*. Charleston, S.C.: Arcadia, 2007.

Langlois, Janet, "The Belle Isle Bridge Incident: Legend Dialectic and Semiotic System in the 1943 Detroit Race Riots." *Journal of American Folklore* 96, no. 380 (April–June 1983): 183–99.

Lee, Alfred McClung, and Norman Daymond Humphrey. *Race Riot*. New York: Octagon, 1943.

Lichtenstein, Nelson. *Walter Reuther: The Most Dangerous Man in Detroit*. Chicago: University of Chicago Press, 1995.

Life. Life on the News Fronts of the World. June 2, 1941.

Lipsitz, George. "The Possessive Investment in Whiteness: Racialized Social Democracy and the 'White' Problem in American Studies." *American Quarterly* 47, no. 3 (Sept. 1995): 369–87.

Lucander, David. "'It Is a New Kind of Militancy': March on Washington Movement, 1941–1946." PhD diss., University of Massachusetts Amherst, 2010. Open Access Dissertations (247).

Marshall, Thurgood. *Supreme Justice: Speeches and Writings*. Edited by J. Clay Smith Jr. Philadelphia: University of Pennsylvania Press, 2003.

Meier, August, and Elliott Rudwick. *Black Detroit and the Rise of the UAW*. New ed. Ann Arbor: University of Michigan Press, 2007.

Moon, Elaine. *Untold Tales, Unsung Heroes: An Oral History of Detroit's African American Community, 1918–1967*. Detroit, Mich.: Wayne State University Press, 1993.

Mullenbach, Cheryl. *Double Victory: How African American Women Broke Race and Gender Barriers to Help Win World War II*. Chicago: Chicago Review Press, 2013.

National Urban League. *Racial Conflict—a Home Front Danger: Lessons of the Detroit Riot*. New York: National Urban League, 1943.

Oates, Joyce Carol. *Them*. New York: Random House, 2000.

Odum, Howard W. *Race and Rumors of Race: The American South in the Early Forties*. Baltimore, Md.: Johns Hopkins University Press, 1997.

Okrent, Daniel. "Detroit: The Death—and Possible Life—of a Great City." *Time*, October 5, 2009.

Omolade, Barbara. "Hearts of Darkness." In *Powers of Desire*, edited by Ann Snitow, Christine Stansell, and Sharon Thompson, 350–70. New Feminist Library. New York: Monthly Review Press, 1983.

Osur, Alan. *Separate and Unequal: Race Relations in the AAF during World War II*. Self-published, CreateSpace, 2012.

Pehl, Matthew. "'Apostles of Fascism,' 'Communist Clergy,' and the UAW: Political Ideology and Working-Class Religion in Detroit, 1919–1945." *Journal of American History* 99, no. 2 (September 2012): 440–65.

Pflug, Warner. *The UAW in Pictures*. Detroit, Mich.: Wayne State University Press, 1971.

Piercy, Marge. *Made in Detroit*. New York: Alfred A. Knopf, 2015.

Platt, Anthony, ed. *The Politics of Riot Commissions, 1917–1970*. New York: Macmillan, 1971.

Randolph, A. Philip. "Call to Negro America 'To March on Washington for Jobs and Equal Participation in National Defense,' July 1, 1941." *Black Worker*, May 1941.

Sacco, Joe. *Footnotes in Gaza*. New York: Metropolitan Books, 2010.

Saldin, Robert P. *War, the American State, and Politics since 1898*. New York: Cambridge University Press, 2010.

Shapiro, Herbert. *White Violence and Black Response: From Reconstruction to Montgomery*. Amherst: University of Massachusetts Press, 1988.

Shockley, Megan Taylor. *We, Too, Are Americans*. Chicago: University of Illinois Press, 2004.

Shogan, Robert, and Tom Craig. *The Detroit Race Riot: A Study in Violence*. Philadelphia, Pa.: Chilton, 1964.

Sitkoff, Harvard. "The Detroit Race Riots of 1943." *Michigan History* 53 (Fall 1969): 183–206.

———. *Toward Freedom Land: The Long Struggle for Racial Equality in America*. Lexington: University Press of Kentucky, 2010.

Steinberg, Stephen. "America Again at the Crossroads." In *Theories of Race and Racism: A Reader*, edited by Les Back and John Solomos, 561–72. New York: Routledge, 2000.

Sugrue, Thomas J. *The Origins of the Urban Crisis: Race and Inequality in Postwar Detroit*. Princeton, N.J.: Princeton University Press, 1996.

Takaki, Ronald. *Double Victory: A Multicultural History of America in World War II*. Boston: Little, Brown, 2000.

Thomas, Richard W. *Life for Us Is What We Make It: Building Black Community in Detroit, 1915–1945*. Bloomington: Indiana University Press, 1992.

Trotter, Joe William, Jr. "From a Raw Deal to a New Deal? 1929–1945." In *To Make Our World Anew: A History of African Americans from 1880*, edited by Robin Kelley and Earl Lewis, 409–44. New York: Oxford University Press, 2005.

Trotter, Joe, and Earl Lewis, eds. *African Americans in the Industrial Age: A Documentary History, 1915–1945*. Boston: Northeastern University Press, 1996.

Turner, Patricia A. *I Heard It through the Grapevine: Rumor in African-American Culture*. Berkeley: University of California Press, 1993.

Tushnet, Mark. *Thurgood Marshall*. Chicago: Lawrence Hill Books, 2001.

U.S. Geological Survey. *State of Florida; Base Map*. 1940. Library of Congress Geography and Map Division, G3930 1940 .U51 TIL. http://hdl.loc.gov/loc .gmd/g3930.ct000499.

Washburn, Patrick S. "The *Pittsburgh Courier*'s Double V Campaign in 1942." *American Journalism* 3, no. 2 (1986): 73–86.

Widick, B. J. *Detroit: City of Race and Class Violence*. Rev. ed. Detroit, Mich.: Wayne State University Press, 1989.

Wilson, Sunnie, with John Cohassey. *Toast of the Town: The Life and Times of Sunnie Wilson*. Detroit, Mich.: Wayne State University Press, 1998.

Wolcott, Victoria. *Remaking Respectability*. Chapel Hill: University of North Carolina Press, 2013.

Zieger, Robert H. *For Jobs and Freedom: Race and Labor in America since 1865*. Lexington: University Press of Kentucky, 2007.

CPSIA information can be obtained
at www.ICGtesting.com
Printed in the USA
LVHW062055290421
685989LV00008B/328

9 781469 663265